THE PRINCETON HISTORY
of MODERN IRELAND

THE PRINCETON

HISTORY

of

MODERN

IRELAND

Edited by

RICHARD BOURKE
& IAN McBRIDE

PRINCETON UNIVERSITY PRESS
Princeton & Oxford

COPYRIGHT © 2016 BY PRINCETON UNIVERSITY PRESS

PUBLISHED BY PRINCETON UNIVERSITY PRESS
41 William Street, Princeton, New Jersey 08540

IN THE UNITED KINGDOM: PRINCETON UNIVERSITY PRESS
6 Oxford Street, Woodstock, Oxfordshire OX20 1TW

PRESS.PRINCETON.EDU

LIBRARY OF CONGRESS CATALOGING-IN-PUBLICATION DATA
The Princeton history of modern Ireland /
edited by Richard Bourke and Ian McBride.
pages cm
Includes bibliographical references and index.
ISBN 978-0-691-15406-0 (hardcover : alk. paper)
1. Ireland—History. I. Bourke, Richard, editor, author.
II. McBride, Ian, editor, author.
DA938.P74 2015
941.5—dc23 2015010402

BRITISH LIBRARY CATALOGING-IN-PUBLICATION DATA IS AVAILABLE

THIS BOOK HAS BEEN COMPOSED IN BELL MT STD

PRINTED ON ACID-FREE PAPER. ∞

PRINTED IN THE UNITED STATES OF AMERICA

1 3 5 7 9 10 8 6 4 2

CONTENTS

PART 2 TOPICS, THEMES, *and* DEVELOPMENTS

ACKNOWLEDGMENTS

THE EDITORS EXPRESS THEIR GRATITUDE to Al Bertrand for commissioning this volume on behalf of Princeton University Press. We are also greatly indebted to Quinn Fusting, Natalie Baan, and Cyd Westmoreland for their help in seeing the book through to completion. Finally, we thank Maggie Scull for her editorial work on a final draft of the typescript, and the anonymous readers for their careful and constructive comments.

CONTRIBUTORS

LAUREN ARRINGTON is Senior Lecturer at the Institute of Irish Studies at the University of Liverpool. She is the author of *W. B. Yeats, the Abbey Theatre, Censorship, and the Irish State: Adding the Half-Pence to the Pence* (2010) and *Revolutionary Lives: Constance and Casimir Markievicz* (2015).

JILL C. BENDER is Assistant Professor in the Department of History at the University of North Carolina at Greensboro. She has written extensively on the relationship between India and Ireland in the mid- to late nineteenth century and on the impact of the 1857–1858 Indian Uprising across the British Empire.

JOHN BEW is Reader in History and Foreign Policy at the War Studies Department at King's College London and Director of the International Centre for the Study of Radicalisation and Political Violence. His books include *The Glory of Being Britons: Civic Unionism in Nineteenth-Century Belfast* (2009) and *Castlereagh: Enlightenment, War and Tyranny* (2011).

ANDY BIELENBERG is Senior Lecturer in the School of History at University College Cork. His publications include *Ireland and the Industrial Revolution: The Impact of the Industrial Revolution on Irish Industry, 1801–1922* (2009) and (with Raymond Ryan) *An Economic History of Ireland since Independence* (2013).

RICHARD BOURKE is Professor in the History of Political Thought in the School of History at Queen Mary University of London. His books include *Peace in Ireland: The War of Ideas* (2009) and *Empire and Revolution: The Political Life of Edmund Burke* (2015).

CIARA BOYLAN is a post-doctoral researcher at Trinity College Dublin. She has published on the Great Famine and nineteenth-century Irish educational and social history and is currently researching aspects of educational publishing in Ireland.

DANIEL CAREY is Director of the Moore Institute at the National University of Ireland Galway and Professor in the School of Humanities. His publications include *Locke, Shaftesbury, and Hutcheson: Contesting Diversity in the Enlightenment and Beyond* (2006). He is currently completing a cultural history of travel in the Renaissance.

ENDA DELANEY is Professor in the School of History, Classics and Archaeology at the University of Edinburgh. Among his publications are *The Irish in Post-War Britain* (2007) and *The Curse of Reason: The Great Irish Famine* (2012).

DAVID DWAN is Associate Professor in English and Fellow of Hertford College at the University of Oxford. He is the author of *The Great Community: Culture and Nationalism in Ireland* (2008) and is currently completing *Liberty, Equality and Humbug: George Orwell's Political Thought.*

DIARMAID FERRITER is Professor of Modern Irish History in the School of History and Archives at University College Dublin. His books include *The Transformation of Ireland, 1900–2000* (2004) and *A Nation and Not a Rabble: The Irish Revolution, 1913–1923* (2015).

ULTÁN GILLEN is Senior Lecturer in European History in the School of Arts and Media at the University of Teesside, England. He has published widely on political culture in late eighteenth-century Ireland and is currently working on a study of the life and political thought of Theobald Wolfe Tone.

MATTHEW KELLY is Associate Professor in the Department of History at the University of Southampton. His books include *The Fenian Ideal and Irish Nationalism, 1882–1916* (2006) and *Finding Poland: From Tavistock to Hruzdowa and Back Again* (2010).

CATRIONA KENNEDY is Senior Lecturer in Modern History at the University of York. She has written extensively on gender in Britain and Ireland in the "long" eighteenth century and is the author of *Narratives of the Revolutionary and Napoleonic Wars: Military and Civilian Experience in Britain and Ireland* (2013).

MARIA LUDDY is Professor of Modern Irish History in the Department of History at the University of Warwick, Coventry. Among her publications are *Women and Philanthropy in Nineteenth-Century Ireland* (1995) and *Prostitution and Irish Society, 1800–1940* (2007).

IAN MCBRIDE is Professor of Irish and British History in the Department of History at King's College London. His books include *Scripture Politics: Ulster Presbyterians and Irish Radicalism in Late Eighteenth-Century Ireland* (1998) and *Eighteenth-Century Ireland: Isle of Slaves* (2009).

FEARGHAL MCGARRY is Reader in Modern Irish History in the School of History and Anthropology at Queen's University Belfast. Among his books are *Irish Politics and the Spanish Civil War* (1999) and *The Rising. Ireland: Easter 1916* (2010).

VINCENT MORLEY was previously a researcher with the Royal Irish Academy and has lectured in Irish history at the National University of Ireland. He is the author of *Irish Opinion and the American Revolution, 1760–1783* (2002) and *Ó Chéitinn go Raiftearaí: Mar a Cumadh Stair na hÉireann* (2011).

MARC MULHOLLAND is Associate Professor of Modern History and a Fellow of St. Catherine's College at the University of Oxford. His publications include *Northern Ireland at the Crossroads: Ulster Unionism in the O'Neill Years, 1960–1969* (2000) and *Bourgeois Liberty and the Politics of Fear: From Absolutism to Neo-Conservatism* (2012).

NIALL Ó DOCHARTAIGH is Senior Lecturer in the Department of Political Science and Sociology at the National University of Ireland Galway. He has written extensively on the Northern Ireland Conflict. His publications include *From Civil Rights to Armalites: Derry and the Birth of the Irish Troubles* (1997).

JANE OHLMEYER is Erasmus Smith's Professor of Modern History at Trinity College Dublin. Among her books are *Civil War and Restoration in the Three Stuart Kingdoms* (1993) and *Making Ireland English: The Irish Aristocracy in the Seventeenth Century* (2012).

MAURICE WALSH is Senior Lecturer in the School of Humanities at Kingston University, London. He is the author of *The News from Ireland: Foreign Correspondents and the Irish Revolution* (2008) and *Bitter Freedom: Ireland in a Revolutionary World, 1918–1923* (2015).

MAPS

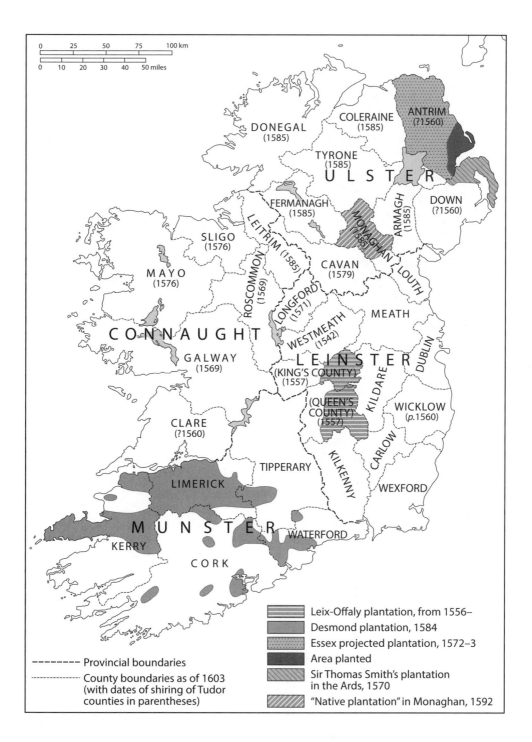

Scale bar:
0 25 50 75 100 km
0 10 20 30 40 50 miles

DONEGAL
(1585)

COLERAINE
(1585)

ANTRIM
(?1560)

TYRONE
(1585)

U L S T E R

FERMANAGH
(1585)

ARMAGH
(1585)

DOWN
(?1560)

SLIGO
(1576)

LEITRIM (1585)

MONAGHAN
1585

CAVAN
(1579)

LOUTH

MAYO
(1576)

ROSCOMMON
(1569)

LONGFORD
(1571)

MEATH

C O N N A U G H T

WESTMEATH
(1542)

GALWAY
(1569)

L E I N S T E R

DUBLIN

(KING'S COUNTY)
(1557)

KILDARE

CLARE
(?1560)

(QUEEN'S
COUNTY)
(1557)

WICKLOW
(p.1560)

TIPPERARY

KILKENNY

CARLOW

WEXFORD

LIMERICK

M U N S T E R

WATERFORD

KERRY

CORK

Leix-Offaly plantation, from 1556–
Desmond plantation, 1584
Essex projected plantation, 1572–3
Area planted
Sir Thomas Smith's plantation
in the Ards, 1570
"Native plantation" in Monaghan, 1592

-------- Provincial boundaries
·········· County boundaries as of 1603
(with dates of shiring of Tudor
counties in parentheses)

MAP 1. Tudor plantations, showing county boundaries as of 1603.

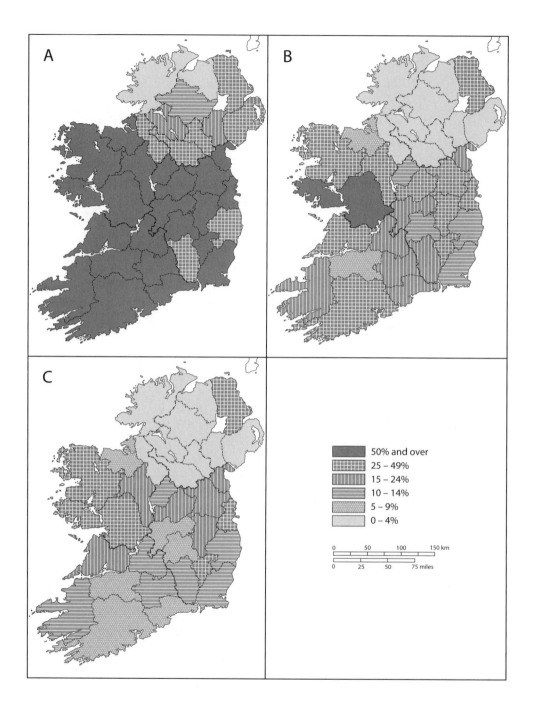

MAP 2. Land owned by Catholics (by county). (A) In 1641 (total Catholic land ownership, 59%). (B) In 1688 (total Catholic land ownership, 22%). (C) In 1703 (total Catholic land ownership, 14%).

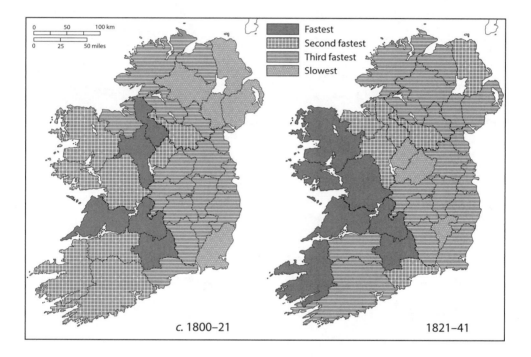

Legend:
- Fastest
- Second fastest
- Third fastest
- Slowest

c. 1800–21

1821–41

MAP 3. Population growth in Ireland, c. 1800–1821 and 1821–1841.

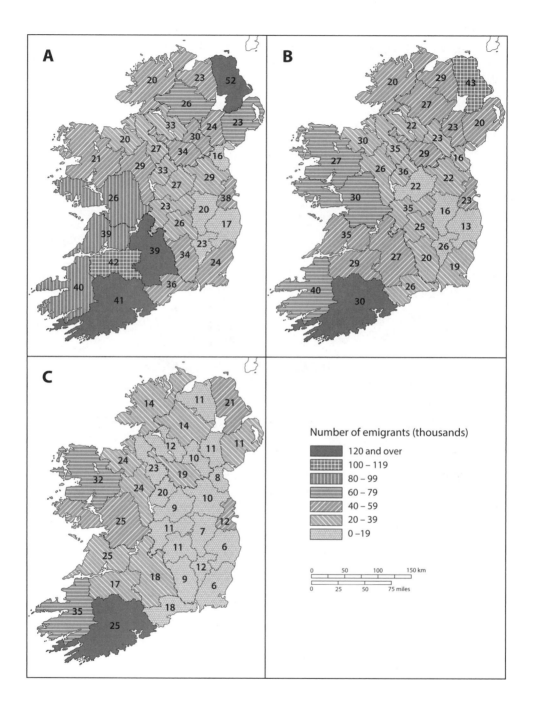

MAP 4. Emigration 1851–1911 (by county). (A) Number of emigrants, 1851–1871.
(B) Number of emigrants, 1871–1891. (C) Number of emigrants, 1891–1911.

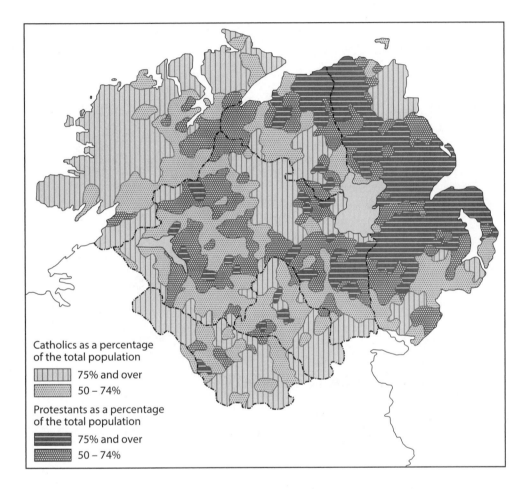

Catholics as a percentage
of the total population

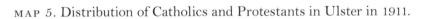

MAP 5. Distribution of Catholics and Protestants in Ulster in 1911.

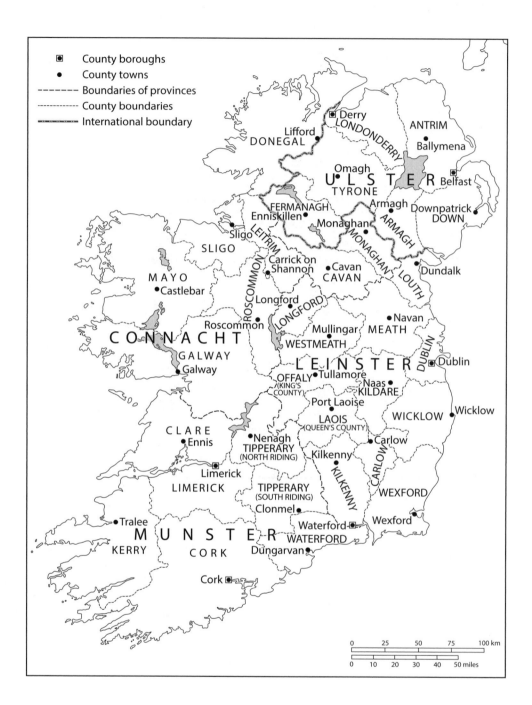

MAP 6. Ireland, North and South: provinces, counties, and county towns.

THE PRINCETON HISTORY
of MODERN IRELAND

INTRODUCTION

Richard Bourke

T HIS VOLUME PROVIDES AN ACCOUNT of modern Irish history from the
sixteenth to the twenty-first century. Its approach is both thematic and
chronological in nature. Part 1 contains six overarching narrative chapters dealing with the main developments in society and politics throughout the
period covered by the book. The aim here is to present readers with an up-to-date
rendition of the course of Irish history. Part 2 then focuses on topics and themes
that played a peculiarly important role in the shaping of that trajectory. These
chapters range from exercises in intellectual, cultural, and literary history to
analyses of formatively significant subjects like religion, nationalism, empire, and
gender. The aim of the volume is to make available the necessary ingredients for
an understanding of Irish history together with a range of insights on pivotal
issues and key controversies.

The contributors to this collection constitute a new generation of historians
whose work seeks to build on the achievements of their predecessors. Historiography in Ireland after the Second World War was devoted to advancing specialized
research, but it can also be seen in part as a reaction against prevailing popular
assumptions rather than a revision of a body of scholarly writing.[1] In this last guise
it aimed to free history from the influence of fable and polemic.[2] Its main achievement was the accumulation of a sizable body of research that enriched the picture
of the Irish past by systematically studying available evidence and archives. Looking back after a quarter century of progress in that direction, T. W. Moody was
eager to draw attention to "unprecedented advances in specialist research, in professional technique, in the organisation of historians and in the publication of
special studies, source materials, bibliographies and aids to scholarship."[3] Members of the succeeding generation of historians were still more focused in their objectives. Writing in the shadow of the Troubles in Northern Ireland after 1968 and

then the accession of the Republic of Ireland to the European Economic Community in 1973, historians from the 1970s through to the 1990s were in general terms more withering in their approach to national traditions. Above all, skepticism about the legitimating narratives that underpinned the establishment of the two jurisdictions on the island of Ireland became pervasive. The principal targets here were the revolutionary ideologies employed to legitimize nationalist and unionist rebellion. Both the Republic of Ireland and Northern Ireland have their roots in popular militancy. The last generation of historians sought to question the justification for this political stance. This could lend their writing a degree of urgency as well as a didactic tone. At times the temptation was to blame rather than explain what was not approved. This volume sets about incorporating the insights of earlier scholarship while moving beyond the more admonitory approach sometimes adopted by precursors.

Few, if any, states have been established by a formal "contract," whereby their populations consented in an orderly way to their formation. Most commonly they have been a product of conquest or revolution. This general observation applies to India and Mexico, as well as to America and France. Much like these last two countries, contemporary Ireland has its origins in revolutionary change, and historians are obliged to account for the process of transition. Recounting major moments of national upheaval, like 1776–1787 in America or 1789–1799 in France, usually involves processes of evaluation as well as reconstruction. Since historians habitually revise their predecessors, they tend to reassess earlier evaluations as they embark on new attempts at reconstruction. In the American, French, and Irish cases, this commonly takes the form of new perspectives on the aims and achievements of the revolutionary generation. Yet it is soon found that this fresh vantage affects perceptions of the antecedent past, meaning the longer history preceding the revolution itself. The reason for this seems clear: revolutions have to justify themselves in relation to their past, and so a reappraisal of a revolution entails a revision of its past. The immediate heirs of the Irish revolutionary generation of 1912–1923 constructed a past that pointed to the legitimacy of their revolution based on two principles: the right to self-determination on the one hand, and the entitlement to assert that right by force of arms on the other. Both principles explicitly depended on one another, because the justification for the resort to violence was taken to follow from the prior existence of a self-determining people.

This position relied on a set of historical assumptions, above all the idea of the unity of a people in a position to proclaim themselves as constituting a state. In 1963, the Belfast historian J. C. Beckett challenged this picture by contrasting the history of Ireland with that of England and France. In the latter cases, Beckett thought, history disclosed a clearly ascertainable pattern based on the facts of political cohesion and continuity. Even Germany and Italy, though late in establishing their own unity, could apparently point to the continuous presence of coherent peoples. For Beckett, the history of Ireland seemed to be lacking on both counts: it was peopled by distinct and often opposing populations who at the same time were deprived of the instruments of self-government. This left Beckett searching for the significance of Irish history while struggling to avoid lapsing into teleology. The projected unity and continuity imposed on the past by republican and unionist militants in early twentieth-century Ireland should be rejected, Beckett argued. But he then wondered whether this exercise in ideological debunking did not at the same time deprive Irish history of any distinguishable subject matter. If there existed no enduring substratum of people whose travails could be collected into a continuous narrative, what was the history of Ireland a history of? Beckett's answer was that continuity was supplied by the "land," which influenced the careers of settlers and natives alike.[4]

Beckett's question at first glance is more promising than his answer. If by "land" he meant landscape, then it is clear that this was continually made and remade by human labor. If, alternatively, he intended the term to refer to territory, then evidently this has not been a singular entity through the Irish past. What is ultimately most interesting about Beckett's question is the extent to which it was fundamentally *mal posée*. Irish history can have no overarching meaning or pattern unless it could be said to be a product of design. The chapters in this book cumulatively show that there was no underlying purpose to which the history of Ireland can be made to conform. What we encounter, instead, is a sequence of attempts at political construction that met with various forms of contingent resistance. For this reason, the subject matter of Irish history is not to be sought in persistence and stability but in discontinuous processes of conflict and conciliation. Given that these processes spilled beyond the geographical boundaries of the island, Irish history should be seen as porous rather than self-contained— affected overwhelmingly by English and British policy, but also by European and American events, as well as developments in the wider diaspora.[5]

The Florentine humanist Niccolò Machiavelli distinguished in his *Discourses* between states established by accident and those created by design.[6] The formation of the Irish polity after 1541 fits neither model. To begin with, it did not come into existence as an independent entity but as a dependent province of an expanding English empire. In addition it was a product of both accident and design. Machiavelli's principal examples were Sparta and Rome: the Spartan commonwealth had been the deliberate creation of a founding legislator, while the Roman republic was brought about by chance. The kingdom of Rome, naturally, had an original founder, but the constitution of the republic was a product of circumstance. Yet despite its contingent origins, Rome was blessed by fortune. In the case of Ireland, accident combined with design to produce a less happy result. This volume opens in the middle of the sixteenth century, with the passage of the Kingship Act of 1541 that established Henry VIII as King of Ireland. This brought an end to English lordship over the country by subjecting the Kingdom of Ireland directly to the imperial crown. It was an act of deliberate constitutional design, yet it collided with the reality of an existing set of forces.[7] In this way, from the Tudor period onwards, statecraft competed with contingency in Ireland. The Irish polity was not so much "constituted" by a harmonious arrangement of orders as marked by a collision of countervailing powers.

The relevant contingencies were determined by the pattern of settlement in Ireland. The attempt to consolidate Henrican power occurred against the background of Norman invasion and occupation, beginning in the twelfth century. After the subjection of Irish territory to the authority of Henry II in 1171, Norman settlement penetrated westwards from Leinster and Ulster as far as Galway and Mayo. This resulted in the establishment of powerful earldoms under the Geraldines, the Burkes, and the Butlers, though these were soon independent of the Dublin government and the crown.[8] This was followed by the relative attrition of Norman power as native Gaelic resurgence diminished the might of settler communities and the authority of administration within the Pale receded. Under these circumstances, Norman colonists, now styled "Old English," were suspected of "degeneration" as their culture merged with that of the "mere Irish."[9] Tudor policy was designed as a response to these developments. This policy began with the scheme of surrender and regrant under Henry VIII, designed to subject the disaffected Irish to common law tenures. However, pledges of allegiance on the part of the Irish nobility were not matched by corresponding acts of subordination. Rebellions were then met by new waves of colonization between the middle of the sixteenth century and the early seventeenth. These occurred in the midst of the spread of Protestant Reformation, dividing the religious loyalties of "New English" planters from the Catholicism of the Old English and native Irish combined. Settlement, from then on, introduced an adverse population as an instrument of imperial consolidation.

Irish history, of course, cannot be understood in terms of the interaction between happenstance and an isolated legislative act. There was no single exercise of political will that set Ireland in a durable constitutional mold. Instead, the country was variously refashioned by a succession of attempts at design. What complicates the picture is that this succession of policies generated new forms of resistance in the process of implementation. Yet in general terms, a dialectical pattern can be discerned over the course of the sixteenth and seventeen centuries. To begin with there was an attempt to transform the medieval lordship into a provincial kingdom, subject to the sovereignty of the English crown. The English monarchy did not govern a passively receptive province but acted through the counsel of an Irish parliament. The problem was that this mixed regime presided over an imperfectly assimilated population. The plantation of Munster from 1586 and the plantation of Ulster from 1606 introduced politically amenable constituencies committed to English government and the Protestant faith. Colonization was an arm of conquest intended as an instrument of pacification. But if this strategy made it possible to secure the territory, it also made the country more diffi-cult to hold. As the seventeenth century progressed, expropriation and sectarian animosity bred disaffection among all sections of the Catholic population.[10] The goal of a "perfect" conquest that would pacify the kingdom eluded every attempt at political subjection. In fact, pacification consistently sparked rebellion, leading to new demands for more effective subordination. A dynamic process of hostile action and reaction became entrenched.

A major push for a final conquest was launched in the aftermath of 1641. In October of that year, a Catholic rebellion against the administration in Ireland culminated in acts of atrocity against English and Scottish planters, drawing the country into the wars of the three Kingdoms that beset England, Ireland, and Scotland through the 1640s and 1650s.[11] Catholic royalist insurgency was met by Cromwellian retaliation between 1649 and 1653. Previous attempts to manage the Irish had been implemented by the crown. Now the new model army was led by Cromwell to deliver control of the country to a rump parliament at Westmin-ster. English victory was accompanied by a dramatic series of confiscations. Before the confederate wars of the 1640s, Irish Catholics still held nearly two-thirds of the land. After the Cromwellian settlement, their tenure was reduced to approxi-mately eight percent, rising again to twenty after the Restoration. This amounted to a drastic social revolution, giving rise to a significant transformation of govern-ment. More than fifty thousand confederate troops piled into continental armies. Prominent rebels were executed or exiled as indentured labor. The remainder, along with compliant Catholics, were systematically expropriated. From now on the Irish parliament was controlled by Protestant lords and gentry. Catholics were excluded from executive offices under the crown.

Migration of population was a standard feature of early modern European history. Much of this occurred against the background of waves of barbarian inun-dation in late antiquity and sequences of settlement and resettlement continuing down through the high middle ages.[12] The Saxon incursions and the Norman con-quest are examples of a widespread European process. In due course, territorial annexation and regnal incorporation became characteristic continental dynam-ics.[13] For this reason, it is interesting to examine the Irish experience in compar-ison with other European attempts at political integration. The union of Spanish crowns and the expansion of the French state are conspicuous examples of these processes of amalgamation. Yet in the English case, consolidation failed to win even minimally comprehensive support. Eastern colonization of Slavic regions by German settlers from the twelfth century led to the coexistence of populations from the Baltic to Slovenia.[14] As in Ireland, the Reformation brought new ten-sions to German and Slavic territories. For example, orthodox Germans were forced to flee Bohemia during the course of the Hussite wars. Thereafter, central-ization was pursued under Habsburg rule from 1526 by building a court party among the Bohemian estates and playing the kingdom against Moravia, Lusatia, and Silesia. Conflict followed, culminating in Habsburg victory over the Bohemian estates on the afternoon of November 8, 1620, the expulsion of Czech nobility, and the confiscation of their estates. The region was then devastated by the Thirty Years' War. At the end of that brutalizing contest, the Habsburg crown asserted its power over depopulated Bohemian territory, yet the diet soon recovered a definite constitutional role. Fifty percent of landed estates changed hands after the Battle of White Mountain, and the German language soon acquired equal status in administration, yet native aristocratic families regained authority in affairs of state.[15] An influx of German settlers buttressed the new regime, while the remaining Slavic ruling families cooperated with Vienna. In Ireland, by comparison, the Catholic nobility was more or less completely disempowered.

That process had not led to peace and prosperity, however. Commenting on Irish conditions in 1672, the political anatomist, William Petty, ascribed continuing discontents to two sources: first, to ongoing disaffection among the Catholic Irish; and second, to the division of imperial sovereignty between distinct legislatures. The solution, he argued, lay in a policy of combining "Union" with "Transmutation." The former was a proposal to incorporate the two kingdoms by reviving the arrangement in operation under the commonwealth, the latter was a scheme for transplanting the majority of Catholics and replacing them with well-disposed settlers from the mainland.[16] In this way, Petty believed, divergent peoples could be blended into a coherent state. The idea of exchanging substantial bodies of population was never pursued beyond the stage of purely speculative projection. However, proposals for a legislative union were ultimately implemented, nearly a century and a half after Petty floated the idea. But if the project of mass transplantation was never seriously contemplated, in a deep sense the attraction of amalgamating nationalities persisted through the seventeenth and eighteenth centuries. Petty's was just a drastic means of effecting a common objective.

The consequences of the Cromwellian conquest along with the Restoration settlement threatened to be reversed after the accession of James II: a Catholic monarch on the British throne allied to the French was not merely an affront to Scottish and English sensibilities, it also undermined the security of the Protestant population in Ireland.[17] Their strength lay in their monopoly of land and therefore power, their weakness in the scarcity of their numbers. The retreat of James II at the Battle of the Boyne on July 1, 1690 followed by the Battle of Aughrim and the Treaty of Limerick that concluded the Williamite War enabled the victors to address this situation.[18] The Protestant monopoly of public life was increased, and the expropriation of rebel forces implemented. Confiscations continued down to the end of the century, reducing Catholic holdings to approximately twelve percent. This was not quite Petty's dream realized by chance, although the flight of Jacobite forces into continental armies was a necessary prerequisite for the allocation of their lands. Since 1641, Catholics had gambled their future on insurrection, leading Petty to conclude that with the victory of "the *English*" they had at least a "Gamester's right" to requisition their opponents' estates.[19] From 1692, with the legislative authority of the Irish parliament more firmly entrenched, the balance of property was underwritten by an exclusive regime of power. Within three years, the Dublin parliament began to enact a series of proscriptions aimed at permanently depriving Catholics of political purchase and reducing the influence of their doctrines, liturgy, and ecclesiology.

These regulations have come to be known as the "popery" or "penal" laws. Their passage was completed in 1728, when Catholics were denied the right to vote in elections to parliament. Over the preceding decades, a series of measures of varying character and significance sought to diminish the threat that popery was felt to pose to the reigning establishment. Most conspicuous among them were attempts to restrict the intellectual commerce between the Catholic clergy and the continent, provisions for further reductions in the Catholic share of the land, and measures to address the suspected evasion of legislation.[20] Between 1649 and 1728, in a succession of sudden and sometimes violent developments, a comprehensive revolution in Ireland had occurred, transforming property relations and the distribution of power. Down to 1782, Ireland was administered by a proscriptive constitution subordinate to the final authority of Westminster. The Church of Ireland enjoyed the status of a national church presiding in the face of widespread religious dissent, most conspicuously among Presbyterians and Catholics. At the same time, despite these apparently stark polarities, Presbyterian industry developed in the north, while Catholic merchants and small farmers prospered in all four provinces.

Rising prosperity occurred against a background of rural and artisanal poverty. In the 1730s, George Berkeley, the bishop of Cloyne, fretted about the viability of social cohesion in the face of a luxury economy driven by the import of foreign commodities. National wealth, for the bishop, ought to include improved conditions among the poor. This, he thought, was best achieved on the basis of industry rather than overseas commerce.[21] From this perspective, the key objective of political economy was not the liberalization of Irish trade restrictions lamented by Irish publicists since the 1690s, but the development of sustainable patterns of domestic consumption. With such a program, Berkeley was disputing the whole tenor of Protestant "patriot" rhetoric that had been mobilized by polemicists between William Molyneux and Jonathan Swift, and that still animated the rhetoric of the parliamentary leader, Henry Grattan, into the early 1780s.[22] The patriot platform amounted to a protest against Irish "slavery" caused by the dependence of the Dublin parliament on the British government. In the 1770s and 1780s, complaints from this constituency were steadily addressed: restrictions on Irish trade were lifted in 1778 and legislative independence granted in 1782. In the same period, the popery laws affecting Catholic property and worship were repealed. Constitutional change was again undertaken in the 1790s: Catholics were admitted to the legal profession in 1792 and granted the electoral franchise in 1793. However, concessions had to be wrung from an "Ascendancy" establishment that persisted in obstructing the right of Catholics to sit in parliament.

Under the diffuse influence of French Revolutionary ideas, the Society of United Irishmen emerged in 1791, seeking parliamentary reform, Catholic emancipation, and political independence from the British parliamentary system. After 1794, the Society went underground. The view that Ireland's difficulties could be traced to British perfidy gained traction among sections of public opinion at this time. From the perspective of the United Irishmen, somewhat paradoxically, national (or "republican") fellowship, retarded by a century of suspicion among domestic sects and parties, would be advanced by allowing these local forces to confront one another directly without the mediation of British parliamentary power. Separation, it was thought, was a necessary prelude to a union of hearts and minds. That idea, of course, was challenged from the start. The best chance that oppressed Catholics had of ameliorating their conditions, Edmund Burke argued, lay in the pressure that Westminster could be induced to bring to bear on local obstructionism.[23] For similar reasons, Adam Smith had underlined the advantages of a parliamentary union: "By a union with Great Britain, Ireland would gain, besides the freedom of trade, other advantages much more important." Above all, he surmised, the lower and middling ranks would gain deliverance from a singularly "oppressive aristocracy," the likes of which could not be found in either England or Scotland. What distinguished Ireland from eighteenth-century Britain, Smith believed, was that its ruling class was differentiated from the mass of the population on the basis of "odious" religious and political distinctions. Given that such distinctions are commonly more potent than rivalry between nations, he concluded, "the inhabitants of Ireland are not likely for many ages to consider themselves as one people."[24]

Irish hostility toward Britain, along with domestic antipathies, came to a head with the rebellion of 1798. Over the summer months, fighting spread through Kildare, Antrim, Down, and Wexford. Captured insurgents were subject to brutal recrimination. The gulf between loyalists and United Irishmen widened. Divergences between Protestants and Catholic Defenders were bridged in the face of common opposition only to be driven apart again under conditions of mutual fear. With the failure of a French naval expedition to Donegal in October 1798, the rebellion was effectively at an end, with one of its leaders, Theobald Wolfe Tone, cutting his own throat in Provost's Prison and dying on November 19. In the aftermath of the uprising, the edifice of Ascendancy rule in Ireland was abruptly dismantled at the behest of British prime minister William Pitt by the introduction of the Act of Union in 1800, which came into effect in January 1801. It has long been debated whether the introduction of full political rights for Catholics in tandem with the imposition of a parliamentary union might have fostered political integration among the populations of Britain and Ireland.[25] What is clear is that emancipation under the existing British franchise would have entailed negligible Catholic representation in the UK parliament. In the absence of a specifiable dynamic leading to consensus, it is difficult to establish how assimilation might have occurred.

Writing at the end of the 1830s, Gustave de Beaumont interpreted nineteenth-century Ireland as the misbegotten offspring of its predecessor. De Beaumont shared with his traveling companion, Alexis de Tocqueville, a comparative interest in the fate of European aristocracies. Like Adam Smith, he contrasted the British system of integrative ranks with the proscriptive culture endemic to the Irish ruling class. Ireland, he wrote, was afflicted by a *"bad aristocracy."*[26] Its principles were singular in European history, acting as a bulwark against assimilation. Throughout the eighteenth century, it had occupied the position of a colonial establishment whose antipathy to the mass of the population whom it governed was perpetuated by its weakness rather than its power. The Protestant insistence on being a "kingdom" and not a "colony" that found expression in patriot discourse for a century after 1698 was the product of a collision between a juridical claim to self-government and the reality of depending for security on the Westminster parliament. Acting as local agents without final responsibility, the Ascendancy, de Beaumont contended, lacked the impulse to seek rapprochement with Catholics. At the same time, in serving as the principal link connecting the two kingdoms, it operated as a screen between the London government and its Irish subjects. This left the majority of the population without representation. In the language of the time, the problem was not simply that they lacked elected deputies but that they were not beneficiaries of even "virtual" representation.[27]

This predicament was not ameliorated by the passage of the Union.[28] Over the next thirty years, sectarian politics in Ireland were exacerbated rather than mollified. When Catholic emancipation was finally introduced by the UK parliament in 1829, the Catholic masses had been organized into a distinct Association for the promotion of the sectional ambitions of their community. After the success of emancipation, Daniel O'Connell proceeded to set up the Repeal Association in 1840 with the aim of repealing the Union of 1801. The main weapon in O'Connell's armory was the show of Catholic numerical strength exhibited during "monster" rallies that appalled the British establishment. Irish politics under the Union was henceforth captured by rival constituencies seeking four opposing goals: durable integration under the existing Union; devolution to an Irish parliament in which Protestants would predominate; the re-establishment of an Irish government in which Catholic fortunes would steadily rise; and the separatist rejection of any link to Britain at all.[29] Taken together, these options looked forward to a variety of arrangements, spanning unionism, various forms of federalism, assorted schemes for self-government, and republican separatism.[30] Through the nineteenth century, three methods were employed for advancing each of these causes: constitutional politics, agitation, and violence.[31] The outlook for each political program and the popularity of the range of methods available to achieve their respective goals depended on political developments in the United Kingdom as a whole. The Irish Famine and electoral reform proved to be the major determinants.

The experience of mass starvation combined with extensive emigration between 1846 and 1852 had a decisive impact on social and political relations in Ireland.[32] By the autumn of 1845, a potato blight had spread through northern and central Europe. Within a year, the devastating effects of the infestation were felt among broad sections of the Irish population dependent on the potato crop as a staple. Between famine, disease, and emigration, the population of Ireland decreased by approximately three million in the space of a decade. Emigration continued over the decades that followed, with the result that the population had fallen to four and a half million by the 1911 census, nearly half the number that had been reached at the outset of the Famine.[33] Over the same period, despite repeated attempts on the part of the British government to improve social conditions among Irish tenant farmers, along with other schemes for winning the allegiance of the Catholic population, turmoil continued to afflict political relationships in Ireland. In July 1848, under the influence of campaigns for national freedom on the European continent, members of the Young Ireland movement staged an abortive rebellion against British rule in Ireland that revived the tradition of insurgent separatism inaugurated in 1798. In the aftermath of this failure, the Irish Republican Brotherhood was formed, dedicated to provisional republicanism in Ireland. Provisionalism was committed to popular sovereignty through revolutionary means. In practice, at least down to 1867, this meant pursuing a program of revolutionary vanguardism: the ideal of democratic self-government was to be implemented by a provisionally unaccountable administration in anticipation of the consent of the people in whose name power was meanwhile exercised.[34] The 1916 Easter Rising in Dublin, when a rebellion organized by seven members of the military council of the Irish Republican Brotherhood was staged against British rule in Ireland, counts as one of the more successful examples of provisional democracy in history: an insurgency was planned by revolutionary partisans in the absence of popular consent, although their actions then won overwhelming support over the course of the years that immediately followed.

The idea of provisional democracy has always been challenging, beginning with its invocation under the French Convention Assembly in 1793. On October 10 of that year, it was declared by deputy Louis Antoine Léon de Saint-Just that "the provisional government of France is revolutionary until there is peace."[35] In other words, democratic constitutionalism would be suspended during the provisional reign of emergency power. Revolution in Ireland in 1916 drew on the same principle: it was assumed by the leaders of the Easter Rising that popular endorsement for a constitutional regime could be claimed by anticipating ratification by the people. Of course, the British government adopted a comparable position at this time. Devolved self-government or "Home Rule" for Ireland had been agreed by regular constitutional procedure in 1912 and was expected to reach the statute book in September 1914, but the provision was suspended in the face of the emergency presented by the First World War. As it turned out, after the War, Irish support for the measure had effectively disappeared under the influence of separatist aspirations represented by Sinn Féin. As a consequence of the general election of 1918, Sinn Féin completely supplanted the Irish Parliamentary Party as the voice of the Irish electorate in all provinces outside Ulster. By this point, northern unionists had already asserted the right to govern their own destiny with a show of plebiscitary and military strength in September 1912. Six years later, two prospectively self-governing communities occupied the island of Ireland—a southern community, overwhelmingly Catholic, that supported the assertion of statehood in arms; and a northern community, predominantly Protestant, that claimed the freedom to pledge its loyalty to the Union.

Both communities were more generally mobilized in the context of the extended franchise created by British parliamentary reforms in 1867 and 1884. Mass enfranchisement empowered the electorate in Britain and Ireland to assert in practice what the people had already enjoyed as a theoretical entitlement: sovereignty over the disposal of its powers. These developments took place alongside further schemes for social and constitutional reform. They comprised, first, the succession of land acts passed between 1870 and 1909, which sought to stimulate national allegiance by bestowing greater security on the tenancy rights of smallholding Irish farmers; and, second, the sequence of bills intended to provide Home Rule for Ireland. These changes were intricately interrelated because, from 1879 onward, agrarian grievances were increasingly inseparable from political mobilization: on the one hand, social protest organized around tenurial rights became a national issue; on the other, political activism aiming at constitutional reform could not avoid the controversy over land.[36] This process is illustrated by the emergence of successive agrarian organizations allied to constitutional campaigns between the end of the 1870s and 1898—from the Land League to the National League and the United Irish League.

It was first argued around the middle of the seventeenth century that a revolution in politics would follow a revolution in property holding: systems of government, in other words, could be expected to reflect the distribution of goods.[37] For most of its history Ireland was largely an agricultural country, with larger scale manufacturing being confined to the northeast of the island. The balance of property therefore substantially consisted of the distribution of land. By the beginning of the nineteenth century, this distribution was affected by the rapid increase in population that took place over the previous fifty years.[38] Numbers at the less prosperous end of the scale continued to expand down to the 1840s, with the result that a considerable proportion of the agrarian community subsisted on twenty-acre farms, while a significant percentage also survived as smallholders, laborers, and cottiers. Over these stood a concentration of landlords and large farmers whose property rights were gradually challenged in the decades after the Famine. Tithe obligations, the welfare of tenants, and pressure on land from tillers and graziers had long triggered agrarian disturbances in Ireland.[39] Yet conflicts developed and sharpened from the middle decades of the nineteenth century, descending into a "land war" from the end of the 1870s and persisting into the period after the Civil War of 1922–1923, down to the 1930s and beyond.[40]

The roots of unrest lay in the dearth of larger "improving" estates combined with the lack of wherewithal among smallholders to upgrade their stock. Obstacles in the way of landlords keen to capitalize on their estates was the focus of legislative intervention in 1848 and 1849 in the form of the Encumbered Estates Acts. But from Gladstone's 1870 Land Act down to the Conservative and then Liberal measures introduced in the first decade of the new century, attempts were made to enable smaller tenant farmers to raise their profits by themselves. This was originally to be achieved by giving what was known as the Ulster Custom the force of law, which in practice meant extending to tenants the possibility of selling their interest in their holdings, a right to fair rent, and fixity of tenure.[41] Yet by the time these measures had been fully achieved in 1881, the Land League under Michael Davitt was demanding the right of outright proprietorship. Vigorous campaigning ultimately bore fruit in the form of a series of major legislative provisions, introduced between 1885 and 1909, which established ownership among tenant farmers by accelerating assisted purchase schemes. In bringing to an end the figure of the landlord in Irish history, this sequence of transfers proved to be perhaps the most significant social change in the country since the 1840s, matched only by the transformation in the standing and roles of women from the middle of the twentieth century.[42] It would also determine the significance of constitutional reform as this began to be introduced from 1886.

Initially, constitutional change was to take the form of a subordinate legislative parliament as advocated by the Irish Parliamentary Party under the leadership of Charles Stewart Parnell along with influential elements inside the British Liberal Party. In the late nineteenth and early twentieth centuries, the Irish Party exercised considerable leverage over the imperial parliament in holding the balance between Britain's mainstream parties. Under this conjunction of forces, Home Rule bills were introduced in 1886 and 1893, polarizing unionists and nationalists in Ireland. This contributed to a crisis of national will, culminating in the conflicts of 1912–1923. At the end of this period, in his Nobel Prize acceptance lecture delivered on December 15, 1923, W. B. Yeats described the era after the death of Parnell in 1891 as a time of "gestation" in Irish life. An "event," Yeats suggested, was then "conceived" that was soon marshaled and advanced by the world of culture as embodied, for example, in the Gaelic League, the National Literary Society, and the Irish Literary Theatre.[43] The event Yeats had in mind was the Anglo-Irish War of 1918–1921, during which the Irish "race" was taken to have realized in practice the national vocation that had first assumed a purely imaginative shape in the wake of Parnell.[44] Yet despite Yeats's retrospective formulation, there had not in fact existed a shared conception of the Irish future that animated the population of the island of Ireland between 1891 and 1912. Instead, a diversity of aspirations found expression in the period. Moreover, in political terms, these had yet to be definitively formed.

It was not the pre-formed characteristics of a "race," to use Yeats's term, that propelled Protestants in Ireland towards an integrated Union. As a matter of fact, before long, the majority would seek a federated arrangement between Britain and Ireland as changing circumstances dictated. Equally, there was nothing integral to Irish Catholic "identity" that drove its protagonists to embrace a particular allegiance. Over the course of a generation, most members of this constituency shifted ground fairly dramatically from endorsing various manifestations of self-government under the Union to supporting competing visions of the separatist ideal.[45] Nonetheless, the trials of the first decades of the twentieth century terminated in the formation of two rival jurisdictions. The partition of Ireland was introduced under the 1920 Government of Ireland Act. Civil War then followed in the South as opinion divided over the terms of the 1921 Treaty designed to replace the 1920 Act. At the same time, in the North, the new Prime Minister, James Craig, moved to consolidate the position of the new six-county polity.[46] These developments gave birth to two opposing and introverted cultures that dominated their respective societies in the North and the South. The Southern government, presiding over what was now termed the "Irish Free State," achieved fiscal autonomy under the provisions of the Anglo-Irish Treaty. This led in the 1930s to the adoption of a policy of economic protectionism that pitched Ireland into conflict with British trade.[47] The policy impacted negatively on industrial growth in a society dominated by its agricultural sector. Through the 1940s and 1950s, national income lagged conspicuously behind the European average. It was not until the 1960s that the economy began to expand and the first bids to join the European Economic Community were made. During the same period, the standard of living in Northern Ireland rose in step with British levels of prosperity. Economic subvention from London eased the blow of industrial decline.

Over the past three hundred years, toleration, prosperity, and population growth have commonly been accepted as indices of a flourishing state of society. Both Irelands—the North and the South—have had interesting difficulties with each of these indicators.[48] In the North since 1920, trade and manufacture underwent decline, forcing the economy into dependence on the British exchequer. At the same time, population increase, instead of boosting assets and promoting optimism, caused alarm about the sectarian demographic balance in anticipation of a rising Catholic vote. Finally, toleration among Catholics and Protestants in the North never became a cherished public virtue, as nationalists resented curtailment of their civil rights while unionists feared a future at the mercy of Catholic democracy. This fear has had two bases: the waning of the British commitment to the permanent survival of the Union and the persistence of Southern claims to the integrity of an island polity. The Southern claim seemed all the more menacing in the context of its enduring culture of religious intolerance, which was not alleviated by the decline in population and relative wealth.[49] In the Republic of Ireland, much like Northern Ireland, moral dogmatism proved a popular habit.[50] Among the Catholic majority on the island, attitudes to sex, gender relations, and ecclesiastical authority bred conformity, submission, and tenacity. A backlash against discrimination followed in the 1970s and 1980s.[51] Because, in general terms, liberalism and democracy have enjoyed distinct though overlapping histories in the West, it is perhaps unsurprising that they can be found in tension in both jurisdictions of Ireland.[52]

That tension came to a head in Northern Ireland between 1966 and 1972. In the mid 1960s, moves to improve relations between the Northern and Southern governments provided leaders of intransigent opinion in the North with an opportunity to resist. Inter-communal hostility became manifest in 1966 surrounding the commemorations of 1916. Within two years, clashes between the authorities and the civil rights movement in Northern Ireland were politicizing society at large. By the summer of 1969, the contest between police and protestors had generated more widespread confrontation. The North soon descended into factional strife. Civil war ensued, lasting for thirty years, contained by the overwhelming force of the British army. By the time that a settlement was agreed to in 1998 among the party and paramilitary leaderships, the desire for peace was matched by a mood of recrimination among the electorate. The long-drawn-out process of implementation bore witness to an attitude of persistent bitterness. By now, the economy had come to flourish in the South, only to be compromised by the credit crisis that unfolded after 2008.[53] Yet under conditions of both boom and bust, suspicion among Northern Protestants for the institutions of the Republic remained entrenched. A jurisdictional war had occurred leaving all jurisdictions intact. In Northern Ireland, the system of government had been reconfigured and the mode of representation reformed, though animosity persisted on the ground. The hope was that, over the longer term, collaboration in government would lead to attitudes among voters beginning to soften.

In a series of lectures delivered in the early 1820s that were then published in 1851 under the title of *The History of the Origins of Representative Government in Europe*, François Guizot marveled at the reconstruction of Europe in the aftermath of the barbarian invasions that destroyed Rome. The central achievement of this protracted process, he believed, was the creation of a collection of "mighty states." The history of modern Europe, he went on, was centrally determined by the "destiny" that shaped these potent political structures.[54] The historical consummation that he had in mind was the gradual modification of centralized power by the reassertion of primitive liberty in modern constitutional forms. The constitutional arrangement that particularly absorbed Guizot was the system of representative government, originally perfected in England and now at last being established in France.[55] This vision would exercise a conspicuous influence on the subsequent writing of European history, which has largely focused on three preeminent themes: state formation, the balance of power, and domestic social and political revolution. Although these dominant narratives have certainly captured discernible aspects of the European past, they were particularly well suited to organizing the histories of England, France, and Spain. At a stretch, Germany and Italy could be fitted into the same mold, albeit as strangely late developers who had been forced to travel along a special path. In each of these cases, the emergence and consolidation of state sovereignty has constituted the central object of historical analysis. The subsidiary themes of the contests between states and the various struggles within them followed as a matter of course. Compared to these leading processes, other developments began to appear peripheral, and their histories have consequently been relegated to the margins. Accordingly, the shifting fortunes of central Europe and the island of Ireland have seemed tangential.

However, instead of viewing the history of Europe in terms of the formation of discrete national units, one might equally see its progress as governed by the inconstant fate of fluctuating empires. From this perspective, volatile frontiers constitute as central a focus as orderly consolidation. It is useful to examine the history of Ireland in this more flexible and complex framework. This reorientation helps us move beyond attempts to plot the story of Ireland as one of trauma or victimhood, both of which assume the existence of a continuous national personality that bore the brunt of this affliction. It also enables us to jettison accounts that depict Irish history as an exception to a norm, most usually portrayed as a case of failed or inadequate modernization. In place of these oversimplified chronicles, a more variegated process comes into view, based on precarious consolidation and oscillating frontiers. From this vantage, states, national rivalry, and revolutions continue to play an important role, but so too does conquest, settlement, and strife as well as diaspora, secession, and partition.[56] This volume throws light on this assortment of topics in a series of chapters that combines fresh insights with sharp analysis and exposition. Although the principal objective of the book is to chart the main lines of development in Irish history, in addition it seeks to present the results of accumulated research while also clearing the ground for new departures.

NOTES

1. See chapter 11 by Richard Bourke.
2. See, for example, R. Dudley Edwards and T. Desmond Williams (eds.), *The Great Famine: Studies in Irish History, 1845–1852* (Dublin: Browne and Nolan, 1956), p. viii: "The political commentator, the ballad singer and the unknown maker of folk-tales have all spoken about the Great Famine,

but is there no more to be said?" This introduction was actually written by Kevin B. Nolan. For the production of the volume, see Cormac Ó Gráda, "Making History in Ireland in the 1940s and 1950s: The Saga of the Great Famine," *Irish Review* 12 (Spring–Summer 1992), pp. 87–107.

3. T. W. Moody, "Twenty-Five Years of Irish Historiography," in *Irish Historiography, 1936–1970* (Dublin: Irish Committee of Historical Sciences, 1971), p. 137.

4. J. C. Beckett, "The Study of Irish History: An Inaugural Lecture," in *Confrontations: Studies in Irish History* (London: Faber and Faber, 1972).

5. See chapter 14 by Jill C. Bender.

6. Niccolò Machiavelli, *Discourses on the First Decade of Titus Livius* (ca. 1517), in *The Chief Works of Machiavelli*, 3 vols., trans. Alan Gilbert (London and Durham, NC: Duke University Press, 1989), vol. I, p. 200.

7. Brendan Bradshaw, *The Irish Constitutional Revolution of the Sixteenth Century* (Cambridge: Cambridge University Press, 1979); Ciaran Brady, *The Chief Governors: The Rise and Fall of Reform Government in Tudor Ireland, 1536–1588* (Cambridge: Cambridge University Press, 1994).

8. The process of migration and castellation is recorded in Giraldus Cambrensis, *Expugnatio Hibernica: The Conquest of Ireland* (1189), edited by A. B. Scott and F. X. Martin (Dublin: Royal Irish Academy, 1978).

9. The outcome of these developments was famously captured and criticized in Edmund Spenser, *A View of the Present State of Ireland* (1596), edited by W. L. Renwick (Oxford: Oxford University Press, 1970).

10. See chapter 1 by Jane Ohlmeyer.

11. Conrad Russell, *The Fall of the British Monarchies, 1637–1642* (Oxford: Oxford University Press, 1991); J.G.A. Pocock, "The British Archipelago and the War of the Three Kingdoms," in Brendan Bradshaw and John Morrill (eds.), *The British Problem, c. 1534–1707: State Formation in the Atlantic Archipelago* (Basingstoke: Palgrave, 1996).

12. Peter Heather, *Empires and Barbarians: Migration, Development and the Birth of Europe* (Basingstoke: Macmillan 2009); Robert Bartlett, *The Making of Europe: Conquest, Colonization and Cultural Change, 950–1350* (London: Allen Lane, 1993).

13. Mark Greengrass (ed.), *Conquest and Coalescence: The Shaping of the State in Early Modern Europe* (London: Edward Arnold, 1991).

14. Charles W. Ingrao and Franz A. J. Szabo, "Introduction," in Charles W. Ingrao and Franz A. J. Szabo (eds.), *The Germans and the East* (West Lafayette, IN: Purdue University Press, 2008).

15. R.J.W. Evans, *The Making of the Habsburg Monarchy, 1550–1700: An Interpretation* (Oxford: Oxford University Press, second ed., 1984), chapters 2 and 6.

16. William Petty, *The Political Anatomy of Ireland*, (1672) in *The Economic Writings of Sir William Petty* (Fairfield, NJ: Augustus M. Kelly, 1986), pp. 157–159.

17. On the European context, see Ian McBride, *Eighteenth-Century Ireland: Isle of Slaves* (Dublin: Gill and Macmillan, 2009), chapter 1.

18. The dating here is according to the Julian calendar. The new style date is July 11, though the battle is usually celebrated on the twelfth.

19. Petty, *Political Anatomy*, p. 154.

20. See chapter 2 by Ultán Gillen.

21. George Berkeley, *The Querist* (1735–1737), in *The Works of George Berkeley*, edited by Alexander Campbell Fraser (Oxford: Oxford University Press, 1901), 4 vols., IV, p. 433: "Whether one may not be allowed to conceive and suppose a society, or nation of human creatures, clad in woolen cloths and stuffs, eating good bread, beef, and mutton, poultry, and fish, in great plenty, drinking ale, mead, and cider, inhabiting great houses, built of brick and marble, taking their pleasure in their parks and gardens, depending on no foreign imports either for food or raiment?"

22. On the intellectual culture of the period, see chapter 7 by Daniel Carey.

23. Edmund Burke to the Rev. Thomas Hussey, May 18, 1795, *The Correspondence of Edmund Burke*, edited by Thomas W. Copeland (Chicago: University of Chicago Press, 1958–1978), 10 vols., VIII, p. 246.

24. Adam Smith, *An Inquiry into the Nature and Causes of the Wealth of Nations*, edited by R. H. Campbell and A. S. Skinner (Indianapolis, IN: Liberty Fund, 1976), 2 vols., II, p. 944.

25. Most recently in Paul Bew, *Ireland: The Politics of Enmity, 1789–2006* (Oxford: Oxford University Press, 2007).

26. Gustave de Beaumont, *Ireland*, edited by W. C. Taylor (Cambridge, MA: Harvard University Press, 2006), p. 134.

27. On this distinction see, conveniently, Hanna Fenichel Pitkin, *The Concept of Representation* (Berkeley and Los Angeles: University of California Press, 1967), chapter 8.

28. See chapter 3 by John Bew.

29. See chapter 19 by Matthew Kelly. For the intellectual context, see also chapter 8 by David Dwan.

30. For nuances along the spectrum, see Colin W. Reid, "'An Experiment in Constructive Unionism': Isaac Butt, Home Rule and Federalist Political Thought during the 1870s," *English Historical Review* 129: 537 (April 2014), pp. 332–361.

31. See chapter 16 by Marc Mulholland.

32. See chapter 17 by Ciara Boylan.

33. Cormac Ó Gráda, *Ireland: A New Economic History, 1780–1939* (Oxford: Oxford University Press, 1995).

34. For the wider European context, see Franco Venturi, *Roots of Revolution: A History of Populist and Socialist Movements in Nineteenth-Century Russia*, translated by Francis Haskell (New York: Alfred Knopf, 1960); Patrick H. Hutton, *The Cult of the Revolutionary Tradition: The Blanquists in French Politics, 1864–1893* (Berkeley and Los Angeles: University of California Press, 1981).

35. Louis Antoine Léon de Saint-Just, "Rapport sur la nécessité de déclarer le gouvernement révolutionnaire jusqu'à la paix" in *Oeuvres Complètes de Saint-Just*, edited by Charles Vellay (Paris: Charpentier and Fasquelle, 1908), 2 vols., II, p. 88: "Le gouvernement provisoire de la France est révolutionnaire jusqu'à la paix."

36. For differing accounts of the priority of economics and politics in the context of agrarian agitation in Ireland, see James S. Donnelly, Jr., *The Land and the People in Nineteenth-Century Cork: The Rural Economy and the Land Question* (London: Routledge & Kegan Paul, 1975); K. Theo Hoppen, *Elections, Politics, and Society in Ireland, 1832–1885* (Oxford: Oxford University Press, 1984); Philip Bull, *Land, Politics and Nationalism: A Study of the Irish Land Question* (Dublin: Gill and Macmillan, 1996).

37. James Harrington, *The Commonwealth of Oceana* (1656) in *The Political Works of James Harrington*, edited by J.G.A. Pocock (Cambridge: Cambridge University Press, 1977).

38. K. H. Connell, *The Population of Ireland, 1780–1845* (Oxford: Oxford University Press, 1950).

39. For an overview, see Maura Cronin, *Agrarian Protest in Ireland, 1750–1960* (Dundalk, Ireland: Dundalgan Press, 2012). On Irish ranch farming, see David Seth Jones, *Graziers, Land Reform, and Political Conflict in Ireland* (Washington, DC: Catholic University of America Press, 1995).

40. Twentieth-century developments are traced in Terence Dooley, *"The Land for the People": The Land Question in Independent Ireland* (Dublin: University College Dublin Press, 2004).

41. See Joseph Lee, *The Modernisation of Irish Society, 1848–1918* (Dublin: Gill and Macmillan, 1973), chapters 2–3.

42. See chapter 15 by Catriona Kennedy. For general comment on the change of women's fortunes in the twentieth century, see Peter Laslett, *The World We Have Lost Further Explored* (1965; London: Routledge, 2000), pp. 269 ff.

43. For the Irish literary revival and its legacies, see chapter 9 by Lauren Arrington; for the Gaelic League, see chapter 13 by Vincent Morley.

44. W. B. Yeats, "The Irish Dramatic Movement: A Lecture Delivered to the Royal Academy of Sweden" (1923–1924), in William H. O'Donnell and Douglas N. Archibald eds., *The Collected Works of W. B. Yeats III: Autobiographies* (New York: Scribner, 1999), p. 410.

45. See chapter 4 by Fearghal McGarry.

46. See chapter 5 by Niall Ó Dochartaigh.

47. See chapter 18 by Andy Bielenberg.

48. J. J. Lee, *Ireland, 1912–1985: Politics and Society* (Cambridge: Cambridge University Press, 1990).

49. See chapter 12 by Ian McBride.

50. See chapter 10 by Maurice Walsh.

51. See chapter 20 by Maria Luddy.

52. Richard Bourke, *Peace in Ireland: The War of Ideas* (London: Pimlico, 2003, 2012).

53. See chapter 6 by Diarmaid Ferriter.

54. François Guizot, *The History of the Origins of Representative Government in Europe*, edited by Aurelian Craiutu (Indianapolis, IN: Liberty Fund, 2002), p. 20.

55. Guizot, *History of the Origins of Representative Government*, pp. 13–15.

56. On the Irish diaspora, see chapter 21 by Enda Delaney.

PART 1

NARRATIVE *and* EVENTS

CHAPTER 1

CONQUEST, CIVILIZATION, COLONIZATION: IRELAND, 1540–1660

Jane Ohlmeyer

OVER THE COURSE OF THE sixteenth and seventeenth centuries Ireland was conquered and colonized. Contemporary observers acknowledged the effectiveness of England's efforts. An early seventeenth-century Ulster poet, Fear Flatha Ó Gnímh, whose family had served as hereditary poets to the O'Neills, wrote a lament ("Pitiful are the Gaels"), which described Ireland as "a new England in all but name."[1] An anonymous pamphlet, dating from 1652 and presumably written by an English parliamentarian, noted how "we have fought to make Ireland English."[2] This chapter explores how, from the mid-sixteenth to the mid-seventeenth centuries, Ireland was conquered, "civilized," colonized, and commercialized. The military, political, economic, religious, social, and cultural initiatives that underpinned these overlapping and interconnected processes began in the 1540s with the passage of the Kingship Act (1541) and a series of surrender and regrant agreements. Thanks to an aggressive policy of plantation, these processes gained momentum during the early decades of the seventeenth century. With the completion of the Cromwellian reconquest and the mid-century revolution in landholding, a new order founded on English legal, administrative, political, landed, and economic structures, the English language, and English culture had become established. Out of this period of profound transition emerged the Protestant Ascendancy and, eventually, the modern Irish state. This was not a linear progression, nor was the outcome predestined. On the contrary, what this

I am grateful to the editors for their comments on an earlier draft of this chapter and to Dr. Eamon Darcy for his research assistance.

chapter highlights is the haphazard, messy, and clumsy nature of the processes surrounding state formation and the very real limitations on central power.

The passage of the Kingship Act in 1541 transformed Ireland's status from a patchwork of feudal lordships to an imperial kingdom. This "constitutional revolution" redefined relations between the English king and his subjects, especially those of Irish provenance who were now accorded the same rights as those of English origin.[3] Though Ireland was a kingdom in name the crown treated it, for much of this period, as a colony whose interests were consistently subverted by those of England. Fear of foreign invasion and concerns about domestic security drove English imperialism in Ireland, as did the determination to populate the island with English, Welsh, and Scottish settlers. Alongside this ran the desire to civilize and anglicize the Irish. Just as Ireland's constitutional status proved fraught with tensions and contradictions, so too were the policies of those who ruled the country. They ranged from some that favored the annihilation of the native people followed by the wholesale colonization of the island to others that promoted the assimilation of the resident population to the culture and religion of the metropole and the introduction of English political, legal, and economic processes. Whether aggressively pursued or not, there was nothing new in these calls for the civilization of Ireland, which dated back to the twelfth century. What distinguished the early modern state from its medieval predecessor was its ability to drive forward an imperial agenda in Ireland in a way not hitherto possible.[4]

James VI and I, who acceded to the throne of the three kingdoms in 1603, needed to capitalize on Elizabeth I's hard-won victory over the earl of Tyrone and his followers at the end of the Nine Years' War. To achieve this, the king sought to reform his unruly subjects, to tame the overmighty lords, to replace "thuggery and feuding" with "law and order," and to channel labor into production rather than destruction. He aimed to establish—at the national, provincial, and local levels—political, administrative, and legal control over all elements of Irish society. Closely linked to this was the determination to secure, wherever possible, religious conformity with the Church of Ireland. Alongside political subjugation and conversion to Protestantism stood cultural assimilation and the need to reform "uncivil" natives and to anglicize their "barbarous" customs, practices, and culture. Finally, the king wanted full control over Irish land. A combination of reform initiatives in the 1540s, 1570s, and 1580s together with official plantation and unregulated colonization transformed the legal basis on which land was held in Ireland and allowed the state to reconfigure Ireland's economic and tenurial infrastructure in accordance with English commercial and improving models, patterns of landowning, and inheritance practices (namely, primogeniture and entail).

The burden of implementing these imperial policies in Ireland fell to the chief governors, government officials, Church of Ireland clergy, and lawyers. The crown also created a "service nobility" or colonial hierarchy loosely modeled on the English aristocracy, akin to what the Habsburgs achieved in Bohemia and Lower Austria after 1620.[5] The Tudor peerage was small and had remained relatively stable for generations with dynasties of Anglo-Norman provenance predominating. During the first three decades of the seventeenth century, the crown embarked on an unprecedented experiment in social engineering. Two hundred and fifty-eight new Irish knighthoods were bestowed, "of which just under a third was awarded to men of Old English or Irish name."[6] Between 1603 and 1640, the resident Irish aristocracy more than doubled, from twenty-nine peers to sixty-nine. The number of Protestant peers increased tenfold over the same period, from three to more than thirty-six. Thus the crown created a new generation of ambitious and avaricious peers, usually Protestant and largely of English and, to a lesser extent, Scottish extraction, who were determined to make their fortunes in Ireland and to secure public reward and social recognition. These "new" lords joined ranks with established ones to form a composite peerage. As Ireland's leading landlords, politicians, military leaders, property developers, entrepreneurs, and philanthropists, these men exercised power and influence locally, nationally, and across the Stuart kingdoms. Land underpinned their status as cultural, economic, and political brokers and provided the wealth needed to sustain their rank. As a result, the aristocratic hierarchy ceased to be determined simply by the rank held by a peer or by other traditional criteria (such as lineage, regional status, or the number of followers over whom a lord wielded power). Instead, lordship came to reflect a peer's financial prowess, his ability to exploit his landed resources, his success in securing high office, and his ability to network at court in particular.[7]

The majority of these imperial agents were Protestant newcomers or converts. However, given the scale of the enterprise and the lack of central funds, Irish Catholics, especially members of the traditional social and ruling elite (many of whom were incorporated into the resident peerage) were encouraged to serve as exemplars of civility and, whether wittingly or not, they collectively facilitated the implementation of civilizing policies on their estates across Ireland. Yet their involvement in these processes also afforded them an opportunity to negotiate compromises that best suited their personal circumstances and political ambitions. Consequently, rather than being seen as passive victims, many Irish Catholics proved reactive and responsive to civilizing schemes. The fact that English imperialism in Ireland lacked any overriding, coherent, and consistent framework allowed some Catholics, together with many Protestant planters, to co-opt the colonial processes to strengthen their regional power bases and even to subvert the original civilizing agenda. As a result, multiple colonizations, occurring at a variety of levels, took place at different times and with varying degrees of intensity throughout this era. Hardly surprisingly, then, no neat imperial or civilizing model can be easily applied to early modern Ireland.

That the political, social, cultural, and economic practices of much of Irish society did not coincide with the norms of Lowland England prompted scorn among the English. The Irish were compared with the ancient Britons (whom the Romans had civilized) and with the Amerindians of the New World. Giraldus Cambrensis had consistently referred to the Irish as "a barbarous people," "a rude people" with "primitive habits," and as "living themselves like beasts."[8] Later observers appropriated this twelfth-century rhetoric. They included members of the Old English community, who had traditionally viewed themselves as the protectors and promoters of the English interest in Ireland against the degenerate native, Gaelic-speaking population. As late as 1614, David Rothe, bishop of Ossory, implored the Catholic synod "to eliminate barbarous customs, abolish bestial rites and convert the detestable intercourse of savages into polite manners and a care for the commonwealth."[9]

Protestant commentators also adopted a discourse of civility, which prevailed in Tudor England. Fynes Moryson, secretary to Lord Mountjoy, traveled extensively throughout Europe, North Africa, the Middle East, and Turkey but saved his greatest scorn for the "meere Irish," whom he regarded as filthy, rude, barbaric, wild beasts. Their women were drunken sluts. Other writers even failed to make a distinction between the Old English and the native or "meere" Irish: both groups were equally uncivil. Thus contemporaries clearly regarded segments of the Irish population as savages and barbarians who had failed to progress, to farm for their food, or to inhabit an ordered polity regulated by the law and Christian morality.[10] As the example of Bishop Rothe highlights, some Catholic writers shared these negative perceptions along with the desire to civilize, but they rejected overt colonization and other, more militaristic, manifestations of imperialism and strongly resisted attempts to associate cultural difference with political disloyalty.

But, of course, Ireland was different. Even by the mid-sixteenth century Ireland remained sparsely populated with widely dispersed settlements, few towns, and difficult internal communications. Pastoralism, especially cattle farming, formed the mainstay of the local economy, with herds moved to high pastures during the summer months, a practice known as transhumance or "booleying." From the perspective of Lowland England, this consumption-oriented, redistributive economy remained relatively unsophisticated. Trade was limited to the exchange of raw materials. Nevertheless, the rudimentary economy played a critical role in sustaining the social and political infrastructure of late medieval Ireland.

A fragmentary patchwork of patriarchal septs (or clans) ruled the country. A small number of powerful Gaelic Irish and Old English overlords not only controlled their own territories but also collected tribute (in the form of military service, food, lodgings, and agricultural labor) and demanded submission from previously independent regions, thereby extending their political control and en-hancing their standing within their own lordships. A number of great dynasties—Desmond, Kildare, Ormond, O'Brien, O'Donnell, and O'Neill—predominated as they vied with one another to exploit to their best advantage the political geog-raphy of their estates and to bring lesser lordships under their protection. By the early sixteenth century there were two dominant factional networks, the Ger-aldines (Fitzgeralds of Kildare and of Desmond) and the Butlers (Ormond), which the crown attempted, with varying degrees of success, to manage in its effort to rule Ireland.[11] English observers were shocked at the extent to which Anglo Nor-man and Gaelic Irish lineages, by the sixteenth century (if not long before), had come together "in kin[d]red, alliance and affinities of bludd" and effectively shared many aspects of the same political culture despite prohibitions against doing so.[12] Rather than being the upholders of civility, critics held these lords to be respon-sible for the degeneration of Ireland into lawlessness as they pursued violent vendettas and became embroiled in factional feuding.

Certainly in the sixteenth century violence proved endemic and escalated into major risings, often led by nobles (Silken Thomas's rebellion of the mid-1530s, the earl of Desmond's of the 1570s, Viscount Baltinglass's of the early 1580s and the earl of Tyrone's of the 1590s). Each of these sixteenth-century rebellions had spe-cific causes, but each one also fed off the widespread lawlessness that afflicted Tudor Ireland. Because military might and robust baronial networks determined dynamic lordship, maintaining and sustaining an effective army became a priority for any sixteenth-century Irish lord. It also underpinned the social order, for a lord's followers were obliged not only to feed and house soldiers but also to offer military service themselves in return for his protection. This elaborate system of extortion, intimidation, and protection was known to the Old English as "coign and livery" and enabled individual lords to field substantial private forces. The rebellious earl of Tyrone and his Ulster allies, for instance, allegedly mustered two thousand *buannachts* (or native mercenary soldiers) in 1594 and between four thousand and six thousand ordinary swordsmen regularly enlisted for service dur-ing the later stages of the Nine Years' War (1594–1603).[13] Scottish mercenaries had long since supplemented these native soldiers and, between the 1560s and the 1590s, some 25,000 Scottish mercenaries found employment in militarized Ul-ster.[14] These mercenary troops received part of their payment in cattle. Since livestock, especially cows, constituted an important form of wealth, cattle raiding, particularly in the long winter evenings, formed an integral part of the local re-distributive economy. Moreover, a successful cattle raid resulted in the submis-sion of a territory, which enhanced the military and political standing of those who led the raids, bringing increased riches in the form of tribute.[15]

Despite the crown's dependence on securing the cooperation of local power brokers for effective governance, criticism of these "overmighty lords" was wide-spread.[16] Civic humanists like Sir Thomas Smith and Thomas Blennerhassett wanted to break the feudal ties that bound common folk to their lords and thereby facilitate Ireland's transition to a civil society.[17] Writers like Edmund Spenser and Sir John Davies particularly resented the power and influence enjoyed by the magnates who "exercise plain tyranny over the common people."[18] Spenser portrayed them as lawless and disloyal princelings, as forces of degeneration, as the principal obstacles to the implementation of government policies and Protestantism, and as upholders of an alien and subversive culture. Matters barely improved over the course of the 1610s and 1620s. The key difference was that these "opposers of justice" included the Protestant newcomers, as well as established lords, and men who were supposedly committed to a "civilizing" agenda. In May 1634 Lord Deputy Wentworth summoned a Scottish planter, Lord Balfour of Glenawley, before the court of castle chamber to account for the outrages he had allegedly committed while he served on an assize circuit. "I do not think there is such another tyrant in the king's dominions," wrote Wentworth, "who [is], utterly drunk with the vice of violence, [and] hath with unequal and staggering paces trod down his majesty's people on every side."[19] Despite these high-profile cases, the Dublin administration maintained that the situation did improve. On the eve of the 1641 rebellion, the lords justice boasted that "the great Irish lords, who for so many ages so grievously infested this kingdom, are either taken away or so leveled with others in point of subjection as all now submit to the rule of law, and many of them live in good order."[20]

For its part, the crown continued to expect the nobility to provide military leadership. The lords, especially the established ones, perceived themselves as a military caste for which service on the battlefield continued to be inextricably linked to a lord's public and private sense of privilege, honor, and virtue. Though the evidence is scare, lords appear to have maintained private baronial armies or retinues and exercised considerable military authority, which became very apparent after the outbreak of war in 1641 as they called their followers to arms, much as their predecessors had done.[21] As the seventeenth century progressed, Ireland remained a violent and highly militarized society especially when compared with its neighbors.[22] Moreover, thanks to the exercise of martial law, which was in operation in Ireland for much of this period, levels of state-sponsored violence were high as the crown and its agents used brute force to exercise power locally.[23]

In addition, the crown maintained thousands of English soldiers in Ireland. Between 1594 and 1599 36,000 troops served against the forces loyal to the earl of Tyrone, and between 1649 and 1651 the English parliament dispatched 55,000 men to serve in Ireland. The cost involved in maintaining a permanent military presence proved prohibitive and helps explain why the Tudors initially favored policies of limited conquest rather than all-out war. In the event the Nine Years' War (1594–1603) cost Elizabeth I nearly two million pounds, an astounding figure that almost bankrupted the English state.[24] That said, each English victory, especially in 1603 and 1653, brought with it a fresh wave of expropriation and colonial activity as the metropole exercised its military and political dominance.[25]

If fighting served as one central pillar on which Irish society rested, feasting was another. The importance in medieval Ireland of guesting (or of demanding hospitality from followers in a practice known as "coshering") and feasting as a public display of a lord's power over his followers cannot be overstated. Though coshering and providing victuals for these lavish feasts placed enormous burdens on followers, especially during times of dearth, these traditions enhanced a lord's standing and status within his lordship in much the same way that maintaining a large household of swordsmen, brehons (or lawyers), hereditary physicians, harpists, bards, minstrels, ballad singers, and storytellers (*seanchaidhthe*) did. In return for rent-free farms and other privileges, they entertained and glorified local lords and their followers. The government effectively suppressed the practice of guesting, but feasting and the provision of hospitality remained a central feature of Irish households and were intimately linked to a lord's honor and reputation, as they were in early modern England and Scotland. Key rites of passage—birth, marriage, and death—provided the occasion for lavish feasts. A text of the masque performed at the wedding of Lord Ridgeway's daughter in 1610 at Rathfarnham castle has survived, and an account of the masque performed in Lord Barrymore's castle in December 1632 is also extant.[26] On the one hand, these were reminiscent of the feasting culture of bygone years, but, on the other, they served as a potent reminder of the continued power and influence of a dynasty and the number of followers a lord might command. During the early decades of the seventeenth century, Gaelic lords continued to maintain large households and kept extensive retinues, which included bards, musicians, poets, priests, and swordsmen.[27]

II

The crown used a variety of devices—legislation, conversion, education, marriage, and the common law—to civilize and anglicize. Legislation that promoted English language, dress, and culture became law in 1537. This aimed to introduce "a conformitie, concordance, and familiarity in language, tongue, in manners, order and apparel" and to cast aside "the diversitie that is betwixt them [the English and Irish] in tongue, language, order and habite."[28] The act also outlawed the Irish language, the wearing of "glibs" (or long fringes) and Irish garments, such as mantles. Later legislation prohibited other Gaelic agricultural, social, political, and cultural practices, and the removal of Irish-speaking "tympanours, poets, story-tellers, babblers, rymours, harpers, or any other Irish minstrels" became a priority.[29]

As the introduction of legislation highlights, great emphasis was placed on the promotion of the English language, which was perceived as an important instrument of empire. During the early decades of the seventeenth century, the use of English increased substantially. By the mid-seventeenth century, bilingualism appears to have been common, and it is likely that one person literate in English lived in each community.[30] Cultural exchange and "cultural hybridity" occurred throughout the country.[31] There are examples of English verse containing Irish words or awkwardly translated phrases from Irish (and vice versa), a fact that illustrates the crossover between the two languages.[32] While English was the language of government, the courts, property, and commerce, a significant proportion of the population, especially ordinary people, continued to speak Irish for much of the early modern period.[33]

By the mid-sixteenth century Protestantism had become a further key index of civilization. The Reformation had, however, failed to convert the Catholic majority to Protestantism.[34] After 1603 James VI and I set out both to revitalize and reform the Church of Ireland with a view to persuading, rather than coercing, the Catholic population to conform. As the Elizabethan clergy died out, he replaced them with able English and Scottish prelates, and by 1625 only three out of twenty-five bishops were of Irish provenance. Since the desire to convert the Irish to the established church often drove colonial impulses, James used Protestant clergymen to spearhead imperial initiatives, much as his Tudor predecessors had done. By 1641 the Church of Ireland had a full complement of bishops who attempted, under the watchful eye of Archbishop Laud, a root-and-branch reform of the fabric and personnel of the church.[35] It remained, however, woefully underresourced, with an insufficient number of ministers to service the church's approximately 2,500 parishes.

In contrast, the Catholic Church went from strength to strength, albeit operating as an underground and clandestine organization. There were thirty Catholic dioceses, and in 1641 fifteen bishops lived in Ireland.[36] It is not known how many recusant clergy ministered to the Irish population, the majority of which was Catholic. Estimates suggest that eight hundred secular clergy and three hundred members of religious orders (largely Dominicans, Franciscans, and Jesuits) were active in Ireland by 1623 and that perhaps one-third of these people had been educated in continental Europe in Counter-Reformation seminaries.[37] By 1641 this number had risen to roughly 1,600 friars (about a thousand of whom were Franciscans).[38] Many of these clergy, especially those trained in Counter-Reformation theology in the continental seminaries, were skilled and experienced preachers capable of offering sermons in both English and Irish on topics that were both spiritually instructive and sufficiently familiar to their listeners that the key messages could be remembered and repeated.[39]

The threat from a resurgent Catholic Church was very real, and given the lack of resources available to the Church of Ireland, the crown did everything possible to secure high-profile conversions from Catholicism, which could result in a cultural reorientation and the introduction of anglicizing initiatives in a region, especially if the convert tried to persuade immediate family members to switch faith and thereby add credibility to the initial conversion. By 1603 there were three prominent converts to Protestantism: Lords Thomond, Courcy of Kinsale, and Ormond, who had been raised at court with Prince Edward VI. In the case of the O'Briens of Thomond, Henry VIII had elevated the Gaelic chieftain, Murrough O'Brien, to the earldom of Thomond in 1543, but it was not until the late sixteenth century that his great-grandson, Donough, the fourth earl (d. 1624), embraced Protestantism. During the course of his lifetime, the fourth earl transformed his vast Connacht patrimony. He sent his sons to Oxford and attempted to convert his kinsmen to Protestantism by offering to educate them. He also encouraged members of his extended family to intermarry with Protestant planters. This process of cultural reorientation was very real, but it took time, and even enthusiasts like the fourth earl of Thomond retained many of the vestiges of a traditional Irish lord. He may have been an improving and anglicizing lord, yet he, like his ancestors, remained a patron to the Gaelic literary classes.[40] In his will, Donough reminded his heir to nurture his native Irish followers, as well as the newcomers. Yet significantly, none of his successors shared the fourth earl's concerns for "the gentlemen and inhabitants of Thomond."[41] By the 1670s, Henry, the eldest son of the seventh earl (and great grandson of the fourth), urged his own heir "to cherish the English uppon his estate and driue out the Irish, and specially those of them whoe are under the name of gentlemen."[42] Thus, 130 years after the original surrender and regrant agreement had been signed, the metropole had finally succeeded in anglicizing this leading native dynasty.

As the Thomond example highlights, contemporaries recognized the significance of schooling as a means of promoting anglicization and Protestantism. Many advocated the establishment of parochial and grammar schools, thereby ensuring, as the Old English writer Richard Stanihurst put it, "to breed in the rudest of our people resolute English hearts" and make them "good members of this commonwealth."[43] According to Sir John Davies, only education could guarantee "that the next generation will in tongue and heart, and every way else, become English; so that there will be no difference or distinction, but the Irish sea betwixt us."[44] Given the fundamental importance of education in shaping young minds and securing religious and political conformity, the state monitored closely where the sons of leading figures were educated and when possible placed them in Trinity College, Dublin. Elizabeth I had founded Trinity in 1592 "to serve for a colledge for lernyinge whereby knowledge and civilitie might be increased by thinstruction [sic] of our people there, wherof many have usually heretofore used to travaille into ffrance, Italy and Spaine to gett lernyinge in such fforraine universities where they may have been infected with poperie and other ill qualities, and so become evill subietts."[45] Oxford, far from the interference of potentially subversive family members, was an even better destination for young Catholic lords whom the king wanted to "civilize." For others the Inns of Court in London served as an exclusive finishing school where young men "may learn qualities fit for a gentle-man."[46] Of course, the education of Catholic heirs was contested. The crown did everything possible to educate them in the Protestant faith, while their fathers and close kin, supported by the clergy, resisted this and if possible dispatched their sons to one of the continental colleges (by 1800 there were forty-one Irish semi-naries and convents across Europe).[47]

In the instances where a lord died leaving a minor, the crown enjoyed even greater control, as the king became responsible for the heir's education and mate-rial welfare.[48] The premature death of a father facilitated the conversion to Prot-estantism of the heirs to the most prestigious and powerful houses of Ormond and Kildare, together with some lesser noble families. When Viscount Thurles died in 1619, his mother placed James, later duke of Ormond, in the Catholic school in Finchley. The king removed young James to the care of George Abbot, archbishop of Canterbury, who raised him as a Protestant. Lord Deputy Went-worth maintained that if Ormond had been reared "under the wing of his own parents," he would have been Catholic like his brothers and sisters. "Whereas now he is a firm Protestant, like to prove a great and able servant to the crowne, and a great assistant ... in the civill government; it being most certaine that no people under the sunne are more apt to be of the same religion with their great lords as the Irish be."[49] The most important pre-war wardship was that of the house of Kildare. The king awarded the wardship of eight-year-old George, sixteenth earl, to the former's favorite, the duke of Lennox. With Lennox's death, the earl of Cork took over Kildare's wardship, promising to revive the family fortunes and "em-ploy all my best endeavours, to reduce [the lineage] to its former lustre."[50] This and the subsequent marriage (August 15, 1630) of the young earl to Cork's daughter, Joan, reinforced the Protestant credentials of the Kildare dynasty.

The central role that both wardship and marriage played in securing key con-versions during the late sixteenth and early seventeenth centuries cannot be over-stated. Marriages across religious boundaries, which helped to forge economic, social, and cultural assimilation, occurred regularly, especially among members of the elite.[51] In 1651 and 1653 the Cromwellian authorities prohibited intermar-riage between Catholics and Protestants, and in 1658 the Catholic synod did like-wise. This suggests that mixed marriages continued to be widespread.[52] Contem-porary observers were conscious of the extent to which marriage with an English woman served as a means of anglicization. Writing in the early 1670s, Sir Wil-liam Petty suggested that marriage between Irish men and English women would facilitate "the transmuting one People into the other, and the thorough and last-ing union of interests upon natural and lasting principles." Petty suggested the exchange of women would, as one historian has observed, "prevent a generation of poor Irish men from marrying poor Irish women, substituting English brides in their place." This would allow the Irish men to embrace English women, who would then raise their children, teach them the English language, culture, and manners and ideally impart the "English religion (though this mattered somewhat less)."[53] In practice, these unions could—and did, especially among the elite—promote assimilation and help make Ireland English.[54]

Of course, under the pressures of war and rebellion, some converts reverted to Catholicism. Despite spending a year at Trinity under Lord Deputy Wentworth's watchful eye and having a Protestant mother, William Bourke, fifth baron of Castle Connell, married a Catholic and took an active role in the 1641 rebellion.[55] One particularly prominent convert was the great parliamentary commander in Ireland Murrough O'Brien, Lord Inchiquin. Born a Catholic, Murrough was ten years old when his father died. Sir William St. Leger, lord president of Munster, took charge of the young man and in 1635 married him to his daughter Elizabeth, having first secured his conversion to Protestantism. Inchiquin reverted to Catholicism in 1657. A personal crisis associated with a serious illness appears to have triggered his conversion, the sincerity of which was not questioned even by hostile commentators.[56] Inchiquin's wife was furious and tried (unsuccessfully, as it transpired) to prevent her husband raising their younger sons as Catholics.[57] His heir, however, conformed, and the lineage remained Protestant. In short, the state used every opportunity and a variety of devices—especially education, wardship, and marriage—to convert lords to the "English religion" and did so with considerable success. By the end of the seventeenth century, most of the leading aristocratic lineages—Clanricarde, Inchiquin, Kildare, Ormond, and Thomond, along with such lesser lords as the Courcys of Kinsale, Dillons of Roscommon, Plunketts of Dunsany, and the St. Lawrences of Howth—had espoused the established church.[58]

Important though education and conversion were to contemporaries, it was the introduction of English common law throughout the island that became the critical prerequisite for the civilization of Ireland and served as the platform from which imperial initiatives could be launched. This was nothing new. From the twelfth century the English kings had attempted to impose the English legal system on Ireland and had introduced a court structure modeled on that of England. From the mid-sixteenth century the state set out with renewed vigor to assert law and order by attacking the military systems on which lordly power rested and by pressuring lords, Old English and native Irish alike, to accept royal authority. Accordingly, legislation proscribed the collection of tribute, cattle raiding, and the maintenance of armed retainers, and it mandated that all lawsuits be settled by English common law, in an attempt to bring the people to "the obedience of English law and the English empire."[59] Equally significant, an "Act for Shiring Ireland" (1569) signaled "the arrival of English property law," the primacy of primogeniture, and the introduction of a culture of "improvement."[60]

After 1603 James VI and I favored reforming initiatives that promoted the maintenance of law and order and minimized the exercise of private violence. It was the law, as his attorney general John Davies noted, that would make Ireland English. A system of courts replicated the English judicial hierarchy. The high court of parliament sat irregularly. The four central courts—exchequer, chancery, king's bench, and common pleas—functioned effectively and were located in Dublin castle, along with the court of castle chamber, which was the judicial arm of the Irish privy council. A parallel structure of prerogative courts—the court of wards and the commission for the remedy of defective titles—emerged in part as a response to the uncertainties associated with a period of war and plantation. Assize and presidency courts were established as part of the surrender and regrant process and provided justice in the localities, alongside manorial courts. By 1624 the country had, one recent scholar suggested, a "full establishment of justices of the peace, constables, sub-sheriffs, bailiffs, gaolers, portreeves, recorders, sovereigns and other local functionaries essential to the task of carrying out litigation."[61] In 1621 James VI and I boasted to his English House of Commons that Ireland had never been more orderly. It had been "one of his masterpieces to reform it."[62]

Despite complaints about the cumbersome nature of the judicial system and gripes about the corruptness of individual lawyers, judges, and juries, levels of litigation appear to have increased significantly, and this, in turn, can be linked to the decline in private violence. Analysis of 415 individual Dublin chancery recognizances dating from 1627 to 1634 reveals that litigants embraced every ethnic and religious group living in early modern Ireland.[63] That a disproportionately large number of Catholic Gaels appear in these legal records is particularly significant and indicates that chancery also acted as a forum whereby suits arising from English common law and Gaelic customary law could be mediated. In other words, the native Irish looked to the common law as a lesser of two evils and as a means of protecting themselves from the traditional obligations associated with the fighting and feasting culture (discussed in section I).[64]

From the crown's perspective, the commitment of local lords to the enforcement of law and the provision of justice was of paramount importance to effective governance. Across early modern Europe, rulers entered into partnership with noblemen, who wielded significant authority in their own localities; Ireland was no exception.[65] James VI and I might have fulminated against the lawlessness of his nobles and twisted traditional, baronial rivalries to his own advantage, but he nonetheless realized that effective and inexpensive royal government would prove impossible without their collaboration. He rewarded loyal administrative, legal, and military service with titles of honor and expected established peers to serve as his counselors and military officers. In fact the system of governing distant and difficult areas through the appointment of a lord president and provincial council dated from 1569 (in Connacht) and 1570 (in Munster). With an army and a large number of officials at his disposal, the lord president enjoyed absolute authority in his own province, and his commissions gave extensive powers, embracing civil, criminal, and ecclesiastical jurisdiction and the innovation of martial law. The presidents appointed their own councils, akin to the councils of the Marches of

Wales or of the North of England, which involved another layer of local grandees, usually of New English provenance. The council book for the province of Munster survives and vividly recaptures the extent to which the council acted as "civilizing" agent as it brought law and order to the province; inculcated English tenurial, economic, educational, cultural, and social practices; and promoted Protestantism. In 1615 the king ordered the council of Munster and Lord President Thomond to cherish "the reformed and civill sorte of subjects" and to instruct the "ignorant and disobedient ... to imbrace knowledge and civillitie."[66] The earl of Clanricarde, lord president of Connacht, received a similar set of instructions.[67] Regional governors were expected to pursue a comparable "civilizing" agenda.

That those who held office were required to take the oath of supremacy was a major grievance and the cause of considerable tensions. Many members of the Catholic ruling elite resented the very real diminution of their influence that occurred as the crown promoted Protestant parvenus. Richard Bellings justified their involvement in the 1641 rebellion on the grounds that they were denied adequate opportunity to serve the king.[68] For its part, the Dublin administration grumbled that the king promoted the interests of the Catholics, especially those who exercised very real influence at court, but had no alternative than to accept this. The compromise that the limited co-option of the Catholic power brokers represented might have proved distasteful to some Protestants, but it nevertheless reflected the realities involved in ruling seventeenth-century Ireland.

III

Land was the basis for political power in seventeenth-century Ireland. Land, inherited through the practice of primogeniture when property passed from a father to his legitimate male heir, also provided the wealth that sustained a lineage. The dissolution of the monasteries (1536–1542), the rebellions of the sixteenth century, and the wars of the seventeenth century resulted in large swaths of Irish land being expropriated and redistributed by the crown to favorites, clients, the "deserving," and those who needed to be paid off. In addition, numerous opportunities—informal land transfers through widespread mortgages and sales—allowed for the purchase of cheap land and facilitated upward social mobility. Greedy speculators of all creeds and backgrounds grabbed lands where they could, which allowed for the creation of vast estates held by a variety of tenures and titles. Whether Catholic or Protestant, native or newcomer, the elite aspired to accumulate landed resources. The widespread adoption of entails—whereby land was settled on a number of persons in succession, so that it could not be bequeathed at pleasure by any one possessor—created relatively stable landed bases and allowed for the emergence of powerful and enduring landed dynasties.[69]

The creation of a landed elite in Ireland represented a significant departure from the medieval past, when status and influence were determined by the number of followers who owed loyalty to a lord, rather than by the size of his estates. Moreover in the medieval Irish system, land belonged to the sept rather than to individuals, and partible inheritance ("gavelkind") was the norm, rather than male primogeniture, which had resulted in the atomization of landholdings.[70] From the 1540s the crown negotiated "surrender and regrant" agreements with leading Gaelic chieftains. Land held by a non-English title was surrendered to the crown and regranted to its holder with title and tenure good in English law. The lord agreed to renounce his Gaelic title for an English one, to accept primogeniture as the basis for succession and inheritance, to recognize the king's writ and courts, and to promise to anglicize his territories.[71] By 1547 some forty Gaelic chieftains, including some of the most powerful magnates, had surrendered their lands.

The particular willingness of Gaelic lords to collaborate and compromise with the crown highlights the extent to which they were "in fact pragmatists concerned with maximizing their power and enhancing their reputation at minimum risk."[72] David Edwards's pioneering study of the FitzPatricks or MacGiollapadraigs of Upper Ossory, one of the middle-ranking Gaelic dynasties, offers a series of fascinating insights into Gaelic attitudes toward English rule and Tudor reform. In 1541 Brian FitzPatrick willingly surrendered his chiefly title ("the Mac-Giollapadraig") and lands, agreed to end the use of Gaelic practices, to adhere to the English common law (including primogeniture), to encourage his followers to use the English language and dress, and permitted his son, Barnaby, to be reared at court with Edward VI (where he embraced Protestantism). He was the first Gaelic chieftain to take his seat in the House of Lords. Despite the rhetoric of the agreement, "the barons of Upper Ossory remained cattle lords in the classic Gaelic tradition."[73] They embraced Tudor reforms as a means of minimizing English interference and of bolstering their own position within the lordship. In the short term, collaboration proved a very effective survival strategy.

Over time, these arrangements became increasingly sophisticated. Throughout the 1570s and 1580s, the state pressured leading powerbrokers to accept "composition" agreements, which sought to demilitarize the local magnates by appealing directly to their principal followers and enhancing the power of the state in the process. Thus, the Composition of Connacht (1585) promoted anglicization in the lordships of Clanricarde and Thomond and paved the way for moderate tenurial and political reform. Ultimately, however, it weakened rather than strengthened the position of the lesser landowners and enshrined in English law the "essential characteristics of the traditional lordships."[74] Thus, these reforming arrangements not only protected, at least in the short term, the estates of leading lords from confiscation but also represented an effective form of unconscious colonization.

Demands for more formal colonial enterprise and expropriation of native lords dated from the later Middle Ages. However, only after the Desmond rebellion of the 1570s did wholesale plantation win widespread acceptance. These windfalls, much like the dissolution of the monasteries in the 1530s and 1540s, provided the crown with an opportunity to hand out vast swaths of Irish land to their favorites or to reward with acres those who supported its wider civilizing agenda. Further rebellions, especially the Nine Years' War (1594–1603) and the Confederate Wars (1641–1653), resulted in fresh rounds of expropriation and colonization. The 1641 rebellion was a central military event, which played a crucial role in shaping the triple Stuart monarchy during the seventeenth century and triggered the onset of a decade of civil war in Ireland. Though Catholic Ireland failed to win lasting political autonomy, the 1640s was the only time before 1922 that Ireland enjoyed legislative independence and Catholics worshipped freely. In contrast, during the 1650s England dramatically reasserted control over Ireland. Cromwellian military victory after 1649, followed by English reconquest, paved the way for another round of expropriation on a scale that not even Edmund Spenser would have imagined possible.

Early attempts at plantation failed in Ireland during the 1550s, on the lands belonging to the O'Connors, O'Mores, and O'Dempseys in King's and Queen's counties. Similarly, in Ulster, efforts in 1571–1572 by Sir Thomas Smith (in the Ards) and the earl of Essex (in Claneboye) to establish private military settlements, which would provide bulwarks against the destabilizing influences exerted by the MacDonnells, ended in disaster.[75] However, after the outbreak of the Munster rebellion, plantation became an instrument of royal policy, and private enterprise was put to work for the purposes of state. In 1585, shortly after the first abortive English attempt to colonize the New World, the government announced an ambitious scheme that aimed to recreate the world of southeast England on the confiscated Munster estates of the earl of Desmond. Grants of land, ranging from four thousand to twelve thousand acres, were awarded to thirty-five English landlords (or undertakers), who undertook to introduce English colonists and to practice English-style agriculture based on grain growing. By the end of the sixteenth century, roughly twelve thousand adult settlers were actively engaged in farming.

The most avaricious and best-documented Munster speculator of all was Richard Boyle, later earl of Cork. A brief examination of his tenurial activities provides a glimpse of what other men on the make were doing across Ireland, albeit not on the same scale. In 1588 Boyle arrived in Ireland virtually penniless, and thanks to the patronage of Sir Geoffrey Fenton, who presided over the Munster confiscations and whose daughter Boyle later married, he secured the pivotal position of deputy escheator. This office provided Boyle with endless opportunities to identify, value, and lease confiscated lands, including those he secured for himself or allocated to his allies.[76] Cork, like the other Munster planters, was fortunate in that he had bought land cheaply in the aftermath of a decade of destructive warfare. Even without investment and improvement, land prices increased significantly during the more peaceful decades of the early seventeenth century.

Improving leases, which included provisions for building a house and enclosing land, were common, as was a requirement to support the militia.[77] Many of Cork's tenants were English. They in turn attracted English subtenants, who also built stone or timber houses and improved their holdings. These men and women brought with them the English language, dress, social customs, and agricultural practices. They helped make parts of Munster English. New English speculators with close contacts to the Dublin administration were ideally placed to subvert tenurial processes to their advantage. Those excluded from government were more vulnerable. Yet continuity of landholding among established Catholic lineages is striking, even in those counties that formed part of the Munster plantation.[78]

In the wake of English victory at the end of the Nine Years' War, Ulster met a similar fate to that of Munster. The unexpected flight of leading native Irish lords to the continent (1607) and the revolt of Sir Cahir O'Dogherty (1608) enabled the state to confiscate vast tracts of Ulster (encompassing present-day Counties Armagh, Tyrone, Fermanagh, Londonderry, Cavan, and Donegal). In particular, the flight of the earls presented the government with an opportunity, as one astute contemporary observed, "not only to pull down for ever these two proud houses of O'Neill and O'Donel, but also to bring in colonies of the English to plant both countries, to a great increase of His Majesty's revenues."[79]

After 1610 land was allocated in relatively small parcels (ranging from one thousand to two thousand acres) to three classes of grantees: undertakers, servitors, and native freeholders. The chief responsibility for plantation fell to the one hundred Scottish and English undertakers and roughly fifty servitors (largely English army officers who had settled at the end of the war, together with servants of the state) in the hope that they would create a British type of rural society. The undertakers were to take possession of their holdings by late 1610 and were obliged to plant twenty-four adult males (English or Lowland Scots) representing at least ten families for every thousand acres they held. Undertakers—who were to be resident for five years—and their tenants had to take the oath of supremacy, and no land was to be leased either to any Irish or to any person who refused to take the oath (this changed in 1622 when the Irish were permitted to become tenants on one-quarter of the undertakers' holdings). All articles concerning building, planting, and residence were to be fulfilled in five years. The servitors received land on the same conditions as the undertakers but could let land to Irish tenants, because there was no requirement to plant. The third group of grantees, the native Irish freeholders (or "deserving Irish," who had served the crown during the Nine Years' War), held their land in the same precincts and on the same basis as the servitors but were required to farm in accordance with Lowland practices. Additional acres were set aside to endow key civilizing institutions—the church, towns, schools, and Trinity College Dublin. Finally, the king obliged the City of London to colonize the entire county of Londonderry in an effort to bring capital and economic prosperity to a commercial backwater.

While significant numbers of Scottish and English settlers—roughly twelve thousand by 1622—were attracted to the escheated counties, the reality of the scheme failed to match the king's intentions. Many settler landlords did not construct the required number of buildings, or exploited their holdings for a quick return. Such colonists as John Rowley, initially chief agent for the Londoners, and Tristram Beresford, mayor of Coleraine, illegally exported timber and illicitly felled trees for pipe-staves, which they then sold. They set up breweries, mills, and tanneries without license, alienated church lands, and rented holdings at extortionate rates to native Irish tenants. More importantly, from the government's perspective, the settlement did not generate substantial revenue, and during the reign of Charles I, the wranglings over how the plantation in County Londonderry should be administered alienated members of the London business community at a time when the king desperately needed their support against his increasingly belligerent English parliament.[80]

More successful in attracting settlers was the informal plantation of East Ulster. James Hamilton, first viscount Claneboye, and James Montgomery, first viscount Montgomery of the Ards, royal favorites, dominated the colonization of County Down. Both men came from Ayrshire, the former the son of a minister and the latter the son of a local laird. In 1605 they carved up the estates of Con O'Neill, lord of Upper Claneboye and the Great Ards, in a tripartite agreement with O'Neill, creating a Scottish Pale. Their plantations quickly prospered, something that the cartographer Thomas Raven vividly captured in his exquisitely detailed, colored maps of the Claneboye estates.[81] Raven portrayed the varied nature of the land (meadow, pasture, moor); depicted how it was farmed and divided (the name of each holder is given); and showed the location of roads, castles, deer parks, orchards, houses, cottages, mills, harbors, and the prospering towns of Bangor (with seventy houses), Killyleagh (with seventy-five houses), and Newtown, together with other natural features, especially bogs and woods.

In neighboring County Antrim, informal plantations also flourished. With an estate of 191,629 plantation acres, the Catholic earl of Antrim was the largest landholder in Ulster and among the top three in Ireland. The first earl's meteoric rise in the peerage was largely due to his enthusiastic support for James VI and I's schemes for the plantation of Ulster. He would have been familiar with this concept, because he had been fostered on the Scottish island of Arran (hence his name, Randal Arranach) and thus exposed to James's unsuccessful attempts to "plant" the troublesome Highlands with Scottish Lowlanders.[82] Like Muskerry in Munster, Antrim recognized the economic advantages of the English system of landlord-tenant relations and of a commercial economy, both of which were introduced with the plantation. Between 1609 and 1626, he leased considerable amounts of land to Lowland Scots, and in a relatively short time, there was a thriving colony of Scottish Protestants living in the baronies of Dunluce and Glenarm.[83] The earl's farsighted policies soon paid off, and in 1629 it was noted that he "hath good tenants and is very well paid his rents."[84] The elaborate nature of the settlement and the scale of the first earl's investment were a tribute to private enterprise. On numerous occasions the king thanked him for "his services in improving those barren and uncultivated parts of the country, and planting a colony there."[85] For his part, Antrim was typical of Catholic Gaels, who quickly realized that, to survive and be considered worthy subjects, they had no alternative but to accept the new commercial economic order inherent in the crown's civilizing and improving initiatives.

In addition, the crown sought to tame "those rude parts" and at the same time enrich itself by interfering in land titles. In 1606 James VI and I established the Commission for the Remedy of Defective Titles, which, on pain of fine or forfeiture, required all Irish landowners to prove their title to their land. Many failed, which resulted in the redistribution of land in Counties Wexford, Leitrim, Longford, and parts of the Midlands between 1610 and 1620. After 1635 Wentworth also attempted, by interfering in land titles, to plant English colonists in parts of Clare, Connacht, and the lordship of Ormond. Ultimately, local vested interests, the tenacity of the Galway lawyers, and the courtly contacts of the local Catholic lord frustrated his plans, but not before he thoroughly alienated large sections of the Catholic population and thereby contributed to the outbreak of rebellion in October 1641.

Whatever form these landed initiatives took, they were underpinned by the need to develop a more commercially oriented, money-driven economy that privileged relationships between a lord and his tenant and focused on the production of marketable goods that could be exchanged for cash. The crown actively encouraged Ireland's transformation from a redistributive economy to one based on money, markets, and consumption as part of its civilizing mission by promoting the development of towns and urban networks. Towns, especially corporate towns on the English model, were regarded as key features of the civilizing and commercializing process.[86] Urban centers also hosted weekly markets and annual fairs. Between 1600 and 1640 the crown issued patents for 560 markets and 680 fairs. Sixty-five new patents were issued for new markets and fairs in south Munster, and in Ulster 153 patents for markets and 85 for fairs were handed out.[87] Irish towns, however, never became fully integrated into the rural economy and often depended for their survival on the activities and connections of local landed grandees. The civil wars of the 1640s shattered these baronial developments and totally disrupted the trade and proto-industry that had grown up around many of the Irish towns. Some never fully recovered from the ravages associated with the conflict; others had to wait until the late 1650s, 1660s, and 1670s before doing so.[88]

Across Ireland, colonial initiatives transformed the physical landscape. A frenzied program of building—castles, mansions, schools, churches, jails, roads, and bridges—together with extensive deforestation, the enclosure of lands, and the planting of orchards and gardens transformed the countryside, resulting in new patterns of rural nucleated settlements and the emergence of major urban ones.[89] An early seventeenth-century poem recorded the change in the Ulster landscape with "the mountain all in fenced fields / fairs are held in places of the chase / the green is crossed by girdles of twisted fences."[90] From the later sixteenth century, regional powerbrokers adopted English and Scottish architectural styles. In 1618 the fourth earl of Clanricarde spent £10,000 he could ill afford building a grand fortified house with mullioned bay windows and an ornate interior at Portumna, near Galway.[91] Though the outer buildings of the earl of Antrim's principal seat at Dunluce remained defensive in character, the inner great house resembled an English manor house with two-storied bay windows and leaded, diamond-shaped panes of glass. Without doubt these residences rivaled any of the other castles that mushroomed up across the country and were very richly furnished—presumably according to the latest London fashions.[92] These "great houses" transformed the physical landscape and stood as powerful testaments to the civility of their owners and the privileged position these power brokers enjoyed.[93] It is little wonder then that the insurgents targeted for destruction these fortified mansions and other symbols of the "improved" and "civilized" landscape after the outbreak of rebellion on October 22, 1641.

The rebellion broke out when the authorities thwarted an attempt to seize Dublin castle but could not prevent Catholic insurgents from capturing strategic strongholds in Ulster. Over the winter of 1641 and spring of 1642 the rebellion spread to engulf the rest of the country. The rising was accompanied by incidents of extreme violence as Catholics attacked, robbed, and murdered their Protestant neighbors. The Protestants retaliated with equal force in what became one of the most brutal periods of sectarian violence in Irish history.[94] The total number of men, women, and children who lost their lives in the aftermath of the rebellion or subsequent war will never be known. Yet it is likely that more people died during the course of the 1640s than in the rebellion of 1798 or in the civil wars of the twentieth century.

The 1641 depositions, which provide a unique insight into this particularly traumatic period of Irish history, record the events that surrounded the outbreak of the 1641 rebellion primarily from the perspective of the Protestant community.[95] In all, about eight thousand depositions or witness statements, examinations, and associated materials, by thousands of men and women of all social classes, amounting to 19,010 pages and bound in thirty-one volumes, are extant in Trinity College Dublin.[96] The depositions record the names of more than ninety thousand victims, assailants, bystanders, and observers and include references to nearly every county, parish, and barony in Ireland. They document losses of goods and chattels, military activity, and the alleged crimes committed by the Irish insurgents, including assault, imprisonment, the stripping of clothes, murder, and atrocities. In short, they reveal as much about debt as they do about death and recapture the biographies, hopes, and fears of ordinary folk, as well the extraordinary.

The 1641 depositions constitute the chief evidence for the sharply contested allegation that the rebellion began with a general massacre of Protestant settlers, something that Aidan Clarke has—after centuries of bad-tempered debate—finally disproved in a recent article.[97] What is immediately clear is the rapidity and extent to which law and order broke down, and people who had previously been neighbors, acquaintances, and even friends engaged in acts of violence against individuals and communities. As far as the English state was concerned, the depositions illustrated the great cruelties inflicted on the Protestant community by the Catholics and formed the basis for convictions in the war crimes tribunals of the early 1650s. In this sense, they must be seen, as William Smyth reminds us, "as documents of conquest."[98]

With the completion of the military conquest after 1649, England subjected Ireland to an unprecedented level of control. The land settlement of the 1650s represented the most ambitious attempt to plant Ireland at any point in the island's history. The Adventurers' Act (March 1642) began the process of expropriation by offering Protestant speculators 2,500,000 acres belonging to Irish delinquents. Legislation the following year allotted parliamentary soldiers serving in Ireland land in lieu of their pay on the same terms as the adventurers. To recompense these soldiers and adventurers, the English parliament stipulated in the Act of Settlement (August 1652) that virtually all land held by Catholics should be confiscated and that many of the dispossessed should be transplanted to Connacht.[99] The revolution in Irish landholding—which began with the plantations of the early seventeenth century and culminated with the Cromwellian and later the Restoration land settlements—resulted in the wholesale transfer of land from Catholic to Protestant hands and was one of the key developments that shaped the face of modern Ireland.[100]

IV

One government official, writing in the early seventeenth century, predicted that "the love of [money] will sooner effect civility than any other persuasion whatsoever."[101] He had a point. On the eve of the Irish rebellion of October 1641, indebtedness plagued power brokers—native, newcomer, Catholic, and Protestant—across the country.[102] When asked why he had wanted to rebel, Lord Maguire, one of the leaders of the 1641 rising, attributed his action to the "the smallness of my estate," which was diminished as a result of plantation, and to the fact that he was "overwhelmed in debt."[103] Maguire, like so many others, had engaged in an orgy of conspicuous consumption during the early decades of the seventeenth century and had mortgaged his estates to fund his spending. The Gaelic intelligentsia commented on the pernicious effect of excessive expenditure and the uncontrolled borrowing that it triggered and how it undermined their position and the traditional culture that they embodied. An anonymous verse, "Blazonry, My

Curse on Thee," ridiculed the Butlers of Mountgarret for their determination to keep up with the latest London fashions, wearing shirts with fancy collars, broad-brimmed hats, narrow shoes, cambric blouses, lace and silk fabrics, and elaborate hair adornments.[104] What a person wore made a powerful statement about who he or she was, and by the early decades of the seventeenth century, "the better sort" were, according to one observer, "apparelled at all points like the English."[105] The obligation to dress like the English, to speak English, and to live in English-style houses was part of the wider "civilizing" agenda, but the "love of money" that this triggered drove many into bankruptcy.

That a handful of prominent Catholic grandees embraced the crown's commercial and civilizing strategies should not suggest that the bulk of the native population shared their enthusiasm. On the contrary, many did not. Extant bardic poetry and vernacular verse help to recapture their responses to these civilizing processes.[106] Many members of the traditional learned classes, reeling in the wake of political (but not intellectual) collapse, clearly abhorred the changes wrought by colonial processes. Some bards criticized the "new methods of fortification, enclosure, and cultivation that followed the displacement of the native Irish by English and Scottish planters."[107] Poets condemned the workings of the Court of Wards, the central and local courts, or members of the Catholic elite who had converted to Protestantism.[108] Others vented their spleen against the newcomers, whom they regarded as lowborn thugs and as "English-speaking bastards" who were drawn, according to John Lynch, "from the barbers' shops, and highways, and taverns, and stables and hogsties of England."[109]

These writers, like the Ulster poet Ó Gnímh, who lamented that Ireland had become "a new England in all but name," may have been appalled by the changes wrought by military conquest and colonization, but they were powerless to stop, never mind to reverse, them.[110] On the contrary, after 1660, as London emerged as a major financial and commercial center and trade increasingly became a determining reason of state, Ireland's colonial status became more apparent still. Priorities shifted from conquest, colonization, and civilization to economic protectionism, but the reality of English imperialism in Ireland remained firmly grounded on English economic and political domination.[111]

FURTHER READING

For the standard narrative account of these years, see the chapters in T. W. Moody, F. X. Martin, and F. J. Byrne (eds.), *New History of Ireland, III: Early Modern Ireland, 1534–1691* (Oxford: Oxford University Press, 1978). For a more recent overview, see Sean Connolly's two-volume history *Divided Kingdom: Ireland 1630–1800* (Oxford: Oxford University Press, 2008) and *Contested Island: Ireland 1460–1630* (Oxford: Oxford University Press, 2007). For discussions of many of the key issues that dominate the early modern period, see the essays in Ciaran Brady and

Raymond Gillespie (eds.), *Natives and Newcomers: Essays on the Making of Irish Colonial Society, 1534–1641* (Dublin: Irish Academic Press, 1986); and Ciaran Brady and Jane Ohlmeyer (eds.), *Making Good: British Interventions in Early Modern Ireland* (Cambridge: Cambridge University Press, 2005). Particularly important for understanding Tudor Ireland are Ciaran Brady, *The Chief Governors: The Rise and Fall of Reform Government in Tudor Ireland* (Cambridge: Cambridge University Press, 1994); and James Murray, *Enforcing the English Reformation in Ireland: Clerical Resistance and Political Conflict in the Diocese of Dublin, 1534–1590* (Cambridge: Cambridge University Press, 2011). Colonial Ireland has been the subject of pioneering studies by Nicholas Canny, *Making Ireland British 1580–1650* (Oxford: Oxford University Press, 2001); and William Smyth, *Map-Making, Landscapes and Memory: A Geography of Colonial and Early Modern Ireland c. 1530–1750* (Cork: Cork University Press, 2006). The plantations have been well covered by Michael MacCarthy Morrogh, *The Munster Plantation: English Migration to Southern Ireland, 1583–1641* (Oxford: Oxford University Press, 1986); Raymond Gillespie, *Colonial Ulster: The Settlement of East Ulster, 1600–1641* (Cork: Cork University Press, 1985); and Michael Perceval-Maxwell, *The Scottish Migration to Ulster in the Reign of James I* (London: Routledge and Kegan Paul, 1973). The role that the aristocracy played in ruling Ireland is discussed in Christopher Maginn, "The Gaelic Peers, the Tudor Sovereigns, and English Multiple Monarchy," *Journal of British Studies* 50 (2011), pp. 566–586; and Jane Ohlmeyer, *Making Ireland English: The Irish Aristocracy in the Seventeenth Century* (New Haven and London: Yale University Press, 2012). For discussions of the wider imperial agenda, see the relevant chapters in Nicholas Canny (ed.), *The Oxford History of the British Empire*, vol. 1. *The Origins of Empire: British Overseas Enterprise to the Close of the Seventeenth Century* (Oxford: Oxford University Press, 1998); and Kevin Kenny (ed.), *Ireland and the British Empire* (Oxford: Oxford University Press, 2004).

NOTES

1. Bernadette Cunningham and Raymond Gillespie, "The East Ulster Bardic Family of Ó Gnímh," *Egise* 20 (1984), p. 108.

2. Anon., *The Present Posture, and Condition of Ireland …* (London: F. Neile, 1652), p. 7.

3. Brendan Bradshaw, *The Irish Constitutional Revolution of the Sixteenth Century* (Cambridge: Cambridge University Press, 1979), pp. 231–257.

4. Explored further in Jane Ohlmeyer, "'Civilizinge of those rude partes.' The Colonization of Ireland and Scotland, 1580s–1640s," in Nicholas Canny (ed.), *The Oxford History of the British Empire*, vol. 1 (Oxford: Oxford University Press, 1998), pp. 124–147; and Jane Ohlmeyer, "A Laboratory for Empire?: Early Modern Ireland and English Imperialism," in Kevin Kenny (ed.), *Ireland and the British Empire* (Oxford: Oxford University Press, 2004), pp. 26–60.

5. G. R. Mayes, "The Early Stuarts and the Irish Peerage," *English Historical Review* 73 (1958), pp. 227–51; and H. M. Scott (ed.), *The European Nobilities in the Seventeenth and Eighteenth Centuries. Northern, Central and Eastern Europe* (London: Longman, 1995), 2 vols., II, pp. 1–11.

6. Victor Treadwell, *Buckingham and Ireland, 1616–1628. A Study in Anglo-Irish Politics* (Dublin: Four Courts Press, 1998), pp. 105–106.

7. Jane Ohlmeyer, *Making Ireland English: The Irish Aristocracy in the Seventeenth Century* (New Haven, CT, and London: Yale University Press, 2012), pp. 34–50.

8. Andrew Hadfield and John McVeagh (eds.), *Strangers to That Land: British Perceptions of Ireland from the Reformation to the Famine* (Gerrards Cross, England: Colin Smythe, 1994), p. 27.

9. Cited in Treadwell, *Buckingham and Ireland*, p. 30.

10. Anthony Pagden, *The Fall of Natural Man: The American Indian and the Origins of Comparative Ethnology* (Cambridge: Cambridge University Press, 1982), p. 26; John Patrick Montaño, "'Dycheyng and Hegeying': The Material Culture of the Tudor Plantations in Ireland," in Fiona Bateman and Lionel Pilkington (eds.), *Studies in Settler Colonialism: Politics, Identity and Culture* (Basingstoke: Palgrave Macmillan, 2011), pp. 47–62; and *The Roots of English Colonialism in Ireland* (Cambridge: Cambridge University Press, 2011).

11. Ciaran Brady, *The Chief Governors. The Rise and Fall of Reform Government in Tudor Ireland* (Cambridge: Cambridge University Press, 1994), pp. 169–208; Vincent Carey, *Surviving the Tudors. The "Wizard" Earl of Kildare and English Rule in Ireland, 1537–1586* (Dublin: Four Courts Press, 2002); Christopher Maginn, *"Civilizing" Gaelic Leinster: The Extension of Tudor Rule in the O'Byrne and O'Toole Lordships* (Dublin: Four Courts Press, 2005); and "The Gaelic Peers, the Tudor Sovereigns, and English Multiple Monarchy," *Journal of British Studies* 50 (2011), pp. 566–586.

12. Quoted in Patrick Duffy, David Edwards, and Elizabeth Fitzpatrick (eds.), *Gaelic Ireland: Land, Lordship and Settlement c. 1250–c. 1650* (Dublin: Four Courts Press, 2001), p. 44.

13. Ciaran Brady, "The Captains' Games: Army and Society in Elizabethan Ireland," in Thomas Bartlett and Keith Jeffery (eds.), *A Military History of Ireland* (Cambridge: Cambridge University Press, 1996), pp. 144–147.

14. Allan I. Macinnes, "Crown, Clan and Fine: The 'Civilising' of Scottish Gaeldom, 1587–1638," *Northern Scotland* 13 (1993), p. 33.

15. Katherine Simms, "Warfare in the Medieval Gaelic Lordships," *Irish Sword* 47 (1975), pp. 98–108; Katherine Simms, *From Kings to Warlords: The Changing Political Structure of Gaelic Ireland in the Later Middle Ages* (Woodbridge: Boydell, 1987); Patricia Kilroy, *Fall of the Gaelic Lords 1534–1616* (Dublin: Éamon de Búrca for Edmund Burke, 2008).

16. Nicholas Canny, *Making Ireland British 1580–1650* (Oxford: Oxford University Press, 2001), chapter 2.

17. Thomas Smith, *A Letter Sent by I.B. Gentleman vnto his Very Frende Maystet [sic] . . .* (London, 1572), no pagination; and Thomas Blennerhassett, *A Direction for the Plantation in Vlster . . .* (London: Ed. Allde for Iohn Budge, 1610).

18. John Davies, *A Discovery of the True Causes Why Ireland Was Never Entirely Subdued* (1612; London, 1968), p. 219.

19. Jon G. Crawford (ed.), *A Star Chamber Court in Ireland. The Court of Castle Chamber, 1571–1641* (Dublin: Four Courts Press, 2005), p. 390; William Knowler (ed.), *The Earl of Strafforde's Letters and Dispatches . . .* (London: W. Bowyer, 1739), 2 vols., I, p. 245.

20. *Calendar of State Papers Ireland, 1633–47* (1901), pp. 275–276.

21. Rory Rapple, *Martial Power and Elizabethan Political Culture: Military Men in England and Ireland, 1558–1594* (Cambridge: Cambridge University Press, 2009); and Jane Ohlmeyer, "The Baronial Context of the Irish Civil Wars," in John Adamson (ed.), *The English Civil Wars* (Basingstoke: Palgrave Macmillan, 2009), pp. 106–124.

22. Roger Manning, *Swordsmen: The Martial Ethos in the Three Kingdoms* (Oxford: Oxford University Press, 2003), p. 18.

23. David Edwards, "Ireland: Security and Conquest," in Susan Doran and Norman Jones (eds.), *The Elizabethan World* (London: Routledge, 2011), pp. 182–200; David Edwards, "Two Fools and a Martial Law Commissioner: Cultural Conflict at the Limerick Assize of 1606," in David Edwards (ed.), *Regions and Rulers in Ireland, 1100–1650: Essays for Kenneth Nicholls* (Dublin: Four Courts Press, 2004), pp. 237–265; and David Edwards, Padraig Lenihan, and Clodagh Tait (eds.), *Age of Atrocity:*

Violence and Political Conflict in Early Modern Ireland (Dublin: Four Courts Press, 2007), pp. 69, 74, 105–106, 120, 127, 207–208.

24. Edwards, "Ireland," p. 188.

25. Scott Wheeler, "The Logistics of Conquest," in P. Lenihan (ed.), *Conquest and Resistance: War in Seventeenth-Century Ireland* (Leiden: Brill, 2001), pp. 177–207.

26. Brian C. Donovan and David Edwards (eds.), *British Sources for Irish History 1485–1641* (Dublin: Irish Manuscripts Commission, 1997), p. 270.

27. Ohlmeyer, *Making Ireland English*, p. 425.

28. *The Statutes at Large Passed in the Parliaments Held in Ireland (1310–1800)* (Dublin, 1786–1801), 20 vols., I, p. 120.

29. Edmund Curtis and R. B. McDowell (eds.), *Irish Historical Documents, 1172–1922* (London: Methuen and Co., 1943), p. 55; Raymond Gillespie, "Seventeenth-Century Irish Music and Its Cultural Context," in Barra Boydell and Kerry Houston (eds.), *Music, Ireland and the Seventeenth Century* (Dublin: Four Courts Press, 2009), pp. 26–39.

30. Brian Ó Cuív, "The Irish Language in the Early Modern Period," in T. W. Moody, F. X. Martin, and F. J. Byrne (eds.), *New History of Ireland, III, 1534–1691* (Oxford: Oxford University Press, 1976), p. 529.

31. Marc Caball, "Culture, Continuity and Change in Early Seventeenth-Century South-West Munster," *Studia Hibernica* 38 (2012), p. 38; and Marc Caball, "Gaelic and Protestant: A Case Study in Early Modern Self-fashioning, 1567–1608," *Proceedings of the Royal Irish Academy* C, 110 (2010), pp. 191–215.

32. Andrew Carpenter, *Verse in English from Tudor and Stuart Ireland* (Cork: Cork University Press, 2003), pp. 11, 210–211, 237.

33. Patricia Palmer, *Language and Conquest in Early Modern Ireland: English Renaissance Literature and Elizabethan Imperial Expansion* (Cambridge: Cambridge University Press, 2001); and James Kelly and Ciarán MacMurchaidh (eds.), *Irish and English: Essays on the Irish Linguistic and Cultural Frontier, 1600–1900* (Dublin: Four Courts Press, 2012).

34. James Murray, *Enforcing the English Reformation in Ireland: Clerical Resistance and Political Conflict in the Diocese of Dublin, 1534–1590* (Cambridge: Cambridge University Press, 2011).

35. John McCafferty, "Protestant Prelates or Godly Pastors? The Dilemma of the Early Stuart Episcopate," in Alan Ford and John McCafferty (eds.), *The Origins of Sectarianism in Early Modern Ireland* (Cambridge: Cambridge University Press, 2005), pp. 54–72.

36. Donal Cregan, "The Social and Cultural Background of a Counter-Reformation Episcopate, 1618–60," in Art Cosgrove and Donal McCartney (eds.), *Studies in Irish History Presented to R. Dudley Edwards* (Dublin: University College, 1979), pp. 85–117.

37. Patrick J. Corish, *The Catholic Community in the Seventeenth and Eighteenth Centuries* (Dublin: Helicon, 1981), p. 26.

38. Moody, Martin, and Byrne (eds.), *New History of Ireland*, pp. 380–381; Brian MacCuarta, *Catholic Revival in the North of Ireland, 1603–41* (Dublin: Four Courts Press, 2007), p. 235.

39. Bernadette Cunningham, " 'Zeal for God and for Souls': Counter-Reformation Preaching in Early Seventeenth-Century Ireland," in Alan J. Fletcher and Raymond Gillespie (eds.), *Irish Preaching 700–1700* (Dublin: Four Courts Press, 2001), pp. 108–126.

40. Bernadette Cunningham, "Political and Social Change in the Lordships of Clanricard and Thomond, 1596–1641" (unpublished MA thesis, NUI, University of College Galway, 1979), pp. 131–132.

41. Brian Ó Dálaigh, "A Comparative Study of the Wills of the First and Fourth Earls of Thomond," *North Munster Antiquarian Journal* 34 (1992), pp. 48–63, 61.

42. John Ainsworth (ed.), *Inchiquin Manuscripts* (Dublin: Irish Manuscripts Commission, 1961), p. 512.

43. Quoted in Raymond Gillespie, "Church, State and Education in Early Modern Ireland," in Maurice O'Connell (ed.), *Education, Church and State* (Dublin: Institute of Public Administration Ireland, 1992), p. 44.

44. Davies, *Discovery*, p. 272.

45. Timothy Cochran, *Studies in the History of Classical Teaching* (Dublin: Educational Company of Ireland, 1911), p. 56.

46. Reginald J. Fletcher (ed.), *The Pension Book of Gray's Inn I 1569–1669* (London: Chiswick Press for the Masters of the Bench, 1901), p. 295.

47. Ohlmeyer, *Making Ireland English*, pp. 435–442.

48. H. F. Kearney, "The Court of Wards and Liveries in Ireland, 1622–1641," *Proceedings of the Royal Irish Antiquaries* C 57 (1955–1956), pp. 29–68.

49. Thomas Carte, *The Life of James Duke of Ormond* (Oxford: Oxford University Press, 1851), 6 vols., VI, p. 214.

50. Public Records Office of Northern Ireland, D.3078/3/1/5, p. 3.

51. Ohlmeyer, *Making Ireland English*, pp. 187–189; Caball, "Culture, Continuity and Change," pp. 55–56; and Colm Lennon, "Religious and Social Change in Early Modern Limerick: The Testimony of the Sexton Family Papers," in Liam Irwin and Gearóid Ó Tuathaigh (eds.), *Limerick: History and Society* (Dublin: Geography Publications, 2009), pp. 114–118, 121–125.

52. Alison Forrestal, *Catholic Synods in Ireland, 1600–1690* (Dublin: Four Courts Press, 1998), p. 105.

53. Ted McCormick, "'A Proportionable Mixture': William Petty, Political Arithmetic, and the Transmutation of the Irish," in Coleman A. Dennehy (ed.), *Restoration Ireland: Always Settling and Never Settled* (Aldershot, England: Ashgate, 2008), pp. 123–139, quotes from pp. 126, 128.

54. Ohlmeyer, *Making Ireland English*, pp. 184–186.

55. Knowler (ed.), *The Earl of Strafforde's Letters and Dispatches*, II, p. 342.

56. Ivar O'Brien, *O'Brien of Thomond. The O'Briens in Irish History 1500–1865* (Chichester, England: Phillimore and Co., 1986), pp. 60, 91–92.

57. John A. Murphy, "Inchiquin's Changes of Religion," *Journal of Cork Historical and Archaeological Society* 72 (1967), pp. 58–68.

58. Ohlmeyer, *Making Ireland English*, pp. 157–168.

59. *Calendar of State Papers Ireland, 1625–32* (1900), p. 58.

60. Montaño, "'Dycheyng and Hegeying,'" p. 51.

61. Crawford (ed.), *A Star Chamber Court in Ireland*, pp. 28–58, quote is from p. 51; John McCavitt, "'Good Planets in their Several Spheares': The Establishment of the Assize Circuits in Early Seventeenth Century Ireland," *Irish Jurist* 14 (1989), pp. 248–278.

62. Maurice Lee, *Great Britain's Solomon. James VI and I in His Three Kingdoms* (Urbana: University of Illinois Press, 1990), p. 226; R. Zaller, *The Parliament of 1621* (Berkeley: University of California Press, 1971), p. 118.

63. Jane Ohlmeyer, "Records of the Irish Court of Chancery: A Preliminary Report for 1627–1634," in Desmond Greer and Norma Dawson (eds.), *Mysteries and Solutions in Irish Legal History* (Dublin: Four Courts Press, 2001), pp. 15–49; and Mary O'Dowd, "Women and the Irish Chancery Court in the Late Sixteenth and Early Seventeenth Centuries," *Irish Historical Studies* 31 (1999), pp. 470–487.

64. Maighréad Ní Mhurchadha, *Fingal, 1603–60. Contending Neighbours in North Dublin* (Dublin, 2005), pp. 36, 142–146; and Raymond Gillespie, "A Manor Court in Seventeenth Century Ireland," *Irish Economic and Social History* 25 (1998), pp. 81–87.

65. Scott (ed.), *The European Nobilities*, I, pp. 35–9; Keith Brown, *Noble Power in Scotland from the Reformation to the Revolution* (Edinburgh: Edinburgh University Press, 2011), chapter 6; and Gerald Power, *A European Frontier Élite: The Nobility of the English Pale in Tudor Ireland, 1496–1566* (Hanover: Wehrhahn, 2012).

66. Margaret Curtis Layton (ed.), *The Council Book for the Province of Munster c.1599–1649* (Dublin: Irish Manuscripts Commission, 2008), p. 240.

67. *Calendar of State Papers Ireland, 1606–1608* (1874), p. 485.

68. J. T. Gilbert (ed.), *History of the Irish Confederation and the War in Ireland, 1641–3* (Dublin, 1882–91), 7 vols., I, pp. 36–38, paraphrase is from p. 36.

69. Ohlmeyer, *Making Ireland English*, chapter 4.

70. K. W. Nicholls, *Land, Law and Society in Sixteenth-Century Ireland* (O'Donnell Lecture) (Dublin: National University of Ireland, 1976), pp. 4–10.

71. Bradshaw, *The Irish Constitutional Revolution*, pp. 193–230; Maginn, *'Civilizing' Gaelic Leinster*, pp. 63–90.

72. Duffy, Edwards, and Fitzpatrick (eds.), *Gaelic Ireland*, p. 45.

73. David Edwards, "Collaboration without Anglicisation: The MacGiollapadraig Lordship and Tudor Reform," in Duffy, Edwards, and Fitzpatrick (eds.), *Gaelic Ireland*, pp. 78–96, quote is from p. 84.

74. Cunningham, "Political and Social Change," p. 168; and Bernadette Cunningham, "The Composition of Connacht in the Lordships of Clanricarde and Thomond, 1577–1641," *Irish Historical Studies* 24 (1984), pp. 1–14.

75. Hiram Morgan, "The Colonial Venture of Sir Thomas Smith in Ulster, 1571–5," *Historical Journal* 28 (1987), pp. 261–78; Phil Withington, "Plantation and Civil Society," in Micheál Ó Siochrú and Éamonn Ó Ciardha (eds.), *The Plantation of Ulster: Ideology and Practice* (Manchester: Manchester University Press, 2011); Victor Treadwell (ed.), *The Irish Commission of 1622. An Investigation of the Irish Administration 1615–22 and Its Consequences 1623–24* (Dublin: Irish Manuscripts Commission, 2006).

76. Michael MacCarthy-Morrogh, *The Munster Plantation: English Migration to Southern Ireland, 1583–1641* (Oxford: Oxford University Press, 1986).

77. Canny, *Making Ireland British*, p. 318; see also pp. 318–326 and *The Upstart Earl: A Study of the Social and Mental World of Richard Boyle, First Earl of Cork, 1566–1643* (Cambridge: Cambridge University Press, 1982).

78. David Dickson, *Old World Colony. Cork and South Munster 1630–1830* (Cork: Cork University Press, 2005), pp. 14–15; MacCarthy-Morrogh, *The Munster Plantation*, p. 185.

79. *Calendar of State Papers Ireland, 1606–1608* (1874), p. 268.

80. Jane Ohlmeyer, "Strafford, the 'Londonderry Business' and the 'New British History,'" in J. F. Merritt (ed.), *The Political World of Thomas Wentworth, Earl of Strafford, 1621–1641* (Cambridge: Cambridge University Press, 1996), pp. 209–229.

81. Raymond Gillespie, *Colonial Ulster. The Settlement of East Ulster, 1600–1641* (Cork: Cork University Press, 1985), p. 56; Michael Perceval-Maxwell, *The Scottish Migration to Ulster in the Reign of James I* (London: Routledge and Kegan Paul, 1973), pp. 56–60.

82. Lee, *Great Britain's Solomon*, p. 212.

83. Perceval-Maxwell, *Scottish Migration*, pp. 231–232; Colin Breen, "Randal MacDonnell and Early Seventeenth-Century Settlement in Northeast Ulster, 1603–1630," in Ó Siochrú and Ó Ciardha (eds.), *The Plantation of Ulster*.

84. British Library, Additional MS 46,188, f. 120.

85. Constantia Maxwell (ed.), *Irish History from Contemporary Sources (1509–1610)* (London: G. Allen & Unwin, 1923), p. 301.

86. Raymond Gillespie, "The Origins and Development of an Ulster Urban Network, 1600–41," *Irish Historical Studies* 24 (1984), pp. 15–16. See also Robert Hunter, "Ulster Plantation Towns 1609–1641," in David Harkness and Mary O'Dowd (eds.), *The Town in Ireland* (Belfast, 1991), pp. 55–80.

87. Dickson, *Old World Colony*, p. 22.

88. Raymond Gillespie, "The Irish Economy at War, 1641–1652," in Jane Ohlmeyer (ed.), *Ireland from Independence to Occupation, 1641–1660* (Cambridge: Cambridge University Press, 1995), pp. 160–180.

89. Canny, *Making Ireland British*; and William Smyth, *Map-Making, Landscapes and Memory: A Geography of Colonial and Early Modern Ireland c. 1530–1750* (Cork: Cork University Press, 2006).

90. Maxwell, *Irish History*, p. 291.

91. Jane Fenlon (ed.), *Clanricard's Castle: Portumna House, Co. Galway* (Dublin: Four Courts Press, 2012).

92. Ohlmeyer, *Making Ireland English*, pp. 407–411.

93. Smyth, *Map-Making*, p. 383; and Montaño, "'Dycheyng and Hegeying,'" p. 57.

94. See the chapters by John Walter, Judith Pollman, Mark Greengrass, and Ben Kiernan in Jane Ohlmeyer and Micheál Ó Siochrú (eds.), *Ireland, 1641: Contexts and Reactions* (Manchester: Manchester University Press, 2013); and the chapters by Brian MacCuarta, Kenneth Nicholls, and Mark Clinton, Linda Fibiger, and Damian Shiels in Edwards, Lenihan, and Tait (eds.), *Age of Atrocity*; Joseph Cope, "The Experience of Survival during the 1641 Irish Rebellion," *Historical Journal* 46 (2003), pp. 295–316; and Eamon Darcy, Annaleigh Margey, and Elaine Murphy (eds.), *The 1641 Depositions and the Irish Rebellion* (London: Pickering and Chatto, 2012).

95. The 1641 Depositions Project aimed to conserve, digitize, transcribe, and make the depositions available online (http://1641.tcd.ie/) in a fully TEI (Text Encoding Initiative)-compliant format. It was a collaborative project between Trinity College Dublin, the University of Aberdeen, and the University of Cambridge working in partnership with IBM LanguageWare and Eneclann. The Irish Manuscripts Commission is publishing serially a twelve-volume edition of the 1641 depositions; edited by Aidan Clarke, vols. 1–3 were published in 2014.

96. The best introduction to the 1641 depositions remains Aidan Clarke, "The 1641 Depositions," in P. Fox (ed.), *Treasures of the Library, Trinity College Dublin* (Dublin: Royal Irish Academy, 1986).

97. Aidan Clarke, "The 1641 Massacres," in Ohlmeyer and Ó Siochrú (eds.), *Ireland, 1641*. Also see Eamon Darcy, *The Irish Rebellion of 1641 and the Wars of the Three Kingdoms* (London: Royal Historical Society, 2013); and John Gibney, *The Shadow of a Year: The 1641 Rebellion in Irish History and Memory* (Madison: University of Wisconsin Press, 2013).

98. Smyth, *Map-Making*, p. 115.

99. John Cunningham, "Transplantation to Connacht, 1641–1680: Theory and Practice" (unpublished PhD thesis, National University of Ireland, Galway, 2009), pp. 344–345, also pp. 212–219. Also see John Cunningham, "The Transplanters' Certificates and the Historiography of Cromwellian Ireland," *Irish Historical Studies* 37 (2011), pp. 376–395.

100. The precise amount of land that Catholics lost is the subject of debate; see Moody, Martin, and Byrne (eds.), *New History of Ireland*, p. 428; Kevin McKenny, "The Restoration Land Settlement in Ireland: A Statistical Interpretation," in Dennehy (ed.), *Restoration Ireland*, pp. 35–52. For the latest statistics, see http://downsurvey.tcd.ie/religion.php.

101. *Calendar of State Papers Ireland, 1611–1614* (1877), pp. 501–502.

102. Ohlmeyer, *Making Ireland English*, pp. 394–401.

103. Charlene McCoy, "War and Revolution: County Fermanagh and Its Borders, c.1640–c.1666" (unpublished PhD thesis, Trinity College Dublin, 2007), pp. 128–129.

104. John C. Mac Erlean, *The Poems of David Ó Bruadair* (London: Irish Texts Society, 1910–1917), 3 vols., I, pp. 133–138.

105. Quoted in S. J. Connolly, *Contested Island. Ireland 1460–1630* (Oxford: Oxford University Press, 2007), pp. 288–289.

106. Cunningham and Gillespie, "The East Ulster Bardic Family of Ó Gnímh"; B. O'Buachalla, "James Our True King. The Ideology of Irish Royalism in the Seventeenth Century," in D. George Boyce, Robert Eccleshall, and Vincent Geoghegan (eds.), *Political Thought in Ireland since the Seventeenth Century* (London: Routledge, 1993), p. 10; Canny, *Making Ireland British*, pp. 426–427.

107. Brian Ó Cuiv, "The Irish Language in the Early Modern Period," in Moody, Martin, and Byrne (eds.), *New History of Ireland*, p. 526.

108. Canny, *Making Ireland British*, pp. 428–431.

109. John Lynch, *Cambrensis Eversus*, translated by Mathew Kelly (Dublin: The Celtic Society, 1851–1852), 3 vols., III, p. 75.

110. Cunningham and Gillespie, "The East Ulster Bardic Family of Ó Gnímh," p. 108.

111. Nicholas Canny, "The Origins of Empire," in *Oxford History of the British Empire*, I, pp. 22–23.

CHAPTER 2

ASCENDANCY IRELAND, 1660–1800

Ultán Gillen

O N JANUARY 1, 1801, CHURCH bells rang out to celebrate the union between the kingdoms of Great Britain and Ireland coming into force that
day. A young Catholic barrister, outraged at what he saw as the violation
of the rights of the Irish nation, reacted to the sound with a mixture of disgust
and fury. Daniel O'Connell would later lead two mass movements that impacted
profoundly on Irish and British history, the campaigns for Catholic emancipation
and for the repeal of the Act of Union of 1800. As generations of Irish school-
children have been told, the bitter memory of those ringing bells inspired him in
later years. A perfect anecdote with which to begin a chapter on the history of
nineteenth-century Ireland, on closer examination it also raises the themes that
shaped Irish history in the period 1660–1800.

The accession of Charles Stuart as Charles II in 1660 saw the end of the brief
union between Britain and Ireland imposed by the Commonwealth regime. For
much of our period, the relationship between the two countries proved contentious,
culminating in the 1798 rebellion and subsequent union decried by O'Connell.
O'Connell personified several of the forces that shaped Irish history at this time.
A speaker of Irish and English, he came from a Munster gentry family that had
been dispossessed of much of its land. Catholics like O'Connell were barred from
practicing law for much of the period; the Catholic Relief Act of 1792 that opened
the legal profession to them reflected the growth of the Catholic professional
classes in the context of a developing economy, changing ideas about toleration in
the era of Enlightenment and revolution, and the increasing political power of
public opinion. Like the Act of Union itself, Catholic relief also reflected the strategic reality of a world in which Britain vied with France for global supremacy.

The connection with England, the ownership of land, religion, economic development, and war: these were the primary forces forging events in Ireland be-

tween 1660 and 1800. They were often so intertwined as to be impossible to separate, either for contemporaries or for historians. Each of them represented the legacy of earlier eras, but none of them was a static and unchanging influence; each was a dynamic, fluctuating, and contingent force. Like many other societies in the Atlantic world, Ireland found itself wrestling with the consequences of past events while at the same time dealing with the early development of the factors that would make the nineteenth and twentieth centuries so very different from what had gone before. By 1800, the power of monarchy, church, and aristocracy had begun to crack under the strain of economic change and the emergence of new forces in society, the realm of ideas, and political life.

The land settlement of the 1660s is the key to much of the subsequent two centuries of Irish history. In a society where ownership brought wealth, prestige, and power, the distribution of land was the central fact of political life; or it would have been, were it not for Ireland's connection with England. This relationship was ultimately the key determinant of Irish politics, and it dictated who won and who lost in the scramble for Irish land during the early years of Charles II's reign.

As the new regime sought to embed itself in Britain and Ireland, Charles II and his governors were faced with competing claims that complicated the already difficult task of coming to a modus vivendi with the formerly Cromwellian elite, whose support had made the Stuarts' return possible.[1] The scale of the land transfer following the Cromwellian conquest is staggering. Land was stripped from those who were loyal to the Stuart monarchy, overwhelmingly Catholics, and transferred to the Protestant supporters of the revolutionary regime. In 1641 Catholics owned about two-thirds of Irish land, with a third in Protestant hands. By the late 1640s, Catholics owned one-tenth. Many of the Cromwellian troops granted land simply sold it. Ownership of land was consolidated in fewer hands than before 1641. The Protestant elite that emerged from the Cromwellian conquest was therefore much more dominant than before. Its royalist and Catholic rivals had been militarily defeated and stripped of much of their land, wealth, and prestige. Land, overwhelming military force, and the state itself were placed firmly in the hands of Cromwell's Protestant supporters.

The re-establishment of the Stuart monarchy threw all this into doubt. The confessional nature of the state seemed open to question, and it was unclear whether the Stuart ruling elite would be composed mostly of Protestants or Catholics. Dispossessed royalists hoped to regain what had recently been theirs; the beneficiaries of the Commonwealth wondered how safe their holdings were. The decisions made by Charles II and his administrators about religious policy and land ownership in Ireland during these years shaped the island's religious, economic, social, and political future.

The land settlement occurred in three distinct phases. First was the Gracious Declaration of November 1660, whereby Charles effectively confirmed the Cromwellian redistribution, partly in recognition of the important role played by

Ireland's Cromwellian elite in placing him on the throne. The king pledged to be "very careful" of their interests, while also recognizing the loyalty of "a considerable part of [the Irish] nation" during his exile. The Declaration noted the "great perplexities" involved in trying to "reconcile these jarring interests," especially when it was impossible to start from scratch.[2] While the current proprietors were largely confirmed in their possessions, land was also promised to those who had fought for Charles I, and fifty-six prominent royalists—about a third of whom were Catholic—were restored to their estates. "Innocent papists" in general were also to have their lands returned. Protestants who lost out from the restorations were to be compensated with land elsewhere on the island. The Declaration calmed the nerves of anxious Protestant landowners, while disappointing the hopes of many Catholic royalists. The new monarch had placed his need for stability, especially in Britain, above the interest of his Irish Catholic supporters, and everyone knew it.

The Act of Settlement (1662) sought to implement the principles of the Declaration. The restored Irish parliament was overwhelmingly Protestant, making Catholic efforts to influence the bill at Charles II's court still more important (and sometimes desperate—Richard Talbot, who had served the Stuarts in exile, was imprisoned in the Tower for over-enthusiastic lobbying). The Act confirmed the essentials of the Declaration and provided for the establishment of a court of claims to judge the innocence of Catholics seeking their lands back. The court began sitting in January 1663, but the government halted its work in August. The reason was simple. Too much was being reallocated—almost 10% of the total. Growing alarm among Protestant landowners forced the government's hand. The lord lieutenant, the Duke of Ormond, a believer in aristocratic hegemony, was trying to balance his (and to some extent the king's) desire to see land restored to reliable families, including Catholics, with the need to placate the formerly Cromwellian elite, whom he regarded as "mean and low aspirers."[3]

The result was the Act of Explanation (1665). The crown had made promises it could not keep. In Ormond's words, "there must be discoveries made of a new Ireland, for the old will not serve to satisfy these engagements."[4] In an attempt to placate enough of the dispossessed without alienating the current owners, soldiers and adventurers were to be stripped of a third of their land to compensate those whose land had been restored to Catholics. A second court of claims was established, which worked at a slower pace than the first and did transfer a significant amount of land. However, new claims were barred. Those with powerful patrons, especially in London, did best at reclaiming or keeping land. By the late 1670s, about one-third of Irish land was in Catholic hands, down from two-thirds in 1641. The Cromwellian and Restoration land settlements, in the view of one historian, constituted a transfer of land "unprecedented in early modern European history." Hence, it has been termed a revolution.[5]

The land question was settled first and foremost with a view to stabilizing the Stuart monarchy, which unsurprisingly placed its interests in Britain far above those of its Irish supporters. The Catholic and Protestant proportions of land ownership had been reversed. The significance was unmistakable. Social and economic power had decisively transferred to Protestant hands along with the land. There was also an element of change in class power, with the traditional aristocracy now sharing power with men who originated further down the social scale, among the middling orders. However, we should not exaggerate the extent of this change. The nobility as a whole gained about a million acres and now owned 40% of the land. Although Catholic ownership had recovered to a level inconceivable in the Cromwellian era, many Catholic hopes for the new monarchy had been shattered, leaving a legacy of bitterness and disappointment. As the Gaelic poet Dáibhí Ó Bruadair put it, those Catholic nobles who had shared the king's exile were left "to gaze at their lands like a dog at a lump of beef."[6] However, many Catholics still harbored hopes that in the longer term the land transfer could be reversed, and that the state run by the Stuarts could be made to work more in their favor. Some Protestants feared they might be proved right.

Charles II favored a policy of religious toleration. Although some legal measures against Catholics remained in force and harassment of Catholic clergy sporadically occurred, the government sought to use Catholics to help stabilize the new regime. Dissenters also benefited from the toleration of the new regime, with the *regium donum* paid to Presbyterian ministers by the crown from 1672. However, toleration had its limits, and both Catholics and Dissenters were subject to repression on occasion, often amid fears of plots. The most famous example was that of Oliver Plunkett, Catholic archbishop of Armagh. During the Popish Plot scare, he was tried for treason but cleared by an all-Protestant jury in Dundalk. Subsequently taken to England, he was convicted and executed despite widespread knowledge of his innocence. Catholic Ireland acquired a new martyr, one who over the centuries often served as shorthand for both religious and national oppression.

In 1673 the English parliament at Westminster introduced a Test Act designed to exclude non-Anglicans from positions of power. James, Duke of York, Lord High Admiral of the Royal Navy and heir to the throne, refused to take the test, thus confirming suspicions he was a Catholic. Somewhat absurdly, while barred from naval command, he remained heir to the throne. The panic that the prospect of a Catholic monarch induced among some British Protestants soon manifested itself in such events as the Exclusion Crisis and the Rye House plot. The Stuarts were able to weather the storm, partly by Charles ruling without parliament for the last few years of his reign. When Charles died, James ascended the throne with great support, with parliament voting him a large income and Monmouth's rebellion easily defeated. Lacking a Catholic heir, James sought to use his time as king to improve the lot of Catholics in the three kingdoms and embed them in the state to such an extent that on his death, their rights and freedoms would be secure. In Ireland, many Catholics hoped that their moment had come. Nevertheless, the succession produced few problems in Ireland. "Everyone is planting, improving and trading ... which is a disappointment to those who do not expect to see the king proclaimed with such genuine joy and conformity," wrote one contemporary.[7]

How did joy give way to civil war within five years? Ultimately, the answer lies in English responses to the birth of a male heir in June 1688, which raised the prospect of a permanently Catholic dynasty. However, events in Ireland were also vital. James II's first appointment as viceroy was the Protestant earl of Clarendon. The king told Clarendon that he expected him to uphold "the English influence" in Ireland, and that although Catholics must enjoy full religious freedom, they should know "that he looked upon them as a conquered people," and that the land settlement would be upheld.[8] James hoped that his policy of religious toleration would gain him allies among the Dissenters, enabling him to base his rule on a wider cross-section of Irish society than his brother had. His determination to reward loyalty and bring Catholics into the administration was symbolized by his appointment of Talbot, later earl of Tyrconnell, to command the army in Ireland in June 1686.[9] Talbot had already successfully lobbied the king to begin appointing Catholics to prominent positions, including the privy council. The state was increasingly being opened up to Catholics, as James intended. However, once Tyrconnell was appointed lord deputy (but not lord lieutenant) in January 1687, he began to exceed James's intentions. Perhaps Tyrconnell was preparing for James's eventual death, and for an Ireland separated from England and Scotland under French protection. Whatever his long-term aims, he persuaded the monarch to back him that August. It was Tyrconnell's policies that finally alienated Protestant opinion from the monarch and ensured that the war of the two kings would also be effectively a religious civil war.

Tyrconnell swiftly began filling the army with Catholics. By September, they formed about two-thirds of the ranks and 40% of the officers. The exclusively Protestant militia was disarmed simultaneously. On becoming lord deputy, he expanded the number of Catholics in the state bureaucracy, and soon they had the majority in the Privy Council and on the bench. He then set his sights on the major prize, the land settlement. A new land act would be necessary, and a new parliament—a Catholic parliament—was needed to pass it. He set about procuring one. When parliament eventually met, the fact that 224 out of 230 members were Catholics testified to his success. Tyrconnell's preferred option was to split estates equally between the former and current proprietors, and James was persuaded to accept this. However, the Dutch invasion of England under William of Orange in November 1688 and James's flight to France and subsequent arrival in

Ireland with a French army had radically altered circumstances by the time parliament met in May 1689.[10]

That parliament—remembered variously as the Jacobite parliament, patriot parliament, pretended parliament, and popish parliament—sought to overturn the land settlement and thus Protestant domination of government and society. Moreover, it asserted Ireland's independence in terms that threatened England's supremacy. These demands reflected the interests of the Catholic elite. James II, anxious to prevent Irish developments reducing his chances of being restored to his other kingdoms, clashed with his Irish supporters even as he acknowledged their "exemplary loyalty."[11] Although an act was passed declaring that Westminster had no right to pass laws for Ireland and that English courts had no jurisdiction there, James prevented the repeal of Poynings's Law. A new law guaranteed religious freedom to all. Tithes were now to go to either the Protestant or Catholic Church as the payer preferred. However, not only did the Church of Ireland remain the established church, with its lands intact, the Acts of Supremacy and Uniformity were also merely suspended, not repealed.

On the land, however, the members of parliament got their way. The act repealing the Acts of Settlement and Explanation began by enumerating Catholic loyalty against Cromwell, the sacrifices made for that loyalty at home and abroad, and the failure of that loyalty to be adequately repaid. It was "high time to put an end to the unspeakable Sufferings" of the loyal Catholics; the only means of doing so was "restoring the former Proprietors to their ancient Right."[12] James II's consent for the bill had to be extorted by withholding financial legislation. Given the centrality of financial legislation in securing the regular meeting of parliament from 1692 onward, this perhaps suggests that had James and not William won, the powers of the Irish parliament vis-à-vis the king might have developed along broadly similar lines despite the supposed Stuart tendency toward absolutism. Political assumptions may have been more similar across the confessional divide than is sometimes realized. An Act of Attainder seized the property of 1,340 Protestants and threatened the same for exiles if they did not return and demonstrate their loyalty. James's response demonstrated the difference between the monarch and his supporters: "What, gentlemen, are you for another 41?"[13] The Irish Protestant memory of 1641 reflected in James's question itself came under legislative attack, with the act commanding official commemorations of October 23, 1641, repealed.

The sense of Catholic *revanche* was unmistakable. Although a small number of Anglicans stayed loyal, Protestants as a whole decided on resistance and to await help from Britain. The Siege of Derry was the most important act of defiance, at least in terms of historical memory. Part rebellion against a monarch, part religious civil war, part power struggle among competing sections of the elite, part local consequence of English events, the military conflict in Ireland was defined by the fact it was also a theater of a major European war. William invaded England to acquire the kingdom, because he feared it becoming a permanent and active ally of his bitter enemy Louis XIV, and because his struggle against Louis would be greatly strengthened by acquiring its resources. In the midst of the war between France and the League of Augsburg, he could not permit an Ireland ruled by James II and garrisoned by French troops. For a short period, Ireland became the main focus of his war effort, as multinational armies led by the Dutch and the French battled for control of Europe's western periphery. In one of Irish history's more entertaining ironies, the pope sided with the Protestant William rather than the Catholic James because of his disputes with His Most Christian Majesty, Louis XIV.

William dispatched twenty thousand troops to Ireland in 1689 but was forced to lead the campaign himself in 1690.[14] The two kings came into conflict at the Boyne on July 12. James fled the losing battle early, earning himself the Gaelic moniker *Séamus an chaca* (James the Shit). William's victory was not as decisive as James himself thought. The war continued for another year despite James's precipitate flight to France three days after the battle. William left Ireland in September. The decisive battle took place on July 22, 1691, at Aughrim, when the Dutch Baron Ginkel defeated an army led by the French Marquis de Saint-Ruth. Ultimately, the Williamite army was better trained, armed, led, and supplied, partly due to geography making logistics easier for William than for Louis, and partly because Ireland mattered much more to William than it did to the French king. The question was now how favorable the terms of surrender would be. As early as September 1690, one Williamite commander quoted the Irish Jacobite leaders as saying they were fighting not for king or faith "but for our estates."[15] If a deal could be struck that protected their possessions, then it seemed that a speedy conclusion to the war could be achieved. William, anxious to liberate resources for the continental campaign, supported such a deal, resulting in the lenient terms of the articles of surrender usually known as the Treaty of Limerick.

Signed on October 3, 1691, the articles of Limerick guaranteed Catholics the same religious liberties as had existed under Charles II. William and Mary pledged to encourage the next Irish parliament to legislate for this. Jacobites taking an oath of allegiance would retain the lands they had possessed under Charles II, and the right to bear arms was guaranteed to nobles and gentlemen. In other words, although lands acquired since 1685 would be lost, the Catholic elite would be free from persecution, even if they would not be full members of the political nation. The articles also provided for transport for those among the Jacobite army "of what quality or condition soever" who wished to go to France and serve Louis.[16] Around 70%, or fifteen thousand men, chose exile. With them went any chance of Irish Catholics fielding an effective military force for decades, although that is more obvious today than it was to contemporaries. As the Williamite army began to withdraw, the English government's desire to micromanage Irish affairs dwindled. Although government would be overseen by English appointees, the Irish Anglican elite had the chance to reshape politics to their liking due to their undisputed possession of parliament and the weakness of their rivals.

William's need to finance the war through tax and borrowing allowed the English parliament to develop a greater role than ever before, and it became a permanent feature of governance. In short, war had made it impossible to rule without parliament. A similar (though less comprehensive) development in the powers of parliament took place in Ireland. It too became a permanent institution. In part its enhanced status stemmed from fiscal need, in part the English example was influential, but the Protestant elite were also determined to control their own affairs as far as possible. This was a response to the articles of Limerick, which they saw as being too lenient, placing them at risk. "The pen's the symbol of our sword's defeat / We fight like heroes, but like fools we treat."[17] The experience of a Catholic-controlled Ireland and then war had been terrifying, even if fears of the attempted extirpation of Protestants had not been realized. The Protestant elite saw their own parliament as a vital bulwark, while realizing that ultimately their position depended on England's military might.

Like their Jacobite predecessors, the Irish parliament's members were also determined to assert their rights. The session of 1692 collapsed when the Commons asserted its sole right to initiate money bills, and the lord lieutenant accused parliament of violating the crown's rights. However, the target was not just the crown but also the claims of Westminster to be able to tax and legislate for Ireland. The subordinate status of the Irish parliament was reflected in the fact that until 1782, it could not draw up bills but only heads of bills for submission successively to the Irish and the English privy councils. Either of these bodies could (and often did) reject or amend legislation, but the bills returned to the Irish parliament could only be accepted or rejected, not amended again. Right from its very first sitting of the new era, the constitutional status of Ireland's parliament, which was to dominate much of political life until 1800, proved controversial.

Parliament quickly turned to the Catholic question, and over the next thirty-five years, it passed a series of measures collectively known as the "penal laws" (or "popery laws" to their enactors). It is worth detailing a few of the more important measures before turning to the question of how to interpret the laws as a whole. Many of the parliamentary elite were convinced that violent conflict with Catholics was inevitable unless their capacity to rebel was permanently removed. "Only the Power of our Enemies is abated, not their Malice or bloody Minds," the bishop of Cork told parliament.[18] This mind-set produced the early penal acts. However, parliament's first action on the Catholic question was inaction—it refused to ratify the articles of Limerick, and did not do so until 1697, and even then only without certain key articles, including that guaranteeing Catholics the same position as under Charles II. The crown, driven by financial motives, accepted this breaking of its word.

The first session of parliament after 1692 was in 1695; the first penal laws were passed at that session. One was the famous law that banned Catholics from keeping weapons and owning horses worth more than £5, and the other restricted Catholic access to education. Its main purpose was to ban foreign education (and thus reduce Irish Catholic contact with continental Catholic religious and political ideas), but it also banned Catholics from keeping schools in Ireland. Catholic education, it stated, was "one great reason of many of the natives of this kingdom continuing ignorant of the principles of true religion … and of their neglecting to conform themselves to the laws and statutes of this realm, and of their not using the English habit or language, to the great prejudice of the publick weal."[19] In 1697 the Bishops' Banishment Act blamed "popish arch-bishops, bishops, jesuits, and other ecclesiastical persons of the Romish clergy" for Catholic rebellions and ordered all bishops and members of regular orders to leave Ireland.[20] Bishops were leaders of the whole Catholic community, not just the clergy, and their removal would weaken its cohesion. Without bishops, moreover, no new priests could be ordained. Further acts regulating the remaining parish clergy were passed in 1704 and 1709.

Perhaps the most important penal law was the 1704 Act to Prevent the Further Growth of Popery, the aim of which was to substantially weaken—if not eradicate—the Catholic landed elite. The pretext for the Act was the belief that Catholics "do daily endeavour to persuade and pervert" Protestants to convert.[21] It banned inheritance by primogeniture among Catholics, with land having to be divided equally among all sons. On conversion to the established church, the eldest son became the owner, the Catholic parent became a mere tenant for life, and primogeniture was restored. Catholics were banned from inheriting land from Protestants, from buying land, and from holding a lease for longer than thirty-one years. The Act also took aim at popular religion, banning pilgrimages. Because the 1704 legislation had been "most notoriously eluded by several papists and others in trust for them," a further act was passed in 1709, reinforcing it.[22] Under this law, a Protestant discoverer could claim Catholic possessions held in violation of the law. English Tory politicians used the 1704 Act to extend the sacramental test to Ireland, thus removing Dissenters from local government. Penal laws barred Catholics from parliament and the legal profession, while marriages carried out by Catholic and Dissenting ministers were not recognized in law. Catholics were finally stripped of the vote, their last political right, in 1728.

The penal laws sought to deprive Catholics of military, economic, and political power and to attack the Catholic Church as an institution; had they been fully enforced, the church would have disappeared from Ireland. Yet a summary such as that above grants the passing of these laws a coherence and clarity of purpose absent at the time. Sean Connolly has argued that rather than being "a systematic 'code' reflecting a consensus among the Protestant elite as to how its security could be best preserved, penal legislation was in fact a rag-bag of measures, enacted piecemeal over almost half a century."[23] The motives behind any individual piece of legislation were mixed, inevitably given that Irish laws were created in both Dublin and London, and were influenced by the interests, ideology, lobbyists, and personalities in both places. Fear, revenge, hatred, parliamentary horse-trading, ambition, European war, invasion scares, Scottish Jacobite rebellion, the crown's desire not to antagonize continental Catholic allies, and differing priorities in Dublin and London all played their part in shaping pieces of penal legislation. So too did hostility toward, and distrust of, the Dissenters.

Some penal laws confirmed what had long been the case; some were immediate responses to short-term pressures. Some were defensive measures, others aggressive. Very few, if any, enjoyed unanimous support from the members of the institutions that produced them. Arguments were raised against severe penal laws almost straight away, including from Protestant stalwarts like Archbishop William King. Some proposals failed, most notoriously a bill of 1719 to castrate Catholic clergy. Ireland was far from unique in having penal laws in this period—an established church and political and civil disabilities for religious minorities were the European norm. They were often harsher than in Ireland (and Irish Protestants never tired of pointing to Catholic countries where discrimination was worse). Ireland may have been exceptional because its laws applied to the majority of the population, but there were territories elsewhere in Europe where regional majorities suffered for being minorities in the state as a whole.

The penal laws, then, were not the deliberate and calculated outcome of a plan by Ireland's Protestant elite to grind Catholics underfoot, as popular memory long had it. Instead, they enacted European assumptions about the relationship between the state, religion, and citizenship, and did so in an often contingent and short-term manner. It is not surprising that they seemed not just necessary but reasonable to their supporters. That said, it is worth remembering Toby Barnard's thesis that a comprehensive penal code only failed to emerge earlier because parliament did not meet after 1666.[24] Ian McBride's recent argument that sermons and pamphlets reveal a more vehement hostility toward Catholicism and Catholics among propertied Protestants than an examination of the legislative process itself suggests is also worth bearing in mind, especially given the intensity of opposition to repealing penal legislation later in the eighteenth century. One thing about the penal laws is indisputable: they aimed to secure the unchallenged political, social, and economic supremacy of Irish Anglicans. This explains why the Dissenters were also the targets of penal legislation. In political terms, these laws worked.

How did the penal laws affect their targets? The popular image of the penal laws is of persecuted Catholics secretly gathered to hear mass at an isolated location, with a rock serving as the altar, and perhaps with the army's redcoats approaching, coming to arrest the priest. In this view, as the Irish historian and Australian cardinal Patrick Moran put it in 1899, the penal laws were "in full force throughout the length and breadth of the kingdom" throughout the eighteenth century.[25] Professional historians, such as Maureen Wall, began questioning these assumptions in the 1950s. Research soon revealed that although attempts were made to enforce the Banishment Act in the early years of the penal laws, to some effect, the Catholic clergy were by the 1720s mostly allowed to operate with impunity, apart from times of crisis or international tension, when rebellion or invasion seemed possible. In such circumstances, senior clerics would be arrested, but the repression quickly ended. Aberrations such as the execution of Father Nicholas Sheehy in 1766 did, however, occur. Irish priests continued to be trained on the continent and were successfully integrated into the church on their return, even if rivalries among the different orders persisted. By mid-century, the laws against religious practice were a dead letter. Even before such laws had been repealed, the church had built itself into a formidable institution closely linked to its flock, on which it depended for financial support in the absence of tithes or state support. The penal laws against religious practice were a failure, but they were never rigorously enforced for a sustained period. The psychological effect of precarious toleration nevertheless marked the Catholic population for much of the century. Complaints from bishops about the poor quality and qualifications of priests were frequent, but the penal laws meant the situation could not be tackled systematically. The penal laws also ensured that the established church dominated public displays of religion.

Where the penal laws were much more successful—perhaps because there was more chance of them being enforced—was in altering the behavior of the Catholic elite. Many of the laws targeted them specifically, to deny them political power and to reduce their ownership of land. Such laws simply did not apply to the majority of Catholics, who would never have exercised political power regardless. More than half of the land-owning families affected by the inheritance provisions of the 1704 act experienced a conversion to the established church. The amount of land owned by Catholics fell from 14% in 1704 to 5% by 1776. However, the story is more complicated than these figures suggest. A variety of legal strategies evolved to get around the laws. One was nominal conversion, which involved only an outward show of conformity sufficient to meet the legal requirements. The heir sometimes converted, but the family as a whole remained Catholic. There were also collusive discoveries, whereby sympathetic Protestants claimed land that actually remained with the Catholics ostensibly dispossessed. When land leased was taken into consideration, there was more land in Catholic hands by 1800 than in 1700. Despite such evasions, the penal laws successfully robbed the old Catholic landowning elite of any political power. Although some Protestants fretted over the supposed Catholic or convert interest in parliament, they need not have worried. Catholic lobbyists in London sometimes were successful, but Ireland's institutions of power had been successfully closed to Catholics. Nor were all conversions merely matters of convenience, as the example of John Fitzgibbon, earl of

Clare, vividly demonstrates—the son of a Catholic convert, as lord chancellor, he was the Ascendancy's most effective leader in the 1790s.

Many Irish Catholics clung to their politics almost as firmly as they clung to their church. Loyalty to the Stuarts and hopes that another restoration would mean the revival of Catholic power persisted for decades. Recent work has used Irish-language poetry to establish the continued appeal of Jacobitism, even as late as the 1770s, by which time the Stuarts had lost the backing of France, leaving the chances of a restoration extremely remote. Jacobitism also revealed itself in recruitment for the Irish regiments in foreign service and in challenges to the cult of William—written, oral, and sometimes physical (such as clashes between Jacobite and Williamite crowds). Given the evidence for widespread Jacobitism, the absence of any Irish rising in either 1715 or 1745 seems strange. It might simply have reflected the military reality that without foreign help, any rising was doomed. However, it also suggests the need for caution about how far rhetorical Jacobitism reflected real commitment to the Stuarts as opposed to discontent with the status quo for religious, national, or socioeconomic reasons. Jacobite poetry may not have been as representative as sometimes claimed. The Catholic elite abandoned Jacobitism by the 1750s, instead seeking accommodation with the state, as the activities of the Catholic Committee from 1757 until 1791 demonstrate. Gaelic poetry also reveals ideological innovation rather than stasis. In 1779, Barry Yelverton was praised as "*lann óir is luiseag na nGaoidheal* [the golden blade and the knife-point of the Gaels]" for his assertion of Irish parliamentary rights by the poet Tomás Ó Míocháin, who also lauded the "*saorarm gáirmhianach na Banban* [glory-seeking free army of Ireland]," the Volunteers.[26] This was the political language of classical republicanism translated into Irish. In the 1790s, several poets mixed traditional complaints about Protestant domination with United Irish rhetoric. For example, Míchael Óg Ó Longáin called on his listeners not to hate Protestants, "but let ye all rise up together."[27] Other works evinced more traditional hostility. An inchoate political message in 1790s Gaelic poetry is no surprise, given other evidence about ambiguous popular attitudes. For much of the century, Jacobitism seems to have expressed genuine discontent but also to have somewhat obfuscated its causes, given the absence of an alternative language of protest.

Cardinal Moran's view that the penal laws barred Catholics "from all means of acquiring either knowledge or wealth" reflected popular understanding of their effects.[28] Wall demonstrated conclusively the existence of a thriving Catholic mercantile bourgeoisie in Ireland's urban centers. By 1792 Ireland's richest man, it was alleged, was Edward Byrne, a Catholic sugar merchant. Modern analysis of agriculture has also revealed the extent to which a class of prosperous Catholic farmers emerged over the course of the eighteenth century. In other words, the notorious poverty of much of the peasantry cannot be ascribed to the penal laws.

An awareness of the outlines of economic history in this period is essential to understand political developments. Economic development and Westminster's restrictions on Irish trade were central to Irish political thought and culture, especially political and economic patriotism. Moreover, the forces from which sprang the revolutionary challenge of the late eighteenth century were to a large extent created by economic development. Broadly speaking, Ireland's economic fortunes fluctuated between 1660 and 1740, when a period of sustained growth began that lasted until the end of the Napoleonic Wars. Famine can serve as a very crude illustration of the difference between the two periods. Individual bad harvests in themselves were not enough to produce famine; usually, a series of poor harvests produced famine as the gradual depletion of the poor's resources left them unable to buy food. This happened sporadically before 1740, when the unprecedented freezing winter of 1739–1740 resulted in a massive famine in 1740–1741 that may have killed as many as one in five of the population. Such a societal disaster might be expected to occupy a larger part of the story of eighteenth-century Ireland, but unlike the Great Famine a century later, it did not fundamentally alter the class structure of Irish society, forge a culture of mass emigration, or leave a bitter political legacy that fueled subsequent political conflict. The surviving evidence is also much thinner. The fact that no famine occurred between 1741 and 1822 despite many bad harvests and downturns is one indication of economic improvement: after "a decisive improvement in living standards" in the 1750s, the rural poor never lacked money to ensure their survival.[29] For a variety of reasons, including falling mortality, higher living standards, changes in diet, subdivision, and increasing fertility in marriage, Ireland's population began to grow beginning in the 1750s, and especially from 1780. By 1800, it stood at about five million. Such growth was unparalleled in Western Europe.

Living standards rose due to the increasing (although uneven) commercialization and specialization of the Irish economy. Ireland's geographical position on Atlantic trade routes and her (limited) access to British imperial markets were vital. The market—domestic and foreign—penetrated more people's lives than before, through both production and consumption, agriculture, the linen trade, and the development of the finance industry. National income increased perhaps fivefold between 1730 and 1815, an increase driven to a large extent by foreign trade. Proto-industrial production centered on spinning and weaving, and was present in many parts of the island. By the end of the century, large-scale industrialization had developed not only in the linen industry in Ulster but also in the provisions trade and associated industries in Munster and in sugar-baking and brewing in Leinster. Ports like Dublin, Cork, and Belfast dominated the economy, and towns were getting bigger. In 1800 Dublin was at least double the size of any city in Ireland or Britain except London and was the sixth-largest city in Europe. Communications greatly improved, with a craze for road building and canals supported by grants from parliament. Print culture expanded dramatically during the century, so that in 1792 at least thirty-five newspapers were being published across the island. The number of readers increased, though the percentage of the population that was literate may actually have declined.

With economic growth came social change. Commercialization encouraged bilingualism. The middle orders—lawyers, doctors, merchants, printers, manufacturers, and the like—grew in numbers, wealth, and influence. The social structure of rural Ireland was also greatly altered, with increasing differentiation among rural dwellers. By 1790, 30% of them were small and medium farmers. At the bottom of the scale, the cottier class was developing rapidly. The increasing mix of commercial agriculture and proto-industrial work gave tenant-weavers greater independence, as well as the means to organize themselves. This factor was crucial in the breakdown of deference in the late eighteenth century in Ulster. Competition in this class has been seen as key to the outbreak of sectarian violence in Armagh in the 1780s, the county where Protestants, Catholics, and Dissenters were most evenly balanced. Perhaps the most significant social change produced by economic growth was the development of public opinion, which, as in other parts of Europe, became an important political force as the century wore on.

Parliament having become an essential institution, government had to learn how to manage it, that is, ensure a majority on important questions, particularly for the money bill. For much of the century, this task was devolved to undertakers, powerful figures who delivered large numbers of votes in the Commons in return for a share of government patronage. The most spectacular case was Speaker William Conolly. Conolly was also chief revenue commissioner and a lord justice, one of those who ran Ireland during the lord lieutenants' lengthy absences. Having made a fortune in post-war land speculation, his political influence made him Ireland's richest man before his death in 1729. The undertaker system broke down in the 1760s, when the lord lieutenants began spending more time in Ireland and took greater control of managing its affairs, building their own parliamentary majorities by the more direct dispensing of patronage. Although taking government patronage could lead to accusations of corruption, in reality the entire parliamentary elite and most of the political nation did not regard it as dishonorable or inappropriate (even if government officials often complained about the scale required). Conolly was also one of a number of men of business, like Nathaniel Clements or John Beresford, in whose hands lay the administration of Ireland's developing state and who brought an increasing professionalism to the task. For most of the century, such men were able to go about their business undisturbed by larger political questions, which flared up into crisis only occasionally.

From 1692 until its abolition, parliament contained an opposition claiming to represent country or real Whig principles. Sometimes, this was a cynical exercise by ambitious politicians eager to secure a government job by making a nuisance of themselves. Even where this was so, they deployed a discourse that had a strong resonance among the political nation and, increasingly, the wider populace. Of course, supporters of government were also keen to claim the mantle of patriotism. Patriotism began as an Irish Protestant version of the Williamite vision of events in England in 1688, but ultimately, it became a highly contested term claimed by everyone from the supporters of Protestant Ascendancy to their enemies in the United Irishmen.

Irish patriotism had two major components, the economic and the political. Economic patriotism centered on improvement, primarily of the economy but also of manners. Ireland was widely believed to have the population, resources, and climate to thrive economically. Toby Barnard has demonstrated the roots of the eighteenth-century "fashionable cult" of improvement in seventeenth-century reform schemes motivated by varieties of Protestantism.[30] The Jacobite parliament passed several acts aimed at securing economic improvement, suggesting that the concept enjoyed widespread acceptance from early on. By the 1760s, "a man has a figure in his county in proportion to the improvements he makes."[31] Improvement took many forms, being institutionalized in the many turnpikes, market towns, canals, and industries funded and encouraged by parliament, other public bodies, landlords, and improving societies like the Dublin Society (1731), which became the model for similar societies across Europe. Self-interest mixed with patriotism as state subsidies often benefited the political elite and their clients. By the end of the eighteenth century, improvement had become subsumed in the concept of Enlightenment. As the government-sponsored *Freeman's Journal* put it when discussing improvement in 1791, "the enlightened spirit of the present times has led the inhabitants of this kingdom to some undertakings infinitely important to society." The "force of reason and the influence of patriotism" would ensure it continued.[32]

Political patriotism was centered on the powers of the Irish parliament. Generally, the viceroys successfully managed parliament, but at times it proved difficult, most often when the rights of the people and parliament of Ireland were seen to be at stake. A clash between viceroy and parliament over the latter's powers ended the first sitting of the new era in 1692. The growing importance of public opinion, which increasingly limited the freedom of maneuver for both politicians and government, was more obvious in such disputes as time passed. The powers of parliament were intimately tied to economic questions because of English restrictions on Irish trade. It was disputes over proposed restrictions on the woolen trade that led William Molyneux to write *The Case of Ireland's Being Bound by Acts of Parliament in England, Stated* (1698). Molyneux made his case using (tortuous) historical precedent, but he also turned the rhetoric and principles of 1688 against the English elite it had secured in power, citing Chapter 16 of John Locke's *Second Treatise* (1689) in defense of inalienable natural rights. Unsurprisingly, politicians in London were deeply unconvinced, while the work produced only a muted response in Ireland. However, its reputation would grow over subsequent decades until it assumed the status of the foundational text of Irish patriotism.[33]

In 1720, annoyed at Irish pretensions, the British parliament (British since the Anglo-Scottish union of 1707) passed the Declaratory Act, which explicitly declared the kingdom of Ireland subordinate and dependent to the crown of Great Britain (really meaning the British parliament). The act explicitly stated that Westminster had the right to pass laws "to bind the People and the Kingdom of *Ireland*."[34] This seemingly settled the issue. However, it soon flared up more virulently than before because of the Wood's halfpence debacle. After the Englishman William Wood acquired the patent to mint coins for Ireland, rumors soon spread that he was using inferior metal. Irish opinion was outraged. Jonathan Swift's *A Letter to the Whole People of Ireland* (1724), part of the *Drapier's Letters* (1724–1725), denied that Ireland was a dependent kingdom and declared that "by the Laws of GOD, of NATURE, of NATIONS, and of your own Country, you ARE and OUGHT to be as FREE a People as your Brethren in *England*."[35] Amid the storm, the government's chief supporters in parliament withdrew their support, and the patent was rescinded. Although motivated in large part by material considerations, the episode reveals the growing influence of patriotism in and out of doors, as well as the increasing power of the press, which turned the Drapier into a national hero. The emerging gap in opinions on Ireland's ideal constitutional status between the Irish and British elites was clear to see. Despite it, most Irish politicians happily worked the system as it stood.

In 1753 the constitutional question was raised once more. The catalyst was a power struggle between the two leading undertakers, Speaker Henry Boyle and George Stone, archbishop of Armagh. Boyle chose to reassert his importance by means of the issue on which both government and public opinion were most sensitive, the money bill. Tellingly named Patriot Clubs appeared across the country to support Boyle, while almost two hundred pamphlets were published on the dispute in three years. Stone feared for his life, and rumors about his alleged homosexuality circulating among the elite and in print reached some members of the lower orders, who pointed at their children's behinds, exclaiming "What a fine pair of buttocks they are."[36] Boyle's abandonment of his new-found patriotism in a deal with government in 1756 produced a profound sense of betrayal among his supporters. The "greatest mob" ever seen in Dublin turned out on St. Patrick's Day with an effigy of Boyle on its way to the gallows; the army dispersed the crowd.[37] Public opinion could be a useful ally for the political elite, providing credibility and status. However, it was also developing the capacity to exceed what the elite considered legitimate bounds: the lower and middle orders (particularly in Dublin) were developing their own distinct interpretation of patriotism, as had been demonstrated in the late 1740s by the popularity of Charles Lucas and his challenge to the oligarchy governing the city. Lord Kildare confessed that "when popularity is on the other side," he could not support the government.[38] Public opinion bared its teeth in December 1759, when rumors of an impending union saw parliament invaded by a large, armed crowd that forced some members to swear that they stood "for the country and against the union."[39] By the mid-eighteenth century, an alternative source of political legitimacy—the appeal to public opinion—was coming into being, as were the conditions for more widespread extraparliamentary political agitation. More political clubs and publications appeared independently of the traditional political elite over the following decades.

War against Louis XIV allowed parliament to become a permanent institution. War against Louis XVI and the American revolutionaries allowed it to achieve legislative independence (i.e., the British parliament accepted that it had no right to legislate for Ireland). Patriots termed this development the "revolution of 1782." It was the product of a popular campaign begun against British commercial restrictions in 1778 that rapidly snowballed into a movement to assert Ireland's rights as an independent kingdom. Independence did not mean separation from Britain, but rather embodied the idea that the two were sister kingdoms, united by the same crown and common interests but each in charge of its own affairs. The war also produced the first formal breach in the penal laws. The Relief Act of 1778 allowed Catholics to hold land on similar terms to Protestants but withheld political rights. London was desperate for military manpower and saw relief as a means to help access the millions of Irish Catholics formally banned from enlisting.

Britain's desperation for manpower in America created the conditions for the events of 1782. Most of the army in Ireland was sent to the colonies. When France formally entered the war in 1778, Irish Protestants feared invasion or rebellion. They founded the Volunteers. The force grew rapidly, peaking at perhaps eighty thousand members. It was a powerful manifestation of classical republicanism—the citizen-soldier defending his homeland in time of need. These armed citizens soon turned their attention from military to political matters. On February 15, 1782, at the famous Dungannon Volunteer convention, they dismissed objections that they should avoid politics: "a citizen, by learning the use of arms, does not abandon any of his civil rights."[40]

The disruption to trade caused by the war, which was beginning to produce real hardship among the urban poor, and opposition from British business interests to concessions for Ireland, focused Volunteer attention on economic restrictions. Their message, as delivered by a Volunteer demonstration on the anniversary of William III's birthday on November 4, 1779, was simple: "A short money bill—A free trade—Or else!!!"[41] That the Volunteers were in this instance merely the armed wing of public opinion was made clear by the popularity of a campaign to buy only Irish goods, by the press, by parliamentary speeches, and by popular demonstrations at parliament. When the Commons voted a short money bill, indicating that government supporters had joined the clamor for free trade, London was forced to give way, and Ireland's right to trade with the colonies (free trade) was recognized.

Patriots in and out of parliament, from all classes, now focused on Ireland's constitutional status. In April 1780 Henry Grattan told parliament: "you, by the assistance of the people, have recovered trade, you still owe the kingdom liberty."[42] The patriot campaign soon stalled but was revivified when parliament met again in October 1781 and by the Dungannon convention, which resolved that "a claim of any body of men, other than the King, Lords and Commons of Ireland, to make laws to bind this kingdom, is unconstitutional, illegal, and a *grievance*."[43] When more traditionally representative bodies—such as county grand juries and meetings of electors—also expressed this opinion, it was clear that the majority of the political nation and wider public opinion supported the patriot demands. The American debacle saw Rockingham replace Lord North as British prime minister, and the new ministry soon repealed the Declaratory Act. Further campaigning led by Henry Flood caused Westminster to explicitly renounce any claim to legislate for Ireland in April 1783.

Vincent Morley has recently argued that it was the American example that influenced Irish patriots, rather than American ideas. This view is supported by the fact that 1782 was presented by its supporters in traditional terms, as Ireland receiving the full benefits of the constitution of 1688 (i.e., civil and religious liberty, with the rights of the people institutionalized in government). Others were more skeptical. In 1791 Theobald Wolfe Tone, a few months before helping to found the Society of United Irishmen, famously described it as "the most bungling imperfect business that ever threw ridicule on a lofty epithet."[44] Why had "Grattan's Parliament" proved such a disappointment to radical patriots?

After 1782 some Volunteers mounted a campaign for reform. Some radical corps had admitted Catholics and the poor, who could not afford to buy the uniform and weapons themselves, to their ranks. Given the link between bearing arms and citizenship, this admission was an assertion that political rights belonged to all, regardless of religion or property, and was a direct challenge to two fundamental principles of the status quo. An angry Grattan claimed arming "the poverty of the kingdom" besmirched the original Volunteers, the "armed property of Ireland."[45] The Volunteer reformers themselves split over religion and property, and the campaign effectively ended when Flood, who went straight to parliament from a Volunteer convention in his uniform, was denounced as a member of an armed force trying to overawe the legitimate representatives of the people. Public opinion, united, armed, and allied to a significant section of the political elite, had proven capable of forcing through change against Westminster's wishes. However, the radical segment of a divided public opinion proved incapable of forcing change from the native parliamentary elite supported by the resources of the state and a substantial segment of public opinion. From 1782 on, this was the rock on which reform plans foundered.

Legislative independence also proved disappointing. The viceroys rapidly proved able to manage parliament once more. Poynings's Law was still used, albeit sparingly. Parliamentary management was made easier by the distribution of seats in the Commons. Fewer than one hundred of the three hundred seats were genuinely open to contest, the rest being pocket boroughs that could be bought and sold. Parliament represented property, not the people as a whole, or even the majority of the political nation. The events of 1782 had not altered this fact. William Drennan lamented the state of Ireland's "helots." "What is the distance between an Irishman and a Freeman? Not less than three thousand miles."[46] The implication of Drennan's extremely popular work was that liberty required a democratic republic, free from the corrupting influence of monarchy and aristocracy.

However, opinion as a whole was determined to protect legislative independence. The British prime minister William Pitt's Commercial Propositions of 1785 for a free-trade area between Britain and Ireland were seen as possibly prefiguring a union and were defeated by vigorous protests in the public sphere. Supporters of both government and opposition saw the Commercial Treaty of 1787 with France, the first to which Ireland was a signatory in its own right, as proof of Ireland's enhanced status. The Regency Crisis of 1788–1789, brought about by King George III's mental incapacitation, showed just how highly Irish independence was valued. A major constitutional crisis whereby Britain and Ireland had the same regent with very different powers in each kingdom was avoided only by the king's timely recovery. The Irish parliament's decision to vote the Prince of Wales full powers in defiance of the British parliament's example and the viceroy's wishes was possible only because many government supporters placed the rights of the Irish parliament above their usual interests.

By mid-1789, Irish politics were frozen. The traditional elite was comfortably in control, while the viceroy could generally control parliament. The parliamentary opposition was better organized after the formation of the Irish Whig Club in June 1789, and there were signs of life among opposition political activists from further down the social scale. But there was no hint that Ireland was about to enter one of the most turbulent and bloody decades in its history, when the whole edifice of the state nearly crumbled under the ideological, political, and eventually, military assault of secular, republican, revolutionary democrats, nor that legislative independence would end in the Irish parliament voting itself out of existence by enacting a union with Britain.

The example, principles, and, later, arms of the French Revolution set Irish politics on the path to attempted revolution. A people had freed itself and set about governing according to the recently proclaimed rights of man. Moreover, it was a Catholic people, convincing many Protestants that Catholics were fit for liberty after all. The French Revolution of course passed through different phases—constitutional monarchy, radical democratic republic, terror, expansionist representative republic, military dictatorship—and Irish attitudes adjusted to them.

Initially, the Revolution seemed to inaugurate a new era of liberty in human history. It was welcomed across the political spectrum, and some quickly argued Ireland should imitate France. "When the people of Ireland see that a nation, which was lately immersed in slavery, are now ably contending for the rights of man, will the Irish ... sit idle," asked one newspaper in August 1789.[47] Such sentiments divided reformers and supporters of the status quo long before the works of Edmund Burke and Thomas Paine appeared. Liberal reformers saw in the early Revolution the creation of a moderate, enlightened government similar, but superior, to their own. Radicals saw something different. The revolutionary principle of the sovereignty of the nation suggested how society and government could be remodeled in the interests of all the people. This belief motivated the foundation of the United Irishmen in October 1791. Their initial resolutions declared the need for a national government free of English influence, for parliamentary reform, and for equal rights for all regardless of religion, at a time when "the rights of man are ascertained in theory, and that theory substantiated by practice."[48] Although couched in the language of reform, their resolutions would mean stripping the aristocratic elite of its political power and religious privileges—revolutionary change, as their opponents understood perfectly. The French Revolution helped motivate opponents of the status quo to renew their efforts, but they were not simply trying to copy France. They were responding to, and trying to change, Irish social, economic, religious, and political conditions.

In late 1791 members of the professional and mercantile bourgeoisie seized control of the Catholic Committee from its clerical-aristocratic leadership and began campaigning more aggressively for political rights. The elite had already considered and completely rejected the idea of change. Reform had been denied after 1782, and an extensive debate in the mid-1780s about the confessional state saw not change but the consolidation of the concept of Protestant Ascendancy (i.e., that the state and its institutions must remain exclusively in the control of members of the established church). The outcome of Catholic claims would depend on who could persuade Pitt that their policy was in Britain's interest. London signaled its intentions by supporting the 1792 Relief Act. This act, however, did not grant political rights, while the new leaders of the Catholic Committee had been roundly abused by government supporters defending Ascendancy.

In response, the Catholic Committee organized elections on the basis of one man, one vote, to what became known as the "Catholic Convention" when it met in December 1792. Wolfe Tone, as secretary to the Committee, had been one of its main organizers. Simultaneously, he was also involved in organizing a new Volunteer unit with republican insignia modeled on the French National Guard. By late 1792, it was clear Britain and France would shortly be at war. Government, fearful that revolution was in the air, moved against the Volunteers, who were effectively suppressed by spring 1793. In 1793 it also brought in a militia act, resulting in massive riots. The Convention Act banned elected assemblies other than parliament, and the Gunpowder Act restricted access to arms and ammunition. The prospect of war led to concessions to public opinion, as well as to coercion, partly to make recruitment easier. London bullied its supporters into passing the 1793 Relief Act, which enfranchised Catholics but excluded them from parliament and senior government positions. Thomas Bartlett has neatly summarized the scale of these changes as "the 1793 revolution."[49] This was defensive modernization, reform to ensure that the aristocratic order as a whole could emerge from the revolutionary wars intact.

Initially, the United Irishmen sought to mobilize public opinion to pressure the government into reform. They embarked on a program of mass politicization, to "make every man a politician."[50] They were supreme propagandists. From 1792 the *Northern Star* was Ireland's most popular paper, and handbills, songbooks, satires, pamphlets, public demonstrations, clothing, badges, even hairstyles and funerals all promoted their message. Mass politicization occurred, also driven by interest in France and the Catholic campaign. However, by 1793, United Irish leaders in Ulster had already begun developing an alternative strategy. Having embraced separatism and republican democracy, they began preparations for a potential military conflict. Before their suppression, moves had begun to better organize radical Volunteers into a coherent force, and arms and ammunition were being secretly stored, including several Volunteer cannon. Secret organizations were also being created. In all these activities, they ran ahead of many of their own members and of public opinion generally. Propaganda, the effects of the war, the government's refusal to deliver either reform or Catholic emancipation, sectarian tensions, and the successes of French arms all helped radicalize opinion in the years that followed.

The Defenders, a Catholic secret society originating from sectarian conflict in 1780s Armagh, were spreading rapidly by 1793. Defender ideology varied from person to person. Secular democratic republicanism inspired by America and France could be found alongside, or fused with, social and economic grievances (such as high prices and tithes) and outright sectarianism. The prominent Protestant United Irishman James Napper Tandy did not swear to restore "the true religion that was lost since the Reformation," unlike some of his fellow Defenders.[51] The Defenders and United Irishmen built on traditions of agrarian popular protest movements like the Whiteboys and Steelboys. The coalescence of the Defenders and United Irishmen in the mid-1790s produced a mass revolutionary underground movement, peaking at perhaps 280,000 members. The United Irish alliance with France, forged during 1796, gave them an invaluable credibility with the populace. The failed attempt at Bantry Bay in December 1796 demonstrated that the French were serious about invasion. Given French victories across Europe, the result of an invasion seemed likely to be a United Irish victory. United Irish recruitment rocketed. The government determined to smash the movement before invasion could occur.

The white terror popularly known as the "dragooning of Ulster" saw the army unleashed on suspect elements of the populace. The United Irish organization in Ulster never really recovered, not least from the suppression of the *Northern Star*. Increasingly, loyalists were mobilized. The yeomanry was established before Bantry Bay. Existing sectarian tensions were exploited, with the recently founded Orange lodges receiving (limited) elite and official patronage. Repressive tactics were employed everywhere. The United Irishmen argued over whether to wait for the French or strike before the movement suffered further. Having decided to act, they were seriously weakened by arrests and the death of the overall military commander, Lord Edward Fitzgerald. The rebellion that broke out on May 23, 1798, was far from that planned. Many United Irishmen never turned out, while the central strategy of taking Dublin failed from the start. Nor did the French arrive in good time or in sufficient numbers. Although the United Irishmen won some significant victories initially, especially in Wexford and, with French help, Connacht, the rebellion was put down relatively easily and quickly. As in the 1690s, the French proved unable to provide sufficient support for their Irish allies, while the rulers of Britain simply could not afford to lose Ireland and poured whatever resources were necessary into keeping it.

What would a successful United Irish revolution have produced? Monarchy, aristocracy, and the church establishment—the three pillars of ancien régime European society—would have been abolished and replaced by a democratic, secular republic. Ireland would have been separate from Britain, but under the protection of France. Some of the major grievances of the lower orders, such as tithes, would have been addressed. The lands of the established church and probably of diehard counterrevolutionaries would have been redistributed. Civic and political equality and meritocracy would have replaced the aristocratic social order. In other words, a political and social revolution placing bourgeois revolutionary democrats in power with the support of the lower orders would have occurred. But not all rebels were motivated by this vision. Sectarian violence broke out in several places, most infamously in the burnings at Scullabogue. Some rebels in Connacht claimed to be fighting for France and the Blessed Virgin. Sectarian tensions remained within the United Irish movement, while disagreements about attitudes toward France and social reform existed. Nevertheless, revolutionary democracy was the main motivation behind the rebellion.

About ten thousand people died, the overwhelming majority killed by the forces of the state, often away from the battlefield. Lord Cornwallis, dispatched to take over the army and the viceroyalty, defeated the rebels and then instituted a policy of considerable leniency, annoying many local reactionaries.

On hearing of the rebellion, Pitt had raised the need for a union to follow its defeat. Although it had long-term origins and was part of a Europe-wide pattern of state centralization, the union of 1800 was a wartime measure, an act of defensive modernization, comparable to, for example, Prussian reforms after 1806. But it was also the moment when the Protestant elite sacrificed their most prized possession, their parliament, which had for a century seemed the best guarantee that their interests would be protected. Why? In part, Edward Cooke was right when he warned that union would have to be "written up, spoken up, intrigued up, drunk up, sung up, and bribed up."[52] Irish politicians drove a hard bargain, rejecting the union at first. Bribery alone, whether in cash, offices, or titles, was insufficient to pass the union. At least the illusion of public support had to be secured. Publications were funded, resolutions of support arranged, and Cornwallis toured the country, receiving pro-union declarations. Catholics were promised emancipation, while Protestants were promised that as a minority in the new state, Catholics would pose no threat. Ultimately, however, fear passed the Union. The Protestant elite feared that without the Union, they would be vulnerable to another rising, or a French invasion, or both. In the past, their parliament seemed to offer the best security for their lives, their church, their property, and their ascendancy— now union did.

The Protestant elite of 1660 maintained their dominance of land, wealth, society, and politics throughout the period. At times it was a close-run thing. The Ascendancy class came under greatest threat at times of major international warfare, when French eyes turned toward Ireland and its supportive population. However, war against the Americans and their allies allowed the Ascendancy to reach its zenith, with legislative independence. The quest for greater control was intimately linked to the desire for economic improvement. Economic improvement became a central part of social and political thought, shaping the Irish Enlightenment and patriotism. Concern over the rights of parliament and the desire for improvement facilitated the elite's adoption of an Irish identity and the rise of public opinion. These concerns also raise the historiographically vexed question of how to characterize Ireland in this period, as a colony or ancien régime kingdom. Ireland's history of colonization is clear, and undoubtedly there were colonial aspects to her government. However, Ireland was recognized as a separate, if for most of the period dependent, kingdom. The often loose and ahistorical use of the colonial model gives further ground for caution. Comparisons with extra-European societies only highlight a fundamental difference. In Ireland, religion was the dividing line and cause of discrimination; unlike skin color, religion could be changed, and entry to the governing elite secured. Moreover, Irish people of all sorts saw themselves as Europeans, and the colonial model risks ignoring this fact. Other concepts from European history are applicable to the governance of Ireland, particularly composite monarchy and state centralization. The 1790s, unlike the 1690s, saw large numbers of Catholics supporting the Protestant state against its challengers, a testament to the success of the elite in acquiring acceptance. The 1790s also saw large numbers of Protestants fight the confessional state in the name of revolution, part of a wider struggle in ancien régime Europe. Throughout the Atlantic world, economic development, the growth of the public sphere, and developments in social and political thought had created the conditions in which monarchy and aristocracy were under threat. The revolutionary democratic challenge to aristocracy sprang from the middle and lower orders; this was class war on an international scale. The events of 1798 were the culmination of that struggle in Ireland, though shaped by its particular national and religious circumstances. The union ended one phase of Ireland's constitutional history; the question now became whether it would prove better at managing the tensions caused by the national, religious, and class questions.

FURTHER READING

The most detailed narrative is found in the *New History of Ireland*, vol. 3 (Oxford: Oxford University Press, 1975) edited by F. J. Byrne, T. W. Moody, and F. X. Martin, and vol. 4 (Oxford: Oxford University Press, 1986) edited by T. W. Moody and W. E. Vaughan. However, both are severely out of date. David Dickson, *New Foundations: Ireland 1660–1800* (Dublin Irish Academic Press, second ed., 2000) is a fine survey of the entire period. Toby Barnard's *The Kingdom of Ireland, 1641–1760* (Houndmills, England: Palgrave Macmillan, 2004) provides excellent insight into key themes. Raymond Gillespie, *Seventeenth Century Ireland* (Dublin: Gill and Macmillan, 2006) is essential. Tim Harris, *Restoration* (London: Allen Lane, 2005) and *Revolution* (London: Allen Lane, 2006) place Ireland in a three-kingdoms perspective. S. J. Connolly's masterful *Divided Kingdom* (Oxford: Oxford University Press, 2008) covers the whole period, reiterates the stimulating and controversial arguments expressed in his *Religion, Law and Power* (Oxford: Oxford University Press, 1992), and casts a skeptical eye on the direction of the recent historiography of the 1790s. Ian McBride's *Eighteenth-Century Ireland* (Dublin: Gill and Macmillan, 2009) is an essential, wide-ranging account and challenges some of Connolly's key arguments. Breandán Ó Buachalla, *Aisling Ghéar* (Baile Átha Cliath (Dublin): An Clóchomhar, 1996); Éamonn Ó Ciardha, *Ireland and the Jacobite Cause, 1685–1766* (Dublin: Four Courts Press, 2004); and Vincent Morley, *Irish Opinion and the American Revolution, 1760–1783* (Cambridge: Cambridge University Press, 2002) are essential reading on the history of Jacobitism and Gaelic poetry. Marianne Elliott, *Partners in Revolution: The United Irishmen and France* (New Haven, CT: Yale University Press, 1982) remains the starting point for the 1790s. Jim Smyth, *The Men of No Property* (Basingstoke: Macmillan, 1998); Nancy Curtin, *The United Irishmen* (Oxford: Oxford University Press, 1994); and Keven Whelan, *The Tree of Liberty* (Cork: Cork University Press, 1996) all develop the recent master theme of popular politicization. P. M. Geoghegan's *The Irish Act of Union* (Dublin: Gill and Macmillan, 1999) is the most up-to-date account of how the union passed.

NOTES

1. See T. C. Barnard, "Conclusion. Settling and Unsettling Ireland: The Cromwellian and Williamite Revolutions," in Jane Ohlmeyer (ed.), *Ireland from Independence to Occupation, 1641–1660* (Cambridge: Cambridge University Press, 1995), pp. 265–291, on the challenges facing, and relations between, the Stuarts and the Irish elites in the decades between the two revolutions.

2. *An Act for the Better Settlement of His Majesties Gracious Declaration for the Settlement of His Kingdome of Ireland* (Dublin: John Crook, 1662), pp. 10, 25.

3. Cited in Raymond Gillespie, *Seventeenth-Century Ireland* (Dublin: Gill and Macmillan, 2006), p. 231.

4. Cited in S. J. Connolly, *Religion, Law and Power: The Making of Protestant Ireland 1660–1760* (Oxford: Oxford University Press, 1992), p. 14.

5. M. Perceval-Maxwell, "The Irish Restoration Land Settlement and Its Historians," in C. A. Dennehy (ed.), *Restoration Ireland: Always Settling and Never Settled* (Aldershot, England: Ashgate, 2008), p. 19. Bottigheimer argued that the Cromwellian and Restoration land settlements were "two halves of a whole" rather than discrete events: K. S. Bottigheimer, "The Restoration Land Settlement in Ireland: A Structural View," *Irish Historical Studies* 18: 69 (1972), p. 21.

6. Perceval-Maxwell, "The Irish Restoration Land Settlement," p. 19.

7. Cited in Gillespie, *Seventeenth-Century Ireland*, p. 272.

8. Cited in Gillespie, *Seventeenth-Century Ireland*, p. 273.

9. See J. Miller, "The Earl of Tyrconnell and James II's Irish Policy, 1685–1688," *Historical Journal* 20: 4 (1977), pp. 803–823, on Tyrconnell's fateful role in Ireland.

10. On Ireland and 1688–1691, see K. S. Bottigheimer, "The Glorious Revolution and Ireland," in L. G. Schwoerer (ed.), *The Revolution of 1688–1689* (Cambridge: Cambridge University Press, 1992), pp. 234–241; D. W. Hayton, "The Williamite Revolution in Ireland," in J. I. Israel (ed.), *The Anglo-Dutch Moment: Essays on the Glorious Revolution and Its World Impact* (Cambridge: Cambridge University Press, 1991), pp.185–213; P. H. Kelly, "Ireland and the Glorious Revolution: From Kingdom to Colony," in Robert Beddard (ed.), *The Revolutions of 1688* (Oxford: Clarendon, 1991), pp. 163–190.

11. *Speech of James II at the Opening of Parliament, 7th May 1689*, reprinted in *Hibernian Mirror* (Dublin, E. Rider, 1751), no pagination.

12. *The Acts of that Short Session of Parliament held on May 7th 1689*, reprinted in *Hibernian Mirror* (Dublin: E. Rider, 1751), p. 51.

13. Cited in Connolly, *Religion, Law and Power*, p. 35.

14. On the war, see R. Doherty, *The Williamite War in Ireland, 1688–1691* (Dublin: Four Courts, 1998); J. Childs, *The Williamite Wars in Ireland, 1688–1691* (London: Hambledon Continuum, 2007); P. Lenihan, *1690: The Battle of the Boyne* (Stroud: Tempus, 2003).

15. Cited in Gillespie, *Seventeenth-Century Ireland*, p. 294.

16. Treaty of Limerick, CELT (http://www.ucc.ie/celt/published/E703001-010/index.html).

17. Cited in Gillespie, *Seventeenth-Century Ireland*, p. 296.

18. Cited in I. McBride, *Eighteenth-Century Ireland* (Dublin: Gill and Macmillan, 2009), p. 196.

19. "An Act to Restrain Foreign Education" (http://library.law.umn.edu/irishlaw/7WIIIc4p254 .htm).

20. "An Act for Banishing all Papists Exercising Any Ecclesiastical Jurisdiction, and All Regulars of the Popish Clergy out of this Kingdom" (http://library.law.umn.edu/irishlaw/9WIIIc1p339 .htm).

21. "An Act to Prevent the Further Growth of Popery" (http://library.law.umn.edu/irishlaw/ 2Anne%20Ch6.htm).

22. "An Act for Explaining and Amending an Act Intituled, An Act to Prevent the Further Growth of Popery" (http://library.law.umn.edu/irishlaw/8Annc3s27-37.htm).

23. Connolly, *Religion, Law and Power*, p. 263.

24. Barnard, "Settling and Unsettling," p. 284

25. Cited in McBride, *Eighteenth-Century Ireland*, p. 215.

26. Cited in V. Morley, *Irish Opinion and the American Revolution* (Cambridge: Cambridge University Press, 2002), pp. 229–230.

27. Cited in B. Ó Buachalla, "From Jacobite to Jacobin," in T. Bartlett, D. Dickson, D. Keogh, and K. Whelan (eds.), *1798: A Bicentenary Perspective* (Dublin: Four Courts, 2003), p. 93.

28. P. F. Moran, *The Catholics of Ireland under the Penal Laws in the Eighteenth Century* (London: Catholic Truth Society, 1899), p. 10.

29. L. M. Cullen, "Economic Development, 1691–1750," in T. W. Moody and W. E. Vaughan (eds.), *New History of Ireland* (Oxford: Oxford University Press, 1986), IV, p. 149.

30. T. C. Barnard, *The Kingdom of Ireland, 1641–1760* (Houndmills, England: Palgrave Macmillan, 2004), p. 80.

31. Cited in R. B. McDowell, *Ireland in the Age of Imperialism and Revolution, 1760–1801* (Oxford: Clarendon, 1979), pp. 6–7.

32. *Freeman's Journal*, October 25, 1791.

33. W. Molyneux, *The Case of Ireland's Being Bound by Acts of Parliament in England, Stated* (Dublin: Joseph Ray, 1698); J. Locke, *Two Treatises of Government* (London: Awnsham Churchill, 1689).

34. *An Act for the Better Securing the Dependency of Ireland upon the Crown of Great Britain. To Which Is Added, J——n T——d, esq; His Reasons Why the Bill for the Better Securing the Dependency of Ireland, Should Not Pass* (London: N.P., 1720), p. 4.

35. [J. Swift], *A Letter to the Whole People of Ireland* (Dublin: John Harding, 1724), p. 15.

36. Cited in B. Harris, *Politics and the Nation: Britain in the Mid-Eighteenth Century* (Oxford: Oxford University Press, 2002), p. 207, n. 69.

37. Cited in S. J. Connolly, *Divided Kingdom: Ireland 1630–1800* (Oxford: Oxford University Press, 2008), p. 248.

38. Cited in E. Magennis, *The Irish Political System, 1740–1765: The Golden Age of the Undertakers* (Dublin: Four Courts, 2000), p. 120.

39. Cited in Connolly, *Divided Kingdom*, p. 386.

40. C. H. Wilson, *A Compleat Collection of the Resolutions of the Volunteers, Grand Juries, &c. of Ireland, Which Followed the Celebrated Dungannon Diet* (Dublin: Joseph Hill, 1782), 2 vols I, p. 1.

41. Cited in Morley, *Irish Opinion and the American Revolution*, p. 224.

42. H. Gratton, *The Speeches of the Right Hon. Henry Grattan*, edited by D. O. Madden (Dublin: James Duffy, 1874), p. 39.

43. C. H. Wilson, *A Compleat Collection of the Resolutions of the Volunteers* (Dublin: Joseph Hill, 1782), vol. 1, p. 1.

44. T. W. Tone, *An Argument on Behalf of the Catholics of Ireland* (Dublin: P. Byrne, 1791), p. 11.

45. *The Parliamentary Register; or History of the Proceedings and Debates of the House of Commons of Ireland* (Dublin: P. Byrne and W. Porter, 1785), vol. 4, p. 41.

46. W. Drennan, *The Letters of Orellana, an Irish Helot* (Dublin: J. Chambers and T. Heery, 1785), p. 12.

47. *Morning Post; or Dublin Courant*, August 15, 1789.

48. W.T.W. Tone (ed.), *Life of Theobald Wolfe Tone* (Washington, DC: Gales and Seaton, 1826), 1, p. 367.

49. T. Bartlett, *The Fall and Rise of the Irish Nation: The Catholic Question, 1690–1830* (Dublin: Gill and Macmillan, 1992), chapter 9.

50. T. A. Emmet, "Parts of an Essay towards the History of Ireland," in W. J. MacNeven, *Pieces of Irish History* (New York: Bernard Dornin, 1807), p. 77.

51. Cited in J. Smyth, *The Men of No Property* (Basingstoke: Macmillan, 1998), p. 113

52. Quoted in Bartlett, *Fall and Rise of the Irish Nation*, p. 257.

CHAPTER 3

IRELAND UNDER THE UNION,
1801–1922

John Bew

> Take then to thy bosom *her* whom heaven seems to have chosen as
> the intimate associate of thy soul, and whom national and hereditary
> prejudice would in vain withhold from thee ... lend your *own individ-
> ual efforts* towards the consummation of an event so devoutly to be
> wished by every liberal mind, by every benevolent heart ...
>
> —SYDNEY OWENSON, *THE WILD IRISH GIRL,* 1806[1]

THE ACT OF UNION, WHICH came into being in January 1801, was imposed on Ireland at a time of severe domestic tumult and European warfare. In contrast to many other acts of state building in eighteenth- and
nineteenth-century Europe, the Union was not the culmination of a social process, related to rapid economic transformation, or a mass cultural or ideological
awakening. Indeed, it was a combination of such forces in Ireland that eventually
broke the Union in the first quarter of the twentieth century. The Anglo-Irish
Union had similarities to the Anglo-Scottish Union of 1707 in that its architects
were cognizant of (and responsive to) recent changes in the social, economic, and
political status quo, rather than simply being intent on suppressing emerging social and political forces.[2] Although a broad base of popular consent for the measure
was preferred, it was not deemed to be essential. From its inception, therefore, the
Union failed to pass the test of being seen to be in line with Irish public opinion.[3]
Unionists were convinced that consent would be forthcoming when the logic of
the Union became clear and its positive effects began to be felt. Yet the definitive

political fact of Ireland under the Union was that it was never consummated in the way that its exponents intended. Indeed, when one considers the intentions of the unionists, it is hard to avoid the conclusion that the Union was ultimately a failure. It may have been a "necessary evil," and it may have been preferable to the alternatives in the wake of the 1798 rebellion. In the end, however, it did not make Ireland easier to govern or "solve" the Irish question. Under the Union, Ireland presented an interminable political problem rather than a project or, consciously at least, a "laboratory" for English social and educational policy.[4]

The failure to pacify Ireland was not for want of many attempts to "do justice" by the country—a phrase to which English statesmen would often revert when legislating on Irish affairs. Tellingly, though, these efforts were protracted, contentious, and bound within the parameters of what was acceptable in British politics. The inability to ameliorate the conditions of Irish discontent—manifested in persistent anti-Union agitation—became a rebuke to the self-image of the British state and the Westminster parliament. As Richard Cobden observed as early as 1835 in his essay *England, Ireland and America*, Great Britain had "an insatiable thirst to become the peace-maker abroad, or if that benevolent task fail her, to assume the office of gendarme, and keep in order, gratuitously, all the refractory nations of Europe." That Ireland, which existed within the purview of the British state, remained a land of "poverty, ignorance and misrule" was, as Cobden noted, "a cancer on the side of England." Cobden's view that the Irish question could only be solved "by a change and improvement of the population" rather than "forms of legislation" was not one shared by most British statesmen in 1835, who believed that the British parliament could legislate effectively for Ireland.[5] Indeed, the publication of Cobden's essay coincided with the first of a number of concerted efforts by English governments to conciliate Ireland to the Union through legislative programs and local government reform. A strong unionist consensus existed among the English governing elite. By the late nineteenth century, however, it was increasingly difficult to make the case that the answer to the Irish question was to be found at Westminster.

Before the 1880s, "constructive" unionists—both liberal and conservative—often complained that their vision was withheld from Ireland for too long and delivered in much less fortuitous circumstances than they had hoped. They could not claim that it was unrealized, however. More than anything, it was this recognition—of the inadequacy of British liberal solutions to Irish problems—that was fatal to the Union. Nationalist political mobilization—in which Charles Stewart Parnell expertly combined extraparliamentary agitation with parliamentary pressure—gave undoubted urgency to the Irish question. Ultimately, however, the Union was born and died in the minds of the British political elite. British solutions to Irish problems did much to shape Ireland over the course of more than a century—particularly in the sphere of education—and left an indelible mark on post-Union Ireland. In an age of European nationalism, however, the Union failed to douse the strength of national feeling in Ireland or to create a compelling alternative to Irish nationalism. While there was an increasingly ideological and emotional attachment to the Union in parts of Irish society, unionism could not match the breadth and depth of Irish nationalist sentiment. Although it was far from inauthentic, the rationalist logic of unionism lacked the sense of historical grievance and future destiny that nationalists harnessed to their movement.

A nation is a "large-scale solidarity, constituted by the feeling of the sacrifices that one has made in the past and of those that one is prepared to make in the future," suggested the French liberal theorist Ernest Renan in 1882—a critical year in the Irish national movement when the lines between constitutional agitation and violence became more blurred than ever before. Consent—what Renan called a "daily plebiscite"—was its "sole legitimate criterion."[6] Ironically, it was the expansion of British democracy in last third of the nineteenth century that confirmed the lack of consent for the Union, despite the efforts of successive British statesmen to conciliate Ireland. As William Gladstone observed when introducing the Home Rule bill in 1886—referring back to decades of "constructive" attempts to legislate on aspects of Irish affairs—the experience of Ireland under the Union proved that "there is something more in this world than even the passing of good laws."[7]

THE ACT OF UNION AS AN
UNCONSUMMATED MARRIAGE

The first clue to understanding the Act of Union is to recognize that it was a top-down act of British *raison d'état* conceived in the wake of the Irish rebellion of 1798. That rebellion, occurring at a critical moment in Britain's war effort against France, presented a grave crisis of British national security. In these exceptional circumstances, the idea of a legislative union was conceived by a relatively small section of the English political elite—chiefly those around Prime Minister William Pitt—who regarded the old colonial structures of Irish governance as a hindrance to national harmony. In pursuing union, they worked in league with an even smaller—and not necessarily the most powerful—portion of the Irish governing classes, who shared the same analysis. For Pitt, who was the driving force behind the measure, the long-term strength and the security of the British Empire was the foremost consideration.[8] It does not quite follow that the Union was "the logical conclusion of a process of consolidation of the British state," however, not least because this assumes some master plan for the construction of the United Kingdom, which never existed.[9] War made for exceptional circumstances. A nation that was fighting an enemy of unprecedented military potency—in the form of Napoleonic France—needed to find a means to restore calm and some degree of social and political harmony in a tumultuous portion of its own body politic. Existing formulas had failed to ensure this. The main aim of the Union was thus to re-establish the authority of the state, stabilize Ireland, and prevent its further drift away from Britain—and potentially into the hands of France.

Liam O'Dowd has argued that unionism, "in its most abstract form," is the "ideology of the British state and empire-building in Ireland."[10] This is accurate only to the extent that the Union was intended to serve the interests of the British state. Equally, however, and in no way contradicting this, the architects of the Union were also convinced that Ireland could, should, and would be governed more judiciously than it had been hitherto. To call this an ideology of "empire-building" is to fail to consider the extent to which the Union was intended to transform the way Ireland was governed—and to break with the old colonial architecture. As Roy Foster has written, interpretations of the Union have often been "brutally simple: colonization as rape, union as shotgun marriage," even though it was an attempt—albeit a flawed one—to "amalgamate the nations."[11] J.G.A. Pocock has suggested that Ireland is in danger of "appearing in the narrative only as part of the 'empire' which the English and their British state exerted over realms not included in its structure."[12] Rather than a conscious ideology of imperialism, or a renewed effort to colonize the country, such alternative intellectual trends as utilitarianism, political economy, and Scottish Enlightenment philosophy had a more profound influence on the thinking of the unionists.[13] The Union may have been a failure when it came to amalgamation and conciliation, but it is more fruitful to evaluate it on those terms than through the prism of twentieth-century constructs of imperialism and colonialism.[14]

To the critics of the Union, the self-interest of the British state and the interests of the Irish people were not so easy to reconcile in practice. Coming in the wake of 1798, the measure was widely perceived to have been "wrung from Ireland in her distress"—the latest incarnation of Britain's "divide-and-rule" approach to the governance of Ireland.[15] That the passage of the act itself was so inglorious—shunted through the Irish parliament by a combination of bribery, intimidation, and skullduggery—was another problem in how it was perceived. Both English and Irish Whigs—particularly those associated with Charles James Fox, the figurehead of the British Whig opposition to William Pitt—objected that unionists had failed to build a sufficiently broad-based consensus in Ireland.[16] It was on similar grounds that as thoughtful and open-minded an Irish member of parliament (MP) as the Whig Richard Lovell Edgeworth opposed the measure, even if he was willing to accept the goodwill of unionists, and accept many of their arguments.[17] This lack of Irish support for the Union was never adequately remedied. This was partly because the logic behind it was never fully understood and partly because the Union failed to deliver on its own terms.

In many ways, the practical experience of early life under the Union seemed to confirm the skepticism of the anti-unionists. The way in which Irish affairs had the capacity to polarize and poison British political debate pointed to a significant miscalculation on the part of the architects of the Union—the assumption that Irish matters would be dealt with more dispassionately and liberally at Westminster once Catholic-majority Ireland was subsumed into a Protestant-majority United Kingdom. The first and most damning example of this mistake was the failure to deal with the question of equal rights for Catholics. It was with bitter disappointment that the most influential pro-unionists—including William Pitt and his Irish chief secretary Viscount Castlereagh—who had steered the Union through the Irish parliament—encountered the fierce opposition of King George III to Catholic emancipation. Pitt's lord lieutenant for Ireland, Lord Cornwallis, commented in February 1801 that it was "mortifying" that the "fatal blow should be struck from that quarter most interested to avert it, and that Ireland is again to become a millstone about the neck of Britain."[18]

Partly because of the failure to complete the Union as intended, the idea of consummation became a motif in post-Union Anglo-Irish literature—a genre that was itself born in this era. In the novels of Richard Lovell Edgeworth's daughter, Maria Edgeworth, Roy Foster has identified a "speculative unionism" and a "disinterested" attempt to create a genuine Anglo-Irish identity, envisaging a successful Union on the Anglo-Scottish model.[19] It has been suggested by other literary scholars that Edgeworth's work was more reflective of traditional pre-Union colonial mind-sets than the type of post-Union re-imagining Foster describes.[20] The imposition of this colonial prism, although having some analytical use, is an ex post facto mode of analysis. It was Foster's version of Edgeworth that contemporaries recognized. Notably, her work was praised by Walter Scott in a postscript to his own novel *Waverly*, as having "done more towards completing the Union than perhaps all but the legislative enactments by which it has been followed up."[21] Viscount Castlereagh was also fond of Edgeworth's 1800 novella, *Castle-Rackrent*, which coincided with the passing of the Union and predicted Irish advancement under it.[22] In the same vein, but less predictable, was Castlereagh's passion for the novels of Sydney Owenson, Lady Morgan. Owenson had been a critic of the Union and was known as an outspoken advocate of Catholic emancipation. In contrast to Edgeworth's utilitarian view of the potential improvement of Ireland under the Union, she articulated a more sentimental and romantic vision of Ireland in her first novel, *The Wild Irish Girl*, published in 1806.[23] On the surface, it may seem surprising that Castlereagh was moved by Owenson's writing, as it articulated feelings of historical grievance and dispossession among Ireland's native population.[24] Yet his fondness for both *Castle-Rackrent* and *The Wild Irish Girl* can perhaps be explained by the fact that both novels ended in marriage and invoked a future in which traditional enmities between England and Ireland, and planter and native, would subside. In Owenson's book, that marriage was perhaps even particularly symbolic, as it took place between a Protestant landowner, Horatia, and a wild Irish Catholic girl, Glorvina, whose family had once been forced off her land by her suitor's ancestors.[25] Even anti-Union novels, such as *The Knight of Gwynne* by Charles James Lever, displayed some sympathy for the intentions of its architects and allowed for their sincerity.[26]

Such literary endeavors provided a space in which alternative political possibilities could be explored, in which the notion of a successful Union could be entertained. However, they did not represent—as some may have hoped—harbingers of future events. This literary moment was fleeting, and the prospects of consummation and conciliation faded every year with the failure to pass Catholic emancipation. In 1830, R. J. Bryce, a liberal Presbyterian educationalist, sought patronage from the Duke of Wellington's government to translate into Gaelic "national" works, such as Edgeworth's *Forgive and Forget,* an unpolemical account of the massacres of 1641.[27] But the fact that the Catholic Relief Act had not passed until 1829—and was forced on Westminster, rather than passed with good grace—meant that this narrative was increasingly difficult to sustain. Attitudes among English MPs had hardened in the first two decades of the nineteenth century, and it could no longer be claimed that George III was the only obstacle to the completion of the unionist project. Indeed, Catholic relief had been refused even after a majority of Irish MPs at Westminster supported it.[28] Instead of generating optimism, the first three decades of the Union came to be regarded as a missed opportunity.[29] More fundamentally, what Castlereagh called "the wisdom of the system" did not function as its architects intended.[30]

IRISH ANOMALIES

The blocking of Catholic emancipation was not the only obstacle to the successful operation of the Union. The governance of Ireland also required the acquiescence of Irish stakeholders, who were not necessarily comfortable with new directives from Westminster—not least the old colonial elites who had been identified as a problem already. In passing the Union through the Irish parliament, for example, Pitt and Castlereagh courted elements of the ultra-Protestant and Orange factions in Ireland. These factions, in turn, were able to exert their influence in their campaign against Catholic emancipation.[31] Thus the logic of the Union turned in on itself. In some respects, the strained relationship the British state had with its own colonial elites in Ireland was symptomatic of the problems it had faced in America before the War of Independence; unionist thinkers were certainly aware of the parallel. As Kanter has described, union was intended to allow for increased control of the periphery of the state, "while simultaneously reconciling that periphery to the fiscal-military demands of the state by extending political and commercial equality throughout the empire." The problem with this ambitious scheme, as was discovered with the American Revolution, was that "it seriously underestimated the assertiveness and self-confidence of colonial elites."[32] Irish peers and MPs sent to England to represent their country were often the greatest opponents of legislation created by English statesmen to improve the condition of Ireland.

Recalling a conversation with Castlereagh in 1821—in which the former chief secretary had reiterated his belief in the importance of Catholic emancipation—the Irish peer Lord Rosse outlined a familiar view of Irish governance, which went against the spirit of the Union but which long outlasted 1801. "For, though the maxim, divide and govern has often been reprobated, it is nevertheless true that the division facilitates the governing of the country," he confessed. Moreover, Rosse also pointed out that the Irish question was much more deep-seated than a simple question of religious liberty and political equality. Referring back to the Plantation, he noted that "notions of aboriginal possession, which are very strong, as well as religion ... are always working in the minds of the [C]atholics against the connection."[33] Ireland was not simply divided between Protestant and Catholic but between settler and native, Saxon and Celt, and landowner and peasant.[34] Although it would be misleading to see every issue through this prism, this divide did give Irish politics its organizing dynamic. Thus many Irish conservatives remained skeptical about the notions of amalgamation and conciliation envisaged by the architects of the Union. In 1849, the *Dublin University Magazine* rebuked the pro-unionists for their naivete in assuming that the Catholic question was the key to solving the Irish question; they had approached the question of religious equality "solely with reference to the tranquility [*sic*] they would produce, and the grounds of discontent they would remove" and could "only see halcyon visions of peace and prosperity."[35]

Problems of sectarianism and social disorder were not unique in a European context, of course. But other ingredients in Irish politics made Ireland both anomalous and particularly combustible. In the late eighteenth century, the country had experienced a unique phenomenon—the mobilization and political awakening of Catholic peasantry, ostensibly in support of a Jacobin rebellion. It was to the horror of the Catholic hierarchy that Ireland had caught "the French disease."[36] As Sir Henry Parnell, grandfather of the future Irish nationalist leader Charles Stewart Parnell, noted early in the life of the Union, anywhere else the French Revolutionary armies marched "armed peasants were their most formidable enemies" and the Catholic religion was traditionally found in support of "arbitrary power." Ireland presented "the only instance where this religion existing in its full force, has been found leagued in resistance to the civil power, and inculcating, at the same time, the dogmas of religious superstition, and the principles of democratical enthusiasm."[37]

The fusion of religious grievance and Jacobinism represented the nightmare scenario of the British governing classes—not only in Ireland but in England too, where the rise of politically conscious Dissenters was of growing concern for those charged with defense of the Anglican constitution.[38] For that reason, the restructuring of the state at the time of the Union was seen as an opportunity to decouple confessional interest groups and Jacobin ideology. The leading Irish advocates of the Union saw an opportunity to reset the relationship between the state and the various religious bodies in Ireland through a dual process of emancipation (the lifting of civil and legal disabilities on Catholics) and endowment (of both the Catholic and Irish Presbyterian Churches).

Although an Anglo-Irish discourse of "benevolence" and "consummation" was enticing to unionists, a colder *realpolitik* rationale was also in operation.[39] It is no coincidence then that some of the most prominent proponents of Catholic emancipation—Pitt, Castlereagh, George Canning, Edward Cooke, and Cornwallis—were also some of the most hawkish members of the political establishment when it came to the prosecution of the war with France. The lengthy document that Castlereagh presented to Pitt's cabinet in favor of Catholic emancipation spoke of "expediency" rather than "justice" and was framed as a measure of security in a time of war. The existence of discontented religious interest groups in the state was a gift to the nation's external enemies.

> Should it be thought that the dissenting interests of the empire at large (the Catholics being so admitted) have not weight, through their lawful operation, to shake the establishment, there can be no question that, in a state of exclusion, they are more naturally open to an alliance with Jacobinism, the enemy of the present day, than in a state of comprehension.

The logic applied not just to Ireland but to all "dissenting" groups (or "sectaries") in the United Kingdom. Government should "adopt a line of conduct towards the sectaries of less distrust, and thereby to put an end to questions affecting the constitutional rights of large classes of the community," Castlereagh stated. The most important question was "what system, without hazarding the powers of the State itself, is best calculated, if not warmly to attach at least to disarm the hostility of those classes in the community who cannot be got rid of, and must be governed."[40]

If emancipation and the removal of disabilities would soothe the relationships, endowment would fasten these groups, Dissenters and Catholics, further to the state and provide the government a channel of communication to the religious hierarchies. A model for this had recently been established by Pitt's endowment of a Catholic seminary at Maynooth in 1795—something that loomed large in the calculations of the pro-unionists after 1798. Indeed, there were notable similarities between the positions of Castlereagh and Sir Henry Parnell, despite their differences over the Union. In support of endowment, Parnell invoked David Hume's *History of England*, which defended the existence of an established church "to bribe the indolence of the clergy, and reduce religious enthusiasms to that degree of temper, which is consistent with the peaceable management of this world." "[T]o weaken the separatist spirit of a sect (and without a spirit of separation a sect is powerless) nothing is done, unless everything is done," Parnell posited, in language that could have been borrowed directly from Castlereagh. The Irish were not "naturally rebels."[41]

Despite the recommendations of such men, the notion of endowment was never explicitly stated in the Act of Union or systematically applied by its exponents. Nonetheless, it is possible to argue that it was implicit in the logic of unionism. The idea certainly struck down roots; it was periodically revived by supporters of the Union. In 1845 the knight of Kerry—who had cooperated closely with Cornwallis and Castlereagh at the time of the Union—wrote to Robert Peel, the prime minister, who was attempting to push through an increase in the government grant to Maynooth. In doing so, Kerry unearthed a letter that Castlereagh had sent him in 1801, confirming that Castlereagh had offered extensive financial support for the "advancement" of the Catholic Church in Ireland at the time of the Union, which dwarfed the amount of money granted to Maynooth. Kerry went so far as to claim that the Catholic hierarchy was "taught to expect it as growing out of the union" and argued—accurately—that the idea of state-funded conciliation with the Catholic Church was at the core the original unionist rationale. Thus, "to object now, *in principle*, to aiding the education of the [C]atholic priesthood, would be to disavow and falsify the union."[42]

At the close of the century, the liberal Home Ruler Viscount Morley suggested that this approach—a "policy of levelling [*sic*] up"—framed the Irish policies of successive Whig and Conservative governments until William Gladstone disestablished the Irish Church in 1869 as part of "a general cessation of endowments for religion in Ireland." At the time of disestablishment, the Conservative leader Benjamin Disraeli had proposed that the state should fund a Roman Catholic university in Ireland as part of his attempt to present a conciliatory alternative to disestablishment. "Mr Disraeli's was at bottom the principle of Pitt and Castlereagh and of many great Whigs," noted Morley, "and doubtless he did not know, how odious it would be to the British householders, who were far more like King George III than they all supposed."[43] Disraeli certainly saw himself as an inheritor of Pitt's policy, which was to "settle Ireland with honour to ourselves, with kindness to the people, and with safety to the realm." The duty of an English minister in Ireland was to "effect by his policy all those changes which a revolution would do by force. That is the Irish question in its integrity."[44]

THE UNION AND IRISH IDEAS

While the Irish question in British politics has been the subject of much scholarship, as K. T. Hoppen has observed, "far less attention has been given to the equally important fact that all aspects of Irish life, not least the political, were constantly obliged to react and reverberate to the imperatives and the dominance of the larger island."[45] The subsuming of Irish affairs into Westminster meant a commingling of individuals, ideas, and political methods between the two islands. Daniel O'Connell and Charles Stewart Parnell were both great British parliamentarians and highly innovative political mobilizers "out of doors." In a similar vein, Gearoid Ó Tuathaigh has called for further exploration of

> the intellectual and psychological ramifications of the Union experience for the Irish ideas market after 1800; the horizons of alternative possibilities ... the "states of mind" conditioned by the Union experience ... the speculative zone—the impact of the Irish Union framework on the imaginative horizons of the nineteenth-century Irish.[46]

As Peter Jupp also noted, particularly after Catholic emancipation (1829) and the Great Reform Act (1832), "trends encouraging incorporation and assimilation co-existed with those emphasising Ireland's distinctiveness."[47]

The Irish parliamentary tradition had its antecedents in College Green, but it was also shaped by the Westminster experience.[48] Both unionists and anti-unionists worked within this system for more than a century. Indeed, it was some-times the case that those presumed to be unionists were less comfortable with the prevailing political mood in England than those whose stated aim was a restoration of the Irish parliament; Orangemen were often deeply uncomfortable about aspects of the post-Union dispensation. While they preferred to side with English Con-servatives on most issues, they viewed the Conservative leadership with some sus-picion.[49] The strength of unionist or nationalist enthusiasm in Ireland was not a fixed commodity; both unionism and nationalism waxed and waned in response to the prevailing political mood in England and the balance of power at Westmin-ster. Thus changes of government in London shaped both unionist and national-ist strategy and discourse. The first illustration of this came with Pitt's death in 1806 and the formation of the "Ministry of all the Talents," in which the Whig leader Charles James Fox was included. William Drennan's 1806 *Letter to Charles James Fox* signaled the willingness on the part of former radical opponents of the Union to be reconciled to the measure on the condition that liberal reforms begin.[50]

The reorientation of Presbyterian radicalism—from being in the vanguard of Irish separatism to an essentially pro-unionist position—was a highly significant development in recasting Irish politics in the nineteenth century. On the one hand, it seemed to demonstrate the possibility of reconciliation to the Union. The sur-vival of the Union for so long would not have been possible without the co-option of this group that had been behind much of the radical separatism of the late eighteenth century.[51] On the other hand, the importance of this development was both outweighed and undercut by a new phenomenon: the emergence of an or-ganized campaign for Catholic rights and its fusion with the cause of Irish nation-alism. It was this campaign that was to become the dominant political force in Ireland—and the biggest threat to the Union.

The extent to which the tone of nineteenth-century Irish nationalism was set by the leader of the Catholic Association, Daniel O'Connell, is hard to overstate.

His leadership bestowed a number of identifiable characteristics. First, O'Connell represented a break from the republican traditions of the 1790s; as a young man, he had been an anti-Jacobin, and it was partly because of his predominance that Irish republicanism remained largely dormant until the 1840s. Second, O'Connell's strategic decision to link the cause of Catholic rights with a campaign to repeal the Act of Union entailed that Catholicism and Irish nationalism became explicitly linked in a way that had been by no means inevitable before 1801. O'Connell's abrasiveness and dominating presence in Irish politics made him a divisive figure across the political spectrum. Not only was he an obvious bogeyman for unionists, he was also much criticized by later generations of nationalists for a variety of perceived sins—including clericalism and his periodic cooperation with English Whigs. Oliver MacDonagh's classic two-volume life of O'Connell published in the 1980s rescued him from many of the late nineteenth- and early twentieth-century nationalist critiques. His version of O'Connell was of a man who combined a strong Catholic faith (after a brief flirtation with Deism) with the characteristics of a clan chief, and who generally adhered to a secular Enlightenment rights-based discourse. Thus O'Connell's conception of the national struggle was one for equality and liberty.[52]

It is also true that O'Connell could depart from this script himself on occasion—lashing out at opponents, falling back on his undoubted powers as a demagogue, and "riding the tiger" of mass Catholic peasant mobilization to challenge the authority of the state.[53] In this respect it is perhaps worth distinguishing between "O'Connellism" and O'Connell himself; Maume has cautioned against an oversanitized version of "The Liberator" that plays down his "verbal violence." Combined with O'Connellite tactics—the tithe war and monster meetings, for example—this meant the Repeal movement, just like the Union itself, also failed to broaden its basis of support much beyond the Catholic Association, which O'Connell had established in 1823, and which he essentially reconstituted into the Repeal Association after 1829.[54] Despite the rights-based framing of the Repeal movement, from the Irish Protestant perspective, it was hard not to view it as a "communal struggle for power."[55]

O'Connellism was as much a symptom as a cause of the polarization of Irish politics in the first three decades of the century. It was the failure to pass Catholic emancipation in the immediate aftermath of the Union that created the conditions for his rise to prominence. As one Irish Tory MP put it in 1828, the Catholic question "embitters every transaction of life, and it is utterly impossible that the country can regain quiet under such a conflict of opinion—An open rebellion would be far preferable for there would be some prospect of a termination of our miseries in the triumph of one party—but now all is suspicion."[56] Coinciding with opposition to emancipation were the political effects of the early nineteenth-century evangelical Protestant revival and renewed efforts at a "Second Reformation" of Ireland.[57] Indeed, even though ultra-Protestants could point to the support that O'Connell received from the Catholic Church, this alliance was partly of their making. Whelan has shown how the Catholic bishops moved in behind O'Connell's campaign partly because of their fears of resurgent evangelical proselytism in Ireland.[58] A related theme was the increasing inadequacy of Irish liberalism—both as a motor for political change and as a conciliating force in Ireland—an important subtext in this story that has been addressed extensively by J. J. Lee for the period after 1848.[59] The Irish liberal tradition, once so robust in the late eighteenth century, never fully recovered from the events of 1798 because of the explosion of sectarian violence that had occurred in the "Year of Liberty." One legacy of the rebellion was that liberals among the Irish gentry were reluctant to embrace "an unrestrained rights-based Enlightenment discourse" predicated on universal suffrage.[60]

Nationalism and liberalism therefore enjoyed a strained relationship in nineteenth-century Ireland.[61] Partly because of their uneasiness about O'Connellism, for example, Ulster liberals in particular sought solace in the broader community of liberal opinion that existed in the United Kingdom. Repeal of the Test and Corporation Acts in 1828 and, finally, the Catholic Relief Act in 1829 were optimistically seized on as representing a new dawn in the life of the Union, particularly as they preceded the fall of the Tory government and the long-awaited return to office of the Whigs. "I must acknowledge that it should not be a Union as we have had hitherto; but let the past be forgotten," declared one prominent liberal at a meeting of the Belfast Reform Society in December 1830, "and let our future Union be one of peace, augmented by the indissoluble ties of equal justice, and reciprocity of interest." As for O'Connell, it was regretted "that the colossal champion of Irish liberty ... should unite his great talents in agitating a question which many patriotic men think calculated to divide our country once more into factions."[62]

Speaking in 1834, when the House of Commons debated Repeal of the Union for the first time, O'Connell could complain with justification that too many of his "fellow countrymen are troubled with a fogginess of intellect, which makes them unable to see their own interests, without the use of British spectacles."[63] He did make periodic attempts to broaden his appeal and reach out to Irish Protestants but with scant success. This was partly because of his tendency to oscillate between rapprochement with and denunciation of such groups—and partly because Irish Protestants were unwilling to reconcile themselves to O'Connellism in any form. In 1830 and 1832, he publicly drank Boyne water and took the Orange oath, only to be criticized by liberals for pandering to the ultra-Protestants for short-term gain.[64] In 1835, conscious that his "tail" of followers in the House of Commons were "almost to a man Catholic," he reached out to the Protestant landowner and radical Chartist William Sharman Crawford by arranging for the latter's election to Dundalk.[65] Yet Crawford spent the rest of the 1830s distancing himself from O'Connell, attempting to outflank him on the left by opposing his alliance with the Whigs, and aligning himself with the radical critics of the government.[66]

By the early 1830s, then, a number of factors—chief among them the emergence of a Catholic nationalist political consciousness and an aggressive Protestant revanchism—had converged to create a division in Irish political life that was rapidly calcifying: that between unionists and anti-unionists ("Repealers"). The period from 1828 to 1833 also saw several important structural changes to the Westminster system that underlined that distinction, such as the broadening of the franchise and an increasing emphasis on party organization. Not all trends pointed toward polarization, however. The arrival of O'Connell and his supporters in the House of Commons meant that Irish political life became further immersed in the wider pool of British politics. Ideas were exchanged, and unlikely alliances were made. This, as Ó Tuathaigh has noted, should guard us "against the danger of oversimplification, of collapsing all parties into a simple story of polarisation."[67]

Recent historiography has established a picture of a more plural, fluid, and diverse political scene after 1832. To give an important example, Joseph Spence's study of the philosophy of Irish Toryism in this period demonstrated both the richness of conservative thought and a degree of unease with the consequences of the Union.[68] Alongside this, Jennifer Ridden has identified a tradition of Protestant liberalism among the Irish gentry (particularly strong in County Limerick) that pushed back against the proselytism associated with the evangelical revival. As she notes, there was a great variety of Irish mentalities that used religious ideas and languages to debate a much wider range of social and political ideas.[69] Studies of individual figures—such as Eve Patten's on Samuel Ferguson—have restored "alternative discourses" and "layered ideology" back into the familiar "nineteenth-century unionist/nationalist dialectic."[70] More than any scholar, Patrick Maume has revealed a genuinely diverse panoply of Irish political thought through the auspices of University College Dublin Press's *Classics in Irish History* series and the *Dictionary of Irish Biography*.[71]

Ironically, one could argue that it was Daniel O'Connell's willingness to participate in British political life—and to recognize the possibility of improvement even under the Westminster parliament—that breathed new life into the Union from the mid-1830s. Departing from their predecessors' overreliance on coercion, the second Melbourne government's approach to Ireland from 1835 to 1841 was characterized by an ambitious campaign of "conciliation." Reliant on O'Connell's parliamentary support for a parliamentary majority, this government developed a "moralistic rhetoric" of doing "justice to Ireland." In practice, this meant a redirection of patronage to Catholic and liberal professionals, a purge of Orange influence in the magistracy, a reduction in the temporalities of the Irish Church, commutation of tithes, and further reform of municipal government. In the words of the Earl of Musgrave, the Irish lord lieutenant, the aim was "to induce a reciprocal feeling of confidence between the governors and the governed ... to treat the English and Irish as 'one nation.'"[72]

The office of the lord lieutenant—which operated from the old colonial garrison at Dublin Castle—was central to efforts at reform. But it also embodied something of a contradiction at the heart of the Union. On the one hand, it underlined Ireland's distinctiveness from the rest of the United Kingdom; on the other hand, the relative autonomy of the lord lieutenant meant that it could be a vehicle for radical reform. Another irony was that it was English liberals who were given to celebrate the virtues of authoritarian, central government when it came to national improvement in Ireland; something that James Mill had prescribed for India could also be recommended by Thomas Macaulay for Ireland.[73] It was a Whig lord lieutenant who suggested that "Ireland wants a Bonaparte" and asked whether it was "fit for a free government."[74] After 1835, under the terms of Melbourne's alliance with O'Connnell, the country became a "Foxite fiefdom" and a stage on which Whigs could apply their notions of "paternal attention" and gestures of "fellow-feeling."[75] The logic of this position was that, in dispensing justice through Dublin Castle, liberals could bypass or undercut local legal and political elites and vested interests that were seen as an obstacle to the successful operation of the Union.

As early as 1803, serious consideration had been given to the reduction of the lord lieutenancy to a ceremonial role—with the English Home Office subsuming the main responsibilities for the governance of Ireland.[76] This debate was revisited again at various points when the governance of Ireland came under scrutiny.[77] Although they were generally more suspicious of state centralization, some Irish conservatives also objected that the lord lieutenancy was "an effectual bar to the complete and virtual recognition of Ireland as part and parcel of the *United* Kingdom, causing her to be looked on rather as a pigmy province, with separate interests, and only fit for the rule of a colonial governor, like that of Trinidad, or Barbados, or Bermuda." Given how often the political spectrum swung in London, it was also a potential source of instability; by 1850 there had been sixteen lord lieutenants since the Union and on average, a new one every three years.[78]

Another unexpected theme of life under the Union is that conservative unionists could be more ambitious and bold in their schemes for Ireland than were liberal unionists. When O'Connell renewed his campaign for Repeal of the Union after the Whigs left office in 1841, the initial response of Sir Robert Peel's Conservative government was unimaginative and reactive—a return to the cycle of coercion and repression that had previously played into O'Connell's hands. However, as Boyd Hilton has described, the reorientation of Peel's approach from 1843 presents another of the "what if" moments under the Union, in which an ambitious campaign of conciliation was interrupted by the arrival of the potato blight in 1845.[79] Peel's three-pronged legislative program consisted of the Charitable Bequests Act (which allowed easier processing of financial gifts and bequests to the Catholic Church), the Maynooth Act (a significant increase in the grant to the Catholic seminary that had been established at Maynooth in the 1790s and support for which had been tied to the original idea of the Union), and the Provincial Colleges Act (which proposed three state-funded nondenominational universities at Cork, Wexford, and Belfast). In the long term it was hoped that this might help foster a new middle-class elite in Ireland that was less welded to sectarian identity politics.[80] In the short term—in a development that Peel was keen to exploit—the initiative highlighted important fault lines in nationalist Ireland that took many years to resolve. Thus it was partly the Irish debates over Peel's program that created the space for a new brand of "Young Ireland" nationalism. This was a cultural and political alternative to O'Connellism that has been seen more in the tradition of the German Romantic movement or as an attempt to revive a civic republican notion of virtue.[81] For the leading Young Ireland intellectual, Thomas Davis, O'Connell's opposition to "Godless Colleges"—Peel's proposals for the extension of nondenominational university education—was opportunistic and damaging to the future progression of the nation.[82]

As Young Ireland never had the democratic weight behind it that O'Connellism did, historians have tended to focus on its cultural and ideological legacy to Irish nationalism. For that reason, sometimes it has been seen as a radicalizing force that fed the political awakening of late nineteenth- and early twentieth-century Irish republicans. Or at least, subsequent generations of republicans read back into the 1840s lessons that seemed apposite to later campaigns—such as Young Ireland's criticism of O'Connell's cooperation with English liberals. Yet the lack of attention paid to the political maneuvering of Young Ireland—behind the pages of the *Nation*—means that a significant aspect of the Young Ireland story is often obscured. Although Davis is remembered as a purist nationalist, perhaps more significant was his unwillingness to treat Repeal of the Union as a zero-sum cause—something absent from other versions of republicanism. His letters on the issue of mixed education indicate a more expansive notion of patriotism. "We have a battle to fight against dangerous bigots and must all do our best," Davis wrote to the Belfast Liberal MP Robert James Tennent, another prominent exponent of mixed education: "If we are beaten the country is ruined."[83]

Davis was also one of the steering hands behind one of the few attempts by nineteenth-century nationalists to genuinely broaden the scope of Irish patriotism—and to address the specifics of how an independent Irish parliament might function. This attempt manifested itself in the brief but highly significant federalist movement (or "moment") of 1844, which has been given remarkably little consideration by Irish historians.[84] Davis repeatedly praised federalists as "men thoroughly national in feeling" and made efforts to help them found their own newspaper.[85] At a private function in Belfast in October 1844, he met with Sharman Crawford, the young Ulster Catholic liberal Thomas O'Hagan, Belfast's Liberal MP David Ross, and the Irish Whig Henry Caulfield to discuss how they might expand their ideas. According to Charles Gavan Duffy, another Young Irelander, if the federalists had actually managed to agree on a united program, Davis would have supported it.[86] For a fleeting moment, O'Connell also saw in federalism a possible compromise position from which to construct a broader national movement. However, he made the mistake of seeing it as a progression toward the nationalist position to which he himself subscribed—remarking that it "annihilates mere Whiggery."[87] What O'Connell failed to realize was that federalism was not the forerunner to but "the shadow of Repeal, he could not get nearer to it or farther from it."[88] "All chance of a Federalist move is gone for the present," complained Davis after O'Connell's public declaration of support for the federalists, "and mainly because of O'Connell's public and private letters" in support of it.[89]

Federalism was one of the few suggested solutions to the Irish national question that engaged those who were, broadly speaking, both in the pro- and anti-Union camps. Nonetheless, in keeping with one motif of this chapter, it would be wrong to claim that it was some sort of missed opportunity in the Irish national story. Before his death in 1845, Davis himself also pointed to more serious obstacles to cooperation across the nationalist-unionist divide. The greatest difficulty in unifying the nation around a reconstituted patriotism was not O'Connellism but the increasingly detached perspective of the northeast of Ireland—particularly Belfast, which had experienced a rapid process of industrialization that gave it more in common with many British cities than the rest of Ireland. Davis believed that Ulster had been infected by "Utilitarianism." This was "the creed of Russell and Peel, as well as of the Radicals" that "measures prosperity by exchangeable values, measures duty by grain and limits desire to clothes, food and respectability."[90]

THE IRISH *SONDERWEG*

When O'Connell died in 1847, *The Spectator*—the embodiment of British compassion fatigue at the time of the Famine—suggested that he had demonstrated the upward limits of Irish nationalism. He

> was supreme only in Ireland and not there among several large and important classes of Irish society: the gentry—witness his cool reception and retreat from the Agricultural Society; the Orangemen—he was their personification of evil; the Irish Whigs—he was sweeping in his retaliatory assaults on the "the Black North"; the Young Irelanders—who were always grinding at his "Whig alliance" and Repeal accounts; and the Ribandmen—whom he was powerless to restrain.[91]

In fact, to an extent that was not immediately obvious, the years preceding the Irish Famine had seen the upward limits of constructive unionism. On the one hand, when Peel left office in 1846, there were reasons to believe that "Irish nationalism appeared to be moribund" and he had "scotched, though not killed, the repeal agitation." On the other hand, however, Peel's government had also carried Irish conciliation as far as it could; at that point he had nearly split his party on the Maynooth grant, and it was only with the support of the Whigs that he had been able to press his Irish measures through parliament.[92]

The gravity of the Famine began to become clear during Peel's last few months in office. "You will see," he wrote to a sympathetic Irish MP in November 1845, "how unfortunately our prospects in Ireland, so far as the present physical comfort of the people is concerned[,] have been clouded by the lamentable disease which has affected the potato crop."[93] As Peter Gray has observed, the lasting impression of 1840s policy toward Ireland was to become one of famine and lost opportunities. Rather than deliberate mendacity or callousness, it was the sheer inadequacy of the Whig government's response to the crisis after 1846 that was to become the greatest indictment of the Union. A blend of Providential evangelical belief and classical economic orthodoxy restricted the government's capacity and willingness to respond effectively. It meant that Britain, the richest nation in Europe, handled its peasant dominions less effectively than did any other European state. The ineffectiveness of the initial response was compounded by another conceptual and analytical shortcoming in English governance. This was the failure to recognize the transformative effect that mass mortality and emigration had on the social and economic structure of the country—particularly how it pertained to the land question. Even by 1850, Whig legislation on land was characterized by a "reassertion of orthodoxy." In addition, Russell's further aggravation of the sectarian problem in Ireland by clashing with the Catholic hierarchy—leading to the Ecclesiastical Titles Bill of 1852—confirmed his reputation as one of the most hapless of British prime ministers when it came to Irish affairs.[94]

The return of a relative period of prosperity and stability in the 1850s and 1860s initially obscured the long-term significance of these events. But the catastrophe of the Famine was to serve increasingly as a symbol of Irish difference, rather than the dawn of a new Victorian age of integration and prosperity.[95] After a lag, the psychological effects of the Famine began to assert themselves alongside a series of other developments that made Ireland increasingly difficult to manage under the Union: the growing problem of religious divisiveness and sectarianism; the infusion of economics into political conflict (above all in the linkage of land and the national question); the emergence of new forms of nationalist organization and ideology; and finally, the spread of prosperity and education, which also helped lay the foundation for the march toward national independence.[96] Above all, as Biagini has put it, "The Irish *Sonderweg* [special path] was shaped, not by colonialism but by the Famine and mass emigration."[97]

In Ireland, rather than giving the nation a common cause around which it could coalesce, the post-Famine period confirmed just how entrenched existing divisions had become. The issue of land reform was something that had the potential to unite liberal political forces in the country and bridge the growing gap between north and south. The Tenant League of North and South partly grew out of cooperation between two newspaper editors and inheritors of the Young Ireland and Presbyterian radical traditions, respectively—Charles Gavan Duffy and James McKneight. Yet divisions over the question of attitudes toward the Union remained a serious stumbling block for further cooperation between them. Indeed, Presbyterians framed their land rights distinctly from those of their Catholic counterparts by invoking customary tenant laws, which dated back to the Plantation, and gave them a more legally privileged position.[98] In some instances, then, in Ulster "tenant right" and "no surrender" could go literally hand in hand as the banner of a form of radical loyalism.[99] Augmenting this divide was the increasing sectarianization of Irish politics. Another burst of popular evangelical revivalism from the late 1850s was paralleled by the increasingly assertive Ultramontane movement, which emerged in the Catholic Church during the same period and was chiefly associated with Cardinal Paul Cullen.[100] The English liberal dream of the emergence of a Whiggish Catholic middle class remained unrealized—at least to the extent that had long been hoped for. The English Catholic intellectual Lord Acton (MP for Carlow between 1859 and 1865) and Thomas O'Hagan, perhaps the embodiment of an Irish Catholic Whig, bemoaned the difficulties of establishing a moderate Catholic journal in Ireland, independent of the hierarchy and of liberal outlook.[101]

It was with good reason that Disraeli saw an opportunity for the Conservatives to cooperate more closely with the Catholic hierarchy in the governance of Ireland. As he told colleagues, he wanted "to break off the connection between Toryism and Orangeism, it was merely accidental, of late growth: the first Orangemen were Whigs."[102] In October 1870, he claimed that the essence of his approach to the Union was to "govern Ireland according to the policy of Charles the First, and not of Oliver Cromwell, to emancipate the political constituency of 1832 from its sectarian bondage."[103] Such a reorientation was much more difficult than Disraeli envisaged, however. In a number of constituencies—particularly in Ulster—traditional Irish Conservative elites were forced to assert their Protestant *bona fides* in the teeth of a rising populist Orange movement, embodied in the figure of the Orange Order agitator William Johnston (though Johnston himself was later bought off by government patronage).[104] The sectarian dynamic was further entrenched by a series of electoral reforms—above all large extensions of the franchise in 1867 and 1884.[105] Although this presented a problem of management for Irish Conservatives, the Irish Liberal party—notwithstanding a brief renaissance between the Second and Third Reform Acts and some success in its adoption of the cause of land reform—was even more vulnerable to confessional polarization. Its survival had traditionally depended on a large fund of Catholic support and an ability to present themselves as the most effective advocates of land reform.[106] As an indication of their vulnerability, the Ulster branch of the Liberal party was severely damaged by William Gladstone's anti-Vatican pamphlets in 1874.[107] As Conor Cruise O'Brien later wrote, the "arrival of mass democracy, in the last quarter of the nineteenth century, made it hard to keep up the pretence that the division had been exaggerated."[108] The sectarian bondage identified by Disraeli was not simply a residue of the past but an organizing dynamic in mass politics.

The two decades following the Famine were a period of reorientation, renewal, or rebirth for Irish nationalism, meanwhile. As the first indication of this, it was a different type of Young Ireland that emerged from the Famine than the movement Thomas Davis had led before his death in 1845. Something of the Davisian spirit of inclusive patriotism—encapsulated in his encouragement of federalism— was lost. What remained was the purist critique of O'Connell's alliance with the Whigs and—because of the botched rebellion of 1848—another staging post in the emergence of a tradition of physical force republicanism. The disproportionate influence of another Young Irelander, John Mitchel, was an indication of the hardening of opinions. In *The Last Conquest of Ireland—Perhaps*, he characterized 1848 as a last act of defiance against British misrule and popularized the view that the Famine had been engineered by the British state as part of a policy of deliberate genocide.[109]

Thus 1848 was an important year in Irish history, but not quite in the way that it was in many European states. In 1935 the American historian Robert C. Binkley suggested that throughout Europe in the period between 1848 and 1871, there was an overarching conflict between an ideal of the "federative polity" (essentially variations on the theme of liberal constitutional governance) and new trends of rationalism and realism that was harnessed by nation-builders, such as Cavour and Bismarck.[110] Ireland did not quite fit the mold, though it did share certain commonalities. As Joe Lee argues, Ireland underwent a period of rapid political and economic modernization after the Famine, which shaped its political path. High emigration rates left behind a generation of tenant farmers engaged in a market-orientated agricultural economy. Rather than pulling away from the British political system in the first instance, this class initially made use of it to secure and improve their position. It was by linking the national question to the self-interest of such groups that nationalists were able to amplify their campaign in the English parliament.[111]

The effects of the Famine—not least a hardening of political attitudes—were not immediately obvious because of the lack of a parliamentary presence for organized nationalism until the establishment of Isaac Butt's Home Rule Association in 1870. Butt's own conversion to Home Rule grew out of the hostility that some Irish Tories had always maintained about the Union. Partly because of this perspective, he might even be regarded as the last genuine federalist in Ireland.[112] The extraparliamentary nationalist awakening that occurred simultaneously was of a markedly different character than the movement led by Butt, though its nature and its potency were not immediately obvious. Thus the establishment of the Irish Republican Brotherhood in 1858 and the emergence of the Fenian movement was watched with interest in England but regarded as a poor cousin of previous incarnations of nationalism—not least because of its strength among the "lower orders." "Once, the only allies to be expected on the side of order were the members of one privileged class; now, we can rely upon every class in Ireland above the lowest," suggested *The Times* in 1865. "When Irish disaffection has dwindled to Fenianism, there is good reason for supposing that it is dying out altogether and must be very near its end."[113] Not for the first time, the anomalous nature of Irish nationalism compared to its European counterparts—not least the importance of a large Irish-American diaspora—obscured the emotional reserves on which it could draw. According to the liberal Presbyterian writer Thomas Croskery in *The Edinburgh Review*, other European patriots were "animated by wider sympathies and antipathies; and however wild their enthusiasm and deplorable their blunders, they set before them a loftier purpose and worship a higher ideal." Fenians were men "of mean education and a narrow mind, whose ambition is restrained by no principle, whose measures are guided by no reflection."[114]

The irony of this was that the very features of Fenianism for which it was mocked were also the characteristics that made it an enduring political force in Ireland. These included its ability to appeal beyond the elite audience reached by Young Ireland, its skill in harnessing nationalist sentiment in the working classes, and its foundation on a loosely defined but strongly felt sentiment of hostility toward England. Taking a more cautious editorial line than *The Times*, in 1868 *The Spectator* recognized that these traits presented "the gravest danger ahead for Liberal statesmanship, a large revolutionary party, with vague and restless cravings for national independence, and without faith in constitutional reforms or Parliamentary agitation."[115] The challenge presented by the Fenians became more complicated because of their willingness to play the parliamentary game after the "New Departure" announced by John Devoy in 1878.[116]

That the government had responded to the Fenian rising of 1867 by resorting to coercion undermined the self-image of liberal English government. It was a theme that Viscount John Morley evoked memorably in his 1868 pamphlet *Ireland's Rights and England's Duties.* "How much longer shall we have the hangman for our ally and the gallows for the symbol of our Government?"[117] It was no coincidence that such liberal angst signaled the beginning of an unprecedented level of English political investment in the Irish question, surpassing the previous legislative programs of the late 1830s and early 1840s. In October 1868, William Gladstone had announced at an election speech in Wigan his intention to take the ax to the tree of the Irish problem in its three branches—church, land, and education.[118] These efforts began with the totemic decision to disestablish the Irish church in 1869. As with Catholic emancipation in 1829, liberal unionists spoke in terms of a new watershed in the life of the Union; it was not only "a measure of justice" but the dismantling of the last pillar of "garrison" rule in Ireland.[119] In Ireland, however, even those who were sympathetic to the measure were not so sanguine that it would make much long-term difference. Although it was a "just and desirable measure," wrote the land reformer Hugh de Fellenberg Montgomery, "those who expect any immediate effect from it on the temper of Ireland will be deceived.... The matter of the Church ... will I imagine soon blow over and make little difference; the land question is much more serious."[120] Yet land reform was more of a domino than a silver bullet. The Liberal Land Act of 1870 did not solve the land question; as the first of five major land reform measures between 1870 and 1909, one might even say that it was the prelude to it.

Having made such concerted efforts to conciliate Ireland, the apparently irreducible nature of Irish nationalism was hard to digest. The bemusement of English liberals when faced with the resilience and the bitterness of these sentiments became a recurrent motif of the 1870s and 1880s. "The majority 4/5th of them are no more H[ome] Rulers than you or I, but they adopted the shibboleth to get into Parliament," boasted the Liberal lord lieutenant Spencer at the end of his tenure in 1874. "I have left your dear country very quiet. I am not depressed about it. I think that we are overcoming the anti-English prejudices gradually."[121] Predictably, this attitude left him rather perplexed at the ferocity of anti-English sentiment articulated by nationalists such as the Young Irelander John Martin:

> I cannot hear how John Martin impressed the House.... It makes my heart sick to think that a man like him sh[oul]d really believe that England looks upon Irishmen as her foes.... If only he knew how devoted and earnest many Englishmen are in the cause of Ireland, and how ready they were to make almost any sacrifices for her good, he would not insult them as he does.[122]

Such willful blindness was in deep reserve. In 1878, reflecting on the decade that had passed since the Fenian Rising of 1867, *The Times* retrospectively celebrated the "sweeping but beneficent legislation of 1869 and 1870" in pacifying Ireland. Although it had taken a number of years, *The Times* haughtily criticized the impatience of those who had complained that its "effects were not visible all at once, just as they are now impatient because Europe is not immediately pacified by the Treaty of Berlin. The mills of politics grind slowly, like those of higher Powers, but in the end they return meal for grain." Both comparisons were as unfortunate as they were Panglossian. The Treaty of Berlin did not solve the Eastern Question, and within months, Ireland was suffering from an acute agricultural depression that led to the formation of the Land League and the Land War from 1879 to 1882. This made a mockery of the 1878 claim that "Fenianism is dead, and nothing has taken its place, though Irish restlessness may still find an occasional outlet in wayward and almost fantastic expressions of imaginary discontent."[123] As if to underline the irony, it was one of the clauses of 1870 Land Act—a provision to protect small farmers from eviction in instances where their rent had been increased significantly—that became the pretext for much of the Land League mobilization. The flood of money from Irish America meant that an increasing number of these cases could be brought to court. This entailed a further politicization of land and law, and was a challenge to the English defense of property rights as sacrosanct. In subsequent land reforms, Ireland's distinctiveness would be increasingly recognized in legislation.[124]

By August 1880, the extent of the agitation—and the "creep of agrarian crime"—had led to a complete change of tone among the English liberal elite. Coercion was countenanced again.[125] Tellingly, it was *The Times*, in its opposition to Home Rule, that led the most visceral and personalized attacks against Charles Stewart Parnell. Disappointment at the failure to pacify Ireland exposed the first cracks in the previously confident unionism of the English governing classes. Parnell's ability to make the Land War tell in terms of parliamentary pressure was particularly disconcerting. Parnellism, according to the liberal constitutional lawyer and opponent of Home Rule, A. V. Dicey, was "organised hypocrisy. It is violence masked under the form of constitutional agitation."[126] Notwithstanding such hyperbole, a substantive change in the nature and strategy of nationalism under Parnell's leadership made the era of Isaac Butt seem very distant. As Maume notes, "the machine politics, opportunistic vaguenesss, and authoritarian leadership which contributed to the growth of Parnell's party," combined with the agrarian violence of the Land War, demonstrated the growing contrast between "Davisian idealism and the seedier aspects of constitutional nationalism."[127]

THE END OF ASSIMILATION

The reversion to coercion in the 1880s weighed heavily on Gladstone's mind—not least the imprisonment of Parnell in Kilmainham Gaol in 1882, reminiscent of Peel's imprisonment of O'Connell almost forty years before. This, as much as anything else, contributed to the gangrene that began to infect the Union in this period. In 1897, Gladstone claimed not to have given much thought to Parnell until relatively late in his career. But the key moment in his reassessment had come with the renewal of agitation. "I do not think that Mr. Parnell or Irish matters much engaged my attention until we came back to Government in 1880," he told Parnell's biographer Barry O'Brien, "You see we thought that the Irish question was settled. There was the Church Act and the Land Act, and there was a time of peace and prosperity, and I frankly confess that we did not give as much attention to Ireland as we ought to have done."[128]

Gladstone's conversion to Home Rule represented the decisive end of the consensus in the British governing classes that the Union, if imperfect, was the least bad option for Ireland. As Hoppen has described, an essentially assimilationist approach had been pursued by successive mid-century administrations. It had been characterized by tithe, poor law and municipal reform, the regularization of the Irish franchise, and the alignment of criminal and civil law with English practice. While assimilation efforts had peaked in the ten years before the Famine, this approach—of equalization—had essentially continued into the 1850s and 1860s. However, Hoppen also argues that a creeping recognition of Ireland's difference began in the late 1860s—manifested in reforms that went against the grain of British political culture and were not replicated in England (disestablishment, land reform, and the acceptance of Catholic control over education). Long before his "Hawarden Kite" (of December 1885, when it was revealed to the press that he had "converted" to Home Rule), Gladstone was bombarding his party with talk of Irish special circumstances. His conversion began, therefore, with an acceptance of the limits of assimilation.

This was a watershed in English attitudes to Ireland from which even anti–Home Rulers recognized it was almost impossible to recover. Both before and after the Home Rule bill, Hoppen suggests, there was a "coherent unity that lay beneath" both Tory and Whig prescriptions for Ireland; before the 1870s, it was assimilationist; after the 1870s, it was increasingly predicated on Irish differentiation. The most significant thing about Gladstone's conversion to Home Rule was not its sincerity or high-mindedness, but the fact that his party's "mode of discourse about Ireland changed to one based upon a general acceptance of Irish difference." And although Lord Salisbury's Conservative-Unionist coalition rejected Home Rule, they too increasingly accepted the logic of Irish difference. Indeed, the result was that policies associated with "constructive unionism"—such as those associated with land reform—were arguably more radical than Gladstone was willing to countenance from an English parliament.[129] Such a conclusion tallies with Andrew Gailey's argument that progressive reform measures under the chief secretaryships of Gerald Balfour and George Wyndham into the early 1900s were sticking-plaster solutions rather than part of a coherent strategy of killing Home Rule by kindness.[130]

The failure of the first and second Home Rule bills in 1886 and 1893, respectively, might be approached as the last "what if" moment in Anglo-Irish relations between 1801 and 1922. Both English liberal historians and sympathizer of the moderate constitutional nationalist John Redmond—who assumed leadership of the Home Rule movement after Parnell—later propounded the view that Home Rule would have prevented the separatism, radicalization, and militarization of Irish politics that occurred in the first two decades of the twentieth century and led to the Easter Rising of 1916 and the War of Independence.[131] Much of this interpretation depends on an assessment of the relationship between Gladstone and Parnell and their leadership of their respective parties. Arguably, Gladstone's approach to the Irish question in the early 1880s was to assess it through the prism of Parnellism, and Parnell himself—the "English face" of Irish national-ism.[132] As an Irish Protestant landowner and the honorary chieftain of a mass movement of Catholic tenants, the paradox of Parnell also provided Gladstone with a potential solution to the problem of Irish discontent and radicalism. Despite his leadership of the Land League, Parnell's discomfort with violence—above all, the Phoenix Park murders of 1882—also suggested a desire to moderate the nationalist movement over which he presided. Gladstone's own conservatism on the question of property rights (his desire to protect the rights of private property ownership) may also have encouraged him to devolve the question to a Home Rule parliament in which the voice of Irish landowners, such as Parnell, would be preserved. This seems to be confirmed in the diaries of Sir Edward Hamilton, who recalls how Gladstone—his close friend—believed that Parnell "appeared to be an altered man" after his release from Kilmainham in 1882 and had demonstrated "evident conservative proclivities which he (Mr. Gladstone) intended to do his utmost to encourage." On another occasion Gladstone also commented to Hamilton that it was a "mistake to suppose that Irishmen were imbued with real democratic tendencies" and that he would not be surprised if, when they had their own legislature, "they might cut a somewhat Tory figure" in the Imperial parliament.[133]

The potential problem with this logic, of course, was that the Home Rule settlement envisaged in 1886 was partly dependent on the preeminence of Parnell, but this ended in 1890 following the acrimony of the O'Shea divorce case (when Parnell was named in divorce proceedings, causing the majority of his party to desert him). Even a unionist writer, such as St. John Ervine, could see the importance of Parnell to the balancing act that was Home Rule: "Parnell was the cornerstone of the Irish arch. When he fell, it fell."[134] The populist Catholic invective against Parnell following his citation in the O'Shea divorce case and the anti-Parnell narrative of the followers of Timothy Healy and the Irish National Foundation under John Dillon internally poisoned nationalist politics in Ireland.[135]

Thus, the missed-opportunity narrative presupposes a number of secondary contingencies that were by no means inevitable. In addition, it would be a mistake to underestimate the extent of British opposition to Home Rule and the absolute rejection of Gladstone's logic on the Irish question. Indeed, as O'Callaghan has observed, British unionists presented the Gladstone-Parnell alliance and land agitation as essentially criminal rather than political.[136] What is more, it was far from inevitable that a federalist solution to the Irish question would have extinguished the growing separatist movement in Ireland. Parnell himself said in a speech in Cork in January 1885 that "no man has the right to fix the boundary to the march of a nation."[137] Kelly's work on the Fenian movement has pointed both to the widespread popularity of separatism and the pragmatism of Fenians in supporting Parnellism as a first step to a fuller political revolution.[138] Perhaps more importantly, neither Parnell nor Gladstone had anything approaching a viable answer to the Ulster question; both the nature and extent of opposition to

Home Rule in the northeast of Ireland made any peaceable settlement to the Irish question very unlikely in 1886.[139]

In another uneven pattern, toward the end of the life of the Union, one could argue that English sympathy for Ireland—expressed both in English support for Home Rule and constructive unionism—increased in parallel with the growth of Irish separatist sentiment in Ireland. Indeed, to a certain extent, the growing dislocation between the English desire for conciliation and the Irish willingness to be conciliated was typical of the story of the Union itself. In *British Democracy and Irish Nationalism*, Biagini has demonstrated how common feeling with the cause of Irish nationalism helped remake English radicalism before 1906. Not only was there a genuine belief in the morality of doing "justice to Ireland," but Home Rule was also identified with broader liberal goods, such as democracy, constitutional freedoms, and humanitarianism.[140] John Redmond's moderate constitutional leadership of the Home Rule movement made such solidarity easier, of course. However, the undercurrents in Ireland suggested that the momentary re-convergence of English liberalism and Irish nationalism was ultimately based on flimsy foundations. In his essays in the *New Ireland Review* between 1898 and 1900, the Gaelic revivalist and essayist D. P. Moran mocked both British self-conscious moralism and Irish eagerness to win British good opinions.[141] Moreover, despite the apparent robustness of Redmond's Irish Parliamentary Party before 1914, the sands of nationalist Ireland were shifting beneath it toward a more radical and separatist stance. From local studies of Leitrum, Longford, Roscommon, Sligo, and Westmeath, Michael Wheatley's *Nationalism and the Irish Party* suggests that the Irish Parliamentary Party was in a stronger position before 1914 than is often assumed. However, he also demonstrates that Irish nationalism was increasingly characterized between 1910 and 1916 by an intensity of grievance and Anglophobia at the micro level. This was reflected in the paramilitarization of the Home Rule campaign and compounded, above all, by the impact of the Great War. The Gaelic revival movement offered further cultural exposition of ethno-religious difference.[142] Meanwhile, of course, the logic of polarization was asserting itself in Irish unionism at the same time: it was slipping out of the realms of British political acceptability in a way that was to have long-term connotations in the bastardized Northern Ireland state. Not only did the unionist campaign become increasingly militarized and extreme; it also began to adopt a tone and a discourse that was increasingly distinct from its sponsors and supporters in the English political mainstream.[143]

OUT OF THE SERBONIAN BOG

Even before the Union was officially ended in 1922, Ireland had defied and defeated the ingenuity of English governance. By 1894, the London correspondent of the *New York Times* claimed that Ireland was regarded by most English MPs at Westminster as "a sort of Serbonian bog, whence proceeded from time to time unintelligible squeaks and groans, and through the obscurity of which vague shadows now and again may be seen flitting about, but no one seriously tried to follow what is going on or to understand what it is all about."[144] That said, this fatalistic attitude to Irish affairs only emerged relatively late in the life of the Union. Indeed, the etymology of the phrase "Serbonian bog," pre- and post-Union, tells a story about how much intellectual effort English statesmen expended on Ireland. First used by Milton in *Paradise Lost*, the phrase had re-entered the English political lexicon in the late eighteenth century through an Irishman, Edmund Burke—whose specter haunted the Union throughout the nineteenth century. Under the Union, English politicians frequently adopted Burke's phrase as shorthand for the complex job of legislating on Irish matters in parliament—on church, education, and land reform. Lord John Russell was the first to do so in a parliamentary debate over Repeal of the Union in 1834, in which he attempted to answer the Irish nationalist case against the Union. In 1835 Peel picked it up and applied it to the vexed question of how to spend the surplus revenues of the established church in Ireland—"a Serbonian bog, in which whole armies of unfortunate logicians had sunk."[145]

Over the course of the century, the phrase increasingly came to denote the fatigue that was beginning to set in when it came to Irish affairs. At the time of the Famine, *The Spectator* objected to Russell's measures of relief on the grounds that "We need not fill up 'the Serbonian bog of Irish destitution' with our hard-earned store of sovereigns, nor make roads to nowhere, nor build work-houses for people to lie down and die in; and it is that conviction which makes the Englishman suddenly tighten his flowing purse-strings."[146] Irishmen from across the political spectrum—including the Orange Order and ultra-Protestant populist William Johnston—were conscious of (and sensitive to) the fact that their concerns were regarded as too provincial for arrogant imperial "senators" at Westminster who wanted to stay clear of "the Serbonian Bog of Irish Polemics."[147] The phrase even found its way into the lexicon of the English supporters of Home Rule for Ireland. In 1891, Viscount John Morley warned William Gladstone that there was a "frightful danger" of the Liberal party finding itself "struggling once more in the Serbonian bog of the land question."[148]

The legacy of the Union is a complex one. Kissane has argued that the Irish experience of the Westminster system—"regular local and national elections, administrative structures increasingly subject to popular control, and a parliament at times responsive to Irish public opinion"—contributed to the political maturation of Irish society and provided the foundations for post-Union Irish democracy.[149] Despite the radicalization of Irish politics after 1914, Townshend has also argued that the influence of the constitutional tradition of O'Connell, Parnell, and Redmond outlasted the hothouse atmosphere of the period from 1916 to 1922.[150] Even though Ireland did succumb to many of the supremacist and violent tendencies common to other forms of European nationalism, Biagini has made the valid point that—both under the Union and after it—the Irish experience also contains remarkable illustrations of the extent to which liberal elites could control and contain such tendencies.[151]

Ultimately, though, the moral of the Union is that the Irish question proved beyond the abilities of a succession of highly imaginative and gifted statesmen. Although "constructive" unionists—a remarkably broad group that encompassed figures as diverse as Castlereagh and Gladstone—complained that their vision was withheld from Ireland for too long and was delivered in much less fortuitous circumstances than they had hoped, they could not claim that it was unrealized. That the high point of the liberal unionist governing vision in the early 1870s formed the prelude to the greatest nationalist campaign of the nineteenth century tells a story in itself. It spoke to the growing—and potentially unbridgeable—gap between legislative ingenuity at Westminster and social and political under-currents in Ireland itself. That is not to say that the end of the Union was only a matter of time after 1870. As Comerford has suggested, the events of 1870—such as land reform and the disestablishment of the Irish church—could even be inter-preted as a new beginning for the Union.[152] It is, however, to posit that the prem-ises of British elite support for the Union had been seriously undermined by the 1890s. Although Irish nationalist mobilization was more formidable than ever be-fore under Charles Stewart Parnell, the real game-changer was the fraying of the pro-Union consensus in the British governing classes.

FURTHER READING

The best starting points for the passage of the Act of Union are Patrick M. Ge-oghegan, *The Irish Act of Union: A Study in High Politics, 1798–1801* (Dublin: Gill and Macmillan, 1999) and D. Keogh and K. Whelan (eds.), *Acts of Union: The Causes, Contexts and Consequences of the Act of Union* (Dublin: Four Courts Press, 2001). For the role of the Union in the eyes of the British governing class, see D. A. Kanter, *The Making of British Unionism, 1740–1848: Politics, Government and the Anglo-Irish Constitutional Relationship* (Dublin: Four Courts Press, 2009). For an excellent article on the death of unionism in the British political elite, see K. Theodore Hoppen, "Gladstone, Salisbury and the End of Irish Assimilation," in Mary E. Daly and K. Theodore Hoppen (eds.), *Gladstone: Ireland and Beyond* (Dublin: Four Courts Press, 2010).

The best general surveys of the nineteenth century are Roy Foster, *Modern Ireland 1600–1972* (Harmondsworth, England: Penguin, 1990); Paul Bew, *Ireland: The Politics of Enmity* (Oxford: Oxford University Press, 2007); and Alvin Jackson, *Ireland, 1798–1998: Politics and War* (London: Wiley Blackwell, 1999). For good guides to political history under the Union, see Ó Tuathaigh, "Political History," in L. M. Geary and M. Kelleher (eds.), *Nineteenth-Century Irish History: A Guide to Recent Research* (Dublin: University College Dublin Press, 2005); and Patrick

Maume, "Irish Political History: Guidelines and Reflections," in M. McAuliffe, K. O'Donnell, and L. Lane (eds.), *Irish History* (Basingstoke: Palgrave, 2009). Also useful is P. Gray (ed.), *Victoria's Ireland? Irishness and Britishness, 1837–1901* (Dublin: Four Courts Press, 2004).

For the movement to repeal the Union, the dominant interpretation has been provided by Oliver MacDonagh, *O'Connell: The Life of Daniel O'Connell 1775–1847* (London: Weidenfeld and Nicolson, 1990). For a superb and more recent account, see Patrick Geoghegan, *King Dan: The Rise of Daniel O'Connell 1775–1829* (Dublin: Gill and Macmillan, 2010); and Patrick Geoghegan, *Liberator: The Life and Death of Daniel O'Connell, 1830–1847* (Dublin: Gill and Macmillan, 2013). For Young Ireland, see R. Davis, *The Young Ireland Movement* (Dublin: Gill and Macmillan, 1987).

For the post-Famine period, the primer remains F.S.L. Lyons, *Ireland since the Famine* (London: Collins/Fontana, 1973). Also seminal are Joseph J. Lee, *The Modernisation of Irish Society, 1848–1918* (Dublin: Gill and Macmillan, 1973); and V. E. Vaughan (ed.), *A New History of Ireland, V: Ireland under the Union, 1870–1* (Oxford: Clarendon Press, 1989). For federalism and the Irish question, the best book is Alvin Jackson, *Home Rule in Irish History, 1800–2000* (London: Weidenfeld and Nicholson, 2003).

A wealth of excellent and relatively new scholarship addresses important questions of sectarianism and the politicization of religion. Among the best studies are: Nigel Yates, *The Religious Condition of Ireland, 1770–1850* (Oxford: Oxford University Press, 2006); James H. Murphy (ed.), *Evangelicals and Catholics in Nineteenth-Century Ireland* (Dublin: Four Courts Press, 2005); David Hempton and Myrtle Hill, *Evangelical Protestantism in Ulster Society, 1740–1890* (London and New York: Routledge, 1992); K. Collins, *Catholic Churchmen and the Celtic Revival in Ireland, 1848–1916* (Dublin: Four Courts Press, 2002); Desmond Bowen, *The Protestant Crusade in Ireland, 1800–1870* (Dublin: Gill and Macmillan, 1978); and Colin Barr, *Paul Cullen, John Henry Newman and the Catholic University of Ireland, 1845–1865* (Notre Dame, IN: University of Notre Dame Press, 2003).

The best insight into the emergence of Ulster (as opposed to Irish) unionism remains Thomas MacKnight's *Ulster as It Is or Twenty-Eight Years' Experience as an Irish Editor* (2 vols., London: Macmillan and Co., 1896). Also important are: Brian M. Walker, *Ulster Politics: The Formative Years, 1868–1886* (Belfast: Ulster Historical Foundation, 1989); and James Loughlin, *Gladstone, Home Rule and the Ulster Question, 1882–93* (Dublin: Gill and Macmillan, 1986).

On Irish nationalism after the Home Rule crisis, there are numerous biographies of Parnell and other key protagonists. The most recent one is by P. Bew, *Enigma: A New Life of Charles Stewart Parnell* (Dublin: Gill and Macmillan, 2012). For Fenianism, the major study remains R. V. Comerford's *The Fenians in Context: Irish Politics and Society, 1848–82* (Dublin: Wolfhound Press, 1985). Matthew Kelly picks up the baton to the Easter Rising in *The Fenian Ideal and Irish Nationalism,*

1882–1916 (Woodbridge, England: Boydell Press, 2006). For early twentieth-century Irish nationalism, see Michael Wheatley, *Nationalism and the Irish Party: Provincial Ireland, 1910–1916* (Oxford: Oxford University Press, 2005). See also David Fitzpatrick, *Politics and Irish Life 1913–1921: Provincial Experiences of War and Revolution* (Oxford: Oxford University Press, 1998).

NOTES

1. Sydney Owenson, *The Wild Irish Girl: A National Tale* (Oxford: Oxford University Press, 1999), pp. 250–252.

2. James Kelly, "The Origins of the Act of Union: An Examination of Unionist Opinion in Britain and Ireland, 1650–1800," *Irish Historical Studies* 25: 99 (1987), pp. 236–263.

3. Daniel Mansergh, "The Union and the Importance of Public Opinion," in D. Keogh and K. Whelan (eds.), *Acts of Union: The Causes, Contexts and Consequences of the Act of Union* (Dublin: Four Courts Press, 2001), pp. 126–139.

4. F.S.L. Lyons, *Ireland since the Famine* (London: Collins/Fontana, 1973), pp. 98–99.

5. Richard Cobden, *England, Ireland and America (1835)*, edited by Richard Ned Lebow (Philadelphia: Institute for the Study of Human Issues, 1980), pp. xii, 74.

6. Ernest Renan, "What Is a Nation," in Geoff Eley and Ronald Grigor Suny, *Becoming National: A Reader* (Oxford: Oxford University Press, 1996), pp. 42–55, 43.

7. 14 April 1886, *Hansard's Parliamentary Debates*, third series, vol. CCIV, p. 1079.

8. Patrick M. Geoghegan, *The Irish Act of Union: A Study in High Politics, 1798–1801* (Dublin: Gill and Macmillan, 1999); D. Keogh and K. Whelan (eds.), *Acts of Union: The Causes, Contexts and Consequences of the Act of Union* (Dublin: Four Courts Press, 2001).

9. Kevin Whelan, "The Other Within: Ireland, Britain and the Act of Union," in Keogh and Whelan, *Acts of Union*, pp. 13–33, 13.

10. Liam O'Dowd, "Republicanism, Nationalism, and Unionism: Changing Contexts, Cultures and Ideologies," in J. Cleary and C. Connolly (eds.), *The Cambridge Companion to Modern Irish Culture* (Cambridge: Cambridge University Press, 2005), pp. 78–95, 79.

11. Roy F. Foster, *Paddy and Mr Punch: Connections in Irish and English History* (London: Penguin, 1993), pp. 81–82.

12. J.G.A. Pocock, *The Discovery of Islands: Essays in British History* (Cambridge: Cambridge University Press, 2005), p. 164.

13. D. A. Kanter, *The Making of British Unionism, 1740–1848: Politics, Government and the Anglo-Irish Constitutional Relationship* (Dublin: Four Courts Press, 2009), pp. 319–320.

14. Stephen Howe, *Ireland and Empire: Colonial Legacies in Irish History and Culture* (Oxford: Oxford University Press, 2001); Terrence McDonough (ed.), *Was Ireland A Colony? Economics, Politics and Culture in Nineteenth-Century Ireland* (Dublin: Irish Academic Press, 2005); A. Jackson, "Ireland, the Union and the Empire, 1800–1960," in K. Kenny (ed.), *Ireland and the British Empire* (Oxford: Oxford University Press, 2004), pp. 123–153. For a discussion of Irish involvement in the British Empire, see K. Jeffrey (ed.), *An Irish Empire? Aspects of Ireland and the British Empire* (Manchester: Manchester University Press, 1996).

15. This was the verdict of former radicals, such as Charles Hamilton Teeling in his *Personal Narrative of the Irish Rebellion* (London: Henry Colburn, 1828), p. 263.

16. Kanter, *The Making of British Unionism*, p. 110.

17. "Maria Edgeworth, Edgeworthstown, to Miss Ruxton, Arundel in Sussex, 29 January 1800," in Maria Edgeworth, *The Life and Letters of Maria Edgeworth*, edited by Augustus J. C. Hare (London: E. D. Arnold, 1893), vol. 1, pp. 67–69.

18. "Marquis Cornwallis to Major-General Ross, 26 February 1801," in Charles Ross (ed.), *Correspondence of Charles, First Marquis Cornwallis* (London: John Murray, 1859), vol. 3, pp. 340–341.

19. Roy Foster, "The Politicisation of Irish Literature," first Clark Lecture, delivered at Cambridge University, February 17, 2009. See also Roy Foster's *Words Alone: Yeats and His Inheritance* (Oxford: Oxford University Press, 2011).

20. Terry Eagleton has pointed out that much of Edgeworth's novel *Castle-Rackrent* was written before the Union, during 1798, when the Edgeworths found themselves threatened by the local peasantry, despite their record as liberal landlords. See Terry Eagleton, *Heathcliff and the Great Hunger: Studies in Irish Culture* (London: Verson, 1995), pp. 161–166. See also Seamus Deane, *Strange Country: Modernity and Nationhood in Irish Writing since 1790* (Oxford University Press: Oxford, 1997).

21. Quoted in M. Butler, "Introduction," in Maria Edgeworth, *Castle-Rackrent and Ennui* (Harmondsworth: Penguin, 1992), p. 3.

22. Edgeworth's account of meeting Castlereagh is in her diary entries for March 9 and April 3, 1822, in Edgeworth, *The Life and Letters of Maria Edgeworth*, vol. 1, pp. 65–67, 71–74.

23. Foster, *Words Alone*, pp. 10–44. Foster sees Owenson and Edgeworth as part of a triumvirate of writers whose works shared loosely connected themes.

24. Mary Campbell, *Lady Morgan: The Life and Times of Sydney Owenson* (Sydney: Pandora Press, 1988), pp. 106–107, 165.

25. Owenson, *The Wild Irish Girl*, pp. xviii, 250–252.

26. Charles Lever, *The Knight of Gwynne* (London, 1872, first published in 1847).

27. "R. J. Bryce (Belfast Academy) to Duke of Wellington, 24 June 1830," Add. Ms. 70992, f. 86, British Library, London, f. 86; "R. J. Bryce to Robert James Tennent, 7 January 1828," *Tennent Papers* D1748/G/76/15, Public Record Office Northern Ireland, Belfast.

28. Kanter, *The Making of British Unionism*, p. 161.

29. J. C. Beckett, *The Making of Modern Ireland* (London: Faber and Faber, 1981), p. 285.

30. Quoted in Paul Bew, *Ireland: The Politics of Enmity* (Oxford: Oxford University Press, 2007), p. 63.

31. For Duigenan, see Bew, *Ireland*, pp. 30–31, 49–51, 59–60.

32. Kanter, *The Making of British Unionism*, p. 320.

33. "Earl of Rosse to Lord Redesdale, 3 May 1822," Redesdale Papers, T3030/13/3, *Eighteenth Century Irish Official Papers in Great Britain*, vol. 2, edited by A.P.W. Malcolmson (Belfast: Public Record Office of Northern Ireland, 1990), pp. 462–464.

34. Frank Wright, *Two Lands on One Soil: Ulster Politics before Home Rule* (Dublin: Gill and Macmillan, 1996).

35. "Lord Castlereagh," *Dublin University Magazine* 249: 39 (October 1849), pp. 433–447.

36. Daire Keogh, *'The French Disease': The Catholic Church and Radicalism in Ireland, 1790–1800* (Dublin: Four Courts Press, 1993).

37. Sir Henry Parnell, *An Enquiry into the Causes of Popular Discontent in Ireland* (London: J. Milliken, [reprint] 1805, second ed.), pp. 2–4.

38. J.C.D. Clark, *English Society 1688–1832: Ideology, Social Structure and Political Practice during the Ancien Regime* (Cambridge: Cambridge University Press, 1985).

39. See J. Bew, "The High Politics of Post-War Reconstruction in Britain after 1815," in Michael Rowe, Karen Hagemann, Alan Forrest, and Stefan Dudink (eds.), *War, Demobilisation and Memory: The Legacy of War in the Era of Atlantic Revolutions* (Basingstoke: Palgrave Macmillan, 2015).

40. "'On the Expediency of Making Further Concessions to the Catholics,' by Lord Castlereagh, 1801," in Charles Vane-Tempest Stewart (ed.), *Memoirs and Correspondence of Viscount Castlereagh* (London: John Murray, 1848–1853), 12 vols., IV, pp. 392–400, 396.

41. Parnell, *An Enquiry into the Causes of Popular Discontent in Ireland*, pp. 3–4, 7, 14–20, 21–22, 71.

42. "The Knight of Kerry, Valentina, to Lord Sandon, 24 March 1845," Harrowby Papers, T3228/7/1, *Eighteenth Century Irish Official Papers in Great Britain*, vol. 2, edited by A.P.W. Malcolmson (Belfast: Public Record Office of Northern Ireland, 1990), p. 147.

43. John Morley, *The Life of William Ewart Gladstone* (London, 1903), II, p. 242.

44. John Pope Hennessy, *Lord Beaconsfield's Irish Policy: Two Essays on Ireland* (London, 1885), pp. 24–25.

45. K. T. Hoppen, *The Mid-Victorian Generation, 1846–1886* (Oxford: Oxford University Press, 1998), p. 559.

46. G. Ó Tuathaigh, "Ireland under the Union: Historiographical Reflections," *Australian Journal of Irish Studies* 2 (2002), pp. 1–21.

47. See Peter Jupp, "Government, Parliament and Politics in Ireland, 1801–41," in J. Hoppit (ed.), *Parliaments, Nations and Identities in Britain and Ireland, 1600–1850* (Manchester: Manchester University Press, 2003), pp. 146–168, 147.

48. B. Farrell (ed.), *The Irish Parliamentary Tradition* (Dublin: Gill and MacMillan, 1973); Alan O'Day, *The English Face of Irish Nationalism: Parnellite Involvement in British Politics, 1880–6* (Dublin: Gill and MacMillan, 1977).

49. H. Senior, *Orangeism in Ireland and Britain, 1795–1836* (London and Toronto: Routledge, 1966); Allan Blackstock, *Loyalism in Ireland, 1789–1829* (Woodbridge: Boydell, 2007).

50. William Drennan, *A Letter to the Right Honourable Charles James Fox* (London, 1806), pp. 30, 34–35.

51. For the classic account, see A.T.Q. Stewart, "The Transformation of Presbyterian Radicalism in the North of Ireland, 1798–1825" (unpublished MA thesis, Queens' University Belfast, 1956). For more recent accounts, see R. F. Holmes, "From Rebels to Unionists: The Political Transformation of Ulster's Presbyterians," in R. Hanna (ed.), *The Union: Essays on Ireland and the British Connection* (Newtownards, Northern Ireland: N.P., 2001), pp. 34–47; and John Bew, *The Glory of Being Britons: Civic Unionism in Nineteenth-Century Belfast* (Dublin: Irish Academic Press, 2007).

52. Oliver MacDonagh, *O'Connell: The Life of Daniel O'Connell 1775–1847* (London: Weidenfeld and Nicolson, 1990). For a more recent account, see Patrick Geoghegan, *King Dan: The Rise of Daniel O'Connell 1775–1829* (Dublin: Gill and Macmillan, 2010) and *Liberator: The Life and Death of Daniel O'Connell, 1830–1847* (Dublin: Gill and Macmillan, 2013).

53. K. T. Hoppen, "Riding a Tiger: Daniel O'Connell, Reform and Popular Politics in Ireland, 1800–1847," *Proceedings of the British Academy* 100 (1999), pp. 121–143.

54. P. Maume, "Irish Political History: Guidelines and Reflections," in M. McAuliffe, K. O'Donnell, and L. Lane (eds.), *Irish History* (Basingstoke: Palgrave, 2009), pp. 1–48.

55. Richard English, *Irish Freedom: The History of Nationalism in Ireland* (Oxford: Oxford University Press, 2006), p. 131.

56. "George Dawson to Sir Robert Peel, Coleraine, 17 August 1828," *Peel Papers*, Add. Ms. 40, 397, f. 244, British Library, London.

57. Nigel Yates, *The Religious Condition of Ireland, 1770–1850* (Oxford: Oxford University Press 2006). See also James H. Murphy (ed.), *Evangelicals and Catholics in Nineteenth-Century Ireland* (Dublin: Four Courts Press, 2005).

58. Irene Whelan, *The Bible War in Ireland: The 'Second Reformation' and the Polarisation of Protestant-Catholic Relations, 1800–1840* (Dublin: Lilliput Press, 2005).

59. Joseph J. Lee, *The Modernisation of Irish Society, 1848–1918* (Dublin: Gill and Macmillan, 1973).

60. Jennifer Ridden, "The Forgotten History of the Protestant Crusade: Religious Liberalism in Ireland," *Journal of Religious Liberty* 31: 1 (March 2007), pp. 78–102, 84.

61. Eugenio F. Biagini, "Liberty and Nationalism in Ireland, 1798–1922," *Historical Journal* 51: 3 (2008), pp. 793–809.

62. *Northern Whig*, December 6, 1830.

63. "17 February 1834," *Hansard's Parliamentary Debates*, third series, vol. XXI, p. 417.

64. *Northern Whig*, July 2, 1832.

65. "Lord Rossmore to O'Connell, 13 December 1834," *The Correspondence of Daniel O'Connell, vol. V, 1833–1836*, edited by M. R. O'Connell (Dublin: The Irish Manuscripts Division, 1977), p. 230.

66. See Bew, *The Glory of Being Britons*, chapter 3.

67. G. Ó Tuathaigh, "Political History," in L. M. Geary and M. Kelleher (eds.), *Nineteenth-Century Irish History: A Guide to Recent Research* (Dublin: University College Dublin Press, 2005), pp. 1–26.

68. Joseph Spence, "The Philosophy of Irish Toryism, 1833–52" (unpublished PhD dissertation, University of London, 1991).

69. Jennifer Ridden, "'Making Good Citizens': National Identity, Religion, and Liberalism among the Irish Elite, c. 1800–1850" (unpublished PhD thesis, London University, 1998). See also Jennifer Ridden's "'Making Good Citizens': Britishness as an Imperial and Diasporic Identity: Irish Elite Perspectives, c. 1820–70s," in P. Gray (ed.), *Victoria's Ireland? Irishness and Britishness, 1837–1901* (Dublin: Four Courts Press, 2004), pp. 88–105

70. Eve Patten, *Samuel Ferguson and the Culture of Nineteenth-Century Ireland* (Dublin: Four Courts Press, 2004), p. 13.

71. See, for example, William Cooke Taylor, *Reminiscences of Daniel O'Connell*, P. Maume (ed.) (Dublin: University College Dublin Press, 2005); and the *Dictionary of Irish Biography* online (http://dib.cambridge.org).

72. *Speech of the Earl of Mulgrave to the House of Lords, on Monday 27 November, 1837, on the Motion of the Earl of Roden* (London: Ridgway, 1837), p. 324. See also M.A.G. Ó Tuathaigh, *Thomas Drummond and the Government of Ireland, 1835–41* (Dublin: National University of Ireland, 1977).

73. Eric Stokes, *The English Utilitarians and India* (Oxford: Oxford University Press, 1959), pp. 25, 73–76, 173, 256; R. Pearson and G. Williams, *Political Thought and Public Policy in the Nineteenth Century, An Introduction* (London and New York: Prentice Hall Press, 1984), pp. 9–38.

74. Cited in Adam D. Kriegel, "Liberty and Whiggery in Early Nineteenth-Century England," *Journal of Modern History* 52: 2 (June 1980), p. 272.

75. Peter Mandler, *Aristocratic Government in the Age of Reform, Whigs and Liberals, 1830–1852* (Oxford: Oxford University Press, 1990), pp. 159–162.

76. Michael Durey, "When Great Men Fall Out: William Wickham's Resignation as Chief Secretary for Ireland in January 1804," *Parliamentary History* 25: 3 (2006), p. 334–335.

77. See Peter Gray, "'Ireland's Last Fetter Struck Off'": The Lord Lieutenancy Debate, 1800–67," in Terrence McDonough (ed.), *Was Ireland a Colony? Economics, Politics and Culture in Nineteenth-Century Ireland* (Dublin: Palgrave Macmillan, 2005), pp. 87–102.

78. *Belfast Newsletter*, March 12, 1850.

79. Boyd Hilton, *A Mad, Bad, and Dangerous People? England, 1783–1846* (Oxford: Oxford University Press, 2006), pp. 542–543.

80. See, for example, L. J. McCaffrey, *Daniel O'Connell and the Repeal Year* (Lexington: University of Kentucky Press, 1996), pp. 214–239.

81. For Young Ireland, see R. Davis, *The Young Ireland Movement* (Dublin: Gill and Macmillan, 1987). See also David Dwan, "Civic Virtue in the Modern World: The Politics of Young Ireland," *Irish Political Studies* 22: 1 (2007), pp. 35–60.

82. See Donal A. Kerr, *Peel, Priests and Politics: Sir Robert Peel's Administration and the Roman Catholic Church in Ireland, 1841–1846* (Oxford: Oxford Historical Monographs, 1984), p. 15; D. Gwynn, *O'Connell, Davis and the Colleges Bill* (Cork: University College Cork Press, 1948).

83. "Thomas Davis to Robert James Tennent, 9 June 1845," *Tennent Papers*, D1748/G/141/5A-B, Public Record Office of Northern Ireland, Belfast.

84. The only study to deal with 1840s federalism in detail is B. A. Kennedy, "Sharman Crawford's Federal Scheme for Ireland," in H. A. Cronne, T. W. Moody, and D. B. Quinn (eds.), *Essays in British and Irish History Presented to J. E. Todd* (London: Frederick Muller, 1949), pp. 235–254. It is only briefly discussed in existing studies of Irish federalism: George Boyce, "Federalism and the Irish Question," in Adrea Bosco (ed.), *The Federal Idea: The History of Federalism from Enlightenment to 1945*, vol. 1 (London and New York: Lothian Foundation Press, 1991), pp. 119–138; J. Kendle, *Ireland and the Federal Solution: The Debate Over the United Kingdom Constitution, 1870–1921* (Kingston and Montreal: McGill-Queen's University Press, 1989), pp. 9–11; and Alvin Jackson, *Home Rule in Irish History, 1800–2000* (London: Weidenfeld and Nicholson, 2003), p. 16.

85. Charles Gavan Duffy, *Young Ireland, Part I, 1840–1845* (Dublin, 1892), pp. 213–214.

86. Charles Gavan Duffy, *Thomas Davis*, edited by B. Clifford (Cork: Anchor Books, 1999), p. 168.

87. "Daniel O'Connell to William Smith O'Brien, 21 October 1844," *Correspondence of Daniel O'Connell, The Liberator*, edited by W. J. FitzPatrick, (London: John Murray, 1888), II, pp. 335–336.

88. Charles Gavan Duffy, *My Life in Two Hemispheres*, 2 vols. (New York: Unwin, 1896), I, pp. 101–103.

89. "Thomas Davis to William Smith O'Brien, undated," *William Smith O'Brien Papers*, Ms. 432/895, National Library of Ireland, Dublin.

90. Duffy, *Thomas Davis*, p. 69.

91. *Spectator*, May 29, 1847.

92. Kanter, *The Making of British Unionism*, pp. 281–282.

93. "Peel to Emerson Tennent MP, 2 November 1845," *Peel Papers*, Add Ms. 40,575, f. 92, British Library London.

94. Peter Gray, *Famine, Land and Politics: British Government and Irish Society, 1843–50* (Dublin: Irish Academic Press, 1999), pp. 139–141, 224–226, 328–338.

95. Peter Gray, "The Making of Mid-Victorian Ireland? Political Economy and the Memory of the Great Famine," in Peter Gray (ed.), *Victorian's Ireland? Irishness and Britishness, 1837–1901* (Four Courts Press: Dublin, 2004), pp. 151–166.

96. Lyons, *Ireland since the Famine*, pp. 16–17.

97. Eugenio F. Biagini, *British Democracy and Irish Nationalism, 1876–1906* (Cambridge: Cambridge University Press, 2007), p. 24.

98. "Seamus Macneactam [James McKneight] to Charles Gavan Duffy MP, 14 October 1847," *Duffy-McKneight Papers*, T1143/1 Public Record Office of Northern Ireland, Belfast.

99. Alexander Dinnen, *Ulster Tenant Right: Mr Jas. Sharman Crawford's Amendment Bill and "No Surrender"* (Belfast: Northern Whig, 1876).

100. David Hempton and Myrtle Hill, *Evangelical Protestantism in Ulster Society, 1740–1890* (London and New York: Routledge, 1992); K. Collins, *Catholic Churchmen and the Celtic Revival in Ireland, 1848–1916* (Dublin: Four Courts Press, 2002), pp. 98–104; Desmond Bowen, *The Protestant Crusade in Ireland, 1800–1870* (Dublin: Gill and Macmillan, 1978); Desmond Bowen, *Paul Cullen and the Shaping of Modern Irish Catholicism* (Dublin: Gill and Macmillan, 1983); Colin Barr, *Paul Cullen, John Henry Newman and the Catholic University of Ireland, 1845–1865* (Notre Dame, IN: University of Notre Dame Press, 2003).

101. "John Emerich Edward Dalberg Acton, first Baron Acton to Lord O'Hagan, undated," *O'Hagan Papers*, D/2777/9/76/3, Public Record Office of Northern Ireland, Belfast.

102. See entry for February 16, 1851, in *Disraeli, Derby and the Conservative Party: The Political Journals of Lord Stanley, 1849–1869*, edited by J. R. Vincent (Hassocks, Sussex: Harvester Press, 1978), pp. 40–41.

103. John Pope Hennessy, *Lord Beaconsfield's Irish Policy: Two Essays on Ireland [1885]* (London: Kessinger reprint 2010), p. 26.

104. For Johnston, see J. Aiken McClelland, *William Johnston of Ballykilbeg* (Lurgan: Ulster Society, 1990). See also Bew, *Glory of Being Britons*, chapter 6; A. Shields, *The Irish Conservative Party, 1852–1868: Land, Politics and Religion* (Dublin: Irish Academic Press, 2007), pp. 207–213.

105. See K. T. Hoppen, "Tories, Catholics and the General Election of 1859," *Historical Journal* 13: 1 (March 1970), pp. 48–67; and K. T. Hoppen, *Elections, Politics and Society in Ireland, 1832–1885* (Oxford: Oxford University Press, 1984).

106. Brian M. Walker, *Ulster Politics: The Formative Years, 1868–1886* (Belfast: Ulster Historical Foundation, 1989); Frank Thompson, *The End of Liberal Ulster: Land Agitation and Land Reform, 1868–1886* (Belfast: Ulster Historical Foundation, 2001).

107. Thomas MacKnight, *Ulster As It Is or Twenty-Eight Years' Experience as an Irish Editor* (London, 1896), 2 vols., I, pp. 303–308.

108. Conor Cruise O'Brien, *States of Mind: States of Ireland* (St. Albans, England: Granada Publishing, 1974), p. 29.

109. Bew, *Ireland: The Politics of Enmity*, pp. 212–213.

110. Robert C. Binkley, *Realism and Nationalism, 1852–1871* (New York and London: Harper and Brothers, 1935).

111. Lee, *Modernisation of Irish Society*.

112. *Speech of Isaac Butt, Esq., MP, at Glasgow November 14th, 1871, on Home Rule for Ireland* (Dublin: Irish Home Rule Association, 1871), pp. 9–11. In one of his earliest speeches on Home Rule, Butt referred back to two previous federalists—Sharman Crawford MP and Thaddeus O'Malley, a Catholic priest and Chartist.

113. *The Times*, May 1, 1865.

114. Thomas Croskery, "The Irish Abroad," *Edinburgh Review* 260: 127 (April 1868), pp. 257–275, 266.

115. *Spectator*, September 26, 1868.

116. Cited in Niall Whelehan, *The Dynamiters: Irish Nationalism and Political Violence in the Wider World, 1867–1900* (Cambridge: Cambridge University Press, 2012), pp. 16, 26.

117. John Morley, *Ireland's Rights and England's Duties* (Blackburn: The Times Office, 1868), p. 18.

118. Kevin McKenna, "From Private Visit to Public Opportunity: Gladstone's 1877 Trip to Ireland," in Mary E. Daly and K. Theodore Hoppen (eds.), *Gladstone: Ireland and Beyond* (Dublin: Four Courts Press, 2010), pp. 77–89.

119. Sir George Young, *The Dis-Establishment of the Irish Church a Measure of Justice; A Letter to the Rev. A. Headley, Rector of Hardenhuish* (Chippenham: S. Spinke, 1868), p. 4. See also J. P. Parry, "Religion and the Collapse of Gladstone's First Government, 1870–1874," *Historical Journal* 25: 1 (March 1982), pp. 71–101.

120. "Hugh de Fellenberg to his cousin, 27 November 1868," *Hugh De Fellenberg Montgomery Papers*, D1121/3, Public Record Office of Northern Ireland, Belfast.

121. "Lord Spencer to Dufferin, 19 March 1874," *Dufferin and Ava Correspondence*, D1071/H/B/S/476/33. Public Record Office of Northern Ireland, Belfast.

122. "Lord Spencer to O'Hagan, undated [circa 1868–1874]" *O'Hagan Papers*, D/2777/8/258B, Public Record Office of Northern Ireland.

123. *The Times*, August 31, 1878.

124. E. D. Steele, *Irish Land and British Politics: Tenant Right and Nationality, 1865–1870* (Cambridge: Cambridge University Press, 1974).

125. *The Times*, August 24, 1880.

126. *The Times*, December 23, 1890.

127. D. P. Moran, *The Philosophy of Irish Ireland*, edited by P. Maume (Dublin: University College Dublin Press, 2006), pp. xx–xxi.

128. "Gladstone, Hawarden Castle, Chester, to Barry R. O'Brien, 11 December 1895," in R. Barry O'Brien, *The Life of Charles Stewart Parnell, 1846–1891* (London, 1897), 2 vols., I, pp. 355–358, 356.

129. K. Theodore Hoppen, "Gladstone, Salisbury and the End of Irish Assimilation," in Mary E. Daly and K. Theodore Hoppen (eds.), *Gladstone: Ireland and Beyond* (Four Courts Press: Dublin, 2010), pp. 45–63, 62.

130. Andrew Gailey, *The Death of Kindness: The Experience of Constructive Unionism, 1890–1905* (Cork: Cork University Press, 1987).

131. For the classic statement of this view, see J. L. Hammond, *Gladstone and the Irish Nation* (London: Cass, 1938).

132. O'Day, *The English Face of Irish Nationalism.*

133. Entries for February 3 and February 11, 1891, in *The Diary of Sir Edward Hamilton*, W. R. Bahlman (ed.) (Hull, England: University of Hull Press, 1993), pp. 110, 138.

134. St. John Ervine, *Parnell* (Harmondsworth, England: Penguin, 1944), p. 244.

135. Frank Callanan, *The Parnell Split* (Cork: Cork University Press, 1993).

136. Margaret O'Callaghan, *British High Politics and a Nationalist Ireland: Criminality, Land and the Law under Forster and Balfour* (Cork: Cork University Press, 1994).

137. Quoted in Albert W. Quill, *The Arguments against Home Rule Unanswered by Mr Morley: A Critical Study* (Dublin: Hodges, Figgis and Company, 1888), p. 20.

138. M. J. Kelly, *The Fenian Ideal and Irish Nationalism, 1882–1916* (Woodbridge: Boydell Press, 2006). For the classic account of Fenianism, see R. V. Comerford, *The Fenians in Context: Irish Politics and Society, 1848–82* (Dublin: Wolfhound Press, 1985).

139. James Loughlin, *Gladstone, Home Rule and the Ulster Question, 1882–93* (Dublin: Gill and Macmillan, 1986).

140. Biagini, *British Democracy and Irish Nationalism, 1876–1906*.

141. D. P. Moran, *The Philosophy of Irish Ireland*, pp. 10–11.

142. Michael Wheatley, *Nationalism and the Irish Party: Provincial Ireland, 1910–1916* (Oxford: Oxford University Press, 2005). See also David Fitzpatrick, *Politics and Irish Life 1913–1921: Provincial Experiences of War and Revolution* (Oxford: Oxford University Press, 1998).

143. George Dangerfield, *The Strange Death of Liberal England* (Serif: London, 1997, first published 1935), pp. 88–90. See also J. Smith, *The Tories in Ireland: Conservative Party Politics and the Home Rule Crisis, 1910–1914* (Dublin: Irish Academic Press, 2000).

144. *New York Times*, September 8, 1894.

145. *Speech of the Right Hon. Sir Robert Peel, Bart., in the House of Commons, on Thursday 2nd April, 1835* (London: John Murray, 1835), p. 14.

146. *Spectator*, May 19, 1849.

147. In this case, William Johnston was referring to his objections to the government's endowment for the Catholic seminary at Maynooth. See *Downshire Protestant*, July 6, 1855.

148. Patrick Jackson, *Morley of Blackburn: A Literary and Political Biography of John Morley* (Madison, NJ: Fairleigh Dickinson University Press, 2012), p. 198.

149. Bill Kissane, *Explaining Irish Democracy* (Dublin: University College Dublin Press, 2002), p. 79.

150. Charles Townshend, "The Meaning of Irish Freedom: Constitutionalism in the Free State," *Transactions of the Royal Historical Society*, sixth series (1998), pp. 45–70.

151. Biagini, "Liberty and Nationalism in Ireland, 1798–1922."

152. Vincent Comerford, "Gladstone's First Irish Enterprise," in V. E. Vaughan (ed.), *A New History of Ireland, V: Ireland under the Union, 1870–1* (Oxford: Clarendon Press, 1989), pp. 431–449. For a critical view of this volume, see the review by Mary E. Daly in *Irish Historical Studies* 27: 106 (November 1990), pp. 171–174.

CHAPTER 4

INDEPENDENT IRELAND

Fearghal McGarry

People talk of the wrongs done to Ireland by England in the past. God knows standing on this holy spot it is not likely any of us can ever forget, though God grant we all may forgive, the wrongs done to our fathers a hundred or two hundred years ago. *But do let us be a sensible and truthful people.* Do let us remember that we today of our generation are a free people (*cheers*). We have emancipated the farmer; we have housed the agricultural labour; we have won religious liberty; we have won free education ... we have laid broad and deep the foundations of national prosperity and finally we have won an Irish parliament and an executive responsible to it (*cheers*).[1]

J OHN REDMOND'S SPEECH, MADE IN Wexford in the autumn of 1914, is a striking reminder of just how different the future of Ireland appeared to contemporaries in the period between the passage of the Home Rule Act and the outbreak of the Easter Rising. Despite Redmond's telling allusion to the spirit of '98, the promised land that his audience (prematurely) celebrated was the product of constitutional politics rather than violent insurrection, and Ireland's national destiny appeared bound up with the peaceful evolution of Home Rule in the United Kingdom rather than with independent statehood.

Redmond's address highlights a major challenge in analyzing a historical period that saw the transformation of Ireland from a poor, Catholic periphery of the United Kingdom to a prosperous independent republic. Hindsight inevitably accentuates processes of change rather than the elements of continuity that were more evident to contemporaries. Successful advocates of change—whether early-twentieth-century separatists or post-1945 economic reformers—are privileged over the more representative figures (like Redmond) that they ultimately vanquished, erasing from history the alternative futures that most contemporaries took for granted. Individual decades are easily presented as watersheds, and the acceleration or prevention of change is attributed to the actions of charismatic individuals.[2] In reality, the agents of change are largely structural, long-term, diffuse, and often transnational: urbanization, for example, reconfigured the "nature and shape of the family, relations between the sexes, patterns of work and of recreation, standards of housing and sanitation, modes of dress, of private and public conduct."[3]

National histories are also fraught with assumptions, beginning with the idea that the nation—or, in Ireland's case, the history of Irish nationalism, the struggle for independence, and the nation-state(s) that emerged from that struggle—should naturally form the principal narrative of history. Although nation-centered accounts remain dominant, the approaches that inform them have changed. The establishment in 1938 of the journal *Irish Historical Studies* marked the emergence of a generation of historians who, under the banner of professional impartiality, dedicated themselves to subverting what they viewed as Ireland's long tradition of mythologized history, a project whose implications were arguably little less politicized than those it sought to revise.[4] Writing against the backdrop of the Troubles from the 1970s, the revisionist generation of historians extended this critique of nationalist historiography into the revolutionary period.[5] While exposing its limitations, they were less successful in liberating the Irish story from moralistic approaches and "the Anglocentric obsession that once led the study of political and economic history so far astray."[6]

Post-revisionist approaches, reflecting both a less polarized climate and revisionist advances, are characterized by a less iconoclastic attitude toward popular nationalism, and a shift from a focus on elites and the state toward the experiences of ordinary people. The emergence of new perspectives, such as gender and social history, has been shaped by the availability of new sources and international historiographical influences; it also reflects a shift in interest from how power was acquired to how it was exercised that coincided with two decades of revelations about corruption and abuse by Irish elites. Given the nature of history as a dialogue between past and present, contemporary history presents particular challenges. While providing historical perspective, accounts of the recent past inevitably reflect current preoccupations. J. J. Lee's influential critique of the state's failure to deliver on the promise of independence was informed by the bleak circumstances of the 1980s; more recent surveys have sought to make sense of the twentieth century in the wake of the Celtic Tiger, the end of the Troubles, or, more recently, the Irish state's worst economic crisis since independence.[7]

Rather than attempting a broad survey, this chapter focuses on four key processes that shaped twentieth-century Ireland: revolution, state-building, economic liberalization, and modernization. Although the violence of the revolutionary decade created the political structures that shape present-day Ireland, the social and economic changes of the final decades of the twentieth century, by rupturing cultural patterns that predated independence, arguably brought about a more profound dislocation. In Southern Ireland—the focus of this chapter—the long era between these periods of upheaval was initially characterized by the pursuit of national sovereignty and self-sufficiency. In contrast, the decades after the Second World War saw the gradual abandonment of that vision in favor of a more pragmatic policy of economic liberalization. The resulting modernization saw many traditional aspects of Irish society replaced by individualistic values more typical of contemporary European society.

REVOLUTION, 1900–1923

How did Ireland's future appear in 1900? Despite the exciting cultural ferment in urban advanced nationalist circles, there was little reason to predict the violent upheavals that followed. The Land War had created a more conservative Catholic bourgeoisie that found political representation in the reunited Irish Parliamentary Party. Under John Redmond's stolid leadership, most Irish nationalists appeared content to await the opportunity to secure a modest measure of home rule from Westminster. Beyond the Protestant-dominated northeast, the Irish Party had few electoral rivals, and some of these—such as the Munster-based nationalist William O'Brien—advocated a more conciliatory political approach: "Seldom had Irish nationalism seemed less revolutionary."[8]

Under the Conservative chief secretary, Gerald Balfour, the British administration in Ireland had sought to kill Home Rule with kindness by advancing reforms that empowered the Catholic majority. His Liberal Party successor, Augustine Birrell, was even more emollient, appointing Catholics to prominent positions in Dublin Castle and treating the Irish Party leadership as the government-in-waiting. Yet nationalist attitudes to Britain remained ambiguous and ambivalent. The royal visits of 1900 and 1903 provoked noisy protest by a separatist minority, apathy, and popular enthusiasm, while Britain's global domination proved both a welcome source of employment and, as during the Boer War, a cause for resentment and agitation.

Nationalist historiography attributed the rise of physical-force republicanism to the disillusionment that followed the Parnell split and the impact of the cultural revival. The success of Sinn Féin in 1918 and the conflict that followed were presented as an inevitable consequence of the Irish Party's betrayal of national ideals. In contrast, subsequent revisionist approaches emphasized the Irish Party's electoral resilience and the marginalization of separatism until the crises triggered by Home Rule, the First World War, and the Easter Rising. What followed has sometimes been presented as a regrettable and counterproductive deviation from the constitutional path. Both interpretations raise questions. If the Irish Party was representative of nationalist opinion, why did it collapse so rapidly? If separatism was a significant political force, why did Redmond's opponents fare so poorly before 1916?

By 1900 it was clear that the Union, lacking legitimacy, was in retreat. Indeed, many aspects of the British administration in Ireland—the viceregal role of the lord lieutenant, its paramilitary police, and the succession of coercion acts required to maintain order—owed more to colonial rule than to British parliamentary democracy. Despite advances by Catholics, the Irish establishment was dominated by Protestant unionists,[9] a reality not lost on propagandists like D. P. Moran, whose sectarian rhetoric expressed the frustration of educated and ambitious Catholics marginalized in their own country.

It was clear also that whatever potential for a political accommodation between Ireland's two traditions may have existed when the Act of Union was implemented had long receded. The presence of a nationalist MP in every constituency with a Catholic majority by the late nineteenth century signaled how "the future of Irish politics lay with the nationalist mobilization of Catholics on the one hand, and the unionist mobilization of Protestants on the other."[10] Yet historians continue to differ on the significance of religion in the Irish question, some emphasizing its role as a cultural marker, others highlighting how religious beliefs shaped political conflict during a period of heightened sectarianism. Revisionist approaches tended to emphasize the confessional dimension of the revolution, arguing, for example, that its political outcome masked "a more far-reaching though informal religious settlement."[11] In contrast, post-revisionist interpretations place greater emphasis on competing claims to popular sovereignty than on confessional identities or communal atavism.[12]

Recent research questioning the dichotomy between constitutional and revolutionary politics helps explain the separatist revival. Despite the Irish Republican Brotherhood's marginalization and the lack of popular support for advanced nationalism before the Ulster crisis, separatist ideals remained "deeply embedded in the texture of Irish identity," achieving an "emotional resonance with the Irish people" that Home Rule failed to inspire.[13] In contrast, Redmondism—with its message of faith in Westminster, conciliation of unionism, and compromise with the Empire—rubbed more against the grain of popular nationalism. The gulf between Redmond's vision and popular sentiment was reflected by the rhetoric of the Irish Party's own provincial activists, which remained steeped in "Catholicity, sense of victimhood, glorification of struggle, identification of enemies, and antipathy to England."[14] Redmond's commitment to parliamentary methods and Ireland's role in the Empire has also distorted perceptions of his party: with one in four of its MPs former Fenians and the Ancient Order of Hibernians providing it with a powerful clericalist machine, the party was both a greener and less enlightened movement than later recalled.[15] Although now acknowledged as a modest attempt to accommodate nationalist aspirations, for some contemporaries on both sides of the political divide, Home Rule symbolized nothing less than the Catholic nation's triumph over centuries of Protestant tyranny.

As in other parts of Europe, the rise of popular movements dedicated to the restoration of native culture strengthened nationalist sentiment. Although formally apolitical, organizations like the Gaelic Athletic Association and Gaelic League sharpened divisions in nationalism by promoting the notion of a distinctive Irish culture, strengthening the position of those who argued that independence necessitated a separate state rather than devolution in the United Kingdom. Arthur Griffith's Sinn Féin, the party that would galvanize revolutionary sentiment after 1916, was a product of this early-twentieth-century cultural nationalist ferment.

There was an important generational dimension to this new nationalism. Although not representative of mainstream opinion, the young men and women who embraced advanced nationalism formed part of a distinctive generation—whose activities spanned language, theater, sports, and politics—and their experiences and aspirations diverged from the older generation that had fruitlessly pursued Home Rule since the 1880s.[16] Drawing on Catholic morality, nationalist purism, and separatist radicalism, their outlook owed as much to the Irish-Ireland movement (and the romantic sensibilities of the European "generation of 1914") as to the historic insurrectionary tradition to which they successfully laid claim in 1916.

It was not only nationalism but also socialism and feminism that challenged the pre-war social order throughout the United Kingdom. The Dublin Lockout of 1913, a bitter dispute over trade-union recognition involving twenty thousand workers, demonstrated the impact in Ireland of the international rise of general trade-unionism and class conflict.[17] It also illustrated the tensions between class and nation: although Jim Larkin's Transport Union won the support of some advanced nationalists, others—notably Sinn Féin's Arthur Griffith—were ambivalent or hostile to what they regarded as a British-backed socialist cause. The strike also highlighted the conditions in Dublin's tenement slums, where a third of the city's population lived in appalling conditions. The workers' defeat, and Larkin's departure to America, made clear that the future of Irish politics did not lie in revolutionary syndicalism.

As in the Irish left, the prominence of the national question proved a source of weakness and division in feminism, with many radical women prioritizing nation over gender. While middle-class, and often Protestant-led, suffragist organizations mobilized around the right to vote at Westminster, such militant nationalist groups as Inghinidhe na hÉireann—which combined republican, feminist, and cultural nationalist aspirations—identified separatism as the key to social and political emancipation.

During the same period, Irish unionism also experienced significant changes, resulting in the geographical and ideological retrenchment of a previously confident movement. The shift in its political leadership from a landed class with interests across Ireland and Britain to Ulster's industrial and commercial entrepreneurs—necessitated by the social and democratic reforms brought about by the Union—created a more militant and democratic unionism, increasingly shaped by the populist impulses of the Orange Order and evangelical Protestantism.[18] At the same time, the Irish question's importance in British politics during these years—and the extent to which the fate of Home Rule was determined by wider political conflicts in the United Kingdom—is easily overlooked. The belief that the Liberals, by breaking the Lords' power of veto, had conspired with Irish Catholics to subvert the British constitution accounted for much of the incendiary tone of Tory rhetoric during the Home Rule crisis. As a result, the Irish question represented a greater threat to the unity of the United Kingdom before the First World War than during the Irish conflict that followed it.[19]

Herbert Asquith's decision in 1912 to introduce Home Rule unleashed the forces that destroyed the Irish Party. Backed by the Conservatives and mutinous elements of the British army, the two-year unionist campaign incentivized by the Liberals' refusal to concede the partition settlement they knew to be necessary destroyed the government's Irish policy. The combination of political mobilization, international propaganda, and paramilitary threat deployed by Ulster unionists was derided, and then emulated, by nationalists. Following gunrunning by both the Ulster Volunteer Force and the Irish Volunteers, violence in Ireland appeared increasingly likely until the dramatic postponement of the Ulster crisis by the Great War.

Throughout these years the Irish Party was consistently outmaneuvered by Asquith and David Lloyd George, who skillfully subordinated the Irish question to their own political ambitions.[20] Having secured Home Rule on September 18, 1914 (albeit with its implementation suspended "for the duration"), Redmond had little alternative but to support the war, particularly given the unresolved status of Ulster. But he was also sympathetic to the war effort, believing that its shared sacrifices might transform sentiment in Ireland, an optimism shared by few of his colleagues. The party's support for enlistment split the Irish Volunteers (which Redmond had reluctantly commandeered), dividing an overwhelming Redmondite majority from a tiny separatist minority, but at the cost of shackling the party to an increasingly unpopular cause.

Despite the Irish Party's difficulties—as fear of conscription, an uncooperative War Office, and the formation of a coalition government comprising diehard unionists eroded its standing at home—the Easter rebels were motivated more by frustration and despair than by optimism. A "legion of the excluded," the militant coalition of republicans, Catholic intellectuals, socialists, and militant nationalists, agreed on little other than the necessity for action.[21] Although nationalist and revisionist historiography—for different reasons—emphasized "blood sacrifice" as its rationale, recent studies have stressed less mystical motivations. This change reflects a shift away from a preoccupation with Patrick Pearse (although his actions have also been more sympathetically reevaluated) as the Rising's figurehead and greater awareness of the motives of both the rebellion's key organizers and its rank-and-file.[22]

The consequences of the rebellion are well established. A military failure, resulting in the death of almost five hundred people and the destruction of much of the center of Dublin, the Rising commanded little public support at the time. Although its violence was dwarfed by the carnage of the Great War, in which two hundred thousand rather than two thousand Irishmen participated, its aftermath transformed Ireland. The authorities' coercive response, particularly the execution of the leading rebels and the internment of several thousand nationalists, aroused popular sympathy—and, later, political support—for the rebels, culminating in Sinn Féin's landslide electoral triumph in 1918. The Rising belatedly became the focus of historiographical controversy from the 1970s. That the rebellion had no democratic mandate, that its principal victims were Dublin's civilians, and that it had no likelihood of military success—thereby rendering partition more likely and the path to independence more violent—came as largely unwelcome insights by revisionist historians. Although echoing criticisms of the insurrectionary mind-set by such contemporaries as Irish Volunteer president Eoin MacNeill, the polemical tone and subtext of the debates that followed owed much to the toxic atmosphere of the Troubles.

Recent historiography has further emphasized the centrality of the First World War to the rebellion's causation, conduct, suppression, and consequences, to the extent that the Rising, and the wider Irish revolution, are now increasingly recognized (and commemorated) as part of the Irish experience of the Great War rather than as a parallel conflict.[23] The rebellion's ideological consequences, particularly the process whereby republicanism (the most extreme and least attainable of competing nationalist visions prior to 1914) became the common goal of Irish nationalism, has received greater attention. Although the radical if incoherent ideals of the organizers found less purchase among the rank-and-file of 1916, the tendency to dismiss the Proclamation as window-dressing has given way to more nuanced explorations of the process by which separatist radicalism was subsumed under a socially conservative Catholic nationalism.[24]

Although the events that followed—the establishment of a parliamentary assembly (Dáil Éireann) by the Sinn Féin Teachtaí Dála (members of the assembly, or TDs) in January 1919; the republican government's attempts to win international recognition and assert its authority in Ireland; the drift to guerrilla war; the truce of July 1921, and the negotiations that led to the Anglo-Irish Treaty—are well established, the dynamics of revolution have been subject to much reinterpretation.[25] That the intertwined strands of political, sectarian, and agrarian violence that occurred during 1919–1921 are inadequately conceptualized by such terms as "Anglo-Irish War" or "War of Independence" is increasingly accepted, but the extent to which the conflict should be considered a civil war remains contested. Nationalist historiography, which initially shaped popular understanding of the conflict, emphasized the idealistic motivations of separatists, the unequal nature of the clash between the Irish Republican Army (IRA) and crown forces, and the depth of public support for republicanism. At the same time, it elided class divisions, popular support for constitutional nationalism, public disquiet about separatist violence, and the strength and integrity of Ulster unionism.

Local studies—the dominant approach to the revolution since the 1970s—reveal greater complexity, emphasizing how the conflict gave rise to intra- as well as inter-communal violence, with separatists imposing their authority over nationalist rivals, and Belfast loyalists targeting Protestant socialists as well as Catholics.[26] Local studies also highlight the uneven nature of the conflict, with more than half of its approximately 2,141 fatalities between 1917 and 1921 occurring in County Cork and the cities of Belfast and Dublin.[27] Analysis of the relationship between revolutionary violence and such factors as social class, religious demography, and previous agitation has shed further light on the geography of revolution, with the importance of nonideological factors—such as collective pressures, communal solidarity, intergenerational tensions, local leadership, and the desire for excitement and status—increasingly evident.

Although the most controversial debates have focused on sectarianism and violence, having few defenders, the egregious behavior of the Black and Tans, Auxiliaries, and Ulster Specials—the paramilitary forces hastily mobilized to restore order in 1920—has aroused relatively little historiographical controversy. In contrast, Peter Hart's groundbreaking study of County Cork—which emphasized the cyclical dynamics of revolutionary violence, the fatal consequences of sectarian enmity in polarized communities, and the high level of violence against noncombatants—trenchantly challenged established narratives of the War of Independence.[28] Although aspects of Hart's research, which overstated the sectarian dimension of the conflict, gave rise to legitimate debates about sources, bias, and the relevance of events in Cork to other parts of the country, the polemical tone of the controversies provoked by his research also testified to the continued politicization of this period of history.

Although they facilitate analysis of change at a popular level, resulting in a more sophisticated understanding of the complexity of the revolution, local studies have been less effective in demonstrating the importance of transnational factors, such as the destabilizing impact of the First World War. The shift of power from imperial to nation-states—which occurred as democratic self-determination emerged as the principal source of political legitimacy in the post-war order—decisively influenced the outcome of what can be seen as a decade-long negotiation of the terms for Britain's disengagement from Ireland.

The tendency to conflate the effectiveness of the challenge to British power with levels of violence has also detracted from appreciation of the importance of the democratic nature of the republican challenge. As during the later Troubles, the propagandistic dimension of armed struggle always outweighed its military potential. The presence of Sinn Féin president Éamon de Valera in the United States throughout much of the War of Independence attested to the importance attached to the mobilization of international sympathy. In Ireland, the harnessing of popular support by Sinn Féin—demonstrated through the success of the republican courts and the less-effective takeover of local government—presented a greater challenge to British rule than did the shooting of small numbers of crown forces. Consequently, the claim that the outcome of the revolution demonstrated "how physical force can prevail over democracy" begs many questions.[29]

In retrospect, the contingent nature of the emergence of a successful challenge to British state power is striking. For example, Sinn Féin's 1918 manifesto had emphasized the importance of political means (notably, an appeal to the post-war Peace Conference) in achieving independence, rather than the violent methods that subsequently came to dominate the struggle for independence. Although drawing on long-established traditions—such as moral force, boycotting, and arbitration courts—it was the combination of the strategies of passive resistance previously advocated by Arthur Griffith—such as abstention from Westminster, the development of a counter-state, and the use of electoral politics—with the violent means and separatist objectives of the republican tradition popularized after 1916 that proved so novel and potent: "Irish republicans invented modern revolutionary warfare, with its mass parties, popular fronts, guerrilla warfare, underground governments, and continuous propaganda campaigns."[30]

The role of the Dáil courts demonstrated both the success and limitations of the republican campaign. The popularity of the courts, and their success in restoring order by mediating agrarian disputes, came to symbolize the Dáil's legitimacy, but their frustration of hopes for radical change also reflected the republican leadership's social conservatism. Nevertheless, the influential argument that Sinn Féin merely decanted the old wine of Home Rule into new bottles and that "there was a thick strand of continuity in political leadership" between republicans and their constitutional predecessors has been vigorously contested.[31] Kevin O'Higgins's much-quoted declaration that his generation was the "most conservative revolutionaries ever" deserves more scrutiny. The conservative outcome of the struggle for independence has allowed the significance of class tensions in the dynamics of revolution to be underestimated. As in other parts of the world, the post-war resurgence of strikes and land agitation emboldened Irish trade-union and socialist leaders, although it remains striking how the most successful trade-union actions were motivated by nationalist rather than by class objectives.

By divorcing the intractable issue of Ulster from the Irish question, the partition of the six northeastern counties in 1920 paved the way for the truce of July 1921 and the subsequent twenty-six-county imperial dominion. Championed by its principal negotiators, Michael Collins and Arthur Griffith, the "Treaty" secured popular support and slender cabinet and parliamentary majorities but was fiercely opposed by a republican minority and a majority of IRA combatants. While the preoccupation of "anti-treatyites" with symbolic issues—such as the oath to the British monarch—has been criticized, British politicians were equally concerned with the implications of these issues for the wider fate of the Empire.

Although some political scientists interpreted the resulting Civil War as a conflict between pragmatic democrats and romantic idealists, historians emphasize how more contingent factors, such as personal rivalries, factionalism, and socio-economic factors, shaped the 1922–1923 Civil War, which—along with communal violence in Belfast—accounted for more fatalities than did the War of Independence. While revisionist approaches often emphasized the anti-democratic nature of anti-treaty opposition, some recent interpretations are less critical, presenting the conflict as one between rival claims of democracy and self-determination.[32] Although such accounts emphasize how the threat of renewed violence by Britain should the Treaty be rejected contributed to the Civil War, in international terms there was nothing unusual about the constraints placed on aspirations for full independence by the geopolitical realities arising from a nation's proximity to a more powerful neighbor.

In comparison with the conflict that preceded it, the nature and dynamics of the chaotic violence of 1922–1923 have received less attention. The involvement of prominent former members of Michael Collins's "Squad" in brutal atrocities against anti-treaty combatants in Kerry, as well as anti-treatyite complicity in murky acts of sectarian and agrarian intimidation,[33] inevitably complicate ideological interpretations of the Civil War as a conflict concerned with the restoration of law and order or defense of the Republic. The extent to which the Free State's military forces, rather than the more widely condemned Irregulars, excelled in the use of terror remains insufficiently acknowledged in the historiography of state-building and in contemporary public discourse.[34] In addition to the execution of at least seventy-seven anti-treatyites (over three times more than the British authorities accounted for in the preceding conflict), "unknown numbers were shot extra-judicially by police and National troops," and "the bodies of at least twenty-five republicans were alleged to have been dumped in Dublin streets."[35]

The Civil War ended with the vanquished anti-treaty IRA's decision to dump arms, but the conflict's traumatic legacy shaped Irish politics for decades. The death of Arthur Griffith and assassination of Michael Collins within a fortnight of each other deprived the treatyite cause of its most talented leaders. Its political effects were most apparent in the emergence of a two-party system defined by civil war divisions. The "unfinished" revolution brought about other enduring consequences. The failure to achieve unity or a republic ensured that the national question long remained—as it does in present-day Northern Ireland—at the center of political discourse. By producing two broad coalitions in which social and economic differences were subordinated to divisions over the Treaty, the Civil War further marginalized the importance of class divisions in Irish politics.

What did the revolution achieve? Republicans failed to resolve the issues that led them to condemn the Irish Party—acquiescence to partition and a continued link with Britain—but they did achieve a far more substantial measure of independence. Although two-thirds of the First Dáil's TDs came from a professional or commercial background, the revolution, in political terms, also facilitated a more egalitarian outcome than Home Rule, installing a well-educated, largely lower middle-class leadership as the new ruling elite. However, few would dispute Joe Lee's assertion that it "brought no significant change in social trends or social attitudes. Home rulers, Sinn Féiners, Cumann na nGaedheal, and Fianna Fáil all shared the same fundamental value system."[36]

An equally important question, as Lee's observation suggests, concerns what the revolution failed to achieve. There is considerable consensus that the key political watershed of modern Irish history "did remarkably little to remould the social, cultural, and psychological features of the country."[37] Indeed, by creating two states that reflected the conservative and often illiberal values of their majority communities, the revolution arguably stymied social reform. The material interests of the nation's aged and infirm, working classes, and impoverished children championed by the First Dáil's Democratic Programme would have been better served had Ireland remained part of a wealthy British state increasingly shaped by Liberal and Labour welfarism. The polarization brought about by revolutionary violence ensured that the losers in both Irish states included not only its religious minorities but also radicals, such as socialists, feminists, and intellectuals. But against these shortcomings stood the momentous achievement of independence: the responsibility for the advances and failures that followed would lie with the elected representatives of the Irish people.

STATE BUILDING, 1923–1948

The most surprising aspect of the Irish settlement was its endurance. Republicans and British policymakers—as well as some unionists—had doubted the permanence of partition. Compared to those of other European successor states that emerged from the wreckage of the First World War, the Irish Free State's democratic structures also proved remarkably stable, particularly given the strength of Civil War animosities and the abstention of anti-treaty republicans from parliament until 1927. Northern stability, necessitating the subordination of political opposition to five decades of one-party rule, proved a less impressive feat. However, the governments of both states agreed on the need to curtail liberal democracy and rely on extensive powers of coercion to ensure their security from internal threats.

Despite occasional fears of a return to civil war, Free State politics remained stable: more than a decade of rule by W. T. Cosgrave's Cumann na nGaedheal (1923–1932) was followed by almost two decades of government by Éamon de Valera's Fianna Fáil (1932–1948). The resilience of parliamentary democracy, the most impressive achievement of the new state, resulted from structural, cultural, and political factors, particularly the acceptance of democratic norms on both sides of the Civil War divide.[38] Although its standard of living was two-thirds lower than that of the United Kingdom, the Irish Free State inherited a relatively modernized society,[39] with a comparatively well-educated population, and levels of socioeconomic development that were more favorable than in other new states in central and eastern Europe. High levels of land ownership and mass emigration contributed to this stability, as did Ireland's sheltered geopolitical position. Although a source of nationalist resentment, partition exported north of the border the potential for ethnic or communal violence so destructive of other European successor states. The principal consequence of partition in the South was to provide republicans with a useful source of political capital, notwithstanding their failure to adopt constructive policies to address it.

The legacy of British rule—not least the skill with which generations of nationalists had mastered political means to overthrow it—also contributed to the state's stability. With its bicameral parliament and cabinet government, the debt owed by the Free State to its predecessor was clear. Key structures of the former administration, such as local government and the civil service, remained largely intact. Such continuity was reinforced by the Civil War: deprived of the possibility of establishing new structures or developing the republican counter-state's divided institutions, treatyites were compelled to build on the foundations of the previous regime. The popular republican courts, for example, were scrapped in favor of a return to the more legalistic *status quo ante*. The Garda Síochána, one of the new state's most successful innovations, saw the replacement of a colonial gendarmerie with an unarmed force closer in spirit to the British model of policing; the emergence of an apolitical meritocratic civil service founded on the principle of ministerial responsibility marked a similar shift toward conventional British practices.

Such continuity reflected the importance of British influences on Irish republicans as well as the ideological limitations of a conflict fought to end British rule rather than transform the state or society. Arthur Griffith had been unusual among Irish revolutionaries in giving the state, rather than the nation, much thought. For many of the revolutionary generation, republicanism was rooted in a nationalist ideology of self-determination rather than any conception of a distinctive mode of government: as a result, ideas about morality, language, and identity tended to outweigh the importance of political ideology in the new state.

Consequently, the most ambitious attempts to distinguish the new regime from its predecessor focused on culture. Institutional continuity reinforced the government's conservatism, disappointing both pro-treaty intellectuals and many Cumann na nGaedheal TDs.[40] The post-revolutionary anticlimax reflected the unrealistic expectations raised by the tendency to blame Irish ills on British rule, and the corresponding assumption that self-government would inevitably lead to prosperity. It also reflected a widespread ideological skepticism about the morality of state intervention by conservative Free State politicians, such as Desmond FitzGerald, whose outlook was steeped in Catholic social thought: "Implicit in our intense nationalism was the supposition that with the coming of a national Government our lives would be radically changed. And how could that be unless the Government took possession of those lives."[41]

The key challenges facing Cumann na nGaedheal included the restoration of order, the rebuilding of the administration and infrastructure of the state, economic regeneration, and the assertion of the Free State's ambiguous constitutional status on the international stage. Unfortunately for Cosgrave's government—which never resolved the contradiction between its unwavering defense of the Treaty settlement, which bound the state to the Empire, and its desire to maximize Irish sovereignty—the state's external sovereignty and internal legitimacy remained intertwined. Despite establishing diplomatic legations, joining the League of Nations, and working with other "restless dominions" to mold the Empire into a more egalitarian Commonwealth, the party's identification with the Treaty undermined its credibility in an international era of resurgent nationalism. Although its successful efforts to integrate the anti-treaty opposition into the political system consolidated the state, the party reaped few dividends and was increasingly criticized as authoritarian because of its reliance on coercion to suppress a renewed IRA threat during its final years in office.

Although its electoral resilience has recently been emphasized,[42] Cumann na nGaedheal never achieved the support of even two-fifths of the electorate. Its appeal was not enhanced by its conservative fiscal policies and prioritization of pastoral farming over the industrialization previously advocated by Griffith. Although rational, its pursuit of free-trade policies was undermined by the Great Depression and the subsequent international shift to protectionism. The abortive mutiny of an ideologically disillusioned and self-interested faction of army officers in 1924, and the quashing of the Boundary Commission the following year, further exposed the government's nationalist credibility, resulting in the departure of several ministers most closely associated with the idea of the Treaty as a stepping-stone to national unity and full independence.

Despite its limitations, Cumann na nGaedheal faced little opposition before de Valera led his anti-treaty supporters into the Dáil in 1927. Notwithstanding a promising showing by the Labour Party in 1922, Civil War politics had prevailed: "alternative patterns of division based on class, sectional, regional, or religious differences played only a subordinate role."[43] Although the absence of political cleavages defined by class differentiated Ireland, north and south, from many European countries, this pattern would later be recognized as characteristic of how the politics of post-colonial states were molded by attitudes to the former ruling power. Nor was the failure of left-wing politics to emerge in a strongly nationalist, Catholic rural state with an underdeveloped industrial base as inexplicable as is sometimes suggested, particularly given Labour's failure to harness the strength of trade-unionism or exploit its limited political opportunities.[44] Consequently, it was Fianna Fáil, which combined a strong appeal to nationalism with a populist social agenda, that won power in 1932. Since its foundation in 1926—when the more modern, moderate, and pragmatic elements of anti-Treaty Sinn Féin had split from an abstentionist majority—Fianna Fáil's combination of nationalist rhetoric, effective organization, and economic protectionism had proved increasingly appealing to Irish voters.

Unsurprisingly, given the enmity between Cumann na nGaedheal and Fianna Fáil, manifested in street violence between pro-Treaty Blueshirts and left-wing IRA supporters during the two years after Fianna Fáil's election, their political differences were more apparent to contemporaries than were their ideological similarities. Despite their revolutionary origins, neither party placed much faith in the people: both favored a centralized approach to government that prioritized state control, and neither curbed the influence of a strong civil service. Republicanism came to be identified with the pursuit of independence from Britain rather than ideas about how the state should be governed. Neither party showed any great interest in redistributing power or wealth, although Fianna Fáil favored land redistribution and a protectionist model that challenged the state's economic dependence on trade with Britain. Although de Valera's "economic war" with Britain (1932–1938) proved counterproductive, his efforts to replace export-led cattle farming with tillage and native industrialization reaped domestic political dividends. Of the two parties, Fianna Fáil was more committed to state intervention, implementing welfare and housing reforms that improved the lives of the urban and rural poor.

The largely unacknowledged consensus underpinning interwar nationalist politics was reflected in the efforts to create a state that enshrined Gaelic culture and a Catholic social order. Both parties prioritized compulsory Irish in schools (seen as key to the restoration of the language) and implemented language tests for public-service employment. The "need to establish the political and cultural identity of the new state" outweighed concerns about alienating the Protestant minority and the consequences of educating children in a language in which they were not proficient.[45]

Although—or perhaps because—some anti-treaty republicans had been excommunicated during the Civil War, Fianna Fáil revealed itself the more sensitive to clerical interests of the two parties. Cosgrave made it impractical to secure a divorce, but de Valera made it unconstitutional; whereas Cosgrave occasionally confronted Catholic chauvinism (refusing, for example, to allow Mayo Country

Council to block the appointment of a Protestant librarian), de Valera viewed Ireland as a Catholic nation. The politics of cultural defense resulted in extensive censorship; few Irish writers of note did not have their work banned prior to the 1960s, although the depiction of independent Ireland as a cultural wasteland has been robustly challenged.[46]

The nationalist consensus reinforced a preoccupation with sexual immorality and facilitated the restriction of women's liberties. Although the 1922 Constitution granted women the vote on the same terms as men, women became less conspicuous in politics, and their status as citizens was eroded by their effective exclusion from civil service examinations and juries, and the introduction of a "marriage bar" for female teachers and civil servants. As elsewhere in interwar Europe, these policies provoked little protest. Although the impact of patriarchal measures, such as the Conditions of Employment Act (1936), which allowed the state to exclude women from certain occupations, was often symbolic (and many Irish Protestants held equally conservative views), the church-state nexus had practical consequences. The Catholic Church's loyalty to the state derived from the understanding that governments would not impinge on its prerogatives in education, health, and welfare. Clerical power was demonstrated not by clashes between church and state but by their absence; the acceptance of the Catholic hierarchy's authority across the political spectrum explained the failure of one of the most ostentatiously Catholic states in Europe to produce a Catholic political party. Although the Catholic Church supplied important services that the state failed to provide, negative long-term consequences of its moral monopoly would later become apparent, both in terms of the stunting of modernization and the treatment of some of the state's most vulnerable citizens.[47]

While both parties sought to assert Irish sovereignty, de Valera's belligerence proved more effective than Cosgrave's diplomacy. By 1938 a series of unilateral initiatives had achieved a degree of independence that few—not least the increasingly redundant IRA—had thought possible in 1932. These included scrapping the oath of fidelity, retention of land annuity payments, abolition of the governor-general's office, removal of references to the monarch and empire from the Free State constitution, and introduction of a new constitution in 1937 that made "Éire" a republic in all but name. Although intermittently outraging the British government, the economic war that these measures provoked was concluded in 1938 with a conciliatory agreement that ceded control of the Treaty ports to the Irish state in exchange for a settlement of outstanding financial issues.

De Valera's 1937 Constitution marked the pinnacle of his efforts to create the Ireland that he dreamed of, although whether the sleight of hand required to bridge the gap between rhetoric and reality should be viewed as ingenious or delusional is debatable. Despite the failure to revive Gaelic, Irish was proclaimed the first official language. Despite the consolidation of partition, the island was declared a single national territory. Notwithstanding the republican framework

of the constitution, the special position of the Catholic Church was explicitly recognized. The distinctive character of the Irish variety of republicanism was further indicated by the acknowledgment of the state's obligation that women should
not neglect their "duties in the home." To avoid sundering links with the North,
Éire (or "Ireland," as the twenty-six-county state became known) was not declared
a republic, but the Irish people's "inalienable, indefeasible, and sovereign right" to
self-determination was proclaimed. No reference was made in the Constitution to
the British monarch or empire, but nor was the president of Ireland formally declared the head of state: the Constitution allowed the government to act as if the
state had left the Commonwealth, while Britain could choose not to notice.

Legitimizing the Southern state in the eyes of all but the most intransigent
of nationalists, de Valera's reshaping of the constitutional relationship with the
United Kingdom marked his greatest achievement. Subsequent republican violence on the island was justified by opposition to partition and northern Catholic
grievances rather than by repudiation of the Southern state. On one level, de
Valera's actions can be seen as remarkably consistent, given how closely their
outcome resembled the external association with Britain that he had insisted, in
the face of considerable skepticism, was possible in 1921; but for his many detrac-
tors, his achievement merely confirmed Michael Collins's assertion that the Treaty
had secured "the freedom to achieve freedom" and the futility of the Civil War for
which de Valera was held responsible.

Accounts of post-revolutionary Ireland acknowledge its state-building achievements while conceding its economic and cultural limitations. There is an increasing focus on the experiences of ordinary people in a "society characterised by a
high incidence of mental disease, by hideous family living conditions in its urban
slums, and by a demoralised casual working class, urban as well as rural."[48] The
depiction of de Valera's Ireland as a priest-ridden hole in memoirs such as *Angela's
Ashes* has inevitably prompted some to question the caricature.[49] Joe Lee has convincingly argued that de Valera's failure was not in articulating a conservative
vision of "cosy homesteads," "sturdy children," and "comely maidens" or his inability to achieve it so much as his pursuit of policies that subverted the possibility
of creating this rural idyll, leading, for example, to some of the highest rates of
female emigration and celibacy in Europe.[50]

The resulting discordance between reality and ideal necessitated an unusual
degree of self-delusion in Irish society: sexual immorality, the only kind to arouse
much concern, was widely attributed to foreign influences, while evidence of
actual sexual abuse was often suppressed.[51] Adoption was banned, but collusion
between church and state permitted babies to be taken from unmarried mothers
for sale abroad.[52] However, such hypocrisy, which partly reflected the material
circumstances of Irish rural society, had long predated independence. The notion
of Ireland as a Catholic gulag, particularly prevalent in literary and film depic-
tions of the era, overlooks how such authoritarianism stemmed less from the abil-

ity of bishops and politicians to impose their values on the public as the popular acceptance of these values as central to national identity (as events such as the Eucharistic Congress demonstrated). It should be noted that similar anxieties about modernity characterized other European societies across the political spectrum, and that in Ireland, as elsewhere, official rhetoric—while indicative of mentalities—was less influential in shaping social mores than were economic realities.[53]

As with de Valera's Ireland, analysis of the Irish experience of the Second World War has often reflected a moralistic approach. The difficulty of objectively evaluating neutrality in its historical context—a policy that must be understood primarily as an expression of Irish sovereignty—was exemplified by the recent public controversy leading to the Irish government's decision to pardon several thousand soldiers who deserted from its own army to serve in the ranks of a neighboring belligerent that occupied what was then regarded as Irish territory and could well have been called on to invade the South. That the policy of neutrality was bolstered by an unattractive moral superiority, underpinned by zealous censorship, is clear. Nor do de Valera's actions—such as the comparison he drew between Germany's claim to the Sudetenland and the status of Ulster, his visit to the German Legation to express condolences on Hitler's death, or his denunciation of the first British reports from Belsen as "anti-national propaganda"—now evoke much understanding.[54]

However, the state's strict public observation of neutrality masked its discreet support for the Allies, which extended to intelligence-sharing, returning downed air crews, and the establishment of overflight corridors. Moreover, some seventy thousand Irish citizens—a greater number than enlisted in Northern Ireland—fought with the Allies.[55] Like Irish veterans of the First World War, the twelve thousand or so who returned received little recognition for their efforts.[56] Although there was more pro-German sentiment than was later recalled, neutrality was a rational, self-interested policy, and one that was pursued where possible by other small states (although not by any other English-speaking British dominion). It was consistent with the policy of avoiding entanglement in Great Power struggles that de Valera had ostentatiously pursued on the international stage as a means of demonstrating Irish sovereignty. Resentment of partition and the memory of the domestic impact of the First World War rendered any alternative policy unlikely, despite the United Kingdom's tentative offers of support for Irish unification in return for entering the war. Nonetheless, it is difficult to disagree with the *Irish Times's* complaint that de Valera had "elevated the idea of neutrality into a principle" by contriving "to convince the people of this country that Irish neutrality had a high spiritual basis."[57]

Although F.S.L. Lyons's influential metaphor of an insular Ireland emerging from the war, as if from Plato's Cave, to a new world order that had left it behind has been persuasively challenged, neutrality did lead to a degree of international isolation.[58] The South's denial of strategic ports to Britain reinforced partition by demonstrating the North's geopolitical value, as did the differing experiences of both parts of the island. By diminishing Civil War animosities and consolidating an emerging twenty-six-county Irish identity, the Emergency also strengthened Southern partitionism. In the longer term, however, this was probably less significant than the growing divergence in living standards that followed northern unionists' somewhat grudging acceptance of the United Kingdom's post-war welfare state.

ECONOMIC LIBERALIZATION, 1948–1972

In popular—and some scholarly—accounts, the 1950s was a lost decade, redeemed only by the heroic modernizing efforts of Seán Lemass, whose embrace of free trade spurred a social and economic transformation that made the 1960s the best of decades. In reality, post-war Ireland was, like most periods, characterized more by gradual change and continuity than by dramatic watersheds, with the most important modernizing trends cutting across established chronological and political boundaries. Economic policy gradually came to take priority over the assertion of national sovereignty. The state's dismal economic performance was increasingly publicly acknowledged, and economic factors became a greater cause of instability, contributing to the collapse of governments in 1954 and 1957. Business interests came to play a greater role in politics and society, as did economic planning. Traditional aspects of society began to be questioned by a more assertive media, and the state became more exposed to external influences. Although usually analyzed in terms of the internal dynamics involved, these changes were largely driven by international pressures.

Despite the formation of Clann na Poblachta, a response to the realization by republicans that Fianna Fáil had reached the limits of its radicalism, Southern politics remained shaped by the two-party system and a socially conservative ideological consensus. Following the IRA's ineffectual "border campaign" (1956–1962), which triggered a temporary wave of anti-partitionist sentiment, militant republicans rediscovered socialism but with little long-term impact, as became clear with the ascendancy of "Provisional" over "Official" republicanism in the early 1970s. Urbanization continued, but without benefiting the Labour Party, introducing new intellectual currents to politics, or altering traditional voting patterns, which remained highly influenced by localism, family tradition, clientelism, and brokerage. Policy formulation continued to be influenced more by a powerful bureaucracy than by party politics.

Despite sustained economic growth across Europe, the Southern economy remained stagnant throughout the golden age of post-war expansion. The importance of pastoral farming (livestock represented more than 70% of the state's exports in 1961) and the lack of industrialization resulted in an exodus of the poor and marginal, as well as the young, frustrated, and talented. A staggering seven hundred thousand citizens emigrated between 1945 and the early 1970s, as the population—an important psychological marker—declined to 2.8 million.[59] Although politicians had long recorded private concerns about the state's economic performance, the increasingly public acknowledgment of the scale of failure marked a new departure that helped facilitate the radical changes to follow.

The formation in 1948 of the Inter-Party government—an unlikely coalition uniting Fine Gael, Clann na Poblachta, a farmers' party, and rival factions of the Labour Party in mutual detestation of de Valera—reflected the instability of post-war politics. Fianna Fáil, the traditional party of government, lost its overall majority in 1943–1944 and governed as a minority between 1951–1954 and 1961–1965. But despite heading two coalition governments in the 1950s, Fine Gael had resumed its traditional position in opposition by the end of the decade.

The first Inter-Party government (1948–1951) is remembered for two reasons: its shambolic declaration of a republic in 1949 and its demise. Although Taoiseach John A. Costello's optimistic claim that the declaration of the Irish Republic would take the gun out of Irish politics was disproved by subsequent events, it did hasten the decline of political and public preoccupation with sovereignty. The British government responded pragmatically to this unwelcome initiative by retaining favorable trade and citizenship links with the South and—more sharply—with the Ireland Act, which guaranteed Northern Ireland's place in the United Kingdom for as long as the Stormont parliament desired. Despite predictable Southern outrage, it is difficult to disagree with British prime minster Clement Attlee's observation that "the government of Éire considered the cutting of the last tie which united Éire to the British Commonwealth as a more important objective than ending partition."[60]

The Inter-Party government's much-quoted assurance to Pope Pius XII of its "firm resolve to be guided in all our work by the teaching of Christ and to strive for the attainment of a social order in Ireland based on Christian principles" demonstrated the continued necessity for deference to the church, not least from a government comprising former gunmen like Seán MacBride (Clann na Poblachta's leader) and his socialist colleague Noel Browne.[61] The centrality of religion in post-war Ireland was reflected not merely by high levels of religious observation but also by the continued role of Catholicism as a marker of communal identity and a source of esteem and meaning for many ordinary people. Personified by the austere archbishop John Charles McQuaid, Catholic power was evidenced by the popularity of devotional sodalities; militant Catholic Action groups, such as Maria Duce; ugly episodes like the boycott of Protestants in Fethard-on-Sea (following a dispute prompted by the *Ne Temere* decree's requirements for religious upbringing in mixed marriages); and, most notoriously, the government's collapse in the wake of clerical opposition to Noel Browne's mother-and-child health proposals.

However, that a dispute between the hierarchy and a government minister (albeit a maladroit one who received little support from his colleagues) became public was significant, as was the passage—in the face of clerical disquiet—of similarly interventionist legislation by the next government. Although it remains difficult to judge whether Ireland became more or less clericalist in the 1950s, the long-term factors that would erode the authority of the church—such as the expansion of the media, urbanization, education, and international influences—were becoming apparent. Although the hierarchy's inflexible attitude to these modernizing pressures has seen the Catholic Church caricatured as a reactionary monolith, internal pressures within the church—whether the international reforms leading to the Second Vatican Council or the role played by Irish journals, such as the Jesuits' *Studies*—also served to diminish clerical authoritarianism.[62]

Much of the historiography of the post-1945 era is concerned with the glacial pace of modernization. Emphasizing cultural over economic factors, Tom Garvin has drawn attention to the ability of entrenched interest groups—including nationalist ideologues, public servants, farmers, trade-unionists, professions, and the church (particularly through its grip on education)—to prevent change in a stable political culture.[63] Other barriers to reform included comparatively low levels of educational investment, low educational attainment (the minimum school-leaving age, at which most children left education, remained fourteen until the 1960s), a fatalistic acceptance of the agricultural structure of the economy, lack of entrepreneurship, and limited state intervention. Like Garvin, Joe Lee has drawn attention to how cultural patterns deeply rooted in society and history elevated the possessor principle—"the dominant ethos not just of a generation, but of a century"—over performance.[64] In contrast, economic historians are more skeptical of cultural explanations and generally less critical of the comparative performance of both the Irish economy and its policymakers.[65]

Change resulted largely from long-term and international factors. The expectations raised in the United Kingdom by the Beveridge Report (1942) had led modernizers, notably Lemass, to advocate the need for economic planning. The decision to abandon economic protectionism was strongly influenced by post-war international circumstances, not least because countries in receipt of Marshall Aid were compelled to formulate a recovery program, join the Organization for European Economic Co-operation (OEEC), liberalize trade practices, and invest in expansionist policies.[66] By 1957 the Republic had joined the World Bank and the International Monetary Fund, whose advice and offer of credit influenced T. K. Whitaker's groundbreaking *Economic Development* proposals. A growing consensus in favor of cooperation between unions and employers led to the founding of the National Industrial Economic Council in 1963 and the subsequent negotiation of the first of a series of national wage agreements.

The expansion of education was pivotal to the modernization of Irish society and its economy.[67] Access to post-primary and university scholarships was extended under Minister for Education Patrick Hillery (1959–1965), whose plans for comprehensive secondary schools and regional technical colleges were gradually implemented. *Investment in Education* (1965), a critical survey of the state's educational policies, laid the groundwork for radical change. In 1966 Donogh O'Malley—one of an emerging generation of politicians that included Brian Lenihan and Charles J. Haughey—announced the introduction of free post-primary education (revealingly, without seeking the approval of his cabinet colleagues).

International influences, such as travel, emigration, and the expansion of the media, undermined the viability of cultural protectionism, contributing to "unprecedented social and psychological change" by challenging contemporary mores and expectations.[68] The impact of cinema, Ireland's most popular pastime, on "the average farm labourer walking five or six miles into Bruff ... in our Irish rain" understandably troubled one contributor to the Jesuits' *Studies*:

> He has seen nightclub queens covered by a few spangles, Chicago gangsters talking a peculiar argot, society playboys babbling aridly of Reno divorce. He has seen crooning cowboys, coal-black mammies, typists clad in Schiaparelli, models living in luxurious flats and millionaires living in Babylonian palaces. He is going home to fall into his bed in the loft, to rise next morning and feed the pigs. What does he make of it all?[69]

Despite such concerns, the censorship of films and books was relaxed in the mid-1960s, and new ideas emerged as intellectual movements, such as Tuairim, challenged traditional orthodoxies.[70] Although deprived of the autonomy from direct state control enjoyed by the British Broadcasting Corporation (BBC), the foundation in 1961 of Telefís Éireann (RTÉ) would have a significant impact. In its first broadcast, President de Valera presciently warned of the "irreparable harm" the new medium might cause; one TD subsequently lamented how there had been "no sex in Ireland before television."[71]

Although the post-war economic reforms were initially associated more with the Inter-Party governments than with Fianna Fáil, political support for economic liberalization cut across political lines, as did resistance to it. In 1949, when the Industrial Development Authority (IDA) was founded, policymakers remained divided between traditionalists, who advocated deflation and continued close economic ties to Britain, and Keynesian expansionists, who championed export-oriented investment. These divisions were replicated in the civil service, with greater support for liberalization in the Department of Industry and Commerce than in Finance or the Central Bank. As a result, the reform process was slow and uneven, with balance-of-payments crises producing a reversion to deflationary policies, austerity, and recession in 1952–1954. Declining industrial employment, high emigration, and stagnant output remained persistent throughout the decade.

The adoption of a strategy of export-led industrialization, outlined in the first of several programs for economic expansion in 1958, marked a decisive shift. The lack of domestic entrepreneurship was addressed by offering capital grants and tax concessions to attract foreign export-oriented manufacturers. Protectionism was gradually dismantled: the Republic applied unsuccessfully for membership of the European Economic Community in 1961 and created an Anglo-Irish free-trade area in 1965. The abandonment of restrictions on the foreign ownership of companies and repatriation of profits by the mid-1960s, combined with a policy of generous state subsidies, transformed the Republic from one of the most protected economies in Western Europe to one of the most dependent on multinational firms. Between 1960 and 1970, for example, foreign capital accounted for 74% of Irish industrial development.[72]

To what extent was this the achievement of Seán Lemass, who succeeded de Valera as taoiseach in 1959, and his influential Department of Finance secretary, T. K. Whittaker? Given that the age of Lemass is now regarded as uncritically as the de Valera era is pejoratively, Lemass's reputation as Ireland's economic savior has inevitably come under scholarly scrutiny. Recent studies have emphasized the limitations of economic management during the 1960s.[73] Lemass was an impatient and somewhat authoritarian leader and, like most successful politicians, fortunate in his timing on coming to power. His radicalism can be overstated. Although personally skeptical of clerical influence, he was cautious in his dealings with the church. Despite his groundbreaking meeting with Northern Irish premier Terence O'Neill in 1965, his revision of anti-partitionist pieties was more pragmatic than substantial.[74] Against this, a certain degree of caution seems understandable, given that Fianna Fáil lost its overall majority in the first test of his leadership in 1961. Recent assessments have highlighted inconsistencies between his earlier role as the architect of protectionism and his subsequent reforming zeal rather than questioning the importance of his contribution to modernization.[75]

MODERNIZATION, 1972–2000

One of the most striking features of the final decades of the twentieth century was the contrast between the socioeconomic and cultural transformation of the era and the lack of political change. Despite the political and economic instability of the 1970s and 1980s, new parties—whether the left-wing Workers' Party or free-market Progressive Democrats—failed to alter established electoral patterns, while the emergence of coalition government as the new norm had little impact on the dominance of Fianna Fáil, which remained the semi-permanent party of government. Women and working-class interests remained poorly represented. Intellectualism in politics—deemed a greater disadvantage than being sexually perverse by Michael D. Higgins (prior to his recent election as Irish president)—remained rare and, as in the case of Garret FitzGerald, the subject of some mockery.[76]

Such was the rapid pace of change during the final decade of the century that the conservatism of Irish politics and society in the 1970s and much of the 1980s is easily overlooked: three cabinet ministers in 1973, for example, held the same posts as their fathers had in 1923.[77] The Republic's embrace of free trade had yet to reap economic rewards. Per capita income in 1973 remained two-thirds that of Britain, with correspondingly low living standards. Stagnant growth, unemployment, high inflation, and high taxation and interest rates blighted the economy. However, the population reached three million for the first time in nearly fifty years; marriage age and family size were declining; and just over half the population lived in urban areas, as demographic trends moved toward international norms.

International oil crises and domestic industrial unrest partly accounted for Ireland's dismal economic performance in the 1970s, but inept fiscal management contributed to it. There was, for example, no budget surplus between 1972 (when a Fianna Fáil government began borrowing to fund current spending) and 1994, and general elections frequently descended into auction politics. The national debt spiraled, and more than 130,000 people emigrated between 1983 and 1988. As in the 1950s, a sense of crisis led to pressure for change. The emergence of bipartisan support for fiscal reform is credited by some for laying the foundation for unprecedented growth rates of between 5% and 10% throughout the 1990s; more speculatively, the precise tipping point in Irish fortunes has been identified as Ray Houghton's winning goal against England in the 1988 European championship. Between 1995 and 2005, personal income doubled, outpacing United Kingdom and United States levels; output increased by 350%; exports quintupled; and immigration replaced emigration as Ireland morphed from banana republic to Celtic Tiger.[78]

As with the Lemass era, there is considerable consensus on the factors responsible but disagreement on where the credit belongs. Few predicted the transformation. *The Economist*—which would rashly declare the Irish Republic to be Europe's shining light at the end of the century—had demonstrated an equal lack of prescience by predicting catastrophe in 1988.[79] Key factors included Ireland's attractiveness to foreign investors as an English-speaking gateway to the Common Market, European structural funds, a skilled and educated workforce, low corporation and personal tax rates, social partnership (corporatist wage agreements between government, employers, and trade unions), and increasing workforce participation rates. Factors over which some indigenous control could be exerted, such as the IDA's ingenuity in attracting foreign investment, remained dependent on international circumstances over which the Republic exercised no control, such as the growth of outsourcing in high-tech and pharmaceutical industries. Some factors proved mixed blessings: the state's widely admired "light-touch regulation" would ultimately fuel property speculation and a construction boom that earned the Republic its reputation as "the wild west of European finance."[80] The argument that good luck, maximized by astute management, was responsible for the Celtic Tiger seems convincing,[81] not least considering the role that bad luck—in the form of the global financial crisis of 2007–2008—maximized by incompetence and negligence played in the dramatic reversal of fortunes that followed.

If change was postponed during the stagnant post-war decades, the boom accelerated social, religious, and cultural shifts, resulting in a disorienting transformation of attitudes. Although the close-fought rivalry between Garret FitzGerald and Charles Haughey that defined the politics of the 1980s illuminated the fault lines of the changes to come, it offered little indication of their pace and scale. Denouncing the "authoritarian desire to enforce private morality by means of public law," FitzGerald articulated—albeit in an endearingly scatty manner—a progressive social democratic vision that Fine Gael had previously spurned.[82] In contrast, Haughey—a charismatic, self-aggrandizing, and menacing opportunist—skillfully mobilized populist impulses against FitzGerald's "constitutional crusade."[83] As with many of the most unsettling aspects of Irish society, the ethical shortcomings of Haughey—the personification of Ireland's post-colonial political culture—were both widely known and largely unacknowledged.

Politicians generally reflect rather than drive social change: notwithstanding FitzGerald's efforts, Irish politicians probably contributed less to the liberalization of society than did the judiciary. While economic prosperity and consumerism also spurred liberalization, international factors were pivotal. Although European Economic Community membership was initially opposed by Labour, which feared its impact on workers' rights, European directives improved the status of women, workers, and minorities. The media and the arts promoted a more critical ethos, as did youth culture. With half of the population aged twenty-six or younger by 1977, pop and rock music and magazines like *Hot Press* provided countercultural voices, attacking—as in the Boomtown Rats' scathing song "Banana Republic"—the hypocrisy of the "Septic Isle."[84] Television—staffed by "young, ambitious, university-educated men and women who were determined to use the medium to hold institutions accountable"—played a liberalizing role, particularly RTÉ's taboo-breaking *Late Late Show* and current affairs programming.[85] Investigative journals, including Vincent Brown's *Magill*, published iconoclastic writers, such as Fintan O'Toole, John Waters, and Colm Tóibín; tragedies that would previously have received little publicity—such as the death of fifteen-year-old Ann Lovett and her baby in a grotto, in Granard, County Longford, in 1985—triggered national debates that challenged public and official attitudes. As in earlier periods, artists and novelists explored the gulf between the ideal and reality but were now occasionally confronted with state patronage and tax breaks rather than suspicion and censorship.

The decline of clerical authority brought about by liberalization (although cause and effect here are not easily separated) and the disintegration of the relationship between Catholicism and nationalism that had shaped Ireland since the mid-nineteenth century constituted the greatest social change of the era. In the early 1970s, when more than 90% of Irish Catholics attended mass, Archbishop McQuaid could respond to demands for liberalization by declaring "there cannot be, on the part of any person, a right to what is evil."[86] In this light, the significance of the removal in 1972 of the church's special position can be overstated. Seen as an anachronistic barrier to good relations with the North, its removal—which was supported by the church—reflected a consensus. Pope John Paul II's triumphant visit to Ireland in 1979 and the conservative outcome of divisive referenda on abortion (1983) and divorce (1986) demonstrated both the collapse of the church-state consensus and the continued strength of Catholicism (although the spate of moving statues in 1985 hinted at the uncertainties of the era). In contrast, the collapse of Catholic power by the end of the century could be gauged by any number of measures: the church's retreat from the provision of education and other social services; the liberalization of moral codes; a collapse in vocations (ordinations in Dublin fell from 129 in 1990 to 1 in 1999); a decline in religious observance (from 85% in 1990 to 65% in 1997); the popularity of *Father Ted*; the elegiac titles of studies, such as Mary Kenny's *Goodbye to Catholic Ireland* (2000); and—most significantly—the church's loss of moral authority following a seemingly endless series of clerical scandals.

As throughout the twentieth century generally, the status of women provides a revealing barometer of wider social attitudes. Its improvement was bound up with economic modernization: the public-sector marriage bar was abolished in 1973, gender discrimination in employment became illegal in 1977, and participation by married women in the workforce rose from 8% in 1971 to 40% in 2000.[87] Advances in women's political and reproductive rights owed more to feminist protest and European and judicial directives than the efforts of the Dáil (where women still accounted for less than 15% of TDs at the end of the century). In 1969 the Irish Family Planning Association opened its first clinic; two years later the Irish Women's Liberation Movement provoked headlines after returning by train from Belfast with illegally imported contraceptives. A bill to permit married couples to access contraception, characteristically prompted by a Supreme Court ruling, was rejected in 1974, when Taoiseach Liam Cosgrave crossed the floor to defeat his own government's measure. By 1980 married couples with medical prescriptions were grudgingly allowed to acquire contraceptives, a measure described by Haughey as "an Irish solution to an Irish problem," but other restrictions remained until 1993, two years after the Virgin Megastore was prosecuted for selling condoms.[88] The liberalization of moral legislation proceeded at a leisurely pace. Homosexuality was not decriminalized until the European Court of Human Rights forced the government to act in 1993, while divorce was permitted in 1996.

During the same period, and not entirely unrelated to the liberalization of society, Northern violence transformed Southern nationalism, most obviously by reinforcing a psychological partitionism. Although sections of Fianna Fáil, for both ideological and opportunistic reasons, sought to exploit solidarity with Northern Catholics at the outbreak of the Troubles, public and political attitudes were increasingly driven by the desire to avoid entanglement in the conflict. The contrast between the extravagant fiftieth and the muted seventy-fifth anniversaries of the Easter Rising demonstrated the impact of the Provisional IRA's violence on nationalist sentiment. Although unity remained a Southern aspiration, the Troubles stripped away much of the self-delusion and hypocrisy that had characterized official and public attitudes to the North, resulting in greater understanding of unionist perspectives and a more realistic appreciation of the consequences of British withdrawal and reunification. It also led to more constructive and (eventually) bipartisan efforts to engage with London and Belfast. In 1998 the revision of core aspects of nationalist beliefs, including the removal of the territorial claim to the six counties (a suggestion that had aroused intense hostility when advocated by intellectuals like Labour Minister Conor Cruise O'Brien in the 1970s), received constitutional endorsement with the Belfast Agreement.

Attitudes to nationality became less brittle. The Gaelic Athletic Association ended its ban on members playing or attending foreign games in 1971. The requirement for Gaelic as an essential subject in state examinations and for employment in the civil service was dropped in 1967 (although it remained compulsory in publicly funded schools and essential for entry into most Irish universities).[89] The retreat from compulsion did not mark the end of the state's commitment to Irish—as was demonstrated by the launch of an Irish-language television service in 1996—so much as an acknowledgment of the policy's failure to prevent the collapse in numbers of fluent speakers (who, by the end of the century, found themselves greatly outnumbered by Polish speakers).[90] Nor did it weaken national identity—compared to indigenous folk culture elsewhere in Europe, Gaelic sports and culture prospered—but it did mark a shift from the tendency to define it in opposition to English values. The emergence of a more confident and pluralistic Southern Irish identity in some respects reversed the politicization of culture that had occurred at the beginning of the century, when the narrowing of national identity and nurturing of sectarian grievances had underpinned the revolutionary generation's efforts to win independence. This willingness to rethink what it meant to be Irish—which overlapped with the onset of significant levels of immigration to Ireland from the 1990s—was evident also in changing popular attitudes to history, exemplified by the transformation of official and popular attitudes to First World War commemoration.

Although benefiting from the spectacular implosion of her principal rival's campaign, the election as head of state in 1990 of Mary Robinson, a feminist intellectual who had devoted her political and legal career to liberal causes came to symbolize the new Ireland that was emerging from the collapse of Catholic nationalism. At the same time, it was significant that she was elected to a largely ceremonial office that reflected how the Irish people liked to see themselves and to be seen by others. In contrast, the actual governance of the country—under the leadership of the personable, populist, and subsequently tarnished Bertie Ahern—remained business-as-usual at the close of the century.

Coinciding with the liberalization of the Republic, a remarkable thirty-two public inquiries into "matters of ethical concern within politics, business, church, police, finance, public service, professions and health" occurred between 1990 and 2010. The resulting scandals about the abuse of children and other vulnerable citizens and the pervasive nature of political, financial, and planning corruption eroded public confidence in the integrity of the state. While provoking understandable outrage at the behavior of politicians, clergy, and other elites, these revelations prompted little reflection on wider responsibility for the shortcomings of Irish society. The decline of the high standards of probity associated with the revolutionary generation was partly a consequence of the expansion of business and property interests that accompanied modernization. As in other Western countries, rising electoral costs necessitated closer relations between politics and business; as far back as the 1960s, the activities of Fianna Fáil's fund-raising body, Taca, had given rise to controversy.[91]

Cultural explanations—including a widespread lack of respect for the legitimacy of the laws of the state that is characteristic of many post-colonial societies—have also been advanced as a means of accounting for poor governance; the electoral success of politicians implicated in unethical behavior demonstrated a feeble public morality that has been attributed to the clientelism and localism of Irish politics. The stifling of democratic accountability by a highly centralized state may have contributed to this, although concerns about the potential for patronage and corruption had been advanced as arguments against local democracy since the establishment of the state. The failure of a strong sense of citizenship to emerge under independence may also reflect the ideological shallowness of Irish republicanism, which came to be defined in terms of antipathy to England and support for irredentist violence rather than commitment to active citizenship, egalitarianism, or accountable government. Although there is little evidence to suggest that the Republic was, by international standards, particularly corrupt at the end of the twentieth century, the cynicism arising from the state's inability to hold corrupt elites to account undermined Irish political culture.

Despite the prosperity of the Celtic Tiger, the Republic continued to be characterized by comparatively high levels of relative poverty and inequality by the end of the century.[92] The long-term impact of the dramatic rise and fall of the Celtic Tiger—and of two decades of inquiries into corruption and abuse—remains to be seen. That many of these revelations coincided with a period of unprecedented prosperity blunted demands for responses to problems that were seen as belonging to the past. In contrast, the economic and political crisis that devastated the Irish state in 2008 has created a stronger awareness of the relationship between the governance of the state and society's contemporary problems.

CONCLUSION

It is now possible to discern the outlines of the major developments that shaped Southern Ireland over the past century. If the first decades of the twentieth century transformed Irish political structures while leaving its society and economy largely intact, something like the reverse occurred during its final decades. Neither upheaval produced a more egalitarian society. The revolution was both liberating and constricting. Although ending imperial rule and empowering a democratic movement that was younger and less bourgeois than the Home Rulers who had grown old waiting in the wings, it produced limited social and economic change. Its polarizing effects reinforced—both North and South—a conservative social order reflecting majoritarian values. The narrow pursuit of national sovereignty and cultural protectionism marginalized liberal and progressive impulses after independence. Following the post-war economic liberalization, a process largely driven by pragmatic considerations and international forces, the Catholic nationalist consensus that had defined Southern politics and society since independence began to unravel. Writing in the 1980s, when the fissures within Catholicism and nationalism were becoming apparent, Joe Lee noted how the "weakening of the twin pillars" that provided "the main barrier between a reasonably civilised value system and the untrammelled predatory instincts of individual and pressure-group selfishness" would confront "the succeeding generations with a fundamental challenge."[93] In an age when the progress of the state is measured in terms of economic growth and global competitiveness rather than the preservation of cultural identity and national sovereignty, it remains to be seen how that challenge will be negotiated.

FURTHER READING

Pre-revolutionary currents are navigated in James McConnel's *The Irish Parliamentary Party and the Third Home Rule Crisis* (Dublin: Four Courts Press, 2013); M. J. Kelly's *The Fenian Ideal and Irish Nationalism, 1882–1916* (Woodbridge: Boydell and Brewer, 2006); and R. F. Foster's *Vivid Faces: The Revolutionary Generation in Ireland, 1890–1923* (London: Allen Lane, 2014). The most recent account of the rebellion is Fearghal McGarry's *The Rising. Ireland: Easter 1916* (Oxford: Oxford University Press, 2010).

David Fitzpatrick's pioneering study of County Clare, *Politics and Irish Life, 1913–1921: Provincial Experience of War and Revolution* (Dublin: Gill and Macmillan, 1977), established the local study as the dominant framework for analyzing the Irish revolution, an approach now reaping diminishing returns. Its most in-fluential successor, Peter Hart's *The IRA and Its Enemies: Violence and Community in Cork, 1916–23* (Oxford: Oxford University Press, 1998), sparked an acrimonious debate, considered in Stephen Howe's article: "Killing in Cork and the Histori-ans," *History Workshop Journal* 77: 1 (Spring 2014), pp. 160–186. The most author-itative overview of the revolution is Charles Townshend's *The Republic: The Fight for Irish Independence 1918–1923* (London: Allen Lane, 2013).

The most innovative interwar survey remains David Fitzpatrick's comparative study *The Two Irelands: 1912–1939* (Oxford: Oxford University Press, 1998). Clair Wills's *That Neutral Island: A Cultural History of Ireland during the Second World War* (London: Faber and Faber, 2007) offers an original take on the Emergency.

The modernizing impact of post-war political developments is addressed by Brian Girvin and Gary Murphy's collection, *The Lemass Era: Politics and Society in the Ireland of Seán Lemass* (Dublin: University College Dublin Press, 2005). Diar-maid Ferriter's *Ambiguous Republic: Ireland in the 1970s* (London: Profile, 2012) ex-plores the upheavals that followed the shift from economic and cultural protection-ism, while R. F. Foster's *Luck and the Irish: A Brief History of Change 1970–2000* (London: Allen Lane, 2007) outlines the transformation wrought by economic prosperity and the collapse of Catholicism and nationalism in the South.

The historiographical shift from a preoccupation with high politics and the role of the State to social, gender, sexual, and family history is reflected in Diar-maid Ferriter's *The Transformation of Ireland 1900–2000* (London: Profile, 2004). Niall Whelehan's edited collection, *Transnational Perspectives on Modern Irish His-tory* (New York: Routledge, 2015), points to another means of widening the lens of Ireland's introspective historiographical tradition.

NOTES

1. *Weekly Freeman's Journal*, October 10, 1914. Quoted in R. F. Foster, *Vivid Faces. The Revolu-tionary Generation in Ireland 1890–1923* (London: Allen Lane, 2014), p. 2.

2. Enda Delaney, "Modernity, the Past and Politics in Post-war Ireland," in Thomas Hachey (ed.), *Turning Points in Twentieth-Century Irish History* (Dublin: Irish Academic Press, 2011).

3. Bernard Wasserstein, *Barbarism & Civilization: A History of Europe in Our Time* (Oxford: Oxford University Press, 2007), p. 205.

4. See chapter 11 by Richard Bourke.

5. Ciaran Brady (ed.), *Interpreting Irish History: The Debate on Historical Revisionism 1938–1994* (Dublin: Irish Academic Press, 1994); Ian McBride, "Ireland's History Troubles," *Field Day Review* 3 (2007), pp. 205–213.

6. Roy Foster, *Modern Ireland 1600–1972* (London: Penguin, 1988), p. ix.

7. J. J. Lee, *Ireland 1912–1985: Politics and Society* (Cambridge: Cambridge University Press, 1989); Diarmaid Ferriter, *The Transformation of Ireland 1900–2000* (London: Profile, 2004).

8. David Fitzpatrick, *The Two Irelands: 1912–1939* (Oxford: Oxford University Press, 1998), p. 13.

9. Fergus Campbell, *The Irish Establishment 1879–1914* (Oxford: Oxford University Press, 2009).

10. Paul Bew, *Ireland: The Politics of Enmity 1789–2006* (Oxford: Oxford University Press, 2007), p. 561.

11. Fitzpatrick, *Two Irelands*, p. 3.

12. Richard Bourke, *Peace in Ireland: The War of Ideas* (London: Pimlico, new edition, 2012).

13. M. J. Kelly, *The Fenian Ideal and Irish Nationalism, 1882–1916* (Woodbridge: Boydell and Brewer, 2006), p. 239.

14. Michael Wheatley, *Nationalism and the Irish Party: Provincial Ireland 1910–1916* (Oxford: Oxford University Press, 2005), p. 266.

15. James McConnel, *The Irish Parliamentary Party and the Third Home Rule Crisis* (Dublin: Four Courts Press, 2013).

16. Fearghal McGarry, *The Rising* (Oxford: Oxford University Press, 2010), pp. 8–43.

17. Pádraig Yeates, *Lockout: Dublin 1913* (Dublin: Gill and Macmillan, 2000).

18. Alvin Jackson, *Ireland 1798–1998: Politics and War* (Oxford: Blackwell, 1999), pp. 215–244.

19. Ronan Fanning, *Fatal Path: British Government and Irish Revolution 1910–22* (London: Faber and Faber, 2013).

20. Fanning, *Fatal Path*.

21. Jackson, *Ireland*, p. 201.

22. Joost Augusteijn, *Patrick Pearse: The Making of a Revolutionary* (Basingstoke: Palgrave Macmillan, 2010); McGarry, *The Rising*.

23. John Horne and Edward Madigan (eds.), *Towards Commemoration: Ireland in War and Revolution 1912–23* (Dublin: Royal Irish Academy, 2013).

24. Foster, *Modern Ireland*, p. 492. In contrast, Foster's recent *Vivid Faces* (p. xx) emphasizes how "the networks, preconditions and processes of the 'pre-revolution'" were characterized by far more radical impulses than the state that emerged from this revolutionary generation's efforts.

25. The most recent, authoritative overview is Charles Townshend, *The Republic: The Fight for Irish Independence 1918–1923* (London: Allen Lane, 2013).

26. The first and most influential local study was David Fitzpatrick's *Politics and Irish Life 1913–1921. Provincial Experience of War and Revolution* (Dublin: Gill and Macmillan, 1977).

27. Eunan O'Halpin, "Counting Terror: Bloody Sunday and *The Dead of the Irish Revolution*," in David Fitzpatrick (ed.), *Terror in Ireland 1916–23* (Dublin: Lilliput, 2012).

28. Peter Hart, *The IRA and Its Enemies: Violence and Community in Cork, 1916–23* (Oxford: Oxford University Press, 1998).

29. Fanning, *Fatal Path*, p. 5.

30. Peter Hart, *The IRA at War, 1916–1923* (Oxford: Oxford University Press, 2003), p. 3.

31. Fitzpatrick, *Politics*, pp. 107, 116; Fergus Campbell, *Land and Revolution: Nationalist Politics in the West of Ireland 1891–1921* (Oxford: Oxford University Press, 2005), pp. 296–304.

32. Tom Garvin, *1922: The Birth of Irish Democracy* (Dublin: Gill and Macmillan, 1996); Bill Kissane, *The Politics of the Irish Civil War* (Oxford: Oxford University Press, 2007).

33. Gemma Clark, *Everyday Violence in the Irish Civil War* (Cambridge: Cambridge University Press, 2014).

34. Brian Hanley, "Terror in Twentieth-Century Ireland," in Fitzpatrick (ed.), *Terror in Ireland*, pp. 15–18.

35. Townshend, *The Republic*, pp. 441–443.

36. Lee, *Ireland*, p. 390.

37. J. H. Whyte, "Economic Progress and Political Pragmatism, 1957–63," in J. R. Hill (ed.), *A New History of Ireland. VII. Ireland, 1921–84* (Oxford: Oxford University Press, 2003), p. 294.

38. Bill Kissane, *Explaining Irish Democracy* (Dublin: University College Dublin Press, 2002).

39. Lee, *Ireland*, p. 69.

40. John Regan, *The Irish Counter-Revolution, 1921–1936* (Dublin: Gill and Macmillan, 1999).

41. Garvin, *1922*, p. 149.

42. Ciara Meehan, *The Cosgrave Party: A History of Cumann na nGaedheal 1923–33* (Dublin: Royal Irish Academy, 2010).

43. Eunan O'Halpin, "Politics and the State, 1922–32," in Hill (ed.), *A New History*, p. 96.

44. Niamh Purseil, *The Irish Labour Party 1922–73* (Dublin: University College Dublin Press, 2007); Donal Ó Drisceoil and Fintan Lane (eds.), *Politics and the Irish Working Class, 1830–1945* (Basingstoke: Palgrave Macmillan, 2005).

45. D. H. Akenson with Sean Farren and John Coolahan, "Pre-university Education," in Hill (ed.), *A New History*, p. 727.

46. Brian Fallon, *An Age of Innocence: Irish Culture 1930–1960* (Dublin: Gill and Macmillan, 1998).

47. Tom Garvin, *Preventing the Future: Why Was Ireland So Poor for So Long?* (Dublin: University College Dublin Press, 2005); Eoin O'Sullivan and Ian O'Donnell (eds.), *Coercive Confinement in Ireland: Patients, Prisoners and Penitents* (Manchester: Manchester University Press, 2012).

48. Lee, *Ireland*, p. 159.

49. Frank McCourt, *Angela's Ashes* (New York: Scribner, 1996); Diarmaid Ferriter, *Judging Dev* (Dublin: Royal Irish Academy, 2007).

50. Lee, *Ireland*, pp. 334, 158–159.

51. James Smith, *Ireland's Magdalen Laundries and the Nation's Architecture of Containment* (South Bend, IN: University of Notre Dame Press, 2007).

52. Diarmaid Ferriter, *Occasions of Sin: Sex and Society in Modern Ireland* (London: Profile, 2012).

53. Finola Kennedy, *Cottage to Creche: Family Change in Ireland* (Dublin: Institute of Public Administration, 2001).

54. Clair Wills, *That Neutral Island: A Cultural History of Ireland during the Second World War* (London: Faber and Faber, 2007). Bew, *Ireland*, p. 474.

55. Eunan O'Halpin, *Defending Ireland: The State and Its Enemies since 1922* (Oxford: Oxford University Press, 1999).

56. Bernard Kelly, *Returning Home: Irish Ex-servicemen after the Second World War* (Dublin: Merrion, 2012).

57. Wills, *Neutral Island*, p. 423.

58. F.S.L. Lyons, *Ireland since the Famine* (London: Fontana, 1971), p. 551; Michael Kennedy, "'Plato's Cave': Ireland's Wartime Neutrality Reassessed," *History Ireland* 19: 1 (2011), pp. 46–48.

59. Enda Delaney, "Emigration, Political Cultures and the Evolution of Post-war Irish Society," in Brian Girvin and Gary Murphy (eds.), *The Lemass Era: Politics and Society in the Ireland of Seán Lemass* (Dublin: University College Dublin Press, 2005), p. 49.

60. Foster, *Modern Ireland*, p. 567.

61. Quoted in Elizabeth Keane, *An Irish Statesman and Revolutionary: The Nationalist and Internationalist Politics of Seán MacBride* (London: I. B. Tauris, 2006), p. 16.

62. Louise Fuller, *Irish Catholicism since 1950: The Undoing of a Culture* (Dublin: Gill and Macmillan, 2002).

63. Garvin, *Preventing the Future*.

64. Lee, *Ireland*, p. 390.

65. D. S. Johnson and Liam Kennedy, "The Two Economies in Ireland in the Twentieth Century," in Hill, *A New History*.

66. Till Geiger and Michael Kennedy (eds.), *Ireland, Europe and the Marshall Plan* (Dublin: Four Courts Press, 2004).

67. John Walsh, *The Politics of Expansion: The Transformation of Educational Policy in the Republic of Ireland, 1957–72* (Manchester: Manchester University Press, 2009); Garvin, *Preventing the Future*.

68. J. H. Whyte, "To the Declaration of the Republic and the Ireland Act, 1945–9," in Hill, *A New History*, p. 261.

69. Ferriter, *Transformation*, p. 429.

70. Tomás Finn, *Tuairim, Intellectual Debate and Policy Formulation: Rethinking Ireland, 1954–1975* (Manchester: Manchester University Press, 2012).

71. Robert Savage, *A Loss of Innocence? Television and Irish Society* (Manchester: Manchester University Press, 2010), p. 52.

72. Lars Mjoset, *The Irish Economy in a Comparative Institutional Perspective* (Dublin: National Economic and Social Council, 1997), p. 273.

73. Ferriter, *Transformation*, p. 544.

74. Stephen Kelly, *Fianna Fáil, Partition and Northern Ireland, 1926–1971* (Dublin: Irish Academic Press, 2013); Michael Kennedy, "Northern Ireland and Cross-Border Co-operation," in Girvin and Murphy (eds.), *Lemass Era*.

75. Bryce Evans's *Seán Lemass: Democratic Dictator* (Dublin: Collins Press, 2013) is more critical than earlier biographies by John Horgan and Tom Garvin. For a balanced assessment, see Girvin and Murphy (eds.), *Lemass Era*.

76. Michael D. Higgins, cited in Diarmaid Ferriter, *Ambiguous Republic: Ireland in the 1970s* (London: Profile, 2012), p. 66.

77. Foster, *Modern Ireland*, p. 575.

78. Roy Foster, *Luck and the Irish: A Brief History of Change 1970–2000* (London: Allen Lane, 2007), pp. 7–36; *Economist*, June 22, 2006.

79. *Economist*, October 14, 2004.

80. *New York Times*, April 1, 2005.

81. Foster, *Luck and the Irish*, pp. 33–36.

82. Garrett FitzGerald, *Towards a New Ireland* (London: Knight, 1972), p. 92.

83. Bew, *Ireland. The Politics of Enmity*, p. 534.

84. Ferriter, *Ambiguous Republic*; Bob Geldof, *Is That It?* (London: Pan, 1986).

85. Savage, *A Loss of Innocence*, p. 384.

86. John Charles McQuaid, *Contraception and Conscience* (Dublin, Lenten Regulations in the Diocese of Dublin, February 17, 1971).

87. Thomas Bartlett, *Ireland: A History* (Cambridge: Cambridge University Press, 2010), p. 542.

88. Foster, *Luck and the Irish*, p. 43.

89. Neil Buttimer, "Language," in Hill (ed.), *A New History*, p. 569.

90. Central Statistics Office, *This is Ireland: Highlights from Census 2011, Part 1* (Dublin: Central Statistics Office, 2012).

91. Elaine Byrne, *Political Corruption in Ireland 1922–2010: A Crooked Harp* (Manchester: Manchester University Press, 2012). Quote is from p. 181.

92. Ferriter, *Transformation*, p. 663.

93. Lee, *Ireland*, p. 657.

CHAPTER 5

NORTHERN IRELAND *since* 1920

Niall Ó Dochartaigh

THE HISTORIOGRAPHY OF NORTHERN IRELAND is dominated by the violent Troubles that broke out in 1968 and continued for the following thirty years. The intensity and duration of the conflict were exceptional in the context of modern Irish history, and the conflict has attracted intensive academic attention across a wide range of disciplines. It became, as was sometimes caustically remarked, the most intensively studied conflict of them all, providing a highly developed and easily accessible English-speaking research site for the study of organized violence.

One element of the British state's normalization project from the mid-1970s on was to emphasize the unexceptional character of the North, the relatively trivial scale of the conflict, and the marginality of those involved in pursuing it—the diplomatic equivalent of the police officer's "nothing to see here, move along, please." But although the scale of violence was far lower than it was in many other contemporary conflicts across the globe, it was utterly exceptional in post-war Western Europe. As O'Leary notes, the death toll between 1969 and 1990 exceeded the toll from political violence in all other European Union countries combined during the same period.[1] More than 3,600 people were killed and over 47,000 injured in a population of a little more than 1,500,000.[2] *Lost Lives*, a dispassionate and comprehensive chronicle of the dead that details every single killing, brings home the relentless toll of human suffering exacted during the conflict.[3] The death toll reached a peak in 1972, when 479 people were killed, but from 1976 on the rate sharply declined as it flattened out to between 50 and 100 per year, occasionally bumping up. This key indicator of declining violence was often cited as evidence that the situation had essentially been brought under control by the late 1970s. But many other indicators of conflict remained high until the very end—most importantly, the huge numbers of soldiers and armed police officers who had to be deployed. The cost of the relative stability was an intensive and open-ended militarization of everyday life in many areas where the Catholic minority predominated. And some indicators of conflict were susceptible to abrupt upward shifts, as with the sharp increase in the financial toll imposed by commercial bombings in Belfast and London in the early 1990s.

The Troubles and the related theme of a peace process with no apparent end point continue to dominate discourse on Northern politics and the writing of the North's history. The long, slow half-century before the Troubles is an object of curiosity to the extent that it helps to explain the outbreak of conflict. From late 1968, time seemed to speed up as the languorous years of Unionist domination—symbolized by the image of Lord Brookeborough treating his premiership as a part-time job[4]—were succeeded by a chaotic, disordered blur of contest and violence. What, then, of those long, slow years before the rush forward—was another future possible? Was the acceleration toward violent disorder a maturing and release of the potential stored up in the state from the beginning? Or was it a contingent outcome explicable by a particular set of events, by the specific but not inevitable form taken by the state?

MAKING NORTHERN IRELAND

If the covenant on which liberal political theory founds its justification of the state is a notional one, Northern Ireland's founding covenant was a contemporary text whose origins could be pinpointed precisely to the communal resistance of Ulster Protestants to Home Rule. Unionists mobilized, armed, and threatened civil war in 1912 to assert the right of a Protestant minority territorially concentrated in the North to reject the authority of a proposed Irish parliament. Northern Ireland was founded on, and mandated by, its Protestant majority, but the new entity included without its consent a Catholic and nationalist minority that formed one-third of the population.

Both unionists and their nationalist and republican opponents invoked democratic principles in support of their positions, but even though both positions had normative force, it was the material capacity of Ulster Unionists to mount a powerful armed challenge to state authority rather than the respective normative weight of the two positions that decided the outcome. Once Northern Ireland had been established, Unionists invoked the principle of majority rule in opposition to any attempt to revisit the settlement. But the new state had been established on principles that undermined its own legitimacy: that a large, culturally distinctive minority should not be coerced to accept a political system it rejected, and that such a minority has the right to resist this system by force of arms if necessary.

With the establishment of a large, armed, and almost exclusively Protestant Ulster Special Constabulary in 1920 (the "B-Specials"), Ulster Unionists acquired a substantial and entirely novel capacity for the autonomous exercise of legitimate force. Combined with the new Unionist-controlled apparatus of government in Belfast, it transformed the balance of power between Unionists and the British state. In 1914 the British government could still seriously consider exerting coercive power against Ulster Unionist resistance. After the establishment of the new Northern Ireland government in 1922 such a course of action became much more difficult.

Although partition strengthened the position of Unionists, it instituted a three-fold weakening of the political position of Northern nationalists. In the first place, they ceased to form part of a political majority in Ireland. Lacking representation in the parliament in Dublin, they had no means of exerting significant influence on the major forces in Irish nationalist politics. Second, the Westminster parliament had also acted as a source of power before partition. The combined impact of the withdrawal of the great bulk of Irish members of parliament (MPs), British determination to keep Irish affairs out of the imperial parliament, and the newly institutionalized power of Unionists nullified Westminster as a source of power for the Northern minority. Finally, Catholics formed an electoral minority in the North large enough that it was important to marginalize and exclude it, but small enough that its representatives were entirely unnecessary for the formation of a government. They were thus doubly absent from the calculus of political power in the new state. Given the absence of any serious threat to order and stability from the minority, only conciliation of the most minimal kind was necessary for the maintenance of public order.[5]

UNIONISM IN A DIVIDED IRELAND

The partition of Ireland led to an abrupt shift in the practice of unionist politics, but it also set in motion a long-term process of ideological change. Despite the cultural distinctiveness of Ulster, unionists in the North had long been accustomed to dealing with Dublin as the administrative center of the country, and the imaginative geographies of Ulster unionism stretched into the deep south and the far west of Ireland. One irony of the increasing centralization of the modernizing British state in nineteenth-century Ireland was that it had knitted Ulster ever more tightly in with the rest of Ireland even as the struggle over Home Rule intensified, circulating people throughout the island more than ever before—bringing policemen from Kerry to Belfast and civil servants from Antrim to Dublin.

Prior to partition, unionists in Ulster and in the rest of Ireland gradually drifted apart as their interests diverged, but unionism retained a strong and significant all-Ireland vision even in the final stages of the struggle to prevent Home Rule. The Irish character of Ulster unionism was personified by its leader, the Dublin lawyer Edward Carson, and was asserted firmly in the 1912 Ulster Covenant, whose opening sentence opposed Home Rule because it "would be disastrous to the material well-being of Ulster as well as of the whole of Ireland." As late as 1921, the year of partition, the Northern prime minister James Craig could declare: "We are very much bound up in the rest of Ireland [and hope for], as Sir Edward Carson said the other day, peace throughout the whole of our land. We must hope not only for a brilliant prospect for Ulster, but a brilliant future for Ireland."[6]

For some time after partition, there was a strong sense among many Ulster unionists that the new entity represented not just the North but also a particular version and vision of Ireland as a whole. This is captured in the *Belfast Newsletter*'s 1963 proposal to rename Northern Ireland as "Royal Ireland."[7] It is evident too in the determination of the Belfast-based and Protestant-dominated Irish Football Association to field an international team called "Ireland" for decades after partition—finally being forced to change to "Northern Ireland" in 1954.

Over the decades, a slow retreat from the broader Irish context took place, and the rest of Ireland became a more hazily imagined and homogenized space beyond the border, losing texture and detail in the Ulster unionist imagination. Unionism shifted from a focus on the maintenance of strong ties between Britain and Ireland to a focus on maintaining the separation between the two jurisdictions in Ireland, from an ideology emphasizing unity and combination to one that emphasized particularity and difference. This shift did not happen all at once. A 1967 survey indicated that almost half a century after partition, 38% of northern Protestants agreed that the reunification of Ireland, within the United Kingdom, would be the best political arrangement for Northern Ireland.[8] The all-Ireland character of the Protestant churches and of many sporting organizations ensured the persistence of all-Ireland spaces and institutions that were significantly unionist and Protestant in composition and outlook, providing institutional expression of a form of Irishness that was comfortable and compatible with unionism and a broader British identification.

The most influential typologies of Ulster unionism are organized around an opposition between two competing territorial frames for action and imagination, between a regional Northern Ireland unionism (or Ulster loyalism) that is more sectarian and retrogressive and a broader UK and British unionism that looks to the metropolis and is more liberal, civic, and inclusive.[9] Building typologies of unionism around these two territorial frameworks tends to marginalize the deepest of the shifts that took place in unionism—its transformation from an ideology concerned with the relationship between all of Ireland and Britain to one concerned primarily to legitimize and defend a six-county unit in Ireland.

The institutionalization of the two new polities in Ireland and the naturalization of partition over time produced powerful pressures for an intensified regionalization of Ulster unionism. The outbreak of violent conflict in 1969 accelerated this process of retreat from the Irish context. The imperative to remove all ambiguity around unionist support for Northern Ireland's membership in the United

Kingdom in the face of the Irish Republican Army (IRA) campaign was a major new factor that worked to close off spaces of ambiguity and openness. The sense of distance from the rest of Ireland was increased too by the intensification of circuits of movement for professional employment and university education in the United Kingdom. They tied the Northern middle class much more tightly into the UK context and increased the distance between them and their contemporaries south of the border.

This gradual but deep generational shift in the Ulster unionist relationship to the Irish context was summed up by Democratic Unionist Party leader and first minister Peter Robinson in his Edward Carson lecture in Dublin in 2012: "I consider myself an Ulster or Northern Ireland unionist not an Irish Unionist. The same would be true of the vast majority of unionists in Northern Ireland. That is a significant change not just from one hundred years ago but even from fifty years ago." Robinson was asserting strongly the regional character of his unionism, but his speech was notable too for acknowledging that the fading of an all-Ireland dimension to Ulster unionism had been a gradual process. It was also notable for linking the decline of unionist identification with Ireland with the concept of regret, albeit in a heavily qualified and indirect way: "Edward Carson was unquestionably an Irish unionist, and while the legacy of Edward Carson lives on, it may be regretted that the idea of 'Irish unionism' in any meaningful sense, as historically defined, does not."[10]

A UNIONIST STATE

After partition the North remained part of the United Kingdom, but the Home Rule government and parliament established in Belfast, with its prime minister, ministries, and cabinet, resembled the Dominion governments then emerging elsewhere in the Empire rather than the arrangements for governance in the components of Great Britain. Treasury oversight and fiscal dependence ensured that Stormont remained dependent on London in a way that the Dominions did not, but the Unionist government was nonetheless insulated to a great extent from the pressures of the British government and parliament.[11]

The politics of the new entity quickly took on a rigid, frozen form. For half a century, the Unionist party won every election, formed every government, supplied every cabinet minister, and took every decision. Membership of the party was almost exclusively Protestant, and virtually every minister who served in government was a member of the Orange Order. Voting patterns followed religious affiliation so predictably that large numbers of constituencies and local councils, where the balance between Protestant and Catholic made the victory of one side or the other entirely predictable, remained uncontested for decades.

Little effort was made to co-opt even the most amenable elements in the Catholic community. The Unionist government had large numbers of public appointments at its disposal but rarely appointed Catholics. It was an indication of the power of populist loyalist pressure for exclusion and, just as importantly, a measure of the political impotence of the minority that the state made so little effort to create a pliable, collaborative Catholic elite. This exclusion at elite level was matched by widespread discrimination in the public service.

However, the image of a monolithically powerful Unionist state does not capture the intensity of internal unionist divisions and the extent to which Protestant unity had to be actively maintained and reproduced. In their scrupulously detailed analysis of the operations of the Stormont government, Bew, Paterson, and Gibbon suggest a continuous struggle between populists and anti-populists.[12] Populists sought increased expenditure, ultimately through the extraction of greater subsidies from the British Treasury, and the maintenance of discrimination against the minority to secure unionism's Protestant, working-class support base. Anti-populists combined a technocratic concern to control spending with the wish to maintain metropolitan standards and resist popular sectarian pressures. The anti-populist position was driven in part by normative considerations but also by the need to keep the money flowing from London and to preempt the exertion of political pressure by the British government. For Bew et al., the dominance of the sectarian populists and the consequent discrimination was a contingent development. It was not a structurally determined outcome of partition. But it is possible to argue that the constant shaping pressure that the populists were able to exert was tied very closely to Northern Ireland's foundational character as a Protestant polity. The partition settlement had produced a drastically unequal division of power between Northern unionists and nationalists. The consequent absence of strong pressure from the minority, from the Irish state, or from London ensured that no significant force balanced the pressure exerted by the unionist right and loyalist ultras. In this sense the consequent exclusion was as much a structural feature of Northern politics as a contingent development.

One significant non-nationalist oppositional force had some success in the late 1950s and mid-1960s. At the height of its power, the Northern Ireland Labour Party took four of the fifty-two seats in the Stormont parliament.[13] But any such third force faced a dilemma produced by the sectarian electoral logic of the state. Such a party could only form part of a winning coalition by allying with the nationalist, republican, and republican labor elements that dominated the politics of the minority. But eroding the power of the Unionist party sufficiently to form an alternative majority and break the Unionist monopoly on power required winning significant support from a Protestant electorate that would be alienated by any such alliance.

Despite the exclusion and discrimination and the disproportionately high levels of Catholic unemployment and emigration, Northern nationalists derived significant material advantages from being on the UK side of the Irish border. With the establishment of the British welfare state in the 1940s, a wide gap began to open up between the level of public services provided in the two Irish jurisdictions. Overt violent repression, although a feature of the state, was only intermittently necessary. Nonetheless, some forms of exclusion and discrimination practiced by the state were so blatant as to ultimately imperil the state itself. The situation in Derry in particular was unsustainable, as certain Unionists recognized. As the civil rights movement gathered momentum in late 1968, Unionist MP Edmund Warnock wrote to Prime Minister Terence O'Neill: "If ever a community had a right to demonstrate against a denial of civil rights, Derry is the finest example."[14] The apparently permanent political exclusion of the minority ensured that even the most biddable, socially conservative, and potentially acquiescent forces in the Catholic community remained at arm's length from the regime. When the Ulster Unionist monopoly on power was finally effectively challenged on the streets, the most socially conservative Catholics were willing to ally themselves with radical oppositional forces rather than with the Unionist government.[15]

MOBILIZATION

In the late 1960s it became apparent that this seemingly impregnable, self-reproducing system had a weak spot that oppositional forces could exploit: the minority was large enough, and territorially concentrated enough, to present a serious challenge to public order and the exercise of state authority in many parts of Northern Ireland.[16] In the right political conditions, a breach of the system at this weak point could bring powerful external forces pouring through the gap. Deep social and economic changes after 1945 helped create a political context in which such a challenge might be effectively mounted and contributed to the emergence of a new cohort of oppositional activists capable of leading such a challenge.

The construction by the British Labour government of a public welfare system that was unprecedented in its ambition and scope transformed the material conditions of everyday life from the late 1940s. Slums were cleared, new houses were built, and free education and medical care were provided universally.[17] Paradoxically, this modernizing state action facilitated a sharp intensification in sectarian discrimination that became a lightning rod for minority discontent. The large-scale housing discrimination that was a central focus for the civil rights movement was no hangover from a bygone age but a novel phenomenon of the post-war era. The practice was intensely concentrated in areas where Unionist control was fragile and where housing-allocation decisions could tip the balance of local political control.

When a massive new program for the building of public housing was launched in the late 1940s, the local councils were put in charge of much of the construction and allocation, significantly increasing the patronage at their disposal. In the most important of the gerrymandered councils—the second city of Derry, where Unionists secured 60% of seats with 33% of the vote—the local council, Londonderry

Corporation, discriminated systematically. By the late 1960s housing construction by the Corporation was grinding to a halt in the city, even though a long waiting list remained. New housing in wards in which Unionists enjoyed a small electoral majority would threaten unionist control of the Corporation and hand this major source of patronage and power to nationalists.[18]

Housing discrimination provided an issue in which the connection between material disadvantage and Unionist political control was immediately apparent. But the mobilizing potential of even this issue was relatively limited. Local activists in Derry and Dungannon, two of the most discriminatory of the gerrymandered local authorities, had been agitating on these issues since 1963. In Derry, activists had staged sit-ins, pickets, and protests through 1967 and 1968. Very few people had been mobilized on the issue of housing, but a cohort of new activists had nonetheless gained experience and had begun to build new networks.[19]

The Civil Rights Association was established in 1967 and provided a focus for mass mobilization on a broad range of issues. The first march, from Coalisland to Dungannon in County Tyrone in August 1968, was a notable success, mobilizing around two thousand marchers. The turnout of about six hundred at the next march, in Derry in October 1968, was disappointingly small, but the TV footage of that march transformed the political climate. Television viewers saw images of a Royal Ulster Constabulary (RUC) baton charge, in which policemen whacked people over the head in a casually random manner—more of a baton stroll than a baton charge, as the raw footage shows.[20] This direct violent confrontation between police and protesters electrified the situation and put the question of the relationship between the Unionist state and its Catholic minority at the top of the political agenda.

The new and powerfully seductive medium of television was central to this shift, providing new channels of influence and communication that connected local oppositional forces with external sources of power, thus changing the balance of forces in the state. It was as if the channels between the Northern minority and both London and Dublin that had been sealed in 1922 had been blasted open.

Now that oppositional forces had found methods that gave them significant political leverage, the question arose of what kind of reordering might be possible. The civil rights mobilization was extremely costly, and as soon as the pressure had abated, external sources of pressure on unionism would ease off. One of the reasons many activists pushed in 1969 for deep changes that went beyond the remedying of the most blatant abuses was the danger that the structural features that had secured Unionist domination for fifty years would once again reassert themselves.

As activists maintained pressure and loyalist counterdemonstrators confronted them, sectarian tensions rose, and clashes between the RUC and people in Catholic working-class areas intensified relentlessly. In January 1969 off-duty B-Specials and other local loyalists attacked a march from Belfast to Derry organized by the radical student group, People's Democracy, as it passed through a predominantly Protestant rural area on the outskirts of Derry. The RUC escort made little effort to stop the attack. Intense, large-scale rioting broke out in Derry that evening after the marchers arrived. Barricades were erected where the working-class nationalist Bogside District met the city center, and the RUC was excluded from the area for three days. In imitation of the "Free Berkeley" slogan of student protesters in the United States, the barricaded zone was dubbed "Free Derry," and the slogan "You are now entering Free Derry" was painted on a wall in the Bogside.[21] This territorial exclusion of state forces was a watershed event. It illustrated the fragility of the Stormont government's control of many of the predominantly Catholic areas under its authority. Derry was also the site of the "Battle of the Bogside," the large-scale rioting in August 1969 that finally triggered the deployment of British troops. The RUC lost control of large areas of the city, and by the third day of clashes, the coercive capacity of Stormont had almost been exhausted. At Stormont's request the British government deployed troops to restore order. The big question now was what kind of order that would be.

ESCALATION

The British state became deeply involved in the day-to-day affairs of Northern Ireland from August 1969 on. This intervention was characterized by a curiously lopsided combination of power and timidity. On the one hand, the state papers convey the impression of an immense and powerful machine overwhelming, infiltrating, and steering the Unionist government. Financially dependent on London since the extension of the welfare state to Northern Ireland in the 1940s and now dependent on London for the maintenance of public order, the Unionist government initially made only half-hearted attempts to bargain against reform and accepted most of the changes recommended by London.[22]

But on the other hand, state papers also depict a British state whose authority was exercised through smoke and mirrors, a Wizard of Oz behind whose curtain lay the reality of limited capacity to enforce its will if faced with resistance. When loyalists and unionists on the streets and in the state apparatus resisted British-sponsored reforms, they discovered it was possible to push back. When the Hunt Report's recommendations for disarming the RUC, for a change of RUC uniform, and for the abolition of the B-Specials were published in October 1969, the subsequent rioting on the working-class streets of Belfast's Shankill Road outlined the limits of the British state's power. Off-duty B-Specials and other loyalists turned their weapons against the troops, and three people were shot dead, including the first RUC officer to be killed in the conflict. The British government retreated from the change of uniform and allowed Stormont to shape the new Ulster Defence

Regiment (UDR) in the image of the B-Specials. From now on the Unionist government could meet any proposal for change with the objection that it would generate violence from the Protestant community.

Resistance to reform on the streets operated in tandem with the braking and shaping power exerted by those in the state apparatus. The implementation of police reform in the two key urban spaces of West Belfast and Free Derry is illustrative of the extent to which overwhelming Unionist and Protestant predominance in the state apparatus constituted an important source of unionist political power and a direct source of political pressure. In West Belfast the new English inspector-general of the RUC, Sir Arthur Young, was met by a wall of hostility from RUC men. The vast majority of them refused to patrol the area under the arrangements negotiated with the local Citizens Defence Association.[23]

In a meeting with Young in Derry, local RUC officers refused to wear the blue uniforms from the London Metropolitan Police that had been delivered to them on the basis that they were not individually tailored. Young yielded. The Derry Citizens Defence Association had made an agreement with Young that the RUC would be accepted back in the area that very day on condition that they were wearing the new uniform.[24] At this crucial juncture, it was not resistance from the Bogside that prevented the return of the police but resistance in the force to the reform package. That these acts of resistance went unpunished showed the limits of the power of the British state. They showed too that Unionist power rested not only with the government but was also diffused throughout the state apparatus and out onto the streets.

With the failure of this truncated reform to secure normal policing of Catholic urban areas, the British army began to settle into a new role as the day-to-day policing agency in large Catholic working-class areas. It was some months before either wing of the IRA launched a campaign. It was above all the failure to resolve the problem of order, which by extension was the problem of the relationship between the minority and the state, that created the space for a violent challenge by the IRA. It was the daily presence of heavily armed troops on the streets rather than the fact of British sovereignty that gave powerful emotional force to the "Brits Out" slogan subsequently adopted by the Provisional IRA.

The army was now holding the ground until a minimally reformed RUC could return to re-establish the authority of a Unionist government that had shown itself capable of setting tight limits to British government action. The army was there to assert state authority and now faced constant pressure from unionists to do so more robustly. The deployment of the army as the agency of day-to-day law and order in Catholic urban areas in October 1969 was a momentous decision. Although many contemporary observers assumed that the subsequent breakdown in relations between local Catholic youths and the troops was manufactured or controlled by the IRA, the intensifying hostility and confrontation had a logic all its own.

In late 1969 and early 1970, a new "Provisional" splinter group broke away from the "Official" republican movement, partly because of dissatisfaction with the perceived reticence of the leadership in pursuing armed action. It is often assumed that nothing would have prevented the Provisionals from launching a determined campaign of violence against the British army. However, that IRA leaders of all shades attempted to maintain good relations with the army into the spring of 1970 indicates that in certain political circumstances, they would have been strongly inhibited from attacking the army. In this respect, the Falls Road curfew of 1970 deserves the prominent place it has been given in explanations of the escalating violence.

In June 1970 rioting and gun battles between the IRA and British troops broke out after a raid for arms in the Lower Falls area of Belfast. The army restored control by imposing a curfew. It is of more than passing significance that primarily the Official IRA fought the troops. Local commander Jim Sullivan had worked cooperatively with the local RUC commander to remove the barricades around the area, and the Officials would lead their movement over the next few years to full support for state security forces and bitter opposition to the Provisional IRA. That this movement found itself involved in gun battles with the British army in mid-1970 is one of the strongest indicators that violent confrontation with the army cannot be explained solely or even primarily in terms of an unalterable determination to launch a major campaign. In the case of the Officials, it happened despite the leadership's intentions rather than because of them.

It is notable too that this crucial escalating event did not originate with a republican provocation of the military—an attempt to draw them into violence—but with a raid for arms that asserted the army's right to control the local territory. The symbolic parade of two Unionist ministers along the Falls in an army jeep after the curfew, sometimes characterized as a publicity error or an act of unfortunate insensitivity, reflected the reality that the British government was indeed acting in response to unionist wishes in asserting the state's authority forcefully in Catholic working-class areas.

ARMED STRUGGLE

Several paramilitary organizations, both loyalist and republican, were active during the Troubles, but the Provisional IRA was far and away the most important. Only the Provisional IRA offered a sustained challenge to the British state's claim to a monopoly of legitimate violence in the North, and only the Provisionals continued as a significant political force after the conflict ended. The relative weight of the various paramilitary organizations in the conflict is most frequently assessed by reference to the death toll. While the Provisionals were responsible for 48.5% of all killings and other republicans for a further 10%, loyalists killed 28.8% of the total.[25] However, the death toll does not accurately reflect the balance of activity between loyalists and republicans. Loyalists in the Ulster Defence Association and the Ulster Volunteer Force engaged primarily in assassinations of Catholic civilians targeted on the basis of their religious background. In contrast, Republicans focused predominantly on attacking the security forces and also carried out many thousands of attacks on infrastructure and economic targets that did not kill anyone. Focusing on the death toll greatly understates the huge gap between the two in terms of capacity, complexity, and level of activity. The security forces accounted for only a tenth of all deaths, but they constituted far and away the largest and most important agent deploying force in the conflict. Their impact is evident not primarily in the death toll but in other figures, such as the three hundred thousand house searches conducted in the early 1970s, the two thousand people interned without charge, and the more than twenty thousand people imprisoned for paramilitary activities. A total of three hundred thousand British troops would serve in Northern Ireland over the course of the conflict. Killings of civilians by the security forces took place infrequently after the mid-1970s. The deployment of overwhelming force by the state had secured a high degree of territorial control by that stage, reducing the need for the kind of measures deployed in the early years and making it possible, and prudent, to control security force behavior much more tightly.

The overwhelming majority of people from Northern Ireland who bore arms did so as members of the RUC and the UDR, whose combined strength by the mid-1980s was almost twenty thousand. Joining the security forces provided a legal and legitimate route for those who sought to sustain the Union through force of arms that had no equivalent on the nationalist side of the divide. The British state emphasized that it combated both republican and loyalist paramilitaries, but even though large numbers of loyalists were imprisoned, the state had an entirely different relationship with the two. Official documents released in recent years present a picture of a deeply ambiguous relationship among loyalists, mainstream unionists, and the British state. In early 1975 an Official Unionist Party delegation led by the party leader met the secretary of state and senior officials shortly after the IRA had called a ceasefire, at a time when loyalists were still carrying out regular killings. One of the three members of the delegation suggested that the government "recruit large numbers of the UDA [Ulster Defence Association] and UVF [Ulster Volunteer Force] to the RUCR [RUC Reserve] and put them into Andersonstown [in West Belfast]." The suggestion was not treated seriously by the British, but the very fact that a member of an Official Unionist Party delegation felt able to make such a suggestion is telling. It is impossible to imagine an equivalent suggestion being made to British officials by a mainstream nationalist.[26]

The Provisional Republican movement's capacity to mobilize and to organize and its ability to maintain a long-term armed campaign against the state are central to understanding the persistence of the conflict and the shape that a settlement eventually took. The Provisionals themselves often represented the movement as an almost mechanical reaction to the structural injustice of partition and state violence, as being forced into their campaign by discrimination and repression. In contrast, much of the historical literature presents the Provisional IRA and its leadership as relentless, driving agents—steering, shaping, and determining the course of the conflict.

In their different ways, both these approaches distort the balance between agency and structure in explaining the role of the Provisionals. The structural explanation fails to acknowledge the range of choices available or to capture the variety of experiences and understandings that underlay the mass mobilization of both the Official and Provisional IRA. In contrast, agential accounts underestimate the extent to which the IRA, like all other actors involved, was constrained and shaped by events and actors over which it had little control. The violence of the Provisionals was an element in a system of conflict in which there were other, far more powerful, forces at work. The coercive capacity of the British state and the shaping pressure of unionist resistance to British policy were much more significant sources of coercive power than was IRA violence.

A direct link exists between the wider political context and patterns of mobilization in the IRA, but the relationship between state repression and militant mobilization was not a linear one. One of the most striking things to emerge from recent interviews with former militants is a pattern of *de*mobilization as repression intensified. Former IRA members recall large numbers of people flooding into the movement in 1969 and 1970, as teenagers of both genders filled the ranks. As violence intensified, many of these recruits dropped out. One teenaged member who in 1969 recruited several of his friends into the republican youth wing, the Fianna, recalls that within a year not one of them remained in the organization.[27] Another recalls that the two friends who were sworn into the Fianna with him had both left within eighteen months.[28] A female volunteer who joined in 1969 at the age of fifteen recalls: "We were all involved, but after a while the numbers fell and a lot of people left, but the people who stayed, stayed for the long haul."[29] They may have left partly because of increasing opposition in the Catholic community to the IRA but also, we must assume, because of the rising cost of involvement. As one former member put it: "A lot of them were in the Fianna and then once people got a bit older they realized this is no joke, you know."[30] Many who joined the IRA cite the experience of state repression as the primary motivating factor. This has provoked the response that most people who experienced such repression didn't join the IRA, that individuals were free to make a choice, and that many resisted the temptation of violence. But for many who joined the IRA, it seemed more like an obligation than a temptation. As one woman volunteer who joined Cumann na mBan after her return from working in London with a Catholic charity put it: "I had thought about it and I had to do it and I feel, it was like I felt compelled to do it ... people had to stand up."[31]

This is not to discount the importance of the excitement of covert armed action in motivating many young recruits, but this was just one of several mobilizing factors. Bosi identifies three pathways to mobilization: those who sought to defend their local areas, those committed to republican ideological goals, and those mobilized by transformative events.[32] Regardless of individual motivation, the political context of an intense ongoing struggle to shape the future of the North was far and away the most important factor in mobilization.

For IRA members who were deeply rooted in neighborhoods where the British army was widely regarded by late 1971 as an army of occupation, it seemed self-evident that the movement enjoyed large-scale popular support and had a popular mandate. One former republican internee remembers his disbelief and the stunned reaction of a fellow-internee in Long Kesh when they read a letter from an uncle of his that fiercely condemned the IRA.[33] They were shocked that someone from an Irish nationalist background could characterize the IRA in such negative terms. As time went on, the Provisionals would find themselves increasingly isolated from the broader Irish nationalist context. The condemnation, exclusion, and calculated isolation of the Provisionals helped give the movement something of the character of an angry militant sect, increasingly isolated and marginalized by the late 1970s.

That a significant core of support remained loyal to the Provisionals throughout it all was the product, in large measure, of direct experience of state repression. The state papers, with their reflective and cerebral tone, rarely convey any sense of the chaotic brutality that security force action often entailed. IRA informer Raymond Gilmour's account of his violent brutalization at the hands of soldiers and the RUC Special Branch at the age of thirteen provides one vivid description of the sense of utter powerlessness and debasement that such encounters could generate.[34] Former IRA member Eamon Collins, who later turned against the organization, also provides a powerful account of the humiliating and radicalizing effects of an army raid.[35] These accounts carry a particular weight, because both books are aimed primarily at criticizing the IRA.

Recent accounts by former IRA members have provided us with novel insights into the IRA as an organization, illuminating its complex bureaucratic character.[36] For example, Eamon Collins provides a deeply disillusioned account of an IRA "court martial," in which he participated.[37] While Collins was appalled by the procedural irregularities and the fact that the accused did not turn up, what is perhaps more striking is that the IRA was organizing such quasi-legal processes in a situation where the risks of arrest for taking part were extremely high. The movement's insistence on attempting to follow judicial norms is testimony to its desire to legitimate itself primarily by reference to the norms of legality and propriety that were dominant in the wider liberal democratic society. But a constant tension existed between these aspirations and the practices of the movement, most evident in the punishment shootings and beatings that were inflicted as penalties for transgression, in the killing of suspected informers and captured security force members, and in the deliberate targeting of off-duty members.

While fanatical mind-sets and frozen ideologies were often identified as the defining features and driving forces behind the IRA, it is its bureaucratic structure, complexity, and the essential modernity of the organization that best explain its strength and persistence. Former IRA commander Martin McGuinness's widely perceived effectiveness in wielding executive power in Northern Ireland's government after 2007 is testimony not so much to the possibilities for individual transformation as to the essential contiguity of the bureaucratic forms of the IRA and the state.

The IRA's legitimation strategies emphasized its legality and the ethical, moral, and even altruistic character of the movement, but the dominant face visible to those outside the movement—particularly as the conflict wore on—was one of appalling and brutal violence. The British government worked hard to demonize and caricature the IRA, but they had plenty of raw material to work with. A huge toll of human life was taken in the random slaughter wreaked by bomb attacks with inadequate or miscommunicated warnings or those that seemed to be carried out with a careless disregard for civilian casualties. Unintentional killings by the IRA took the lives of 376 civilians in Northern Ireland, more than all of those killed by the security forces.[38] For even the most liberal and reflective of unionists, the IRA's campaign was an affront, a carnival of brutality that was not in any sense justified by the levels of injustice present in the state.

Although the death toll inflicted by state forces and loyalists roughly balanced the death toll inflicted by republicans until 1976, the imbalance became quite pronounced after that. The IRA and the Irish National Liberation Army accounted for the great majority of killings between then and 1985, when loyalist killings began to increase and then overtake republican killings in the wake of the Anglo-Irish Agreement. A powerful consensus developed south of the Irish border in the late 1970s that the violence was being driven overwhelmingly by the IRA rather than by state repression or loyalist violence. *The Northern Ireland Question*, poet Desmond Egan's angry challenge to those who endorsed the IRA campaign, distilled that sense of moral outrage:

> two wee girls
> were playing tig near a car ...
>
> how many counties would you say
> are worth their scattered fingers? [39]

From this perspective, the question of "what then?"—what kind of political settlement should follow the end of the IRA campaign—was an insignificant one in the face of appalling human suffering. But the Provisionals were not alone in placing immense weight on the question of "what then?" Unionists were scarcely any more willing to concede significant political ground in the interests of a peace settlement than were the Provisionals, but they were in a holding pattern, seeking to maintain the status quo rather than transform it. Unionists exerted influence on the conflict primarily through pressure on the British state to use its coercive resources more aggressively to secure a defeat of the IRA, which would obviate the need for major compromises.

NEGOTIATION

It is difficult to penetrate the haze of obfuscation and propaganda surrounding contact between the British government and the Provisional leadership during the Troubles. To a certain extent, this haze was a collaborative product, as both parties had a shared interest in maintaining their ideological purity and their bargaining positions in the event of failure.

A stereotype of republican ideological purity was valuable to the Provisionals, but it was also of use to the British government. If the republicans were extreme, rigid, and uncompromising, then no amount of concessions would bring peace. If compromise were impossible, then those who wanted peace had only one clear path to that goal: full support for the military efforts of the British state to secure the defeat of the IRA. The oft-repeated observation that the 1972 talks between Secretary of State for Northern Ireland William Whitelaw and an IRA delegation at Cheyne Walk in London were fruitless because the republicans laid out a set of impossible demands perpetuates a contemporary British government interpretation aimed at winning the blame game. The 1972 talks didn't founder over Provisional ideological rigidity but because of a local confrontation at a peaceline in Belfast. The pattern was repeated in subsequent ceasefires: violence resumed not because of a refusal to compromise on the big issues but because of difficulties in achieving progress that made a difference on the ground.

The exclusion of republicans, loyalists, and the Democratic Unionist Party from the negotiations at Sunningdale that led to setting up a power-sharing executive in 1974 was explained too on the basis that compromise with extremists was impossible. The Belfast Agreement (Good Friday Agreement) of 1998 would subsequently be dubbed "Sunningdale for slow learners," but in certain respects, Sunningdale was the opposite of the Good Friday Agreement: the former agreement was aimed at securing moderate nationalist support for repression of the IRA and offered no major concessions on security-related issues.[40] Reporting on a meeting with the Social Democratic and Labour Party (SDLP) leader Gerry Fitt as negotiations began in late 1973, key British official James Allan noted that "Mr Fitt will have been reminded forcefully [at the recent SDLP annual conference] … that the electorate wanted to see early dividends on the emotional issue of internment rather than simply to read that the party leaders were occupying themselves in sharing out the jobs."[41] The SDLP failed to secure significant movement on police reform or internment, and the Council of Ireland provided a symbolic victory in compensation. Without the Council of Ireland, Sunningdale offered the SDLP no more than ministerial seats in return for supporting a big push against the IRA that would have stretched the party's electoral support base to its limits. The SDLP brought together civil rights leaders, nationalists, and Labour politicians who were united by their opposition to both Official and Provisional republicans. It enjoyed the electoral support of the majority of Catholic voters throughout the conflict, but the party suffered from a certain lack of coherence. In John Hume, however, it had an exceptionally astute leader who played a major role in shaping the policy of both the British and Irish governments.

The proximate cause of the collapse of the power-sharing executive in 1974 was a massive Ulster Workers Council strike, which demonstrated the power of loyalists to bring the North to a standstill when running with the tide of unionist public opinion.[42] Protestant predominance in the workforce of key facilities, including the power stations, allowed the Ulster Workers Council to exert immense pressure on the British government. Also important was the persistence of the IRA campaign (although at a deliberately reduced level), which provided a backdrop against which unionists rejected compromise. Sunningdale was a project of a previous Tory government, which meant that the new Labour prime minister Harold Wilson had no great political capital invested in it. His strong personal preference for withdrawal was also important in determining his attitude.

The argument was later made that Sunningdale collapsed primarily because of the Council of Ireland and that responsibility for failure therefore lay primarily at the door of insistent nationalists. Power sharing and equality within the state were viable, the argument went, but in pursuing a nationalist agenda that inspired fear in unionists, nationalists pushed unionists too far. This was emphatically not the lesson that the British government drew at the time. A recurrent mantra of post–Sunningdale British policymakers was that power sharing was not practical politics, because unionists would not accept it.

After the collapse of Sunningdale, and particularly as the 1970s wore on, there was significant pressure for the co-option of the SDLP to a minimalist British government agenda whose parameters were set by unionist opinion. Throughout this time, John Hume continued to advocate an overarching settlement to end the conflict and was able to draw on his strong alliances with the Irish government and U.S. politicians to ensure that the political space for this position was maintained.[43]

In the months that followed the collapse of Sunningdale, the British prime minister Harold Wilson authorized the opening of secret contact with the IRA leadership.[44] As in 1972, many of those involved on both sides sought political cover after the talks came to nothing. Because the air had been thick with talk of

British withdrawal in the wake of Sunningdale's collapse, the British government subsequently went to great lengths to insist that withdrawal had formed no part of its plan in 1975. What can be said with some certainty is that this engagement began as a serious attempt to achieve a negotiated settlement of the conflict through the inclusion of paramilitaries. What is also clear is that Wilson viewed British military and political withdrawal from Ireland as the optimal outcome of a settlement. The contradictions of the 1975 talks and their ultimate failure arose to a great extent from the weakness of Wilson's divided government, the narrowness of his parliamentary majority, and the fading of his power as he entered a phase of personal and political decline.[45]

Many state papers present a picture of British officials trying to do their best to choose between difficult alternatives rather than following a relentlessly imperialist or repressive agenda. Some scholars working with the papers have found it irresistible to identify with those perspectives and to treat the development of policy as the outcome of a terribly difficult situation where much of the time decision makers effectively had no choice. We do not have access to equivalent records from the republican movement. However, the diaries of the 1975 negotiations kept by Brendan Duddy, the intermediary who acted as the primary channel of contact between Britain and the IRA then and later, provide a rare contemporary insight into the perspective of senior Provisionals. Duddy's account of the 1975 talks conveys a powerful sense of a Provisional leadership dealing with external constraints, impossible dilemmas, and choices among unpalatable alternatives that strongly echo the themes evident in the state papers. As the Provisional IRA ended its ceasefire in late 1975, for example, Duddy wrote in his diary: "I told the British that the Provos had really no choice. They had backed peace, but the corridors of power had ensured that no progress was possible."[46]

As the state secured greater control of the streets from 1976 on, expectations of a negotiated end to the conflict gave way to the hope among many that the conflict might end as all previous IRA campaigns against partition had done: with a dwindling of IRA violence and capacity and a victory for the state.

LONG WAR

The standard account of the Troubles has the British government adopting a policy from late 1975 of normalization, criminalization, and Ulsterization. The policy was aimed at treating the conflict as a criminal problem to be dealt with by policing measures while minimizing the impact on British public opinion by withdrawing British troops. External political pressure would be held at bay through an emphasis on the problem of violence rather than on politics, and there would be no need for engagement or negotiation with the "men of violence." At the same time, the IRA settled into a Long War, reorganizing to ensure that they could sustain a campaign long enough to eventually "sicken"[47] the British into withdrawal. The two parties settled into a long struggle.

But the sequence of events that later came to be characterized as a policy of criminalization and normalization might usefully be characterized instead as the opening up of a policy vacuum that was filled by the priorities and agenda of the security forces. Roy Mason, the secretary of state who succeeded Merlyn Rees in 1976, epitomized this turn away from politics. Perhaps the most quietly damning comment on Mason's tenure is that of the most senior civil servant in the Northern Ireland Office, Permanent Under Secretary Brian Cubbon. In a letter accompanying a 1979 paper in which he discussed possible political ways forward, Cubbon refers to a few of the possible courses of action and then adds: "Or the new Secretary of State might seek to avoid the political whirlpool altogether, as Mr Mason has. Is this possible?"[48]

In the absence of any clear political vision or policy, those in charge of security began to drive policy by setting operational goals. And those goals had a clear political color. Writing to the head of the Northern Ireland Office and the General Officer Commanding (GOC) in 1976, the incoming RUC chief constable Kenneth Newman, presented the normalization of policing as a sharply focused political project to defeat the IRA:

> My first priority must be to create a strong and efficient crime fighting machine designed to erode and ultimately overthrow the power of the PIRA ... the primacy of the police can not be established until the PIRA is weakened and ultimately eliminated ... my concept of police primacy involves: i) full mobilisation of manpower and resources for the investigation and detection of crimes generally and, in particular, the defeat of the PIRA.

Over the previous two years, loyalists had killed almost exactly as many people as republicans had. The Provisional IRA on the other hand had spent much of 1975 on ceasefire, negotiating secretly with the British government. But Newman's sixteen-point memo was dominated almost entirely by the aim of defeating the IRA. Loyalists finally get a secondary mention in point 13, which makes passing reference to dealing with "republicans *and* loyalists."[49]

Perhaps the most damaging consequence of the policy vacuum was the steep escalation of confrontation in the prisons. Far from seeking to criminalize IRA prisoners in the process of moving them into the H-Blocks of the new Maze prison, Secretary of State Merlyn Rees had actually sought in 1975 to retain special category conditions by extending all but one of these conditions to all prisoners, but his view had not prevailed.[50] If it had, one of the most important elements subsequently sustaining the conflict would have been removed. As IRA and Irish National Liberation Army prisoners protested against the removal of those conditions in 1976, prison authorities responded with steadily harsher measures, to which the prisoners responded by escalating the protest.[51]

The intensity of the pressure placed on the prisoners aroused the concern even of Roy Mason. In late 1978 his private secretary wrote to the prison authorities on his behalf to say that correspondence about the prison

> has raised a query in his mind—why is it necessary to conduct these close body searches of protesting prisoners in the H Blocks? It occurs to the Secretary of State that if these men are naked in their cells for 24 hours a day, then they have very little scope to hide anything. If this is the case, then why subject them to this further, apparently unnecessary, indignity?... As you know the Secretary of State is not in general disposed to be over-sympathetic to these men ... but he does rather wonder about the question of searching.[52]

In a lengthy and assertive reply, the Director of Prison (Ops) insisted that "the Governor must be allowed to exercise his professional judgment of what is required to maintain the security of his prison." Explaining the rationale behind the searches, he explained that "As in any contest, the participants aim to destroy their opponents' morale" and that it was important that there be no change that the prisoners could see as an advance in their position.[53] By this logic, no escalation in punishment could be reversed until the prisoners had been defeated.

Cheered by the emphasis on defeating the IRA rather than achieving a compromise political settlement, unionists took great heart from what appeared to be a new departure. In fact the emphasis on security reflected an exhaustion of political will and energy that is distilled in the response of one civil servant to Cubbon's suggestions in 1979 for a new departure: "Since there are no foreseeable solutions to the Irish problem (and HMG have anyway no ultimate objective), we are only seeking to pass the time decently."[54]

The displacement of politics by security created a sense of complacency among some senior unionists that was extremely dangerous to the unionist position in the long term. If indeed there was no political conflict, only a criminal problem, then the state had an obligation to tackle it through the criminal justice system. The British government would fund, organize, and fight an open-ended war against the IRA, while unionists resisted almost all movement toward compromise with nationalists. Under direct rule, unionists could shape British policy through a constant exertion of pressure at the level of elite politics and at the operational level of a state apparatus in which unionist opinion was overwhelmingly dominant: in the civil service and the prison service, in the police and the UDR. Finally, unionist politicians could repeatedly invoke the prospect of loyalist paramilitary violence or large-scale resistance by the Protestant majority as an argument against change. An underestimation of the British state's need for political progress was unionists' most damaging political miscalculation.

A sense that the defeat of the IRA was within reach helps explain how the British government allowed the prison dispute to escalate to the stage where the IRA launched a hunger strike. On the eve of the first hunger strike in October 1980, Permanent Under Secretary Ken Stowe told his colleagues:

> Senior Northern Ireland civil servants believed that the Catholic community considered the war to be over. Although the position might be affected by the H Block hunger strike there did appear to be a real chance that over the next few months the men of violence would find themselves increasingly isolated ... and the security forces would be able to mop them up gradually.[55]

When the Provisionals called off their first hunger strike in December 1980 on the basis of a promise of very modest changes, Secretary of State Humphrey Atkins regarded this as an act of capitulation, a sign of weakness and of republican desperation to end the protest. When the prison authorities subsequently implemented these changes in a minimal and restrictive fashion, the British government did not make strenuous efforts to avert a second hunger strike.

Only after the first four hunger strikers had died; after one of them, Bobby Sands, had been elected as a Westminster MP; and after two other IRA prisoners had been elected to the Irish parliament did the British government secretly begin negotiating with the Provisionals in July 1981. This move was a measure of the political damage the strike was inflicting. The failure of these talks to produce a negotiated compromise settlement and the deaths of six more hunger strikers remain the focus of intense contemporary debate.[56] Both the IRA and the British government were engaged in intense negotiations during the impending death of the fifth hunger striker, Joe McDonnell, both sides being aware that the imminent deadline that his approaching death imposed produced heightened pressure for last-minute concessions.

The failure to negotiate a compromise settlement over the prison issue had disastrous consequences. Much recent commentary identifies the hunger strikes as the beginning of Sinn Féin's politicization and the route to compromise. But failure to find a negotiated compromise on the prison issue radicalized a new generation of republicans, reenergized the IRA campaign, reconnected the movement with a mass support base, and hardened opinion in the movement. It helped push the eventual political compromise far into the future.

PEACE PROCESS

Analysis of the 1985 Anglo-Irish Agreement generally emphasizes that the Irish government wanted it for political reasons and the British for security. But a much broader set of concerns drove the Agreement on the British side. The initial policy documents in 1979 that proposed dealing with the conflict in a broader

Irish context focused on the aim of building a partnership with the Irish state to share the political burden. Implicit in this model was a shifting of the balance of British policy in the direction of Irish nationalism. That this would involve confrontation with unionists was recognized from a very early stage. As one civil servant put it in 1979, "HMG [the British government] could not offer 'partnership' to the Irish Government <u>unless</u> we were prepared to face the Unionist reaction and deal with it."[57] The Agreement was clearly intended to exert pressure for compromise on unionists and to shatter the assumption that the British government would follow a unionist security agenda regardless of the political position that unionists adopted.

The Agreement opened up a range of avenues for progress. Although the Provisionals rejected it, it contributed to movement in Sinn Féin's negotiating position. In a series of policy documents in the late 1980s and early 1990s, the party nudged forward the outer edge of its negotiating position. Engagement with the SDLP and the Irish government in 1987 and 1988 provided early signs that the Provisionals would be willing to settle for something far short of their stated aims.[58] In November 1989 a journalist asked new secretary of state Peter Brooke if he could envisage a British government talking to Sinn Féin. Brooke replied that it was "difficult to envisage a military defeat" of the IRA and that the government would need to be "imaginative" in dealing with a possible end to the IRA campaign, throwing in a reference to Cyprus for good measure. It provided a public glimpse of some of the more adventurous conversations that were taking place at senior levels of the Northern Ireland Office.[59]

Despite the hail of criticism from Unionists that this apparently inadvertent kite-flying generated, reaction on the whole was sufficiently encouraging that Brooke subsequently gave a carefully considered speech in which he gave a clear public signal to the Provisionals that an inclusive negotiated compromise was possible, that if they "renounced violence," they "would be able, like other parties, to seek a role in the peaceful political life of the community."[60] However, it took another eight years to reach the formal peace agreement of 1998 and a further nine years before the Executive finally began to operate on a firm footing in 2007.

The fraught negotiations surrounding the Belfast Agreement were characterized by a multilayered mutual suspicion. Both republicans and Ulster Unionists argued that they were sincere in wishing to reach a settlement in which they would ultimately allay their opponents' concerns, but they doubted the sincerity of their opposite numbers. Republicans argued that Unionists demanded decommissioning before a political settlement because they knew it was impossible. Unionists argued that republicans were cynically holding on to weapons and maintaining the capacity of the IRA for as long as possible because it gave them a powerful (and illegitimate) bargaining chip.

The compromise eventually imposed by U.S. Special Envoy Senator George Mitchell called for parallel processes for the establishment of new structures of government and the decommissioning of IRA weapons. Both parties would jump at the same time. The intense distrust surrounding the choreography of these acts of simultaneity is captured neatly in comedian Eddie Izzard's 2001 take on the process:

> the IRA was going "If you just sign your name on the declaration there, we will be taking our hands off the guns right now, if you could just put your signature there ..."
>
> [UNIONISTS]
> We will sign this piece of paper if you will take your hands away from the guns—the signature is so close to going on to the thing—If you could just remove ...
>
> [IRA]
> I've got my nail on the gun now. That's all I have. The ball is in your court. If you could just put that ink on to that thing—it's hardly a nanometer away ...
>
> [UNIONISTS]
> If you could just fuckin' take your fuckin' finger away. I'm dripping the ink down there. I'm putting ink on. It's not actually making any sentences yet, but I'm ...
>
> [IRA]
> You fuckin' ... Alright, it's all fuckin' off. Forget about it![61]

In many respects, unionist and republican arguments on decommissioning were not contradictory. If the possibility for resumption of an IRA campaign had been eliminated near the beginning of the talks process, it would have greatly eased the pressure on unionists to compromise. They would have been in a much stronger position to exert pressure on the British government for their optimal outcome: a settlement that left Sinn Féin marginalized and perhaps subject to a long "decontamination" process that might split and destroy the movement. Unionists were right to think that delaying the process strengthened the republicans' hand. But given the history of unionist approaches to compromise settlements in the past, republicans were probably right that unionists would have pressed for a much less inclusive settlement if they had the opportunity and that unionists were quite relaxed about the possibility of an IRA split. Ulster Unionist Party leader David Trimble ultimately agreed to take part in a (short-lived) executive with Sinn Féin, the IRA decommissioned its weapons, and Sinn Féin eventually signed up to support policing. The Provisionals had moved to entirely peaceful means, while Ulster Unionists, and later the Democratic Unionist Party, had agreed to share power. These key parties to the negotiations ultimately proved willing to make far-reaching and fundamental compromises, but the intense pressure placed on them played a major role in generating this outcome.

CONCLUSION

In a 1990 *Star Trek* episode about an armed rebellion, Lieutenant Commander Data—the android crew member who embodies scientific rationality—points out to Captain Jean-Luc Picard that armed rebellion and terrorism sometimes succeed. He reminds him of "the independence of the Mexican state from Spain, the Irish unification of 2024, and the Kenzie rebellion." "Yes, I'm aware of them," Picard replies briskly, amplifying the impact of this pseudo-historical list with his offhand confirmation.[62]

The playful reference to Irish unity reflected a widespread assumption that history and the force of natural boundaries were on the side of Irish republicanism. But the century that began with the hardening and militarization of the central cleavage in Irish politics and the subsequent partition of the country has given way to a twenty-first century in which that partition persists and seems likely to persist for some time to come.

For many unionists the question of partition has now been finally settled. The 1998 Agreement is valued above all because it sealed the border, ended the dispute, and locked republicans into the United Kingdom. The bitter cost of this achievement is the toleration of tamed republicans, but the prize of Northern Ireland has been secured. In one sense there is good reason to interpret the Agreement in these terms. Its cross-border elements have proven to be marginal and trivial.[63] If Ireland is ever politically reunited, it will certainly not be through a gradual process of increasing cross-border collaboration. In addition polls suggest that although the Catholic proportion of the population in the North has increased, enthusiasm for reunification is far from strong—although it is subject to sharp fluctuations. However, the combined unionist vote dipped below 50% in the early years of the twenty-first century, foreshadowing a deep transformation in the political dynamics of Northern Ireland. The transition to a double-minority situation for the first time since partition has direct implications for the future constitutional status of the North. Northern nationalists may be cautious about the prospect of reunification, but they do not have the same deep-rooted objections as unionists do to a possible future reordering of relationships on the island.

Whatever relationship develops between the two parts of Ireland and between both parts of Ireland and Great Britain in the twenty-first century, it will be powerfully shaped by wider European and international currents. It will also be shaped by both Irish nationalism and unionism. Despite the powerful discourses that treat the question of the relationship between unionism and nationalism as one that is internal to Northern Ireland, the question is one that stretches across the Irish border and remains intertwined with broader questions of sovereignty, legitimacy, and political power in Ireland.

The great structural themes of class and nation long dominated the historiography of the Northern Ireland state. They were threaded through the two earliest full-length histories of the state, Patrick Buckland, *A History of Northern Ireland* (Dublin: Gill and Macmillan, 1981) and Michael Farrell, *Northern Ireland: The Orange State* (London: Pluto, 1980). The most fully developed theoretical project focused on class was Paul Bew, Henry Patterson, and Peter Gibbon, *The State in Northern Ireland 1921–1972: Political Forces and Social Classes* (Manchester: Manchester University Press, 1979). Brendan O'Leary and John McGarry asserted the importance of nationality and the nation-state in the spirit of Ernest Gellner and insisted on the need to address these issues in any peace settlement in *The Politics of Antagonism: Understanding Northern Ireland* (London: Athlone Press, 1993) and *Explaining Northern Ireland: Broken Images* (Oxford: Blackwell, 1995). Also important in this tradition are Frank Wright's groundbreaking comparative work *Northern Ireland: A Comparative Analysis* (Dublin: Gill and Macmillan, 1987) and Joseph Ruane and Jennifer Todd, *The Dynamics of Conflict in Northern Ireland: Power, Conflict and Emancipation* (Cambridge: Cambridge University Press, 1996).

The ending of the conflict and the opening up from 1998 on of the relevant archives has seen a distinct shift in focus from structure to process, from class and nationalism to violence and decision making. This work tends to focus on untangling the threads of responsibility and on analyzing choices rather than on deep structural forces. Examples are Simon Prince and Geoffrey Warner, *Belfast and Derry in Revolt: A New History of the Start of the Troubles* (Dublin: Irish Academic Press, 2012) and Thomas Hennessey, *Northern Ireland: The Origins of the Troubles* (Dublin: Gill and Macmillan, 2005). In the context of a compromise peace settlement that undermined the narratives that both republicans and unionists had confidently pressed during the conflict, much of this work is bound up with the ongoing struggles of political actors to assert legitimacy and to shape the settlement. There is some irony in the fact that as the conflict recedes further into the past, the struggles around its interpretation seem to become ever more intense.

NOTES

1. Brendan O'Leary, "Mission Accomplished? Looking Back at the IRA," *Field Day Review* 1 (2005), pp. 216–246.

2. Martin Melaugh, Fionnuala McKenna, and Brendan Lynn, "Background Information on Northern Ireland Society—Security and Defence," CAIN web service (http://cain.ulst.ac.uk/ni/security.htm). Accessed July 4, 2013.

3. David McKittrick, Séamus Kelters, Brian Feeney, Chris Thornton, and David McVea, *Lost Lives, the Stories of the Men, Women and Children Who Died as a Result of the Northern Ireland Troubles* (Edinburgh: Mainstream, 2004).

4. Terence O'Neill, *The Autobiography of Terence O'Neill* (London: Hart-Davis, 1972), p. 40.

5. Henry Patterson, "Party versus Order: Ulster Unionism and the Flags and Emblems Act," *Contemporary British History* 13: 4 (1999), pp. 105–129.

6. Dennis Kennedy, *The Widening Gulf: Northern Attitudes to the Independent Irish State, 1919–49* (Belfast: Blackstaff, 1988), p. 59.

7. Marc Mulholland, "Assimilation versus Segregation: Unionist Strategy in the 1960s," *Twentieth Century British History* 11: 3 (2000), pp. 284–307. Term is from p. 290.

8. Mulholland, "Assimilation versus Segregation."

9. Paul Bew, Henry Patterson, and Peter Gibbon, *The State in Northern Ireland 1921–1972: Political Forces and Social Classes* (Manchester: Manchester University Press, 1979); Jennifer Todd, "Two Traditions in Unionist Political Culture," *Irish Political Studies* 2: 1 (1987), pp. 1–26.

10. Peter Robinson, "Reflections on Irish Unionism," Edward Carson Lecture, Dublin, March 29, 2012 (http://cain.ulst.ac.uk/issues/politics/docs/dup/pr290312.htm).

11. Patrick Buckland, *The Factory of Grievances: Devolved Government in Northern Ireland, 1921–39* (Dublin: Gill and Macmillan, 1979); Bew, Patterson, and Gibbon, *The State in Northern Ireland 1921–1972*; Michael Farrell, *Northern Ireland: The Orange State* (London: Pluto, 1980).

12. Bew, Patterson, and Gibbon, *The State in Northern Ireland 1921–1972*.

13. Aaron Edwards, *A History of the Northern Ireland Labour Party: Democratic Socialism and Sectarianism* (Manchester: Manchester University Press, 2009).

14. Marc Mulholland, *The Longest War* (Oxford: Oxford University Press, 2002) p. 54.

15. Niall Ó Dochartaigh, *From Civil Rights to Armalites: Derry and the Birth of Irish Troubles* (Basingstoke: Palgrave Macmillan, second ed., 2005).

16. Niall Ó Dochartaigh and Lorenzo Bosi, "Territoriality and Mobilization: The Civil Rights Campaign in Northern Ireland," *Mobilization* 15: 4 (2010), pp. 405–424.

17. Sabine Wichert, *Northern Ireland since 1945* (London: Longman, 1991).

18. Niall Ó Dochartaigh, "Housing and Conflict: Social Change and Collective Action in Derry in the 1960s," in Gerard O'Brien (ed.), *Derry and Londonderry: History and Society* (Dublin: Geography Publications, 1999).

19. Bob Purdie, *Politics in the Streets* (Belfast: Blackstaff, 1990); Simon Prince, *Northern Ireland's '68: Civil Rights, Global Revolt and the Origins of the Troubles* (Dublin: Irish Academic Press, 2007).

20. "Protest in Full Swing," *Civil Rights Movement 1968–69 Exhibition: RTÉ Archive* (http://www.rte.ie/archives/exhibitions/1031-civil-rights-movement-1968-9/1034-derry-5-october-1968/319387-derry-civil-rights-demonstration/?page=1).

21. Eamonn McCann, *War and an Irish Town* (Harmondsworth, England: Penguin, 1974), p. 53.

22. Marc Mulholland, *Northern Ireland at the Crossroads* (Basingstoke: Macmillan, 1999); William Beattie Smith, *The British State and the Northern Ireland Crisis, 1969–73: From Violence to Power Sharing* (Washington, DC: U.S. Institute of Peace Press, 2011); Geoffrey Warner, "Putting Pressure on O'Neill: The Wilson Government and Northern Ireland 1964–69," *Irish Studies Review* 13: 1 (2005), pp. 13–31.

23. "Narrative and extracts from personal diary (Sir Arthur Young) Sept 26 1969 to 14 Oct 1970," CJ4/153, National Archives, London.

24. "Narrative and extracts from personal diary (Sir Arthur Young) Sept 26 1969 to 14 Oct 1970," CJ4/153, National Archives, London.

25. McKittrick et al., *Lost Lives*.

26. "Note of a meeting between the Secretary of State and a delegation from the Official Unionist Party 17 February 1975," CJ4/858, National Archives, London.

27. Interview with former Belfast Provisional IRA Volunteer "A," July 6, 2011.

28. Interview with two former Belfast Provisional IRA Volunteers "G" and "H," March 23, 2012.

29. Rosaleen McCorley, *Mná an IRA* [women of the IRA], TG4, broadcast February 9, 2012. Original interview in Irish: "Bhí muid uilig ann but i ndiaidh tamaill thit na huimhreacha agus d'imigh cuid mhaith daoine but na daoine a d'fhan, d'fhan said don long haul."

30. Interview with two former Belfast Provisional IRA Volunteers "G" and "H," March 23, 2012.

31. Rosaleen Walsh, *Mná an IRA* [women of the IRA], TG4, broadcast February 2, 2012.

32. Lorenzo Bosi, "Explaining Pathways to Armed Activism in the Provisional Irish Republican Army, 1969–1972," *Social Science History* 36: 3 (2012), pp. 347–390.

33. Interview with former Belfast Provisional IRA Volunteer "A," March 28, 2012.

34. Raymond Gilmour, *Dead Ground: Infiltrating the IRA* (London: Little, Brown, 1999), p. 53.

35. Eamon Collins (with Mick MacGovern), *Killing Rage* (London: Granta, 1997), pp. 49–53.

36. Collins (with MacGovern), *Killing Rage*; Gerry Bradley (with Brian Feeney) *Insider: Gerry Bradley's Life in the IRA* (Dublin: O'Brien Press, 2009).

37. Collins (with MacGovern), *Killing Rage*, pp. 246–247.

38. O'Leary, "Mission Accomplished," p. 240.

39. Desmond Egan, *Midland* (Newbridge: Goldsmith, 1972).

40. Michael Kerr, *The Destructors: The Story of Northern Ireland's Lost Peace Process* (Dublin: Irish Academic Press, 2011).

41. James Allan, "Meeting with Mr Fitt," 6 Sept 1973, PREM 15/1695, National Archives (UK).

42. Don Anderson, *Fourteen May Days: The Inside Story of the Loyalist Strike* (Dublin: Gill and Macmillan, 1994); Robert Fisk, *The Point of No Return: The Strike Which Broke the British in Ulster* (London: Times Books, 1975).

43. Peter McLoughlin, *John Hume and the Revision of Irish Nationalism* (Manchester: Manchester University Press, 2010).

44. Niall Ó Dochartaigh, "Everyone Trying. IRA Ceasefire 1975: A Missed Opportunity for Peace?" *Field Day Review* 7 (2011), pp. 50–77.

45. Philip Ziegler, *Wilson: The Authorised Life of Lord Wilson of Rievaulx* (London: Weidenfeld and Nicolson, 1995).

46. "1975 diary, entry for 21/11/75," Brendan Duddy papers at NUI Galway, POL 35/62.

47. As Martin McGuiness put it in a 1988 speech. Cited in Brendan O'Brien, *The Long War: The IRA and Sinn Féin* (Dublin: O'Brien, third ed., 1999).

48. "Letter from Brian Cubbon 7 Feb 1979," CJ4/2710, National Archives, London.

49. "Newman to PUS and GOC, 16/4/76," CJ4/1780, National Archives, London.

50. Stuart Aveyard, *No Solution: British Government Policy in Northern Ireland under Labour 1974–79* (Manchester: Manchester University Press, forthcoming).

51. Liam Clarke, *Broadening the Battlefield: The H-Blocks and the Rise of Sinn Féin.* (Dublin: Gill and Macmillan, 1987).

52. "A. R. Brown to Mr Jackson, 30 October 1978," CJ4/2728, National Archives, London.

53. "W. R. Truesdale to Secretary of State, 15 November 1978," CJ4/2728, National Archives, London.

54. "P.W.J. Buxton, 20th February 1979," CJ4/2710, National Archives, London.

55. "Political developments in Northern Ireland—the next steps, notes of a meeting held on 14 October 1980," FCO 87 /1036, National Archives, London.

56. Richard O'Rawe, *Blanketmen: An Untold Story of the H-block Hunger Strike* (Dublin: New Island, 2005).

57. "W. R. Haydon to Brian Cubbon, 28 February 1979," CJ4/2710, National Archives, London, emphasis in the original.

58. Ed Moloney, *A Secret History of the IRA* (London: Allen Lane, 2002).

59. Peter Taylor, *Provos: The IRA and Sinn Féin* (London: Bloomsbury, 1998), p. 316.

60. Taylor, *Provos*, p. 318.

61. Eddie Izzard, *Circle* (New York: Ella Communications and Line by Line Production, November 2002), DVD.

62. This fleeting reference was deemed sufficiently sensitive that all mainstream British and Irish TV channels then showing the series dropped this episode. Seventeen years later the BBC showed it.

63. John Coakley, "The North-South Relationship, 1998–2013," unpublished paper delivered at "The Agreement, 15 Years on," Symposium at the University of Ulster, Belfast, April 19, 2013.

CHAPTER 6

TWENTY-FIRST-CENTURY IRELAND

Diarmaid Ferriter

THE FIRST DECADE OF THE twenty-first century in Ireland witnessed significant economic, social, and political optimism, ultimately overtaken by a calamitous crash that by the end of 2010 left the Irish Republic bereft of meaningful sovereignty and reliant on bailout funds to finance the state. It was a decade of economic expansion, relative peace, and stability, but also of greed, revelations of historic misdeeds and abuses, severe incompetence in governance, and failures in financial regulation.

Prior to the economic crash, some historians tentatively sought to assess the impact of the transformations witnessed during the economic expansion (the "Celtic Tiger" period) of the mid-1990s to the mid-2000s in a state long accustomed to economic malaise. The big changes that had evolved from the 1970s, according to Roy Foster, were "perhaps decisively and forever ... a question of attitude," and he traced these shifts through economics, politics, the decline of religion, women's liberation, the cementing of partition, and the impact of Irish literature. Whether the collective transformations represented Ireland's Great Leap Forward or were the product of a series of interconnected crises, he decided, it was too early to conclude.[1]

Foster's assessment is a reminder of the perils of contemporary history and the obvious caution that is necessary in drawing conclusions about recent events due to the lack of source material and perspective. This is an even more salient point now, as the convulsions since 2008 have added more complexity and layers for historians and analysts to sift through to grasp the essence of the Irish experience. But it can be fairly asserted that the following themes should loom large in any attempt to understand Ireland in the twenty-first century so far: politics, the Celtic Tiger economy, the Northern Ireland peace process, the fortunes of the

Catholic Church, the Republic's relationship with the European Union (EU), and the economic collapse and its consequences. This chapter deals with each of these themes in turn.

POLITICS

The last general election of the twentieth century was fought in the Republic in 1997, largely on the grounds that excessive taxation of middle-class incomes was an unacceptable form of persecution, and this issue was to dominate political thinking and strategy for the next ten years. In terms of party politics, no ideological reasons prevented all the main political parties from serving in a grand coalition; there was little debate concerning equality or redistribution of wealth, but rather a preoccupation with who could manage the wealth most effectively to benefit the middle classes. Fianna Fáil (FF) won the 1997 election, but to govern, it needed the support of a smaller party, the Progressive Democrats, which championed a deregulated economy, low personal taxation, and social liberalism. Five years later, campaigning during the 2002 general election, the leader of the Progressive Democrats, Mary Harney, suggested "the country cannot afford a lurch to the left," which was a reaction to the Labour Party's promise to improve public services.[2]

Two years previously, Harney had made a speech at the Law Association of Ireland in which she addressed the issue of fiscal restraints being imposed by the European Central Bank and concluded defiantly: "Our economic success owes more to American liberalism than to European leftism ... geographically we are closer to Berlin than Boston. Spiritually we are probably a lot closer to Boston than Berlin."[3] These words entered the Irish political lexicon as a shorthand for a battle of ideas, but in truth their significance was more because the notion of addressing political philosophy was not part of mainstream Irish political discourse. Bertie Ahern, for example, leader of FF from 1994 to 2008, and electorally the most successful politician since Éamon de Valera in the 1930s and 1940s, made it clear in his autobiography that he was hostile to the notion of ideas in politics: "I kept my appeal very simple ... I would turn up at Supermarkets, to flirt with the housewives and joke about football with the husbands." For him, the oldest rule in politics was that "the other lot are the opposition but you actually find your enemies on your own side ... from the moment I won in 1977 the only plotting I was doing was about how to hold on to the seat at the next election."[4] On such sophisticated foundations was built the career of a three-time prime minister (1997–2008). But it was also built on short-termism, accompanied by "an almost manic desire to cultivate ... a myriad of constituencies," and

for all the economic and political successes of the government, it never articulated a vision of what it was all for.... Showtime politics was ruled by the electoral cycle ... everything—policy, economics, government personnel and coalition choices—was subjected to the overwhelming importance of maintaining power. It was the retention of political power above all else to which Bertie Ahern's Fianna Fáil was dedicated.[5]

This did not mean that the opposition parties, including the largest, Fine Gael (FG), were offering much that was different; the opposition did not propose "anything of substance or distinctive appeal. The outstanding performance of the Irish economy was not matched by a politics of equal calibre."[6] Nor was the Labour Party urging radical new departures; by 2005, it was insisting it would not increase income or corporation taxes.[7]

Although it was clear in the 1990s that the era of single-party government had come to an end—FF, it seemed, went from a position where it had all of the power most of the time to having most of the power all the time after 1997—the continued domination of FF meant that there was much reference to the notion of crisis within FG.[8] Notwithstanding this dominance, FF's position was clearly not impregnable; in 2004 its share of the vote fell to 32% in the European and local elections, the lowest since 1927. There was a justifiable skepticism in 2009 that the result of the local elections, when FF again polled poorly, could be labeled revolutionary, as the continuing battle between two large conservative parties that date from the Civil War era of the 1920s took a new, albeit dramatic, turn. But the result did raise questions: Just what did FF now stand for? Was it in danger of losing its self-proclaimed status as a national movement rather than just a political party? In 1985 it polled 47% of the vote in the local elections; in June 2009 it polled 25%.

In contrast to Bertie Ahern and his predecessors, Brian Cowen, who took over the leadership of FF in 2008, inspired no cult of leadership, meaning that the party, for the first time, had a serious leadership dilemma on its hands.[9] The main problem for FG remained its lack of experience in government and policies that were indistinguishable from FF, and even though in November 2007 the leader of the Labour Party, Eamon Gilmore, made a declaration of his socialism, it was deliberately cautiously defined: "I believe that every person is equal. It is as simple as that. That's what makes me a democrat. That's why I am a socialist. And why I belong to a social democratic party."[10] When Gilmore elaborated on what motivated him, the result was an overtly careful balancing act, offering little depth or candor.[11]

One of the most dramatic political events of this era was the general election of February 2011 that led to what the victors, FG and Labour, suggested was a democratic revolution.[12] Since its foundation in 1926, FF had not only dominated Irish politics, being in power for almost sixty of the next eighty years, but it had also been one of the most successful political parties in the world. Over the course of all general elections that it contested from 1927 to 2007, it secured an average of almost 45% of first-preference votes. To lose to the extent it did in 2011—its vote went down to 17.4%, and it lost fifty-one of its seventy-one seats in parliament—represented defeat on a historic scale, with echoes of the seminal December 1918 general election, when Sinn Féin routed the Irish Parliamentary Party, winning seventy-three seats to the Irish Parliamentary Party's six, down from sixty-nine at the dissolution of parliament. But in a sense, the 2011 general election result was about revenge rather than revolution. Irish political culture—involving an excessively centralized state, weak local government, and national parliamentarians focused on local constituency work to secure their reelection—was not at all transformed by the 2011 election, and it is also questionable if it really represented a "revolution in mood."[13] The main beneficiary of the collapse in the FF vote was FG, hardly a radical alternative.

In the context of economic convulsions, loss of sovereignty, and the demise of FF from 2008 to 2011, there was no shortage of assessments of the cumulative failures of Irish political culture. Fintan O'Toole, for example, suggested Ireland "needs to lose every last vestige of hope in our governing culture" in the sense of a state that was conducted for the public interest, as opposed to a state that was a separate entity from the people.[14] The state was depicted as a failed entity and a parody of democracy: local government did not in any meaningful sense exist; 94% of decisions on public expenditure were made at the national level; no link existed between local taxation and local services; and the national parliament passed already-decided-on legislation rather than initiating it, with no transparency provided for the benefit of its citizens.[15] In relation to these failings, there also seemed to be much food for thought in the observations of historian Tony Judt on the international financial meltdown in his final collection of essays: "we have substituted endless commerce for public purpose and expect no higher aspirations from our leaders."[16]

Although Irish culture had developed a sense of the permanence and robustness of the nation, it tended to see the Republic and nation as coterminous as opposed to seeing a republican citizenship that was conscious, active, and needed to be watched over with the vigilance of civic virtue.[17] There also developed a certain nostalgia for the Civil War generation and its idealism and sense of public service that had been seemingly abandoned by the subsequent generation. Journalist John Waters, for example, reflected on the failure to question the moral basis of the Celtic Tiger version of modern Ireland, which was rooted in the inadequacies of those who sought to modernize the country "on exclusively materialist principles since the 1960s." The result was a country never sustained by its own resources. Added to this, he maintained, was an Irish self-hatred, preventing the imagining of a new beginning and regret at the absence of "a national father figure to show us the way." Waters framed his argument by pointing to the loss of an idealism and honesty associated with the Irish revolutionaries who fought the war of independence from 1919 to 1921.[18] Some of this criticism was unduly simplistic and ignored many historic ambiguities in relation to Irish political culture, but Waters was accurate in his conclusion about contemporary Irish politics: "politics today is not politics at all, but something more like management of a minor company with an uninteresting product."[19]

ECONOMIC EXPANSION

As was observed in a special feature in *The Economist* magazine in October 2004, "surely no other country in the rich world has seen its image change so fast." Various explanations were offered as to the reasons for the economic expansion. The Industrial Development Authority had been successful in attracting foreign investment, and the education system had supplied a corpus of skilled workers who made a significant contribution to the information technology sector (more than one-third of all personal computers sold in Europe were manufactured in Ireland, and it was the world's biggest software exporter, highlighting its globalization). Pharmaceutical and health-care companies also found Ireland an attractive base; for these foreign companies, a well-educated English-speaking workforce combined with low corporation and capital gains taxes made Ireland highly desirable. By 2004 the more than 1,100 multinationals in the Republic were exporting goods worth $60 billion a year.

Low taxes were a boost to home-grown enterprise, while women's participation in the workforce increased dramatically, and with the European single currency, lower interest rates became the norm. But *The Economist* also identified problems in 2004, principally the lamentable state of some public services "and a dangerous obsession with property"; average house prices in Dublin had quadrupled over the previous decade. Nonetheless, it concluded that "Ireland has grown up."[20] Economic historian Cormac Ó Gráda argued that Ireland's low tax, low public debt economy, and development of social partnership were the result of the Celtic Tiger rather than its cause, while Roy Foster observed in the midst of the economic boom "a sometimes spectacularly unequal prosperity."[21]

For its champions, social partnership was a crucial factor in creating the stability and industrial peace needed to sustain economic expansion, but to its critics it was about a smothering protectionism between privileged groups.[22] At the end of the 1980s, social partnership had been seen as a necessary response to despair about the Irish financial crisis, resulting in the Programme for National Recovery (1987–1990), an accepted strategy to escape the cycle of stagnation, rising taxes, and unmanageable debt. Partnership was continually widened, and the benefits of industrial peace were much touted; it created an interesting interdependence but also complacency and aspirations that could not always be delivered on as well as problems of monitoring. The titles of the agreements in the early twenty-first century give an indication of how the partnership mission was officially viewed:

Prosperity and Fairness (2003–2005) and Sustaining Progress (2003–2005). The program Towards 2016, agreed on in 2006, was effectively abandoned because of the economic crisis after 2008 and the imposition of pay cuts in 2009.

During the boom social mobility increased, as did disposable income; average gross weekly household income in the state in 2004–2005 was €989.53, 48.4% higher than the €666.72 recorded in 1998–1989, and disposable income (after tax and social insurance) increased by almost 53%.[23] Higher earners had a variety of opportunities to avoid paying substantial tax; in 2003, the statistical branch of the Irish Revenue Commissioners listed the incomes of the top four hundred earners in Ireland without naming the individuals. Fifty-one of them had an effective tax rate of less than 5%, while of the 117 highest earning, twenty-nine had no tax liability at all, suggesting that tax shelters were protecting the wealthiest to an extraordinary degree.[24] Figures in relation to public spending as a proportion of the country's national wealth were also revealing of Irish priorities: in 2000 the proportion for Ireland was 32% compared to the United Kingdom's 40.2%, Belgium's 49.9%, and Germany's 45.9%; the average across the EU was 47%.[25] Three years later, Ireland was twenty-seventh out of thirty Organisation for Economic Co-operation and Development countries for social transfers, meaning the redistribution of wealth through welfare payments or pensions.[26] In the midst of extraordinary economic growth (which witnessed, for example, the Irish economy growing by 11% in 2000) came observations from a UN Human Development Report suggesting, in light of social spending falling as a share of gross domestic product (GDP) from 1997 to 2001, that the Republic had the second-highest level of poverty in the developed world.[27] Another interesting aspect of the boom was the proportion of new jobs that were being filled by migrant workers; of the 90,000 jobs created between September 2004 and September 2005, for example, 40,000 of these went to such workers.[28] The following year, there were 420,000 foreign nationals in the Republic, up from 200,000 in 2002, out of a total population of 4.2 million, the highest Irish population since 1861.

But it was the reliance on the construction sector that was truly alarming. By 2006 construction amounted to nearly one-quarter of Irish GDP, compared to less than 10% "in a normal economy, and Ireland was building half as many new houses a year as the UK which had 15 times as many people to house."[29] There is no doubting the importance of land and property ownership as a driving force in post-Famine Irish history; the land war of the late nineteenth century was a defining campaign that was ultimately to result in the breaking of the power of the landlord class, the transfer of property to former tenants, and legislation that enabled ownership to be entrusted to a new class. Perhaps what was ironic was that one hundred years after that revolution in land ownership had been largely completed, it was replaced by a native class of landowners and speculators who, with external speculators, were to exercise their domination of land and the Irish economy in an even more invidious way than some of the most wretched of the nineteenth-century landlords.[30] Ireland in the twenty-first century was consumed by a property boom and bubble that was ultimately to be its undoing.

NORTHERN IRELAND PEACE PROCESS

Despite the broad welcome for the Belfast Agreement in 1998 that did much to bring thirty years of the Northern Ireland Troubles to an end, its allowing for a power-sharing executive and assembly has resulted in negative assessments of the Agreement. For example, Henry Patterson has argued that it was "an elite brokered settlement that balanced precariously on deep reserves of communal distrust and antagonism." Much attention was also focused on the resentment that unionists felt about nationalists benefiting much more from the Agreement, such sentiment rising on the unionist side from 31% of those polled in 1998 to 55% in 2002.[31] In addition, Eamon McCann and others consistently argued that the 1998 solution institutionalized sectarianism.[32]

During the long path to a relative peace in Northern Ireland, there was much desire for and talk of the normalization of politics and society, and many wished for the days when economics rather than violence would dominate discussion. Though the Democratic Unionist Party and Sinn Féin found a way to work together as part of a power-sharing executive and assembly, a great deal of division and sectarian hatred was still apparent in Northern Ireland in the first decade of the twenty-first century, while dissident republicans showed no sign of disappearing and remained a serious threat to peace. Historically, given the cyclical nature of violence, there was no reason to expect it would disappear completely as a result of the 1998 Agreement, and it did not, but it was massively reduced.

In 2009, George Quigley of the Institute of British Irish Studies suggested that some of the stridency had gone out of the tone of debate in Northern Ireland and that "there is mutual civility there never was before."[33] But it was quite fragile: a frosty tolerance that was easily unhinged. Many physical barriers dividing communities remained, as did the segregated housing estates and the education divide. After the sheer horror of the Real Irish Republican Army's (IRA) Omagh bomb that killed twenty-eight people in 1998, the number of killings dramatically declined, which was cited as a vindication for the choice of politics over violence. The years after 1998 also witnessed the eclipse of the Social Democratic and Labour Party and the Ulster Unionist Party, and the end of the era of the respective leaders of those parties, John Hume and David Trimble (who won the Nobel Peace Prize for their efforts in laying the groundwork for the Belfast Agreement). In 1997 the Ulster Unionist Party had ten members of parliament; by 2005 it had just one. The Social Democratic and Labour Party went from being the largest party in terms of votes in Northern Ireland to the fourth-largest party. Sinn Féin secured a strong presence in the Dáil as well as in the North; Ian Paisley and his successor, Peter Robinson, leaders of a resurgent Democratic Unionist Party, were converted to power sharing.

Along the way, there were postponed assembly elections and numerous claims that the Belfast Agreement was dead, as well as the firm IRA statement of July 2005 ("All volunteers have been instructed to assist the development of purely political and democratic programmes through exclusively peaceful means").[34] These steps were followed by verifiable arms decommissioning and numerous twists and turns before acceptance of a new police force and a power-sharing government in 2007. John Hume's replacement as Social Democratic and Labour Party leader, Mark Durcan, had asked: "what hope is there that those who delivered the worst of Northern Ireland's past will deliver the best of its future?"[35] The short-term answer came in the form of the "chuckle brothers"—the Democratic Unionist Party's Ian Paisley as first minister and Sinn Féin's Martin McGuinness as deputy first minister. Paisley was on the losing side in 1998 but was the long-term winner. It seemed in 1998 that the Belfast Agreement had vindicated the moderates, but in the long run the so-called "extremes" were the beneficiaries. There was an element of history repeating itself in this regard, as a similar transformation happened in the south during 1922–1932, when the anti-Treaty republicans lost the vote over the Treaty agreed with Britain following the War of Independence and were crushed in the Civil War, only to win power less than ten years later.

After the Belfast Agreement, Sinn Féin and the IRA profited from internal discipline and ruthless centralization, in contrast to the loyalist paramilitaries, who imploded, the irony being that it was the republicans' opponents who got more out of the Agreement by securing the Union, the principle of consent, and the eradication of the Republic's territorial claim to Northern Ireland in its constitution. The republicans obtained a share of power, cross-border bodies, the disbandment of the Royal Ulster Constabulary, and acceptance that they had fought a war and prisoners could be released. The path to power sharing was long and winding, precisely because both sides needed to make it so, unionists because of divisions in their ranks, and republicans because, in the words of historian and Trimble adviser Paul Bew, "how could a revolutionary movement settle for such a prosaic, even dull outcome, which fell so drastically short of its stated objectives? Perhaps this helps to explain the IRA's consistent compensating adventurism in this period" (including controversies about an alleged republican spy ring at Stormont and the Northern Bank robbery in 2004, a massive heist that suggested "the IRA was still committed to running a criminal empire").[36]

The British interest in Northern Ireland was not as deep as unionists would have liked, which was also the case during the War of Independence era. Historically, there have always been pragmatic reasons for British politicians wanting to get the Irish question off the table at Downing Street, reasons that could take precedence over ideological commitment. For example, during the War of Independence, despite what was said in public, British policy, while initially focused on defeating the IRA's military campaign, ultimately became about engineering a deal with Irish republicans. While this aim was complicated at various stages by surges in violence from 1920 to 1921, as it has been in more recent times, it remained the central goal in both eras.[37]

In relation to the contemporary Irish republican project, while Gerry Adams moved south and won a seat in the Dáil, Sinn Féin's bold move to have Martin McGuinness elected president of Ireland in 2011 did not go as well as it wished (he received 13.7% of first-preference votes). The voting results revealed that the legacy of the Troubles was still raw, partitionist mind-sets were still entrenched, and republicans were worried about lack of interest in Irish unity.[38]

Ultimately, the most obvious thaw was in Anglo-Irish relations. This was encapsulated in Bertie Ahern's words at the Palace of Westminster in 2007, when he addressed a joint session of parliament: "We are now in an era of agreement—of new politics and new realities ... reconciliation has brought us closer."[39] The visit of Queen Elizabeth II to the Republic in May 2011 was also an indication of confidence on the British and Irish sides that both were ready for a gesture of this significance. The British government took this development very seriously; the presence of Prime Minister David Cameron and Foreign Secretary William Hague was testament to that. At the outset of her speech in Dublin Castle during that visit, President Mary McAleese declared: "this visit is a culmination of the success of the peace process."[40] That was certainly underlined by the warmth of Anglo-Irish relations, but those sharing power in Northern Ireland were less effusive about what held them together and their capacity to overcome what still divided them.

THE CATHOLIC CHURCH

The collapse of the authority, credibility, and influence of the Catholic Church—a process that had begun in the 1960s and 1970s and was given added momentum by the revelation of scandals in the 1990s—continued unabated in the first decade of the twenty-first century. In November 2009 the Report of the Commission of Investigation, Catholic Archdiocese of Dublin, chaired by Justice Yvonne Murphy, was published (the Murphy Report). It had its origins in the 2002 broadcast by Radio Telefís Éireann (RTÉ, the national public-service broadcaster) of a television series produced by the acclaimed Irish documentary maker Mary Raftery, *Cardinal Secrets*, which investigated the handling of child sex abuse allegations in the Dublin Catholic archdiocese. Following the broadcast, the government pledged to establish a full independent judicial inquiry into the archdiocese's handling of abuse allegations, which led to the setting up in 2006 of an investigation into the handling of those allegations by church and state authorities from 1975 until

2004. It found that four successive archbishops of the Catholic Archdiocese of Dublin handled allegations of child sexual abuse badly, with "denial, arrogance and cover-up," and did not report their knowledge of abuse to the Irish police over a period of three decades. The structures and rules of the Catholic Church facilitated the cover-up of abuse. Auxiliary bishops of Dublin were also aware of complaints of child sex abuse, yet assignments of priests to parishes were often made without any reference to child sex abuse issues. The report detailed cases involving forty-six priests and more than 320 children, most of them boys. Senior members of the Irish police force regarded the actions of priests as being outside their remit, and some of them reported complaints to the archdiocese instead of investigating them. Although some priests did bring allegations of abuse to their superiors, there was, it was found, a "don't ask, don't tell" policy.[41]

The Murphy Report was the third devastating report—following the Ferns Report of 2005 in relation to the abuse of children in a Wexford Diocese and the Ryan Report of 2009 into child abuse in institutions run by religious orders and funded by the state—that vindicated the abused child and revealed much about how power was used and abused in the past. In providing such an overwhelming body of evidence about an "obsessive concern with secrecy and the avoidance of scandal" and "little or no concern for the welfare of the abused child," these reports provided a corrective to the atmosphere of secrecy and shame that surrounded these experiences for so many years. The Murphy Report also made it clear that the extent of the sexual assaults on children could not be explained by maintaining that the country was too poor and ignorant; there were calculated cover-ups by the church and a deliberate abdication of state responsibility. The documentation available and the decision in 1986 to protect church assets from abuse victims by taking out an insurance policy gave lie to the claims that there was not enough knowledge of what was going on and that the church hierarchy "was on a learning curve," as it maintained.[42]

The abuse scandals were just one indication of a church in crisis; many other factors were relevant, including the decline in Marianism (devotion to Mary, mother of God), a loss of credibility in relation to contraception, and a decline in mass attendance and religious vocations. Between 1990 and 1998, ordinations to the priesthood fell by 66% and by 1998 deaths and departures from the priesthood outnumbered ordinations by a factor of almost five to one. In 2000 the historian James Donnelly suggested the need for an "effective repositioning of the institutional Catholic Church in Ireland."[43] The decline of its authority also raised questions as to the church's continuing ability to staff the schools and hospitals it had controlled for so long.

There were also calls for the cutting of historic links between church and state. When the Ferns Report was published, its contents prompted some of the most explicit denunciations of the church from Irish politicians regarding its role and status in Irish society. In November of that year, Progressive Democrat Teachta Dála (a member of the Irish parliament) Liz O'Donnell went further than most by asserting that the church was incapable of self-regulation and unworthy of consultation on any issue affecting reproduction, relationships, sexuality, or family planning. It was time, she insisted, for a clear division between church and state, the implication being it was time to assert that Ireland should be a secular state in practice.[44] Politicians gradually came to reject, in the words of Barry Desmond, former minister for health, the idea that "the common good" was the same as "the Catholic good."[45] But others also wondered about the gap left; in 2003 former taoiseach Garret FitzGerald wrote about the decline of the influence of religion in the Republic and the "inadequacy of any alternative lay or civic ethic, especially in the face of the double hazard of the siren call of individualist liberalism on the one hand and the off-putting face of fundamentalist Catholicism on the other."[46]

During this period other indicators of change were also evident; a referendum on abortion to prevent suicide being grounds for a termination of pregnancy was defeated in 2002, and Dick Walsh suggested this was the first occasion "in which the alliance of Fianna Fáil, the Catholic bishops and lay activists were defeated, largely by social democrats." Brian Girvin concluded that "those in a minority in the 1970s now represented a majority."[47] Girvin also pointed to another shift in the church/state equilibrium, when the Minister for Children Brian Lenihan insisted it was his responsibility to ensure that the church's guidelines with respect to children were compatible with the state's.[48] But the state made some strange decisions in this regard also; despite the assertion in the Ryan Report that "it is impossible to determine the full extent of sexual abuse committed in boys' schools," an indemnity deal between some religious orders and the state was patently inadequate and was agreed on without enough external scrutiny. In 2011 Taoiseach Enda Kenny excoriated the Vatican for its alleged lack of cooperation with Irish inquiries into child abuse, while the Irish embassy at the Vatican was closed down, supposedly on grounds of cost.

In terms of the practice of religion and mass attendance, an opinion poll in April 2005 revealed average weekly mass attendance was 44% among Irish adults (and only 28% in Dublin); the figures were 78% in 1992 and 65% in 1997.[49] It was also clear that a laissez-faire approach to Catholicism was now firmly and irreversibly established: three-quarters of Irish adults agreed in 2005 that the Catholic Church should allow women priests; support in vitro fertilization treatment for couples; and relax its views on sex before marriage, divorce, and having a child outside marriage. An even higher proportion—83% and 87%, respectively—did not accept the church's view on the use of artificial contraception and believed it should change its stance on the prohibition of condoms in Africa to prevent the spread of AIDS. Quite simply, many Irish adults decided to be Catholics on their own terms.

It has been estimated that over the course of the forty years of Irish membership in the EU, GDP per capita in Ireland rose from 53% of the EU average to 140% in 2008. During the same period, €67 billion worth of transfers from the EU to Ireland took place, at one point amounting to 5% of gross national product.[50] Overall, it has been estimated that Irish farmers benefited from Common Agricultural Policy funds to the value of €44 billion between 1973 and 2008, while structural funds amounted to €17 billion up to 2012.[51]

Given the size of these figures, it is hardly surprising that membership of the EU was largely seen as positive during the years of Irish economic underdevelopment. What changed significantly in the first decade of the twenty-first century was the extent to which the euro-skepticism apparent for so long in Britain resonated with many in Ireland. In the first twenty years of membership, this factor was not significant. The early Eurobarometers, taken twice a year to monitor feelings about the Community in the member states, suggested that it was economics rather than politics that was foremost in the minds of the Irish.[52]

There was rarely any evidence that Irish enthusiasm for European integration could be taken at face value as an expression of a European identity; Irish attitudes were essentially pragmatic and related to how much money Ireland could get out of membership. In 1997 political scientist Tom Garvin had argued that "Ireland has become a rather well plugged-in periphery of Europe and America rather than a periphery of Britain. She probably prefers it that way."[53] A Eurobarometer in 1994 revealed that 79% of the Irish surveyed responded positively to the question of whether they viewed membership as a good thing, compared to 58% in the community as a whole. That same year, Dermot Scott, an official in the EU parliament, suggested that in Ireland,

> for want of information, public opinion has not understood the EU and has therefore not genuinely taken the EU to its heart, having a somewhat semi-detached attitude, willing to go along, but having little knowledge or conviction about the goals of integration, little vision of what a European Union might become. The corollary is also true: that there seems to be little enough genuine opposition and that each dose of integration, however balefully received, is swallowed and ingested, though the patient may scowl at the next spoonful.[54]

But that was to change, and by 2001, turnout for the Nice referendum was only 35%, which resulted in the rejection of that treaty, which had been designed to reform the institutional structure of the EU to cope with expansion of its membership. In reacting to this, political commentator Dick Walsh suggested "It has taken us 30 years to hold our most thorough debate on Ireland's role in the EU and what Europe means to us."[55] The rerun of that referendum in October 2002 resulted in the passing of the treaty after many pro-Europe heavyweights were called on to hammer home the message that Ireland was doomed if it was rejected again. Some on the No side had been consistently drawing attention to the undermining of Irish autonomy due to accelerating European integration. Anthony Coughlan argued in 1999 that with the embrace of the euro and "by ceding to Brussels and Frankfurt the power to control credit in the economy, decide interest rates and the currency exchange rate, the politicians of our main parties are abandoning fundamental interests for advancing the Irish people's welfare."[56]

Certain trends and sentiments were made clear from the Nice campaigns and subsequently the referendums on the Lisbon Treaty, the stated aim of which was to enhance the efficiency, legitimacy, and coherence of the EU, which was rejected in the first referendum in 2008 but passed in another referendum in 2009. Accusations of a "democratic deficit"—deliberate marginalization of smaller states by arrogant EU officials—and an alleged undermining of Irish neutrality resulted in the assertion in 2008 by those campaigning against the Lisbon Treaty that "The New EU Won't See You, Won't Hear You, Won't Speak for You."[57] The main political parties struggled to confront these sentiments effectively, while the "No" campaigners, though they made exaggerated and sometimes disingenuous claims, marketed their message much more effectively.

The longer Ireland was a member of the EU, the more questionable it became as to whether membership was a foreign policy issue at all; Irish interaction with the EU fell "into a new intermediate area where foreign and internal policy-making blend into one another," a development further underlined by the acceptance of a severe austerity program in return for EU/European Central Bank (ECB) and International Monetary Fund (IMF) support.[58] In 2010 Irish dependence on the EU was clear in terms of financing the state, but there was much confusion and uncertainty about Ireland's status in the midst of domestic bankruptcy and international credit fears. In 2011 a leading historian of Irish foreign policy, Patrick Keatinge, suggested that

> among the major political and bureaucratic actors in this drama is an exotic mix of Finance Ministers and their officials, bankers both public and private, external institutions (the European Central Bank and the International Monetary Fund), as well as more remote and menacing entities, such as markets and investors.... It is necessary to get to grips with the story of negotiations of a highly technical nature, conducted in terms of a grotesque mix of euphemism, denial and apocalyptic threat.... It is a sobering realisation that in such an environment the European Union itself is on the defensive; this is a crisis for the euro as well as for Ireland's financial and economic credibility. Amidst this confusion, positive attitudes towards EU membership—arguably the most significant Irish policy strategy of the past fifty years or so—can no longer be

taken for granted. Adaptation to this situation in the short term has already involved negotiating from a position of great weakness, in the context of a formal suspension of full economic sovereignty. Beyond that, there will be a need at the very least to restore a severely damaged international reputation.... There are many imponderables in all of this.[59]

THE ECONOMIC COLLAPSE AND CRISIS

How had all this come to pass? Or as economist Morgan Kelly put it in 2011: "What happened to Ireland?" It was, he said, a "natural question," given "the meteoric trajectory of the Irish economy over the past 25 years from basket case to superstar and back to basket case."[60] He looked at the long-term factors relevant to the economic boom—including free secondary education and expansion in the numbers at third level in the 1970s, more competitive costs, and currency devaluations—but by 2000, while Irish incomes had risen to average European levels, competitiveness was affected as wages rose faster than increased productivity: "at this stage it might have been expected that Irish growth rates would fall back to ordinary European levels. Instead, growth continued at the rapid rates of the 1990s with one difference, that it was now driven by a credit-fuelled building boom rather than by competitiveness."[61]

In the 1990s 5% of the Republic's national income came from building—"the usual level for an industrialised economy"—but by 2006 this had reached 15%, with bigger mortgages and rising bank lending. Kelly then summarized the origins of the collapse:

> While most banks abroad lent about 80% of national income, Irish banks in 2000 lent only 60%. Between 2000 and 2008, during what economists used to call the "Great Moderation", banks found that they could borrow almost any amount on international markets without security, at rates only slightly above central bank rates. This led to an international lending boom where bank lending in most European economies rose to around 100% of national income. In Ireland, lending rose from 60 to nearly 200% and most of this was funded by borrowing from overseas banks. Everything that happened in Ireland between 2000 and 2008 stems from this simple fact.[62]

Of the €1.8 billion of taxes collected in excess of expectation in the first nine months of 2006, €1 billion of this was tax from property transactions.[63] But for all the focus on revenue generated, there was not enough concern expressed about the borrowing underpinning it: personal debt as a percentage of disposable income increased from 89% to 140% between 1996 and 2006.[64] One of the failures of the era was the determination not to act on the Kenny Report of 1974 on the price of building land; it had recommended that development land should be compulsorily acquired by local authorities at a 25% premium above its existing use value and that a register of property sale prices be established. The report's recommendations were essentially ignored, because restrictions on land speculation threatened powerful pressure groups and vested interests.[65] The Kenny Report, a reaction to the housing shortages, land prices, and land rezoning practices of the 1960s and early 1970s, was frequently invoked in the decades after its publication; it had highlighted that the demand for housing would continue to grow, and that if nothing was done about it, prices would rise "at an even more rapid rate than previously." But as was observed twenty-five years after the report, "one administration after another failed to meet the challenges of profiteering."[66]

In 1997 Irish banks were funded entirely by Irish deposits, but by 2005 most of their funding came from abroad and could be easily withdrawn.[67] From 2000 to the collapse, lending to construction and real estate rose from 8% to 28%, and banks loaned in the region of $100 billion to speculators to gamble with. The acclaimed American financial journalist Michael Lewis characterized what was going on as in effect a Ponzi scheme. Much that was built was simply not needed; between 2000 and 2004, for example, an extra 987 hotels were built with a tax subsidy of €196 million. Nonresident companies in the Irish Financial Services Centre found that they would be facilitated in what was in effect a low tax enclave. In April 2005 *The New York Times* remarked on the "light hand" of corporate regulation that made Dublin "the wild west of European finance." The Office of Director of Corporate Enforcement set up in 2001 was not staffed properly (it had only thirty-six employees in 2006) and was not taken seriously enough.[68] Gene Kerrigan concluded, accurately, that those in government "just wanted something that would pass for a regulatory system if you didn't look too closely at it," and the ECB looked the other way.[69]

Lehman Brothers collapsed and filed for bankruptcy in the United States in September 2008 with debts of €440 billion, and the first stage of the Irish crisis also came to a head that month when Anglo Irish Bank suffered a run in wholesale funding markets. Although it is true that Lehman's collapse precipitated the Irish crisis, it did not cause it; the reckless loans by Irish banks had been made well before the collapse. Anglo had used lending to developers to dramatically transform its market share and was left woefully exposed. Minister for Finance Brian Lenihan was put under considerable pressure to guarantee the Irish banks and their bondholders. The bank guarantee that was then agreed on "sank Ireland," as bondholders were protected. From November 2007 to October 2010, Irish banks borrowed €97 billion from the ECB to repay private creditors, many of whom had not even expected to get back all their money. All public deposits in banks were guaranteed, as well as most existing bonds issued to other financial institutions. Private debts became public debts, with devastating consequences.[70]

The role of the ECB in all this was controversial. In one of the many books on the onset of the crisis and the reaction to it, this role was summed up by one of Ireland's leading journalists: "It was the ECB that had put a loaded gun to the

Irish government's head" with an implied threat that it would withdraw liquidity support for the banks if the Irish government did not move to calm market fears. The ECB, of course, had a bigger concern with the stability of the wider euro-zone, but according to journalist Matt Cooper, the ECB subsequently "conveniently forgot its own enormous failings in dealing with the crisis, as well as its responsibilities."[71] This was the same ECB whose president, Jean Claude Trichet, in Dublin in May 2004 heralded Ireland as a "model for the millions of new citizens of the European Union."[72] But by 2008 Trichet's main concern regarding Ireland was that no European bank would be seen to collapse and subsequently, in 2011 he put undue pressure on the Irish government to abandon its plan to enforce burden-sharing on senior bondholders in Anglo Irish Bank by threatening to withdraw ECB emergency funding from Irish banks.[73]

Morgan Kelly described the bank guarantee as "an astonishingly stupid move: these bonds had been bought by sophisticated investors who knew that they stood to lose if the banks did badly."[74] There was a determination to continue to honor this guarantee even after it became clear that the bank losses were beyond the resources of the state. Some have argued it should have been revoked, though others have challenged this narrative and warned against the simplification of the blame-game narrative. The absence of regulation dominated the world's financial markets and was not just an Irish issue—the Lehman Brothers' implosion involved the largest financial default in world history—and there was no alternative to the bank guarantee beyond a run on the banks and the complete implosion of the banking system.[75] Nonetheless, the idea that bondholders did not have to take any of the pain remained one of the striking and controversial aspects of the Irish crisis.

International lenders stopped lending to Ireland, and the country was forced to accept an EU/ECB/IMF bailout at the end of 2010. The program provided for up to €50 billion in fiscal needs and up to €35 billion in banking support measures from 2011 to the end of 2013, contingent on action to clean up the financial sector, put the public finances on a sustainable path, and implement a structural reform package. Forecasts of bank losses of €40 billion were shown to be ridiculously underestimated; Morgan Kelly suggested in 2012 that the bank losses would eventually cost the state in the region of €100 billion and that along with capital invested in worthless banks, "Irish national debt is likely to rise closer to €240–250 billion. There would also be the need for new capital for the banks and there was the danger of widespread defaulting on personal mortgages: the chance that such sums can be repaid by a nation with 1.8 million employed people is zero."[76]

By 2009 the National Asset Management Agency, a state-funded "bad bank" was in place, and unemployment, which had been 4.8% in 2007 rose to 13.1%.[77] By 2013 the unemployment rate had trebled since 2008 to more than 14% and the annual rate of emigration increased by more than 350% in the same period; 68,000 emigrated from April 2009 to April 2011, while 46,500 Irish people left the state between April 2011 and April 2012.[78] In early 2011, estimates put the drop in house prices at 55–60%, and it was difficult to avoid the conclusion that "the performance of the Irish political and economic system during the property price crash, the banking crisis and the deficit debacle revealed many unsavoury truths about Ireland that the unregulated growth and wealth of the Celtic Tiger obscured."[79] Three reports commissioned by the government on the collapse of the economy suggested the burden of responsibility was broad, with insufficient surveillance, warnings not heeded, and a "national speculative mania," which was another misdirected exaggeration and exacerbated the tendency toward what Conor McCabe dubbed "pseudo-historical analysis."[80] Crucially, no comprehensive official inquiry into the failings of the banks had been conducted up to the time of the writing of this chapter (2014), and there was no accountability with regard to their practices, meaning that "the public narrative about what actually happened remains vague and incomplete."[81]

The financial crisis did not lead to civil unrest as it did in Greece, and Irish politics in 2010 had, according to Michael Lewis, a "frozen-in-time quality."[82] A country that fought a war of independence in the early twentieth century became, it seemed, compliant and docile in the face of the exposure of systemic corruption and the destruction of that independence nearly a century later; those responsible were not made accountable and punished for their misdeeds. Many answers and theories were offered as to why this was the case, including the post-colonial mind-set, the underlying political stability of Ireland over an extended period with an accompanying lack of ideological debate, the dominance of the Catholic Church, and the resultant absence of a strong civic culture and dissent.[83] But the crisis led to considerable reflection on the nature of Irish decision making, political leadership, the lack of distribution of power, and links between business and politics. Morgan Kelly argued that FF had become "the political clients of property developers ... the building boom suited everyone that mattered."[84]

In the last few years of his life, Garret FitzGerald occasionally broached the issue of corruption in Irish politics, suggesting in 2010 that the Civil War generation through its "unselfish patriotism" provided a barrier "to the spread to politics of the socially inadequate value system that we, as a people, had inherited from our colonial past."[85] This assertion may be too sweeping, but there is some truth in it. In 2012 the Mahon Report, which examined allegations of corrupt payments to politicians, concluded that such corruption was systemic and endemic.[86] The network of alliances, powerful vested interests, and pressure groups that was built up and facilitated corruption did not just emerge in recent decades. The network thrived initially in a small, protected economy and in a society that was snobbish and hierarchical.

The existence of such groups is a reminder that because of the way in which political culture evolved after independence, it bred a cynicism and selfishness about how to do business and make money in Ireland and the hierarchy of influence. Alongside attachment to the tradition of parliamentary democracy was a parallel devotion to a culture of self-advancement, which was about whom you knew and what you could pay. Many venal people were willing to buy Irish politicians, and politicians who were exposed as corrupt or untruthful continued to be elected and endorsed; those who called for accountability in this culture experienced fear, menace, and intimidation.[87]

In relation to the decision-making processes in the state since its foundation, Conor McCabe argued that the economic crisis was not just the result of unregulated, reckless bankers or because Irish people were obsessed with home ownership but was the consequence of the rottenness of the governing culture and vested interests over many decades, which allowed public money to be funneled into profits for private shareholders along with the surrender of rights to minerals, gas, and oil for a pittance. The privileging of Irish banks to influence the state's finances was also something that had been building over decades.[88] In addition, some politicians seemed determined to discourage a robust questioning of the past in this regard—a popular phrase became "we are where we are."[89] The notion of collective responsibility was also used when convenient to distract from the failures of leadership. For example, Brian Lenihan asserted that "we decided as a people collectively to have this property boom. That was a collective decision we took as a people."[90] This statement is a simplification to the point of distortion of reality; people did not collectively decide to "have" a property boom; a relatively small number were able to skew the market through speculation, reckless lending, and a refusal to reduce the inflation of the property market, and many were encouraged to borrow beyond their means or were panicked into buying through warnings that if they did not move with speed they would fail to get a foot on the much-vaunted property ladder.

What did the journey from boom to bust in the first decade of the twenty-first century mean for Irish identity? Was there a sense that materialism had come at the expense of a traditional Irish value system? It may have been the case, as argued by a sociologist in 2007, that "the issue of identity ... crystallizes around the issue of whether Irishness, as we understand it today, is fundamentally determined by an oppressed past or a privileged present."[91] The challenge after the crash was not just to get to the truth of what had happened and why but also to respond to it with some new vision; in that regard, those running the country were found wanting. Crucial themes—fairness, public service, and the nature of society—were undoubtedly neglected during the boom; it became commonplace for cultural commentators to assert that it had never been more fashionable to be Irish but for the more skeptical, what this amounted to was "the baleful influence that modernization theory has exercised over Irish cultural commentary."[92]

In 2007 Gearóid Ó Tuathaigh, while lauding the positive changes witnessed in Celtic Tiger Ireland, also suggested that "what is striking is the almost total absence of any clearly articulated or elaborated coherent social vision by political leaders in recent decades.... The general run of statements of social policy have rarely ventured too far from the safe zone of economic managerialism which has become the general zone of political discourse." While Ó Tuathaigh acknowledged the progress politicians made in overseeing economic expansion and bedding down the peace process in Northern Ireland, he made the fair point that

> the failure to articulate, still less to systematically take steps of achieving a coherent and persuasive vision of social solidarity, based on a set of values and principles that would enjoy wide public endorsement, has resulted in a series of confused, inconsistent or contradictory strategies being announced and pursued—in regional planning, health and housing, integrated planning of infrastructure, crime and the causes of crime—an incoherence which continues to cause widespread frustration, confusion, disappointment and anger among different sections of the community.[93]

Six years after these observations, in the midst of austerity, high unemployment, and mass emigration, and as the centenary of the events that composed the revolution of the early twentieth century was fast approaching, the stark reality was that the Irish Republic was bereft of meaningful sovereignty due to its bankruptcy, and its governing culture over the previous few decades had been exposed as rotten.

FURTHER READING

For obvious reasons there is no extensive historical literature on the Irish experience of the past fifteen years. The enlarged and updated edition of T. W. Moody and F. X. Martin's popular general history of Ireland, *The Course of Irish History* (Dublin: Mercier Press, 2011) includes a balanced overview in "Turning Corners: Ireland 2002–11" by Patrick Kiely and Dermot Keogh. The economic crisis that afflicted the Republic from 2008 on has generated a large volume of titles, most hurried, journalistic, and reactive rather than historical or nuanced, though some are biting, honest, and accurate, including Gene Kerrigan's *The Big Lie: Who Profits from Ireland's Austerity?* (Dublin: Random House, 2012) and Conor McCabe's *Sins of the Father: Tracing the Decisions That Shaped the Irish Economy* (Dublin: History Press Ireland, 2011). Other crisis titles incorporate a more long-term appraisal, including the collection edited by one of Ireland's foremost commentators and journalists, Fintan O'Toole, in *Up the Republic! Towards a New Ireland* (London: Faber and Faber, 2012). As a visitor's response and a comparative perspective, Michael Lewis's *Boomerang: The Meltdown Tour* (London: Allen Lane, 2011) is both informative and entertaining.

Before the crash, one of Ireland's leading novelists, Colm Tóibín, brought an original slant to bear on the evolution of the new Irish materialism in "Selling Tara, Buying Florida," *Eire-Ireland* 43: 1&2 (Spring/Summer 2008), pp. 11–26; Brian Girvin did likewise in relation to the waning influence of the Catholic Church, in "Church, State and Society in Ireland since 1960," *Eire Ireland* 43: 1&2 (Spring/Summer 2008), pp. 74–79. After the full extent of the economic crisis became apparent, academic economists began to produce measured titles in response, including Donal Donavan and Antoin E. Murphy in *The Fall of the Celtic Tiger: Ireland and the Euro Debt Crisis* (Oxford: Oxford University Press, 2013). In relation to Northern Ireland, the later parts of Paul Bew's *Ireland: The Politics of Enmity 1789–2006* (Oxford: Oxford University Press, 2007) offer a learned and insightful—if hardly detached—overview. The nature of Irish foreign policy is soberly analyzed up to the very recent past in Ben Tonra, Michael Kennedy, Noel Dorr, and John Doyle (eds.), *Irish Foreign Policy* (Dublin: Gill and Macmillan, 2012).

NOTES

1. Roy Foster, *Luck and the Irish: A Brief History of Change, 1970–2000* (London: Allen Lane, 2007), pp. 1–7.

2. *Irish Times*, February 16, 2002.

3. Richard Aldous (ed.), *Great Irish Speeches* (London: Quercus, 2007), pp. 184–185.

4. Bertie Ahern and Richard Aldous, *Bertie Ahern: The Autobiography* (London: Hutchinson, 2009), pp. 23–34.

5. Pat Leahy, *Showtime: The Inside Story of Fianna Fáil in Power* (Dublin: Penguin Ireland, 2009), p. xi.

6. Leahy, *Showtime*, p. xi.

7. Henry Patterson, *Ireland since 1939: The Persistence of Conflict* (Dublin: Penguin Ireland, 2006), p. 308.

8. Patterson, *Ireland since 1939*.

9. Diarmaid Ferriter, "Fianna Fáil Has Lost Its Self-proclaimed Status as a National Movement," *Irish Times*, June 13, 2009.

10. *Irish Examiner*, November 22, 2007.

11. Eamon Gilmore, *Leading Lights: People Who've Inspired Me* (Dublin: Liberties Press, 2010), pp. 7–17.

12. Patrick Kiely and Dermot Keogh, "Turning Corners: Ireland 2002–11," in T. W. Moody and F. X. Martin (eds.), *The Course of Irish History* (Dublin: Mercier Press, 2011), pp. 358–398.

13. Kiely and Keogh, "Turning Corners," p. 382.

14. Fintan O'Toole, *Enough Is Enough: How to Build a New Republic* (London: Faber and Faber, 2010), p. 6.

15. O'Toole, *Enough Is Enough*, p. 45

16. Tony Judt, *The Memory Chalet* (London: William Heinemann, 2010), pp. 1–33. Quote is from p. 23.

17. Fintan O'Toole (ed.), *Up the Republic! Towards a New Ireland* (London: Faber and Faber, 2012).

18. John Waters, *Was It for This? Why Ireland Lost the Plot* (Dublin: Transworld Ireland, 2012), pp. 271–298. Quote is from p. 109.

19. Waters, *Was It for This?*, p. 277

20. *Economist*, October 14, 2004.

21. Foster, *Luck and the Irish*, p. 35.

22. Kieran Allen, *The Celtic Tiger: The Myth of Social Partnership* (Manchester: Manchester University Press, 2000).

23. Fergus Finlay, *Notes from the Margins: A Decade of Irish Life* (Dublin: Hachette Books Ireland, 2009), p. 301.

24. Finlay, *Notes from the Margins*, p. 220.

25. Finlay, *Notes from the Margins*, p. 275.

26. Colm Tóibín, "Selling Tara, Buying Florida," *Eire-Ireland* 43: 1&2 (Spring/Summer 2008), pp. 11–26.

27. Patterson, *Ireland since 1939*, p. 306; and *Irish Times*, February 14, 2001.

28. Tóibín, "Selling Tara."

29. Morgan Kelly, "What Happened to Ireland?: The 2011 Hubert Butler Annual Lecture," *Irish Pages* 6: 1 (2011), pp. 7–19. Quote is from p. 9.

30. Diarmaid Ferriter, "'The Stupid Propaganda of the Calamity Mongers': The Middle-Class and Irish Politics, 1945–1997," in Fintan Lane (ed.), *Politics, Society and the Middle Class in Ireland* (Basingstoke: Palgrave Macmillan, 2011), pp. 271–289.

31. Patterson, *Ireland since 1939*, p. 348.

32. Eamon McCann, *War and Peace in Northern Ireland* (Dublin: Hot Press Books, 1998), p. 241.

33. George Quigley, "The Impact of Devolution on Everyday Life: 1999–2009," *Institute of British Irish Studies Working Paper 84* (Dublin: University College Dublin, 2009), p. 1.

34. Brian Hanley, *The IRA: A Documentary History 1916–2005* (Dublin, 2010), p. 208.

35. Stephen King, "In from the Cold: The Rise to Prominence of the Democratic Unionist Party since 2003," *Irish Review* 38 (Spring 2008), pp. 1–13. Quote is from p. 12.

36. Paul Bew, *Ireland: The Politics of Enmity 1789–2006* (Oxford: Oxford University Press, 2007), pp. 486–556. Quotes are from pp. 551–553.

37. Ronan Fanning, *Fatal Path: British Government and Irish Revolution 1910–1922* (London: Faber and Faber, 2013).

38. Diarmaid Ferriter, "Frosty Tolerance of Powersharing in the North Is a Far Cry from the Thaw in Anglo-Irish Relations," *Irish Times*, April 10, 2013.

39. Aldous (ed.), *Great Irish Speeches*, p. 214.

40. *Irish Times*, May 21, 2011.

41. Diarmaid Ferriter, *Occasions of Sin: Sex and Society in Modern Ireland* (London: Profile, 2012), pp. xi–xii.

42. Ferriter, *Occasions of Sin*, p. xii.

43. James S. Donnelly, "A Church in Crisis: The Irish Catholic Church Today," *History Ireland* 8: 3 (Autumn 2000), pp. 12–27. Quote is from p. 27.

44. *Irish Times*, November 12, 2005.

45. Ferriter, *Occasions of Sin*, p. 425.

46. Garret FitzGerald, *Reflections on the Irish State* (Dublin: Irish Academic Press, 2003), p. x.

47. *Irish Times*, March 9, 2002.

48. Brian Girvin, "Church, State and Society in Ireland since 1960," *Eire Ireland* 43: 1&2 (Spring/Summer 2008), pp. 74–99. Quote is from p. 98.

49. *Sunday Tribune*, April 24, 2005; and Donnelly, "Church in Crisis."

50. *Irish Times*, January 10, 2013.

51. "EU 2013, 40 years of EU Membership," *Irish Times* Supplement, January 10, 2013.

52. Joe Lee, *Reflections on Ireland in the EEC* (Dublin: Irish Council of the European Movement, 1984), pp. 32–35.

53. Tom Garvin, "Reflections: The Periphery-dominated Centre," *European Journal of Political Research* 31 (1997), pp. 63–71. Quote is from p. 64.

54. Dermot Scott, *Ireland's Contribution to the European Union* (Dublin: Institute of European Affairs, 1994), 57.

55. *Irish Times*, October 26, 2002.

56. Anthony Coughlan, "Why the Euro Is Bad for Ireland," *An Phoblacht*, January 7, 1999.

57. *Irish Examiner*, May 22, 2008.

58. Noel Dorr, "Ireland in an Interdependent World: Foreign Policy since 1973," in Ben Tonra, Michael Kennedy, Noel Dorr, and John Doyle (eds.), *Irish Foreign Policy* (Dublin: Gill and Macmillan, 2012) pp. 54–70.

59. Patrick Keatinge, "Making Sense of Irish Foreign Policy," in Tonra et al. (eds.), *Irish Foreign Policy*, pp. vii–xvii.

60. Kelly, "What Happened to Ireland," p. 7.

61. Kelly, "What Happened to Ireland," p. 8.

62. Kelly, "What Happened to Ireland," p. 9.

63. Tóibín, "Selling Tara, Buying Florida."

64. Tóibín, "Selling Tara, Buying Florida."

65. Diarmaid Ferriter, *Ambiguous Republic: Ireland in the 1970s* (London: Profile Books, 2012), p. 596.

66. *Irish Times*, February 6, 1999.

67. Michael Lewis, *Boomerang: The Meltdown Tour* (London: Allen Lane, 2011), p. 90.

68. Gene Kerrigan, *The Big Lie: Who Profits from Ireland's Austerity?* (Dublin: Random House, 2012), p. 52.

69. Kerrigan, *The Big Lie*, pp. 71–87. Quote is from p. 70.

70. Lewis, *Boomerang*, p. 114.

71. Matt Cooper, *How Ireland Really Went Bust* (Dublin: Penguin Ireland, 2011), pp. 6–8.

72. Kerrigan, *The Big Lie*, p. 71.

73. Pat Leahy, *The Price of Power: Inside Ireland's Crisis Coalition* (Dublin: Penguin Ireland, 2013), pp. 123–125.

74. Kelly, "What Happened to Ireland," p.11.

75. Donal Donavan and Antoin E. Murphy, *The Fall of the Celtic Tiger: Ireland and the Euro Debt Crisis* (Oxford: Oxford University Press, 2013).

76. Kelly, "What Happened to Ireland," p. 15.

77. Moody and Martin (eds.), *Course of Irish History*, p. 376.

78. *Irish Times*, March 21, 2013.

79. Moody and Martin (eds.), *Course of Irish History*, p. 378.

80. Conor McCabe, *Sins of the Father: Tracing the Decisions That Shaped the Irish Economy* (Dublin: History Press Ireland, 2011), p. 33.

81. Colm McCarthy, "Suspicions of Cover-up Will Remain without Inquiry into Financial Crisis," *Sunday Independent*, September 15, 2013.

82. Michael Lewis, *Boomerang*, p. 85.

83. Diarmaid Ferriter, "History Will Ask How We Could Be So Docile in the Face of Such Betrayal," *Irish Independent*, July 1, 2013.

84. Kelly, "What Really Happened."

85. *Irish Times*, October 16, 2010.

86. *The Final Report of the Tribunal of Inquiry into Certain Planning Matters and Payments* (Dublin, 2012).

87. Diarmaid Ferriter, "State Now Morally as Well as Economically Bankrupt," *Irish Times*, March 26, 2012.

88. McCabe, *Sins of the Father*, pp.17–43, 189.

89. Kerrigan, *The Big Lie*, p. xiii.

90. Kerrigan, *The Big Lie*, p. 104.

91. Mary Corcoran, "Consumption and Identity," *Field Day Review* 3 (2007), pp. 239–243.

92. Colin Coulter and Steve Coleman (eds.), *The End of Irish History* (Manchester: Manchester University Press, 2003), pp. 2–32.

93. *Irish Examiner*, September 20, 2007.

PART 2

TOPICS, THEMES, *and*
DEVELOPMENTS

CHAPTER 7

INTELLECTUAL HISTORY:
WILLIAM KING *to* EDMUND BURKE

Daniel Carey

THE PERIOD OF GREATEST ACHIEVEMENT in Irish intellectual history occurred in the long eighteenth century when a remarkable group of figures emerged with very different religious, philosophical, political, and economic orientations, ranging from Archbishop William King to William Molyneux, Jonathan Swift, Robert Molesworth, John Toland, George Berkeley, Francis Hutcheson, and Edmund Burke. Over the course of this period, religious controversy dominated discussion, whether it came in the form of deist agitation against established religion; the response of Anglican authorities, who attempted to shore up the status of the church; internal disputes within confessional groups (such as the subscription controversy that gripped Presbyterians or tussles over orthodoxy among Anglican churchmen); and arguments regarding the prospect of religious toleration and its limits. The vast array of interventions on these issues—in the form of sermons, treatises, pamphlets, satirical forays, and innovative contributions—demonstrates the intellectual vitality of the country in an era of cultural, economic, and political transition.

At the outset of the period under review, the victory of Williamite forces in the Battle of the Boyne (1690) and Aughrim (1691) defined the context of much of what ensued, fostering an Anglican establishment, limiting political participation, and occasioning the fact that Catholic involvement in intellectual life transpired largely on the Continent. The consolidation of an elite in the Church of Ireland, many of whom received their training at Trinity College Dublin (TCD), gave employment opportunities, economic means, and the leisure to pursue their intellectual interests,

I am grateful to Richard Bourke and Andrew Carpenter for comments on versions of this chapter.

whether in rural or urban parishes, deaneries, bishoprics, or the prebendary stalls of cathedrals. At the same time, the political relationship with Britain opened up spaces for cosmopolitan activity in a wider sphere, as the careers of Molesworth, Swift, Toland, Berkeley, Burke, and R. B. Sheridan testify. Burke's most famous text, *Reflections on the Revolution in France* (1790), addressed another defining political moment, which he explored in British terms, although its consequences would later be felt in the activities of the United Irishmen at home.

Tempting though it is to frame this discussion around the Enlightenment and its enemies, close attention to the range of productions in Irish intellectual history suggests an immersion by participants in more immediate concerns and a variety and inconsistency of approach depending on the issue at hand. We can, for example, reframe debates between Deists and their opponents along these lines, but the real skirmish is one over political power and government more than upholding abstract attachments to reason for its own sake.

THEOLOGY, PHILOSOPHY, AND
RELIGIOUS CONTROVERSY

With the exception of William King, who published significant works on the question of predestination and theodicy, few theological writings of frontline international importance appeared in an Irish context in the eighteenth century.[1] The distinguished churchman Edward Synge II (1659–1741) produced *A Gentleman's Religion* (1698), which covered basic issues of church government, scriptural interpretation, and the role of reason in religion, while positioning advocates of alternative views as implicitly lacking in civility, but the work did not break especially new ground. Outside the country, meanwhile, Irish Catholic authorities continued to contribute to the scholastic tradition in places ranging from Prague to Paris and Valladolid.[2] The real center of gravity back home lay in the art of wrangling, both between confessions and within them. King again had a leading role. He embodied some of the central conflicts in himself, as the child of an Antrim Presbyterian family who then converted to Anglicanism at TCD, which he entered in 1667. King's oft-reprinted *Discourse concerning the Inventions of Men in the Worship of God* (1694)—produced while he was dean of Derry—addressed the dissenting community he had abandoned on points of ecclesiology, initially in a tone of reverend care before becoming decidedly patronizing. His position elicited two responses from the notable Presbyterian divine Joseph Boyse. Charles Leslie, the energetic, Trinity-educated non-juror, took on an array of targets, attacking Dissenters and Deists as well as members of his own church, whom he branded as Socinians denying the divinity of Christ. In the 1720s, Irish Presbyterians became locked in dispute between subscribers and nonsubscribers. The question here was whether the Synod of Ulster should continue to make it a requirement for ordination that licensed ministers subscribe to the articles of the Westminster Confession. A group known as the Belfast Society, including John Abernethy and James Kirkpatrick, rejected the insistence on endorsing a manmade creed of this kind.[3] The conflict led to a split, with the Presbytery of Antrim expelled from the General Synod in 1726.[4]

John Toland (1670–1722) entered the fray in 1696 with *Christianity not Mysterious*, initiating a long-lasting controversy with orthodox theologians and defenders of the religious establishment. The protean array of interests pursued by Toland does not lend itself to easy summary, but they were organized around a political agenda informed by republican and Whig principles, in which his often polemical mode of scholarship challenged inherited assumptions in the name of radical reform. In *Christianity not Mysterious*, he teased out the consequences of available philosophical arguments to produce a radical conclusion, drawing on resources made available by John Locke's *Essay concerning Human Understanding* (1690). Toland achieved this by following Locke's theory of ideas and language and insisting that alleged Christian mysteries contained in scripture had no meaning if, as Toland maintained, they had no clear and distinct ideas attached to them.[5] At the same time, he intervened where Locke had treaded very lightly, in Book IV of the *Essay*, to dispute the viability of Locke's category of "things above reason." Toland claimed that Christian doctrine contained nothing "mysterious," that is, nothing contrary to reason, and that reason therefore regulated the meaning and interpretation of those doctrines held by some to be above it. Revelation in itself had no special authority to make unintelligible doctrines subject to faith; rather, it spoke only to the means by which they were communicated and could not displace reason. His refutation, finally, allowed him to trace the origins of religious mysteries to priestcraft. Toland was well aware of the provocation contained in his argument, but he could always point to unattractive alternatives to what he argued, either religious enthusiasm or alien religions that gained support from false and irrational claims.

Toland's position is all the more interesting because he began his life in the Irish-speaking area of the Inishowen peninsula in County Donegal and was raised as a Catholic. Indeed, he acknowledged in the Preface that some had suggested that "the Credulity of Popery has frighted me to an unwarrantable Distance from it."[6] He rejected this faith at the age of 16, but he was eminently capable of offending across the religious spectrum. The Irish House of Commons ordered the book to be burned by the common hangman, and in England it was debated and condemned by the lower house of convocation. He produced some spirited defenses of his position, suggesting that he delighted in the controversy, the most substantial of which was *Vindicius Liberius* (1702).

The fullest Irish response to Toland came in 1697 from Peter Browne, a fellow of TCD and future provost (appointed in 1699 on the back of his answer to Toland). Browne's purpose was to reinstate the place of mysteries in the Christian religion, which arose from their containing "something we do understand, and something that we are wholly ignorant of." He objected to Toland's account of clear and distinct ideas as excessively narrow; our knowledge of the divine consisted of analogical imaginings of perfections, which likewise explained the necessity for revelation to communicate truths in this fashion. Provided that we understood the words, discerned no contradiction in them, and were assured of their divine source, then mysteries conveyed by revelation should raise no objection, and acceptance of them should not merit the charge of *"blind Credulity."*[7] Of course Toland had repudiated all these premises, so the argument merely restated oppositions rather than resolving the matter.

The dispute between Toland and Browne testifies to the deep impact of Locke's *Essay* in Ireland, although in Browne's case this became more apparent in his later work, *The Procedure, Extent and Limits of Human Understanding* (1728). Locke's emergence as a major philosophical resource occurred early on in the country, in part through the influence of William Molyneux (1656–1698), the major natural philosopher, founder of the Dublin Philosophical Society, historian, and translator of Descartes. Molyneux persuaded the provost of Trinity, St. George Ashe (his former classmate in the college), to adopt Locke's *Essay* in the curriculum. Molyneux had in fact formed a close friendship with Locke through correspondence and arranged for a Latin translation of the *Essay* by a TCD graduate and chancellor of the diocese of Down, Ezekiel Burridge, whose writing in support of William of Orange in the Glorious Revolution made him a politically congenial candidate.[8] But Molyneux also had his own significant impact on Locke, suggesting topics for him to develop in the *Essay* (including identity and diversity, among other additions and modifications).[9] Locke sought Molyneux's advice on the inclusion of a possible chapter on the problem of enthusiasm, which Molyneux encouraged him to pursue, although Locke declined to give "an historical account of the various ravings men have embraced for religion," which would, he feared, "be enough to make an huge volume."[10] Molyneux's most valuable contribution to the *Essay* was his introduction of the thought experiment known as the "Molyneux Problem" into philosophical discussion, which became a staple of Irish philosophical reflection. He raised the question of whether a person born blind who suddenly gained the sense of sight would have the capacity to recognize objects known formerly only by the sense of touch. For David Berman, this is the root metaphor of Irish philosophy.[11] George Berkeley, the most exceptional philosophical mind in eighteenth-century Ireland, provided an important answer to this question, while Francis Hutcheson and others also intervened in the debate.

Elsewhere Locke exerted a kind of negative influence by stimulating the formulation of objections to his position. Berkeley openly disputed Locke's treatment of abstraction in the *Essay*, as the introduction to *A Treatise concerning the Principles of Human Knowledge* (1710) makes clear.[12] There is also evidence that his philosophy of language sought, in contrast to Locke, to carve out an area of legitimate meaning based on the emotive potential of language and not on its strictly representational function. Because Berkeley nonetheless grounded knowledge in the senses, he has typically been included in the canon of empiricist philosophers along with Locke and Hume, but his central argument depended on denying the intelligibility of the concept of matter and the restriction of his ontology to two categories—ideas and spirits (as that which "thinks, wills, and perceives").[13] Thus he is equally entitled to a place in the tradition of idealism. He advanced the immaterialist position by maintaining that the existence of things depends on their being perceived (*"esse* is *percipi"* [to be is to be perceived], as he famously put it, Part I, §3). He regarded the notion of matter as contradictory and indeed unnecessary. By ridding himself of it, Berkeley made room for an expansive role for the divine: if matter did not cause ideas, then God must be the figure responsible for our experience and for the magnificence and uniformity of nature's operations.[14] He considered his argument as one that actually preempted the skepticism introduced by the existing view of matter.

Berkeley's work as a whole confirms the interpenetration of religion and philosophy in Ireland. The subtitle of his *Principles* announced it as inquiring into the *Grounds of Scepticism, Atheism, and Irreligion,* while he presented his elaboration of the work in *Three Dialogues between Hylas and Philonous* (1713) as written *in Opposition to Sceptics and Atheists.* His approach in the *Principles* had the advantage, he emphasized, of thwarting systems of atheism built on materialist assumptions (as well as undermining idolaters).[15] Socinians and others who caused trouble over the notion of the resurrection, based on the supposed identity of body and material substance, would lack a foundation for their objections (§95). The theological underpinning of his *New Theory of Vision* (1709) became more apparent in his vindication of the work in 1733. Having shown that the senses of sight and touch produce separate ideas, the question was "how one idea comes to suggest another belonging to a different sense" (§14) (without treating the source as a substrate of matter with supposed primary qualities). For Berkeley, the "arbitrary connexion" between these ideas of different senses was introduced by "the Author of Nature" (§43). His most extended consideration of specifically religious issues occurred in *Alciphron* (1732), but we can see the pattern of interrelationship conspicuously in his *Siris* (1744), which advocated the virtues of tar-water as a panacea. In a text devoted ostensibly to a medical cure, demonstrating considerable erudition in contemporary chemistry and experimental science generally, the occult virtues of this entity led him to discuss the nature of fire, with which it had affinities, and thence to God, the being with whom fire has the closest association, making tar-water, as Berman puts it, tantamount to "drinkable God."[16]

In Irish moral philosophy, the major voice was that of Francis Hutcheson (1694–1746), who was born in County Down, the son and grandson of Presbyterian ministers, and educated in Glasgow where he trained for the ministry. He returned to Ireland and was licensed to preach, but he chose instead to set up a Dissenting academy in Dublin, made possible by the Toleration Act of 1719. His

Dublin decade—ending in 1730 when he became professor of moral philosophy in Glasgow—provided the occasion for publication of his major works, *An Inquiry into the Original of Our Ideas of Beauty and Virtue* (1725) and *An Essay on the Nature and Conduct of the Passions. With Illustrations on the Moral Sense* (1728). Inspired by the work of the third Earl of Shaftesbury, Hutcheson departed from a traditional Presbyterian view of fallen nature (in ways that continued to attract criticism well into the nineteenth century from some northern Irish commentators).[17] He articulated a sociable view of human nature, predicated on Stoic conceptions of the beauty and uniformity of creation. According to Hutcheson, God endowed mankind with internal senses, including a moral sense that generated consensus in perceptions and judgments of morality. Benevolence represented the key impulse of human beings and the ultimate criterion of virtue. He thereby answered the two principal alternative positions of the time, put forward by exponents of egoism, either in its prudential formulation by Locke and Samuel von Pufendorf (in which rewards and punishments structure morality) or in the cynical take of Bernard Mandeville (who reduced everything to self-interest). Hutcheson also answered the rationalist position upheld by Samuel Clarke. In matters of doctrine and discipline, Hutcheson sided with the Moderate movement among Presbyterians in Ireland and Scotland. He shared with a group of fellow Glasgow graduates in Dublin an enthusiasm for Viscount Molesworth, the exponent of Whig and commonwealth ideology, around whom a literary circle formed, which included James Arbuckle, editor and leading contributor to the *Dublin Weekly Journal* from 1725 to 1727. At the same time, Hutcheson made inroads with Anglican authorities, suggesting grounds for considerable rapprochement with Dissenters at a key moment in relations between the communities.

Hutcheson maintained his Irish connections after he took up his Glasgow professorship and in fact died in Dublin on a return visit in 1746. The subscription list of his posthumous *System of Moral Philosophy* (1755) indicates the continuity of support he enjoyed. A significant number of prominent Irish figures subscribed, including his friend Edward Synge III (for ten copies). The reception of his work in Ireland includes a poem by Constantia Grierson (d. 1732), who participated in the salon of Martha Perceval. She evidently gave a copy of Hutcheson's *Inquiry* to Martha Perceval and praised her in verse for providing a model of virtue that excelled Hutcheson's portrait.[18] Not all of the reaction was favorable. Laetitia Pilkington—never short of an opinion—commented in her memoirs that Hutcheson should have quit while he was ahead after his discussion of beauty. She complained that his *Essay* of 1728 "overturned his scarce established Praise" by its obscurities. She added, in a rather doubtful claim, that she had known Synge himself to "declare he did not understand it."[19]

More serious objections came from Philip Skelton (1707–1787), who was born in Antrim and entered TCD in 1724, before taking holy orders and gaining employment variously as a tutor and priest in parishes in several northern counties. In his best-known work, *Ophiomaches, or Deism Revealed* (1749), he presented a rival system predicating morals on the will of God. Skelton disputed the existence of the moral sense proclaimed by Hutcheson and followed Locke in rejecting innateness; revelation alone established moral duty.[20] Hutcheson found a defender in Dublin in the Huguenot minister Charles-Louis de Villette in 1755, who affirmed the reality of the moral sense and dismissed those critics who questioned its validity on the basis that it represented an "occult quality."[21]

Hutcheson also contributed significantly to eighteenth-century aesthetics, though his influence was not equal to Shaftesbury's in this domain. In parallel with his account of morals, Hutcheson argued for an internal sense of beauty. Shapes that exhibited what he called "Uniformity amidst Variety" (whether in nature or in geometry) had the effect of generating ideas of beauty and aesthetic pleasure, which occurred prior to calculation of personal interest. Pastor Villette was unpersuaded on this occasion; for him, judgments of beauty depended on reason and reflection rather than being immediate and adequate in themselves. The sentiment of beauty was in truth a moral sentiment and therefore part of the operation of the moral sense itself.[22]

The most remarkable Irish contribution to the field of aesthetics came from the young Edmund Burke in his *Philosophical Enquiry into the Origin of Our Ideas of the Sublime and Beautiful* (1757; second ed. 1759). Burke (1729–1797), the child of a Protestant father and Catholic mother, attended TCD from 1744 to 1748. His analysis of the sublime in the *Philosophical Enquiry* marked a crucial transition between a classical taste in which the sublime corresponded to moments of elevation, heightened experience, and transcendence, to a darker account in which it was bound up with terror, which Burke called the "ruling principle of the sublime," through its association with danger.[23] Vastness, darkness, "vacuity," silence, the "gloomy forest" and "howling wilderness," and the threat posed by wild animals— all were productive of the sublime,[24] in a clear anticipation of Romantic taste that came to dominate literature and painting through the conventions of the Gothic. He connected these responses with the desire for self-preservation and aesthetic play with what brought it under threat.[25] Burke achieved this breakthrough by relying on a number of analytical tools inherited from Locke. Locke's "way of ideas," for example, informs his view that the imagination, however creative, must rely on ideas supplied by the senses and that the method for interpreting experience is bound up with an analysis of ideas.[26] In his account of taste and beauty, Burke offered a range of criticisms of Hutcheson without naming him. In his view, judgments of taste derived from the understanding, not a sudden reaction of the senses. When he turned to the subject of beauty, Burke argued that the equation between beauty and virtue represented a "loose and inaccurate manner of speaking."[27] Nor had it anything to do with utility, as Berkeley had maintained. Instead, he identified beauty with certain qualities that affected the senses, including small-ness of size, delicacy, and smoothness. Thus he introduced an implicitly gendered differentiation between the masculine sublime and the feminine beautiful.

ANGLICANISM AND THE DEIST CHALLENGE

As we have seen, in Ireland questions of philosophy rarely detached themselves from underlying religious concerns. The enduring preoccupation with deism rep-resents an important case in point. Edward Synge II produced a philosophically serious response in 1698, and he was joined by the indefatigable Charles Leslie (1650–1722), who published (an oft-reprinted) *Short and Easie Method with the Deists* in the same year.[28] The scale of engagement with this phenomenon by rep-resentatives of the Church of Ireland indicates how seriously the threat was taken. The satirical response by Jonathan Swift (1667–1745), in which he used a charac-teristic technique of occupying the position of his opponents, only partly conceals his strength of feeling on the mischief done by underminers of ecclesiastical au-thority. His traditional adherence to Christian mysteries and matters above rea-son (apparent in his undated "Sermon on the Trinity") demonstrates that philo-sophical attachments of his own were under attack. Among his rejoinders, Swift's most effective piece was *An Argument against Abolishing Christianity* (1708; pub-lished 1711), which took as its premise the idea that Matthew Tindal was right and that Christianity consisted of nothing more than a civil religion, with no spiritual or transcendental claims to make. The narrator then defends the reten-tion of Christianity on limited grounds rather than proposing to abandon it al-together. Its utility resided in offering a target for wits who might dangerously turn their attention to other objects of critique. Thus he accepts that nothing more than "nominal" Christianity survives in the world and invites a rejection of this position by drawing out its extremity. In his answer to Anthony Collins, *Mr. C———'s Discourse of Freethinking, Put into Plain English, by Way of Abstract, for the Use of the Poor* (1713), Swift parodied the ostensibly sound logic of his antagonist. The train of inferences accumulated by Collins becomes a series of weak-minded fallacies, such as the claim that the loss of some books of the Bible invalidates those that survive.[29] This chicanery simply masks the real point of freethought, which is to advance the Whig cause. In the end Swift exposes the freethinker as a social type, smirking at conventional wisdom in a complacent fashion.[30] Swift re-sumed his criticism in *Gulliver's Travels* (1726). The occasion of Gulliver's account of the state of England to his Houyhnhnm master provided ample satirical oppor-tunity; according to Gulliver, the consumption of luxury goods caused a drain of specie, which led the population to seek its living by pursuing a range of activ-ities from "Begging, Robbing, Stealing, Cheating, Pimping" to "Whoring, Canting, Libelling, Free-thinking."[31]

There are similarities of approach to be found in Berkeley's *Alciphron*, which advanced its satirical questioning of freethought in dialogue form, pitting two "minute philosophers" (his preferred designation for freethinkers) against two balanced representatives of more orthodox and reasonable opinion. Berkeley chooses an English setting for the discussion and positions freethought as a social phenomenon, led, as Swift had shown, by shallow men who fancy themselves as part of an intellectual avant-garde. Alciphron, the exponent of this position in the work, confidently remarks: "Take my word for it, priests of all religions are the same: wherever there are priests there will be priestcraft: and wherever there is priestcraft there will be a persecuting spirit."[32] In a telling autobiography, he explains that he began as a member of the Church of England and moved to the Latitudinarian wing; from there he became a deist, and is now, he openly admits, an atheist.[33] The difference between Berkeley and Swift is that Swift's satirical strategy made it virtually impossible for him to advocate a position positively without making it seem untenable, as the structure of *A Tale of a Tub* makes clear (with its relative silence about the figure of Martin). In contrast, Euphranor, who speaks for Berkeley, must arrive at something more constructive; he exposes the weakness of Alciphron's position through a process of Socratic questioning and gradual accumulation of logically connected premises. Nor was freethinking a purely philosophical threat alone. The social danger was underscored when Berkeley excoriated members of two notorious Dublin clubs known as the Blasters and the Hellfire Club, composed of various dissolute aristocrats and others, for promoting irreligion in his *Discourse Addressed to Magistrates* (1738).[34]

Philip Skelton proved an energetic participant in this ongoing controversy, taking a Swiftian approach in *Some Proposals for the Revival of Christianity* (1736) before taking up the dialogue form in *Ophiomaches, or Deism Revealed* (1749) to reprove exponents of the "Deistical Creed." His view chimed with Browne, Swift, and Berkeley by upholding such mysteries as the Trinity, grace, the incarnation, and the resurrection and maintaining that they required revelation to make them known.[35] However, no one could compete with John Leland (1691–1766) for the sheer extent of his commitment to drowning Deists with replies. That Leland was a Presbyterian minister—he led the New Row congregation in Dublin (later in Eustace St.) from 1716—demonstrates that it was not the Anglican establishment alone that perceived a threat. Leland's corpus includes a two-volume answer to Tindal's *Christianity as Old as the Creation* (1730) in 1733; a reply (also in two volumes) to Thomas Morgan's *The Moral Philosopher* (1737) in 1739–1740; two replies to Henry Dodwell (the younger)'s *Christianity not Founded in Argument* (1741) in 1744; a reply to Viscount Bolingbroke (1753); and finally *A View of the Principal Deistical Writers*, published in two volumes (1754–1755) and a supplement (1756).

Edmund Burke (1729–1797) joined the argument in 1756 in his satirical *Vindication of Natural Society*, his first extended published work, directed against Lord

Bolingbroke, among others. The purpose was largely to undermine the notion that the deficiencies of existing political forms made them not only artificial but also inferior to "natural" society, but this feeble line of thinking was equally bound up with a view of religion as an objectionable bulwark of government on the grounds that "artificial Laws receive a Sanction from artificial Revelations."[36] If the satirical pitch left any doubt about Burke's views, he made them clear in his *Reflections on the Revolution in France* (1790), where he dismissively asked "Who, born within the last forty years, has read one word of Collins, and Toland, and Tindal, and Chubb, and Morgan, and that whole race who called themselves Freethinkers? Who now reads Bolingbroke?"[37] In Ireland, certainly, controversy had continued in mid-century with the work of Robert Clayton (1695–1758), author of the anonymous anti-Trinitarian *Essay on Spirit* (1750). Educated at TCD, Clayton was an unusual Irish participant in freethinking debates, as he had taken holy orders and served as bishop of Clogher at the time of the work's publication (although its appearance denied him the archbishopric of Tuam). It went through many editions, generating a significant response in Ireland and England, and eliciting various defenses from Clayton.[38]

If freethought represented a pernicious threat to the establishment, the challenge posed by Dissenters was of another order, given the size of these communities and their historic role in radical politics. The question of toleration was addressed at length in the Irish parliament, with a particular focus on the position of Presbyterians, in part as a result of the pattern of Ulster emigration to the American colonies. In 1719, after much argument and dispute, a toleration bill was passed (without including Catholics in its compass), bringing measures for Protestant Dissenters in line with English legal arrangements (and receiving notable support from English-born bishops in Ireland), but it did not remove the sacramental test clause that excluded Dissenters from political office.[39] Archbishop King, a tireless opponent of toleration, lamented the development nonetheless and maintained that it opened the door to "Jews, Turks, deist[s], Socinians and all the most wild and fanatic sects" to set up in Ireland without having to make an account of themselves before ecclesiastical officials.[40] King was supported in his views by Edward Synge II, archbishop of Tuam, who, at an early stage of his career had published *A Peaceable and Friendly Address to the Non-Conformists: Written upon Their Desiring an Act of Toleration without the Sacramental Test* (1697). The purpose of that work was to persuade Dissenters that they should join the established church on the grounds that it taught all that was necessary for salvation and that its forms of worship were indifferent (although necessary for "Decency and Order") and therefore constituted no bar to participation. He suspected that the real motive behind their appeal for toleration was, in fact, "to lay a foundation for the overthrow of the Established Church, and to get, in time, the whole Ecclesiastical and Civil Power into your own hands, as is already done by those of your persuasion in *Scotland*."[41] The danger of factionalism created by toleration was too great to allow it. He harkened back to 1641 and noted that Presbyterians continued to show no regret for disestablishing the church. The Belfast Presbyterian minister John McBride (or MacBride) responded anonymously in 1697, observing that Synge had "snappered on a piece of disingenuity" in the title itself, because the peaceable and friendly pose only masked a desire to libel Dissenters as schismatics. McBride denied the charge that Dissenters sought political power and argued that Synge's encouragement of the domination by his own party fanned the flames of political conflict more than toleration would do, and, among other things, would make it impossible to draw on Dissenters in a time of future crisis, an allusion presumably to the events of the Glorious Revolution.[42] Synge was moved to reply in a text five times longer than his original contribution.[43]

In 1721, two years after legislation passed in favor of toleration, Synge preached a sermon before the lord lieutenant (the Duke of Grafton) in a somewhat more conciliatory vein, affirming that persecution of those of a different faith, even a false one, was inconsistent with Christianity. However, "bare exclusion" from public office did not constitute persecution. He reiterated the danger of introducing rival political forces in the state. The position of Catholics led him to emphasize that no persecution was involved in laying down laws against those whose religion contained principles of rebellion or sedition. The authority claimed by the pope and the prospect of disturbance justified "the restraint of strict laws."[44]

Synge's son Edward preached a sermon on toleration of his own in 1725. He was then a prebendary of St. Patrick's Cathedral and chaplain to the new lord lieutenant, John Carteret. He argued on Lockean grounds for extended toleration, holding that conscience could not be dictated by the magistrate, whose penalties would only produce hypocrites or dissemblers.[45] He departed from the views expressed in his father's 1697 foray into the topic when he claimed that severities adopted by civil authority caused factions to form, and that historic abuses committed by a previous generation on religious grounds did not warrant penalties against later adherents to the same religion. Yet the younger Synge still regarded it as legitimate to deprive people of their property, in whole or in part, if they did not conform; to supervise their education of children; and, if some remained intractable, to *remove them out of the Society.*[46] The purpose of the discussion was to lay a foundation for addressing the problem caused by Catholicism. A religion that posed a civil threat was not tolerable, a point underlined by the ongoing Jacobite danger, but he proposed to distinguish between Catholics who supported the unjust authority to depose princes claimed by the pope and those who repudiated it.[47] Synge's strategy was evidently to expose those Catholics who remained politically problematic by drawing up an oath of abjuration that would expose the troublemakers and consolidate those worthy of inclusion in the state.[48] Nonetheless, he met with sarcastic criticism from the vicar of Naas, Stephen Radcliffe, who replied with amazement that Synge could preach a sermon proposing Catholic toleration on the anniversary of the Irish Rebellion.

Among Dissenters, the issue of toleration received close attention, as one would expect. Two prominent representatives of the Presbyterian cause, Joseph Boyce and John McBride, tackled the question in print in the late seventeenth century, from their positions in Dublin and Belfast, respectively.[49] An unusual contribution came later from John Abernethy, the Glasgow-educated minister at Wood St. in Dublin and friend of Francis Hutcheson. He preached a sermon on *Persecution Contrary to Christianity* on October 23, 1735, once again on the anniversary of the Irish Rebellion. Although he rounded at length on the errors, faults, and abuses of Catholicism, Abernethy asserted that to extirpate the faith by force would smack of Catholicism itself; penal laws had a justification for civil protection, although the milder the better, but to attempt to convert through this means was impossible. The Huguenot pastor of French reformed churches in Lucy Lane and Peter Street in Dublin, Gaspar Caillard, did not share this softening stance toward Catholics. He gave two sermons on toleration printed in 1728, the first on the lines of scripture "contrain-les d'entrer" famously explored by Pierre Bayle, while the second considered the just limits of toleration. In the latter, Caillard acknowledged that the sovereign was entitled to protect his preferred religion against the threat of arms by its opponents, to perpetuate it by erecting schools to teach it, and to favor it by distributing some of his benefits to those adhering to it. No toleration should extend to religions that permitted blasphemy, treason, murder, or other crimes, since their followers would clearly not submit to the laws of the state. "Papisme" clearly qualified for this exception to general toleration. Otherwise, those who professed "false" religions should not be subject to corporal punishment or enforcement that they embrace the "true" one; no penal laws should oblige them to contradict their consciences. Rather, they should enjoy free exercise of their religion and the benefits of the law as members of the state. Nor should ecclesiastical authorities stir up trouble for other religious groups.[50]

Of course the cause of toleration was not championed exclusively by prospective beneficiaries among the Dissenting population. The "true Whig" position on the matter was succinctly expressed by Robert Molesworth (1656–1725), who supported toleration while maintaining his suspicion of organized religion and priestcraft. He professed himself a member of the Church of England (which had the merit of relying less than other faiths on "Miracles, Martyrs, Inspirations, Merits, Mortifications, Revelations") but wished for others to enjoy freedom of religious opinion, including pagans, Quakers, Socinians, and Presbyterians, as well as "Papists." The issue with Catholics was not that they prayed to saints or believed in the real presence in the Eucharist but rather that they owed obedience to a foreign jurisdiction. For this reason, they could not qualify as true governors of the commonwealth (referring to James II) or as true subjects.[51]

Later in the century, the effort to repeal the penal laws received important support from the Catholic scholar Charles O'Conor (1710–1791), best known for his antiquarian interests, in a series of anonymous pamphlets published from the late 1740s to the early 1760s. Edmund Burke also turned to this issue in the 1760s and dismantled the arguments used against Catholics in his unfinished "Tracts on the Popery Laws." His systematic critique observed that regulations relating to property discouraged industry and improvement of land by Irish Catholics. Rebellions in the country had resulted not from tolerating Catholics but by engaging in "the most unparalleled oppression" of them. He dismissed the notion that the pope would somehow lead a conquest over the British as a "wild chimera"; the suggestion that the pope might otherwise stir up a revolt (in a post-1745 context) was an "exploded idea."[52] In 1791, Theobald Wolfe Tone addressed these questions in his widely distributed pamphlet, *An Argument on Behalf of the Catholics of Ireland.* He suggested that the "days of illumination" at the end of the eighteenth century invited an end to the oppression of Catholics, whose political predicament created their attachment to priest and pope, which would diminish with the extension of property rights and enfranchisement of Catholics. Nor would their inclusion in parliament lead to Catholic domination, because property and therefore power still predominated in the country, especially if a condition of possessing a £10 freehold were adopted for electors. He made an impassioned appeal on the basis of Paine's *Rights of Man* (1791) and drew on the language of Shakespeare's Shylock to defend the humanity of Catholics.[53]

POLITICS AND ECONOMIC THOUGHT

Political thought was shaped at both ends of the long eighteenth century by revolutionary moments. At the outset of the period, the defeat of James II and installation of William and Mary confined the political nation in Ireland to an Anglican elite, but this fact did not supply consensus on the management of Irish affairs or how best to configure the country's relationship with Britain. At the close of the period, the rebellion led by the United Irishmen in 1798—based on a complex coalition and inspired by the writings of William Drennan, among others—spoke to the reverberations of the French Revolution in Ireland. At the same time, the integration of Ireland and Britain afforded ongoing opportunities across the century for participation in political argument in a wider setting. As we shall see, the greatest of these contributions came from Edmund Burke, whose *Reflections on the Revolution in France* (1790) defined a tradition of political thought that celebrated the British constitution and deplored the French experiment.

The Treaty of Limerick (1691) and the end of the Jacobite military cause left some, like Edward Wetenhall (1636–1713), bishop of Cork and Ross, with the embarrassing problem of explaining how they could have sworn an oath to James II only to reconcile themselves with his overthrow. As Wetenhall presented the matter, William of Orange had taken Ireland by conquest and therefore enjoyed a right of allegiance, delivering the Protestant population not only from popery but also, as he put it, from *"all Scruple."*[54] The future archbishop, William King, took up the challenge in a typically vigorous and unapologetic fashion in *The State of the Protestants of Ireland* (1691). In effect he pleaded that Protestants had no choice: they faced destruction, he maintained, due to the "Invasions made on our Liberties, Properties, Lives and Religion." He devoted considerable space to detailing the many grievances against James II that made deserting him and seeking the protection of William and Mary legitimate.[55] The norm of passive obedience made such a position intrinsically difficult to maintain, but King drew support from Grotius and other jurists to defend it. However, some Protestants remained unconvinced. The non-juror Charles Leslie composed a lengthy *Answer* to King in 1692.[56]

Not all those who supported William III believed that the Revolution resolved Ireland's political dilemmas vis-à-vis Britain. William Molyneux's *The Case of Ireland's Being Bound by Acts of Parliament in England, Stated* (1698) opened with an address to King William, which remarked on his rescuing of "these Nations" from "Arbitrary Power" and urged him to defend the rights and liberties enjoyed by Ireland under the crown that it had acquired over five centuries. In contrast to Wetenhall, Molyneux maintained that Ireland had never undergone a conquest parallel to the Norman Conquest. Even if such an event had occurred, the people who participated in the conquest could not suffer as a result of it; only the "*Antient Race* of the *Irish*" ought to endure penalties. But even in this case the implications were limited, as he argued on grounds that Locke had developed in the *Second Treatise of Government*.[57] From matters of jurisprudential principle Molyneux turned to history and legal precedent to establish Irish legislative authority. The debate over Molyneux's book in the English House of Commons, where it was condemned, indicates the unwelcome nature of his assertion of Irish privileges.[58] The work attracted a number of negative rejoinders, including one from the unstoppable Charles Leslie.[59] Nonetheless, *The Case of Ireland's Being Bound* was reprinted nine times in the ninety years between its first appearance and 1782, meriting Patrick Kelly's conclusion that it constitutes "the most significant Irish political pamphlet of the seventeenth and eighteenth centuries."[60]

Agitation over the issue of Irish legislative independence continued in various quarters in the eighteenth century. Although the Declaratory Act of 1720 did not spur an enormous literature, Robert Molesworth encouraged John Toland to compose a pamphlet addressed to the British parliament on the subject.[61] The argument continued to be put forcefully in the fourth and fifth of Swift's *Drapier's Letters*. It was not until 1782 that the British parliament surrendered the legislative privilege under political pressure led by Henry Grattan (with further support in the British parliament from Richard Brinsley Sheridan), although the independence would only survive for twenty years with the imposition of the Act of Union in 1801 following the Irish Rebellion.

The political ties between Britain and Ireland provided opportunities for engagement at the highest levels, as the careers of Burke and Sheridan testify in the second half of the eighteenth century. In the earlier period, Robert Molesworth established a high profile in both countries for his politically radical position. Molesworth was born in Dublin and possessed an estate near Swords in addition to extensive lands elsewhere. Among his classmates at TCD were Molyneux and St. George Ashe. Molesworth's republican and Whig credentials brought him into close contact with a spectrum of figures from the third Earl of Shaftesbury to Toland. Molesworth announced his convictions forcefully in *An Account of Denmark* (1694), a widely reprinted and translated work that established his reputation. Composed after a challenging period as English envoy to Denmark, he commented on the danger of tyranny, which was clearly not confined to Catholic Europe but pointedly existed under Protestant princes.[62] Liberty remained under threat from priestcraft and doctrines of passive obedience and divine right, as the lessons of travel made clear.[63] His rousing preface to the work provided a call to virtue, lamenting the current enslavement of Europeans under different regimes and reminding them of past freedom under various forms of ancient constitution. Molesworth's most succinct statement of his political credo occurred in the "Translator's Preface" to the second edition of François Hotman's *Franco-Gallia* (1721). Here Molesworth took occasion to enunciate the principles of a "True Whig," a position he did not distinguish, provocatively, from being a "*Commonwealthsman.*"[64] He was not exactly apologetic about revolutionary action, noting that princes who disregarded the law committed treason against the constitution. "To affirm," he remarked, "that Monarchy, Episcopacy, Synods, Tythes, the Hereditary Succession to the Crown, *etc.* are *Jure Divino*, is to cram them down a Man's Throat."[65] In his political "profession of faith," he stated that true Whigs supported toleration, a general naturalization, frequent parliaments, and a citizen army as opposed to a standing army of mercenaries (also condemned in his earlier discussion of Denmark), among numerous other commitments. The republican side of Molesworth's thought took inspiration, of course, from James Harrington, another enthusiasm he shared with Toland, who prepared an edition of Harrington's works in 1700.

The circle that Molesworth formed around himself at his Dublin estate, following his failure to secure election to the British parliament in 1722, included Francis Hutcheson. Hutcheson's own political thought was clearly sympathetic to Molesworth's mixture of Whig and republican convictions. Hutcheson used the final section of his *Inquiry* to provide a deduction of obligations and rights from the moral sense itself and thereby built a foundation for natural rights within human nature. The intention was to establish the deep congruence between moral virtue and natural law, an aspiration he shared with Richard Cumberland, author of *De legibus naturae* (1671), together with Cumberland's esteem for benevolence and emphasis on sociability in reply to Hobbes.[66] Hutcheson's most elaborate account of his jurisprudence came in his *System of Moral Philosophy* (1755), published in Glasgow after his death, which presented an influential set of arguments articulating a contractual conception of government, rights of resistance, a critique of the grounds for slavery, and a rationale for colonies to gain their independence.[67] Hutcheson's thought and reputation survived among the United Irishmen later in the century; he also reached an audience in America, with influence on Thomas Jefferson and prominence in the pantheon of anti-slavery authorities.[68]

Political questions were rarely separate from economic ones, particularly in an era still dominated by mercantilist assumptions. The stance adopted by Swift in the *Drapier's Letters*—in which he fomented against the award to William Wood of a patent in 1722 to import low-value copper coinage—remains the best-known intervention. Swift used to his advantage the ostensible consensus among jurists that "Copper is not Money" to claim that the British crown had no authority in the matter, because Wood's halfpence did not constitute legitimate currency under their control.[69] The patriot argument created unexpected alliances, particularly apparent in Swift's dedication of the fifth Drapier's Letter to Molesworth, whose political position was otherwise anathema to him. Nonetheless there are grounds for questioning the wisdom of his economic strategy. The endemic problem of small change in a marginal or colonial economy necessitated a circulating medium of some kind (whether paper or base metal). Berkeley provided a more imaginative solution in his economic work *The Querist* (1735–1737) by distinguishing the concept of money from its intrinsic value as a precious metal. Part of his remedy involved advocating the establishment of a national bank. Berkeley recommended an institution that would remain, unlike the Bank of England, not private but national, backed by the value of land and underwritten by the Irish parliament, with the paper money issued by it subject to tight controls. The bank would become a national asset by reinvesting profits in the country and ensuring a wide distribution of credit throughout the four provinces.[70] Like his Bermuda project, this was another scheme that failed to gain support (it was not until 1783 that the Bank of Ireland came into being). The most sophisticated Irish commentator on economic matters was Richard Cantillon (1687?–1734?), who came from a Catholic Kerry family and spent significant periods of his career in France (where he anticipated the collapse of the Mississippi Scheme and profited in the process). His *Essai sur la nature du commerce en général* (1755, composed between 1728 and 1730) provides a remarkably lucid theorization of technical issues of trade, prices, income, value, and markets. As a monetary theorist, in particular, he sharpened notions developed by Sir William Petty and John Locke relating to the velocity of money in circulation and the quantity theory of money, while he conceived of the specie flow mechanism (undermining a central tenet of mercantilism) independently of Hume, who is usually credited with the idea.

Cantillon's European career drew on family connections and followed an established diasporic pattern among Irish Catholics. In fact the scenario of cosmopolitanism and multiple identification was familiar across a wide spectrum of Irish intellectual figures, from Swift to Toland and Burke. In the latter cases the crucial consideration was the close political relationship between Ireland and Britain. For Burke this laid the groundwork for his trajectory from TCD graduate to private secretary, initially for William Gerard Hamilton in his capacity as chief secretary to Ireland and then, in England, for Lord Rockingham, briefly prime minister and leader of a Whig faction. Burke entered parliament in 1766, where his oratorical brilliance defined his reputation in the midst of a turbulent set of political conflicts over the next twenty-eight years (as a member of parliament, successively, for Wendover, Bristol, and Malton). His speeches and writings in the lead-up to the American War of Independence and later his attempts to impeach the governor of Bengal in India, Warren Hastings, form key parts of his political and intellectual profile, but the French Revolution undoubtedly provided the occasion for his greatest work, the *Reflections*. Here Burke eschewed an Irish identity; the "we" of the text is a British "we," even at times a specifically English one.[71]

Given Burke's lengthy career espousing Whig causes and, in an earlier moment of rebellion, defending the American interest, it was not a straightforward assumption that he would oppose the French Revolution. Indeed the critical position he took led to the sacrifice of relations with former Whig allies in Charles James Fox and Sheridan. One of the key questions for Burke, initially, was to clarify the difference between the Glorious Revolution and its French counterpart, as commentators in England (notably his main target, the Unitarian minister and advocate for France Richard Price) had confused them, in his estimation. Burke maintained that the Glorious Revolution was undertaken not to assert the right of the people to choose their governors but simply to settle the succession, based on an acceptance of hereditary monarchy. He described the removal of James II as a "small and temporary deviation" and an "act of *necessity*" performed under special circumstances, which merely qualified hereditary succession by introducing Protestantism as a criterion. In any case the move had not required the "decomposition of the whole civil and political mass" and the creation of a new civil order as occurred in France.[72]

This revolutionary undertaking was aberrant in Burke's view, because it encouraged deplorable attributes of human nature—not only vanity, greed, envy, and revenge, but also the megalomania of the present, which failed to understand human relations and politics as conditioned by inheritance. Each generation acquired things, from property to the political constitution itself, which it handed on to its successors. This was an inherently conservative model of trusteeship, not one of radical reform. Burke regarded the revolutionaries in France as "metaphysicians" for whom theory prevailed over experience and practice as the great sources of instruction. He spoke of this tendency with contempt and associated it openly with an Enlightenment infatuation with reason, in contrast with the notion that political institutions constituted the repository of wisdom. Thus he described as "our old settled maxim" in Britain the injunction "never entirely nor at once to depart from antiquity."[73]

One of Burke's strategies is to identify his position with the impulses of moral sensibility. In England, he maintains, "we still feel within us" and allow moral sentiments to provide guidance in matters of duty, in contrast with France, where the appalling spectacle of October 6, 1789, when a crowd forced the departure of the king and queen from Versailles, caused a "revolution in sentiments, manners, and moral opinions." He identifies Louis XVI as a man of feeling, forced to witness the suffering of his wife and children, and he naturalizes our relationship with kingship by introducing shared responses to a melancholy scene. Burke ties this moral capacity to an antique age of chivalry, which once gave its character to Europe but has now been sacrificed to an era of "sophisters, economists and calculators" devoid of authentic moral passion.[74]

Burke's political analysis could overlook the problem with the French monarchy, the abuses of which he attributes to the absence of "constant inspection" from popular representatives. Thus the problem is ultimately the familiar one of absolutism, the answer to which is a slower approach to reform and not the extreme measure of destroying the fabric of the state in the name of a "theoretic, experimental edifice." The sense of outrage permeating the text stems in part from his perspective on France as a country at the heart of civilized Europe, not a Turkish or Persian monarchy worthy of condemnation.[75] The British constitution—a mixed monarchy with distributed powers and balances—supplies a norm and a stable position with which to test the activities of the revolutionaries and to resist the spread of their doctrines. As Burke puts it, "We are resolved to keep an established church, an established monarchy, an established aristocracy, and an established democracy, each in the degree it exists, and in no greater."[76] The new French constitution arrogated sovereignty to the National Assembly, neglected the provision of a senate, reduced the role of the executive to a cipher, undermined the independence of the judiciary, and threatened its own position by detaching the army from necessary structures of authority. Burke reserved some of his strongest vituperations for the revolutionaries' attack on religion, suspecting them of deep intolerance.[77] They were animated not by simple anticlericalism but by an atheistic desire, at least among a literary vanguard, to destroy Christianity, whereas Burke maintained that "We know, and what is better, we feel inwardly, that religion is the basis of civil society, and the source of all good and of all comfort."[78] The confiscation of church property in France not only undermined the security of property in general, making the government despotic, but also the proceeds were used to fund a "fictitious" and pernicious paper currency, the depreciated *Assignats*. Burke condemned this as chicanery at some length, regarding it as a trick that handed political control over to moneyed individuals and made the nation into a set of "gamesters." He set the British system in opposition, which employed paper currency only on the basis that it was fully convertible to precious metal.[79] What he made of the suspension of cash payments by the Bank of England in 1797, during the outbreak of war with France, is another question.

Burke's analysis enabled him to configure the British constitution as the guardian of liberty, particularly in relation to the protection of property, and France, for all its declaration of rights, as the enemy of such freedoms. Thus he rejoined his conservative account to his original Whig proclivities.

In Ireland, Wolfe Tone—writing anonymously as "A Northern Whig" in 1791—remained an enthusiast for the French Revolution, which he described as a "stupendous event," before asking "who can praise it as it merits?" He regarded the Irish "Revolution" of 1782, which obtained legislative privileges for the Irish parliament, as "a bungling, imperfect business."[80] At the end of the period under review, the United Irishmen failed to bring about the political transformation they aspired to in the Rebellion of 1798. William Drennan, who had agitated with Wolfe Tone, responded to the prospect of the Union with two acerbic letters addressed to William Pitt in 1799. He quoted the opponent of Scottish union from the start of the century, Andrew Fletcher of Saltoun, and condemned Pitt's initiative as creating a military machine for war with France, in which Ireland would be "shaped and rounded into a Buckler for Britain" and turned into a barracks with no political mediation between monarchy and military rule.[81] His sister, Martha McTier, who helped distribute the first *Letter* in the North, perused the piece with "eager sensibility," while noting that "no lady (except perhaps those of a certain rank) could acknowledge they had read it."[82] So came to a close an exceptional time of ferment that constituted Ireland's greatest era of intellectual history.

FURTHER READING

Irish intellectual history in its richest period, from 1690 to 1800, has largely been studied through its major figures—Berkeley, Burke, Hutcheson, King, Molesworth, Molyneux, Swift, and Toland. Among wider interpretations, David Berman's discussion of Irish philosophy up to the 1750s represents the leading account, emphasizing Enlightenment and Counter-Enlightenment oppositions and right- and left-wing Lockeanism, in articles reprinted in *Berkeley and Irish Philosophy* (London: Continuum, 2005). For a perceptive survey, see Thomas Duddy, *A History of Irish Thought* (London: Routledge, 2001). For a wide-ranging account see Ian McBride, *Eighteenth-Century Ireland: The Isle of Slaves* (Dublin: Gill & Macmillan, 2009), esp. ch. 2. Among the vast writings on individual authors, see especially Kenneth P. Winkler, *Berkeley: An Interpretation* (Oxford: Clarendon Press, 1989); Richard Bourke, *Empire and Revolution: The Political Life of Edmund Burke* (Princeton, NJ: Princeton University Press, 2015); James Moore, "The Two Systems of Francis Hutcheson: On the Origins of the Scottish Enlightenment," in M. A. Stewart (ed.), *Studies in the Philosophy of the Scottish Enlightenment* (Oxford: Clarendon Press, 1990); Daniel Carey, *Locke, Shaftesbury, and Hutcheson: Contesting Diversity in the Enlightenment and Beyond* (Cambridge: Cambridge University Press,

2006); Philip O'Regan, *Archbishop William King of Dublin (1650–1729) and the Constitution in Church and State* (Dublin: Four Courts, 2000); Caroline Robbins, *The Eighteenth-Century Commonwealthman* (Cambridge, MA: Harvard University Press, 1959); Patrick Kelly, "Recasting a Tradition: William Molyneux and the Sources of *The Case of Ireland … Stated* (1698)," in Jane H. Ohlmeyer (ed.), *Political Thought in Seventeenth-Century Ireland: Kingdom or Colony* (Cambridge: Cambridge University Press, 2000), pp. 83–106; Laurent Jaffro, "Abolition ou réformation du christianisme? L'argument de Swift contre les libres penseurs," *La Lettre clandestine* 3 (2005): 15–33; Justin Champion, *Republican Learning: John Toland and the Crisis of Christian Culture, 1696–1722* (Manchester: Manchester University Press, 2003). For entries on obscure and well-known figures, see David Berman, Thomas Duddy, and M. A. Stewart (eds.), *Dictionary of Irish Philosophers* (Bristol: Thoemmes Continuum, 2004). On political, religious, and economic thought, see D. George Boyce, Robert Eccleshall, and Vincent Geoghegan (eds.), *Political Thought in Ireland since the Seventeenth Century* (London: Routledge, 1993); S. J. Connolly (ed.), *Political Ideas in Eighteenth-Century Ireland* (Dublin: Four Courts, 2000); D. George Boyce, Robert Eccleshall, and Vincent Geoghegan (eds.), *Political Discourse in Seventeenth- and Eighteenth-Century Ireland* (Houndmills: Palgrave, 2001); Daniel Carey and Christopher J. Finlay (eds.), *The Empire of Credit: The Financial Revolution in the British Atlantic World, 1688–1815* (Dublin: Irish Academic Press, 2011). For Irish Catholic scholarship on the Continent, see Martin W. F. Stone, "Punch's Riposte: The Irish Contribution to Early Modern Scotism from Maurice O'Fihely OFMConv. to Anthony Rourke OFMObs.," and Liam Chambers, "Irish Catholics and Aristotelian Scholastic Philosophy in Early Modern France, c. 1600–c.1750," in James McEvoy and Michael Dunne (eds.), *The Irish Contribution to European Scholastic Thought* (Dublin: Four Courts, 2009). Patterns of women's intellectual history can be traced in Amy Prendergast, "Irish Literary Salons of the Long Eighteenth Century," in *The Literary Encyclopedia*, first published April 10, 2013 (http://www.litencyc.com/php/stopics.php?rec=true&UID=19346); and in the text and notes of *The Memoirs of Laetitia Pilkington*, 2 vols., edited by A. C. Elias, Jr. (Athens: University of Georgia Press, 1997) and *The Drennan-McTier Letters*, 3 vols., edited by Jean Agnew, general editor, Maria Luddy (Dublin: Irish Manuscripts Commission, 1999). On Huguenot culture, see Máire Kennedy, *French Books in Eighteenth-Century Ireland* (Oxford: Voltaire Foundation, 2001).

NOTES

1. William King, *Divine Predestination and Fore-knowledge, Consistent with the Freedom of Man's Will* (Dublin: Andrew Crook, 1709); William King, *De origine mali* (Dublin: Andreas Crook, 1702); the latter work was translated with extensive commentary by the Cambridge philosopher Edmund Law in 1731. For a later contribution on theodicy published in Dublin, which argued against King,

see the Huguenot pastor Charles-Louis de Villette's *Dissertation sur l'Origine du Mal* (Dublin: Richard James, 1755).

2. See the work of Michael Moore (Paris); Francis O'Devlin (Prague); and Anthony Rourke (Valladolid).

3. See A.W.G. Brown, "Irish Presbyterian Theology in the Early Eighteenth Century," (unpublished PhD thesis, Queen's University Belfast, 1977); A.W.G. Brown, "A Theological Interpretation of the First Subscription Controversy (1719–1728)," in *Challenge and Conflict: Essays in Irish Presbyterian History and Doctrine* (Antrim, UK: W. & G. Baird, 1981), pp. 28–45.

4. The nonsubscribing position was stated in print by, among others, Abernethy, Michael Bruce (cousin of Francis Hutcheson), and Samuel Haliday, with significant support from Boyse. Defenders of the Synod's decision included John Malcome and Charles Mastertown. The issue poignantly separated Francis Hutcheson, who aligned himself with the nonsubscribers, from the views of his father, the Presbyterian minister John Hutcheson, whose verdict on the matter appeared after his death, in 1730. For references and discussion, see James Moore, "Presbyterianism and the Right of Private Judgement: Church Government in Ireland and Scotland in the Age of Francis Hutcheson," in Ruth Savage (ed.), *Philosophy and Religion in Enlightenment Britain: New Case Studies* (Oxford: Oxford University Press, 2012), pp. 141–168; and A.G.D. Steers, "Samuel Haliday (1685–1739): Travelling Scholar, Court Lobbyist and Non-Subscribing Divine," in Ruth Savage (ed.), *Philosophy and Religion in Enlightenment Britain*.

5. John Toland, *Christianity not Mysterious: Text, Associated Works and Critical Essays*, edited by Philip McGuinness, Alan Harrison, and Richard Kearney (Dublin: Lilliput Press, 1997), pp. 31, 34.

6. Toland, *Christianity not Mysterious*, p. 8.

7. Peter Browne, *A Letter in Answer to a Book Entitled Christianity not Mysterious* (Dublin: Joseph Ray, 1697), pp. 14, 74.

8. E. B. [Ezekiel Burridge], *Historia nuperae rerum mutationis in Anglia: in quâ res à Jacobo rege contra leges Angliae, & Europae libertatem, & ab ordinibus Angliae, contra regem patratae* (London: Sam. Buckley, 1697).

9. Locke added a chapter on "Identity and Diversity" to the *Essay concerning Human Understanding* for the second edition (Book II, chapter xxvii as it became). *An Essay concerning Human Understanding*, edited by Peter H. Nidditch (Oxford: Clarendon Press, 1975).

10. *The Correspondence of John Locke*, edited by E. S. de Beer (Oxford: Clarendon Press, 1976–1989), 8 vols., V, p. 352 (letter of April 26, 1695, replying to Molyneux's letter of March 26, 1695).

11. David Berman, *Berkeley and Irish Philosophy* (London: Continuum, 2005), p. 87. For a study, see Marjolein Degenaar, *Molyneux's Problem: Three Centuries of Discussion on the Perception of Forms* (Dordrecht: Kluwer, 1996).

12. George Berkeley, *A Treatise concerning the Principles of Human Knowledge*, "The Preface," §§11–13, in *Philosophical Works*, edited by M. R. Ayers (London: Dent, 1975), pp. 68–70.

13. Berkeley, *Treatise*, Part I, §138; see also §27; on these as the sole objects of human knowledge, see §86.

14. See Berkeley, *Treatise*, Part I, §§29, 31, 96, 146–151. See also George Berkeley, *Siris: A Chain of Philosophical Reflexions and Inquiries concerning the Virtues of Tar Water* (Dublin: Printed by Margaret Rhames for R. Gunne, 1744), §§160, 243.

15. See Berkeley, *Treatise*, §§87–89; 92; on idolaters, 94.

16. David Berman, *George Berkeley: Idealism and the Man* (Oxford: Clarendon Press, 1994), pp. 173, 176.

17. See James Seaton Reid, *History of the Presbyterian Church in Ireland*, with additional notes by W. D. Killen (Belfast: William Mullen, 1867), 3 vols., III, pp. 296–298.

18. Constantia Grierson, "To the Honourable Mrs. Percival, with Hutcheson's Treatise on Beauty and Order," in Mary Barber, *Poems on Several Occasions* (London: C. Rivington, 1734), p. 155.

19. *The Memoirs of Laetitia Pilkington*, edited by A. C. Elias, Jr. (Athens: University of Georgia Press, 1997), 2 vols., I, pp. 304–305.

20. [Philip Skelton], *Ophiomaches: or, Deism Revealed* (London: A. Millar, 1749), 2 vols., I, pp. 133–135.

21. Villette, *Dissertation*, pp. 50–51. Villette was born in Lausanne in 1688. He served at French churches in Carlow and Kilruane before arriving in Dublin as minister of the French church at St. Patrick's in 1737. Máire Kennedy, *French Books in Eighteenth-Century Ireland* (Oxford: Voltaire Foundation, 2001), p. 77n.

22. Charles-Louis de Villette, *Oeuvres mêlées, dont les Sujets sont le Stile, le Théatre Moderne, le Beau, et le Goût* (Dublin: S. Powell, 1750), pp. 130, 134.

23. Edmund Burke, *A Philosophical Enquiry into the Origin of Our Ideas of the Sublime and Beautiful*, edited by Adam Phillips (Oxford: Oxford University Press, 1990), p. 47.

24. Burke, *Philosophical Enquiry*, pp. 60–61, 65, 66, 69.

25. Burke, *Philosophical Enquiry*, pp. 35–37, 47, 79.

26. Burke, *Philosophical Enquiry*, pp. 16–17.

27. Burke, *Philosophical Enquiry*, pp. 85, 101–102.

28. A century later, it appeared in revised form under the title *Deism a Madness* (London: for the editor [Rev. Griffith Williams], 1797).

29. *The Prose Works of Jonathan Swift*, edited by Herbert Davis (Oxford: Blackwell, 1939–1968), 14 vols., IV, p. 40.

30. For further discussion, see Daniel Carey, "Swift among the Freethinkers," *Eighteenth-Century Ireland* 12 (1997), pp. 89–99; Laurent Jaffro, "Abolition ou réformation du christianisme? L'argument de Swift contre les libres penseurs," *La Lettre clandestine* 3 (2005), pp. 15–33.

31. Jonathan Swift, *Gulliver's Travels*, edited by Paul Turner (Oxford: Oxford University Press, 1998), p. 244.

32. George Berkeley, *Berkeley's Alciphron: English Text and Essays in Interpretation*, edited by Laurent Jaffro, Geneviève Brykman, and Claire Schwartz (Hildesheim: Georg Olms Verlag, 2010), p. 29.

33. *Berkeley's Alciphron*, pp. 31, 33–34. See also Berkeley's *The Theory of Vision ... Vindicated and Explained* (1733), in *Philosophical Works*, pp. 231–233.

34. See David Ryan, "The Dublin Hellfire Club," in James Kelly and Martin J. Powell (eds.), *Clubs and Societies in Eighteenth-Century Ireland* (Dublin: Four Courts, 2010), pp. 332–352.

35. Skelton, *Ophiomaches*, pp. 43, 114, 219–220.

36. Edmund Burke, *Pre-Revolutionary Writings*, edited by Ian Harris (Cambridge: Cambridge University Press, 1993), p. 16.

37. Edumund Burke, *Reflections on the Revolution in France*, edited by Frank M. Turner (New Haven, CT: Yale University Press, 2003), p. 76.

38. Nigel Aston, "The Limits of Latitudinarianism: English Reactions to Bishop Clayton's *An Essay on Spirit*," *Journal of Ecclesiastical History* 49 (1998), pp. 407–433.

39. The campaign to remove the test only prevailed in 1733, led by Abernethy. See his *The Nature and Consequences of the Sacramental Test Considered* (Dublin: N.P., 1731). Energetic support for the test had earlier come from William Tisdall and Jonathan Swift. For discussion of the political context, see D. W. Hayton, *Ruling Ireland, 1685–1742: Politics, Politicians, and Parties* (Woodbridge: Boydell Press, 2004), chapter 6.

40. Quoted in Philip O'Regan, *Archbishop William King of Dublin (1650–1729) and the Constitution in Church and State* (Dublin: Four Courts Press, 2000), p. 259.

41. [Edward Synge II], *A Peaceable and Friendly Address to the Non-Conformists: Written upon Their Desiring an Act of Toleration without the Sacramental Test* (Dublin: John Foster, 1697), pp. 5, 8.

42. [John McBride], "An Answer to A Peaceable & Friendly Address to the Non-Conformists," in *Animadversions on the Defence of the Answer to a Paper, Intituled, The Case of the Dissenting Protestants of Ireland* ([Belfast]: N.P., 1697), pp. 95, 115, 116, 117.

43. Edward Synge II, *A Defence of the Peaceable and Friendly Address to the Non-Conformists against the Answer Lately Given to It* (Dublin: J. B. and S. P., for John Foster, 1698).

44. Edward Synge II, *A Sermon against Persecution on Account of Religion* (Dublin: J. Carson, for Jer. and Sil. Pepyat, 1721), pp. 7, 11, 15, 13, 28.

45. Edward Synge III, *The Case of Toleration Consider'd with Respect both to Religion and Civil Government* (Dublin: A. Rhames for Robert Owen, 1725), p. 21.

46. Synge, *The Case of Toleration*, pp. 34, 39.

47. Synge took heart from a recent work by the Catholic theologian Francis Martin, based in Louvain. Born in Galway, Martin had at one time advocated the assassination of William of Orange, but he softened his position in his *Scutum fidei contra haereses hodiernas* (Louvain: Michael Zangrius, 1714), by emphasizing the duty owed to established authority.

48. Synge issued a defense of the sermon: *A Vindication of a Sermon Preach'd before the Honourable House of Commons of Ireland. On Saturday the 23d of October, 1725* (Dublin: A. Rhames for Robert Owen, 1726).

49. See Ian McBride, "Ulster Presbyterians and the Confessional State, c. 1688–1733," in D. George Boyce, Robert Eccleshall, and Vincent Geoghegan (eds.), *Political Discourse in Seventeenth- and Eighteenth-Century Ireland* (Houndmills: Palgrave, 2001), p. 177.

50. Gaspar Caillard, *Sermons sur divers textes de L'Ecriture Sainte* (Dublin: J. Smith and W. Bruce, 1728), pp. 1–60.

51. Robert Molesworth, *An Account of Denmark with Francogallia and Some Considerations for the Promoting of Agriculture and Employing the Poor*, edited by Justin Champion (Indianapolis, IN: Liberty Fund, 2011), pp. 177–178.

52. Burke, *Pre-Revolutionary Writings*, pp. 99, 101.

53. [Theobold Wolfe Tone], *An Argument on Behalf of the Catholics of Ireland* (Dublin: P. Byrne, 1791), pp. 34–35, 43–44, 47.

54. [Edward Wetenhall], *The Case of the Irish Protestants: in Relation to Recognising, or Swearing Allegiance to, and Praying for King William and Queen Mary, Stated and Resolved* (London: Robert Clavel, 1691), p. 6.

55. William King, *The State of the Protestants of Ireland* (London: Robert Clavell, 1691), pp. 225, 5.

56. For further discussion, see S. J. Connolly, "The Glorious Revolution in Irish Protestant Political Thinking," in S. J. Connolly (ed.), *Political Ideas in Eighteenth-Century Ireland* (Dublin: Four Courts Press, 2000), pp. 27–63.

57. William Molyneux, *The Case of Ireland's Being Bound by Acts of Parliament in England, Stated* (Dublin: Joseph Ray, 1698), p. 19. He cites Locke's *Two Treatises* (pp. 27–28).

58. J. G. Simms, *William Molyneux of Dublin 1656–1698*, edited by P. H. Kelly (Dublin: Irish Academic Press, 1982), pp. 111–112.

59. [Charles Leslie], *Considerations of Importance to Ireland in a Letter to a Member of Parliament There; upon Occasion of Mr Molyneux's Late Book* ([London]: N.P., 1698). Leslie used Locke against Molyneux (p. 3).

60. Patrick Kelly, "Recasting a Tradition: William Molyneux and the Sources of *The Case of Ireland ... Stated* (1698)," in Jane H. Ohlmeyer (ed.), *Political Thought in Seventeenth-Century Ireland: Kingdom or Colony* (Cambridge: Cambridge University Press, 2000), p. 83.

61. [John Toland], *Reasons Most Humbly Offer'd ... Why the Bill ... Entitul'd, an Act for the Better Securing the Dependency of the Kingdom of Ireland upon the Crown of Great-Britain, Shou'd Not Pass into a Law* (London: R. Franklin, 1720).

62. Molesworth, *An Account*, p. 157.

63. Molesworth, *An Account*, p. 17.

64. Molesworth, *An Account*, p. 175; see also p. 189.

65. Molesworth, *An Account*, p. 179.

66. Evidence of Cumberland's appeal in Ireland appears in John Maxwell's translation in 1727 of the *Treatise of the Laws of Nature*. Maxwell was a TCD-educated prebendary of Connor and chaplain to Lord Carteret. John Towers, prebendary of St. Patrick's Cathedral and vicar of Castleknock, produced his translation of Cumberland in 1750/1; both Maxwell and Towers included lengthy treatises of their own on natural law in their editions of Cumberland.

67. Some of this work can be traced back to the Latin classroom texts that Hutcheson developed for the dissenting academy he ran in Dublin during the 1720s and the Glasgow curriculum in which he was formed.

68. See Ian McBride, "The School of Virtue: Francis Hutcheson, Irish Presbyterians and the Scottish Enlightenment," in D. George Boyce, Robert Eccleshall, and Vincent Geoghegan (eds.), *Political Thought in Ireland since the Seventeenth Century* (London: Routledge, 1993), pp. 73–99; Daniel

Carey, "Francis Hutcheson's Philosophy and the Scottish Enlightenment: Reception, Reputation, and Legacy," in Aaron Garrett and James A. Harris (eds.), *Scottish Philosophy in the Eighteenth Century* (Oxford: Oxford University Press, 2015), I, pp. 36–76.

69. *Swift's Irish Pamphlets*, edited by Joseph McMinn (Gerrards Cross: Colin Smyth, 1991), p. 95.

70. See Patrick Kelly, "Berkeley and the Idea of a National Bank," in Daniel Carey (ed.), *Money and Political Economy in the Enlightenment* (Oxford: Voltaire Foundation, 2014), pp. 163–184.

71. Burke, *Reflections*, pp. 73, 76, 209. For the expression of Burke's "English" identity, see also "An Appeal from the New to the Old Whigs," in *Further Reflections on the Revolution in France*, edited by Daniel E. Ritchie (Indianapolis, IN: Liberty Fund, 1992), p. 77.

72. Burke, *Reflections*, pp. 15, 16, 19. See also p. 22.

73. Burke, *Reflections*, p. 85. See also pp. 28, 67, 73.

74. Burke, *Reflections*, pp. 73, 69, 65. On moral feeling, see also pp. 123, 143.

75. Burke, *Reflections*, pp. 107–108. On absolutism, see p. 114.

76. Burke, *Reflections*, p. 78.

77. Burke, *Reflections*, pp. 94, 121, 127. The accusation is made openly in Burke, "An Appeal from the New to the Old Whigs," p. 84.

78. Burke, *Reflections*, pp. 77, 94.

79. Burke, *Reflections*, p. 196. Burke was consistent in condemning the theft of Church property by the "tyrant" Henry VIII (p. 98).

80. Wolfe Tone, *An Argument*, pp. 39, 11.

81. [William Drennan], *A Letter to the Right Honorable William Pitt* (Dublin: James Moore, 1799), pp. 7, 19. Fletcher of Saltoun is quoted on pp. 31–32.

82. Martha McTier to William Drennan, postmark January 22, 1799. *The Drennan-McTier Letters*, edited by Jean Agnew, general editor Maria Luddy (Dublin: Irish Manuscripts Commission, 1999), 3 vols., II, p. 459.

CHAPTER 8

CULTURAL DEVELOPMENTS: YOUNG IRELAND *to* YEATS

David Dwan

T HE ORIGINS OF "NATIONAL FEELING" in Ireland may be difficult to trace, but according to W. B. Yeats, such sentiment was "expressed for the first time in a definite political philosophy" by a group known as "Young Ireland." Those who failed to engage with the ideas of this patriotic coterie would possess "no understanding of modern Ireland."[1] Yeats exaggerated the originality and coherence of the band of journalists and poets that gathered under the banner of the *Nation* newspaper in the 1840s: it is far from clear that an output so diverse and unsystematic as the *Nation*'s is reducible to a "definite political philosophy," even if there are clear patterns in the journal's pronouncements about politics. And as for Young Ireland's historical significance, Yeats later implied that this was an aftereffect of the way the group was commemorated—most notably, by one of its erstwhile leaders, Charles Gavan Duffy. In his various acts of fond remembrance throughout the 1880s and 1890s, Duffy often cited the judgment that "a new soul came into Ireland" with the foundation of the *Nation* newspaper; the repetition of the phrase may have bolstered a general impression of its truth.[2] Even Yeats applauded the *Nation*'s feat of soul-production and hoped to produce a similar awakening in Ireland, albeit through a more sophisticated type of art.[3] Yeats was not alone in modeling himself on the example of Young Ireland. Many of his contemporaries—from Arthur Griffith to Patrick Pearse—engaged in a frequently competitive program of emulation, and it yielded very different interpretations of Young Ireland's principles. This chapter examines the group's more important ideas and their contested legacy in Ireland.

The legacy pointed in two distinct but not irreconcilable directions. Though the Young Ireland rebellion of 1848 was a risible failure, the group successfully rekindled, for some, a tradition of physical force republicanism that stretched back to the United Irishmen of the 1790s. However, the Young Irelanders were also credited with the invention of a particular form of cultural or—as Patrick Pearse would have it—"spiritual" nationalism. If Theobald Wolfe Tone was the evangel of "political" nationalism for Pearse, the Young Irelander Thomas Davis—whose early and sudden death in 1845 facilitated his swift beatification—was the first modern Irishman to view the nation as "a spiritual unity."[4] The nation's spiritual attributes were—perhaps, by definition—difficult to pin down, but they were reflected and sustained by a "body of traditions" and by the possession of a common language (Pearse made much of Davis's assertion that a "people without a language of its own is only half a nation").[5] On the eve of his own rebellion in 1916, Pearse insisted that political and spiritual forms of nationalism were co-dependent—"true political independence requires spiritual and intellectual independence as its basis"—but he had earlier maintained that they were largely independent objectives.[6] In 1905, for instance, he declared that the "language movement" was more important than the "political movement" and insisted that "political autonomy ... is not, in itself, an essential of nationality."[7]

Subsequent interpreters of nationalism would continue to make a strong distinction between its political and cultural forms—understandably so, as the differences are in some ways trivially apparent. Words like "politics" or "culture" connote different practices and institutional settings: most people can tell the difference between a parliament and a playhouse and the discursive rules and pragmatic function that characterize both. But attempts to produce a more ideologically substantive dividing line between political and cultural nationalisms in Ireland have proved problematic.[8] Such efforts often beg the question about what politics is, or they overlook some of the political reasons behind the turn to culture. This chapter explores the political logic behind key cultural movements from the 1840s to 1916. The logic is by no means unitary and is, I shall argue, a response to different things: the advent of popular sovereignty and the attendant need to give a cultural form to the notion of a sovereign people; the search for a cultural salve to democratic factionalism and to older habits of sectarian hatred; the need to instill civic virtues in an increasingly commercial age. But if cultural nationalism represents an aesthetic approach to political questions, this transfiguration has a political meaning: it reflects the fact that modern political institutions and social structures can no longer adequately house an ancient tradition of politics—a tradition that is, I shall argue, broadly republican. Under Young Ireland, republicanism increasingly assumes an aesthetic form. It does so partly because modern society can no longer fully actualize this vision of politics. This shortfall would be viewed by some as indictment of modern society; for others, of course, it merely exposed the wrongheadedness of such politics.

I. AESTHETIC REPUBLICANISM

Thomas Davis may have been the first man, in Patrick Pearse's eyes, to assert "the spiritual fact of nationality."[9] Yet Davis would trace his spiritual conception of nationality (a nation, as he put it, is a "spiritual essence") back to Edmund Burke.[10] Indeed, on many issues the Young Irelanders were far from being radical innovators. For a start, much of the *Nation*'s initial policies and rhetorical tactics depended heavily on Daniel O'Connell and his preexisting campaign for repeal of the Act of Union.[11] Moreover, the paper's celebrated fusion of politics and poetry had several precedents: a similar type of experiment had been attempted by the United Irishmen and later by Thomas Moore (a figure denounced by Young Ireland as a sellout, even as his melodies were enthusiastically mimicked).[12] Ten years before the foundation of the *Nation* (launched in October 1842) the *Dublin Penny Journal* had hoped to foster an inclusive sense of nationality and to sink party divisions by focusing on the country's cultural achievements. The *Dublin University Magazine* also championed a distinctive Irish culture, although its message was interestingly mixed: it called for the "repeal of the literary union" in its first issue, but some of its contributors continued to insist that true civilization in Ireland was "substantially English."[13] Moreover, Young Ireland's enthusiasm for Irish antiquities reflected a much greater antiquarian revival sparked off, in part, by the Ordinance Survey Project and the pioneering work of George Petrie, John O'Donovan, and Eugene O'Curry.

So the *Nation*, as Roy Foster has put it, "did not spring out of a vacuum."[14] The nationalism of Young Ireland was, in fact, a self-consciously commemorative enterprise and repeatedly hearkened back to the Volunteers of the 1780s and the United Irishmen of the 1790s. But even though the United Irishmen drew much of their inspiration from the French Revolution of 1789, the Young Irelanders were highly ambivalent about this epochal event. The group was eventually swept up in the revolutionary enthusiasm of 1848, staging their own shambolic uprising in July of that year. Before this, however, Young Ireland had tried to dissociate themselves from charges of being a "French Party" ("We are Irish, and Irish alone").[15] Both Duffy and Davis, in particular, were suspicious of the abstraction and universal scope of the *Droits des Hommes* (in a speech to the Historical Society of Trinity College, Davis emphasized "the utter hopelessness of universalism") and preferred to ground their claims for Irish independence on historical precedent rather than on natural right.[16] For instance, Davis traced the pedigree of Irish freedom to the Patriot Parliament of James II; he also cast "Repeal of the Union" as no more than a return to the constitutional arrangement of 1782. No Young Irelander consistently applied Davis's injunction against universals—who coherently could?—but it informed their distrust of French abstraction and British pretensions to global dominion. For similar reasons, they shrank from grandiose schemes of cosmopolitan benevolence ("We like not the cosmopolitans who, in embracing universal mankind, forget their closer affinity with their country").[17] Even O'Connell's criticisms of slavery exemplified the moral hazards of global philanthropy in Young Ireland's eyes.[18]

If the politics of Young Ireland were aggressively particularist, they were also decidedly republican. The group ransacked the idioms of an earlier patriot tradition, endlessly emphasizing the need for civic virtue and political friendship to defeat the dark forces of corruption.[19] The group's obsessive emphasis on unity went hand in hand with diatribes against faction and party. However, when accused of being a faction themselves in their quarrels with O'Connell, Young Ireland emphasized another strand of republican thought: namely, the need for vigilance and the value of civil dissension ("it was a safeguard against apathy and social torpor").[20] The *Nation*'s weekly indictments of both individual and collective slavery can seem extravagant in retrospect, but it was also a conventional motif of republican rhetoric. In this tradition, slaves—and enslaved countries— were pitiable not because they were necessarily ill-treated but because they were dependent on the will of another. As the *Nation* explained: "It is the condition of *receiving laws*, bad or good, at the hands of another, that makes the true description, essence and proper difference of servitude."[21] Young Ireland's emphasis on martial ardor and its furious defense of the citizen's right to bear arms was also self-consciously republican.[22] Much of the sword-waving was purely verbal, and they initially endorsed O'Connell's prioritization of moral over physical force. Here, at least, the message was clear: "We want no swords."[23] But Young Ireland's eventual split with O'Connell over the question of violence was not simply a question of strategy: war was a forum for the virtues, and to fight for one's country was an intrinsically noble act. O'Connell's total injunction against bloodshed was not simply impolitic, it was immoral. Young Ireland's belief in the moral substance of conflict was clearly set out by Davis—often cast as the most pacific of the Young Irelanders—in his article "The Morality of War."[24] According to John Mitchel, wars and revolutions were "the truest moral force" and were "needed to purify and vivify a comatose world."[25]

The ostentatious republicanism of the Young Irelanders destabilizes some standard oppositions drawn between eighteenth-century patriotism and nineteenth-century nationalism—a historical rationalization of earlier efforts to distinguish between civic and ethnic nationalisms. The magic mist of romanticism is sometimes held accountable for the fall from a civic-minded patriotism to an ethnically oriented nationalism, but, in practice, ethnic and civic attitudes were never perfectly discrete: patriot accounts of "English liberty" or the "French Disease" (absolutism) could breed their own type of chauvinism and often fused ethnic (a vague concept in its own right) and civic properties. Nonetheless, Young Ireland is frequently linked with a nationalist fall into ethnicity—a fact that betrays, for some, the Germanic origins of the group's nationalism.[26] But there is very little evidence to suggest that Young Ireland got its bearings from German Romantics.

Nor is the ethnic question clear-cut. Thomas Davis could recycle clichés of Saxon perfidy and Celtic virtue as fluently as any other bigot: his poem "Celts and Saxons" begins with a spasm of contempt ("We hate the Saxon and the Dane, / We hate the Norman men"), but it also longs for a moment when "every race and creed / Might be by love combined." Ultimately, it explicitly disavows a racial or sectarian basis for patriotism: "We heed not blood, nor creed, nor clan," once Ireland's cause is served.[27] This inclusive message (for those serving the cause) was endlessly repeated in the *Nation* and would prove to be one of its most enduring attractions to later bands of patriots.

This is not to suggest that no disjunctions exist between eighteenth-century patriotism and nineteenth-century nationalism, but the difference has as much to do with the advent of popular sovereignty as it has with nineteenth-century racism. Edmund Burke famously mocked conceptions of the people under the Revolution: a people, he argued, was a product of political association, not its legitimizing condition.[28] Be that as it may, the increasing emphasis on the "people" or the "nation" as the source of the state's legitimacy raised questions about who the people or nation were, independently of the political institutions that they would authorize or overturn. So although Davis may have tried to derive legitimacy from specific, historical parliaments, he also attempted to base it on a unitary people that was independent of all parliaments. This partly explains Young Ireland's cultural (or what some might call "ethnic") emphasis: it was a fraught attempt to give historical substance to a juridical fiction, namely, the people. The aim was to become "a nation once again," but its rediscovery was indistinguishable from its invention—a fact partly acknowledged by the *Nation*'s own mission statement ("to create and to foster public opinion" in Ireland) or the title of one of Davis's articles: "We want a history."[29]

Young Ireland's cultural program also reflected their belief that democracy was the imminent political future of Europe. Alexis de Tocqueville had made this prediction throughout the 1830s, while Daniel O'Connell's extraordinary experiments in mass mobilization had struck many commentators as a democratic dawn. But O'Connellism vindicated all the classical objections to democracy in the eyes of some: it was an intrinsically factional form of politics that cast the many against the few—a particularly worrying prospect in Ireland, where huge economic disparities were accompanied by religious differences. Protestant oligarchy, as Burke had argued, was no monument to religious inclusiveness; nonetheless, the defenders of Anglican interests in the *Dublin University Magazine* repeatedly worried about the illiberal features of democratic trends: "In Ireland alone, the more democratic its political predilections are found to be, the more undisguised is its religious intolerance."[30] The Anglican divine, Samuel O'Sullivan, was a particularly virulent critic of O'Connell's mobilization of the masses: "*that* democracy, being ferociously anti-Anglican and anti-protestant; and *for all purposes of evil* under the influence of the Popish priests."[31] In 1844 the editor of the

Dublin University Magazine, Charles Lever, insisted that there "never was a people less disposed to democracy than the Irish"—a form of wishful thinking that was also played out in his novels, where neofeudal loyalties occasionally prevail over the "democrat and the destroyer."[32] Isaac Butt—later to become leader of the Home Rule party—was deeply concerned about the prospect of political and social revolution in Ireland; he was adamant that "an intolerant and bigoted democracy would be the inevitable result of Repeal of the Union."[33]

The Protestant Thomas Davis was a firm advocate of Repeal, but he also worried about becoming "a tool of Catholic Ascendancy, while apparently the enemy of British domination."[34] His emphasis on literary and artistic nationality needs to be situated in this context: it was a fraught attempt to forge a common sense of Irishness that would transcend the sectarian rancor that had been the bane of Ireland's past and threatened to undermine its political future.[35] His investment in the solidarity-bestowing effect of culture was also an attempt to resist wider problems of social fragmentation in a democratic age. Davis outlined the problem in apocalyptic terms: "on the shore of democracy is a monstrous danger—the violence and forwardness of selfish men, regardful only of physical comfort, ready to sacrifice to it all sentiments—the generous, the pious, the just ... till general corruption, anarchy, despotism, and moral darkness shall re-barbarise the earth."[36] Equality, according to its critics, eroded hierarchical forms of solidarity built on deference and *noblesse oblige*, but it did little in itself to produce alternative forms of fellowship. According to the *Dublin University Magazine*, Tocqueville had effectively shown that democracy kills "sympathy."[37] The attendant result was a dangerous individualism—a blinkered preoccupation with private concerns at the expense of the public freedom on which all personal liberties depended. For this reason, Davis placed a strong emphasis on civic education, explicitly calling on the advice of the "great man" (Tocqueville): "if you would qualify Democracy for power, 'you must purify their morals and warm their faith, if that be possible.'"[38]

Davis's resistance to individualism was also reflected in his attacks on "Benthamism"—a pretty elastic term for a host of evils.[39] This partly explains Irish nationalist interest in a number of British ideologues—from the Young England group (from which the initially mocking ascription "Young Ireland" was derived) to Thomas Carlyle ("the profoundest of living philosophers"), who had fulminated for years against the "Benthamee species."[40] Thus, many of the standard objections to Bentham in England reappeared in the *Nation*: that he was a narrow rationalist, offensively dismissive of sentiment; that he recognized no intrinsic goods outside of pleasure itself and was thus as philistine as he was amoral; that his approach to politics was ahistorical and naively universalistic; that he consequently had no sense of how national character might dictate or constrain policy.[41] The Young Irelanders also associated Benthamism with the harsher aspects of political economy—although up to and even during the Famine, they were as skeptical of state-sponsored welfare programs as any card-carrying Benthamite (the Irish

Poor Law, for instance, converted "the whole population of the country into paupers, by taking away the produce of their labour and giving it to idlers").[42] The attacks on individualism could also degenerate into a simple-minded anglophobia. Mitchel repeatedly upbraided English civilization with idioms supplied by Carlyle, "the ultimate idea of English civilization being that 'the sole nexus between man and man is the cash payment.'"[43] Echoing Carlyle's frequent invocations of Native Americans, Mitchel insisted that Thomas Davis would "rather have been a Cherokee than English."[44] It could certainly sound that way at times: "Oh, no! oh, no!" Davis cried out, "ask us not to copy English vice, and darkness, and misery, and impiety; give us the worst wigwam in Ireland and a dry potato rather than Anglicize us."[45]

Underneath the histrionic chauvinism was a serious point about the moral substance of politics: the object of government was not simply to generate material well-being, but to secure, in broad terms, "the good." For Young Ireland, it was a disastrous loss of perspective to conflate the good with pleasure, wealth, or even peace. Many contemporaries would conclude the same, but some were also prepared to accept that the relationship between individual endeavor and the attainment of the good was extremely indirect—thanks to an invisible but helpful hand, public well-being was often judged to be better secured by the individual's pursuit of self-interest rather than through concerted benevolence. However, Young Ireland was highly reluctant to surrender the direct connection between the good individual and the public good—a link lived out in a life of virtuous citizenship. If, as Pearse maintained, the Latin word "*virtus*" summed up Davis's career, then many of the Young Irelanders were similarly committed to a very Roman concept of valor.[46] Unfortunately, this civic and distinctly martial ethos was not easily accommodated in the contemporary world: modern states were large, centralized, and representative; warfare was highly specialized and delegated to professional armies; political economy—denounced by Mitchel as "the creed and gospel of England"—was in key respects the new science of politics and involved a specialized knowledge not easily attained by even the most ardent citizen.[47] Indeed, the most basic principles of modern social organization—namely, the specialization and delegation of function—could make the cult of the citizen-soldier seem sadly anachronistic, lending republican principles a peculiarly romantic cast.

Young Ireland made significant attempts to convert their ideals of citizenship into a practical reality: they sponsored a policy of decentralization and local government; they made less promising bids for the revival of a militia. But much of this zeal culminated in a type of toy-soldiery and a bellicose poetry that sometimes seemed like a sublimation of politics rather than an expression of citizenship. Young Ireland yearned for the country's economic advancement, and the commercial benefits of independence were repeatedly stressed. Yet the values of republican virtue and commercial well-being were sometimes cast as a stark either–or, culminating in the joyless primitivism of Davis—an Ireland of wigwams and potatoes. Indeed, the group's obsession with political virtue could itself seem apolitical in a commercial age, not least in the ways that it failed to acknowledge the economic limits of politics. The *Nation's* explanation of the Famine, for instance, was extremely crass: it was divine retribution for "a national sin," namely, dependence on a foreign ruler.[48] But in the face of mass hunger, the Young Irelanders made some strides to promulgate an *Irish* form of political economy. This proposal, according to its critics, was as implausible as an "Irish mathematics or Irish astronomy": political economy was a science and *qua* science its "truths are of universal application."[49] In Young Ireland's eyes, however, the methods of political economy did not apply universally and had to be attuned to the historical circumstances of specific countries. To this extent they anticipated the principles of the historical school of economics championed by the professor of jurisprudence and political economy at Queen's, Cliffe Leslie, and the Trinity professor John Kells Ingram—who had sympathized with the cause of Young Ireland in his ardent youth. The *Nation* also sponsored a policy of protectionism, drawing heavily on Butt's economic writings to do so. The system of self-preference—in which the Irish were encouraged to buy Irish products—was, perhaps, a useful way of healing the rift between virtue and commerce. But, not everyone, as we shall see, was convinced by this pragmatic synthesis.

II. YOUNG IRELAND ONCE AGAIN

In a speech to the Young Ireland Society in the Rotunda in January 1885, the returned exile John O'Leary admitted that the Young Irelanders had in some senses "done nothing." They did not achieve Irish freedom, "they did not even disestablish a Church"; nor did they "get a Land Act." But they had bequeathed a moral and literary example to Ireland, which made the achievements of later groups seem paltry. "The Fenian movement," in O'Leary's estimate, "did comparatively little for Irish literature and the Land League one has done far less."[50] This assessment seriously overlooked the significance of his Fenian colleague Charles Kickham—after all, Kickham's *Knocknagow* (1873) was the most widely read novel in Ireland in the late nineteenth century. But partly through the auspices of O'Leary, who traced "all that was Irish" in himself to Davis, and partly due to Gavan Duffy's commemorative program, which began in the 1880s—the Irish literary revival initially started off as a revival of Young Irelandism.[51] As Yeats put it, the "Ireland of Mitchel and Davis had returned."[52] Yeats joined the Young Ireland Society in 1885 and featured prominently in *Poems and Ballads of Young Ireland* (1888)—a collection dedicated to O'Leary and containing a number of other patriot-poets from John Todhunter and Katherine Tynan to Ellen O'Leary and T. W. Rolleston. The volume also contains a pugnacious contribution from Douglas Hyde ("Different from the Saxon / We are men of other minds").[53] In

1892 Hyde preached the famous "Necessity of de-Anglicising Ireland" and pro-ceeded to found the Gaelic League in the following year.

Yeats—who would always remain ignorant of Irish—was keen to defend the principle of a "national literature, which shall be none the less Irish in spirit from being English in language."[54] Moreover, over time he sympathized with those who would call for "the de-Davisisation of literature" (though he distanced him-self from such proposals when they were first voiced) and grew increasingly im-patient with the legacy or, indeed, "wreckage of Young Irelandism."[55] The most obvious grounds of dissatisfaction were aesthetic. Davis was a lackluster poet, and Yeats was not afraid of saying so ("it was I alone," he later boasted, "who found certain flaws in Thomas Davis").[56] As such poems as "September 1913" or "Easter 1916" make clear, Yeats was a stridently political poet, but his quarrels with Young Ireland often saw him defending the autonomy and intrinsic value of art against its political co-option. However, he also tried to outflank the group's patriotism, suggesting it was not radical or inclusive enough: Young Ireland's cult of "the good citizen" was, he intimated in 1899, a tepid middle-class ethos.[57] The citizen and the bourgeois had struck some republicans (namely, Rousseau) as distinct and even antagonistic entities—a tension Yeats preserved by showing how they had been so thoroughly conflated by Young Ireland.[58] The phrase "good citi-zen" could thus operate, for Yeats, as both a bohemian and a patriotic slur.

Here he capitalized on the mood of the times. If Yeats was inclined to exagger-ate the popular disillusionment with constitutional politics after the fall of Charles Parnell and the breakup of the Home Rule party, criticisms of conventional poli-ticking were certainly common in nationalist circles throughout the 1890s.[59] Pat-rick Pearse dismissed the Irish Parliamentary Party as a vast "Anglicising agency," while Arthur Griffith—editor of the *United Irishman* and future founder of Sinn Féin—exulted in the fact that every day "Parliamentarianism is becoming more discredited by [those] whom it befooled for over twenty years."[60] This could make the meaning and basic location of both politics and citizenship appear quite elusive—a fact that would also worry figures like Griffith. But it was a situation that Yeats exploited to the full, allowing him to play the anti-political aesthete and the nationalist radical in the same breath. In an interview in 1902, he insisted that the Parnellite split had "removed the air of romance that had gathered round Parliamentary politics." He regarded the "fading of romance" as a good thing: it had "liberated all the other pent-up forces of the nation."[61] He also supplied some telling analogies: the parliamentarian John Redmond continued the political tra-dition of O'Connell, while the Irish literary revival maintained the cultural em-phasis of Young Ireland.

So Yeats would repeatedly avow and disavow the influence of Young Ireland throughout his career. To a Protestant poet, and to some extent a Londoner, op-erating in a country in which Catholicism was sometimes conflated with Irishness (D. P. Moran put it bluntly in 1901: "the Irish *Nation* is *de facto* a Catholic nation"), the inclusive character of Young Ireland's nationalism had a deep appeal: its thought may have been "artificial," but it was also "synthetic" in the best sense.[62] Yeats applauded the group's communitarian vision of social life—they were "not separated men; they spoke or tried to speak out of a people to a people; behind them stretched the generations"—and he initially shared their hostility to individualism or "the greed and pride of the counting-house."[63] He also cast the war between virtue and commerce as a battle between two civilizations: his ambition was to "transmute the anti English passion into a passion of hatred against the vulgarity of a materialism whereon England founds her worst life & the whole life that she sends us."[64] Indeed, if Davis advocated a scorched-earth policy of wigwams and potatoes to secure republican virtue from luxury and corruption, Yeats was only too happy to declare Ireland "a primitive country."[65] But it was a country inhabited by Arnoldian Celts rather than Young Ireland's Cherokees: a people engaged in "a futile revolt against the despotism of fact" and a "necessary revolt against political and moral materialism."[66]

Yeats's portraits of a "romantic and spiritual" people reflect his ambition to fuse his patriotism with wider metaphysical commitments: broadly, a Neoplatonic idealism whereby the patriotic campaign against "materialism" led ultimately beyond the pseudo-realities of the physical world.[67] Thus the Irish combined "love of the Unseen Life and love of country."[68] Yeats also sponsored a metaphysical theory of unity—a unity so perfect that it transcended (in his Neoplatonic moments) all plurality or temporal and spatial difference.[69] This exacting theory of integration was not perhaps the most promising model for terrestrial forms of association, but it informed his social views as much as it did his art. "I always rouse myself to work," he wrote in 1909, "by imagining an Ireland as much a unity in thought and feeling as ancient Greece and Rome and Egypt."[70] He was acutely aware that this form of cohesion—or what contemporaries would call "mechanical solidarity" or "solidarity by similarities"—strained against some basic features of modern social organization, most notably the modern division of labor and function.[71] Civilization, he admitted, replicated itself "by division like certain low forms of life," destroying in the process its own conditions of unity, while also depriving individuals of a coherent sense of themselves.[72] In these circumstances, he regarded Ireland's uneven economic development as a relative boon.

Yeats's interest in Young Ireland is thus bound up with his obsessive quest for unity. The group had produced an inspiring model of a national community unified in its pursuit of a common good. The social and moral coherence presupposed by this model was its great attraction, but it could also seem naïve, deeply at odds with the complexity of the contemporary world, or what Yeats identified as "the leprosy of the modern—tepid emotions and many aims."[73] Primitivism sustained his hopes, but Yeats gradually conceded that the country lacked the preconditions for even Young Ireland's version of patriotism. This was because modern nations were not communities of "feeling and thought"; they lacked, therefore, the type of solidarity enjoyed, in Yeats's mind at least, by traditional societies. Here "Unity of Being," organized around some shared set of principles, was no longer possible. Modern states, it seemed, were too populous and too complicated to allow for anything more than the most basic agreement on what should operate as a common good. To insist on a more thoroughgoing moral consensus was foolish or authoritarian or both. The ideals of Young Ireland were a "conscious simplification" of social existence and could "only perish or create a tyranny."[74] Yeats was not necessarily opposed to tyrannical solutions to modern problems (in 1933 "he found himself constantly urging the despotic rule of the educated classes as the only end to our troubles").[75] But against coercive forms of nationalism, he often adopted a liberal position. Young Ireland's model of nationhood, he concluded, was an outdated and illiberal dream.[76]

In the face of oppressive forms of unity, Yeats increasingly emphasized the civic value of discord. Division, he insisted in 1904, was the sign of a nation's health, for it was not "natural for any country to be united." Such unity, he insisted, precluded "individuality of thought," and in his various defenses of this principle—particularly during the controversy surrounding the plays of his colleague J. M. Synge—he adopted an aggressively iconoclastic and individualistic pose.[77] His new delight in autonomy and conflict was bolstered by his reading of Nietzsche, but it also owed something to the local climate. Griffith's *United Irishman* had published several articles outlining the need for independent thinking in Ireland, while the pugnacious editor of the *Leader*, D. P. Moran, repeatedly emphasized the need for dissent.[78] As Moran put it:

> Uniformity is soul-destroying, and leaves more than half the faculties of a man dormant. It is in strife of all kinds that men are drawn out for what they are worth; and free play of strife and competition is an essential condition if we are to get the greatest net energy out of any community.[79]

Moran was a glaring embodiment of this agonism. His newspaper supplied Ireland with a new lexicon of offense—involving Sourfaces (usually Loyal Protestants), Shoneens (apes of English ways), or West Britons (a related species of ape)—in the name of "national self-criticism."[80] Nor would Yeats escape derision: "he is a bigot who thinks he is broadminded; a prig who thinks he is cultured; he does not understand Ireland."[81]

Moran was the scourge of misty-eyed patriots and repeatedly rebuked the "spirit-wearing flow of romances about '48 and '98 and other periods, in all of which, of course, Ireland was painted spotless white."[82] "Sentiment" and "sentimentality" were excoriated; the "plain, unvarnished truth" was esteemed.[83] He was dismissive of Wolfe Tone and the entire physical force tradition: "rebel clap-trap" about fighting for Ireland entirely overlooked the complexity and technological sophistication of modern warfare.[84] His invocation of Edmund Burke in this context was particularly revealing: Irish people needed reminding that the days of chivalry were gone. Moran took particular pains to emphasize the second part of Burke's ruminations about a lost age—"That of sophisters, economists and calculators has succeeded."[85] At first glance Moran seems to be restaging Mitchel's war against Mammon—"For many years the Irish nation has been breaking up before the inexorable forces of political economy"—but his general point was to stress the irresistibility of these economic forces.[86] According to Moran, "the age of economics has come," but it was a fact lost on Ireland's advanced patriots.[87] The pursuit of "heroic politics" in the country had led to a dangerous neglect of economic science and allowed backwardness to be miscast as virtue.[88]

Young Ireland's criticisms of political economy (before and despite its sponsorship of an Irish version) were an attempt to assert the priority of political virtue over the secondary values of economic husbandry, but Moran inverted these priorities. He did so under the broad auspices of nationality, insisting that this was something independent of politics: "From the great error that Nationality is politics a sea of corruption has sprung."[89] In Moran's eyes, Young Ireland were naïve sponsors of heroic politics or "large-hearted, well-intentioned fools."[90] Moran commended the group's inclusive concept of nationhood: "No one wants to fall out with Davis' comprehensive idea of the Irish people as a composite race drawn from various sources they like."[91] Yet there was a significant caveat: "The foundation of Ireland is the Gael, and the Gael must be the element that absorbs."[92] And although Davis may have enthused over the Irish language, he was clearly not enthusiastic enough. Moran condemned Young Ireland's sponsorship of "a mongrel thing which they called Irish literature, in the English language."[93] Arthur Griffith was incensed by Moran's attacks and condemned his sectarianism, his linguistic fundamentalism, and his denigration of politics. Moran and his ilk may "cry 'no politics,' but they mean no nationalism." Moreover, in their cynical assaults on nationalism's cult of the hero, they failed to see that "an Irish Ireland means an heroic Ireland."[94]

Griffith was a born-again Young Irelander.[95] He derived the title of his own newspaper from Mitchel and published editions of the writing of Mitchel, Davis, Thomas Francis Meagher, and Michael Doheny. Against those who would query the value of what he called "Davisism," Griffith insisted that "everything National during the past forty years from Fenianism ... to the present revival owed its inspiration to Davis."[96] Indeed, in the Treaty debates of 1921–1922, Griffith presented Davis as "the prophet who [he] followed throughout [his] life," and in his endorsement of the Treaty, he claimed to be "following Thomas Davis still."[97] Like Davis, Griffith was a critic of utilitarianism, universal benevolence, and the "barbarous fetish of cosmopolitanism."[98] He was a strong advocate of active citizenship, sustained by programs of political education in which the modern newspaper played an important role. He was an enthusiast of martial valor (though he was highly skeptical about the prospects of armed insurrection against England) and placed a republican emphasis on individual and collective self-dependence.

Griffith's economic model was consequently autarchic: drawing on the economic theories of Friedrich List and Henry Carey, he argued that national industry vouchsafed by protective tariffs would thrive in an independent Ireland. This theory of economic self-help had much in common with the *Leader*'s program—indeed, Griffith's journal repeatedly condemned Moran for "having stolen all its ideas on an Irish industrial revival and the de-Anglicisation of Ireland."[99]

The system of economic self-preference was perhaps a useful means of integrating virtue with commerce, although it also risked conflating them, allowing mercenary values to masquerade as republican ideals. The logic of such policies was vividly set out by the outfitting specialist T. J. Loughlin, in the advertising sections of *An Claidheamh Soluis* and the *Leader*: here the consumption of "Irish Poplin Scarfs, Irish-Made Shirts, Irish Hosiery, Irish-Made Football Jerseys" was extolled as "practical patriotism."[100] However, the philosophy of practical patriotism struck some interpreters as wildly impractical—it expressed an autarchic fantasy that overlooked the intrinsically cosmopolitan features of capitalism; according to others, it was cynically complicit with capitalist injustices. As Fred Ryan argued, there was nothing intrinsically virtuous about "Irish millionaires and Irish factory-hells." Moran may have preached "the necessity of inducing Irishmen to buy sweated-made suits at 21s each because the employers who profit by them are Irish," but he revealed his "intellectual barrenness" when he cast this as a general panacea for Ireland.[101] Indeed, Ryan repeatedly criticized the shallowness of contemporary nationalist thought:

> Nationalism to the majority of people in Ireland merely means the hoisting of the Green Flag in place of the Union Jack over a society resting on a basis of competitive capitalism differing in no vital or essential particular from any other such society or from our own condition now.[102]

The mature Yeats was no socialist, and his famous critique of a meanly acquisitive Ireland in "September 1913"—a poem published during the famous industrial dispute known as the "Lockout"—could apply to grasping workers as much as it did to selfish owners. But by invoking the patriotic largesse of men like Wolfe Tone and Robert Emmet, Yeats, nevertheless, raised salient questions about the health of republicanism in modern Ireland. Surveying the different brands of Irish patriotism in his *Memoirs*, he had found much of it wanting: "Neither the grammars of the Gaelic League nor the industrialism of the *Leader*, nor the attacks on the Irish Party in *Sinn Féin* give any sensible image for the affections."[103] For all of its errors, Young Ireland had supplied Ireland with these inspirational images—symbols "vivid enough to follow men on to the scaffold." The group had constructed a crude but effective "model of the nation"—a type of "moral diagram" that had served as a basis for committed citizenship. According to Yeats's estimate, the Irish literary revival "began by trying to do the same thing in a more profound and enduring way."[104] But events like the death of Synge—and his ugly manhandling by the nationalist press—appeared to indicate that the revival had stalled. Indeed, by 1909 Yeats was convinced that national feeling was dying. Over time he situated the reasons for this demise in a wider theory of social change: since the fall of Parnell, Irish society was increasingly dominated by a Catholic middle class—a class that mixed a dogmatic piety with a mean acquisitiveness. Adding "halfpence to the pence / And prayer to shivering prayer," these hucksters had destroyed romance in Ireland—or so Yeats informed readers of the unionist *Irish Times* in September 1913.[105]

III. CONCLUSION

Yeats's famous lament for a lost Ireland ("Romantic Ireland's dead and gone") entrenched perceptions of nationalism as essentially a romantic credo.[106] The description implies a sense of high principle but also—tacitly for its adherents, explicitly for its critics—an attendant impracticality or cognitive indiscipline (even Yeats identifies the romantic outlook as a type of delirium). The abstract contrast between virtue and commerce, which sustains "September 1913," adds to this sense of romantic exorbitance. Similarly bald contrasts between idealism and materialism were staple features of Young Ireland's polemic, even if in practice the group was firmly committed to Ireland's economic advancement. It is hardly a surprise, therefore, that Yeats chose to model "September 1913" around aspects of Davis's "Green above the Red," thus re-enacting a form of high-minded patriotism while simultaneously declaring it to be dead. Romantic nationalism, at least as Yeats presents it, is a self-consciously anachronistic force; if it survives at all, it does so primarily as an aesthetic artifact—namely, the poem itself—and less as a viable form of politics. The practical object of "September 1913" is a testimony to this atrophy: the memory of violent revolution now services a bid for an art gallery on the Liffey, not an assault on Dublin Castle. But the events of Easter 1916 would significantly complicate the picture. Yeats deemed the Rising an act of "heroic lunacy," but he also believed that it had made the refrain of "September 1913" ring false: Romantic Ireland, it now appeared, was alive and kicking.[107] Toward the end of his life, Yeats wondered whether his own works had provided the ideological fuel for 1916—a speculation that some critics have taken seriously, seeing in the event itself and in nationalism more generally a dangerous conflation of aesthetics and politics.[108]

"Romantic nationalism" is the name given to this aestheticized politics, and Young Ireland are often credited with its invention—at least in an Irish context. The activities of this group may easily be labeled "romantic," triggering all the value judgments that have inhered in that word since the eighteenth century (it has served as another term for the atavistic, sentimental, imaginative, and false). But such labels can also beg the question of the politics they ostensibly describe—depriving it of political rationality before analysis of its content has really started.

I have argued that the politics that issued from Young Ireland was an intellectually creditable form of republicanism, but it was also a republicanism in crisis. The discourse of civic virtue was difficult to integrate with the realities of modern commerce; primitivism—Spartan, Cherokee, or Celtic—was not much of a solution, whereas autarchy could seem economically naïve or morally impoverished. The realities of making a living in the modern world pulled against the ethos of political participation, as did the representative and centralized nature of modern government. Moreover, the professionalization of the arts of politics and of war could make the days of the citizen-soldier seem like a distant dream.

Figures like Patrick Pearse—for whom no dream, perhaps, was too distant—would take succor from the appearance of the Irish Volunteers in 1913 and even from the mass mobilization of World War I ("Heroism has come back to the earth").[109] Pearse wanted "to see any and every body of Irish citizens armed," convinced, as he was, that the right to bear arms was a fundamental condition of citizenship.[110] After all, "a citizen who cannot vindicate his citizenship," Pearse insisted, "is a contradiction in terms."[111] But this would remain the problem: despite the continuous luster of guns in Ireland, republican citizenship proved difficult to practice in a functionally differentiated world. "Cultural nationalism" was an expression of the problem as well as an attempt to mitigate it: it was a synthetic ethos, which fused—promisingly in the eyes of some, disastrously in the estimate of others—two ostensibly distinct types of function: one aesthetic, the other political. It re-energized republican citizenship by giving it a refracted expression in the domain of civil society rather than in particular institutions of the state. Yeats spelled out the practical values of this strategy in 1904:

> A political movement can only give occupation to some two or three thousand of the people of a nation. The others can only join an organization and subscribe a little money. But a movement like that of Irish Ireland and the intellectual awakening of the people gives occupation to every man and woman and child in the country.[112]

So the civic values sponsored by Young Ireland and reanimated during the Irish Literary Revival had, it would seem, an immense impact. Yeats viewed this as an intellectual awakening, but he would eventually regard the cult of Young Ireland as a type of dogmatic slumber.

FURTHER READING

As I argue above, the pedigree and ideological constitution of cultural nationalism is far from straightforward, but the most ambitious attempt to treat it as both a coherent and distinct type of nationalism is John Hutchinson's *The Dynamics of Cultural Nationalism: The Gaelic Revival and the Creation of the Irish Free State* (London: Allen and Unwin, 1987). See also David Dwan, *The Great Community: Culture and Nationalism in Ireland* (Dublin: Field Day, 2008). An influential account of Young Ireland, which focuses in detail on the group's conflicts with Daniel O'Connell, is Richard Davis's *The Young Ireland Movement* (Dublin: Gill and Macmillan, 1987). There are also several studies of individual Young Irelanders. For assessments of Davis, see John Molony, *A Soul Came into Ireland: Thomas Davis 1814–45* (Dublin: Geography Publications, 1995) and Helen Mulvey, *Thomas Davis and Ireland: A Biographical Sketch* (Washington, DC: Catholic University of America Press, 2003). For a treatment of Dillon, see Brendan O'Cathaoir, *John Blake Dillon, Young Irelander* (Dublin: Irish Academic Press, 1990). A good introduction to Mitchel's views may be found in James Quinn's *John Mitchel* (Dublin: University College Dublin Press, 2008). See also Bryan P. McGovern, *John Mitchel: Irish Nationalist, Southern Secessionist* (Knoxville: University of Tennessee Press, 2009). For a recent study of McGee, see David A. Wilson, *Thomas Darcy McGee*, 2 vols. (Montreal and Kingston: McGill-Queen's University Press, 2008–2011). William Smith O'Brien's involvement is discussed in Robert Sloan's *William Smith O'Brien and the Young Irelander Rebellion of 1848* (Dublin: Four Courts Press, 2001). For a discussion of the group's lurch toward revolution, see Christine Kinealy, *Repeal and Revolution: 1848 in Ireland* (Manchester: Manchester University Press, 2009). There are several overviews of cultural movements from Young Ireland to Yeats, but among the most useful are Malcolm Brown's *The Politics of Irish Literature* (London: Allen and Unwin, 1972) and Roy Foster's *Words Alone: Yeats and His Inheritances* (Oxford: Oxford University Press, 2011). Foster's *W. B. Yeats: A Life*, 2 vols. (Oxford: Oxford University Press, 1997–2003) provides an excellent sense of Yeats's political and cultural contexts. On the political significance of drama see his recent *Vivid Faces: The Revolutionary Generation in Ireland* (London: Allen Lane, 2014), particularly chapter 3.

NOTES

1. W. B. Yeats, *Uncollected Prose*, edited by John P. Frayne and Colton Johnson (London: Macmillan, 1970–75), 2 vols., II, p. 33.

2. Charles Gavan Duffy, *Young Ireland: A Fragment of Irish History, 1840–1850* (London: Cassell, Petter, Galpin and Co., 1880), p. iii; Charles Gavan Duffy, *My Life in Two Hemispheres* (London: Macmillan, 1898), 2 vols., vol. I, p. 69.

3. Yeats, *Uncollected Prose*, II, p. 223.

4. Patrick Pearse, *The Coming Revolution: The Political Writings and Speeches of Patrick Pearse* (Cork: Mercier Press, 2012), p. 239.

5. Pearse, *The Coming Revolution*, p. 240; Thomas Davis, *Essays Literary and Historical* (Dundalk: Dungalgan Press, 1914), p. 98.

6. Pearse, *The Coming Revolution*, p. 235.

7. Quoted in Ruth Dudley Edwards, *Patrick Pearse: The Triumph of Failure* (London: Gollancz, 1977), pp. 70–71.

8. Hutchinson believes that cultural nationalists have "a politics," but he insists—somewhat confusingly—that it is "very different from that of the political nationalist." See John Hutchinson, *The Dynamics of Cultural Nationalism* (London: Allen and Unwin, 1987), p. 15.

9. Pearse, *Political Writings*, p. 240.

10. *Nation*, December 17, 1842. Burke had insisted that a nation was a "moral essence," not a purely "geographical arrangement." See Edmund Burke, *The Writings and Speeches of Edmund Burke. Volume 9. 1: The Revolutionary War, 1794–1797, II: Ireland*, edited by Paul Langford, R. B. McDowell, and William B. Todd (Oxford: Clarendon, 1991), p. 253.

11. For an account of Young Ireland that largely concentrates on its fractious relationship with O'Connell, see Richard Davis, *The Young Ireland Movement* (Dublin: Gill and Macmillan, 1987).

12. For an appraisal of Moore, see the *Nation*, October 29, 1842. On the United Irishmen's cultural pursuits, see Mary Helen Thuente, *The Harp Re-Strung* (Syracuse, NY: University of Syracuse, 1994).

13. *Dublin University Magazine*, January 1833, p. 41; *Dublin University Magazine*, March 1937, p. 369.

14. Roy Foster, *Words Alone: Yeats and His Inheritances* (Oxford: Oxford University Press, 2012), p. 67.

15. *Nation*, February 4, 1843.

16. Davis, *Essays*, p. 35.

17. *Nation*, September 2, 1843.

18. For more on these debates, see Maurice O'Connell, "O'Connell, Young Ireland, and Negro Slavery," *Thought* 64: 2 (1989), pp. 130–136.

19. For a fuller account of this, see David Dwan, *The Great Community: Culture and Nationalism in Ireland* (Dublin: Field Day, 2008), chapter 2.

20. *Nation*, April 13, 1844.

21. *Nation*, July 25, 1846 [*Nation*'s emphasis].

22. See the *Nation*'s attacks on "The Slaves Disarming Bill," May 6, 1843, or "The Philistine Bill," July 1, 1843.

23. *Nation*, October 15, 1842.

24. *Nation*, June 10, 1843.

25. John Mitchel, *Jail Journal* (New York: Press of The Citizen, 1854), p. 109.

26. See Joep Leerssen, *Remembrance and Imagination: Patterns in the Historical and Literary Representation of Ireland in the Nineteenth Century* (Cork: Cork University Press, 1996), p. 22.

27. Thomas Davis, *The Poems of Thomas Davis* (Dublin: James Duffy, 1846), pp. 27–28.

28. Edmund Burke, *The Works of the Right Honourable Edmund Burke* (London: Bohn, 1854–1889), 8 vols., III, p. 96.

29. Davis, *Poems*, p. 73; *Nation*, October 14, 1843.

30. *Dublin University Magazine*, April 1838, p. 526.

31. *Dublin University Magazine*, April 1841, p. 509.

32. *Dublin University Magazine*, November 1844, p. 509; Charles Lever, *The Martin's of Cro' Martin* (London: Chapman and Hall, 1859), 2 vols., II, p. 446.

33. *Dublin University Magazine*, April 1847, p. 515.

34. Charles Gavan Duffy, *A Short Life of Thomas Davis* (London: T. Fisher Unwin, 1895), p. 194.

35. Davis, *Essays*, p. 367.

36. Davis, *Essays*, p. 45.

37. *Dublin University Magazine*, November 1840, pp. 555–556.

38. Davis, *Essays*, p. 367. Here Davis drew on the introduction of Tocqueville's *Democracy in America*.

39. Daniel O'Connell, however, had declared himself a "humble disciple of the immortal Bentham." See Jeremy Bentham, *The Works of Jeremy Bentham*, edited by John Bowring (Edinburgh: William Tate, 1838–1843), 11 vols., X, p. 594. Quoted in James E. Crimmins, "Jeremy Bentham and Daniel O'Connell: Their Correspondence and Radical Alliance, 1828–1831," *Historical Journal* 40: 2 (June 1997), p. 368.

40. *Nation*, October 29, 1842; Thomas Carlyle, *Chartism* (London: James Fraser, second ed., 1840), p. 92.

41. See Dwan, *The Great Community*, pp. 40–50.

42. *Nation*, November 26, 1842.

43. Mitchel, *Last Conquest*, p. 117.

44. Mitchel, *Last Conquest*, p. 85.

45. Davis, *Essays*, 75.

46. Pearse, *Political Writings*, p. 257.

47. John Mitchel, *The Last Conquest of Ireland (Perhaps)*, edited by Patrick Maume (Dublin: University College Dublin Press, 2005), p. 107.

48. *Nation*, February 6, 1847.

49. W. N. Hancock, "On the Economic Views of Bishop Berkeley and Mr. Butt, with Respect to the Theory that a Nation May Gain by the Compulsory Use of Native Manufacturers," *Transactions of the Dublin Statistical Society* (1847–1849), p. 3. Quoted in Thomas A. Boylan and Timothy P. Foley, "A Nation Perishing of Political Economy?" in Chris Morash and Richard Hayes (eds.), *New Perspectives on the Famine*, (Dublin: Irish Academic Press, 1996), pp. 138–150, p. 139. J. A. Lawson, "On Commercial Panics," *Transactions of the Dublin Statistical Society* (1847–1849), p. 3. Also quoted in Boylan and Foley, "A Nation Perishing," p. 139.

50. *Freeman's Journal*, January 20, 1885.

51. John O'Leary, *Recollections of Fenians and Fenianism* (London: Downey and Co., 1896), 2 vols., I, p. 3.

52. W. B. Yeats, *Memoirs*, edited by Denis Donoghue (London: Macmillan, 1972), p. 58.

53. W. B. Yeats and John O'Leary (eds.), *Poems and Ballads of Young Ireland* (Dublin: Gill and Son, 1888), p. 78.

54. Yeats, *Uncollected Prose*, II, p. 255.

55. John Eglinton, *Bards and Saints* (Dublin: Maunsel and Co., 1906), pp. 36–43. For Yeats's initial criticisms of Eglinton, see *Uncollected Prose*, II, pp. 255–260.

56. W. B. Yeats, *Tribute to Thomas Davis* (Cork: Cork University Press, 1947), p. 12.

57. Yeats, *Uncollected Prose*, II, p. 185.

58. Jean-Jacques Rousseau, *The Social Contract and Later Political Writings*, edited and translated by Victor Gourevitch (Cambridge, Cambridge University Press, 1999), p. 51.

59. Yeats, *Uncollected Prose*, II, p. 320.

60. *An Claidheamh Soluis*, October 19, 1901. Quoted in Joost Augusteijn, *Patrick Pearse: The Making of a Revolutionary* (Basingstoke: Palgrave, 2010), p. 222. *United Irishman*, February 3, 1900.

61. Yeats, *Uncollected Prose*, II, p. 288.

62. *Leader*, July 27, 1901. Cited in Conor Cruise O'Brien, *Ancestral Voices: Religion and Nationalism in Ireland* (Chicago: University of Chicago Press, 1994), p. 59; Yeats, *Memoirs*, pp. 53, 180.

63. W. B. Yeats, *Essays and Introductions* (London: Macmillan, 1969), p. 353.

64. W. B. Yeats, *The Collected Letters of W. B. Yeats. Volume 2: 1896–1900*, edited by Warwick Gould, John Kelly, and Deirdre Toomey (Oxford: Oxford University Press, 1997), p. 537.

65. Yeats, *Uncollected Prose*, I, p. 258.

66. Yeats, *Uncollected Prose*, II, p. 91.

67. Yeats, *Uncollected Prose*, II, p. 159.

68. Yeats, *Essays and Introductions*, p. 204.

69. For a fuller account, see David Dwan, "Yeats's Thought," in Edward Larrissy (ed.), *Irish Writers and Their Time: B. Yeats* (Dublin: Irish Academic Press, 2010), pp. 109–126.

70. Yeats, *Memoirs*, p. 251.

71. Emile Durkheim, *The Division of Labour in Society*, translated by H. D. Hall (Houndmills, Basingstoke and London, 1984), pp. 31–67.

72. W. B. Yeats, *Autobiographies* (London: Macmillan, 1955), p. 194.

73. Yeats, *Uncollected Prose*, I, p. 104.

74. Yeats, *Memoirs*, pp. 250–251.

75. Letter to Olivia Shakespear, July 13, 1933, Yeats, *Collected Letters*, Accession letter 5915, Oxford University Press (InteLex Electronic Edition), 2002.

76. Yeats, *Memoirs*, p. 251.

77. W. B. Yeats, "Four Lectures by W. B. Yeats," edited by Richard Londraville, in Warwick Gould (ed.), *Yeats Annual No. 8* (Houndmills, Basingstoke, and London: Macmillan, 1991), p. 105.

78. See "A Plea for Independence of Thought," *United Irishman*, April 28, 1900; or "The Need for Independent Thinking in Ireland," *United Irishman*, June 8, 1901.

79. D. P. Moran, *The Philosophy of Irish Ireland*, edited by Patrick Maume (Dublin: University College Dublin Press, 2006), pp. 77–78.

80. Moran, *Philosophy of Irish Ireland*, p. 79.

81. *Leader*, July, 27, 1901. Quoted in O'Brien, *Ancestral Voices*, p. 59.

82. Moran, *Philosophy of Irish Ireland*, p. 102.

83. Moran, *Philosophy of Irish Ireland*, pp. 85, 84, 83, 72.

84. Moran, *Philosophy of Irish Ireland*, p. 19.

85. Moran, *Philosophy of Irish Ireland*, pp. 13–14.

86. Moran, *Philosophy of Irish Ireland*, p. 21.

87. Moran, *Philosophy of Irish Ireland*, p. 15.

88. Moran, *Philosophy of Irish Ireland*, p. 76.

89. Moran, *Philosophy of Irish Ireland*, p. 99.

90. Moran, *Philosophy of Irish Ireland*, p. 40.

91. Moran, *Philosophy of Irish Ireland*, p. 36.

92. Moran, *Philosophy of Irish Ireland*, p. 37.

93. Moran, *Philosophy of Irish Ireland*, p. 43.

94. *United Irishman*, June 8, 1901.

95. See Patrick Maume, "Young Ireland, Arthur Griffith, and Republican Ideology: The Question of Continuity," *Eire-Ireland* 34: 2 (1999), pp. 155–174.

96. *United Irishman*, September 14, 1901.

97. Quoted in Michael Tierney, "Thomas Davis: 1814–45," *Studies: An Irish Quarterly Review* 34: 135 (1945), p. 301.

98. *United Irishman*, October 5, 1901.

99. *United Irishman*, December 21, 1901.

100. Quoted in John Scally and Claire Nally, *Advertising, Literature and Print Culture in Ireland* (London: Palgrave, 2012), p. 42.

101. *United Irishman*, May 4, 1901.

102. Frederick Ryan, "Young Ireland and Liberal Ideas," *Dana* 1: 2 (1904), p. 64.

103. Yeats, *Memoirs*, p. 184.

104. Yeats, *Memoirs*, p. 184.

105. See W. B. Yeats, "Romance in Ireland (On Reading Much of the Correspondence against the Art Gallery)," *Irish Times*, September 8, 1913. The poem was later titled "September 1913."

106. Yeats, "Romance in Ireland."

107. Yeats to Lady Gregory, May 9, 1916, *Collected Letters*, Accession letter 2945, Oxford University Press (InteLex Electronic Edition), 2002. He commented on the anachronistic features of "September 1913" in a note added to the poem in 1916. See Yeats, *Poems*, p. 820.

108. Yeats wondered about his own impact on the Rising in "The Man and the Echo," *Poems*, p. 632. See, in particular, Conor Cruise O'Brien, *States of Ireland* (London: Hutchinson, 1972), pp. 48–64; *Irish Times*, August 22, 1975; *Ancestral Voices*, pp. 61–72.

109. Pearse, *Political Writings*, p. 169.

110. Pearse, *Political Writings*, p. 84.

111. Pearse, *Political Writings*, p. 155.

112. Yeats, *Uncollected Prose*, vol. II, p. 326.

CHAPTER 9

IRISH MODERNISM *and* ITS LEGACIES

Lauren Arrington

T HE IRISH REVIVAL LAID THE foundations for the emergence of a simultaneously local and cosmopolitan literature that emerged during the formation of the modern Irish nation-state and in its aftermath. Partitioned, nominally free but not completely independent, the question of what Ireland was, and who the Irish were, was as politically charged as ever. Writers developed new, often abstract, forms of expression as a means of responding to political and cultural instability. The most recent scholarship on Irish Modernism has addressed the collaboration of writers and other artists and emphasizes the interrelationship of literature with the visual and plastic arts.[1] This chapter focuses exclusively on literary Modernism, which includes a range of techniques and movements, from impressionism to expressionism, symbolism to surrealism. In their classic study, *Modernism: a Guide to European Literature, 1890–1930*, Bradbury and MacFarlane argue that "the Modernist writer is not simply the artist set free, but the artist under specific, apparently historical strain."[2] Locating that particular historical strain is essential to understanding the way that Irish Modernism operates. In the *Oxford Handbook of Global Modernisms* (2010), Ireland is never considered in its own right but is mentioned alongside "postcolonial nations," including Jamaica, "Trinidad, Africa [*sic*], and India."[3] Such arguments ignore the complex historical relationship between Britain and Ireland, which is most accurately considered in imperial and not in colonial terms. A more nuanced understanding of the relationship between Ireland and the British Empire allows stylistic affinities between Irish writers with very different politics to surface; similarities between Irish and British writers also come into view. Such an approach illustrates how Irish Modernism is distinct from and interrelated to transnational literary Modernism.

Among the Irish Revival's most important innovations was the creation of cultural activities and literary forms in which the nation, as it was aesthetically rendered, could accommodate divergent and even antagonistic attitudes to politics and class. The Abbey Theatre is exemplary in this regard. The theater's first directors, W. B. Yeats, Lady Gregory, and Edward Martyn, asserted in their manifesto for the Irish Literary Theatre a "freedom to experiment which is not found in theatres of England" and their ambition to carry out "a work that is outside all the political questions that divide us."[4] Yet from the beginning of the enterprise, there was a tension between high culture and popular will. This could be sublimated for periods of time, but it surfaced in important flashpoints, such as the famous riots over J. M. Synge's *The Playboy of the Western World* in 1907, which W. B. Yeats believed were symptomatic of narrow-minded cultural nationalism. Yeats's growing disenchantment with the legacies of the Revival precipitated a shift in his poetic style, beginning with *The Green Helmet and Other Poems* (1910). This disillusionment increased over the next decade, culminating in a sense of alienation from Irish political and cultural life, as the new Irish Free State enshrined conservative Catholic orthodoxy in its policies.

Other Modernists experienced a similar sense of alienation and disillusionment with the culture and politics of the Irish state, and many were driven abroad by a sense of claustrophobia. For the most part, Yeats remained in Ireland throughout his life, although he stayed intermittently in England and Italy, and the relationships that he formed abroad with musicians, dancers, designers, and fellow poets were essential to his changing style. James Joyce and Samuel Beckett are Ireland's most famous literary émigrés, but avant-garde networks in London and Paris were equally important to the work of the poet Thomas MacGreevy; the novelist Liam O'Flaherty; and, of course, the novelist and short-story writer Elizabeth Bowen, who is more often considered to be a British author than an Irish one. Writers who remained in Ireland developed cryptic and even parodic experiments in subject and form, which reached their zenith in the plays of Denis Johnston and the novels of Flann O'Brien.

Scholars generally regard a focus on the city as a characteristic of Modernist writing. This concentration was shaped, in part, by Joyce, whose *Dubliners* (1914) and *Ulysses* (1922) transformed the cityscape into palimpsests of meaning, layering private and public histories in a new epic form. Yet the city as a defining characteristic of Modernism is problematic when considering other Irish experimental writing of the 1910s and 1920s, in which rural landscapes are prevalent. Apart from the eruption in Dublin of the 1916 Easter Rising, it was in the Irish countryside that sudden cultural change was most keenly felt. The concentrated wealth and power of the landed estates was destabilized; the Anglo-Irish and the Irish Civil Wars fractured the countryside, and modernization brought stark changes to the vast pre-industrial landscape.[5] As will be shown, Yeats and Bowen both responded through their literature to the destabilization of the Anglo-Irish class and consequent questions of identity. Yeats moved further into abstraction, using images and archetypes to encode his political philosophies and to impose a sense of order on the disturbed landscape of the west of Ireland. O'Flaherty, who at first glance appears to be the antithesis of Yeats and Bowen, uses landscape similarly in his most experimental novel, *The Black Soul* (1924).

The Black Soul interrogates the gap between modernity and the lives of the Irish peasantry. The novel is set on the island of Inverara, a fictional representation of Inis Mór in the Aran Islands, where O'Flaherty was born and brought up. His protagonist, The Stranger (a phrase that is the vernacular for a visitor to the islands as well as an anticipation of Camus's *L'Étranger*) has traveled to the island to seek answers to the existential questions that have been provoked by his experience of war on the Western Front. The psychological trauma of the returning soldier, also explored in such British Modernist fiction as Rebecca West's *The Return of the Soldier* (1918) and Virginia Woolf's *Mrs Dalloway* (1925), is doubly suppressed in the Irish subject because of the hostility and outright aggression that many returning Irish soldiers faced. O'Flaherty's outcast Stranger attempts to repress his experience of the war, but—in an important rejection of the Revivalist pastoral—O'Flaherty uses the rural landscape to evoke the traumatic event:

> He listened for a full minute, breathing gently, perfectly motionless. In that minute he felt that he was a pure soul being judged by wicked demons. Then his mouth gaped as the picture of the night he was buried by a shell in France flashed before his mind. A cormorant called dismally passing over the house. He listened to the swishing wings.... He gasped and his eyeballs started. As he ran headlong forward, fantastic visions crowded into his mind. He saw millions of dying men, worlds falling to pieces, continents being hurled into the air, while he himself wandered among the chaos, the only living atom in the wrecked universe.[6]

O'Flaherty's imagery here is very similar to Woolf's description in *Mrs Dalloway* of the shell-shocked Septimus Smith, who believes that an airplane, benignly advertising toffee in the sky above central London, is attempting to communicate with him: "The sparrows fluttering, rising, and falling in jagged fountains were part of the pattern."[7] The similarity in O'Flaherty and Woolf's evocation of the trauma of aerial bombardment illustrates the way that Modernist style connects writers across national boundaries and vastly different politics.

Other novels by O'Flaherty are in the realist mode, but the *Black Soul* is existentialist, Modernist, and explicitly Irish. The Stranger seeks solace from the horrors of modernity by escaping to the furthest reaches of the west to live among people whom he expects to find uncorrupted, in accordance with the Revivalist aesthetic. However, he soon learns that Inverara's inhabitants are afflicted by the same corruption, self-interest, and violence that degrade "civilization."[8] His attitude toward the peasants changes, as he disparages them for their ignorance and backwardness: "like all peasants and rustics and small townspeople, [they] loved the sensation of somebody in their village being dead or sick or murdered or accused of murder or gone mad. They did not read newspapers."[9] He perceives the peasants as having an "ape likeness," with "weak minds" and "strong bodies [that] were like crippled machines without a motive power. They were like wild beasts in a cage."[10] A strong critique of Revivalist primitivism colors the Stranger's perceptions, but his mentality is most fully explained in the context of O'Flaherty's Marxism.[11]

O'Flaherty fought as a republican in the Irish Civil War, was a founding member of the Communist Party of Ireland, and later traveled to Russia so that he could write about Bolshevism firsthand.[12] His representation of the peasantry in the *Black Soul* reflects his commitment to Marxist industrial progress. In the section of the novel titled "Summer," the Stranger finds in the brutality of nature a model for regenerating a civilization that has become "a cursed quagmire that sucked everything good into its bosom."[13] Standing by a tide pool, the Stranger watches a starfish attack a periwinkle, "slow and calculated as that of hired labourers working in a State factory."[14] The strange juxtaposition provides a model from nature for industrialization and collective action. The war has provoked a deep disillusionment, but collectivity provides at last a sense of progress: "Men, starfish, crabs, motion without purpose. But it is motion."[15] The novel ends without a resolution to the Stranger's existential crisis. Nevertheless, in the closing scene, he flees Inverara with Little Mary, a "civilized savage" who is ultimately rejected by her fellow islanders. The pair leaves—not on a traditional boat, a currach—but on a "yacht": a word that O'Flaherty uses twice at the novel's close, reinforcing a return to modernity and a rejection of the island and its backward present.

Protestant unionist Elizabeth Bowen's politics are antagonistic to Liam O'Flaherty's worldview, yet both writers use the Irish landscape to express the unspeakable or the unacknowledged, and both are also concerned with a perceived crisis of civilization and the questions of identity that are common themes of Modernist literature. Bowen's *The Last September* (1929) was her first novel to be set exclusively in Ireland, but the country is also important to her other most accomplished work, particularly *The House in Paris* (1935) and *The Heat of the Day* (1948). In those later novels, Ireland is a place that her characters go to escape—but when there, they never feel quite settled. *The Last September* is set in 1920 and deals with the rapid historical change that followed the Better Government of Ireland Act, which led to the suspension of judicial process, the introduction of martial law, and a guerilla war. County Cork, hotbed of the Irish Republican Army (IRA), is the location of her own ancestral house Bowen's Court and is the setting of the novel and its fictional Big House, Danielstown. Throughout the novel, violence seeps through the surrounding landscape, leading to the ultimate destruction of the house. Although most of the action is indirect, there is an important reference to an actual historical killing in December 1920, when a group of British Auxiliary soldiers opened fire on civilians in Cork city center, set fire to several buildings, and shot two IRA men in their beds. The event surfaces in the novel when Laurence, a visitor to Danielstown, and Gerald, an Englishman and junior officer in the British army, discuss the killing of a local man, Peter Connor, who has been shot by British soldiers in his own house. The patriarch of Danielstown, Sir Richard, is flustered by the news, but he only replies blithely: "His mother is dying. However, I suppose you must do your duty. We must remember to send up now and inquire for Mrs Michael Connor. We'll send some grapes."[16]

Bowen writes from the perspective of the Anglo-Irish landed class, but she makes clear in *The Last September* that this is not personal "opinion" but a collective "point of view."[17] The epigraph to the novel is from *Time Regained*, Proust's seventh volume of *In Search of Lost Time*: "They suffer, but their sufferings, like the sufferings of virgins and lazy people...." She leaves the sentence unfinished, but the ellipsis alludes to the conclusion of Proust's statement: "are of a kind that fecundity or work would cure." Bowen's indictment of the failures of the Ascendancy is oblique, as indicated by the epigraph and by the way that the most important political questions in the novel are raised by Lois, an adolescent and orphan living at Danielstown. She asks, for example, "What is it exactly ... that they mean by freedom?"[18] Yet Lois can only approach the idea of Ireland indirectly: "She could not conceive of her country emotionally: it was a way of living, an abstract of several landscapes, or an oblique frayed island, moored at the north but with an air of being detached and washed out west from the British coast."[19]

In *The Last September*, the landlords perceive Ireland to be anchored by the solidity of Ulster unionism, in contrast to the instability that they believe has been instigated by republican violence in the south. In *The House in Paris*, which is set ambiguously some time after the First World War, the whole country is perceived as unmoored; to the Michaelis family, "Florence had seemed less distant.... 'Abroad' was inside their compass."[20] For that family, Ireland is neither home nor abroad. The place is marked by absence and paralysis. Nature is inert—"Cork consumes its own sound: the haze remained quite silent"—and so are the people: "Aunt Violet ... [was] becoming each year more like an ageless primitive angel."[21] It is a place outside of time: "All the ticking clocks did little to time here."[22]

In *The House in Paris*, Aunt Violet and her husband, Colonel Bent, attempt to recreate in the Protestant enclave of Rushbrook the identity that they lost when their Big House was burned "in the troubles," a euphemism that allows the Bents to avoid the reality of historical and political change.[23] The Bents' newfound sense of security lacks foundation and, as Bowen suggests, is rooted in an imaginary past: "The nineteenth-century calm hanging over the colony makes the rest of Ireland a frantic or lonely dream."[24] The history of nineteenth-century Ireland with its violent land agitations and campaigns for parliamentary reform was anything but calm. Yet this history is available only to readers who are already historically informed, because Bowen refrains from directly pointing out the fallacies in the Bents' perceptions. The overriding atmosphere of repression is reinforced by Bowen's description of the Bents' new "place" as "unstrange," a neologism that hints at the Freudian *unheimlich*, the basis for the psychoanalytic uncanny: "this unstrange place was never to lose for Karen [the Bents' niece] a troubling strangeness, a disturbing repose. Marshes threaded with water, pale tufts of pampas, grey bridges, a broken tower lie for some flat miles between here and Cork."[25] The image of the marsh, neither solid ground nor waterway, underlines the Bents' untenable position.

In *The Heat of the Day*, set during the London Blitz, neutral Ireland and the question of what to do with the "white elephant" of the ancestral house, Mount Morris, provide an interlude to the war.[26] Roderick, who inherits Mount Morris and travels from London to see it, perceives that "by geographically standing outside war it appeared also to be standing outside the present," an observation that applies equally to the house and to the country.[27] To his mind, the house presents "an historic future."[28] However, this future is impeded by the perspective of his relatives who live in Ireland and are unable or unwilling to acknowledge the historical realities that led to their class's disenfranchisement. Cousin Nettie, to whom Roderick feels obligated to offer the house, psychologically transfers her traumatic experience of the end of the Ascendancy onto a failed romantic relationship, and these feelings are in turn imposed onto the landscape. Her psychological repression ultimately manifests itself in the supernatural: "Nature hated us; that was a most dangerous position to build a house in—once the fields noticed me with him, the harvests began failing, so I took to going nowhere but up and downstairs, till I met my own ghost."[29] She adds, there was "nothing to be frightened of in the garden," but even that cultivated, controlled space "has all run wild now, I dare say."[30]

Bowen uses the themes of instability and fragmentation that are common to Modernism generally to give voice to specifically Irish concerns. Because of her social class, her work as a British agent in the neutral south of Ireland during the Second World War, and the English settings of most of her other novels, critics have been reluctant to claim Bowen as a wholly Irish writer. Yet she proclaimed without qualification, "I regard myself as an Irish novelist. As long as I can remember I've been extremely conscious of being Irish—even when I was writing about very un-Irish things such as suburban life in Paris or the English seaside."[31] A close reading of Bowen's work illustrates her deep concerns with the ethics of the Anglo-Irish attitude to Ireland, which is closely related to her ideas about the ethics of the novel as a form. Bowen rejected what she regarded as the author's "preassumption" of a particular morality, and instead she demands that readers excavate the "poetic truth" from her texts.[32] In *The Heat of the Day*, Stella asks,

> Whatever has been buried, surely, corrupts? Nothing keeps innocence innocent but daylight.... Dug up again after years and laid on the mat, it's inconvenient, shocking—apart from anything else there's no place left in life for it any more. To dig up somebody else's truth for them would seem to me to be sheer malignancy; to dig up one's own, madness.[33]

Truths can be told, Bowen suggests, but only indirectly. *The Last September* ends with an epiphany, as the flames of the burning Danielstown light up the night. It is this destruction that enables the Naylors to see briefly and "too distinctly."[34]

Yeats's attitude to the Anglo-Irish class is far less nuanced in his writing than in Bowen's. Yeats shared T. S. Eliot's and Ezra Pound's elite attitudes to class and tradition, and his poetry exhibits a similar tendency in form: the use of Classical references (many of which are intended to be inaccessible to the general reader), shifting personae, and a rejection of the conventional uses of rhyme and meter. In his earliest work, which was foundational to the Irish Revival, Yeats used characters and stories from Irish folklore to represent a heroic past on which he believed the Ireland of the present day should be modeled. He hoped that by representing to urban audiences and readers the virtues that he believed were preserved in the peasantry, Irish people could recover a unique national identity. This belief worked in tandem with his early experiments in the occult. For example, in "A Dramatic Poem," which was dedicated to Lady Gregory and served as his preface to the verse play *The Shadowy Waters* (1906), he enumerates the "seven woods of Coole," from Kyle-dortha to "Dim Pairc-na-tarave, where enchanted eyes / Have seen immortal, mild, proud shadows walk." He continues, "I had not eyes like those enchanted eyes," but he is nevertheless enchanted in his dreams, where the images he has "woven" move among elemental powers.[35] Yeats believed that his poetry could be a medium for enchantment, and he collaborated with the actress and musician Florence Farr to develop methods of rhythmic recitation that would heighten his poetry's magical qualities. This is important for understanding the extent of Yeats's disenchantment with the beliefs he held so strongly in the 1890s and in the first decade of the new century.

The *Playboy* riots were a catalyst for Yeats's political and artistic disenchantment, as the audience's rejection of Synge's drama was also a rebellion against Yeats's and Gregory's authority as directors of the Abbey Theatre and as shapers of Irish cultural identity. Several poems in *The Green Helmet* (1910) reflect Yeats's anxieties about the destabilization of Anglo-Irish power. "At the Abbey Theatre" asks "Craoibhin Aoibhin" (the pen name of the founder of the Gaelic League, Douglas Hyde) to explain how to "bridle" the fickle crowd "That turns and changes like his draughty seas?" The irony of the question is reinforced by the concluding couplet, "Or is there none, most popular of men, / But when they mock us, that we mock again?" Yeats's attitude to the Abbey's insurgent audiences is expressed most directly in "On Those that Hated the *Playboy of the Western World*, 1907" from *Responsibilities* (1914). There, John Synge is figured as Don Juan whose poetic prowess—always related in Yeats's imagination to sexual power—overrides the emasculated crowd.

Out of Yeats's individual sense of alienation from the course of Irish history emerged his conviction that Irish society was detaching itself from a great tradition. He believed that this tradition had been preserved through the Anglo-Irish Ascendancy, which was symbolized by the image of the Big House. "Upon a House Shaken by the Land Agitation" from the *Green Helmet* introduces the house as the nest of inherited wisdom, "the sweet laughing eagle thoughts that grow / Where wings have memory of wings." This theme comes to the fore in the titular poem of *The Tower* (1928) and in "Meditations in Time of Civil War" from the same volume. During the 1910s and 1920s, Yeats's poetic forms became increasingly fragmented. The long poems in *The Tower* are composed of shorter movements, which reflect the fracture of the structure of society that is their subject. The first movement of "Meditations in Time of Civil War," "Ancestral Houses," opens with images of abundant nature, but as in Bowen, this is not celebrated but instead used to express a threatening wildness. Rejecting the "levelled lawns and graveled ways" that now seem tainted with violence and bitterness, the poet imagines a new beginning in the next movement, "My House," where "an ancient tower" rises up out of "An acre of stony ground." The only ornaments to adorn "My Table," the subject of the third movement, are the tools for writing and an ancient Japanese sword, which is an emblem in this poem and elsewhere in Yeats's work of a changeless tradition that is passed from one generation to the next. In the final line of that movement, the scream of Juno's peacock heralds anxieties about "My Descendants" (the fourth movement), whom the poet worries are at risk of "natural declension of the soul," involvement in politics, or miscegenation. Through the images of the peacock and the owl, symbols of governance and wisdom, the poet sets the scene for the appearance of political figures in the fifth movement, "The Road at My Door." Here Yeats uses the pejorative word "irregular," rather than "republican," to describe the first soldier who arrives: "A heavily-built Falstaffian man." However, the poet is not wholly confident in the Free State's "brown Lieutenant and his men," who next appear and are described as only "Half dressed in national uniform." The poem returns to nature in the following movement, "The Stare's Nest by My Window," but the scene is unstable: "My wall is loosening.... somewhere / A man is killed, or a house burned, / Yet no clear fact to be discerned." The final movement, "I see Phantoms of Hatred and of the Heart's Fullness and of the Coming Emptiness," ascends into phantasmagoria with clouds like "white glimmering fragments," self-obliterating images of war, rage, and vengeance. "Meditations in Time of Civil War" concludes with a retreat into the tower, where the poet weighs briefly the possibility of a life dedicated to action against a life of contemplation, and he concludes that his mind is best satisfied with "abstract joy."

Yeats's disenchantment with public life is closely related to his disenchantment with the creative act, which is the theme of "The Circus Animals' Desertion" in *Last Poems and Two Plays* (1939). As early as the *Green Helmet*, in "The Fascination of What's Difficult," Yeats expresses frustration with work that has merely "dried the sap out of my veins, and rent / Spontaneous joy and natural content / Out of my heart." Rather than the noble Pegasus that was imagined by the founders of the Abbey, the theater is figured as a carthorse "under the lash, strain, sweat and jolt / As though it dragged road metal." The harsh, modern image grates against the romantic Ireland that Yeats laments in "September 1913" is "dead and gone." Yeats sought refuge from his disappointments in spiritualism and took instruction from his communicators from the other world, many of whom appear as the voices of his poems; the volume *Michael Robartes and the Dancer* (1923) is named for one of these otherworldly personae. However, the "abstract joy" that he hoped to find in the occult was elusive, and at the end of his life, the question of his legacy, which had concerned him throughout his career, began to weigh more heavily. In "Are You Content" from *New Poems* (1938), he calls on his ancestors to judge his achievements: "Have I, that put into words, / Spoilt what old loins have sent?"

The class politics that are so strongly associated with Yeats's middle and late work do not define Irish Modernist poetics. Throughout his career, Louis MacNeice was in dialogue with Yeats, from his study *The Poetry of W. B. Yeats* (1941) to his posthumous collection *The Burning Perch* (1963). In "Budgie" from that volume, MacNeice responds to Yeats's "Lapis Lazuli" from *Last Poems* through the image of a budgerigar, twittering in his cage, self-obsessed—"'I twitter Am'"— while "the human / Race recedes and dwindles."[36] The line break disrupting "human" and "race" reinforces MacNeice's democratic poetic voice against Yeats's abstracted and aristocratic tone.[37] Another line of Yeatsian influence extends through the Modernist poetry of Denis Devlin and Brian Coffey, whose *Poems* (1930) is indebted to Yeats for its forms but which takes leave of him in important ways. Devlin and Coffey were both Catholics, so the spiritual elements of their poetry have more precise and more public meanings than the obscure private codes in Yeats's work. Coffey's "The Eternal Thought" uses the dialectical formation of Yeats's "A Dialogue of Self and Soul," but the self in Coffey's poem is a "body," a "machine giv'n to me / for the service of God."[38] Devlin is generally considered to be a superior poet to Coffey; in contrast to the overt statements of "The Eternal Thought," Devlin's "O Paltry Melancholy" combines Catholic, classical, and Irish mythologies in a way that equally echoes and subverts Yeats. Robert Graves, who with Laura Riding published the influential *A Survey of Modernist Poetry* (1927), described Devlin's work in *Poems* as indicative of a "natural intelligence," and he hoped that Devlin "would unrelate [himself] further."[39] In his account of Graves's statement, Coffey suggests that Graves's attitude of "I-distrust-and-dislike-the-Irish" was what compelled him to urge Devlin toward abstraction. Devlin resisted this advice and instead works, in Coffey's summation, "at the level of things deindividualised."[40]

Apart from Yeats and Joyce, the most important influence on Irish Modernism was Thomas MacGreevy. A close friend of Beckett and Joyce, MacGreevy was important to transatlantic Modernism and corresponded with major figures, including T. S. Eliot, Wallace Stevens, and Richard Aldington. Although he is best known for his criticism, MacGreevy was also an important poet, if not a prolific one. His single volume, *Poems* (1934) distinguished him as "a modern" whose work was praised for its "revolutionary intensity."[41] MacGreevy fought at the Somme, but this was just one of the cataclysmic events that provoked his response to what Beckett described as the "rupture of the lines of communication."[42] Wars in Ireland and wars abroad are evoked with a similar diction. The "wheeling stars" of the short poem "Nocturne," which is dedicated to Geoffrey England Taylor, second lieutenant RFA, who "Died of Wounds," resonate with the "withering world" of the poem "Autumn, 1922" about the Irish Civil War. His long poem "Crón Tráth na nDéithe," an Irish phrase that is equivalent to the German Götterdämmerung, lurches from "Nineteen-sixteen perhaps / Or fierce, frightened Black-and-Tans / Like matadors!" through the "Rain, rain" to "Remember Belgium! / You cannot pick up the / Pieces / But, oh, Phoenicians, who on blood-red seas / Came sailing." The image of the Phoenician sailor underscores the poem's similarity to "The Waste Land" and illustrates how neither MacGreevy nor Irish Modernism can be sequestered from their international contexts.

MacGreevy moved to Paris in 1927, where he was Beckett's predecessor at the École Normale Supérieure, work that enabled him to move in the vibrant expatriate circles in the city, including the coteries of important patrons, such as Richard Aldington and Nancy Cunard. MacGreevy soon became part of Joyce's inner circle. He read to him and assisted with the research for *Work in Progress*, the future *Finnegans Wake*. When Beckett arrived to take MacGreevy's place at the École, MacGreevy introduced him to Joyce, initiating a relationship that is crucial to Irish Modernism and to the history of literature in English. Although Joyce and Beckett both chose to live the rest of their lives outside of Ireland and are often considered as part of an international avant-garde, their work is nonetheless a reaction to the Irish Revival.

In *A Portrait of the Artist as a Young Man*, Stephen struggles against the "nets" of "nationality, language, religion," which he feels are the means by which Ireland attempts to hold the soul "back from flight."[43] The word "tundish"—which Stephen uses to refer to the object that the Jesuit dean, an Englishman, calls a "funnel"—is the occasion for Joyce's deep and ironic critique of the relationship of language to identity. The dean marvels, "That is a most interesting word. I must look that word up. Upon my word I must." His teacher's response makes Stephen feel a stranger in his own country and provokes a sense of dejection:

> The language in which we are speaking is his before it is mine. How different are the words *home*, *Christ*, *ale*, *master*, on his lips and on mine! I cannot speak or write these words without unrest of spirit. His language, so familiar and so foreign, will always be for me an acquired speech. I have not made or accepted its words. My voice holds them at bay. My soul frets in the shadow of his language.[44]

In an unexpected turn, Stephen learns near the novel's close that "tundish" is "English and good old blunt English too." The discovery liberates him from scholastic, religious, and cultural authority: "What did he come here for to teach us his own language or to learn it from us? Damn him one way or another!" Stephen is transformed, free to sally forth, "to forge in the smithy of my soul the uncreated conscience of my race."[45]

Beckett described Joyce's work as a "heroic achievement" but said, "I realized that I couldn't go down that same road."[46] In his essay, "Recent Irish Poetry" (1934), Beckett criticized writers' failure to respond to the "thing that happened." Other Modernists, like MacGreevy, wrote in response to identifiable cataclysmic events, but Beckett leaves the actual historical "thing" unspecified and instead describes it as "the breakdown of the object, whether historical, mythical, or spook." He makes it clear that this problem is not "peculiar to Ireland or anywhere else," but it is particularly evident in the work of writers who continued to prop up Irish Revivalism. He specifically indicted Austin Clarke, whom he sarcastically praised for his consummate command of "The fully licensed stock-in-trade from Aisling to Red Branch Bundling."[47] Clarke is also satirized in Beckett's novel *Murphy* (1935) in the thinly veiled guise of Austin Ticklepenny, whose poetry is lampooned:

> as free as a canary in the fifth foot (a cruel sacrifice for Ticklepenny hiccupped in end rimes) and at the caesura as hard and fast as his own divine flatus and otherwise bulging with as many minor beauties from the gaelic prosodoturfy as could be sucked out of a mug of Beamish's porter.[48]

Murphy is a goodbye to the Revival and all that; at the end, Murphy hopes that his ashes will be flushed down the toilet of the Abbey Theatre.

Whereas Joyce's experiments soared to greater and greater linguistic feats in the attempt to know and to communicate as much as possible, Beckett was concerned with the impossibilities of knowing and communicating. As early as his 1931 essay *Proust*, he articulated the linguistic problem:

> There is no communication because there are no vehicles of communication. Even on the rare occasions when word and gesture happened to be valid ex-

pressions of personality, they lose their significance on the passage through the cataract of the personality that is opposed to them.... The only fertile research is excavatory, immersive, a contraction of the spirit, a descent.[49]

This is the trajectory of the trilogy, *Molloy* (1951), *Malone Dies* (1951), and *The Unnamable* (1953), in which the unstable self that is the subject of Modernist writing dissolves entirely. The dissolution of the "I," Beckett's interest in the philosophy of language, and his move toward nonverbal expression in the theater lend his work to post-Modernist and post-structuralist modes of academic enquiry. However, Beckett's earlier work—such as his poem *Whoroscope* (written in response to a competition sponsored by Nancy Cunard), and his novel *Murphy*—is clearly Modernist in subject, in style, and in the contexts out of which it arose.

Beckett redefined twentieth-century theater with *Waiting for Godot* (1953), but there was also important—and often critically overlooked—experimental theater happening in Ireland in the 1920s. Although the founders of the Abbey Theatre had imagined bringing the best of European drama to the Dublin stage, the theater was limited in its repertoire because of financial pressures and its status as the national theater, with its burden of formulaic and remarkably popular peasant plays. In 1918, with financial support from the poet and novelist James Stephens and the literary historian Ernest Boyd, W. B. Yeats and Lennox Robinson organized the Dublin Drama League, which—unsubsidized and unambiguously avante-garde—would have far greater artistic freedom than the Abbey. Several actors from the Abbey company were involved, including Arthur Shields, whom Yeats and Robinson encouraged to explore expressionist techniques. Yeats also used the League to stage some of his own work; the dance plays *The Only Jealousy of Emer* and *The Cat and the Moon* were performed as a double bill in 1924. The young Modernist painter Norah McGuinness designed the costumes and masks for that production, and she danced the role of Fand in *The Only Jealousy of Emer*.[50] Working with McGuinness, who was good but was nonetheless an amateur, prompted Yeats to pursue a collaboration with Ninette de Valois, a professional with whom he established the Abbey School of Ballet at the new Peacock Theatre, which was designated as a permanent space for the Abbey's more experimental productions.

The Dublin Drama League, not restricted to Irish drama, staged avant-garde work by Ernst Toller and Eugene O'Neill, and there is evidence that Sean O'Casey attended those productions.[51] The influence of Modernist expressionist drama on O'Casey's theater is clear in his play *The Silver Tassie* (1928). The play opens in the central room of an urban family home, a setting that would be familiar to audiences of his Dublin Trilogy: *The Shadow of a Gunman* (1923), *Juno and the Paycock* (1924), and *The Plough and the Stars* (1926). The content of the first act would be equally familiar, as O'Casey mocks the religious and political pieties that compel a family to send their son to fight in the First World War. A change in style is evident near the end of the first act, when O'Casey's stage directions instruct the characters Simon, Sylvester, and Susie to speak together "You must go back," and the Voices of the Crowd Outside to echo "They must go back!"[52] This signals the play's departure from a naturalistic mode, which is wholly broken in the second act. Set "in the war zone," this scene is described as a "jagged and lacerated ruin of what was once a monastery. At back a lost wall and window are indicated by an arched piece of broken coping pointing from the left to the right, and a similar piece of masonry pointing from the right to the left."[53] This formation gives the impression of a broken proscenium, behind which are the trenches. The characters are therefore pushed out into the no-man's-land between the proscenium arch and the audience. On one side of the stage hangs a broken crucifix, damaged by an exploded shell, and "almost opposite" is a gun-wheel to which the character Barney has been tied in punishment. In the center, "where the span of the arch should be," is the "shape of a big howitzer gun." O'Casey's use of the word "shape" is another marker of anti-naturalistic theater—a far cry from the spinning wheel and pampooties that Synge sourced from the Aran Islands for the Abbey's production of *Riders to the Sea* (1904). O'Casey's setting, his use of chanting and song, the stylized movements described in the stage directions of the second act, and his symbolic use of color throughout the play situate the *Tassie* in the expressionistic Modernist theatre. Ironically, O'Casey's innovations in the *Tassie* were prompted by Yeats and Robinson's Dublin Drama League, but Yeats rejected the play for the Abbey, because he failed to understand O'Casey's technique.[54]

The Dublin Drama League was also important to the work of Denis Johnston, who made Irish theater history when his play *Shadowdance* was rejected by the Abbey Theatre, prompting him to give it the new, acerbic title *The Old Lady Says No!* Johnston uses similar techniques to O'Casey's *Tassie*: vignettes, verse, and dance; however, Johnston denied that he had written an expressionist play and preferred the term "experimental," probably an attempt at preventing the establishment of rigid generic categories that would inhibit innovation. In *Shadowdance/ The Old Lady Says No!* Johnston stages a pastiche of Irish heroes in a heavy-handed critique of the Revival. At the beginning of the play, an actor (the Speaker) who is playing the role of Robert Emmet on the night of Emmet's arrest receives a blow to the head and wakes up believing that he *is* Emmet. The Speaker/Emmet is taken on a tour of 1920s Dublin, where he meets Cathleen ni Houlihan (now hawking flowers on the street), historical figures, and abstract shadows who have come "to dance at a wake." Johnston's attack offended Yeats, mostly because Yeats believed that the eighteenth century represented the height of Anglo-Irish power and was a model for the modern nation. On reading the script, Yeats commented, "rubbish. 'cynicism' was a worn out commonplace thirty years ago."[55] Rejected by the Abbey, *The Old Lady Says No!* (1932) was staged instead by the newly formed Gate Theatre, a permanent company that was inspired by the Dublin Drama League to dedicate itself to producing experimental drama. The Dublin Drama League, the Peacock Theatre, and the Gate Theatre offer counter-histories to a narrative of

Irish drama that focuses on the Abbey, and taken together they provide a dynamic picture of Irish Modernist theater that is in dialogue with the Continental avant-garde and the experimental theaters of the United States.[56]

Another bourgeoning area of research in Irish Modernism is Irish-language literature. The popularity of Flann O'Brien's novels in English, *At Swim-Two-Birds* (1939) and *The Third Policeman* (published posthumously in 1967), means that he is one of the few Irish-language Modernists to receive widespread critical attention. His novel *An Béal Bocht* (1941), published in English as *The Poor Mouth* (1961), satirizes Irish autobiographies of poverty and hardship, exemplified in the work of Tomás Ó Criomhthain, Peig Sayers, and Muiris Ó Súilleabháin, which helped to create a post-Revival mythology of an authentic anti-modern national identity. Other important Irish-language Modernists, including Máirtín Ó Cadhain, Breandán Ó Doibhlin, and Eoighan Ó Tuairisc, are only beginning to be considered alongside Anglophone Irish Modernists.[57] As in Anglophone Irish writing, the tensions between avant-garde internationalism and local contexts are still being negotiated. In his recent essay, Louis de Paor argues that the similarities between Ó Cadhain's *Cré na Cille* (1949) and Joyce's *Ulysses* (1922) that have been noted must also take into account the way that Ó Cadhain "owes as much to the verbal jousting that is a characteristic feature of Gaeltacht culture as it does to avant-garde experimentalism."[58]

The study of Irish Modernism has much to contribute to an understanding of the forms and networks of transnational Modernism, but the terms of inclusion must be carefully scrutinized. As Pamela Caughie cautions in her introduction to *Disciplining Modernisms*, modernity as a philosophical concept is generally dated from the seventeenth century; modernity for historians generally commences in the nineteenth century, and for literary scholars, Modernism is separate from modernity and denotes an experimental style that reacts against conventional forms.[59] If these terms are not carefully defined, then Modernism becomes a useless aesthetic category and is synonymous with the modern. The writers surveyed here responded to a perceived crisis in culture through literature that exhibits the stylistic qualities of instability, contingency, and fracture. This survey is by no means exhaustive, yet by adhering strictly to this stylistic criterion, several important points are illustrated. First, not all Irish literature written after the Revival was Modernist. This is not to disparage Irish writing but instead is a comment on the variety and richness of the literature of the period. Sean O'Faolain could simultaneously publish realist novels and edit the little magazine *The Bell*, in which radically avant-garde work by the poet Freda Laughton, the novelists Elizabeth Bowen and Flann O'Brien, and painter and playwright Jack B. Yeats appeared. While Denis Johnston was being staged at the Gate Theatre, Modernist dance drama was performed in the Peacock, and realist plays set in rural Ireland were on the Abbey's main stage. Just as Irish literary histories have focused on describing a national literature that took realism and naturalism as its dominant modes, Ireland's history must not be rewritten to define Lady Gregory's plays or the novels of Katherine Cecil Thurston as Modernist, if the integrity and usefulness of Modernism as an aesthetic category is to be preserved.[60] This survey also illustrates the stylistic affinities among writers who held radically different political views. The imposition of such categories as Anglo-Irish Modernism, or the assertion that the Anglo-Irish monopolized Ireland's Modernism, elides these similarities and inhibits the inclusion of Irish Modernism in a transnational literary movement.[61] From the Irish Revival through the early years of the new state, Ireland underwent wars, class conflict, partition, and modernization, and it was these historical changes that provoked the sense of crisis and fracture to which Irish Modernism gives voice.

FURTHER READING

The most comprehensive survey to date is *The Cambridge Companion to Irish Modernism*, edited by Joe Cleary. Essays by Rónán McDonald on "The Irish Revival and Modernism" and Ben Levitas on "Modernist Experiments in Irish Theatre" are particularly useful. *The Cambridge Companion to European Modernism* (Cambridge, 2011) is important for context. For post-colonial approaches, see Mark Quigley, *Postcolonial Irish Writing and the Politics of Modern Literary Form* (New York: Fordham University Press, 2012) and Michael Rubenstein, *Public Works: Infrastructure, Irish Modernism, and the Postcolonial* (Notre Dame, IN: University of Notre Dame Press, 2010). For a post-imperial approach, see Terence Brown's "Ireland, Modernism and the 1930s" in *The Literature of Ireland: Culture and Criticism* (Cambridge: Cambridge University Press, 2010). Essays by Adrian Frazier, Terence Brown, and Vera Kreilkamp in *The Cambridge Companion to the Irish Novel* (Cambridge: Cambridge University Press, 2006) discuss Modernist themes in Irish fiction. For a study of Irish Modernists during the Second World War, including MacNeice and Bowen, see Clair Wills *That Neutral Island* (London: Faber, 2007). For a full bibliography of Irish Modernism and particular Irish Modernist writers, see my entry, "Irish Modernism" for *Oxford Bibliographies Online*.

NOTES

1. Joe Cleary (ed.), *Cambridge Companion to Irish Modernism* (Cambridge: Cambridge University Press, 2014).

2. Malcolm Bradbury and James MacFarlane (eds.), *Modernism: a Guide to European Literature 1890–1930* (London: Penguin, 1976), p. 26.

3. Eric Bulson, "Little Magazines, World Form," in Mark Wollaeger (ed.), *The Oxford Handbook of Global Modernisms* (Oxford: Oxford University Press, 2010), pp. 267–287, 269.

4. Lady Augusta Persse Gregory, *Our Irish Theatre: A Chapter of Autobiography* (London: G. P. Putnam's Sons, 1913), p. 10.

5. For Irish Modernism arising out of "uneven" development, see Joe Cleary, "Toward a Materialist-Formalist History of Twentieth-Century Irish Literature," *Boundary* 2: 31 (2004), pp. 207–241.

6. Liam O'Flaherty, *The Black Soul* (Dublin: Wolfhound, 1981 [1924]), pp. 46–47.

7. Virginia Woolf, *Mrs Dalloway* (London: Hogarth, 1929 [1925]), pp. 34–36.

8. O'Flaherty, *Black Soul*, p. 136.

9. O'Flaherty, *Black Soul*, p. 87.

10. O'Flaherty, *Black Soul*, pp. 220–228.

11. For primitivism, see Sinéad Garrigan Mattar, *Primitivism, Science, and the Irish Revival* (Oxford: Clarendon, 2004).

12. Liam O'Flaherty, *I Went to Russia* (London: Jonathan Cape, 1931).

13. O'Flaherty, *Black Soul*, p. 52.

14. O'Flaherty, *Black Soul*, p. 190.

15. O'Flaherty, *Black Soul*, p. 191.

16. Elizabeth Bowen, *The Last September* (London: Vintage, 1998 [1929]), p. 91.

17. Bowen, *Last September*, p. 92.

18. Bowen, *Last September*, p. 62.

19. Bowen, *Last September*, p. 34.

20. Elizabeth Bowen, *The House in Paris* (London: Vintage, 1998 [1935]), p. 76.

21. Bowen, *House in Paris*, pp. 72, 75.

22. Bowen, *House in Paris*, p. 81.

23. Bowen, *House in Paris*, p. 75.

24. Bowen, *House in Paris*, p. 75.

25. Bowen, *House in Paris*, p. 76.

26. Elizabeth Bowen, *The Heat of the Day* (London: Vintage, 1998 [1948]), p. 82.

27. Bowen, *Heat of the Day*, p. 50.

28. Bowen, *Heat of the Day*, p. 50.

29. Bowen, *Heat of the Day*, p. 217.

30. Bowen, *Heat of the Day*, p. 217.

31. Victoria Glendinning, *Elizabeth Bowen: Portrait of a Writer* (London: Penguin, 1977), p. 165.

32. Elizabeth Bowen, "Notes on Writing a Novel," in Hermione Lee (ed.), *The Mulberry Tree: Writings of Elizabeth Bowen* (London: Virago, 1999), pp. 35–48.

33. Bowen, *Heat of the Day*, p. 229.

34. Bowen, *Last September*, p. 206.

35. All lines from Yeats's poetry are quoted as they appear in W. B. Yeats, *The Poems*, edited by Daniel Albright (London: Everyman, 1992).

36. Tom Walker, "MacNeice's Byzantium: the Ghosts of Yeats and Eliot in *The Burning Perch*," *Review of English Studies* 62: 257 (November 2011), pp. 785–804, 788–789.

37. Walker, "MacNeice's Byzantium"; and Peter MacDonald, "Louis MacNeice: Irony and Responsibility," in Matthew Campbell (ed.), *The Cambridge Companion to Contemporary Irish Poetry* (Cambridge: Cambridge University Press, 2003), pp. 59–75, 60.

38. Brian Coffey and Denis Devlin, *Poems* (Dublin: Printed for the authors, 1930).

39. Brian Coffey, "Of Denis Devlin: Vestiges, Sentences, Presages," *Poetry Ireland Review* 75 (Winter 2002–2003), pp. 82–100, 84.

40. Ibid.

41. Susan Schreibman, *Collected Poems of Thomas MacGreevy: An Annotated Edition* (Dublin: Anna Livia, 1991), p. xx.

42. Tim Armstrong, "Muting the Klaxon: Poetry, History and Irish Modernism," in Alex Davis and Patricia Coughlan (eds.), *Modernism and Ireland: The Poetry of the 1930s* (Cork: Cork University Press, 1995), pp. 43–74, 52.

43. James Joyce, *A Portrait of the Artist as a Young Man* (London: Penguin, 1985 [1916]), p. 203.

44. Joyce, *Portrait*, pp. 188–189.

45. Joyce, *Portrait*, pp. 251, 253.

46. James Knowlson, *Damned to Fame: The Life of Samuel Beckett* (London: Bloomsbury, 1996), p. 105.

47. Samuel Beckett, "Recent Irish Poetry," in Ruby Cohn (ed.), *Disjecta: Miscellaenous Writings and a Dramatic Fragment* (London: Calder, 1983), pp. 70–76, 72–73.

48. Samuel Beckett, *Murphy* (London: Pan Books, 1973 [1935]), p. 53.

49. Samuel Beckett, *Proust and Three Dialogues with Georges Duthuit* (London: Calder, 1987 [1931]), pp. 64–65.

50. Richard Allen Cave, *Collaborations: Ninette de Valois and William Butler Yeats* (Alton: Dance Books, 2011), pp. 4–5. Louis Le Brocquy also designed scenery for the League's early productions.

51. Christopher Murray, *Seán O'Casey: Writer at Work* (Dublin: Gill and Macmillan, 2004), pp. 145, 153, 160, 191, 193.

52. Sean O'Casey, *The Silver Tassie: A Tragicomedy in Four Acts* (London: Macmillan, 1928), p. 37.

53. O'Casey, *Silver Tassie*, p. 41.

54. Carol Kleiman, *Sean O'Casey's Bridge of Vision* (Toronto: University of Toronto, 1982), pp. 8–14.

55. TS (copy of original in library of University of Victoria, BC, Canada), *Shadowdance*, Ur. B, second script (as finally rejected), annotations by Yeats, TCD MS 10066/2/4.

56. Elaine Sisson, "'A Note on What Happened': Experimental Influences on the Irish Stage: 1919–1929," *Kritika Kultura* 15 (2010), pp. 132–148.

57. Mark Quigley, *Empire's Wake: Postcolonial Irish Writing and Modern Literary Form* (New York: Fordham University Press, 2013) and Louis de Paor, "Irish Language Modernisms," in Cleary (ed.) *Cambridge Companion to Irish Modernism*, pp. 161–173.

58. De Paor, "Irish Language Modernisms," p. 168.

59. Pamela L. Caughie (ed.), *Disciplining Modernism* (Basingstoke: Palgrave, 2009).

60. For this interpretation, see Anne Forgarty, "Women and Modernism," in Cleary (ed.), *Cambridge Companion to Irish Modernism*, pp. 147–160; similarly, Cleary's construction "women's Modernism" must be interrogated.

61. For the argument that the Anglo-Irish "monopolized" Irish Modernism, see Terry Eagleton, *Heathcliff and the Great Hunger* (London: Verso, 1995), pp. 299–300.

CHAPTER 10

MEDIA *and* CULTURE *in* IRELAND, 1960–2008

Maurice Walsh

I
N 1971 BRIAN CLEEVE PUBLISHED his well-received novel, *Cry of Morning*, anatomizing "the new Irish revolution." The blurb on the cover advertised the novel as a story of "money and expensive cars and towering office blocks among the Georgian slums." It opens in a Dublin television studio crackling with tension as the countdown begins for another live edition of the popular current affairs show, *Friday at Ten*. The host, suave and handsome John Lennox, is the only person at ease under the fierce studio lights. His guests, property developers and conservationists united in enmity in a superheated space, can barely think beneath the beams, which glare with the intensity of a tropical sun. The floor manager's countdown provides Cleeve with markers to introduce the main characters and cue meticulous descriptions of the normally concealed artifice of television production—the swiveling cameramen, the whispered commands of the director, the stagehand arranging the captions. Behind his apparently confident smile, John Lennox is assessing the chances that the discussion he is about to chair will descend into a brawl too undignified even for television. At this point in the novel, Lennox is uncommitted in the controversy between development and conservation. His passion is television itself; "he believed in nothing except shadows flickering on the screen." Lennox knows that half a million people in Ireland will be tuning in to watch the discussion, partly with an inchoate hope that there will be a disaster, an unseemly row that will be the topic of conversation for weeks, but mainly because they had become enthralled by the idea that television, and *Friday at Ten* in particular, was inviting them to share the previously hidden secrets of how the world worked. "It showed you things, told you things you wouldn't have heard before television came."[1]

Although establishing the verisimilitude of the scene would have come easily to Cleeve, who when he wrote the novel was a reporter on Telefís Éireann's (RTÉ's) main current affairs program, *7 Days*, his fascination with television was not just a question of an author writing what he knew. The mystique and excitement he conjured up in his depiction of the pre-transmission studio captured something of the sense in which television in the 1960s and 1970s was a source of popular fascination and a major influence on Irish life, a force field reconfiguring other media, the practice of politics, and culture more widely. Despite the unusually lengthy disclaimer in its title pages that *Cry of Morning* was a work of pure fiction unrelated to any living person or institution, its central character, John Lennox, could not fail to remind contemporary readers of David Thornley, a dashing political scientist at Trinity College who in 1966 became RTÉ's first star political interviewer. During the lunch at which he recruited Thornley as a presenter, the producer Muiris MacConghail had overcome the academic's reservations about the ephemeral qualities of television by telling him that he must "break out of Trinity and into Ireland."[2] Television made this possible: a college magazine of the time described the "swaggering, pink-shirted" Thornley as "one of the few Trinity academics … the mention of whose name in the remoter corners of Tipperary or Cork is liable to provoke more than an uninterested grunt."[3] Handsome, debonair, and an effortless performer with a purring English accent, Thornley imagined himself as another Robin Day, but his academic training and feel for Irish politics equipped him with an authority that would never allow him to be dismissed as a mere television personality. Reflecting on his first year as a broadcaster, Thornley wrote in 1967 that although he understood the resentment of politicians who felt they were being made to seem like fools by "a mickey taking [ridiculing] interviewer who had never been elected to anything" their feelings were, in the end, "archaic." Hard questioning on television was now one of the added prices of power, Thornley argued. "The public wants information, and the excitement of confrontation; the party or TD [member of Irish parliament] who gives it to them sets the pace for others who must reluctantly follow suit."[4]

This diagnosis of a whole political style suddenly rendered obsolete by television appeared to vindicate the severe misgivings with which Ireland's leaders reluctantly accepted the arrival of the medium. To President Éamon de Valera, if he had chanced to read Thornley's article, the word "archaic," dropped with such casual judgmental finality, would have confirmed his anxieties that the new era would deliver a death sentence on the embattled cultural vitality of Ireland's revolutionary generation. In his broadcast to inaugurate the new service on New Year's Eve 1961, de Valera had delivered the remarkable confession that he felt "somewhat afraid" when he thought of television's "immense power."[5] As de Valera was associated more than any other politician with the idea of the Irish nation as a rural, anti-materialist oasis of Catholic frugality, proudly aloof from the currents of modern vulgarity, he had good reason for his anxiety. But his words were even more revealing of how Ireland embraced television not as a wondrous new toy but as a modern phenomenon that could no longer be avoided. By the late 1950s television was no longer a distant abstraction, because households along the east coast were able to receive broadcasts from the British Broadcasting Corporation (BBC). A decision was being forced on Ireland's politicians. There is a striking similarity between the arguments voiced in Ireland in the late 1950s for launching a television service and those aired in South Africa, another (radically different) cultural oasis, which waited another sixteen years before finally succumbing to television. A commission of inquiry established by the South African government in 1970 reported that it would not be possible to hold out much longer. "If, for instance, it were possible for a hostile power to transmit television programmes to South Africa via satellites," the commission argued, "South Africa could only counter this effectively by introducing its own service."[6] A similar defensive strategy seemed the most persuasive rationale to the guardians of Irish culture in 1959. If Ireland did not have its own version of the technology, the argument went, the country would end up being swamped by British stations. The sense in which this decision was regarded as an inevitable, unavoidable outcome of progress came with an implicit fear that television might not be amenable to control. Strongly advanced arguments that the new television station should be run as a private, commercial operation on the American model were overridden by a fear that Irish culture might be overwhelmed and that only state control could protect it.

There was also an attempt to convert anxiety into optimism. Rather than finally demolishing the faltering project to de-anglicize Ireland, perhaps this powerful new medium could be enlisted to revivify national culture and make it more adaptable to the modern age. And not only cultural guardians had instrumental designs on RTÉ. Television's arrival coincided with a major break with economic nationalism, the reigning orthodoxy since the revolution. Protectionism had been abandoned, and Ireland was opening up to free trade and foreign investment. Although largely indifferent to the conservative cultural idea of a Catholic, self-sufficient, and rural people, the architect of these changes, the taoiseach Sean Lemass, still had very prescriptive ideas of how television should serve his new vision of Ireland. Lemass had to be dissuaded from issuing public directives to the authority running the new service, but he drafted memos and speeches for his ministers and officials, leaving them in no doubt what he expected. Television, Lemass insisted, must cultivate the image of a vigorous and, above all, efficient Ireland, "a progressive, scientifically inclined, modern industrial nation." Social problems, he advised, should be treated "constructively," and programs should not highlight faults "under the pretext of objectivity."[7]

Lemass was certainly onto something here. His suspicion that the public-service remit of the new generation of broadcasters would entitle them to subject Ireland to documentary scrutiny rather than act as the cheerleaders for an updated, more utilitarian, version of a national ideal were well founded. Any young social critic embarking on a career in television had a powerful inspiration for such an approach: *The Bell* magazine founded by the writer Sean O'Faoláin in 1940. Although it was a literary journal that never enjoyed the reach of television, throughout its fourteen-year existence *The Bell* possessed a strong documentary strain in the widest cultural sense. Its aim was to reveal a more complex, less harmonious Irish reality than the officially sanctioned version, a republic characterized by urban-rural divides, class antagonisms, and impure enthusiasm for exotic and material foreign influences. The magazine strove to make contact with its Irish readers, to provide a forum for their actual—as opposed to their piously avowed—concerns. In its second issue, *The Bell* published under the title "I Live in a Slum" the testimony of a thirty-six-year-old man describing how, with his wife and five children, he shared a Dublin tenement house with fifty-six other people, all using the same water tap and lavatory and cooking on an open fire.[8] It was the kind of exposé that Lemass would have scorned, another indictment of the unfulfilled republic at odds with its founding ideals. But it was precisely the kind of reportage that RTÉ television would pursue in the first decade of its existence. Indeed, the kind of people who might have contributed to *The Bell*, or read it if they were old enough, were now being recruited to the national television station. They saw their job as transforming the perceptions of Irish society. Once this role was undertaken by a relatively small and venerated coterie of writers, a "cultural priesthood" on the margins of Irish society.[9] Now a much wider range of creative talents—journalists, producers, performers, actors—were being given license by the state to use one of the most powerful mediums of the twentieth century and to form a cultural priesthood in their own right.

In a perceptive survey of the changes engulfing Ireland published in 1964, before he became a broadcaster, David Thornley had registered his incredulity at the passivity exhibited by the Irish public in the face of major cultural and economic upheavals. Civil servants were rewriting economic policy so that growth, not national self-sufficiency, was the new lodestar; signs of affluence and urbanization were emerging in the wake of this historic rupture. And yet, Thornley wrote, this transformation was passing undocumented. "We are shown a country which has somehow managed to combine uniquely a revolution in its attitudes to growth and productivity with the preservation of the simple unsophisticated and familial virtues of a rural and deeply Catholic community. In fact, of course, this is nonsense. Remarkably little is known of the social breakdown of the country in which we live."[10] The first generation of television program makers saw their task as rousing the country from passivity to self-awareness. Just as the American muckrakers in the progressive era at the end of the nineteenth century believed that public knowledge of the facts would of itself be enough to cure social ills, such as municipal corruption and the abuses of big business, so the program makers in the 1960s believed that merely revealing Ireland to itself would change it for the better. Their mission, as Paul Durcan put it in another context (a poem written in admiration of the reports from Northern Ireland by the RTÉ correspondent Liam Hourican), was to "reach truth through language."[11]

Within two years of the launch of the television service, a close associate of Sean Lemass could marvel at how "a rare crew" had found a berth in RTÉ's headquarters in Montrose, a building whose design, as Chris Morash has noted, was "iconic of the quickstep modernisation and impatience with the past"[12] that characterized the era. In this case "rare" was not meant as a compliment. Neither did it describe a nucleus of Marxists or rigorous ideologues; the spread of views among the program makers was broadly liberal. Although it has by now acquired a patina of myth, the spirit animating the early days of RTÉ television was adventurous and intoxicating. The program makers were clearly enjoying themselves. Recollections of those who worked there at the time speak of an atmosphere of audacity and invention in which creatively talented people were encouraged to be as daring as they wished. Janet Moody, a researcher on 7 Days at the age of twenty-four, found that many of her colleagues were also very young, and they all possessed a sense that "we could do anything we wanted." Their sense of ambition and boldness was encouraged. "I think in many ways we wanted to sail as close to the wind as possible, that is the nature of that type of journalism ... to see how far you can go."[13] They also shared a sense that, in the words of Lelia Doolan, (a producer who would eventually resign and co-author a book on how the station's bureaucracy was killing creative vitality), "people who worked in television were in touch, in some 'universal' sense, with Irish society at large."[14]

This sophisticated approximation of de Valera's famous declaration that he only needed to look into his own heart to discover the desires of the Irish people was a sign of how power had shifted. It turned out that Lemass had been right: under the guise of objectivity and the notion that television served the public and not the state, RTÉ program makers set about a critical appraisal of institutions long accustomed to deference. There is no better illustration of the extraordinary presumptuousness of authority in Ireland at this time than the fact that the simple juxtaposition in a news bulletin of a statement by Minister for Agriculture Charles Haughey and that of the leader of farmers protesting over agricultural prices became one of the catalysts for the first major clashes between the government and the new television station. The response of Lemass was indicative of his despair at how things were turning out. In the debate in the Dáil over the controversy, he rejected the idea that RTÉ should be completely immune to government supervision. "Radio Telefís Eireann was set up by legislation as an instrument of public policy and as such is responsible to the Government."[15] It must, he argued, sustain public respect for the institutions of government.

It was not only politicians who found television inherently disrespectful. The other great source of authority in Ireland, the Catholic Church, was deeply concerned about the prevalence of unbelievers and bad Catholics among the production staff. The archbishop of Dublin, John Charles McQuaid, was a consistent meddler and critic. On-screen comments construed as critical of the church often produced days of outrage and public controversy. For traditional Catholics, the corrosive power of television was to be seen in the ruination of the customs of Marian devotion that had flourished even into the era of new prosperity. Until television, many rural families had said the rosary at home at night, and enthusiastic crowds had turned up in parish halls for lectures and slide shows on the Virgin. But by the late 1960s the director of the National Rosary Crusade, Father Gabriel Harty, had become used to gazing down on sparse audiences for his talks; the people who should have been there were "all at home watching television," he concluded bitterly.[16] Significantly, the solution traditional Catholics reached for was not a campaign against the evil influence of television but an appeal to RTÉ itself to repair the damage. "Up to now television has done immense harm to the rosary," an old IRA man from County Westmeath wrote to in a letter to the *Irish Catholic*. "If they decide now to televise the rosary every night, it would reverse the situation."[17] Father Harty concurred. The rosary would be saved for the next generation if it was shown on television. Although RTÉ's decision to reject the proposal to make the rosary part of its schedule was the subject of angry exchanges with traditionalists, the real importance of the controversy was the acceptance by Catholic activists, and gradually by the leadership of the church generally, that television had to be dealt with on its own terms. In retrospect it could even be argued that television began to dictate the terms on which the authority of the Catholic Church was communicated to the audience. Thus, of necessity, a series of clerical personalities emerged who came across well on the small screen. If nightly transmissions of the rosary were a step too far, the jovial Bishop Eamon Casey—a showman with radical views on the Third World—and Father Michael Cleary—the singing priest who was au fait with *Top of the Pops*—would do instead (the innocence of the times is illustrated by Casey's popular reputation as a wild man because of his predilection for speeding).

Both of these men became popular public figures through their appearances on the *Late Late Show*, a live, American-style, Saturday night chat show that captured enormous audiences. The compère, Gay Byrne, was an admirer of Johnny Carson and the famous American talk-show hosts—and on the strength of the show's reputation was even courted by the American networks. But the *Late Late Show*'s formula relied, not on rehearsed predictability, but on the risk of an unexpected or unruly passionate opinion. This might come from members of the audience as much as from the guests or the presenter, and entire families tuned in in ambivalent anticipation of being shocked or embarrassed. "If the *Late Late Show* had not existed," the novelist Colm Tóibín wrote, recalling staring at the screen in the presence of his parents, tense with embarrassment, "it is highly possible that many people would have lived their lives in Ireland in the twentieth century without ever having heard anyone talking about sex."[18] Gay Byrne's talent as presenter and producer lay in his ability to keep the program interesting over two hours, balancing interviews with visiting Hollywood actors, musical acts, and serious discussion about contraception or Northern Ireland. He was not a crusader like some of the program makers in RTÉ but an impresario of controversy. Tóibín observed Byrne off-screen, preparing the show, and compared him to a parish priest managing the affairs of the parish. It is an apt metaphor for the subtle—and more gradual than sometimes asserted—shift in influence between the church and not just television but the media in general.

If those working in television could regard themselves as, in John Horgan's phrase, "masters of the media universe,"[19] it did not mean that Ireland's news-papers and magazines were left behind. As managing director in the 1950s of *The Irish Press*—the newspaper founded by de Valera to represent the Fianna Fáil view, if not to be strictly speaking a party organ—Sean Lemass had subtly turned it into a mouthpiece for his arguments that Ireland should abandon import sub-stitution and open the country to free trade. The biggest-selling Irish daily, *The Irish Independent*, had replaced advertisements on its front page with news in 1961, and its sister paper, the *Sunday Independent*, introduced its first color sup-plement two years later. Gradually, lengthy coverage of bishops' pastorals and pilgrimages (on August 15, 1954, the front page of *The Sunday Press* was domi-nated by the headline "IRISH THRONG LOURDES FOR A GREAT MARIAN CLIMAX" and the report below began, "Fervently demonstrating their Faith, Irish pilgrims prayed late into the night and the early hours of yesterday morning at the Grotto here") were replaced by more racy news. When a bishop asked the new editor of the *Irish Independent*, Aidan Pender, what he was trying to do with the paper, Pender replied, "Sell it, my Lord."[20] And although the transformation of *The Irish Times* from the almost moribund house journal of Protestant union-ists into the crusading newspaper of the intelligentsia is often portrayed as an ideological shift, this too was spurred by commercial necessity. Its new editor, Douglas Gageby, recognized that the paper's survival depended on broadening its appeal to the growing employed population of working age. Advertising on radio and television was crucial to its success.

It was in this period that Gageby established his reputation as a legend of Irish journalism. A Protestant from Belfast who had served as an intelligence officer in the army of the Irish Republic ("not so much a token Protestant as a trophy Prot-estant" in the words of his colleague, James Downey),[21] his romantic nationalism and Anglophobia tended to overshadow a keen grasp for the business of journal-ism. The remarkable success of *The Irish Times* in the years he was associated with it—its circulation trebled between 1963 and 1986—was testament to his under-standing of how to offer new generations of university-educated Catholics the attractive idea that the paper was an essential guide to understanding—and align-ing themselves with—the changes sweeping Ireland. He recruited journalists whose interests were at an angle to the traditional profile of an *Irish Times* writer.

For instance, Donal Foley, who as news editor was the controlling intelligence in the daily assembly of the paper, came from the Ring Gaeltacht in County Waterford and had spent most of his time in London after emigrating at fifteen. He was intensely curious about the reforms in the Catholic Church emanating from Vatican II, the rapid expansion of education, the Irish language, and the burgeoning renewal of interest in Gaelic sports and traditional music largely fostered by television. Foley helped recruit a cadre of women who turned *The Irish Times* into a platform for the women's movement.

They were helped by Gageby's conviction that objectivity in journalism was an illusion. Not only did Gageby appear to regard women as equal to men, Maeve Binchy recalled, but he also conveyed no sense that as a reporter she was required to confine herself to merely recording debates about what was wrong with Irish society: "In our minds we did not have to restrict ourselves to talking about righting wrongs: we could get out and right them."[22] Women at the paper extended themselves beyond the women's movement. Eileen O'Brien wrote about poverty in "A Social Sort of Column." And Nell McCafferty's column, "In the Eyes of the Law," pioneered a form of court reporting that broke free of the established convention of desiccated transcription to use the dialogue of judges, witnesses, barristers, and officers of An Garda Síochána, the Irish police force, to dramatize the issues of class, poverty, and privilege. Michael Viney wrote several series on social issues in the spirit of *The Bell* or RTÉ. Reporters were given the time to develop authority about civil rights in the United States or the Cuban revolution.

Gageby's paper ("his republic" in the words of Olivia O'Leary)[23] had a reputation for being particularly welcoming to liberal views. But in an important sense, at this time journalists in Dublin across all media shared many of the same opinions and an expanded (arguably exaggerated) sense of their own mission and entitlement. They formed their own republic through a sensibility that was bohemian and literary. Maeve Binchy captured a sense of this when she wrote about her time working for Gageby. "It was a lovely time.... We could go to meet anyone we wanted to in Ireland. We didn't have to go home to our tea at six o'clock because there were always press receptions offering us drink and canapés. We had power, huge power to get things out into the open."[24] This feeling of confidence and excitement was partly a function of expanded university education. A new generation of journalists did not perceive themselves as trade stenographers drilled in convention during apprenticeships on provincial newspapers but as professionals with ideas and knowledge about politics, economics, and history. This notion that journalism offered a voice in shaping history was not only the preserve of university graduates but could also inspire people like Donal Foley, who had never been to university but who found in newspapers a place where they could pursue their intellectual curiosity. Gageby once remarked that many journalists were eccentrics and misfits, and the media scene in Ireland in the 1960s and

1970s opened up possibilities for many people who would not have thrived in conventional careers.

The Dublin media community overlapped with artistic, academic, legal, and political circles. Graduates from University College Dublin and Trinity College made friends with people who went on to become politicians and barristers. For journalists newly arrived from the provinces, life in the Dublin media was an intoxicating experience where writers, actors, television personalities, and ministers would drink and debate in the same pubs and turn up at the same parties. When the RTÉ producer Muiris MacConghail took David Thornley to lunch in a Dublin hotel to persuade him to become a television presenter in the summer of 1966, they found three government ministers, including Charles Haughey, dining in the same restaurant. Later that year after the standoff between the government and RTÉ over coverage of the farmers' protests, Haughey invited MacConghail and Thornley to a late supper in a Dublin restaurant, after which they adjourned—despite a heated argument over whether RTÉ was insulting Haughey—to the minister's mansion in north Dublin, where he invited them to inspect his wine cellar and finally sent them home, following a convivial discussion about history and painting, carrying bottles of vintage French red.[25]

The media in Ireland in the 1960s and 1970s exuded such glamor and its practitioners were so possessed by their own sense of importance that it was only toward the end of this period and into the 1980s that anything resembling a critique began. Until then, the dominant theme in cultural debate was censorship and, in particular, the restrictions imposed on RTÉ's coverage of the developing troubles in Northern Ireland under Section 31 of the Broadcasting Act of 1960. Largely ignored when the bill was first introduced, Section 31 gave the government the power to instruct the RTÉ Authority at any time to prohibit any specific broadcast it deemed to undermine the national interest. It was first invoked in September 1971, when RTÉ defied a government request not to broadcast interviews with two IRA spokesmen. The station was ordered "to refrain from broadcasting any matter that could be calculated to promote the aims or activities of any organization which engages in, promotes, encourages or advocates the attaining of any political objective by violent means."[26] RTÉ protested that this instruction was too vague but pledged to continue providing balanced coverage of the northern troubles. A little over a year later, when a reporter broadcast a detailed account of an interview he had conducted with the leader of the Provisional IRA, the government sacked the entire authority. A writer friend suggested to Taoiseach Jack Lynch that the government's critics would accuse them of restricting freedom of speech, and Lynch replied: "Fuck them."[27] A new minister, Conor Cruise O'Brien, provided some of the clarification RTÉ sought in 1974 by specifying the organizations whose members were to be banned from broadcast, most notably Sinn Féin and the IRA, but his name was forever after associated with censorship.

Until these provisions were eventually lifted in 1994 after the IRA ceasefire and the beginning of the peace process, journalists and program makers continually argued that they created a climate of self-censorship that discouraged any controversial investigations, particularly on security policy.

Beyond this persistent debate about Section 31 and some perceptive comment in television reviews, there was little serious debate about the media as a whole. Taking its cue from the work of such cultural studies pioneers as Raymond Williams and Stuart Hall, a new intellectual journal, *The Crane Bag*, devoted a series of issues to exploring the media and Irish culture in the early 1980s. A dominant theme in the articles and roundtable discussions was whether Irish audiences deferred to the new authority of television, reduced to passive consumers of its encoded values and images, or were encouraged to be active partners in a genuine cultural conversation. Luke Gibbons in particular argued strongly that both the *Late Late Show* and the popular rural serial *The Riordans* represented a significant Irish subversion of the talk show and soap formats, adapting them to local cultural idioms so that audiences were enabled to explore and reconsider their own experiences.[28] The value of public-service broadcasting and the general high quality of the Irish media were taken for granted. The next step was to extend the education of the audience about the media, so that they became not only critical consumers but also eventually active producers themselves.

By the time these discussions began, Ireland was no longer the optimistic place that had nurtured the creative dreams of the first wave of RTÉ program makers. From being a land of possibility to which emigrants like Gay Byrne returned, because "we seemed to be leaping forward,"[29] the Ireland of the 1980s had become stagnant and depressing. In the 1980s unsustainable levels of foreign debt, unemployment of almost 20%, and the relentless violence in Northern Ireland created a deep sense of crisis.[30] The popular success of a 750-page survey of Ireland's twentieth century by the historian Joe Lee—who concluded that the country's economic performance had been the worst in modern Europe and that this failure could no longer be blamed on British colonialism or partition—suggested an appetite for new thinking. The crisis spawned a vigorous discussion of Irish identity among newspaper columnists largely centered on the competing claims of modernity and traditionalism and what those terms might mean. This bitter polemical debate, in which the media in general were characterized as a metropolitan clique out of touch with the common people, was fueled by the referenda on abortion and divorce, in which Catholic traditionalists appeared to win lasting victories. It was some distance from Lelia Doolan's idea of a creative communion between program makers and Irish society. RTÉ was no longer seen as the source of innovation. This now came from magazines like *In Dublin* and *Magill*, both influenced by American traditions of new journalism, in which in-depth reportage on drug culture or the power of the Irish judiciary was combined with attention to writing.

But even as this Irish debate about media and culture had begun, an epochal international shift had occurred that would radically alter its terms. By the end of the 1970s, the foundations of a new economic model had taken hold in Britain and the United States, propagated by a self-conscious and well-funded "counterintelligentsia," who seized the opportunity presented by the successive oil crises to launch a successful assault on the welfare economies of the golden age of prosperity in the previous three decades.[31] The election of Margaret Thatcher and Ronald Reagan represented the political victory of a set of ideas that would transform public life in more ways than the obvious vogue for privatization and deregulation. In place of public service, community, and the idea of "society" (famously dismissed by Thatcher), the new intellectual ideas were about individualism, choice, free trade, and markets. These catchcries appeared incontrovertible after the fall of Communism (hence "the end of history") and were further validated by the exponential development of the internet from the mid-1990s. They provided the compass for Ireland's path out of its own crisis into an unprecedented economic boom. In the process, globalization and the creative destruction of the digital age threatened to overturn the idea of media and culture that energized the Irish 1960s.

Revisiting the attempt by *The Crane Bag* to start an evaluation of the Irish media, it is striking how little attention was paid to the launch of the *Sunday World* in 1973, Ireland's first color tabloid newspaper. It was as if Ireland was assumed to be immune to tabloid culture, even though such British Sunday papers as the *News of the World* had enjoyed healthy sales for decades. Throughout the twentieth century, the tabloid newspaper and its values had always represented not just a scandalous affront to Catholic prudery but also the worst features of vulgar materialism; Yeats regularly decried the "base idioms of the newspapers."[32] While there was no Irish equivalent, both Catholic prudes and acolytes of Raymond Williams could hold on to the belief that Irish society was predisposed to a more exalted engagement with modern communication than the masses elsewhere. The arrival of the *Sunday World* broke the spell. Marketed with the slogan "We go all the way," by the end of its first year it was selling two hundred thousand copies a week and had established itself as a success.[33] Tabloid culture could no longer be seen as an alien import. Within a decade the *World* had eaten into the sales of the *Sunday Press*, the emblematically wholesome and nationalist Sunday paper of the de Valera stable. In its own way, it was acting as a kind of force field on other media in the same way as television had done in its early years. In 1980 the editor of the *Sunday Press* urged his long-standing agony columnist, Angela McNamara, a devout Catholic whose problem page had enabled many of her devoted readers to explore confusions over their sexuality for the first time, to match the more salacious and explicit copy of the tabloids. When she refused, the column was dropped.[34]

In the face of steadily falling sales over the next decade, the broadsheet daily *Irish Press* was redesigned as a tabloid in 1988 under the guidance of British consultants, a fate that was doubly ironic. Leaving aside the de Valera connection, with its pages devoted to new fiction, incisive film, book and television criticism, and above-average sportswriting, the *Press* was arguably even more representative of the high standards of popular reading than the increasingly fashionable *Irish Times*. When this less-than-convincing metamorphosis failed to arrest the decline, the de Valera family turned first to the American newspaper magnate Ralph Ingersoll and, after a spectacular falling-out, sought investment from the Daily Mirror group (in vain). In the midst of appalling industrial relations all the *Press* newspapers shut down in 1995, never to re-open. The turmoil at the *Press* group was symptomatic of the upheaval in the newspaper industry caused by the introduction of electronic production, which opened up new opportunities for British newspapers to compete in the Irish market. The disappearance of the *Press* titles coincided with the introduction of the *Star*, a hybrid Irish-British daily produced with the latest computer technology, which, after a faltering start, turned out to be the template for other British media to enter the Irish market. Soon there was an Irish edition of *The Sun* and *The Sunday Times*. Such was the scale of the British invasion that in 1996 Tony O'Reilly, head of Independent Newspapers, wrote to the taoiseach John Bruton urging government action to protect the Irish newspapers. "If Ireland is to have an indigenous print industry, it is going to have to have support from every quarter if it is to repulse the long-term efforts of Rupert Murdoch and his lieutenants in Ireland from simply taking over the Irish media."[35] The irony of his request for protectionism was that O'Reilly himself had embarked on acquisitions that would make the Independent group not only the most powerful Irish media company but also turn him into a mini-Murdoch owning hundreds of newspapers, magazines, radio stations, and websites in Britain, South Africa, India, Australia, and New Zealand. By the beginning of the twenty-first century, the Irish media was no longer much discussed in terms of cultural values and national conversations but in reference to market share and revenue models, the language of the global media business.

In this new world, RTÉ—the crucible of Ireland's cultural redefinition for thirty years—faced even bigger challenges. Under the guise of deregulation and greater choice, Fianna Fáil Minister for Communications Ray Burke legalized commercial radio stations at the end of the 1980s and capped the amount of money RTÉ could earn from advertising. Many saw this specific constraint as an attempt to tame the broadcasters who had been so troublesome since the state had given them a platform for dissent. But the general direction of policy was part of an international trend. All across Europe deregulation spurred the creation of private television networks, fragmenting the audience for previously revered public service stations, forcing them to compete on the same terrain and thereby diluting their essential claim to be delivering a service the market could not provide. Ireland's first commercial television station, TV3, was launched in 1998 and owned by a Canadian company. The availability of cable and satellite channels across borders put further pressure on publicly funded broadcasters. Sky Sports screens now dominate in pubs throughout Ireland. In place of defending indigenous culture, popular protest in the 1990s was organized around the right to gain access to foreign television, with supporters of a campaign against the removal of illegal devices that deflected British television signals into rural homes pressing their "inalienable right" to multi-channel television.

The proliferation of television channels and twenty-four-hour news coincided with spectacular revelations of corruption and abuse scandals in politics and the church. Trails of secret bribes—most sensationally a payment of a million pounds to Charles Haughey by the supermarket tycoon Ben Dunne—offshore bank accounts, and cash-filled envelopes to fix planning applications were uncovered by judicial tribunals. The hearings provided ready-made factual drama to fill the ever-expanding hours of news coverage but raised questions as to why judges and not investigative reporters were exposing the workings of a political underworld long suspected to be flourishing. Libel laws and a culture of secrecy were significant barriers. But the further emergence of shocking stories of decades of systematic physical and sexual abuse by Catholic clergy suggested that the notion of the ascendancy since the beginning of the television era of a mercilessly probing media, fearlessly disrespectful of authority and convention, needed some revision. The first scandal to undermine the moral prestige of the Catholic Church also revealed how much it was feared by the newspaper many would have regarded as its most confident adversary.

In 1992 *The Irish Times* received a tip that the bishop of Galway, Eamon Casey, was the father of a grown child, the product of a long affair with an American woman. Even after the paper's North American correspondent had interviewed the woman and her son and convinced himself of the truth of their story, the editor Conor Brady still hesitated to publish. Partly he was concerned to obtain corroboration of the woman's story (without it he feared the bishop could just deny its truth), and he was also influenced by a culture of restraint in the Irish media about invading the private lives of public figures. But he was also wary that publication would be construed as an unfair assault by Ireland's liberal newspaper on the church. He even considered the possibility that the whole story was an attempt to trap the newspaper in a catastrophic error. Brady sought the advice of an expert on canon law to find out whether the church might have found a way to regularize the bishop's transgression of his vows of celibacy. His informant told Brady that if the story were published and turned out to be wrong, or even if it were true but the paper could not provide incontrovertible proof, "the church will destroy *The Irish Times*."[36] Before the paper was able to publish details of payments Casey had made to his former lover, the Vatican announced the bishop's resignation and the one-time star of the *Late Late Show* fled the country for a secret destination in South America.

This incident was only the beginning—and in retrospect maybe the least invidious—of a series of revelations that fatally undermined the church's moral prestige. A year after Bishop Casey disappeared in South America, the death of another *Late Late* performer, Father Michael Cleary, prompted the disclosure that the singing priest, sometimes risqué on stage but always severely doctrinaire when it came to sexual morality, had a secret family—two sons and their mother who had lived with him for twenty-six years, ostensibly as his housekeeper. Then in April 1999 RTÉ broadcast a three-part documentary by the producer Mary Raftery containing harrowing testimony from former inmates of industrial and reformatory schools, who described sadistic sexual and physical abuse inflicted on them by members of religious orders paid by the state to take custody of difficult and emotionally disturbed children from poor backgrounds. Using previously unseen archives from the Department of Education, Raftery was able to show that officials were aware of the abuse for decades but had covered up or ignored most of it. The series provoked such an outcry that before the final episode, Taoiseach Bertie Ahern apologized to victims of the abuse "for our collective failure to intervene, to detect their pain, to come to their rescue."[37] In 2002 Raftery produced another documentary for RTÉ revealing the repeated failures by Cardinal Desmond Connell and the Dublin archdiocese to control priests who were sexually abusing young children. This program led to the appointment of an official inquiry by the government.

It is striking that for all the anxiety in the 1960s about the corrosive influence of television, the Catholic Church was able to retain considerable power and guard its most egregious secrets. As many commentators pointed out, much of this abuse was hidden in plain sight; the industrial schools were well-known local landmarks in towns and cities, not closely guarded camps. When he worked at *7 Days*, Brian Cleeve, author of *Cry of Morning*, had tried to make a program about them in 1965, but after the head of the best-known institution in Artane, in Dublin, had sought prior approval of the script, the program was dropped, much to the relief of the archbishop of Dublin. Remarkably, Cleeve sought to persuade Dr. McQuaid to co-operate by explaining to the archbishop that his aim "was to combat in some small way the recent and not so recent allegations made against what was being done for these children in Ireland."[38] The Catholic Church had become so strongly associated with Irish identity that it was impregnable. Hence, during the 1980s criticism of the church was easily construed as criticism of the common people by a metropolitan elite. All the fury about an omnipotent media concealed its weakness. When the pope visited Ireland in 1979, Douglas Gageby called all *The Irish Times* journalists to his office and told them that this was a historic occasion for the people of Ireland. "I don't want any of you fashionable liberals sneering at the Pope. You will cover this seriously as the great occasion it is for the people of this country and most of our readers." It was, Olivia O' Leary noted, the only time she remembered him instructing his staff how they should write.[39]

RTÉ was, despite appearances, in the same position as *The Irish Times*. And because of its umbilical relationship with the state, it was also vulnerable to straightforward political pressure. The deeper and more pervasive constraints on the Irish media were only revealed when the church and the political classes themselves began to self-destruct. It was a commonplace of attacks on the Dublin media during the 1980s that its members formed a privileged, self-referential class of liberals intent on destroying Irish life. But the events of the past two decades suggest that the media had never been as autonomous as its reputation suggested. In 1984 the late Nuala O' Faolain, who then worked as a producer at RTÉ, remarked that the station was so implicated in Irish life that it was virtually incapable of challenging the consensus.[40] In retrospect, even the vaunted *Late Late Show* is perhaps better viewed as much as a unifier of public consensus as a challenger of traditional culture, allowing the nation to see itself in a tolerably more pleasing light. It could be both challenger and unifier at the same time. Colm Tóibín wrote that Gay Byrne had spent decades dramatizing a war between reality and perception, "between de Valera's vision of Ireland and Patrick Kavanagh's 'The Great Hunger.'"[41] But the audience was reluctant to choose, and the history of the media in Ireland shows the extent to which it could never entirely escape from the nets of self-delusion flung by its own society.

Perhaps this ambivalence also underlies Ireland's remarkable adaptability to global media. Chris Morash has noted how "startlingly fast" mobile phones, Facebook, YouTube, satellite television, and a surge in the sales of *Playboy* (only legalized in Ireland in 1996) came to be a normal part of Irish life. He suggests that the "defining feature of Irish culture in the early twenty-first century is … a deeply engrained, mediated connectedness between Ireland and the rest of the world."[42] Many traditional features of Irish culture have adapted and indeed flourished in this mediated universe. The Gaelic Athletic Association is a perfect illustration of this. Since its foundation in 1884, it had been associated with a narrow "Irish-Ireland" view of the world that was hostile to foreign (British) games and practices. In 2007, for the first time, it allowed the Irish rugby and soccer teams to play at Croke Park, its hallowed stadium in Dublin, which was the site of an infamous massacre of civilians by crown forces in 1920. The occasion of this historic shift was used to show the world media that Ireland's most modern stadium was home to its most traditional sporting organization, still successfully committed to amateurism in Gaelic hurling and football, when most elite sport is professional. Now hurley sticks are often made in Poland, Pakistan, and Taiwan, and local GAA teams have often been crucial in integrating the new wave of immigrants.

As is often the case, much of this engagement with the world is not new. In the 1920s and 1930s the GAA's nationalist principles did not get in the way of allowing British Pathe newsreels to film hurling and football matches and thus open up a new way of popularizing them with cinema audiences. Ireland was always ready for openings to the world offered by the media. Writing in *The Bell* in 1953, Anthony Cronin pointed out that Irish girls danced to same tunes as London debutantes. Obscurantism and censorship drove people to react by developing "a curious nostalgia" not for some idealized Ireland of the past but for mass entertainment pleasures they might find in Birmingham, "the vitality of the dance-hall and the dog-track, the sad gaiety of the Odeon and the skating rink."[43]

From 1961 television provided this vitality. In doing so, RTÉ played its part (with Ireland's entry into the European Economic Community in 1973) in making the Republic of Ireland seem to its citizens a more complete state than the unfinished, unrealized, and unwanted outcome of a thwarted revolution. It is remarkable that RTÉ has survived at all in the era of borderless media. Visiting Dublin in 1969 during the creative row which saw Lelia Doolan and others resign from RTÉ, Raymond Williams found the program makers he met as both Irish and international in an "authentic" sense, "deeply responsible to their own people, rather than to an Irish sector of the international market."[44] Much of Irish popular culture could now be described as the local version of a global product. The president of Ireland, Michael D. Higgins, a former minister for culture, has devoted several speeches to the need for media policy to regulate the borderless market. "A mass media characterized by the rise of large trans-national media players brings new challenges for journalists," he told an international communications conference in Dublin in 2013. "Media becomes less diverse, and less willing to challenge received wisdom or the interests of those in power, be that through direct editorial challenge or through less obvious measures."[45] Although it is under huge pressure, Irish public television can still be deeply responsive to Irish audiences; it was Mary Raftery's television documentaries on the church and child sex abuse that achieved the biggest impact. That to bring her films to the screen she had to struggle mightily with opposition within RTÉ demonstrated that public service broadcasting could still be a powerful idea when deployed by a determined program maker.

FURTHER READING

Two essential surveys of the media in modern Ireland are John Horgan, *Irish Media: A Critical History Since 1922* (London: Routledge, 2001) and Chris Morash, *A History of the Media in Ireland* (Cambridge: Cambridge University Press, 2010). The best account of the birth and development of RTÉ is found in Robert J. Savage's *Irish Television: The Political and Social Origins* (Cork: Cork University Press, 1996) and *A Loss of Innocence: Television and Irish Society 1960–72* (Manchester: Manchester University Press, 2010). John Bowman's *Window and Mirror, RTÉ Television: 1961–2011* (Cork: Collins Press, 2011) is a fascinating account benefiting from his historian's eye and insider's knowledge as one of the station's most respected current-affairs broadcasters.

Mark O' Brien has written the definitive histories of two major Irish newspapers: *The Irish Times: A History* (Dublin: Four Courts Press, 2008) and *The Truth in the News: De Valera, Fianna Fáil and the Irish Press* (Dublin: Irish Academic Press, 2001). He has also edited with Kevin Rafter a collection on Ireland's most commercially successful media group, *Independent Newspapers: A History* (Dublin: Four Courts Press, 2012). Some recent memoirs have provided insights into the social history of Irish journalism. Andrew Whittaker's collection on Douglas Gageby, *Bright, Brilliant Days: Douglas Gageby and The Irish Times* (Dublin: A & A Farmar, 2006) is full of suggestive gems. And though much concerned with institutional politics, two memoirs by senior *Irish Times* executives—Conor Brady, *Up with The Times* (Dublin: Gill and Macmillan, 2005) and James Downey, *In My Own Time: Inside Irish Politics and Society* (Dublin: Gill and Macmillan, 2009) are good on Irish journalism and politics more generally. Both Michael O' Toole, *More Kicks than Pence: A Life in Irish Journalism* (Dublin: Poolbeg Press, 1992) and John Waters, *Jiving at the Crossroads* (Belfast: Blackstaff Press, 1991) have written nonfiction *bildungsromans* about the journey from provincial Ireland to a metropolitan media life.

NOTES

1. Brian Cleeve, *Cry of Morning* (London: Corgi Books, 1972), p. 22.

2. Muiris MacConghail, "'He boxed lightly in the interviews but intended to land a punch': David Thornley at RTÉ, 1966–69," in Yseult Thornley (ed.), *Unquiet Spirit: Essays in Memory of David Thornley* (Dublin: Liberties Press, 2008), p. 115.

3. "Who is David Thornley?" in *TCD*, February 29, 1968, pp. 6–7.

4. David Thornley, "Television and Politics," *Administration* 15: 3 (Autumn 1967), pp. 219–220.

5. Quoted in Robert J Savage, *A Loss of Innocence? Television and Irish Society 1960–72* (Manchester: Manchester University Press, 2010), p. 52.

6. *Report of the Commission of Inquiry into Matters Relating to Television to the State President of the Republic of South Africa* (Pretoria: Government Printer, 1971), p. 1.

7. John Horgan, *Broadcasting and Public Life: RTÉ News and Current Affairs 1926–1997* (Dublin: Four Courts Press, 2004), p. 28.

8. Kelly Matthews, "'Something Solid to Put Your Heels On': Representation and Transformation in *The Bell*," *Éire-Ireland* 46: 1&2 (Spring/Summer 2011), p. 111. For an excellent account of the magazine's history, see Kelly Matthews, *The Bell Magazine and the Representation of Irish Identity: Opening Windows* (Dublin: Four Courts Press, 2012).

9. Matthews, "'Something Solid to Put Your Heels On,'" p. 112.

10. David Thornley, "Ireland: The End of an Era?" in Thornley (ed.), *Unquiet Spirit*, p. 168.

11. Quoted in John Bowman, *Window and Mirror, RTÉ Television: 1961–2011* (Cork: Collins Press, 2011), p. 128.

12. Christopher Morash, *A History of the Media in Ireland* (Cambridge: Cambridge University Press, 2010), p. 173.

13. Savage, *A Loss of Innocence*, p. 139.

14. "A Debate on the Media and Popular Culture: Richard Kearney talks to Lelia Doolan, Nuala O'Faolain, Ciaran Carty & Luke Gibbons," *The Crane Bag* 8: 2 (1984), p. 176.

15. John Horgan, *Irish Media: A Critical History since 1922* (London: Routledge, 2001), p. 85.

16. James S. Donnelly, "Opposing the 'Modern World': The Cult of the Virgin Mary in Ireland, 1965–85," *Éire-Ireland*, 40: 1&2 (Spring/Summer 2005), p. 184.

17. Donnelly, "Opposing the 'Modern World,'" p. 184.

18. Colm Tóibín, "Gay Byrne: Irish Life as Cabaret," *The Crane Bag* 8: 2 (1984), p. 66.

19. Horgan, *Broadcasting and Public Life*, p. 64.

20. John Horgan, "The Changing of the Guard at Middle Abbey Street," in Mark O' Brien and Kevin Rafter (eds.), *Independent Newspapers: A History* (Dublin: Four Courts Press, 2012), p. 143.

21. James Downey, "Irish Catholics' Favourite Protestant Editor," in Andrew Whittaker (ed.), *Bright, Brilliant Days: Douglas Gageby and The Irish Times* (Dublin: A & A Farmar, 2006), p. 22.

22. Maeve Binchy, "Something Magical" in Whittaker (ed.), *Bright, Brilliant Days*, p. 17.

23. Olivia O'Leary, "Mr Gageby's Republic," in Whittaker (ed.), *Bright, Brilliant Days*, p. 45.

24. O'Leary, "Mr Gageby's Republic," p. 17.

25. MacConghail, "He boxed lightly," pp. 120–121.

26. Bowman, *Window and Mirror*, p. 123.

27. Bowman, *Window and Mirror*, p. 124.

28. Luke Gibbons, "From Kitchen Sink to Soap: Drama and Serial Form on Irish Television" and "From Megalith to Megastore: Broadcasting and Irish Culture," in Luke Gibbons, *Transformations in Irish Culture* (Cork: Cork University Press in association with Field Day, 1996), pp. 44–81.

29. Gay Byrne, *To Whom It Concerns: Ten Years of the Late Late Show* (Dublin: Torc Books, 1972), p. 48.

30. For a survey, see Terence Brown, *Ireland, A Social and Cultural History 1922–2002* (London: Harper Perennial, 2004), pp. 316–354.

31. Daniel T. Rodgers, *Age of Fracture* (Cambridge, MA: Belknap Press of Harvard University Press, 2011), p. 7.

32. Quoted in David Dwan, *The Great Community: Culture and Nationalism in Ireland* (Dublin: Field Day in association with the Keough-Naughton Institute for Irish Studies, University of Notre Dame, 2008), p. 160.

33. Horgan, *Irish Media*, p. 109; and Mark O'Brien, "Independent Newspapers and Irish Society, 1973–98," in O'Brien and Rafter (eds.), *Independent Newspapers*, p. 173.

34. Paul Ryan, "Asking Angela: Discourses about Sexuality in an Irish Problem Page, 1963–1980," *Journal of the History of Sexuality* 19: 2 (May 2010), p. 338.

35. Quoted in Colum Kenny, *Moments that Changed Us* (Dublin: Gill and Macmillan, 2005), p. 251.

36. Conor Brady, *Up with The Times* (Dublin: Gill and Macmillan, 2005), p. 146.

37. Dermot Keogh, "The Catholic Church in Ireland since the 1950s," in Leslie Woodcock Tentler (ed.), *The Church Confronts Modernity: Catholicism since 1950 in the United States, Ireland and Quebec* (Washington, DC: Catholic University of America Press, 2007), p. 143.

38. Horgan, *Broadcasting and Public Life*, pp. 32–33.

39. O'Leary, "Mr Gageby's Republic," p. 47.

40. "A Debate on the Media and Popular Culture," p. 180.

41. Tóibín, "Gay Byrne," p. 69.

42. Morash, *History of the Media in Ireland*, p. 225.

43. Anthony Cronin, "Nationalism and Freedom," *The Bell* 8: 11 (Summer 1953), p. 16.

44. Raymond Williams, "Introduction," in Jack Dowling, Lelia Doolan, and Bob Quinn (eds.), *Sit Down and Be Counted: The Cultural Evolution of a Television Station* (Dublin: Wellington Publishers, 1969), p. xii.

45. Remarks by President Michael D. Higgins at the International Federation of Journalists, 28th World Congress, Dublin June 4, 2013 (http://www.president.ie/en/media-library/speeches/remarks-by-president-michael-d.-higgins-at-the-international-federation-of).

CHAPTER 11

HISTORIOGRAPHY

Richard Bourke

I<small>N</small> 1969, T. W. MOODY, then professor of modern history at Trinity College
Dublin, published an article outlining a plan for a "New History" of Ireland.[1]
This was to be a multi-volume collaborative enterprise, synthesizing the results of a generation of specialized research. Some of the inspiration for the project derived from Lord Acton's *Cambridge Modern History*, also a work of many
hands that cultivated a detached perspective.[2] Acton's venture looked back, in turn,
to European scholarship: to Georg Weber's *Allgemeine Weltgeschichte* of 1857, and
to Lavisse and Rambaud's *Histoire générale* of 1893–1902.[3] In an obvious yet crucial respect, each of these enterprises was very different in conception from the
New History of Ireland as it was first imagined and ultimately executed: the earlier experiments were universal histories, European in focus but global in scope.
Weber's fifteen-volume study was a single-authored *magnum opus* that aimed at
the instruction of "educated ranks" (*gebildete Stände*).[4] What it offered was a model
of cumulative scholarship, based on the synthesis of previous research. To that
extent it exuded the ethos of professionalization pioneered in nineteenth-century
German universities.[5] It was part of an academic culture whose goal was to offer
guidance and improvement to the professional and administrative classes of the
modern bureaucratic state.[6] Viewed in this context, Moody's project exemplified
a long-established program of providing public education by synthesizing historical research.

However, Moody's public was already different from that envisaged by his
European predecessors. His audience was not limited to civil servants and the
cultured elite but included all who passed through a program of national education. By comparison, a dominant strand in the British historical profession of the

My thanks go to Ultán Gillen and Ian McBride for their comments on this chapter.

late nineteenth century saw itself as equipping a clerisy for leadership, including the class of future politicians.[7] This was to be achieved with the tools of the German professoriate: the critical examination of sources and the spirit of impartiality (*Unparteilichkeit*).[8] Seeley, for example, saw the Historical Tripos at the University of Cambridge as a seminary for statesmanship, not a resource for guiding the public imagination. In contrast, the *New History of Ireland* was to be a history for the population at large: it was supposed to be intelligible "to men as such."[9] But while the history planned by Moody had to be relevant to the general public, it would not be a means of confirming existing prejudices and opinions. Its mission was to "study human thought and action in the stream of time" insofar as this could be recovered from "the surviving evidence."[10]

"Evidence" was the key term in the sentence, pointing to the scientific ambition of Moody's project. That ambition certainly bore considerable fruit—in the cataloging of archives and the production of printed editions of sources; in the work of Moody himself along with contemporaries like Robert Dudley Edwards, J. C. Beckett, and R. B. McDowell; among the students of T. D. Williams, from F. X. Martin to Ronan Fanning; and in outstanding research conducted from the 1950s to the 1980s by historians ranging from Kenneth H. Connell and Maureen Wall to A.T.Q. Stewart, Thomas Bartlett, Sean J. Connolly, and K. Theo Hoppen. The goal of genuinely historical research derived, again, from the nineteenth century: history should aspire to the condition of a science. Because historical research resulted in some form of knowledge, a broad claim to the status of science (*scientia*) was uncontroversial. However, it was not clear what kind of science might be intended: "science" was a poor translation of the German *Wissenschaft*, and, whatever it was, historical study was not a natural science.[11] What Leopold von Ranke, the most renowned exemplar of the scientific approach, had in mind was the simultaneous application of a number of methods. These included the philological scrutiny of documents, a marshaling of the complete range of evidence, and a critical examination of sources. Each task was to be pursued with rigorous independence of mind. Of course, none of these techniques was new to the nineteenth century: they were developed among Renaissance humanists and deployed by scholars of the *ars historica* through the seventeenth century.[12] What was new was the critical investigation of state archives. However, ironically, many of Ranke's disciples, like Heinrich von Sybel and Johann Gustav Droysen, drew their data from national archives with a view to justifying public policy.[13] The scientific historian proved to be as politically partisan as the trained rhetorician of the fifteenth century. Von Sybel offered perhaps the best illustration of this pattern. Part of his legacy to modern historical writing is less the rigorous sifting of evidence than the instrumental collection of data from public archives, a procedure easily confused with historical method proper.[14] This leads to an important conclusion about the history of historiography: despite the standard genealogies of historical research, professional methods and nonpartisan perspectives are only contingently related, and they might just as readily conflict as mutually support one another.

The mastery of state archives is a potent political weapon, fed by a powerful fantasy. Its attraction lies in the promise of penetrating national secrets, giving access to *arcana imperii*.[15] However, classified documents present evidence, not facts; and evidence should offer a means of inferring valid conclusions, not a way of assembling testimony to fit the facts one likes. This last pitfall presents a constant temptation for the historian. The lure of previously unseen statements can lend a veneer of authority to the mere assertion of belief. However, the collection of data to confirm beliefs does not so much yield historical conclusions as what Moody liked to call "myth."[16] Resort to the term "myth" to mean a set of historically unsubstantiated commitments was a curious choice of expression. Its use is partly explained by its provenance in the historical profession. The word supplied the British historian Ian R. Christie with the title for his inaugural lecture at University College London in 1967, and then for the collection in which it appeared two years later.[17] Christie had been an admirer of Lewis Namier in the 1950s, producing his first monograph for Namier's "England in the Age of the American Revolution" series in 1958.[18] One of the things that had enabled Namier to distinguish himself was his extraordinary command of the manuscript sources for British high politics around 1760. Deploying new evidence, he exploded the assumptions of previous Whig historians—Macaulay, Lecky, Trevelyan—all of whom had misconstrued the character of political parties in parliament in the aftermath of the Seven Years' War.[19] He effectively depicted his predecessors as captivated by "myth": their conclusions were predetermined by their picture of the period. This picture had been derived from pamphlet literature and memoirs: it was, in truth, an extension of propaganda. Deploying the evidence of manuscript correspondence against the misperceptions generated by published polemics, Namier powerfully illustrated how research could correct misconceptions generated by ideology.

For Moody, ideology could be "benign or malignant," depending on whether it destroyed or sustained those who employed it.[20] In the Irish case it had largely been destructive, perpetuating sectarianism and conflict. By way of contrast, history promised deliverance in the form of liberation, an escape from servitude to habits of mind that research could reveal to be without foundation. In this way, Moody's program was based on the assumption that a professional cadre of historians could effectively instruct contemporary society while remaining aloof from the pressures that condemned the public to ideological confusion. Ideology inclined the popular mind to enmity and recrimination, whereas the dispassionate art of historical reconstruction spread a message of ecumenism. Moody drew inspiration from Herbert Butterfield's injunction to historians to cultivate a tragic sense of the past.[21] This was a call to view the drama of the past as a conflict between equally flawed actors. As Moody recognized, the moral force of Butterfield's agenda derived from the Pauline ethic to be found in the *Epistle to the Ephesians* urging fellowship among our "flesh and blood."[22] The point was not that historians should embrace religious doctrine, but that the process of historical research created a disposition to hear both sides that coincided, as it happened, with the Christian message.

Butterfield saw the historical profession in Britain as having advanced along a path to greater understanding since the days of Acton's triumphant righteousness.[23] This gave the impression that the ideal of historical detachment had particularly blossomed with the advent of professional historiography. The truth is, however, that the goal of historical impartiality was first championed by skeptics from Pierre Bayle to David Hume aiming to promote properly philosophical history, written *sine ira et studio*.[24] Moody followed Butterfield in thinking of objectivity as the achievement of modern research. This, in turn, has encouraged the idea that proper historical writing only emerged in the twentieth century—or even later, in the Irish case, with the establishment in 1938 of *Irish Historical Studies*. One of Moody's greatest successes was in reproducing this perspective in subsequent historians.[25] For a succeeding generation schooled in the 1960s, Irish historical writing began in the 1940s. It might be acknowledged that figures like Eoin MacNeill and Edmund Curtis contributed to the study of medieval Ireland, but historians of the post-Tudor period were in general dismissed as having produced "vintage cowboy and Indian stuff."[26] Accordingly, the aim of the Irish historical establishment became one of dismantling still-prevailing myths, and its method was to challenge abiding pieties with the tools of professional research. In the South, as illustrated by the attempt to produce a centenary volume on the Famine, this largely meant debunking popular assumptions, often peddled by committed propagandists.[27] As Dudley Edwards put it in 1955, national opinion, which had largely been formed in accordance with the teachings of Southern Ireland's Civil War parties, stood urgently in need of "a different attitude" to recent history.[28] In seeking to provide this new perspective, historians offered less a revision of previous research than a critique of popular perceptions. As a consequence of this approach, generations of Irish historians were consigned to oblivion: Lecky barely figured, John Curry was forgotten, and Charles O'Conor was rarely read.

Moody's opposition between myth and history, which subsequently pervaded Irish historiography, was informed by a fundamental intuition. This was the idea that political communities are sustained by their sense of "corporate identity" over time.[29] By thinking of a people in corporate terms, its current existence could be connected to a collective past. The question for Moody was how that connection was established. It might either spuriously be fabricated, or it might accurately be charted. Whereas the mythographer was disposed to produce a fictitious version of community with the past, the historian could recover the real thing. The remainder of this chapter first tries to show that skepticism about corporate ideas of nationality long predates the "historical revolution" in Ireland, inaugurated by Moody and celebrated since. The chapter then proceeds to question the underlying premise: namely, the idea that "corporate" entities form the subject matter of history, providing a substratum of continuity in the midst of perpetual change. The subjection of the idea of corporate succession to historical scrutiny began with Edmund Burke, and so I turn first to his handling of the idea of corporate blame and then to its wider use in eighteenth-century historiography.

II

In the *Reflections on the Revolution in France*, dismayed by the partisanship of Revolutionary propaganda, Burke reflected on the use and abuse of history. Under the right circumstances, he noted, history could instruct us regarding the errors of the past as a means of guiding policy in the future. Too often, however, it was perverted for ideological gain. In this misbegotten form, history could serve as an arsenal of attack, supplying "offensive and defensive weapons for parties in church and state, and supplying the means of keeping alive, or reviving dissensions and animosities, and adding fuel to civil fury."[30] Burke was thinking of the contemporary use that was being made of historically remote injustices to condemn the current nobility and clergy of France. However, he was keenly aware that the same process had operated in Ireland. In the France of 1789, past crimes were being revivified and ascribed to collective perpetrators identified with the upper ranks of society. These, as the Abbé Sieyès famously claimed, were the beneficiaries of conquest, and consequently bore the marks of a criminal usurpation.[31] By a strange process of transubstantiation, Burke contended, the living were being held responsible for the misdeeds of the dead. What made this possible was the idea of corporate blame. It was an idea that played a prominent role in the writing of Irish history. For instance, Roman Catholics were often condemned for the treachery of their forefathers. Censure of this kind involved a curious mystification, which carried with it an insidious mischief. It condemned contemporary groups on account of their corporate affiliation, linking their mortal existence to a continuous life in the past. This fiction of continuity made it possible to attribute the sins of the fathers to their remotest progeny. "It is not very just to chastise men for the offences of their natural ancestors," Burke wrote, "but to take the fiction of ancestry in a corporate succession, as a ground for punishing men who have no relation to guilty acts ... is a sort of refinement in injustice."[32]

What Burke was complaining about was the invocation of corporate identities across history. A corporation was an idea of collective existence. Ideas of the kind were historical fictions: in reality, there were no such transhistorical entities as "the Irish" and "the French." Historical fictions of the kind had their uses in sustaining national cultures, but they could not reasonably be used to blacken their individual members in one age for the activities of their members in another. For example, in an Irish context, both native and settler populations might sustain themselves by imagining their possession of a corporate past. Nonetheless, it was an affront to blame "descendants" by association with their "ancestors." "Corporate bodies are immortal for the good of the members," Burke argued, "but not for their punishment."[33] It was an argument keenly felt by John Curry, a founding member of the Catholic Committee established in 1757 to seek the repeal of anti-Popery legislation. Curry's objective was to liberate the writing of Irish history from the ongoing influence of sectarian passion. It was an ambition that inaugurated historical revisionism in Ireland. Previously, from Sir John Davies to Richard Cox, history served as an instrument of colonial policy. This, of course, did not mean that the events narrated were deliberately distorted or untrue. Nonetheless, in both Davies and Cox, no attempt was made to recover the reasoning of the government's opponents. Curry, however, sifted evidence from Catholics and Protestants as a means of revising unwarranted historical assumptions.

Curry's project certainly had a political purpose: if successful, it would free the current generation of Catholics in Ireland from being implicated in the presumptive guilt of their forebears. He focused on the events surrounding the 1641 rebellion, beginning with the Catholic insurgency that triggered the Confederate Wars. Accounts of 1641, particularly those of John Temple and Edmund Borlase, had served to fan the flames of sectarianism in church and state through the seventeenth century, and their legacy continued deep into the eighteenth.[34] In his *Historical Memoirs of the Irish Rebellion*, which he published in 1758, Curry recalled how the Jacobite rising of 1745 affected denominational relations in Ireland. In that year, a raft of pamphlets appeared, trumpeting the disposition to rebellion among the native Irish.[35] Many of these raised the specter of the rebellion of 1641 as a means of casting aspersions on Catholic loyalty in the 1740s. In response, Curry published his *Brief Account of the Rebellion of 1641*, a piece of historical criticism in dialogue form.[36] His *Historical Memoirs* was designed to counter objections that had been made against the *Brief Account*, above all by Walter Harris, a member of the Dublin Physico-Historical Society, who openly accused Curry of seeking to incite his fellow Catholics to insurrection by exonerating their predecessors for 1641.[37] As Curry presents it, the purpose of his counterblast was to offset the "Rage of Party" by correcting willful distortions of the historical record. This rage had dominated the whole era of modern Irish history, extending from the Tudor conquest to the Glorious Revolution. It sustained the continuous struggle for power on the island along with its accompanying ecclesiastical rivalries. The constant recapitulation of the perfidy of the native Irish served the purpose of perpetuating hatred and bitterness. It therefore managed to "oppress the Living by the Abuse of the Dead."[38]

By implication, correcting the historical record would restore harmonious relations. "Restore," however, was not quite the word. Curry never dreamed of a return to pre-conquest conditions. These, in fact, revealed a scene of relentless strife and anarchy.[39] Curry accepted an intuition of Sir John Davies in proposing that the advent of pacification would generate a common allegiance under a shared framework of law.[40] Although consensus was not to be expected through a reunion of churches, "yet an Union on civil principles" might well be secured.[41] Curry followed William Molyneux in stipulating that civil concord would depend on the antecedent existence of consent: "the right of being subject *only* to such Laws, as receive our own Consent, is … inherent to all Mankind, and founded on … immutable Laws of Nature and Reason."[42] Consent had to be established in two stages, according to Curry. First came a basic disposition to allegiance, then came an active endorsement of the regime. What inhibited the transition from the one to the other in Ireland was the ongoing fear of rebellion fomented by propaganda based on the false testimony of past histories. Particularly unsettling for Curry was the recent boost that this process had received from the publication of Hume's *History of England.* The two volumes covering the Stuart reign originally appeared under the title of the *History of Great Britain* between 1754 and 1756. In the first of these volumes, Hume confirmed the dominant interpretation of 1641, largely basing his account on John Temple's representation. The brutality of the attacks on English settlers in Ulster was depicted with horror: "Without provocation, without opposition, the astonished English, living in profound peace, and full security, were massacred by their nearest neighbours, with whom they had long upheld a continued intercourse of kindness and good offices."[43]

One of Burke's nineteenth-century biographers presents an account of an early encounter with Hume: "on religion and politics their sentiments were too diametrically opposed ever to approach to agreement." Among the main points of contention was "the Irish massacre of 1641."[44] For Curry, Burke, and Charles O'Conor, the treatment of 1641 constituted one of the great failings of Hume's *History,* undermining its claim to philosophical detachment. Hume's celebrity as a historian derived from his refusal to prostitute his craft before the idols of party-minded propagandists.[45] Disappointment with his depiction of the 1641 massacre stemmed from the sense that he had betrayed his own ideals in caving in to the partisanship of seventeenth-century publicists. For his Irish opponents, two things were suggested by the available evidence: first, that the rebellion was not an unprovoked vendetta, proceeding from unaccountable bitterness; second, that the extent of the massacre had been wildly exaggerated, with lurid accounts of "enormities" that could only encourage recrimination.[46] From the 1750s through to the 1770s, Burke promoted the idea of challenging this orthodox myth, collaborating with Charles O'Conor and encouraging Thomas Leland to that end.[47] According to O'Conor himself, much was to be expected from the "enlightened" Leland, whose intellect was definitively above party.[48] However, when Leland's three-volume *History of Ireland from the Invasion of Henry II* finally appeared in 1773, neither Burke nor O'Conor could disguise their disappointment.[49] The hope of finding an Irish exemplar of philosophical history had been defeated.

Leland reminded his readers that there had been no account of the various "commotions" in Ireland since Richard Cox produced his "hasty" and "indigested" chronicle in 1690.[50] Moreover, it was generally the case that prejudice and animosity continued to pervade accounts of Irish history long after the disputes that originally bred them had subsided. However, after extended peace and prosperity since 1691, it was now to be hoped that "reflection, and an encreasing liberality of sentiment, may have sheathed the acrimony of contending parties."[51] Nonetheless, Leland confessed that when tackling the events of 1641, it was next to impossible to describe what took place without offending some or all of the "discordant parties" who had an investment in how it was represented.[52] For his part, Curry was so dismayed by the content of Leland's account that he hurried out his *Historical and Critical Review of the Civil Wars in Ireland*, openly assailing Clarendon and Hume, but aiming above all to refute Leland.[53] In his *Review*, Curry pursued a relentless campaign of exoneration, identifying an antecedent "dread of … extirpation" as the proximate cause of the Rebellion.[54] He then proceeded to refute claims that the Irish clergy had disseminated subversive doctrines, that the insurgents were activated by instantaneous malice, and that the numbers of those massacred could be numbered in the hundreds of thousands. He also sought to undermine the authority of previous historians from Temple to Leland and to question the credibility of the depositions.[55]

As Curry set about exculpating his co-religionists, he neglected to contextualize the behavior of their opponents. Ultimately, the *Review* resembled more a compendium than a history. It collected and cited sources, but it failed to probe the deeper causes of action and belief. Catholic reactions were endlessly vindicated. As a result, Protestant antagonism was deprived of every conceivable remnant of rationality. Reluctantly, Charles O'Conor objected to the performance: "it is a mere justification on one side and a disguised invective on the other," he complained.[56] O'Conor's diagnosis was acute: together with Curry, he had set out to revise the history of 1641, but the enterprise had culminated in a Catholic apology. Explanation took the form of exculpation, which implicitly fixed guilt on the opposing side. From this perspective, although the *Review* was an exercise in historical criticism, it offered absolution rather than sober revision. Curry chose the precept "*audi alteram partem*" as the epigram to his 1775 volume, but it was an injunction that his history failed to observe.

Nonetheless, the attempt to develop a philosophical history from the middle of the eighteenth century represents an inaugural moment in Irish historical writing. The determination to rise convincingly above party now receded for almost a century. The main achievements of the early nineteenth century lay in the study of antiquities, building on eighteenth-century predecessors like O'Halloran, O'Conor, Vallancey, and Ledwich.[57] This led to the development of scholarly source criticism and a commitment to linguistically grounded philological study.[58] Running in parallel with these developments, modern history fell under the spell of 1798, resulting in rival narratives of the causes of past rebellions. In 1810, Curry's *Review* was reissued to service Catholic polemic. Once again, 1641 acquired a symbolic status that persisted for another eighty years. Most dramatically, the controversy was reignited in the 1880s by James Anthony Froude: *The English in Ireland in the Eighteenth Century* reproduced the venom of Temple and Borlase.[59] Froude's work, however, was not conceived as a work of historical inquiry so much as a staunch polemic directed against Home Rule.[60] Even so, it shortly acquired an iconic status among rival historians in Ireland as an exemplification of unhistorical moralism and vituperation. For W.E.H. Lecky, the aim of Froude's work had been to enforce "certain political doctrines."[61] His complaint was instructive: first he derided Froude as having produced a political work, but he also derided his arguments as politically objectionable.

III

Early on Lecky became a devotee of Burke, but he was also a keen admirer of Young Ireland.[62] His first historical work, *Leaders of Public Opinion in Ireland*, was published anonymously in 1861. It offered a spirited defense of the sentiment of nationality understood in terms of a revival of popular consent. In a concluding chapter on clerical influence in Ireland, it extolled "the will of a united people" as a precondition for successful government.[63] On Lecky's understanding, sectarianism was the antagonist of a united popular will, and he set about examining its causes. The term "sectarian" was deployed with its usual nineteenth-century meaning to denominate antagonism born of religious antipathy. Above all since O'Connell, not just sectionalism, but religious sectionalism—dubbed "sectarianism"—distracted and enervated national sentiment in Ireland: "blind hatred is the actuating principle of the people."[64] This called for some form of political redress, but Lecky also trusted in the "spirit of the age": it was clear, he thought, that the tendency of the times was toward the disassociation of religion from politics, accompanied by the decline of theological dogmatism.[65] Accordingly, Lecky turned from Ireland to the European scene, and from biography to intellectual history. Under the influence of Henry Thomas Buckle, he got to work on "the history of a mental tendency," which finally appeared in 1865 as *A History of the Rise and Influence of the Spirit of Rationalism in Europe*.[66] Its aim, he wrote, was to examine "the causes of the decline of the sense of the miraculous."[67] He then turned to writing a *History of European Morals from Augustus to Charlemagne*, which he opened with a long, schematic essay on the transhistorical significance of intuitionist and utilitarian principles in ethics.[68] It was then that Lecky turned to political history, as he embarked on an ambitious narrative of English politics through the eighteenth century. The history of policy and government formed the central plank of Lecky's account. This made the work an imperial as much as a national history, involving detailed coverage of the American and Indian empires. In the process, Lecky was inevitably brought back to the history of Ireland, whose role bulked ever larger as the book progressed.

Lecky began work on what was to become his *History of England in the Eighteenth Century* in 1872. Eighteen years later, the eighth and final volume was published to critical acclaim. Although the work was structured around a core political narrative, it nonetheless gave due weight to social and economic developments; to the history of political ideas; and to the history of art, manners, and belief. Its aim was to pick out the enduring characteristics of national life and to identify dominant themes—the "growth or decline of the monarchy, the aristocracy and the democracy, of the Church and Dissent, of the agricultural, the manufacturing, and the commercial interests."[69] Lecky's research drew him ever more deeply into the archives, especially in connection with Ireland. Determined to supersede the investigations of Froude, he immersed himself in the records of Dublin Castle, the Four Courts, and the Royal Irish Academy.[70] By the time he got started on the new work, his attention had already turned to the peculiar plight of the Irish: in 1871, he brought out a revised edition of *The Leaders of Public Opinion in Ireland*. This carried, inter alia, a new introduction that again traced the deepening dissensions in Ireland to the state of public opinion. As with Hungary, opinion in Ireland was divided and disaffected. Parliament in Britain served as a means of focusing and refining the mass of public attitudes. In Ireland, however, power was forced to operate without consent, while the population itself was partitioned into hostile constituencies. This predicament came with an additional complication: the only solution available threatened to exacerbate the problem. Self-government was necessary to establish popular consent, yet cohesion among the people was a precondition of Home Rule.[71] What was required, therefore, were "slow, cautious, and gradual steps" toward some measure of devolution.[72] Public spirit needed to be fostered by exemplary leadership in the country, which meant decentralizing at least some institutions of the Union. This step, however, would have to be secured without aggravating factionalism.

Through the 1870s and 1880s, the prospect of rejuvenating public opinion gradually receded. As Lecky saw it, a great antagonist to progress appeared in the form of William Ewart Gladstone. In the aftermath of the Fenian outrages of the late 1860s, the disendowment and disestablishment of the Church of Ireland was carried out. The first Irish Land Act followed in close succession. But in the 1880s the situation deteriorated rapidly, partly through a series of successor Land Acts that attacked the rights of landlord proprietorship, but also on account of Gladstone's conversion to a policy of Home Rule. In the context of disaffection and mass enfranchisement, these measures threatened the integrity of the Empire. Writing in 1891, after the defeat of the first Home Rule bill, Lecky estimated that about a third of the population regarded self-government under current conditions as an unmitigated catastrophe.[73] He increasingly drew inspiration from Burke: the author of the *Reflections* had more to offer than Machiavelli or Montesquieu, Lecky wagered.[74] What Burke had demonstrated was the detrimental effect of mass popular politics. This was exemplified, in Lecky's opinion, by the

Irish Parliamentary Party under the influence of Parnell. O'Connell's plans for repeal and Butt's for self-government had hoped to reconcile devolution with two necessary preconditions for any successful system of rule: a common allegiance among the population and an ethic of responsibility among its representatives. In the Preface to the final 1903 edition of *Leaders of Public Opinion in Ireland*, Lecky recollected how these plausible schemes of national administration had given way to populist rancor.[75] The period between 1885 and 1893 were marked by attacks on the principle of property in Ireland, rising hostility to the English connection, and the enfranchisement of the democratic mass. These developments prognosticated not only the dissolution of the Union but also the emergence of civil faction in the secessionist polity.

All this had occurred in the wake of the Union that brought a close to eighteenth-century Ireland. Lecky recognized that an explanation of the status quo could only be developed by recounting the history of the past. The popular demand for a cogent account of the pre-history of the late nineteenth-century impasse encouraged Lecky to distinguish his treatment of Ireland in his *History of England in the Eighteenth Century*. This effort resulted in the separate publication of his *History of Ireland in the Eighteenth Century* in 1892. Its sympathetic treatment of opposition to the Union, together with Lecky's habitual defense of the "sentiment of nationality," ensured that the committed unionist became an intellectual resource for the Home Rule movement. On the eve of the 1911 Parliament Act that removed a final legislative impediment to the introduction of self-government in Ireland, Francis Cruise O'Brien and W.E.G. Lloyd reissued the final chapter of the 1861 edition of *Leaders of Public Opinion in Ireland* as a pamphlet with a commendatory preface. Home Rule, it was now contended, would dispel animosity rather than feed it.[76] Lecky accepted that his arguments had helped arm his enemies, but he still remained committed to the principle of nationality.

Lecky reiterated that commitment in *Democracy and Liberty*, a historico-philosophical meditation in the tradition of Sumner Maine and Fitzjames Stephen that lamented the impact of modern democracy on the cast of British politics.[77] Lecky accepted the Tocquevillian thesis that the aspiration to democracy was an inescapable element in modern political life, but he also believed that its injurious consequences ought to be counteracted.[78] In this context, he supported the democratic "doctrine of nationalities" that he associated with the spirit of 1789, although he noted that, having peaked around 1848, it was generally on the decline by the 1870s, except in Ireland.[79] Yet even though he endorsed the principle of popular sovereignty in terms of the "inalienable right of every people to choose its own form of government," he recoiled at the idea that democratic government was the best vehicle for popular consent. The danger involved in expressing national sovereignty through a system of popular rule had been steadily illustrated in Ireland by the process of franchise reform. To begin with, the extension of the suffrage since 1867 had progressively compromised the viability of parliamentarism.

Having occurred in tandem with the emergence of the party caucus, the decline of parliamentarism was liable to end in democratic Caesarism.[80] This line of thought led Lecky to the disconsolate conclusion that government by consent, based on popular sovereignty, was incompatible with mass electoral politics. His thesis was to be tested by twentieth-century Irish politics, though it has largely been ignored by subsequent historians, disposed to assume that their discipline began in the 1930s.

IV

Elements of Lecky's analysis nonetheless remained. In 1971, in the preface to his magisterial survey, *Ireland since the Famine*, F.S.L. Lyons accepted that a "historiographical revolution" had occurred over the course of the preceding forty years.[81] What he meant was that the bitterness of 1912–1923 had sufficiently subsided by the 1930s for dispassionate historical study to be undertaken again. At the same time, his own rendition of the Irish story took up where Lecky had left off: with the centrality of the "national question" to modern Irish history. However, the debt went even deeper, whether knowingly or not. Lyons examined the vicissitudes of this question over the course of nearly a thousand pages in relation to Lecky's major themes: public opinion, property relations, and the emergence of newer "forms of nationalism."[82] It was not entirely clear, in Lyons's phraseology, how the "national question" related to "newer forms of nationalism." What this had meant, in Lecky's terms, was the relationship between national sovereignty and democratic government under conditions of mass enfranchisement and popular representation. Lecky's comparative analytical precision meant that he could offer a political and constitutional account of what he saw as the deterioration of "public opinion," by which he understood the emergence of antagonism in society. With Lyons, however, this was mainly ascribed to opposing attitudes. In his 1977–1978 Ford Lectures, *Culture and Anarchy in Ireland*, hostile attitudes were largely described in terms of rival "cultures," yet the same *petitio principii* remained: what, in concrete terms, had caused these attitudes to clash?[83]

Lyons's closest disciple in the study of Irish attitudes is Roy Foster, who, with the publication in 1988 of *Modern Ireland, 1600–1972*, offered the most comprehensive single-volume overview of Irish history for a generation. One of the undisputed achievements of *Modern Ireland* was its addition of layers of cultural analysis to the established narrative of high politics, combined with a summation of advances in scholarship accumulated since Moody. Above all, while criticizing deterministic assumptions often found in Lyons, Foster brought to the writing of Irish history a predilection for vigorous judgment and irreverence.[84] Both the vigor and the irreverence were largely directed against the "pieties" of Irish nationalism, defined in terms of a set of "exclusivist" cultural beliefs.[85] In Foster's earlier work, this verdict was most sharply formulated when deployed in connection with the Irish revolutionary generation who participated in the events of the Easter Rising, the War of Independence, and the Civil War. Here the motives for rebellion and secession were usually compressed into the capacious term "Anglophobia," which designated a form of mindless opposition to the British connection.[86] This habit of pithy judgment captured something of the mood of a generation of Irish historians, fatigued by the heroic postures in which the founders of the Irish Free State had hitherto been cast.[87] Frequently, this fatigue gave rise to an assertive moralism underpinning what claimed to be "value-free" analysis, sparking controversy about the bona fides of historical revisionism.[88] The impetus behind such moralism lay in a determined effort to delegitimize the assumptions of revolutionary politics in twentieth-century Ireland. In some of its more credulous incarnations, this could take the form of charting contests between "cultures," with "Britishness" doing battle with various forms of "Irishness."[89] In the process of surveying rival "identities," whose collision conflicted with the aspiration to toleration, the historian was transmuted into a purveyor of "pluralism," lamenting, but never explaining, the advent of discord.

The animus against the revolutionary generation, which climaxed in the 1980s and 1990s, finding perhaps its most sophisticated formulation in the writings of Peter Hart, began to relent with the advent of the new millennium when younger historians like Matthew Kelly, Senia Pašeta, and Fearghal McGarry set about recovering the intricate range of motives that drove Irish politics after 1886, the year of the first Home Rule bill.[90] By 2014 Irish historical revisionism itself had more or less come to an end when Foster returned in *Vivid Faces* to describe the assorted "mentalities" of protest that animated society after the fall of Parnell. The so-called "long gestation" between 1891 and 1919, which W. B. Yeats had retrospectively construed as a preparation for national self-assertion, was recast in the form of a "pre-revolution," in which a variety of rebellious ideals of freedom jostled for position.[91] The supposed conspiratorial alliance between Catholicism and nationalism, which had dominated so much Irish historiography since the 1970s, was over.[92]

In the decades between 1938 and the present, the great achievement of Irish historical writing has been the steady and systematic accumulation of new research, with the early work of Marianne Elliott and David Fitzpatrick epitomizing fastidious scholarship.[93] Large, paradigmatic innovation has been a scarcer commodity, although women's history as pioneered from Margaret MacCurtain to Maria Luddy conspicuously broke new ground. In contrast, the *Annales* School produced few imitators, and Marxism secured only a handful of disciples. Paul Bew, Peter Gibbon, and Henry Patterson are apparent exceptions, yet the truth is that the significance of their work is only marginally indebted to Marxist categories of analysis. In Bew, for example, politics tends to be given decisive primacy, operating against a background of social strife.[94] Accordingly, his principal contribution, along with Gibbon and Patterson, has been in exposing Irish nationalist myopia concerning the unionist determination to resist.[95] As we have seen, Lecky's principal historiographical themes were national sentiment, new political movements, and the fate of property. For the twentieth century, the leading account of relations between property and power did not derive from Marxism; instead, it is to be found in the work of J. J. Lee. In his powerful study, *Ireland, 1912–1985*, he largely focused his attention on the failures of the South in terms of national expectations of social and economic performance.[96] Lee's approach was ambitiously comparative in nature, situating Ireland alongside smaller European nations: Denmark, Finland, and Norway repeatedly featured. Because its main emphasis was on the relationship between the rhetoric and the reality of Irish independence, its focus tended to disregard the legacy of the Famine. By way of contrast, for Cormac Ó Gráda, the leading economic historian of the nineteenth century, this perspective is liable to appear truncated. The Famine, Ó Gráda argued, still has to be seen as the central event in modern Irish history, which decisively shaped society and politics over the century and a half that followed.[97]

Since Lecky opted to print his Irish history separately from his history of England, the history of Ireland has largely been placed in a national framework. With rare exceptions like Fernand Braudel and Marc Bloch, this has been the European norm since the nineteenth century. It is mainly among early modern historians that this emphasis has been challenged, beginning with the work of D. B. Quinn. It was Quinn who first integrated sixteenth-century Irish history into a wider British pattern, which he placed in turn in the context of European expansion.[98] His leading disciple is Nicholas Canny, who capitalized on Quinn's insights in a series of important studies that have appeared since 1976.[99] More than any of his contemporaries, it was Quinn who broke old molds in the writing of Irish history, not least by raising the question of what the focus of history should be. In the case of Ireland, it could not, in the first instance, be a history of the state. For Quinn, "Ireland" after 1534 was an assemblage of principalities with overlapping authorities. Its history could be encapsulated neither as the biography of a people nor in terms of the trajectory of an administration. It could not therefore be assimilated to the annals of a nation. From the early 1970s, a series of attempts was launched, above all by J.G.A. Pocock, to reconcile this insight with British imperial history.[100] Yet for the most part, with the exception of figures like Jane Ohlmeyer, Quinn's message went largely unheeded.

In the 1970s and 1980s, debate about Ireland's histories became a matter of ideological contention, focused on whether the island was inhabited by two nations or one.[101] As Alvin Jackson, the leading Irish historian of Ulster Unionism, has shown, by the late nineteenth century Protestant politics in the northeast of the island of Ireland was already largely bound up with the fate of local constituencies.[102] Did the sum of these constituencies add up to a national community? In the end, this amounted to asking whether the Protestants of Ulster formed a people with a right to establish a polity of their own.[103] As with the French debates on the legacy of the Revolution in France and the German *Historikerstreit* around the same period, historical analysis displayed its power as a form of political argument.[104] In the Irish case, assorted anxieties concerning the constitutional status of Northern Ireland deepened already existing intellectual confusion. Confusion centered on the character of a self-determining people, a pivotal theme in the history of natural law since Hugo Grotius.[105] The issues involved are integral to basic problems in jurisprudence, above all the question of how a community comes to constitute a people, and whether a people can preexist the creation of a state.

If the term "nation" designates any pre-political community, then, by the criteria stipulated by natural law doctrine, a nation is reducible to the dimensions of the family, with the result that there were roughly 1.8 million nations in Ireland by the time of the 1981 Hunger Strikes.[106] If, however, a nation is constituted by the aspiration to form a political community, then the number of nations in Ireland was coterminous with the electorates on both parts of the island. However if, finally, the term "nation" refers to a population under a political leadership aspiring to sovereignty and wielding the means of coercion, then there were at least three nations on the island of Ireland in 1981: the Southern Irish community, the Northern community comprising both British and Irish affiliates, and the constituency supporting the Provisional Irish Republican Army (IRA).[107] This last nation was derisory in terms of its actual numbers, commanding the allegiance of just a tenth of the Northern electorate, but for all that, it was a powerful contender in the game of politics.

In this vein, one might readily proliferate answers to the question of how many peoples inhabited the island of Ireland during the heyday of historical revisionism. If our answers were to be properly historical in nature, then they ought to avoid two fallacies at once. The first is the fallacy of continuity: the idea that political claims to ancestry represent real historical continuities. In this genre, one could single out as examples the claim that Irish republicanism has its roots in the United Irishmen, or that the origins of Ulster nationalism are to be found in the Volunteers. These misconceptions are related to a second aberration, the fallacy of composition. Of all Irish historians, Louis Cullen stands out as the most stringent critic of this particular of heresy. Writing of the eighteenth century, he has pointedly argued that, abstractly conceived, the Irish Catholic "did not exist." Equally, he went on, the "abstract" Protestant was less a reality than a political fabrication.[108] The same might be said of the seventeenth-century "Old English," the eighteenth-century "Ascendancy," and the nineteenth-century "landlord." The fallacy of composition is often combined with the fallacy of continuity to constitute the fiction of corporate identity. The idea of corporate agency began as a Roman legal category, adopted for political purposes by modern theorists of the state.[109] Its legacy to historical writing has been powerful and pervasive, giving us the history of the "Germans" and the "Irish," just as it supplied the history of the "Greeks" and the "Celtic races." History is often tempted to trade in these abstractions; at its best, it is prepared to scrutinize and dismantle them.

FURTHER READING

Modern Irish historical writing has, understandably, largely been concerned with establishing authoritative narratives of the development of society and politics. The history of historiography has therefore been a relatively marginal pursuit. There is consequently little available on eighteenth-century historiography, although Clare O'Halloran's *Golden Ages and Barbarous Nations: Antiquarian Debate and Cultural Politics in Ireland, c. 1750–1800* (Cork and Notre Dame, IN: Notre Dame University Press, 2005) is an important exception to this generalization. For the nineteenth century the main studies were undertaken by Donald McCartney, "The Writing of History in Ireland 1800–30," *Irish Historical Studies* 10: 40 (September 1957), pp. 347–362; "James Anthony Froude and Ireland: A Historiographical Controversy of the Nineteenth Century," *Irish University Review* 1: 2 (Spring 1971), pp. 238–257; and *W. E. H. Lecky: Historian and Politician, 1838–1903* (Dublin: Lilliput Press, 1994). In addition, there is an important essay by Roy Foster, "History and the Irish Question" (1988), in Roy Foster, *Paddy and Mr. Punch: Connections in Irish and English History* (London: Faber and Faber, 1993, 2011). For the twentieth century, there are revealing accounts and observations in J. J. Lee, *Ireland, 1912–1985: Politics and Society* (Cambridge: Cambridge University Press, 1989, 1992). The starting point for controversy about the politics of Irish historiography is Ciaran Brady (ed.), *Interpreting Irish History: The Debate of Historical Revisionism* (Dublin: Irish Academic Press, 1994), containing influential essays by Theo Moody, F.S.L. Lyons, and Ronan Fanning. The most recent contribution to decades of debate on the subject is John M. Regan's *Myth and the Irish State: Historical Problems and Other Essays* (Kildare: Irish Academic Press, 2013). D. George Boyce and Alan O'Day (eds.), *The Making of Modern Irish History: Revisionism and the Revisionism Controversy* (London: Routledge, 1996) offers a collaborative overview of the impact of revisionism on various periods of Irish history, while Evi Gkotzaridis, *Trials of Irish History: Genesis and Evolution of a Reappraisal, 1938–2000* (Oxford: Routledge, 2006) presents a useful narrative of developments since 1938. The impact of the Troubles on Irish history is further explored in Ian McBride, "The Shadow of the Gunman: Irish Historians and the IRA," *Journal of Contemporary History* 46: 3 (July 2011), pp. 686–710; and in Richard Bourke, "Languages of Conflict and the Northern Ireland Troubles," *Journal of Modern History* 83: 3 (September 2011), pp. 544–578.

1. T. W. Moody, "A New History of Ireland," *Irish Historical Studies* 16: 63 (March 1969), pp. 241–257.

2. Josef L. Altholz, "Lord Acton and the Plan of the Cambridge Modern History," *Historical Journal 39*: 3 (September 1996), pp. 723–736.

3. Georg Weber, *Allgemeine Weltgeschichte unter besonderer Berücksichtigung des Geistes- und Kulturlebens der Völker und mit Benutzung der neueren geschichtlichen Forschungen für die gebildeten Stände bearbeitet* (Leipzig: Engelmann, 1857–1880), 15 vols.; Ernest Lavisse and Alfred Nicolas Rambaud (eds.), *Histoire générale du IVe siècle à nos jours* (Paris: A. Colin, 1893–1902), 12 vols.

4. As indicated by its unwieldy title.

5. See Georg G. Iggers, *The German Conception of History: The National Tradition of Historical Thought from Herder to the Present* (Middletown, CT: Wesleyan University Press, 1968); John Burrow, *A History of Histories: Epics, Chronicles, Romances and Inquiries from Herodotus and Thucydides to the Twentieth Century* (London: Allen Lane, 2007), p. 455.

6. Fritz Ringer, *The Decline of the German Mandarins: The German Academic Community, 1890–1933* (Cambridge, MA: Harvard University Press, 1969, 1990), pp. 14–42.

7. Sheldon Rothblatt, *The Revolution of the Dons: Cambridge and Society in Victorian England* (1968) (Cambridge: Cambridge University Press, 1981), chapter 5. Compare to Stefan Collini, Donald Winch, and John Burrow, *That Noble Science of Politics: A Nineteenth-Century Intellectual History* (Cambridge: Cambridge University Press, 1983, 1987), pp. 362–363.

8. Leopold von Ranke, "On the Character of Historical Science," in Georg G. Iggers and Konrad Von Moltke (eds.), *Leopold von Ranke: The Theory and Practice of History* (Indianapolis, IN: Bobbs-Merrill, 1973). For the impact of the Germans on British historical research, see Lord Acton, "German Schools of History," *English Historical Review* 1: 1 (January 1886), pp. 7–42; J. W. Burrow, *A Liberal Descent: Victorian Historians and the English Past* (Cambridge: Cambridge University Press, 1981, 1983), pp. 119–125.

9. Moody, "New History of Ireland," p. 246.

10. Moody, "New History of Ireland," p. 245.

11. On these distinctions, see R. G. Collingwood, *The Idea of History* (Oxford: Oxford University Press, 1946, 2005), pp. 165 ff.

12. Anthony Grafton, *What Was History? The Art of History in Early Modern Europe* (Cambridge: Cambridge University Press, 2007).

13. Wolfgang J. Mommsen, "Objektivität und Parteilichkeit im historischen Werk Sybels und Treitschkes," in Reinhart Koselleck, Wolfgang J. Mommsen, and Jörn Rüsen (eds.), *Objektivität und Parteilichkeit in der Geschichtswissenschaft* (Munich: Deutscher Taschenbuch Verlag, 1977); Wilfried Nippel, *Johann Gustav Droysen: Ein Leben zwischen Wissenschaft und Politik* (Munich: C. H. Beck, 2008).

14. Georg G. Iggers, "Nationalism and Historiography: The German Example in Historical Perspective," in Stefan Berger, Mark Donovan, and Kevin Passmore (eds.), *Writing National Histories: Western Europe since 1800* (London and New York: Routledge, 1999).

15. A goal first articulated in Tacitus, *Annales*, II, 36.

16. T. W. Moody, "Irish History and Irish Mythology," (1978) in Ciaran Brady (ed.), *Interpreting Irish History: The Debate on Historical Revisionism* (Dublin: Irish Academic Press, 1994).

17. Ian R. Christie, "Myth and Reality in Late-Eighteenth-Century British Politics," in Ian R. Christie, *Myth and Reality in Late-Eighteenth-Century British Politics and Other Papers* (Berkeley and Los Angeles: University of California Press, 1970).

18. Ian R. Christie, *The End of North's Ministry, 1770–1782* (London: Macmillan, 1958). See the preface, p. v, for the tribute to Namier.

19. Lewis Namier, *The Structure of Politics at the Accession of George III* (London: Macmillan, 1929).

20. Moody, "Irish History and Irish Mythology," p. 71.

21. Herbert Butterfield, "Tendencies in Historical Study in England," *Irish Historical Studies* 4: 15 (March 1945), pp. 222–223, cited by Moody, "Irish History and Irish Mythology," p. 86.

22. *Epistle to the Ephesians*, VI, 12, cited in Moody, "Irish History and Irish Mythology," p. 86n, following Butterfield, "Tendencies," p. 223.

23. Butterfield, "Tendencies," p. 219.

24. On philosophical history in the eighteenth century, see J.G.A. Pocock, *Barbarism and Religion: Narratives of Civil Government* (Cambridge: Cambridge University Press, 1999).

25. F.S.L. Lyons, "The Meaning of Independence," in Brian Farrell ed., *The Irish Parliamentary Tradition* (Dublin: Gill and Macmillan, 1973), p. 223; Ronan Fanning, "'The Great Enchantment': Uses and Abuses of Modern Irish History" (1988), in James Dooge (ed.), *Ireland and the Contemporary World: Essays in Honour of Garret Fitzgerald* (Dublin: Gill and Macmillan, 1988), passim.; Roy Foster, "History and the Irish Question" (1988) in Roy Foster, *Paddy and Mr. Punch: Connections in Irish and English History* (London: Faber and Faber, 1993, 2011), p. 19.

26. J. J. Lee, *Ireland, 1912–1985: Politics and Society* (Cambridge: Cambridge University Press, 1989, 1992), pp. 588–589.

27. The long-overdue volume appeared as R. Dudley Edwards and T. Desmond Williams eds., *The Great Famine: Studies in Irish History, 1845–1852* (Dublin: Browne and Nolan, 1956).

28. [Robert Dudley Edwards], "The Future of Fianna Fáil," *Leader: Current Affairs, Literature, Politics, Art and Industry*, January 29, 1955, p. 7. Copy at University College Dublin Archives, File LA 22/1204.

29. Moody, "Irish History and Irish Mythology," p. 71.

30. Edmund Burke, *Reflections on the Revolution in France*, edited by J.C.D. Clark (Stanford, CA: Stanford University Press, 2001), pp. 310–311.

31. Emmanuel Joseph Sieyès, *What Is the Third Estate?* (1789) in Emmanuel Joseph Sieyès, *Political Writings*, edited by Michael Sonenscher (Indianapolis, IN: Hackett, 2003), p. 99.

32. Burke, *Reflections*, p. 310.

33. Burke, *Reflections*, p. 310.

34. John Curry, *A Brief Account from the Most Authentic Protestant Writers of the Causes, Motives, and Mischiefs of the Irish Rebellion* (London: N.P., 1747), p. 60, where Temple's *The Irish Rebellion* (1646) and Borlase's *History of the Irish Rebellion* (1679), are described as having inaugurated a genre with peculiar "Malice."

35. See, for example, Henry Brooke, *The Farmer's Six Letters to the Protestants of Ireland* (Dublin: George Faulkner, 1745); [Anon.], *Seasonable Advice to Protestants: Containing Some Means of Reviving and Strengthening the Protestant Interest* (Cork: George Harrison, 1745); [Anon.], *A Caveat against the Papists* (Dublin: N.P., 1746).

36. Curry, *A Brief Account*.

37. Walter Harris, *Fiction Unmasked: or, An Answer to a Dialogue Lately Published by a Popish Physician* (Dublin: N.P., 1757). On the activities of the Physico-Historical Society, see Eoin Magennis, "'A Land of Milk and Honey': The Physico-Historical Society, Improvement and the Surveys of Mid-Eighteenth-Century Ireland," *Proceedings of the Royal Irish Academy* C 102: 6 (2002), pp. 199–217.

38. John Curry, *Historical Memoirs of the Irish Rebellion in the Year 1641* (London: N.P., 1758), p. xi.

39. Curry, *Historical Memoirs*, p. xi.

40. Curry, *Historical Memoirs*, p. xix.

41. Curry, *Historical Memoirs*, p. xiv.

42. Curry, *Historical Memoirs*, xvii.

43. David Hume, *The History of England* (Indianapolis, IN: Liberty Fund, 1983), 6 vols., V, p. 342.

44. James Prior, *Life of the Right Honourable Edmund Burke* (1824) (London: N.P., 5th ed., 1854), pp. 60–61.

45. See Karen O'Brien, *Narratives of Enlightenment: Cosmopolitan History from Voltaire to Gibbon* (Cambridge: Cambridge University Press, 1997, 2005), chapter 3.

46. See Hume, *History of England*, V, p. 343.

47. Walter D. Love, "Charles O'Conor of Belanagare and Thomas Leland's 'Philosophical' History of Ireland," *Irish Historical Studies* 13: 49 (March 1962), pp. 1–25.

48. O'Conor to Curry, May 26, 1772, cited in Love, "Charles O'Conor," p. 12n26.

49. Edmund Burke to Richard Burke, Jr., March 20, 1792, *The Correspondence of Edmund Burke*, ed. Thomas W. Copeland (Chicago: University of Chicago Press, 1958–1978), 10 vols., VII, p. 104.

50. Thomas Leland, *The History of Ireland from the Invasion of Henry II, with a Preliminary Discourse on the Antient State of that Kingdom* (Dublin: R. Marchbank, 1773), 3 vols., I, i–ii. Leland is referring to Richard Cox, *Hibernia Anglicana, or the History of Ireland from the Conquest thereof by the English to this Present Time* (London: H. Clark, 1689–1690),

51. Leland, *History of Ireland*, I, p. iii.

52. Leland, *History of Ireland*, II, p. 86.

53. John Curry, *An Historical and Critical Review of the Civil Wars in Ireland* (Dublin: J. Hoey, 1775), on Clarendon and Hume at pp. xiii–xv.

54. Curry, *Review*, p. 99.

55. Curry, *Review*, pp. 100 ff.

56. Charles O'Conor to Denis O'Conor, April 11, 1775, *Letters of Charles O'Conor of Belanagare: A Catholic Voice in Eighteenth-Century Ireland*, edited by Catherine Coogan Ward, Robert E. Ward, and John F. Wrynn (Washington, DC: Catholic University of America Press, 1988), pp. 322–323.

57. Clare O'Halloran, *Golden Ages and Barbarous Nations: Antiquarian Debate and Cultural Politics in Ireland, c. 1750–1800* (Cork and Notre Dame, IN: Notre Dame University Press, 2005).

58. Donald McCartney, "The Writing of History in Ireland 1800–30," *Irish Historical Studies* 10: 40 (September 1957), pp. 347–362; Oliver MacDonagh, *States of Mind: Two Centuries of Anglo-Irish Conflict, 1780–1980* (London: Allen and Unwin, 1983), pp. 1–9.

59. James Anthony Froude, *The English in Ireland in the Eighteenth Century* (London: Longmans, Green and Co., 1872–1874), 3 vols.

60. Donal McCartney, "James Anthony Froude and Ireland: A Historiographical Controversy of the Nineteenth Century," *Irish University Review* 1: 2 (Spring 1971), pp. 238–257.

61. W.E.H. Lecky, "Mr. Froude's English in Ireland," *Macmillan's Magazine*, 1873, p. 266.

62. Donal McCartney, *W.E.H. Lecky: Historian and Politician, 1838–1903* (Dublin: Lilliput Press, 1994), chapter 1.

63. [W.E.H. Lecky], *The Leaders of Public Opinion in Ireland* (London: Saunders, Otley and Co., 1861), p. 308.

64. Lecky, *Leaders of Public Opinion*, p. 307.

65. Lecky, *Leaders of Public Opinion*, p. 305.

66. W.E.H. Lecky, *A History of the Rise and Influence of the Spirit of Rationalism in Europe* (London: Longman, Green and Roberts, 1865), 2 vols., I, p. xix.

67. Lecky, *History of the Spirit of Rationalism*, I, p. xxii.

68. W.E.H. Lecky, *History of European Morals from Augustus to Charlemagne* (London: Longmans, Green and Co., 1869), 2 vols.

69. W.E.H. Lecky, *History of England in the Eighteenth Century* (London: Longmans, Green and Co., 1878–1890), 8 vols., I, pp. vi–vii.

70. MacCartney, *Lecky*, p. 88.

71. W.E.H. Lecky, *The Leaders of Public Opinion in Ireland* (London: Longmans, Green and Co., 1871, pp. xix–xx.

72. Lecky, *Leaders of Public Opinion in Ireland* (1871), p. xx.

73. W.E.H. Lecky, "Ireland in the Light of History" (1891) in W.E.H. Lecky, *Historical and Political Essays* (London: Longmans, Green and Co., 1910), p. 79.

74. Speech at the centenary of Burke's death cited in Elisabeth van Dedem Lecky, *A Memoir of the Right Hon. William Edward Hartpole Lecky, by His Wife* (London: Longmans, Green and Co., 1909), p. 305.

75. W.E.H. Lecky, preface, *The Leaders of Public Opinion in Ireland* (London: Longmans, Green and Co., 1912), 2 vols., I, pp. vi–xii.

76. W.E.H. Lecky, *Clerical Influences: An Essay on Irish Sectarianism and English Government*, edited by W.E.G. Lloyd and F. Cruise O'Brien (Dublin: Maunsel and Co., 1911), p. 13.

77. Benjamin Evans Lippincott, *Victorian Critics of Democracy: Carlyle, Ruskin, Arnold, Stephen, Maine, Lecky* (Minneapolis: University of Minnesota Press, 1938).

78. W.E.H. Lecky, *Democracy and Liberty* (1896) (Indianapolis, IN: Liberty Fund, 1981), 2 vols., I, p. 217.

79. Lecky, *Democracy and Liberty*, pp. 397, 425.

80. Lecky, *Democracy and Liberty*, pp. 127–128, 217.

81. F.S.L. Lyons, *Ireland since the Famine* (1971) (London: Fontana, 1973, 1990), p. 7.

82. Lyons, *Ireland since the Famine*, p. 17.

83. F.S.L. Lyons, *Culture and Anarchy in Ireland* (Oxford: Oxford University Press, 1979).

84. For criticism of Lyons, see Roy Foster, "'Colliding Cultures': Leland Lyons and the Reinterpretation of Irish History," in *The Irish Story, Telling Tales and Making It Up in Ireland* (London: Penguin, 2001).

85. R. F. Foster, *Modern Ireland, 1600–1972* (London: Penguin, 1988), p. 454.

86. Foster, *Modern Ireland*, pp. 473, 474, 480, 484, 493. For assorted additional applications of the term, cf. pp. 449, 450, 456, 459, 506, 508.

87. In this genre see, for example, Tom Garvin, *Irish Revolutionaries in Ireland, 1858–1928* (Oxford: Oxford University Press, 1987).

88. "Revisionism" itself is a contested term. For discussion, see D. George Boyce and Alan O'Day, "Introduction: 'Revisionism' and the 'Revisionist Controversy,'" in D. George Boyce and Alan O'Day (eds.), *The Making of Modern Irish History: Revisionism and the Revisionism Controversy* (London: Routledge, 1996); and, more recently, Robert Perry, *Revisionist Scholarship and Modern Irish Politics* (Farnham, Surrey: Ashgate, 2013), chapter 1.

89. Hugh Kearney, *The British Isles: A History of Four Nations* (Cambridge: Cambridge University Press, 1989, 2007), pp. 8–9, 281.

90. Peter Hart, *The IRA and Its Enemies: Violence and Community in Cork, 1916–1923* (Oxford: Oxford University Press, 1998); Matthew Kelly, *The Fenian Ideal and Irish Nationalism, 1882–1916* (Woodbridge: Boydell, 2006); Senia Pašeta, *Irish Nationalist Women, 1900–1918* (Cambridge: Cambridge University Press, 2013); Fearghal McGarry, *The Rising: Easter 1916* (Oxford: Oxford University Press, 2010).

91. Roy Foster, *Vivid Faces: The Revolutionary Generation in Ireland, 1890–1923* (London: Allen Lane, 2014).

92. For an indicative judgment about the impact of the Troubles on the writing of Irish history, see Ronan Fanning, "Introduction," in *Fatal Path: British Government and Irish Revolution, 1910–1922* (London: Faber and Faber, 2013).

93. Marianne Elliott, *Partners in Revolution: The United Irishmen and France* (New Haven, CT: Yale University Press, 1982); David Fitzpatrick, *Politics and Irish Life, 1913–1921: Provincial Experience of War and Revolution* (Dublin: Gill and Macmillan, 1977).

94. Paul Bew, *Land and the National Question, 1858–1882* (Dublin: Gill and Macmillan, 1978); Paul Bew, *Conflict and Conciliation in Ireland 1890–1910: Parnellites and Agrarian Radicals* (Oxford: Oxford University Press, 1987).

95. Paul Bew, Peter Gibbon, and Henry Patterson, *Northern Ireland, 1921–2001: Political Forces and Social Classes* (London: Serif, 2002).

96. Lee, *Ireland, 1912–1985*, pp. 511–521.

97. Cormac Ó Gráda, *Ireland: A New Economic History, 1780–1939* (Oxford: Oxford University Press, 1004), p. 173.

98. D. B. Quinn, "Agenda for Irish History: Ireland from 1461 to 1603," *Irish Historical Studies* 4: 15 (March 1945), pp. 258–269. For discussion, see Nicholas Canny, "Writing Early Modern History: Ireland, Britain, and the Wider World," *Historical Journal* 46: 3 (September 2003), pp. 723–747.

99. Nicholas Canny, *The Elizabethan Conquest of Ireland: A Pattern Established* (Hassocks: Harvester, 1976).

100. Richard Bourke, "Pocock and the Presuppositions of the New British History," *Historical Journal* 53: 3 (September 2010), pp. 747–770.

101. The debate first emerged after the first Home Rule bill of 1886, spawning a literature of its own. It resurfaced after 1969 under the influence of the British and Irish Communist Organisation, entering mainstream historical debate thereafter.

102. Alvin Jackson, *The Ulster Party: Irish Unionists and the House of Commons, 1884–1911* (Oxford: Oxford University Press, 1989), pp. 1–21.

103. For a political and historiographical overview of this question, see Michael Gallagher, "How Many Nations Are There in Ireland?" *Ethnic and Racial Studies* 18: 4 (1995), pp. 715–739.

104. Comparisons, especially between Ireland and post-Gaullist France, are drawn in Evi Gkotzaridis, *Trials of Irish History: Genesis and Evolution of a Reappraisal, 1938–2000* (Oxford: Routledge, 2006), p. 4.

105. For ready access to the relevant debates, see Richard Bourke and Quentin Skinner eds., *Popular Sovereignty in Historical Perspective* (Cambridge: Cambridge University Press, 2016).

106. This figure comprises the number of households, North and South. For statistics, see *The Northern Ireland Census 1981: Summary Report* (Belfast: Her Majesty's Stationery Office, 1981); *Census of Population of Ireland 1981: Household Composition and Family Units* (Dublin: Central Statistics Office, 1985).

107. The Irish National Liberation Army is a possible fourth contender. Neither the Ulster Volunteer Force nor the Ulster Freedom Fighters consistently aimed to reconfigure established sovereignty.

108. Louis Cullen, "Catholics under the Penal Laws," *Eighteenth-Century Ireland* 1 (1986), pp. 23–36. Statement from pp. 24–45.

109. See David Runciman, *Pluralism and the Personality of the State* (Cambridge: Cambridge University Press, 1997).

CHAPTER 12

RELIGION

Ian McBride

A WELL-WORN IRISH JOKE BEGINS WITH a stranger being stopped on the streets of Belfast and asked whether he is a Protestant or a Catholic. To hear these words in Northern Ireland, as surely everyone knows, is not a good omen. Normally the natives go to great lengths to avoid this explosive question, preferring to work out the answer by the subtle code of nods and winks that one anthropologist has called "the telling."[1] In this case, our unfortunate visitor replies, "Neither, I'm an atheist." "Aye," insists the Belfast man, "but are ye a Protestant atheist or a Catholic atheist?"

Like much of the black comedy that thrived during the Troubles, this old joke invites us to despair at the intractability of Ulster's sectarian division and its apparently irrational character, as well as the persistent connection between violence and religious intolerance. Not surprisingly, perhaps, a version of it turns up in Christopher Hitchens's *God Is Not Great* (2007), where the author recalls interviewing the relatives of those "kidnapped and killed or tortured by rival religious death squads, often for no other reason than membership of another confession."[2] It also appears in Richard Dawkins's best-selling polemic, *The God Delusion* (2006). Although Dawkins clearly understands that the Troubles revolved around political issues rather than theological controversies, he maintains that there would have been no conflict without religion. Indeed he believes that intractable violence all across the world—Israel/Palestine, Iraq, Kosovo—can be attributed to the prevalence of religious mentalities.[3]

In contrast, for historians and sociologists, religious difference is not an adequate explanation of violence, but rather something that must itself be explained. And, as it turns out, there is no evidence that individuals who are more inflexible in their religious beliefs or more regular in church attendance are also more militant in their politics.[4] But recent controversies concerning the multiple cases of child abuse concealed by the Catholic Church have provided further reasons for hostility toward organized religion, in this case south of the border. The domineering figure of John Charles McQuaid, archbishop of Dublin between 1940 and 1971, is now viewed as the personification of everything that was wrong with independent Ireland—a society that was authoritarian, philistine, and conformist; that regarded material wealth and modernity with suspicion and encouraged a fatalistic acceptance of poverty; a society whose churches and schools seethed with sexual exploitation and petty brutality. Looking back at the decades of economic stagnation that followed Irish independence, some scholars have also suggested that Catholicism, at least in its Irish manifestations, is incompatible with capitalist enterprise. Tom Garvin recognizes that what he calls Catholic "fundamentalism" cannot, on its own, account for the fact that the Irish missed out on the unprecedented economic growth that characterized post-war Europe. Avoidance of the Second World War, with its attendant social and cultural convulsions, is surely one important factor. Others include the demographic legacy of the Great Famine of the 1840s, and the undoing of landlordism by the Land Acts of the later nineteenth century, which created an entrenched social order dominated by a large class of small farmers, whom economic reformers were afraid to confront. There is also the inconvenient fact that, during the same period, Irish-Americans remained devout Hiberno-Roman Catholics, and yet they managed to enjoy worldly success without the inhibitions attributed to their old-world cousins. Yet the villains of Garvin's influential book *Preventing the Future* are preeminently the clerics. Garvin quotes approvingly Horace Plunkett's view that Catholicism in Ireland was "in some of its tendencies non-economic, if not actually anti-economic," because it elevated the prospect of justice in the next world above human betterment.[5] The resulting portrait of independent Ireland is disturbingly reminiscent of Ulster Unionist denunciations of the priest-ridden Free State.[6]

It would appear that St. Patrick has a lot to answer for. But a survey of recent historical controversies—over the failure of the Reformation in Ireland, the impact of the penal laws, the timing and extent of the devotional revolution—makes possible a much more complex understanding of the impact of religion on political division, violence, and economic behavior. If anything, it suggests that the criticisms of Irish religion outlined above have mistaken cause for effect. Most historians, for example, have concluded that the sexual puritanism of modern Ireland is the product of a highly distinctive social structure rather than Catholic clerical power. Similarly, the intransigent character of Irish faith can plausibly be attributed to political polarization rather than the reverse. But to think of religion as simply a convenient kind of boundary marker between two ethnic or national groups, as if religious belief were interchangeable with language or skin color, is equally inadequate. How the churches have been structured and governed, their relationship with schools and the state, and their theological and social outlooks all have important implications for the internal experiences and values of the two main communities, as well as the functioning of the boundary itself.[7]

Religious hostility between Protestants and Catholics reflects a combination of theological tradition, ecclesiastical organization, and differing experiences of authority. For militant Protestants, such as "Roaring Hugh Hanna" in the 1860s or Ian Paisley in the 1960s, "popery" was not viewed simply a set of religious doctrines but as a sinister and powerful *political* organization bent on eradicating heresy. Nationalist resentment at Protestant dominance was not focused on the church—there is no single Protestant church—but on its political and social manifestations, such as the Orange Order. Such fears reflect the actual behavior of the two constitutional entities established in the 1920s. Southern Protestants were permitted to maintain their social privileges in a state that nevertheless gave legislative backing to Catholic teachings on divorce and contraception. In contrast, Northern Catholics suffered widespread political and social discrimination in a state that was—in its outward forms at least—secular. Anti-Catholic stereotypes in the North combined psychological attributes (Catholics lacked the industry and independence of the "Ulsterman"), social prejudice (Catholic poverty was attributed to lack of family planning and other forms of self-discipline), as well as political disloyalty.[8] While anti-Catholicism is an established field of historical and sociological research, there has yet to be an academic study of "anti-Protestantism." The materials for such a study are nevertheless abundant. In the Free State of the 1920s and 1930s, for example, Protestantism was often equated with paganism, materialism, sexual immorality, and birth control—then identified as "the crime of race suicide," which thankfully had not established a footing among "the plain people of Ireland, that is, among the Catholic people."[9]

The most celebrated revolt against Irish religion generated *A Portrait of the Artist as a Young Man*, first serialized in 1914; but Joyce's mind remained "supersaturated" with the beliefs he had disavowed.[10] *Ulysses* is suffused with references to religious orders, saints, Catholic rituals, devotions, and doctrines.[11] Correspondingly, the occult preoccupations of W. B. Yeats (and other literary revivalists) have been interpreted as a form of specifically Protestant mysticism, a fin-de-siècle response on the part of Anglo-Irish bohemians to the "superstitious" Catholicism they regarded with a mixture of contempt and fascination.[12] Joyce himself suspected that the craze for Theosophy was an escape route for lapsed Protestants, and retorted that the literary mystics of Dublin could not "compare either for consistence, holiness, or charity with a fifth-rate saint of the Catholic Church."[13] Even ex-Protestants and ex-Catholics have been divided by the creeds they have repudiated. As our Irish atheist joke reminds us, religion means many things. It has helped construct enduring collective identities as well as providing personal assurance and a sense of salvation.

Compared with their European neighbors, or with the English-speaking societies of North America and Australasia, the single most striking feature of Irish
people is surely their obstinate religiosity. In the now voluminous literature on
secularization, Ireland is regularly cited as the outstanding exception to general
trends. During the 1960s the reverence displayed in Ireland toward the priesthood was unmatched anywhere in the Western world. An astonishing 78% of
Dublin Catholics identified with the following statement, which today seems
almost incomprehensible: "if I had a son, I would surely wish him to be a priest,
above and beyond everything else in the world." This figure is taken from a sociological survey carried out by an American Jesuit, Bruce Francis Biever, with the
cooperation of Archbishop McQuaid. The results now seem more damaging than
the rabid outpourings of Ian Paisley's *Protestant Telegraph*. In the event of a conflict between church and state, 87% of respondents rejected the proposition that
their primary allegiance should be given to the state. Biever also found that 73%
of his respondents did not believe that the pleasurable feelings associated with sex
were good, while 69% objected to the statement that what a person does in his
heart is more important than going to mass.[14]

For much of the twentieth century the Irish Catholic was a fixed point of reference in a sea of bewildering change, rivaled only by the *Polak-Katolik*.[15] The
Irish and the Poles were three times more likely to be regular church-attenders
than the French, Germans, or Dutch; they also provide the only two cases where
the number of religious vocations actually increased after the sixties rather than
plummeted.[16] How far this national exceptionalism can be projected back beyond
the 1960s, into an era before large-scale surveys of belief and practice, is less clear.
We tend to forget that the decade after 1945 was an era of religious revival in the
United States and many parts of Europe, when Christianity was regarded as a
defining feature of the free world, in contrast to Nazi Germany or global Communism. We need to remember also that Catholicism was intensely political all
across post-war Europe, whether in Italy and parts of France (where politics polarized between Catholics and Communists) or in the "pillarized" society of the
Netherlands (where Catholics and Protestants formed regional subcultures alongside Socialists and Liberals). In the first half of the twentieth century it is arguable that England, where religious practice had been in decline since the 1890s,
was more anomalous than Ireland.[17] Yet foreign visitors to Ireland, like Louis
Paul-Dubois in 1908, were generally struck by "the intensity of Catholic belief
there, and by the fervour of its outward manifestations."[18] What made Ireland
unusual, moreover, was not just high levels of sacramental observance but also
the ideological and organizational power of the church. Its vigor and endurance
can only be understood if we bear in mind that in Ireland (as, again, in Poland)

fidelity to the church had become intertwined with a long-standing struggle for national liberation.

The religious topography of Ireland in the 1960s reflects surprisingly faithfully the patterns of national or ethnic settlement established by the plantation schemes of the seventeenth century (see table 12.1). During the early modern period, Irish people did not, with relatively few exceptions, become Protestant; instead Protestant people were imported into Ireland, on a scale with no obvious contemporary European parallels. The first religious census was attempted in 1732–1733, based on information supplied by the collectors of the hearth tax. There are good reasons for thinking that these tax returns understated the number of households in general and the number of Catholic families in particular. Scholars have suggested that the size of the Catholic majority, estimated at 73%, was probably closer to 80%. Yet the regional pattern is instantly recognizable. The hearth tax returns revealed that Protestants were vastly outnumbered in the three provinces of Leinster (4:1), Munster (9:1), and Connacht (11:1). In the six counties that would later compose Northern Ireland, however, Protestant families enjoyed substantial majorities in Antrim (4:1), Down (3:1), Londonderry (3:1), and Armagh (2:1); while in Fermanagh they outnumbered Catholic families by three to two, and in Tyrone they were "near Equal." In the northeast, today, Church-of-Ireland congregations are still clustered where English colonists settled, along the Lagan Valley into north Armagh and Fermanagh; while Presbyterians are most numerous in the heartland of Scots settlements in Antrim and north Down. When William Shaw Mason compiled his three-volume *Statistical Account or Parochial Survey of Ireland* (1814–1819), the first work of its kind, the imprint of seventeenth-century settlement was still evident at the level of the individual parish. Maghera in County Derry is a typical example: the survey reported "the usual division of its inhabitants into English, Irish, and Scotch," noting that the differences of dialect, customs, and creed coalesced to demarcate "distinct races of people."[19]

Since the seventeenth century the spatial distribution of the main denominations has altered in two obvious ways. One reflects the gradual erosion of Protestantism, a comparatively recent development. In the first quarter of the twentieth century the minority denominations in the South were depleted by higher rates of emigration, lower birth rates, and intermarriage; the dismantling of British rule and the violence of the Irish revolution also contributed to the decisive drop that took place between 1911 and 1926.[20] Since the 1960s the Protestant majority in the Six Counties has also contracted as a result of lower fertility and intensified communal segregation. The effects of urbanization have been even more dramatic. Plans to expel all Catholics from cities and towns were implemented under Cromwell in the 1650s but abandoned as impractical in subsequent decades. In Georgian Dublin and in Victorian Belfast rapid urban expansion meant that these two Protestant bastions came to reflect the denominational balance of their respective

TABLE 12.1. PERCENTAGE OF CATHOLICS, 1732

Year	East Ulster	Mid-Ulster	South Ulster	Rest of Ireland	Total
1732	23	51	61	86.57	73
1732 (adjusted)	24.84	55.08	65.88	93.50	79

Source: David Bindon, *An Abstract of the Number of Protestant and Popish Families in the Several Counties and Provinces of Ireland* (Dublin, 1736).

Note: East Ulster here refers to Antrim, Down, and Belfast; Mid-Ulster to Londonderry, Armagh, Tyrone, and Fermanagh; South Ulster to Cavan, Donegal, and Monaghan.

hinterlands. When Jonathan Swift took up residence as dean of St. Patrick's in 1715, the Catholic population of Dublin was around a third of the total, but these proportions had already been reversed by the end of the century.[21] When Wolfe Tone visited Belfast in 1791—the town he called his "adopted mother"—its eighteen thousand inhabitants were overwhelmingly Presbyterian; a century later Catholics accounted for just over a quarter of the population, having increased rapidly in the first half of the century and then fallen after the Famine (see table 12.2).[22]

Adjustments in the boundaries between confessional communities have generally resulted from social and economic shifts rather than the accumulation of individual decisions to change sides. The most obvious exceptions derive from the eighteenth-century "penal times," when it was hoped that social pressures, reinforced by discriminatory legislation, would rectify the imbalance between the Anglican and the Catholic populations. In fact only 5,800 Catholics conformed to

TABLE 12.2. PERCENTAGE OF CATHOLICS, 1834–1991

Year	East Ulster	Mid-Ulster	South Ulster	Rest of Ireland	Total
1834	31.4	50.5	74.9	92.8	80.9
1861	29.7	51.6	76.3	91.1	77.7
1911	24.3	50.5	81.8	93.8	75.0
1991	29.3	54.8	87.6	91.8	75.1

Source: John Coakley, "Religion, National Identity and Political Change in Modern Ireland," *Irish Political Studies* 17: 1 (2002), p. 10.

Note: East Ulster here refers to Antrim, Down, and Belfast; Mid-Ulster to Londonderry, Armagh, Tyrone, and Fermanagh; South Ulster to Cavan, Donegal, and Monaghan.

the established church, roughly a third of them from landed families. Even at their peak, in the 1760s, conformities numbered just 131 annually. In the short term, moreover, converts were treated as a distinct category or "interest," mistrusted by many members of the established church. Far from abandoning their own communities, many converts had simply opted for a pragmatic accommodation with the Protestant regime and used their influence to shield their Catholic relatives from persecution.[23]

II

Contemporaries who reflected on the character of Ireland's Protestant Ascendancy recognized that religious affiliation, ethnic attachment, and social status had overlapped to produce an antagonistic relationship more profound and enduring than any single factor. The Williamite war (1689–1691) saw the last formal military campaigns on Irish soil and was followed by the final transfers of confiscated Catholic estates. After the battles of the Boyne and Aughrim the victorious Protestants, such as Sir Richard Cox, spoke of the Irish as "Enemies by Nation, Manners, Religion and Interest."[24] Differences of national origin and of "interest" (i.e., those created by the redistribution of landed property) were not, by themselves, viewed as insurmountable: indeed Cox looked forward to a day when they would be *"buried and annihilated."* It was the religious bar, he believed, *"the Irreconcilable Antipathy that is between the Roman Catholick Religion and Heresie,"* that obstructed reconciliation:

> This great concern has so silenced all the rest, that at this Day we know no difference of Nation but what is expressed by *Papist* and *Protestant*; if the most Ancient Natural Irish-Man be a Protestant, no Man takes him for other than an English-Man; and if a Cockny be a Papist, he is reckoned, in *Ireland*, as much as Irish-man as if he was born on Slevelogher [Sliabh Luachra].[25]

The extension of the Reformation in Ireland, where the power of the English crown had been severely restricted, was dependent on repeated bursts of English conquest and colonization stretching over more than a century and culminating in the military campaigns fought by Cromwell and William III. The emergence—between roughly the 1550s and the 1640s—of two distinct and mutually hostile religious blocs was more the product of violence than its cause. There were certainly other reasons the Irish Reformation failed, most obviously the poor resources and inadequate organization of the existing church.[26] As in many other parts of Europe, the attempt to replace a religion of ritual observance with a bibliocentric faith based on scriptural authority and personal salvation also confronted the formidable obstacles of illiteracy and linguistic difference. For at least a century after Luther's defiance of Rome, the Reformation everywhere remained a largely urban phenomenon; and where it eventually triumphed—in England,

Scotland, parts of Germany, and the Netherlands—it was often weakened by ferocious internal divisions.[27] Catholic Ireland also benefited from the system of Irish colleges scattered through Spain, France, Italy, and the diverse territories that made up the Holy Roman Empire, which produced the standard ideological defenses of the Irish nation in addition to a regular supply of priests. There is nevertheless much truth in Edmund Burke's view that religious reform was fatally compromised by its entanglement in the contest between settlers and natives that could be traced all the way back, through the reign of Elizabeth, to a period "before the words Protestant and Papist were heard of in the world."[28] Crucially, the sporadic imposition of Protestantism was bound up not only with the military conquest of Gaelic Ireland but also with the marginalization of the Old English nobility and gentry—the older colonial community descended from Anglo-Norman settlement of the twelfth century, who had been the traditional agents of anglicization in Ireland.

That religious differences were a consequence of political polarization, rather than its cause, has been borne out by those few adventurous Irish historians who have attempted comparative analyses. Where the Reformation thrived—in parts of France, in the Netherlands, in Bohemia and Hungary under the Hapsburgs, and in the Polish-Lithuanian commonwealth—Protestantism had become allied with the defense of noble privileges and representative institutions against a centralizing monarchy; in Ireland the situation was the other way round. A fruitful comparative survey of Ireland, Bohemia, and Hungary carried out by Tadhg Ó hAnnracháin has identified a range of other significant factors. In each case an imperial monarchy sought to impose its official religion on a subordinate kingdom by coercion. But in central Europe the Habsburgs benefited from more compelling push-and-pull factors. Military coercion against Protestant rebels in Bohemia was systematic and sustained, whereas religious persecution in Ireland ebbed and flowed as priorities shifted in London. At the same time, Protestant Ireland lacked the resources to mount the extensive missionary enterprise introduced in Bohemian lands, where nineteen new Jesuit colleges were founded. Above all, however, Ó hAnnracháin confirms that the relationship between metropolitan authority and the local elites was the key element in determining the success or failure of conversion. In Hungary and Bohemia the imposition of new office-holders from the Habsburg court was tempered by the retention of native Magyar, Croatian, and Czech magnates; in Ireland the religious conformity of the landed class was achieved by replacing it with another.[29]

Although Ireland's conflicting communities were increasingly divided along religious lines, this is not the same thing as saying that religion *caused* the divisions.[30] To illustrate this distinction we have only to examine that paradigmatic case of "sectarian" violence, the 1641 rising, which became the key foundation myth of the Protestant Irish. The most notorious atrocities took place in the triangle formed by the mid-Ulster towns of Dungannon, Armagh, and Lurgan. The area of fertile land and dense English settlement around Loughgall and Legacorry (present-day Richhill) formed the epicenter; in contrast, the Scots settlements were, initially at least, left alone. A careful study of the depositions for Armagh reveals that the minimum figure for Protestants killed in this county alone was roughly five hundred out of a settler population numbering somewhere between three thousand and five thousand. The vast majority of the victims were unarmed civilians. Contrary to Protestant legend, however, there is no evidence of any plan for a general massacre of planters. The insurrection was initiated by the seizure of Charlemont Castle and other fortifications by a group of Gaelic lords led by Sir Phelim O'Neale, their declared aims being "the libertie of their religion," and "the recouery of those lands ... vniustly held from them."[31] Over the next two or three weeks settler families were robbed, stripped of their clothes, and expelled from their homes by groups of yeomen, laborers, and servants who were often their own neighbors or employees. For O'Neale, who was not only a substantial land-owner, but also a London-trained lawyer and member of parliament, this explo-sion of popular grievances was clearly a very unpleasant surprise.

Sometime around the middle of November the first recorded massacres took place. The common feature was the apparently spontaneous slaughter of convoys of Protestant prisoners being transported by insurgents. Once again the violence was uncoordinated, reflecting the failure of O'Neale's planned coup rather than its success: the frenzied attacks on defenseless Protestants were carried out in the knowledge that the Catholic conspiracy to seize Dublin Castle had failed, and that settlers were mobilizing in various parts of the North and had already repulsed an insurgent force at Augher in Country Tyrone. The drowning of about one hundred Protestant men, women, and children at Portadown, and the burning of a group of prisoners in a thatched cottage at Kilmore, seem to have been precipi-tated by a bloody defeat inflicted on the rebels at Lisnagarvy (now Lisburn).[32] As with Scullabogue in 1798, the most notorious killings occurred not in areas where rebel forces were attempting to solidify their control, but where the improvised structures of rebellion were on the point of total collapse.

Religion played a vital role in the atrocities committed in Ulster and through-out the island, although it was not the *primum mobile* described in Sir John Tem-ple's *History of the Irish Rebellion*, first published in 1646, and periodically re-printed, recycled, and updated over the next two and a half centuries. The crisis in Ireland was intertwined with events in the other kingdoms of Charles I, whose pretensions to royal absolutism had already provoked an uprising of Scots Cove-nanters in 1637 and deadlock with Puritan parliamentarians in England. The rad-icalization of religion in Scotland and England was a menacing development for Irish Catholics, who were increasingly excluded from political office on the grounds of confessional allegiance and were already fearful for the security of their landed estates. At the high-political level, the collapse of order throughout the British Isles was caused by what Conrad Russell called "the problem of multiple kingdoms," that is, the attempted centralization of three separate kingdoms, each with its own distinctive political and social structures, and the resistance provoked by administrative innovations. But in the British case (as in the Spanish Netherlands), a political crisis in a multiple kingdom was combined with a crisis of religious division with particularly toxic results. The impact of the Reformation and the consequent re-ordering of European states along confessional lines had produced a world where religious uniformity was regarded as essential to political stability. For a ruler to tolerate in one of his kingdoms religious beliefs that were prohibited in another was asking for trouble. To maintain, as the Gaelic and Old English lords had done, that adherence to the Church of Rome was compatible with loyalty to the English crown was to walk an increasingly precarious tightrope.[33]

The carnage of 1641 became so deeply embedded in the Protestant imagination, and has been exploited so tirelessly as evidence of Irish disloyalty and savagery, that historians have been deterred until recently from investigating the eight thousand witness accounts collected in its aftermath. Perhaps the most striking revelation in this extensive archive is the relative absence of the plantation itself as a motivating factor in the insurrection.[34] As order collapsed in mid-Ulster, the rebels began driving English settlers off their farms and taking their money, animals, clothes, and possessions. A frequent object of these house raids was the destruction of leases and other legal documents, particularly records of native debt, which suggests that the rebels were focused on redressing immediate economic grievances rather than the confiscation scheme that had been implemented more than thirty years earlier. Even in these early skirmishes, however, several depositions state that "their cheife malice was against Churchmen."[35]

As the disturbances spread across the island the "visceral hatred" of the settlers was evident in the humiliation of victims by stripping them of their clothes, but also in specifically sectarian forms of abuse.[36] Deponents recalled rebels urinating on bibles and prayer books as well as burning them, and the exhumation of Protestant remains from churchyards at the bidding of priests who would not consecrate the ground until "the hereticks bones were removed."[37] Although priests were sometimes singled out as the instigators of violence, some testimony recognized that they acted as a restraining influence, directing popular animosity against the symbols of Protestant worship rather than their persons. The familiar intersection of ethnic and religious hostility is clear in the deposition of William Wood, a yeoman from West Cork, who was warned by a band of insurgents that "all those that did not turne to their holy Masse, were damn'd; & that our religion was a new found religion inuented by Martin Luther and Caluin ... and that they would neuer trust an Englishman vpon any occasion whatsoeuer, no more than they would a Turke."[38] The recurring insistence that settlers "turn to Mass" (another anticipation of 1798) was sometimes successful. If the geography of the rebellion can be explained by the extent of plantation in different parts of the island, and the resultant disruption of customary landholding practices, the ritualized character of the violence reveals the mobilization of local communities—men, women, and children—who seem to have defined their boundaries in essentially religious terms and who acted collectively to eradicate the pollutant of Protestant heresy from Ireland's soil.[39]

III

During the eighteenth century many Protestants in Ireland continued to see themselves—in Burke's words—as "a sort of colonial garrison to keep the natives in subjection." It was unsurprising that Catholics continued to identify the reformed faith with the power structures that had dispossessed them. "The religion of this country," as William King lamented, "is rather a national faction than conscience."[40] This was as true of the cohesive Ulster-Scots communities of the north as of the native Irish elsewhere. Like King, archbishop of Dublin between 1703 and 1729, the more energetic bishops and pious laymen welcomed the penal statutes enacted during the reigns of William and Anne as a serious opportunity for Anglicans to remake Irish society in their own image. Recent historical research has uncovered powerful reformist impulses in the clergy, with spiritual renewal sought through episcopal visitations, the revival of convocation (the governing body of the church), voluntary societies, and charity schools—all vying for attention. The urgency of converting the natives was a frequent theme of Anglican sermons and presumably was a goal to which most thinking Protestants in some sense subscribed. Yet the scale of the problem and the economic sacrifices involved were dimly perceived.

Matters were complicated by the fact that many Anglican clergymen regarded the Presbyterian Synod of Ulster as a more pressing challenge than the dispersed and depleted Catholic hierarchy. Scotland's Reformation had been "radical" rather than "magisterial" in character in the sense that key phases of its development were carried out in opposition to the monarch. A long history of struggle with civil authority encouraged the adoption of what is sometimes called the "doctrine of the two kingdoms," the view that the powers of church and state are quite distinct and are strictly confined to their respective spheres. In a world where political obligation was usually grounded on religious duty, this was an explosive notion (and completely incapable of realization). Deprived of the backing of the civil magistrate, Presbyterians fell back on an ascending theory of power that grounded the authority of ministers in the will of their congregations rather than the top-down model of episcopacy. Their insistence that ecclesiastical government should remain free from state interference and should be organized on a sort of republican model set Presbyterians in Ireland, as in Scotland, at odds with the Anglican church.[41] On these issues each side detected in the other the very negation of true Christianity—or, as they were inclined to put it, the remnants of "popery."

Anglican reformers were hopelessly divided over priorities. Even the most conscientious bishops suspected independent initiatives, such as the reformation societies, which were reliant on laymen and sometimes involved Dissenters. Although some lay enthusiasts, such as the memorably named Abel Ram of Wexford, cultivated the Society for the Promotion of Christian Knowledge in London, the predominantly Tory clergy looked to convocation as the proper instrument for restoring the dignity of the established church. While John Richardson of Belturbet drew up ambitious plans for a missionary drive led by Irish-language preachers, others believed that anglicization was the indispensable prelude to evangelization. In the meantime, surely Protestant backsliding, rather than popish superstition, was the proper target of a church with such meager resources? Consequently only two of the twenty-six charity schools in Dublin catered specifically to the Catholic poor.[42] By the 1720s King was leading a group of disillusioned Anglican bishops who attempted to block further penal legislation in the House of Lords. The contrast between the House of Commons's tenacity in seizing and redistributing Catholic estates and their failure, session after session, to improve the maintenance of Anglican curates provoked King to complain that the penal code had become a mechanism for controlling the natives rather than converting them: "Papists make the best Tenants," he observed sardonically, since "they pay more rent and are greater slaves to their landlords than protestants wou'd be."[43]

None of this is to argue that religious belonging was simply a convenient means of excluding Ireland's colonized populations from political and social power. The Protestant Ascendancy of the eighteenth century pitted its resources against a theological threat and against the ritual practices of Catholics, especially popular pilgrimages; above all it was locked in a struggle with an international organization supported by the great imperial monarchies of Europe. Protestants anxiously watched the trials of vulnerable Protestant communities on the continent. In 1580 roughly half of Europe had been Protestant; by 1680 the proportion had fallen to about one-fifth as Protestant princes were converted and grants of religious toleration revoked. It was King's consistent belief that the survival of Irish Protestantism was bound up with the fate of the "Protestant Interest" in Europe, and he compared the sufferings of Irish Protestants under James II to those of the Vaudois under the Duke of Savoy, the Hungarians under the Emperor Leopold, and the Huguenots under Louis XIV.[44] Conversely, the suppression of the Jesuits in all Catholic states between 1759 and 1773 and the introduction of toleration for Protestant, Greek Orthodox, and Jewish minorities throughout the Habsburg dominions by Joseph II broke apart the Protestant consensus on the penal code. Even before the French Revolution it seemed to some reformers that "popery" was decaying all over Europe and could not survive among the Irish "unless we prop up their superstition with their resentment, and keep their prejudices alive by maintaining our own."[45]

The Catholic hierarchy was even more likely to view Irish developments in a European context, not least because of its dependence on continental seminaries for education, intellectual creativity, and print. The Franciscan scholars who flourished at Louvain during the first half of the seventeenth century had reworked Irish historical sources into a new national narrative that stressed the continuity of Ireland's faith from the early Christian era, its unswerving loyalty to the papacy, and its resilience in the face of foreign persecution. It was at Louvain that the word *eithriceacht* ("heresy") was introduced into the Irish language.[46] The coalescence of political discontents and Counter-Reformation theology during the revolts of Elizabeth's reign left a difficult legacy for later generations of Catholic landowners and merchants keen to reach an accommodation with the Stuarts and Hanoverians. In 1727 and again in 1757 Catholic noblemen drew up statements repudiating the notorious deposing power claimed by the papacy; in both cases attempts at compromise foundered on the opposition of the Holy See itself as well as that of orthodox controversialists at home.[47] It mattered little that no pope had actually released his subjects from their duty of obedience since Elizabeth was excommunicated by Pius V in 1570. Theories of political obligation, monarchical power, and rights of resistance were now so entangled in Europe's wars of religion that Ireland's divisions could not easily be resolved within its own national boundaries. As the age of confessional states gave way to the age of revolutions, ecclesiastical leaders continued to view domestic politics through continental lenses. Both of the two great modernizers, John Thomas Troy (1739–1823) and Paul Cullen (1803–1878), spent their formative years in Rome, returned to Ireland determined to impose a more sanitized and ultramontane faith on their people, and consistently subordinated local demands for national self-government to the overriding struggle against the revolutionary creeds unleashed in 1789 and 1848.

The church that emerged from the penal era was a remarkable phenomenon: a fully functioning underground organization, maintained on a voluntary basis in direct opposition to the regime. By the middle of the century the full "titular" hierarchy of some twenty-six bishops had been re-established. Even more impressive, there was an effective parish school system over much of the island, operating in defiance of the penal laws, in which the Catholic catechism was taught. The Catholic Church was already a uniquely powerful alternative center of legitimacy and discipline, a shadowy state within the state. Its only significant rivals for popular allegiance were the secret oath-bound fraternities of the Whiteboys, Rightboys, and Defenders, who erected their own alternative structures of power on behalf of the oppressed; on occasion these groups attempted to regulate clerical dues and even the administration of the sacraments, threatening their priests with the same ritual punishments they applied to land agents. The ecclesiastical organization was also vital to a series of "national" bodies, including the Catholic Convention of 1792, the first democratically elected body in Irish history, and O'Connell's Catholic Association of the 1820s.

It was the French Revolution that convinced British statesmen that Ireland's Catholic hierarchy, for so long a potential source of subversion, might become a powerful stabilizing influence. In the aftermath of the 1798 rebellion Dublin Castle worked closely with Archbishop Troy on the passage of the Union, convinced that the benevolent neutrality of the hierarchy was essential to its success.[48] The political and social influence acquired by the Catholic Church enabled it to impose a confessional system of education on the British government in the 1830s. In addition to primary and secondary schools, the clergy effectively controlled reformatories, industrial schools, and orphanages. More than any other single factor, the church's direction of educational and welfare provision would ensure its extraordinary dominance in independent Ireland.

IV

The main challenge to "official" church doctrine was not Protestant heresy but the resilience of popular religious customs, which revolved around the seasonal calendar and the ritualized practices surrounding holy wells and other places of local pilgrimage. The following description of a pilgrimage was written in 1682 by Sir Henry Piers, an associate of the Dublin Philosophical Society (and a Protestant), but the essence of the passage and the unease of the author were typical of the two centuries between 1650 and 1850. At Lough Derravaragh in County Westmeath there was an ancient chapel cut out of a nearby rock, where the "natives" made their way on the first three Sundays of the harvest season, barefoot for some of the stages and walking on their knees for others, over stone and gravel. Having paid their devotions, the mood of the people was quickly transformed:

> they return with speed to a certain green spot of Ground and here fall a dancing and carousing the rest of the day for the Ale sellers in great numbers on these days have here their booths as in a Fair and to be sure y[e] Bagpipes fail not to play their attendance. Thus in Lewd and obscene dances with Excess of drinking the day of their devotion is ended so as one who now should see y[m] would think they had been celebrating a Feast to Backus rather than their penitentialls or the memory of any pious saint.[49]

What particularly disturbed observers of these local community rituals was the promiscuous combination of solemn devotion and libidinal energy. Here the orthodox Catholicism of the Counter-Reformation overlapped untidily with older means of imposing order on the common people's relationships with the natural world and with one another.

How far was Catholic doctrine actually internalized by the laity? Unfortunately Irish historians do not have the visitation returns available for some European kingdoms, where special commissioners were dispatched to assess the beliefs of both the clergy and their congregations. It was a basic requirement of the episcopal office that a *relatio status* describing the material and spiritual condition of each diocese be submitted to the Holy See every ten years. In the fifty years between 1720 and 1770, however, only seven of these documents were returned for the entire country, causing the cardinal prefect at Propaganda Fide to lament *"una quasi generale mancanza in tutti i vescovi Irlandesi."*[50] In Dublin the first archbishop to fulfil this obligation was John Carpenter, as late as 1780. The mixture of complaints and consolations he records is broadly representative of the hierarchy's sentiments between roughly the 1730s and the 1830s:

> Quoad populi mores haul [*recte* haud] mirum videbitur quod in urbe regni totius principe, ea que tam conferta ac nimia popinarum multitudine scatente in tanta hominum colluvie non obstantibus q[ui]bus-c[u]mque increpationibus ac monitionibus grassetur plurimum vitium ebrietatis, aliaque inde nata, q[ua]lia sunt blasphemiae, imprecationes, praecipites ac temerariae Divini nominis usurpationes, jejunii violationes etc. Ad n[imi]rum tamen accredit solamen quod non exigius [*recte* exiguis] fidelium numerus ab his aliisque vitiis ab horrens vitam ducat vere Christianam, ac Sacra[me]nta Paenitentiae et Eucharistiae semel singulis mensibus ac saepius devote frequentet.

> [Concerning the behaviour of the people, it will hardly seem strange that in the capital city of the whole kingdom, so densely packed and teeming with such an excessive multitude of inns, in such a vile confluence of people, notwithstanding all sorts of rebukes and warnings, the vice of drunkenness is most rampant and the other faults arising from it, such as blasphemy, swearing, and taking the Lord's name in vain, and breaches of fasting. But it is certainly a consolation that no small number of the faithful shuns these vices, and they are leading a truly Christian life, faithfully attending confession and Eucharist once each month or more.][51]

The progress of Tridentine reform is rather like the rise of the bourgeoisie, detected by scholars in a bewildering variety of periods, ranging anywhere from the beginning of the seventeenth century to the 1770s to the post-Famine era, when it becomes subsumed within the concept of the devotional revolution. Such terms as "the Tridentine ideal" are employed so casually by Irish historians that it is worth considering what compliance with the standards defined by the Council of Trent (1545–1563) might actually have entailed. Annual meetings of bishops were instituted in Tuam (1752), Cashel (1775), and Armagh (1779); regular meetings of the four metropolitans were held from 1788. But central aspects of Tridentine reform, such as the strengthening of episcopal control over diocesan priests, were achieved slowly, retarded by the penal restrictions of the eighteenth century. Others, such as the provision that each diocese should have a seminary for clerical training, were impossible. For many bishops the greatest struggle was to establish clerical control over marriage, hitherto constituted simply by the private exchange of promises and sexual intercourse, preferably in that order. If we turn to mass attendance we have no statistical evidence before the 1830s, when D. W. Miller has demonstrated that only 43% of Catholics attended on a given Sunday.[52] Although that figure might have been higher a century before, when the ratio of priests to people was more favorable, the overall picture cannot have been very different. Catholic revival, whether measured by the building of mass-houses, the keeping of parish registers, or the introduction of new devotions and religious fraternities, did not extend far beyond Dublin and the wealthy ports of Galway, Limerick, Cork, Waterford, and Wexford, together with their hinterlands.[53]

In understanding how the noticeably lax canonical practices of the pre-Famine era were transformed into the prodigious piety discovered by Francis Biever in the 1960s, the starting point is still Emmet Larkin's essay, "The Devotional Revolution in Ireland, 1850–75" (1972), probably the most famous article ever published by an Irish historian. Although its timing and extent are fiercely contested, the transformation of religious observance described by Larkin has fascinated scholars ever since. The decades after the Famine saw the extension and improvement of church buildings, the achievement of almost universal mass attendance, and regular communion and confession. More intense, personal forms of devotion were facilitated by the new popularity of the rosary, forty hours, devotion to the Sacred Heart and the Immaculate Conception, benediction, stations of the cross, novenas, and lay fraternities and sodalities. This was the origin of the extraordinary Marian piety that peaked at the height of the Cold War era, when Larkin embarked on his research. These new devotions coincided with a dramatic increase in the power and professionalism of the clergy, and the rigid discipline they apparently imposed on their congregations, manifested above all in a strict code of sexual morality.

What accounts for the extraordinary success of the devotional revolution in turning the mass of the Irish people into practicing Catholics within a generation? One obvious answer was the psychological impact of the Great Famine, but Larkin rightly dismissed that tempting suggestion as too neat. Unfortunately his preferred explanation was suspiciously convenient and equally unverifiable. This centered on the idea of an identity crisis brought about by the erosion of the Irish language and culture, creating a need for a new "cultural heritage" for the Irish.[54] Most subsequent historians have turned instead to the peculiarities of the demographic regime produced by the Famine. The trend toward the impartible inheritance of land produced a predominantly agrarian society ruled by large and middling farmers; it was characterized by the unusually high and persistent emigration of surplus children, relatively late marriage, and high celibacy (the term still preferred by demographers for those who never married). The Irish "match" became a highly regulated mechanism for transferring property between two farmers in which physical desire or affection between the bride and groom was a distinct bonus rather than a shared expectation.[55] The rigidities of the typical Irish family strategy created a society based on repression: large numbers of young people were raised for the inevitability of the Atlantic passage; parents were separated from their children; sexual gratification was deferred, forsworn, and consequently despised. On this reading the church simply supplied the moral and psychological rationalization for emotional austerity. As Paul Blanshard (a Protestant atheist if ever there was one) caustically observed in 1953, Irish priests had "exalted virginity to the point where it is almost a national catastrophe."[56]

The restructuring of Irish rural society after the Famine has become the default explanation for Ireland's devotional *Sonderweg*. Like most explanations for large-scale shifts in popular belief, this one is frustratingly incapable of being either proved or disproved, in spite of its attractions. Disconcertingly, no scholar has ever outlined the sort of mechanism by which a moral code derived from the social organization of *rural* Ireland could have been transferred to the inhabitants of towns and cities who lived at some remove from the matrimonial bargains struck by country people. In accounting for Ireland's fidelity to Roman discipline and devotion from Cullen's time, we might do better to return again to the long penal era, which had consolidated a kind of "popery" no longer sustainable in countries where Catholicism was the established religion. Everywhere in early modern Europe, and not only in Protestant territories, rulers had increased their control over church affairs in their borders, not least in the area of ecclesiastical appointments.[57] In eighteenth-century Ireland, in contrast, the hierarchy operated a kind of counter-establishment that directly opposed the institutions of the British state while sometimes working alongside them. The clergy remained dependent on the voluntary contributions of their people. Gallican tendencies were consequently muted. Irish students in Paris periodically got into trouble for their vitriolic attacks on Jansenist theology and their embarrassingly zealous support for the papal bull *Unigenitus* (1713). Here, as in other continental controversies, Irish priests acquired a reputation for extreme orthodoxy or, as it were, ultra-ultramontanism.

If the driving force behind the devotional revolution remains uncertain, there is a clear consensus among historians on two fundamental points. One is that there is nothing primordial about Irish Catholic devotion. The popular notions that Catholic piety is somehow rooted in Gaelic tradition, or that Catholicism was the religion of the poor, courageously preserved through a century of persecution, do not stand up. In the 1830s mass attendance was weakest among the Gaelic speakers of the west, where it varied between just 20% and 40%. In contrast, the more anglicized and urbanized regions of the east and southeast achieved rates of between 40% and 60%, with pockets of higher concentration already emerging: the Wexford coast in particular already boasted attendance figures of 80–100%.[58] Among the determining variables the most important was the larger proportion of laborers and cottiers in the west—those sections of the population where canonical standards were lowest. The catastrophic collapse of this agrarian underclass brought about by the Famine of the 1840s decisively accelerated the social and cultural dominance of the respectable farmers and shopkeepers from whose ranks the priests—whose numbers by 1870 had increased to 3,200—tended to come. The timing certainly supports the theory: both the distinctive social organization of rural Ireland and the Irish cult of self-denial stretched from the Famine to the 1960s. By the 1990s it was being superseded by the cult of self-realization so prevalent among its European neighbors, that is, of shopping and sex.

Second, we should not assume that the strict regulation of "company-keeping," which observers came to see as a defining feature of Catholic Ireland, was an external imposition. Sean Connolly's careful study of pre-Famine Catholicism found that sexual discipline was already well established in the decades after the Union and that the role of the Catholic priest was "to articulate and reinforce an outlook whose roots lay far deeper in the structure and assumptions of the society of which he was himself a product."[59] Its foundation was the threat posed by sexual irregularity to the efficient transmission of the family holding from one generation to the next. Indeed the fact that similar patterns of marriage existed among Protestants strongly suggests Catholic teaching did not determine marriage strategies but simply reflected them.

The more personal and inward spirituality of the devotional revolution existed in dynamic interaction with the rise of evangelicalism among the Protestant denominations. Evangelical revivalism experienced its first significant growth spurts in the predominantly Anglican communities of Fermanagh and Armagh in the 1790s. Like the Orange Order, such early bodies as the Methodist mission and the Evangelical Society of Ulster seem to have been stimulated by the eruption of sectarian violence in the Ulster borderlands. Decades later the great revival of 1859 convulsed the Presbyterian recesses of Antrim and Down, complete with prostrations and other exotic manifestations of enthusiasm, particularly among females, which produced the same combination of elation and consternation among the local clergy as the apparition of the Virgin Mary in the unlikely location of Knock, County Mayo, twenty years later. Evangelicalism brought a new emphasis on religious activism, on godly living, on biblical orthodoxy, and above all on the centrality of the conversion experience. Its effects were particularly significant among the Presbyterians, where it contributed to the marginalization of the fading "New Light" tradition of the eighteenth century, which had identified itself with the cause of religious toleration to the point of rejecting all established religion. From the 1820s, the activities of Irish-speaking missionaries, gospel preachers, Bible societies, and town missions provoked the anger of the Catholic Church by crossing long-established communal boundaries. At the same time the emphasis on the cross and on scriptural authority, and the emotional intensity of conversion helped dissolve the differences over church government that had divided Anglicans and Presbyterians in the past.

In explaining the success of evangelical enthusiasm in nineteenth-century Ulster, David Hempton and Myrtle Hill have rejected the focus on "modernization" offered by older accounts, opting for a more subtle blend of economic tensions, psychological needs, cultural and regional characteristics, and the individual labors of true believers. They echo recent interpretations of British and American religion in allowing a generous measure of autonomy to the internal dynamics of religious faith. It is all the more telling, then, that Hempton and Hill repeatedly find that revivalism was linked to political upheaval. They demonstrate how the good news flourished in those areas shaken by industrial change and the revolutionary upheavals of the 1790s, where it counteracted social and political radicalism. They view 1859 as evidence for the theory that revivals flourish in "societies whose identity or cohesion is perceived to be under threat."[60] Like other regional subcultures in the north of England, south Wales, or parts of Scotland, Ulster Protestants experienced the social dislocations created by rapid industrialization. Uniquely, however, they also confronted the "sheer vigour of Irish ultramontanist Catholicism," its close connection with nationalist mobilizations, and the willingness of successive British administrations to renegotiate the constitutional guarantees previously offered to Protestants in order to conciliate the majority population.

Evangelical confidence in the moral superiority of Protestantism was apparently vindicated by the increased prosperity and material progress of the northeast. It connected local conflicts in the streets of Belfast with the global extension of the British Empire. A new mythology developed around the superior virtues of the Ulsterman, generally portrayed as dour, dogged, and democratic in spirit, "above all things, able to stand alone, and to stand firmly on his own feet."[61] When Home Rule threatened, the unionists responded that there was no homogeneous national community in Ireland, but two antagonistic populations separated by confessional allegiance, ethnic origins, political loyalty, culture, values, and economic development. If one of these merited special political arrangements, then so did the other. The barrister and historian Thomas Dunbar Ingram, onetime professor of jurisprudence of Hindu and Mohammedan Law in Calcutta, lamented the failure of the English and Scots to understand that "there are in Ireland, included under the generic term of Irish, two separate nations differing in origin, in religion, and in traditions."[62] That Protestants were actually outnumbered in five of its nine counties did not prevent "the Protestant province of Ulster" from becoming the trump card of unionist propaganda. Unfortunately "the Protestant province of Ulster," defined largely in terms of its allegedly superior moral fiber, was even less capable of territorial realization than the Irish nation, which demanded Home Rule and, after 1918, full self-determination.

V

The identification of church and state after independence was close but never absolute. For one thing, the heritage of Protestant patriotism was too valuable to be discarded. Republicanism had been primarily a Presbyterian invention, after all, while the Gaelic revival of the nineteenth century had been pioneered by Anglican intellectuals. The memory of Wolfe Tone, the United Irishmen, and the rebellion of 1798 was a vital weapon in the propaganda war over the Six Counties, apparent evidence that under his tough skin the northern Protestant was essentially Irish. The imperative of national reunification thus provided a counterweight to the confessional tendencies of the southern state. Although the 1937 constitution recognized the "special position" of the Catholic Church, de Valera rejected the full Catholic polity urged by the bishops and the Vatican, ostensibly because it would antagonize Protestants, particularly north of the border. When Garret Fitzgerald embarked on his constitutional crusade in the 1980s, proposing to liberalize social attitudes in the South, the rationale offered for reform was the unconvincing notion that Ulster Protestants would find unification a more appealing prospect once divorce was available in the Republic. Even the young Charles Haughey, galvanized by the first clashes between Northern Catholics and British troops, vowed that there was "nothing he would not sacrifice, including the position of the Catholic Church in order to get a United Ireland."[63]

The assumption that there was an almost umbilical relationship between Irish nationality and the Catholic faith was nevertheless evident in the intimacy between successive governments and the hierarchy. When Costello's coalition government took power in 1948 it sent a telegram to the Vatican assuring Pope Pius XII "of our devotion to Your August Person as well as our firm resolve to be guided in all our work by the teaching of Christ."[64] Such declarations of fidelity had become routine. The annual military parades marking the invocation of the Blessed Virgin as the patroness of the Irish army, navy, and air corps were rather more bizarre, even by contemporary standards. The first of these took place on October 7, 1951, when the president and the taoiseach joined Archbishop McQuaid in a solemn high mass at Arbor Hill Barracks, and the Irish military dedicated themselves to Mary, Our Lady, Queen of the Holy Rosary.[65]

McQuaid's influence with party leaders was formidable. The opening of his monumental archive has revealed the full extent of his role in the drafting of de Valera's 1937 constitution. The preamble and the definition of the national territory bear his fingerprints, as well as the prohibition on divorce, the articles dealing with educational and social policy, and the assertion that the proper place of the mother was in the home. During the "Mother and Child" affair of 1950–1951, when a scheme for the provision of free medical care for mothers and children under sixteen was vetoed by the hierarchy, McQuaid not only composed the bishops' attack on "Socialised Medicine" but helpfully drafted the government's response.[66] An extraordinary system of moral surveillance now radiated outward from the archbishop's palace in the suburb of Drumcondra. The archbishop's Vigilance Committee, established in 1954 to monitor Communism and "other anti-Catholic activities, such as Liberalism," included influential members of trade unions, the universities, the media, and the State Intelligence Services. McQuaid was regularly supplied with confidential information from Garda Special Branch and Army intelligence, including, on occasion, surveillance reports acquired from the London police. The amount of energy devoted to countering the Communist threat seems all the more remarkable when we consider that a U.S. Senate report in 1953 found that the main Communist group in the Irish Republic had a membership of about one hundred people.[67]

In explaining the vast power of the church and the remarkable efflorescence of Marian devotions between the 1930s and 1960s, the pressures of the Cold War have some role to play.[68] Just as much as Troy or Cullen, McQuaid was focused on the continental struggle to preserve Catholicism, this time in the face of Soviet Communism. The show trials of Archbishop Stepinac in Yugoslavia and Cardinal Mindszenty in Hungary prompted a demonstration in Dublin in 1949 attended by 150,000 Catholics in total, with thousands kneeling in the streets to recite the rosary, a devotion that had become associated with the crusade against Communism. But the enabling conditions of Catholic hegemony were created by the Irish revolution of 1916–1922. Secession from the United Kingdom removed the most obvious secularizing agent, the British government, which alone had the resources to expand the educational system—an alarming prospect for the hierarchy, whose overriding political priority was always the retention of clerical control over schools. The Easter Rising and its aftermath also eliminated a generation of experienced politicians habituated to operating in alliance with nonconformist Liberals at Westminster. The presence of Archbishop Walsh of Dublin and 200 priests in the funeral cortège of the republican hunger striker Thomas Ashe in 1917 signaled the switch from the constitutional politics of the Irish Parliamentary Party to a revolutionary movement, which, rather perversely, reinforced the forces of social conservatism and Catholic puritanism.[69]

Partition meanwhile severed the industrialized northeast from the Free State, further accentuating the dominance of the small farmers and their distinctive moral ethos. The division of the island into two mutually hostile jurisdictions weakened professional elites, already incapable of challenging the clergy in the South—at least until the expansion of the media in the 1960s. Even in academic circles there was no overt challenge to orthodox belief. At University College Dublin, McQuaid nominated the chairs of Ethics and Politics, Logic and Psychology, Education, Sociology and Metaphysics, all occupied by Catholic priests. The first lay lecturer in the Department of Politics was the eirenic scholar (and orthodox Catholic) John Whyte, who resigned his position when he was told by McQuaid to discontinue research on what became his classic study, *Church and State in Modern Ireland* (1970).[70] Some of the social sciences professors at University College Dublin—such as Father Fergal O'Connor, who had become a popular guest on the *Late Late Show*, or Father Conor Martin—were nevertheless quiet modernizers, and they had counterparts elsewhere in the clerical firmament. There was no Irish equivalent of *Slant*, the English journal founded in 1964 by Catholic Marxists including the literary critic Terry Eagleton, but the spirit of *aggiornamento* found echoes in such local journals as *Christus Rex, Doctrine and Life*, and *The Furrow* even before the Second Vatican Council completed its work. Combined with the new medium of television, the emergence of tensions between traditionalists and modernizers did much to puncture the air of mystique that had protected episcopal authority.[71]

In retrospect the stir surrounding John McGahern's *The Dark* (1965) appears as the emblematic cultural confrontation of the period. McGahern's precise, self-effacing prose described the close-knit communities of rural Ireland—their guilt complexes and hypocrisies, their commonplace civilities, and their apparently timeless funeral rituals. McGahern had admired Joyce's *Dubliners*, because it was written in a style that "never draws attention to itself" but enters the imagination by stealth; this is something that could equally be said of his own later novels, particularly *Amongst Women* (1990) and *That They May Face the Rising Sun* (2001), which made him the most celebrated Irish writer of his day.[72] The setting for *The Dark*, his second novel, was the oppressive, patriarchal Irish countryside of the 1950s. Controversially, the word "fuck" appeared on its very first page—just six months before the theater critic Kenneth Tynan notoriously used the f-word on the British Broadcasting Corporation (BBC). (To be exact, McGahern spelled out "F-U-C-K," while Tynan stammered "f-f-fuck.") Worse still, the book describes the adolescence of a boy torn between habitual masturbation and a vocation for the priesthood. The boy's fantasies are first ignited by a newspaper advertisement for ladies' depilatory cream. (The erotic potential of such advertisements was clear to McQuaid, who once complained that advertisements for women's underwear in the *Irish Press* revealed the *mons pubis*—if scrutinized through a magnifying glass.)[73] McGahern consequently lost his job as a national schoolteacher, apparently at the insistence of McQuaid himself. Any hopes of reversing the decision were scuppered by his recent marriage to a Finnish theater director and translator, which had taken place in a London registry office: "And what anyhow entered your head," asked the general secretary of the Irish Teachers Union, "when there are hundreds of thousands of Irish girls going around with their tongues out for a husband?"[74]

Reading McGahern's account of his dismissal today, what stands out most is the unspoken compromises and complicities that characterized a society where overt confrontation with Catholic dogma was still unthinkable. McGahern was treated sympathetically by his school colleagues, while the discomposed headmaster advised him to apply for a job in London, promising to supply the necessary references. England was, by the 1950s, the preferred destination of the deviant and disruptive elements in Irish society—the intellectuals and iconoclasts, single mothers, homosexuals, and eventually the pop stars—along with its large surplus laboring population. Without this pressure valve, it is unlikely that the tensions in Catholic Ireland could have been contained for so long. But England was also the source of such magazines as *Women's Own*, with their inflammatory advertisements for the removal of "unwanted hair."[75] From England, too, came the Catholic periodical *The Tablet*, sufficiently progressive to outrage McQuaid and Bishop Browne of Galway.[76] The traffic of people across the Irish Sea had important cultural implications, long before cheap air fares made regular visits affordable. Reports reached Drumcondra that a "disturbingly large proportion" of Irish immigrants in Britain lost their "purity" in boarding houses and dance halls across the water, the problem being that the Irish were innocent of sexual matters while the English youth were "saturated in unwholesome knowledge" and corrupted by the prevalent "atmosphere of paganism."[77]

Post-war Ireland is probably best seen as a distinctive variant of a Western pattern rather than an exception to it. Reflecting on the dominant explanations offered by scholars of secularization—the unprecedented affluence of the long 1960s, the new independence and mobility of young people, and decline of community pressures on individual behavior, the transformation of gender roles and sexual behavior, even the conflicts in the churches themselves over modernization—it seems arguable that the main difference between Ireland and its neighbors is principally one of timing.[78] A survey of Catholic university students in the mid-1970s found that although eight in ten attended weekly mass, a clear majority (56%) rejected the church's position on contraception. Fewer than three in ten accepted the doctrine of papal infallibility or the proposition that the Catholic Church is "the one true Church."[79] If, as cultural historians often observe, much of Europe did not actually experience the Sixties until well into the Seventies, then most of Ireland had to wait until the Nineties.

Responsible historians should pause before writing obituaries for Catholic Ireland. Yet the forces ranged against the old faith are formidable. Even without the extraordinary catalogue of clerical abuse, corruption, and hypocrisy uncovered in the Ferns Report and other public inquiries, conventional Catholicism was unlikely to thrive in the era of Ryanair, Father Ted, and the condom vending machine. Optimists might object that the Republic of Ireland census of 2011 showed that 84% of the population regard themselves as a Roman Catholics. But those with "no religion" had almost doubled their numbers in just five years and now reached 13% among twenty-five- to twenty-nine-year-olds. Meanwhile it has been suggested that national identity in the South has lost the Catholic communal basis so striking in the early decades of independence and has become refocused on the institutions of the twenty-six-county polity; Southerners accordingly express a greater sense of political and psychological distance from *both* communities in the North.[80]

In Northern Ireland too there is a significant trend toward disaffiliation from the churches, with more than 10% of the population choosing "no religion" in the 2011 census. Although the figures for weekly church attendance remain high—60% among Catholics and 34% among Protestants—there is a clear generational shift: the corresponding figures for those younger than thirty-five fall significantly to 42% for Catholics and 16% for Protestants. A detailed study of Belfast suggests that it conforms to the classic secularizing pattern, with churchgoers on both sides of the divide more likely to be female and middle-aged or elderly, with those younger than twenty-five and the unemployed poorly represented. Among Catholic women there is also a conspicuous difference in patterns of religious observance between housewives and women in paid employment (51% attending mass weekly compared to 37%).[81]

In their experiences of religious decline, as in so many other respects, analysis of the two Northern communities continues to reveal contrasting patterns. Although the overwhelming majority of Catholics attend church regularly, the clear tendency, among the young especially, is towards an *à la carte* approach to doctrine and away from regular confession. Almost half of those surveyed in the 1990s agreed with the view that individual conscience is more important than church teaching.[82] Half of all Protestants, meanwhile, attend church infrequently or not at all; but theological conservatism characterizes those who do and is particularly noticeable among young churchgoers, who overwhelmingly accept that biblical inerrancy and the experience of being "born again" are essential to true Christianity. Taken as a whole, Ulster Protestants have slipped behind their Catholic neighbors in their attachment to the key points of Christian faith—except for belief in the existence of hell, where, perhaps reassuringly, the steadfastness demonstrated by the two communities is more-or-less equal.[83]

FURTHER READING

The history of the Irish churches was first written by Irish churchmen. J. S. Reid, *History of the Presbyterian Church in Ireland*, ed. W. D. Killen (3 vols., Belfast: William Mullan, third ed., 1867) is an outstanding achievement. The case for the established church is made by Richard Mant, *History of the Church of Ireland* (3 vols., London: John W. Parker, 1840). Perhaps the most influential work on the Catholic side was W. P. Burke's *The Irish Priests in the Penal Times, 1660–1760* (Waterford: Printed for the author, 1914): although it greatly overestimated the severity of the penal code, it contains rich information from the Irish Public Records destroyed in 1922. In the past fifty years the best denominational historians have kept pace with historiographical currents, as demonstrated by R.F.G. Holmes, *Our Irish Presbyterian Heritage* (Belfast: Presbyterian Church in Ireland, 1985) and P. J. Corish, *The Irish Catholic Experience: A Historical Survey* (Dublin: Gill and Macmillan, 1985).

Modern scholarship, often sociological in its methodology and less reverent in tone, really begins with Emmet Larkin's seminal article, "The Devotional Revolution in Ireland, 1850–75," *American Historical Review* 77: 3 (June 1972). Larkin's student, D. W. Miller, produced an equally bold, wide-ranging, and controversial thesis in "Presbyterianism and 'Modernization' in Ulster," *Past & Present* 80 (1978). Some of Larkin's arguments are qualified in S. J. Connolly's exemplary *Priests and People in Pre-Famine Ireland* (Dublin: Four Courts Press, second ed. 2001).

Tom Inglis, *Moral Monopoly: The Rise and Fall of the Catholic Church in Modern Ireland* (Dublin: Gill and Macmillan, second ed.,1998) proceeds at a level of generalization that will displease many historians but contains important insights, including his analysis of the Catholic mother. Reading Louise Fuller's *Irish Catholicism Since 1950: The Undoing of a Culture* (Dublin: Gill and Macmillan, 2004) will cure the common misconception that the Catholic Church was monolithic. Roy Foster's sparkling *Luck and the Irish: A Brief History of Change 1970–2000* (London: Allen Lane, 2007) relates secularization to the social and cultural ferment of the late twentieth century, rightly highlighting changing attitudes to gender and sexuality as a key driver of change. Steve Bruce's classic *God Save Ulster: The Religion and Politics of Paisleyism* (Oxford: Oxford University Press, 1986), explores the centrality of evangelicalism to what many Ulster Protestants still take to be the British way of life.

NOTES

1. Frank Burton, *The Politics of Legitimacy in a Belfast Community* (London: Routledge and Kegan Paul, 1978), chapter 3.

2. Christoper Hitchens, *God Is Not Great* (London: Atlantic, 2007), p. 18.

3. Richard Dawkins, *The God Delusion* (London: Black Swan, 2007), pp. 23–24, 294.

4. Claire Mitchell, *Religion, Identity and Politics in Northern Ireland* (Aldershot, England: Ashgate 2006), especially chapters 2–3.

5. Tom Garvin, *Preventing the Future: Why Was Ireland So Poor for So Long?* (Dublin: Gill and Macmillan, 2005), p. 52.

6. Dennis Kennedy, *The Widening Gulf: Northern Attitudes to the Independent Irish State 1919–1949* (Belfast: Blackstaff, 1988).

7. As brilliantly demonstrated in T. K. Wilson, *Frontiers of Violence: Conflict and Identity in Upper Silesia 1918–1922* (Oxford: Oxford University Press, 2010), especially chapter 4.

8. Marc Mulholland, "Why Did Unionists Discriminate?" in Sabine Wichert (ed.), *From the United Irishmen to Twentieth-Century Unionism: A Festschrift for A. T. Q. Stewart* (Dublin: Four Courts Press, 2004), pp. 187–206.

9. Senia Pašeta, "Censorship and Its Critics in the Irish Free State," *Past and Present* 181 (November 2003), p. 211.

10. James Joyce, *A Portrait of the Artist as a Young Man*, edited with an introduction and notes by Jeri Johnson (Oxford: Oxford University Press, 2000), p. 202.

11. Best pursued in Don Gifford with Robert J. Seidman, *Ulysses Annotated: Notes for James Joyce's Ulysses* (London: University of California Press, second ed., 1988).

12. R. F. Foster, "Protestant Magic: W. B. Yeats and the Spell of History," in *Paddy and Mr. Punch: Connections in Irish and English History* (London: Allen Lane, 1993), pp. 212–232.

13. Richard Ellman, *James Joyce* (Oxford: Oxford University Press, 1982), p. 99.

14. B. F. Biever, *Religion, Culture and Values: A Cross-Cultural Analysis of Motivational Factors in Native Irish and American Irish Catholicism* (New York: Arno Press, 1976), pp. 268, 306, 308.

15. James E. Bjork, "Beyond the Polak-Katolik: Catholicism, Nationalism, and Particularism in Modern Poland," in U. Altermatt and F. Metzger (eds.), *Religion und Nation: Katholizismen im Europa des 19. und 20. Jahrhunderts* (Stuttgart: Kohlhammer, 2007), pp. 97–118.

16. A. M. Greeley, *Religion in Europe at the End of the Second Millennium* (New Brunswick, NJ: Transaction, 2003), pp. 70–71.

17. S.J.D. Green, *The Passing of Protestant England: Secularisation and Social Change, c. 1920–1960* (Cambridge: Cambridge University Press, 2011).

18. L. Paul-Dubois, *Contemporary Ireland* (London: Unwin, 1908), p. 492.

19. William Shaw Mason, *A Statistical Account or Parochial Survey of Ireland* (Dublin: Graisberry and Campbell, 1814–1819), 3 vols., I, p. 591.

20. Andy Bielenberg, "Exodus: The Emigration of Southern Irish Protestants during the Irish War of Independence and the Civil War," *Past and Present* 218 (February 2013), pp. 199–233.

21. David Dickson, "The Demographic Implications of the Growth of Dublin 1650–1850," in Richard Lawton and W. R. Lee (eds.), *Urban Population Development in Western Europe* (Liverpool: Liverpool University Press, 1989), pp. 178–189.

22. Tone to Russell, 1 Sept. 1795, National Archives of Ireland, Rebellion Papers, 620/16/3; A. C. Hepburn, *A Past Apart: Studies in the History of Catholic Belfast, 1850–1950* (Belfast: Ulster Historical Foundation, 1996), p. 4.

23. Thomas P. Power, "Converts," in T. P. Power and Kevin Whelan (eds.), *Endurance and Emergence: Catholics in Ireland in the Eighteenth Century* (Dublin: Irish Academic Press, 1990), pp. 101–127.

24. Edward [Wetenhall], *A Sermon Setting Forth the Duties of the Irish Protestants, Arising from the Irish Rebellion, 1641 and the Irish Tyranny, 1688* (Dublin: Joseph Ray,1692), p. 13. This was a common formulation.

25. Richard Cox, *Hibernia Anglicana: or, the History of Ireland from the Conquest Thereof by the English, to This Present Time* (London: Joseph Watts, 1689), vol. 1, [C2ʳ].

26. The literature is reviewed in Karl S. Bottigheimer and Ute Lotz-Heumann, "The Irish Reformation in European Perspective," *Archiv für Reformationsgeschichte* 89 (1998), pp. 268–309.

27. Geoffrey Parker, "Success and Failure during the First Century of the Reformation," *Past and Present* 136 (August 1992), pp. 43–82.

28. Edmund Burke, *A Letter from the Right Hon. Edmund Burke, M.P. in the Kingdom of Great Britain, to Sir Hercules Langrishe* (London: J. Debrett, 1792), p. 43.

29. Tadhg Ó hAnnracháin, "The Consolidation of Irish Catholicism within a Hostile Imperial Framework: A Comparative Study of Early Modern Ireland and Hungary," in Hilary M. Carey (ed.), *Empires of Religion* (Basingstoke: Palgrave Macmillan, 2008), pp. 25–40.

30. For a similar argument about the English Civil War, see Conrad Russell, *The Causes of the English Civil War* (Oxford: Clarendon, 1990), p. 59.

31. Deposition of John Kerdiff, TCD, MS 839, f. 15r, 1641 Depositions Project (http://1641 .tcd.ie/deposition.php?depID<?php echo 839012r013?>) accessed January 14, 2015.

32. M. Perceval-Maxwell, *The Outbreak of the Irish Rebellion of 1641* (Dublin: Gill and Macmillan, 1994), chapter 10.

33. Russell, *Causes of the English Civil War*, chapters 2 and 3.

34. The fullest treatment is now Nicholas Canny, *Making Ireland British, 1580–1650* (Oxford: Oxford University Press, 2001), chapter 8. But see also Eamon Darcy, *The Irish Rebellion of 1641 and the Wars of the Three Kingdoms* (London: Royal Historical Society, 2013), especially pp. 53–54.

35. Deposition of Henry Boyne, TCD, MS 839, f. 10r, TCD, 1641 Depositions Project, (http://1641.tcd.ie/deposition.php?depID<?php echo 839010r012?>) accessed January 14, 2015.

36. Canny, *Making Ireland British*, p. 541.

37. Deposition of Thomas Huetsonn, TCD, MS 813, fol. 260v, TCD, 1641 Depositions Project, http://1641.tcd.ie/deposition.php?depID<?php echo 813260r192?>) accessed January 14, 2015.

38. Deposition of William Wood, Beare and Bantry, TCD, MS 823, f. 55, TCD, 1641 Depositions Project, (http://1641.tcd.ie/deposition.php?depID<?php echo 823055r053?>) accessed January 15, 2015.

39. For European comparisons, see Graeme Murdock, Penny Roberts, and Andrew Spicer, *Ritual and Violence: Natalie Zemon Davis and Early Modern France: Past and Present Supplement* 7 (Oxford: Oxford University Press, 2012).

40. J. C. Beckett, "William King's Administration of the Diocese of Derry 1691–1703," *Irish Historical Studies* 4 (1944), p. 173.

41. Ian McBride, "Ulster Presbyterians and the Confessional State, 1689–1733," in D. G. Boyce et al. (eds.), *Political Discourse in Early Modern Ireland* (Basingstoke: Macmillan, 2001), pp. 169–192.

42. D. W. Hayton, "Did Protestantism Fail in Eighteenth-Century Ireland? Charity Schools and the Enterprise of Religious and Social Reformation, c. 1690–1730," in Alan Ford, James McGuire, and Kenneth Milne (eds.), *As By Law Established: The Church of Ireland since the Reformation* (Dublin: Lilliput, 1995), pp. 166–186.

43. King to Edward Southwell, 12 Nov. 1719, TCD MSS, 790/5/210–12.

44. William King, *The State of the Protestants of Ireland under the Late King James' Government* (London: Robert Clavell, 1691), pp. 7, 13, 14–15.

45. [Peter Burrowes,] *Plain Arguments in Defence of the People's Absolute Dominion over the Constitution* (Dublin: Thomas Webb, 1784), p. 53.

46. Bernadette Cunningham, "The Culture and Ideology of Irish Franciscan Historians at Louvain 1607–1650," in Ciaran Brady and Iván Berend (eds.), *Ideology and the Historians* (Dublin: Lilliput, 1991), especially p. 19.

47. Ian McBride, "Catholic Politics in the Penal Era: Father Sylvester Lloyd and the Devlin Address of 1727," *Eighteenth-Century Ireland* (2011), pp. 115–147.

48. Thomas Bartlett, *The Fall and Rise of the Irish Nation: The Catholic Question, 1690–1830* (Dublin: Gill and Macmillan, 1992), pp. 244–259.

49. Sir Henry Pyerce, account of Westmeath in "Common Place Book of Papers Relating to the Natural History of Ireland," TCD, MS 883/1, 299.

50. [Cardinal Leonardo Antonelli] to Archbishop Troy, 1 Oct. 1785, Archivio Segreto Vaticano, Fondo Missioni, 117.

51. M. J. Curran, "Archbishop Carpenter's Epistolae (1770–1780)," part ii, *Reportorium Novum*, I: 1 (1956), p. 397.

52. D. W. Miller "Mass Attendance in Ireland in 1834," in Stewart J. Brown and David W. Miller (eds.), *Piety and Power in Ireland 1760–1960: Essays in Honour of Emmet Larkin* (Belfast: University of Notre Dame Press, 2000), pp. 158–178.

53. Kevin Whelan, "The Regional Impact of Irish Catholicism 1700–1850," in W. J. Smyth and K. Whelan (eds.), *Common Ground: Essays on the Historical Geography of Ireland Presented to T. Jones Hughes* (Cork: Cork University Press, 1988), p. 253.

54. Emmet Larkin, "The Devotional Revolution in Ireland, 1850–75," *American Historical Review* 77: 3 (1972), p. 649.

55. The best discussion is David Fitzpatrick's "Marriage in Post-Famine Ireland," in Art Cosgrove (ed.), *Marriage in Ireland* (Dublin: College, 1985), pp. 116–131.

56. Paul Blanshard, *The Irish and Catholic Power: An American Interpretation* (Boston: Beacon Press, 1953), p. 149.

57. Robert Bireley, *The Refashioning of Catholicism, 1450–1700* (Basingstoke: Macmillan, 1999), p. 74.

58. Miller, "Mass Attendance in Ireland in 1834," figure 7.5. Delightfully, one small pocket even appears on Miller's map as "over 100%."

59. S. J. Connolly, *Priests and People in Pre-Famine Ireland* (Dublin: Four Courts Press, second ed., 2001), p. 207.

60. David Hempton and Myrtle Hill, *Evangelical Protestantism in Ulster Society 1740–1890* (London: Routledge, 1992), p. 160.

61. T[homas] C[roskery], "Ulster and Its People," *Frazer's Magazine* xiv (1896), p. 221.

62. Thomas Dunbar Ingram, *A History of the Legislative Union of Great Britain and Ireland* (London: Macmillan and Company, 1887), p. 21.

63. Quoted in Briege Rice, "British and Irish State Responses to Militant Irish Republicanism, 1968–1971" (Thesis, Queen's University Belfast, 2014), p. 161.

64. Dermot Keogh, *Ireland and the Vatican: The Politics and Diplomacy of Church-State Relations 1922–1960* (Cork: Cork University Press, 1995), p. xix.

65. See John Cooney's rather sensationalist *John Charles McQuaid: Ruler of Catholic Ireland* (Dublin: O'Brien Press, 1999), pp. 288–289.

66. Cooney, *McQuaid*, p. 15.

67. David Connolly, "The 'Red Scare' in 1950s Dublin: Genuine or Generated? The Role of Archbishop McQuaid's Vigilance Committee" (Thesis, Trinity College Dublin, 2011).

68. James S. Donnelly, Jr., "The Peak of Marianism in Ireland, 1930–60," in Brown and Miller (eds.), *Piety and Power*, pp. 252–283.

69. The best account is now Charles Townshend, *The Republic: The Fight for Irish Independence, 1918–1923* (London: Allen Lane, 2013).

70. Tom Garvin, "The Strange Death of Clerical Politics in University College Dublin," *Irish University Review* 28: 2 (1998), pp. 308–314.

71. Best explored in Robert J. Savage, Jr., *A Loss of Innocence?: Television and Irish Society 1960–72* (Manchester: Manchester University Press, 2010).

72. John McGahern, "Dubliners," *Canadian Journal of Irish Studies* 17 (1991), p. 36.

73. Cooney, *McQuaid*, p. 282.

74. John McGahern, *Memoir* (London: Faber and Faber, 2005), p. 251.

75. Pašeta, "Censorship," p. 204.

76. Cooney, *McQuaid*, p. 380.

77. Catholic Social Welfare Bureau (Emigrant Section): Report on Various Aspects of Conditions Obtaining in Great Britain and on the Progress of Welfare Work on behalf of Irish Catholic Immigrants (Dublin Diocesan Archive, McQuaid Papers, XIX/12G/2), p. 16.

78. Compare the cases of Quebec and the Netherlands, where Catholicism was also implicated in wider political and social divisions: Callum G. Brown and Michael Snape (eds.), *Secularisation in the Christian World* (Farnham, England: Ashgate, 2010), chapters 7 and 11.

79. T. F. Inglis, "Dimensions of Irish Students' Religiosity," *Economic and Social Review* XI (1980), pp. 244, 247.

80. See John Coakley's excellent survey, "Religion, National Identity and Political Change in Modern Ireland," *Irish Political Studies* 17: 1 (2002), pp. 4–28.

81. Frederick W. Boal, Margaret C Keane, and David N. Livingstone, *Them and Us? Attitudinal Variation among Churchgoers in Belfast* (Belfast: Institute of Irish Studies, 1997).

82. Boal, Keane, and Livingstone, *Them and Us*, p. 27.

83. Mitchell, *Religion, Identity and Politics*, p. 69.

CHAPTER 13

THE IRISH LANGUAGE

Vincent Morley

I RISH IS THE MEDIUM FOR one of the oldest vernacular literatures in Europe. Annals and legal tracts in Old Irish are among the most important primary sources for the history of early Ireland. From the thirteenth century until the final overthrow of independent lordships around 1600, the compositions of professional poets shed light on the outlook of the lords they served. Pseudo-historical texts compiled during the Middle Irish period constituted the raw materials from which a national and Catholic narrative of the Irish past was constructed in the seventeenth century. The cultivation of a manuscript-based literature in Irish during the eighteenth and early nineteenth centuries allowed opinions that were frequently hostile to the establishment to be disseminated without recourse to print. Although a precipitate decline in the number of Irish speakers took place from the middle of the nineteenth century, a language-revival movement helped foster a climate conducive to the growth of radical nationalism: contemporary publications and later memoirs in Irish afford insights into the cultural context of the early twentieth century. After independence, Irish became an official language of the new state. Although the radical goal of replacing English was not achieved, the rapid abandonment of the language that characterized the post-Famine decades was halted, and a vibrant literature gradually emerged. If the use of Irish as a community language is now largely confined to scattered rural districts along the western seaboard, it nonetheless retains considerable importance for students of Irish history and culture.

Modern forms are used for Irish terms throughout this chapter (e.g., *"filí"* rather than Old Irish *"filid"* or Middle/Early Modern Irish *"filidh."* The spelling of pre-1650 quotations is preserved; that of post-1650 quotations is normalized.

BACKGROUND

Irish belongs to the Celtic group of the Indo-European family of languages. It is closely related to the Gaelic of Highland Scotland, and speakers of one language can acquire a reading knowledge of the other with little effort, although differences in accent and pronunciation make oral communication more problematic. In contrast, the relationship of Irish to Welsh and Breton was not recognized until the publication of Edward Lhuyd's pioneering linguistic survey, *Archaeologia Britannica*, in 1703.

Speakers of Celtic cannot have arrived on an island on the edge of the Atlantic for some time after they began to migrate from their homeland in central Europe around the beginning of the first millennium BC. One can only speculate about the circumstances in which the language was introduced to Ireland and came to be adopted by its people, but there is unlikely to have been a large influx of Celtic speakers, because the island supported a populous agricultural society since the Neolithic period and the archaeological record reveals no major discontinuity in its material culture during the first millennium BC.[1] Nonetheless, Irish was the only language spoken in Ireland when history began in the fifth century AD, it showed no obvious signs of a pre-Celtic substrate, and it was already distinct from the Celtic tongues then spoken in Britain. The establishment of an Irish colony in Argyll in the same century introduced Irish to Scotland, where it supplanted Pictish over a period of five centuries—a process that probably owed much to its association with Christianity and literacy, as exemplified by the Irish-speaking monks of Colum Cille's foundation at Iona.

With the exception of short memorial inscriptions in Ogham, some of which may be as early as the fourth century and attest to an archaic form of the language, the earliest Irish texts now extant are believed to date from the late sixth century. A former consensus that much of the literature of the Old Irish period (c. 600–900) was pre-Christian in origin has been subjected to telling criticism in recent decades.[2] While admitting the possibility that certain texts may have drawn on oral traditions, recent scholarship has stressed that the literature was composed by clerical authors who were literate in Latin.[3] None of it is manifestly pre-Christian, and much of it is overtly Christian: for example, the earliest datable composition appears to be *Amra Choluim Cille* ("Colum Cille's eulogy"), which was composed shortly after the saint's death in 597 and is attributed to Dallán Forgaill, himself a founder of churches.

A corpus of unadorned lyric verse that displays a disarmingly modern sensibility may be the Old Irish genre of greatest appeal to modern readers, although the earliest prose narratives—including heroic tales of Cú Chulainn and other champions of the Ulster cycle—were also composed in Old Irish.[4] The compendium of legal tracts known as the *Senchas Már* ("great tradition") and the annals are of more interest to historians. The *Senchas Már*, fancifully reputed to have been redacted from a pre-Christian original by Saint Patrick, was compiled by monastic scribes in the seventh and eighth centuries and provides important insights into the structure of early Irish society.[5] The annals, which recorded noteworthy political and ecclesiastical events, were also produced in monastic scriptoria, and their earliest entries can be traced to the monastery of Iona in the late seventh century. Originally written in Latin, the Iona chronicle was continued in Ireland, and entries in Irish became common from the ninth century. The text of the resulting Irish chronicle has not survived in its original form, but it was the common stem from which the early medieval annals (*Annals of Ulster*, *Annals of Tigernach*, *Annals of Innisfallen*) diverged in the tenth century.

Old Irish showed surprisingly little variation across the various literary genres, but the written standard, which can only have been devised and maintained in the monastic schools, began to break down in the tenth century—possibly under the impact of Norse raids on the monasteries. In contrast to the standardized idiom of earlier centuries, the Middle Irish period (c. 900–1200) was characterized by linguistic variety, with obsolescent and contemporary forms being employed according to the taste or learning of individual scribes. The impression of cultural disarray conveyed by the diversity of language is consistent with the instability of Irish society in the four centuries between the first Norse incursions and the English invasion, but this impression is belied by the substantial volume of writing in Middle Irish that has survived. Furthermore, the literature of the period includes several works that were to have a profound influence on Irish thought.

The most important of these is *Lebor Gabála Érenn* (the "book of the taking of Ireland"), a pseudo-historical compendium in which more than a hundred poems are linked by passages of prose. The *Lebor Gabála* enumerates the various peoples that successively colonized Ireland (the followers of Cessair, of Partholón, of Nemed, the Fir Bolg, and the Tuatha Dé Danann), describes the migrations of the Gaels from Egypt to Spain by way of Scythia, and recounts the ultimate invasion of Ireland by the sons of Milesius and their victory over the treacherous Tuatha Dé Danann. The *Lebor Gabála* drew on earlier traditions, some of which were recorded by Nennius in his ninth-century *Historia Brittonum*, but it appears to have assumed its final form in the eleventh century. The poem *"Ériu ard inis na rríg"* ("Noble Ireland, isle of the kings"), composed by Gilla Cóemáin in the late eleventh century, may have formed part of the compendium from the beginning. The poet listed 136 pre-Christian kings who had reigned over Ireland from the mythological Sláine, first king of the Fir Bolg, to Lóeguire, king of Tara when Patrick began his mission:

> Sé ríg déc sé fichit ríg
> ría tíachtain Pátraic co fír;

dar éis Sláine na ngal ngrind,
is é lín ro gab Hérind.[6]

(Sixteen and six score kings before the arrival of Patrick with truth; after Sláine of the fierce combats, this is the number who took Ireland.)

This regnal list was extended by a later addition to the *Lebor Gabála*: "*Ériu óg inis na náemh*" ("Chaste Ireland, isle of the saints"), a poem composed by Gilla Mo Dutu in 1143, counted a further forty-eight high kings from Lóeguire to Máel Sechnaill II (✝1022).

If the *Lebor Gabála* established the concept of Ireland as an ancient kingdom with a roll of kings stretching back to remote antiquity, an ideal of patriotic kingship was presented in *Cogadh Gaedhel re Gallaibh* ("War of the Gaels against the foreigners"), a prose saga about the Norse wars composed in the early twelfth century. The king concerned was Brian Bóruma, high king of Ireland from 1002 until his death in 1014, and the original purpose of the work was to shed reflected glory on the O'Briens, descendants of Brian who formed the ruling dynasty in Thomond. This text elaborated on the terse accounts of the annals and portrayed Brian as a wise, heroic, and devout monarch who freed Ireland from a foreign yoke.

Acallam na Senórach ("the colloquy of ancients"), a major compilation containing both prose and verse, is the oldest substantial work devoted to the mythical hero Fionn mac Cumhaill and his roving band of warriors, the *fianna*. Written near the end of the Middle Irish period, it describes an encounter between Patrick and two aged survivors of the *fianna*, Fionn's son Oisín (the "Ossian" of James MacPherson) and Caoilte mac Rónáin, who regaled the saint with accounts of their late comrades' adventures. Tales of the *fianna* would continue to be popular in Ireland and Scotland until modern times, and the *Acallam* may represent an attempt by a monastic author to apply a Christian veneer to a genre that was hitherto largely oral and resistant to clerical manipulation.

EARLY MODERN IRISH

The extension of English rule over much of Ireland in the decades following the arrival of Henry II in 1171 introduced English to the island for the first time. The new language took root in the major towns but had little impact in rural areas, and only two districts—in north Dublin and south Wexford—were English-speaking before the sixteenth century. Although the gentry of Old English origin generally retained a knowledge of English, they became bilingual with the passage of time, and in 1366 a law (the statute of Kilkenny) was enacted in an attempt to proscribe the use of Irish among those of English descent. The greatest impact of English rule on the language in the short term arose from the impetus it gave to a process of ecclesiastic reform that was already under way: by introducing continental religious orders, this reform severed the long-standing link between Irish monasticism and vernacular learning.

From the early thirteenth century, the cultivation of Irish literature was transferred to a hereditary learned caste whose original members appear to have been recruited from laicized personnel of the monastic schools; by the fourteenth century, new secular schools were flourishing.[7] The emergence of Early Modern Irish as a literary medium coincided with the passing of the baton from clerical to lay hands, and a considerable volume of pedagogic material on the new literary standard, generally known as "Classical Irish," has survived.[8] Although the Classical norm was based on the spoken language of the thirteenth century, it continued to be used by professional poets throughout Ireland and Highland Scotland until the seventeenth century, by which time the vernaculars of both countries had evolved so much that the Classical idiom was no longer readily intelligible to those who lacked a literary training. In contrast, the language of prose texts from the Early Modern Irish period (c. 1200–1650) was less uniform and could be either more conservative or more modern than the standard of the poets.

The learned caste on which the cultivation of Irish letters devolved included *breitheamhain* (jurists), *seanchaíthe* (chroniclers), and *filí* (poets) who were retained by native lords. If the *breitheamhain* largely restricted themselves to writing glosses and commentaries on increasingly obscure legal texts in Old Irish, the *seanchaíthe* compiled annals in the time-honored style of their clerical predecessors (examples include the *Annals of Connacht* and the *Annals of Loch Cé*) and constructed genealogies to validate the legitimacy of ruling dynasties by tracing their descent from one or another of the sons of Milesius. Translations from Latin and English were increasingly common and included both devotional texts, such as *Smaointe Beatha Críost* (a translation of *Meditationes Vitae Christi*), and purely secular works, such as the *Buke of John Maundeville*. However, the characteristic literary genre of Early Modern Irish is the poetry of the *filí*, a genre composed in strict meters defined by the number of syllables in each line and by complex patterns of alliteration and rhyme within and between lines.[9] Although it is commonly known as "bardic" poetry in English, the term is unfortunate, as the *bard* was a figure of lower status than the poet. The usual expression in Irish is *filíocht na scol* ("poetry of the schools"), which conveys the elite nature of the material while suggesting an element of continuity with the monastic *scholae* of the Old and Middle Irish periods. Syllabic verse was unsuitable for singing, but it could be recited by a *bard* to a musical accompaniment.

The *filí* could, and frequently did, address both religious and personal themes, but their professional function was to eulogize their patrons. Much of their poetry is encomiastic and extols the distinguished ancestry, military prowess, piety, and generosity of particular lords in conventional terms. The following example from an ode composed by Fearghal Óg Mac an Bhaird to mark the inauguration of Ó Ruairc, lord of Bréifne in the sixteenth century, employs the common literary conceit that the poet and his patron were lovers. It is exceptional only in its conciseness:

> Brian Ó Ruairc mo rogha leannán
>   lór a bhuga ag bronnadh séad;
> 's is lór a chruas i gcrú chaoilshleagh,
>   an cnú do chnuas Ghaoidheal nGréag.[10]

(Brian Ó Ruairc is my choice of lovers, ample is his tenderness in gifting jewels, and ample is his firmness in a palisade of slender spears, this nut of the Grecian Gaels' hoard.)

As might be expected, the resistance of native lords to English expansion forms a notable theme in the literature of the period. For example, Gofraidh Fionn Ó Dálaigh incited Domhnall Óg Mac Carrthaigh (✝1391), king of Desmond, to recover his ancestral lands around Cashel:

> Mar do bhuail Maoise an Muir Ruaidh
> don tslait le rug gach robhuaidh
> sdiuir, a Dhomhnaill, na sluaigh soir
> buail do ghoirmloinn ar Ghallaibh.[11]

(As Moses struck the Red Sea with the rod by which he secured each great victory, direct, O Domhnall, the hosts eastwards; strike your steely blade against foreigners.)

However, the same poet struck a very different note in a poem composed for another magnate, Gerald Fitzgerald (1338–1398), third earl of Desmond, who was of English descent:

> I ndán na nGall gealltar linn
> Gaoidhil d'ionnarba a hÉirinn;
> Goill do shraoineadh tar sál sair
> i ndán na nGaoidheal gealltair.[12]

(In the foreigners' poem we promise to expel Gaels from Ireland; the scattering of foreigners eastwards over the sea is promised in the Gaels' poem.)

The recipient, who is better known under the soubriquet "Gearóid Iarla," was himself an amateur poet and the author of Irish verse that displays the chivalric sensibility of *amour courtois*.

The continuity of themes and motifs throughout the Classical Irish period has led some writers to conclude that the world view of the *filí* was remarkably resistant to innovation.[13] As one scholar put it, "the poetry prior to 1640 is largely apolitical, because responding to outside influences, including New English influences, was no part of its traditional function."[14] The idea that the *filí* may have retained an antiquated and static worldview specific to their craft is not inherently implausible, as they received a professional training and constituted a hereditary caste in Irish society. Nonetheless, it must be remembered that their raison d'être was to extol their patrons. The contradictory attitudes expressed by Gofraidh Fionn Ó Dálaigh in the quatrains quoted above is evidence, not of confusion or indifference, but of professionalism. Yet if the poetry can shed little light on a putative "bardic mentality," it may still provide insights into the images that lords of the period wished to project to their contemporaries.

In contrast to the foregoing, other scholars have detected "the first stages of development of a national political consciousness" in certain poems composed from about 1560 on.[15] The evidence adduced for this development is suggestive but inconclusive. This is hardly surprising: new ideologies rarely appear fully formed or achieve general acceptance in a short space of time. Yet it is clear that one development of great importance took place in the late sixteenth century: by the reign of Elizabeth I, hostility to the Reformation and loyalty to the church of Rome was being proclaimed in Irish literature. A eulogy by Fearghal Óg Mac an Bhaird has already been quoted; around 1581 the same poet composed a more personal poem in which he expressed his grief at being unable to hear Mass while on a visit to Scotland:

> Dámadh liom uile a hór bog
> dá bhfaghuinn a bhfuil d'argod
> i gcrích bhraonuair na mbeann bhfionn
> do b'fhearr aonuair an t-Aifrionn.[16]

(If all her soft gold were mine, were I to obtain all the silver in the cool moist land of the fair peaks, a single Mass would be better.)

The closing decades of the sixteenth century also saw the appearance of a new class of author: the Catholic cleric who dabbled in poetry. One such figure, a Franciscan named Eoghan Ó Dubhthaigh, stressed the hostility of the state toward the Virgin Mary in a poem of 1578:

> 'S ar mháthair Airdríogh na ndúl,
>> ríoghan úr dárab oighre Dia—
> ní fhuighe acht dorn ar a dúid,
>> istigh i gcúirt Átha Cliath.[17]

(As for the mother of the High-King of creation, a young queen whose heir is God—she'd get nothing but a blow to her head, inside in the court of Dublin.)

Clerical authors like Ó Dubhthaigh would play a decisive role in shaping the literature of the following century; they may originally have been inspired by religious devotion, but their work was fraught with political implications.

The Protestant response was slow and uncertain. Although the use of vernacular languages was a Reformation principle, the act of uniformity that restored a Protestant liturgy following the Marian interlude prescribed the use of Latin whenever a priest was unable to officiate in English: the political imperative of anglicization took precedence over the religious imperative of evangelization. But in 1567, John Carswell's *Foirm na nUrrnuidheadh*, based on John Knox's *Book of Common Order*, was published at Edinburgh. The book contains few Scotticisms, and it is clear from Carswell's address to the reader that he hoped it would circulate in both Ireland and Scotland. Possibly in response to this initiative, a translation of the catechism from the Anglican *Book of Common Prayer* was issued at Dublin in 1571; it was the first book in Irish to be printed in Ireland. A collaborative translation of the New Testament followed in 1602. Although a translation of the Old Testament was prepared in the 1630s, it was not until 1685 that an Irish Bible finally appeared in print—more than a century after Carswell deplored its absence.

SEVENTEENTH CENTURY

The sixteenth century had seen the spread of English in south Leinster with the plantation of Laois and Offaly. The "flight of the earls" in 1607 (an event chronicled by one of the earls' party, Tadhg Ó Cianáin, in the earliest surviving journal in Irish) facilitated a more extensive plantation in Ulster and this, together with spontaneous migration from Lowland Scotland to Antrim and Down, established English as the dominant language in eastern and northern Ulster by the second quarter of the seventeenth century. The early years of James I's reign also witnessed the extension of effective royal government throughout Ireland for the first time: English common law was imposed, rendering the *breitheamhain* redundant and reducing the surviving members of former ruling families to the status of gentry. Native landowners felt a pressing need to acquire a competent knowledge of English and came to regard Irish eulogies and genealogies as items of purely antiquarian interest.

The native *literati* did not disappear at once, however, and praise poems in the traditional style continued to be composed with declining frequency in districts where native gentry survived. A recent anthology of 500 previously unpublished bardic poems contains about 150 works from the seventeenth century.[18] Striking evidence of the residual vitality of the hereditary learned class is provided by *iomarbhágh na bhfileadh* ("contention of the poets"), a dispute in verse that erupted in 1617 when Tadhg mac Dáire Mac Bruaideadha, a Munster poet, asserted the seniority of the southern nobility, descendants of the eldest son of Milesius, over the northern nobility, who descended from a younger son. This provoked an indignant response from an Ulster poet, Lughaidh Ó Cléirigh, and more than a dozen poets participated in the resulting controversy. The distinction between *Leath Choinn* (Connacht, Ulster, and the former province of Meath) and *Leath Mhogha* (Munster and Leinster proper) was deeply rooted in Irish mythology, but the polemics may have been given an added edge by the contrasting fortunes of the two halves in the early seventeenth century: while the northern poets lost their most important patrons with the flight of the earls, Donough O'Brien, fourth earl of Thomond, was raised to the presidency of Munster in 1615.[19] Indeed, Lughaidh Ó Cléirigh was also the author of *Beatha Aodha Ruaidh Uí Dhomhnaill*, a laudatory biography of Red Hugh O'Donnell, which is an important source for the Nine Years' War. Some observers felt that the energy expended in the debate was misdirected, and one critic passed the following acerbic judgment on the proceedings:

> Lughaidh, Tadhg agus Torna
> ollaimh oirrdheirce ar dtalaimh,
> coin iad go n-iomad feasa
> ag troid fa an easair fhalaimh![20]

(Lughaidh, Tadhg and Torna, renowned master-poets of our land, they are hounds of great learning fighting over the empty litter!)

The author of this quatrain was Flaithrí Ó Maoil Chonaire (Florence Conry); a member of a learned family, he was also the Catholic archbishop of Tuam and played a leading role in the foundation of Saint Anthony's College, Louvain, in 1607.

The association of clergy from Old Irish and Old English backgrounds in the continental Irish colleges helped to assuage inherited animosities. The most important of these foundations was the college at Louvain, from whence a steady stream of publications in Irish, English, and Latin flowed into Ireland. One such work was *Scáthán Shacramuinte na hAithridhe* (1618), a tract on the sacrament of penance by Aodh Mac Aingil (Aodh Mac Cathmhaoil), a former tutor to the sons of Hugh O'Neill, earl of Tyrone, and subsequently archbishop of Armagh. This text illustrates the extent to which Catholicism was already identified with Irish identity by the early seventeenth century:

> As ní deimhin dearbhtha do réir an chomhráidh si go bhfuil Éire 'na hóigh fhírghlain san ccreideamh 's gur choimhéd a maighdionas do Chríosd ón am fár ghlac a chreideamh tré sheanmóir ár n-absdail uasail iongantuigh gan aon aonta do thabhairt d'earráid ná d'eiriceachd ríamh go beag nó go mór.[21]

(It is certain and definite from this exposition that Ireland is a most pure virgin in the faith and that she preserved her virginity for Christ from the time she received His faith through the preaching of our wonderful noble apostle [Patrick] without ever agreeing with any error or heresy in part or in whole.)

Several figures associated with the Louvain foundation were accomplished Irish scholars. Examples include Giolla Brighde (Bonaventura) Ó hEodhasa, whose

Irish catechism appeared at Antwerp in 1611, and Tadhg (Mícheál) Ó Cléirigh, who was sent to Ireland in 1626 to copy manuscript sources. The chief product of Ó Cléirigh's labors was the compendium now known as the *Annals of the Four Masters*. This work is of enduring value, because several of the sources used by Ó Cléirigh are no longer extant, but its dry annalistic format, archaic language, and the inaccessibility of manuscript copies all ensured that it had little contemporary impact. Instead, it was a Catholic priest of Old English origin who created a historiographical synthesis that captured the imagination of the native intelligentsia.

His English ancestry notwithstanding, Geoffrey Keating (Seathrún Céitinn) graduated from one of the surviving schools of poetry in his native Tipperary before traveling to France for clerical training and returning to Ireland around 1610. The author of verse in both the traditional syllabic and modern stressed meters, he also wrote two theological tracts that circulated in manuscript. However, his most important work was *Foras Feasa ar Éirinn* ("a foundation of knowledge about Ireland"), a narrative history extending from the earliest antediluvian settlement to the arrival of the English under Henry II. Keating drew on *Lebor Gabála Érenn, Cogadh Gaedhel re Gallaibh*, and the annals, among other sources, to fashion an integrated account of the Irish past in stately prose that retained elements of the Classical idiom without impairing its intelligibility for contemporary readers. Keating presented Ireland as a distinct and ancient kingdom, a kingdom whose people had always remained faithful to the religion introduced by Saint Patrick, and a kingdom that was now ruled by a royal house of Milesian descent.[22] Keating gave full vent to his hatred of the New English in his poetry:

> A Fhódla phráis, is náir nach follas díbhse
> gur córa tál ar sháirshliocht mhodhail Mhíle;
> deór níor fágadh i gclár do bhrollaigh mhínghil
> nár dheólsad ál gach cránach coigríche.[23]

(O brazen Ireland, it is shameful you don't see that it would be fitter to suckle the noble gracious race of Milesius; not a drop was left in the surface of your smooth white bosom that wasn't sucked by the litter of every foreign sow.)

By the time these lines were composed, the identification of the Old English with the native population was approaching completion. Further evidence of this evolution is provided by the poetry of Pádraigín Haicéad, an Old English priest from Tipperary who spent some time at Louvain and who hailed the outbreak of the 1641 rebellion in verse:

> Caithfid fir Éireann uile
> ó aicme go haonduine,
> i dtír mbreic na mbinncheann slim,
> gleic 'na timcheall nó tuitim.[24]

(All the men of Ireland must, as groups and individually, in the dappled land of the smooth mountain-tops, fight for her sake or fall.)

In later compositions, Haicéad gave unequivocal support to the papal nuncio, Giovanni Battista Rinuccini, when the Confederate Catholics split on the issue of the Ormond peace.

A journal kept by Toirdhealbhach Ó Mealláin, a Franciscan priest attached to the Confederate army in Ulster, is arguably the most important source in Irish for the war of the 1640s. However, the most characteristic literary genre of the period is represented by a series of long narrative poems composed in contemporary language and in *caoineadh* (elegy) meter—a stressed meter that is rhythmical yet almost prosaic in its simplicity. Although the earliest example may date from around 1640, most were composed in the 1650s and reflect the traumas of the Confederate war and the Cromwellian conquest. One of the best-known poems in the series, *An Síogaí Rómhánach* ("the Roman fairy"), composed by a northern author around 1650, illustrates the intimate link that had been forged between religious and national feeling. The poet directed his prayers to the three patrons of Ireland—Patrick, Colum Cille, and Brigid:

Guímse Dia, más mian leis m'éisteacht,
guím Íosa do-chí an mhéid seo,
is an Spiorad Naofa arís d'aontoil,
Muire mháthair is Pádraig naofa,
Colm croí is Bríd déidgheal,
go ndaingníd sin Gaoil dá chéile
is go dtige dhíobh an gníomh so a dhéanamh:
Gaill d'ionnarbadh is Banba a shaoradh.[25]

(I pray to God if he deigns to hear me, I pray to Jesus who sees all this, and again to the Holy Spirit with deliberation, to mother Mary and holy Patrick, to beloved Colum Cille and white-toothed Brigid, that they may consolidate Gaels together so that they may be able to do this deed: to expel foreigners and to free Ireland.)

Another poem in the series, *Tuireamh na hÉireann* ("Ireland's dirge"), was composed by a Catholic cleric named Seán Ó Conaill and provided a concise and memorable account of Irish history, which followed Keating's history until the twelfth century but continued the narrative as far as the Cromwellian conquest. This work became phenomenally popular, and at least 250 manuscript copies survive—more than for any other text in Irish.[26]

If the tone of literary compositions from the 1650s is understandably bleak, the accession of a Catholic monarch in 1685 was hailed by Irish poets, among whom Dáibhí Ó Bruadair and Diarmuid mac Sheáin Bhuí Mac Cárthaigh are the best known. Their euphoria was short-lived, and the defeat of James II produced a crop of elegies for fallen Jacobite officers. The War of the Two Kings also generated a number of anonymous songs in colloquial diction—songs that either originated in, or quickly entered, the oral tradition. One of these extolled Patrick Sarsfield, a Jacobite commander who had frustrated the first attempt by Williamite forces to capture Limerick city:

> A Phádraig Sáirséal, is duine le Dia thu,
> is fearrde an talamh ar sheasadh tu riamh air;
> do bhuainteá allas as clanna na striapach,
> 's do sciob an bharr ó láimh Rí Uilliam leat.[27]

> (O Patrick Sarsfield, you are a man of God, any ground you ever stood on is the better for it; you used to make the whore-sons sweat, and you snatched the advantage out of King William's hand.)

Irish literature was still dominated by professionally trained poets in 1600, and the graduates of continental seminaries were prominent at mid-century, but by the 1690s the voice of the populace had become audible.

EIGHTEENTH AND NINETEENTH CENTURIES

With rare exceptions, the authors of the eighteenth century were not descended from the learned caste of previous centuries. The Catholic clergy continued to be well represented in the first half of the new century but were less noticeable thereafter. Instead, the authors of the eighteenth century were recruited from a wide range of occupations. In social status, they ranged from landless laborers like Art Mac Cumhaigh to minor members of the gentry like Piaras Mac Gearailt, but a large majority belonged to the middling sort: they were substantial tenant farmers, priests, publicans, artisans, and—most importantly—schoolteachers. These amateur poets were overwhelmingly Catholic, largely rural, and almost exclusively male. Lacking professional training, they wrote in language close to their native dialects. Irish prosody was also transformed: the syllabic meters employed by professional poets in earlier centuries were discarded in favor of *amhrán* (song) meters, and it became increasingly common for scribes to note the airs of songs from the 1730s on.[28] Older texts would continue to be copied for as long as the manuscript tradition endured, but contemporary literature in Irish had been thoroughly popularized in both language and form by 1750.

Few books in Irish were published during the eighteenth century; there was no legal prohibition, but any such publication would have attracted unwelcome attention to the printer in the early decades of the century. It is striking that the first Irish grammar (1728) in English was published at Louvain and that the first English-Irish (1732) and Irish-English (1768) dictionaries were issued at Paris.[29] Similarly, when a Catholic catechism was published in 1748 it appeared without an imprint.[30] The extent of official hostility toward the language can be gauged from the arguments advanced by John Richardson, a minister of the established church, who in 1711 promoted a scheme to convert Catholics by publishing Bibles, catechisms, and prayer books in the vernacular:

> Preaching in the *Irish* Language is not an Encouragement of the *Irish* Interest, any more, than preaching in *French* in *England*, is an Encouragement of the *French* Interest; For the *Irish* Papists, who can speak *English*, ever were, and still are as great Enemies to the *English* Interest, as the *Irish* Papists who cannot speak *English*.[31]

Richardson encountered strong opposition from his co-religionists, although he did succeed in having a book of sermons and a catechism published.

If printing in Irish was uncommon, an upsurge in manuscript production took place in the early decades of the eighteenth century. This can probably be attributed to the economic expansion and more settled conditions of the period. Although a mere 250 manuscripts have survived from before 1600, and only a further 250 are extant from the seventeenth century, 1,000 and 3,000 manuscripts survive from the eighteenth and nineteenth centuries, respectively, with the great majority of the latter written before 1850.[32] The manuscripts provide a unique insight into the culture of the society in which they were produced—a better insight than could ever have been provided by printed sources, as the barriers to manuscript production were much lower. This scribal culture was geographically restricted, however, and two areas predominated: the province of Munster and a region straddling the Ulster-Leinster border. Dublin city, which was a pole of attraction for migrants from all parts of Ireland, also hosted a coterie of scribes. The areas of scribal activity correlate well with regions where a substantial Irish-speaking middle class existed. More than a century ago, Eoin MacNeill, the distinguished historian of early Ireland, surveyed the contents of the O'Laverty manuscript collection held in Saint Malachy's College, Belfast.[33] The collection contained 333 discrete compositions, and MacNeill categorized them as follows: eighty-five items were religious and a further seven were "purely controversial," a description that probably signified anti-Protestant polemics; 38 pieces were heroic in nature and mainly concerned tales of Fionn and his *fianna*; seventeen items related to "contemporary politics," and a further sixteen dealt with "past history"; twenty-six pieces were characterized as "amorous," a small proportion of which MacNeill acknowledged to be "indecent"; "humorous literature" was represented by eighteen pieces, and a further eleven were described as "satirical"; twenty pieces praised persons who were recently deceased, and seven were composed in honor of living subjects. MacNeill's sample was small and a northern bias is likely, given the provenance of the manuscripts, but it is not possible to cite a more recent or more representative analysis, as later historians have paid scant attention to Irish popular culture. Of the various themes identified by MacNeill, religion and politics may be the topics of greatest historical interest, and they will be briefly considered in turn.

The most widely circulated printed book in Irish in the eighteenth century was a collection of sermons by James Gallagher, Catholic bishop of Raphoe, which went through several editions after its first publication in 1736. New devotional works continued to circulate in manuscript, and notable examples include *Beatha Chríost*, an anonymous account of Christ's life running to four thousand lines (which may have been inspired by the fifteenth-century *Smaointe Beatha Críost*), and an anonymous northern translation of *De Imitatione Christi* by Thomas à Kempis. A considerable proportion of the poetry and song of the eighteenth century deals with religious themes, and most poets of the period made some contribution to the genre. The devotional verse of Tadhg Gaelach Ó Súilleabháin is particularly significant, as it was collected and published posthumously under the title *Timothy O'Sullivan's Pious Miscellany* in 1802. This anthology went through several later editions and replaced Bishop Gallagher's sermons as the most popular printed volume in Irish. Polemical texts condemning Luther, Calvin, Henry VIII, Elizabeth I, and other Protestant reformers were also common, while members of the Catholic clergy who conformed to the established church were often excoriated in verse.[34]

Jacobitism was the dominant ideology in the political literature of the period, but it was a distinctively Irish Jacobitism that emphasized the Milesian ancestry of the Stuarts, their loyalty to Catholicism, and Ireland's status as a kingdom with a crown of its own.[35] Although Jacobite sentiment was expressed in a variety of literary genres, the *aisling* (vision) is especially identified with the ideology. In *aislingí*, the poet typically encounters a *spéirbhean*, a beautiful otherworld woman personifying Ireland, and either receives from her, or imparts to her, an assurance that the Stuart pretender is coming with an army to liberate Ireland. The popular appeal of the *aisling* made it an excellent vehicle for disseminating a range of political views. The following example has been attributed to Liam Dall Ó hIfearnáin and illustrates the messianic tone of eighteenth-century Jacobitism. The *spéirbhean* who appeared to the poet made the following prediction:

Gidh fada faoi dhaorbhroid laochra Chaisil
    i ngéibheann galair gan áitreabh,
gan talamh gan tréad gan réim gan rachmas
    gan scléip gan aiteas gan áthas,
dá ngreadadh dá gcéasadh dá gcréimeadh ag Gallaibh
    's dá séideadh thar caladh ina dtáintibh,
ní fada go réidhe an laoch gan ainm
    ár bpéin, ár bpeannaid 's ár ngá-na.[36]

(Although the heroes of Cashel have long been in bondage, in miserable fetters without a dwelling, with no land, herd, power or wealth, without gaiety, delight or happiness, being pounded, tormented and ground down by foreigners, and being expelled overseas in great numbers, it won't be long until the nameless champion relieves our pain, our torment and our need.)

After a republican interlude in the 1790s, the *aisling* was again employed to foretell the imminent arrival of another liberator from overseas. In the early nineteenth century, Donncha Ó Súilleabháin addressed the *spéirbhean* who appeared to him as follows:

Dá dtiocfadh trúp go cuan an Daingin
   is súgach mar a léimfinn,
ba radharc sa dúthaigh búir á dtreascairt
   agus póirt dá lasadh in éineacht;
mar go deimhin táid siúd ar a gcúrsa ag teacht
   le cúnamh ceart an Aonmhic,
is domhain do chumha gan fonn, a bhean,
   go dtí Bonaparte lá gréine.[37]

(If an army were to come to Dingle bay I'd leap for joy, the destruction of the boors would be a sight in the countryside, with fortresses blazing simultaneously; for assuredly they are coming on their voyage, with the righteous assistance of the Only Begotten Son, deep will be your listless gloom, O woman, until [Napoleon] Bonaparte arrives one sunny day.)

Later still, the *aisling* was pressed into service to extol a homegrown liberator. The following anonymous example is taken from a printed broadsheet:

Do fhreagair sí mise go tapa le meidhir,
   "I'm none of those damsels, O'Kelly, you mean,
   ach Éire, cé fada mé ag taisteal i gcéin
but now I'll come over to my own native isle."
Á insint le mórtas go mbeidh Dónall faoi mheidhir,
exalted, victorious, most glorious in style,
ag rúscadh clann Luther go tapa thar faill,
   agus fágaimis siúd mar atá sé.[38]

(She answered me quickly with spirit, "I'm none of those damsels, O'Kelly, you mean, but Ireland, though I've long been traveling abroad but now I'll come over to my own native isle." Asserting with pride that Daniel [O'Connell] will be lively, exalted, victorious, most glorious in style, quickly flinging Luther's offspring off a precipice—and let's leave that as it is.)

Such macaronic compositions in which passages of Irish and English alternated became increasingly common as bilingualism spread in the early nineteenth century.

Certain authors have portrayed the Irish language and its associated culture as being effectively moribund by the start of the nineteenth century.[39] This view is untenable. The production of Irish manuscripts continued to increase in the early years of the new century, scribes continued to copy the literature of earlier centuries for their own use or that of clients, and new works continued to be written in a range of genres.[40] Poets of the period who have had modern anthologies published include Antaine Raiftearaí, a blind musician whose compositions were preserved in the oral tradition of Galway; Máire Bhuí Ní Laoire, a rare female author whose songs are still sung in west Cork; Pádraig Cúndún, who continued to write after he emigrated to New York in 1826; Aodh Mac Dónaill, who also compiled a manuscript natural history in 1853; and Art Mac Bionaid, who also completed a manuscript history of Ireland from the Norse wars to the Williamite revolution in 1858.[41] The journal of Amhlaoibh Ó Súilleabháin (Humphrey O'Sullivan) furnishes a vivid account of small-town life in County Kilkenny in the years 1827–1835.

In the absence of contemporary statistics, estimates of the numbers who spoke Irish in the eighteenth century can only be impressionistic. At the beginning of the period, the language may have been spoken by 70% of the population, a proportion that had fallen to about 60% a hundred years later, but this modest decline masked a significant increase in the number of those who were bilingual. Although it is true that English spread from east to west, it also spread from the top to the bottom of society: if the gentry acquired English in the seventeenth century, the rural middle class followed suit in the eighteenth century. In an analysis of census data, Garret FitzGerald estimated that "something approaching half—perhaps even half or more—of the children in Ireland at the start of the nineteenth century spoke Irish."[42] Language change accelerated in the early nineteenth century, especially in north Leinster and south Ulster, and English also began to penetrate into east Connacht and east Munster. This development was facilitated by the establishment in 1831 of a state-funded system of primary education from which Irish was excluded, both as a subject and as a medium of instruction. Nonetheless, on the eve of the Great Famine of 1845–1852, Irish remained the vernacular language all along the western and southern seaboard. Crucially, however, Famine-related mortality was highest among the poor in remoter parts of Connacht and Munster—precisely the demographic group that was least likely to know English. About one million died, and an even larger number emigrated to Britain or North America. With the disappearance of a large pool of monoglot Irish speakers, those who were bilingual no longer needed to transmit the language to the next generation. Instead, a command of English was seen as essential by parents who realized that many of their children would emigrate. Copying of manuscripts also declined rapidly after 1850 and had virtually ceased by 1860. Writing after his appointment as professor of Celtic in the Queen's College, Belfast, in 1849, the distinguished scholar John O'Donovan predicted the death of the language within a lifetime:

The taste for Irish language and literature will become less and less every year, and therefore I think it of more consequence to work steadily and assiduously to preserve in an intelligible form what historical materials we have than anything that could be done in the way of teaching the language, which will become obsolete in about fifty years.[43]

This was a realistic estimate at the time of writing. The census of 1851, conducted in the immediate aftermath of the Famine, found that 23.3% of the general population could speak Irish, but only 12.7% of those aged ten or younger knew the language. Forty years later, the census of 1891 revealed that a mere 3.5% of those aged ten or younger were Irish speakers.

REVIVAL

The formation of the Society for the Preservation of the Irish Language in 1876 marked the start of sustained efforts to arrest the language's decline. The Society concentrated its efforts on lobbying to improve the position of Irish in the educational system and obtained permission for it to be taught outside of normal hours in primary schools and its recognition as an optional subject in secondary schools. A more activist group, the Gaelic Union, was formed in 1880, and two years later it took the important step of establishing a literary journal, *Irisleabhar na Gaedhilge*, which survived the demise of its parent body. In 1893 the Gaelic League was founded under the presidency of Douglas Hyde, and it grew rapidly in the first decade of the twentieth century. The League employed itinerant organizers to form branches and teach evening classes, while original works and editions of the literature of earlier centuries were published under the League's imprint. A bilingual weekly paper, *An Claidheamh Soluis*, was established as the League's official organ in 1899 and introduced many native speakers to the experience of reading their own language. The League defied the Catholic hierarchy by successfully campaigning to make Irish an essential subject for matriculation to the National University of Ireland, thereby ensuring that it would be widely taught in secondary schools. Following the establishment of the Irish Free State, the language became a core part of the school curriculum. The League's most important achievement was less obvious and more gradual: the growing stream of students visiting Gaeltacht areas and the increased cultural prestige attaching to Irish convinced a critical mass of native speakers that knowledge of the language would be an asset rather than a liability for their children. Most of those districts where Irish was spoken by all age groups in 1920 are still Irish-speaking today.

The absence of a standard form of Irish posed a difficulty in the early years of the revival, as native speakers from Ulster, Connacht, and Munster each championed the claims of their own dialect. Those who learned Irish as a second language were particularly vulnerable to the criticism of purists. Patrick Dinneen, a lexicographer from Kerry, penned the following critique of a short story in Connacht Irish by the Dublin-born Patrick Pearse:

> I have tasted Connemara butter before now: it has its defects ... It may at times be over-salted and over-dosed with the water of *"béarlachas"* [anglicism] but it is genuine mountain butter all the same and not clever margarine. I am afraid the storyette about the *Píobaire* smacks more like the margarine of the slums.[44]

Few literary works of lasting value emerged in the early decades of the century, although the short stories and novels of Pádraic Ó Conaire and Seosamh Mac Grianna, natives of Galway and Donegal, respectively, stand out as exceptions. Two autobiographies by natives of the Blasket Islands, *An tOileánach* (*The Islandman*) by Tomás Ó Criomhthain and *Fiche Bliadhan ag Fás* (*Twenty Years A-Growing*) by Muiris Ó Súilleabháin, attracted international attention in translation, but their significance is more anthropological than literary; these and other Gaeltacht autobiographies would be mercilessly satirized by "Myles na gCopaleen" (Brian O'Nolan) in *An Béal Bocht*. The small readership made it impossible for writers to earn a living from writing in Irish: Liam O'Flaherty, a native of Aran, produced a fine collection of short stories, *Dúil*, but otherwise concentrated on English. It was only in the 1940s, with the emergence of the poets Máirtín Ó Direáin, Máire Mhac an tSaoi, and Seán Ó Ríordáin and the prose writer Máirtín Ó Cadhain, that a foundation was laid for a modern literature of high quality. About the same time, the state finally addressed the sensitive issue of standardization. In 1945 the translation service of Dáil Éireann published recommendations for a reformed orthography that eliminated consonants that had been silent since the demise of Classical Irish. This modernized spelling was universally adopted and was complemented by the publication of a standard grammar in 1958. Originally intended for official purposes, the grammar was widely adopted in journalism and the education system and had the unintended effect of diminishing the status of the spoken dialects. However, a revised standard grammar was issued in 2012 that is less prescriptive and gives official sanction to many common provincial forms for the first time.

Contemporary texts in Irish written by the cultural nationalists of the early twentieth century are an important primary source for historians of the Irish revolution; several prominent figures, including Douglas Hyde, Ernest Blythe, and Seán T. O'Kelly, left memoirs in Irish.[45] Later memoirs of historical interest range from those of a communist who fought for the Spanish Republic to those of a Nazi sympathizer who spent the Second World War in Berlin.[46] Historical biography has been a significant genre, some of the more notable subjects including Robert Emmet, James Fintan Lalor, and Jeremiah O'Donovan Rossa.[47] Medieval historians have generally acknowledged the importance of sources in Irish, but they have rarely been used by historians of the seventeenth century or later—a neglect that can be attributed to the historians' lack of the necessary linguistic and paleographic skills. The resulting vacuum has been partly filled by literary scholars who have a historical perspective. Several imposing monographs have been written: the weightier tomes include Liam Ó Caithnia's social history of hurling between the seventeenth and nineteenth centuries, Breandán Ó Buachalla's analytical survey of Irish royalist literature in the seventeenth and eighteenth centuries, and Pádraig Ó Siadhail's biography of the nationalist revolutionary Piaras Béaslaí.[48] Scholarly essays are, naturally, more numerous, and the outlets include academic journals that publish entirely in Irish, such as *Irisleabhar Mhá Nuad* and *Léachtaí Cholm Cille*, and others, including *Éigse, Studia Hibernica*, and *Eighteenth-Century Ireland*, which have a bilingual policy. In recent years, *Festschriften* for Irish-language scholars have also provided a forum for research with a historical dimension. The task of cataloging manuscripts and publishing editions of literary texts is ongoing: texts in Old and Middle Irish are invariably accompanied by English translations, as is frequently the case for Classical Irish texts, but editions of texts from the seventeenth century on are generally published without translations.

What is the current state of the language itself? If census returns were a reliable indicator, one would have to conclude that it is in good health. The 2011 census for the Republic of Ireland found that 1.77 million people, representing 40.6% of the population aged three and older, claimed to know Irish. Passive comprehension of the language is widespread, and this figure may reflect the number of those who understand news bulletins in Irish, but it is a gross overestimate of the number who speak it. A more realistic measure of linguistic competence is provided by the numbers who reported that they speak Irish on a daily or weekly basis outside of the education system: these groups numbered 77,185 and 110,642 respectively, equivalent to 1.8% and 2.5% of the population aged three and older. The Northern Ireland census of 2011 did not ask about language use, but 10.6% of the population claimed to have "some ability in Irish." This result should be accorded the same credibility as the 40.6% figure reported for the Republic, but it seems reasonable to conclude that the proportion of the population who speak the language in Northern Ireland may be about a quarter of that in the Republic. The total number of Irish speakers on the island can therefore be estimated at about 200,000.

If the condition of the language is assessed using other criteria, plausible cases can be made for the glass being either half full or half empty. In the field of communications, Raidió na Gaeltachta, a Gaeltacht-based radio station established in 1972, has been an unqualified success: it put widely dispersed Gaeltacht communities in contact with one another and made problems of comprehension among the speakers of different dialects a thing of the past. The record of TG4, an Irish-language television service established in 1996, has been more equivocal, but its programming for children is critical for language maintenance. In the field of publishing, newspapers and magazines have struggled in recent years, a development that partly reflects the growing importance of digital media. Book publishing remains vigorous, however, with 100–150 titles appearing annually. The historical novel has been particularly successful in recent years: subjects include the fourteenth-century "Gearóid Iarla," the Cromwellian conquest, the "Wild Geese," and the Civil War in Kerry.[49] Interestingly, a website that uses software to monitor blogs written in lesser-used languages reports that the incidence of blogging in Irish is only half of that in Welsh, but it is considerably higher than for Faeroese, Occitan, Friulian, Frisian, Gaelic, or Breton.[50] In the field of education, the standard of Irish in primary schools has fallen sharply in recent decades.[51] This in turn has affected teaching at the secondary level, where the focus is now on the acquisition of basic linguistic skills; as the same curriculum is followed in all schools, Irish-speaking students find the course unchallenging. Yet even as the standard of Irish in English-medium schools has declined, demand for Irish-medium education has grown steadily: in 1972, only eleven primary and five post-primary schools outside the Gaeltacht taught through the medium of Irish, but the corresponding figures for 2013 were 180 and forty-one.[52] The greatest threat to the future of the language may be the decline in use that has been noted in the major Gaeltacht areas of Galway and Donegal in recent years, especially among teenagers and young adults.[53] At the same time, the influence of English pronunciation, grammar, and idioms on the speech of the younger generation is giving rise to concern.[54] Yet it must also be acknowledged that some of the smaller Irish-speaking districts have shown remarkable resilience and that all living languages constantly evolve.

The future of Irish remains uncertain, but it is spoken as a first language by children who were born in the present century; we can therefore be assured that the last native speakers will not pass away until the twenty-second century at the earliest. John O'Donovan would have been surprised.

FURTHER READING

For a linguistic analysis, see Mícheál Ó Siadhail, *Modern Irish: Grammatical Structure and Dialectal Variation* (Cambridge: Cambridge University Press, 1989). Kim McCone, Damian McManus, Cathal Ó Háinle, Nicholas Williams, and Liam Breatnach (eds.), *Stair na Gaeilge* (Maynooth: Roinn na Sean-Ghaeilge, 1994) provides the only detailed account of the language's evolution. Brian Ó Cuív (ed.), *A View of the Irish Language* (Dublin: Dublin Stationery Office, 1969), is a dated but still useful collection of essays. The chapters by Paul Russell, James Carney, Brian Ó Cuív, Neil Buttimer, and Máire Ní Annracháin in successive volumes of *A New History of Ireland* (Oxford: Oxford University Press, 1976–2005) provide the fullest historical treatment of the language's literature and sociolinguistics, but the series narrative concludes in 1984. For a more concise account that extends to the present millennium, see the relevant chapters in Margaret Kelleher and Philip O'Leary (eds.), *The Cambridge History of Irish Literature* (Cambridge: Cambridge

University Press, 2006). Tony Crowley (ed.), *The Politics of Language in Ireland 1366–1922* (London: Routledge, 2000) is a convenient anthology of relevant texts. Caoilfhionn Nic Pháidín and Seán Ó Cearnaigh (eds.), *A New View of the Irish Language* (Dublin: Cois Life, 2008) offers an assessment of the language's current condition. Katharine Simms, *Medieval Gaelic Sources* (Dublin: Four Courts Press, 2009) is an excellent guide for students of history. Éamonn Ó Ciardha, "Irish-Language Sources for the History of Early Modern Ireland," in Alvin Jackson (ed.), *The Oxford Handbook of Irish History* (Oxford: Oxford University Press, 2014) considers the seventeenth and eighteenth centuries but is largely focused on political literature. Aidan Doyle, *A History of the Irish Language: From the Norman Invasion to Independence* (Oxford: Oxford University Press, 2015) appeared after the present chapter was completed.

NOTES

1. J. P. Mallory, *The Origins of the Irish* (London: Thames & Hudson, 2013), chapter 9.

2. For a concise presentation of the traditional view, see Proinsias Mac Cana, *Literature in Irish* (Dublin: Department of Foreign Affairs, 1980).

3. The "anti-nativist" case is stated in Kim McCone, *Pagan Past and Christian Present in Early Irish Literature* (Maynooth: An Sagart, 1990).

4. See Gerard Murphy, *Early Irish Lyrics* (Oxford: Clarendon, 1956) and Jeffrey Gantz, *Early Irish Myths and Sagas* (Harmondsworth: Penguin, 1981) for anthologies of Old Irish verse and prose, respectively.

5. Fergus Kelly, *A Guide to Early Irish Law* (Dublin: Dublin Institute for Advanced Studies, 1988), is an accessible introduction to the subject.

6. Peter J. Smith, *Three Historical Poems Ascribed to Gilla Cóemáin* (Münster: Nodus, 2007), p. 166.

7. The transition is discussed in Proinsias Mac Cana, "The Rise of the Later Schools of *filidheacht*," *Ériu* 25 (1974), pp. 126–146.

8. Brian Ó Cuív, "The Linguistic Training of the Mediaeval Irish Poet," *Celtica* 10 (1973), pp. 114–140.

9. For details of the meters, see Eleanor Knott (ed.), *An Introduction to Irish Syllabic Poetry of the Period 1200–1600* (Dublin: Dublin Institute for Advanced Studies, 1994), pp. 1–12.

10. Knott, *An Introduction to Irish Syllabic Poetry*, p. 23; "nut" is a term of endearment.

11. Láimhbheartach Mac Cionnaith (ed.), *Dioghluim Dána* (Dublin: Oifig an tSoláthair, 1938), p. 231.

12. Mac Cionnaith, *Dioghluim Dána*, p. 206.

13. T. J. Dunne, "The Gaelic Response to Conquest and Colonisation: The Evidence of the Poetry" in *Studia Hibernica* 20 (1980), 7–30; Bernadette Cunningham, "Native Culture and Political Change in Ireland" in C. Brady and R. Gillespie eds., *Natives and Newcomers* (Dublin: Irish Academic Press, 1986), pp. 148–70; Michelle O Riordan, *The Gaelic Mind and the Collapse of the Gaelic World* (Cork: Cork University Press, 1990); Joep Leerssen, *Mere Irish and Fíor-Ghael* (Cork: Cork University Press, 1996), pp. 151–202.

14. Cunningham, "Native Culture and Political Change in Ireland," p. 164.

15. Brendan Bradshaw, "Native Reaction to the Westward Enterprise: A Case-Study in Gaelic Ideology" in K. R. Andrews, N. P. Canny, P.E.H. Hair (eds.), *The Westward Enterprise* (Liverpool: Liverpool University Press, 1978), p. 75. See also Breandán Ó Buachalla, "Poetry and politics in early modern Ireland," *Eighteenth-Century Ireland* 7 (1992), pp. 149–175; and Marc Caball, *Poets and Politics: Reaction and Continuity in Irish Poetry, 1558–1625* (Cork: Cork University Press, 1998).

16. Lambert McKenna (ed.), *Aithdhioghluim Dána*, vol. I (Dublin: Irish Texts Society, 1939), p. 204.

17. Cuthbert Mhág Craith (ed.), *Dán na mBráthar Mionúr*, vol. 1 (Dublin: Institiúid Árd-Léinn, 1967), p. 134.

18. Damian McManus and Eoghan Ó Raghallaigh (eds.), *A Bardic Miscellany* (Dublin: Department of Irish, Trinity College Dublin, 2010).

19. Joep Leerssen, *The Contention of the Bards* (London: Irish Texts Society, 1994). For a contrasting assessment, see Breandán Ó Buachalla, *Aisling Ghéar: na Stíobhartaigh agus an tAos Leinn, 1603–1788* (Dublin: An Clóchomhar Tta, 1996), pp. 54–57.

20. Mhág Craith, *Dán na mBráthar Mionúr*, vol. 1, p. 126.

21. Cainneach Ó Maonaigh (ed.), *Scáthán Shacraiminte na hAithridhe* (Dublin: Institiúid Árd-Léinn, 1952), p. 190.

22. For a summary of Keating's ideology, see Brendan Bradshaw, "Geoffrey Keating: apologist of Irish Ireland" in Brendan Bradshaw, Andrew Hadfield, and Willy Maley (eds.), *Representing Ireland: Literature and the Origins of Conflict, 1534–1660* (Cambridge: Cambridge University Press, 1993), pp. 166–190.

23. Pádraig de Brún, Breandán Ó Buachalla, Tomas Ó Concheanainn (eds.), *Nua-Dhuanaire I* (Dublin: Institiúid Ardléinn, 1971), p. 18.

24. Máire Ní Cheallacháin (ed.), *Filíocht Phádraigín Haicéad* (Dublin: An Clóchomhar Tta, 1962), p. 35.

25. Cecile O'Rahilly (ed.), *Five Seventeenth-Century Political Poems* (Dublin: Institiúid Árd-Léinn 1952), pp. 31–32.

26. Vincent Morley, *Ó Chéitinn go Raiftearaí: Mar a Cumadh Stair na hÉireann* (Dublin: Coiscéim, 2011), pp. 127–138.

27. Tomás Ó Concheanainn, "Slán chum Pádraic Sáirséal," *Éigse* 14 (1971–1972), p. 226.

28. Breandán Ó Buachalla, "Ceol na filíochta," *Studia Hibernica* 32 (2002–2003), pp. 99–132.

29. Hugh MacCurtin, *The Elements of the Irish Language Grammatically Explained in English* (Louvain: Martin Van Overbeke, 1728); Conchobhar Ó Beaglaoich, *The English Irish Dictionary: An Focloir Bearla Gaoidheilge* (Paris: Seamus Guerin, 1732); [John O'Brien], *Focalóir Gaoidhilge-Sax-Bhearla, or an Irish-English Dictionary* (Paris: Nicolas-Francis Valleyre, 1768).

30. [James Pulleine], *An Teagasg Criosdaidhe Angoidhleig* (N.P.: 1748).

31. John Richardson, *A Proposal for the Conversion of the Popish Natives of Ireland to the Establish'd Religion* (Dublin: E. Waters, 1711), p. 6. The episode is described in Nicholas Williams, *I bPrionta i Leabhar: Na Protastúin agus Prós na Gaeilge 1567–1724* (Dublin: An Clóchomhar, 1986), chapter 9.

32. Brian Ó Cuív, "Ireland's Manuscript Heritage," *Éire-Ireland*, 19: 1 (1984), pp. 90, 104.

33. Eoin MacNeill, "The O'Laverty Manuscripts" in *Irisleabhar na Gaedhilge*, November 1906, pp. 226–7.

34. This topic awaits detailed investigation, but see Vincent Morley, "The Penal Laws in Irish Vernacular Literature," in John Bergin, Eoin Magennis, Lesa Ní Mhunghaile, and Patrick Walsh (eds.), *New Perspectives on the Penal Laws* (Dublin: Eighteenth Century Ireland Society, 2011), pp. 173–96.

35. Breandán Ó Buachalla, "James Our True King: The Ideology of Irish Royalism in the Seventeenth Century" in George Boyce, Robert Eccleshall, Vincent Geoghegan (eds.), *Political Thought in Ireland since the Seventeenth Century* (London: Routledge, 1993), pp. 7–35; Breandán Ó Buachalla, *The Crown of Ireland* (Galway: Arlen House, 2006).

36. Risteárd Ó Foghludha (ed.), *Ar Bruach na Coille Muaire* (Dublin: Oifig an tSoláthair, 1939), pp. 78–79.

37. Diarmuid Ó Muirithe (ed.), *An tAmhrán Macarónach* (Dublin: An Clóchomhar Tta, 1980), p. 112.

38. Ó Muirithe, *An tAmhrán Macarónach*, p. 103.

39. See, for example, John Hutchinson, *The Dynamics of Cultural Nationalism: The Gaelic Revival and the Creation of the Irish Nation State* (London: Allen and Unwin, 1987), p. 50; and Joep Leerssen, *Remembrance and Imagination: Patterns in the Historical and Literary Representations of Ireland in the Nineteenth Century* (Cork: Cork University Press, 1996), p. 1.

40. For the continuity of the scribal tradition between the eighteenth and nineteenth centuries, see Meidhbhín Ní Úrdail, *The Scribe in Eighteenth- and Nineteenth-Century Ireland: Motivations and Milieu* (Münster: Nodus, 2000).

41. For the prose works by Mac Dónaill and Mac Bionaid, see Colm Beckett (ed.), *Fealsúnacht Aodha Mhic Dhomhnaill* (Dublin: Clóchomhar, 1967); and Réamonn Ó Muirí (ed.), *Lámhscríbhinn Staire an Bhionadaigh* (Monaghan: Éigse Oirialla, 1994), respectively.

42. Garret FitzGerald, "Estimates for Baronies of Minimum Level of Irish-Speaking among Successive Decennial Cohorts: 1771–1781 to 1861–1871," in *Proceedings of the Royal Irish Academy* C 84 (1984), p. 126.

43. Breandán Ó Buachalla, *I mBéal Feirste Cois Cuain* (Dublin: An Clóchomhar Teoranta, 1968), p. 239.

44. Proinsias Ó Conluain and Donncha Ó Céileachair, *An Duinnníneach* (Dublin: Sáirséal agus Dill, 1958), p. 211.

45. Dubhghlas de hÍde, *Mise agus an Connradh* (Dublin: Oifig Dhíolta Foillseacháin Rialtais, 1931) and *Mo Thuras go hAmerice* (Dublin: Oifig Díolta Foillseacháin Rialtais, 1937); Earnán de Blaghd, *Trasna na Bóinne* (Dublin: Sáirséal agus Dill 1957), *Slán le hUltaibh* (Dublin: Sáirséal agus Dill, 1971) and *Gaeil á Múscailt* (Dublin: Sáirséal agus Dill, 1973); Seán T. Ó Ceallaigh, *Seán T.*, vol. 1 (Dublin: FNT, 1963) and vol. 2 (Dublin: Cló Morainn, 1972).

46. Eoghan Ó Duinnín, *La Niña Bonita agus an Róisín Dubh* (Dublin: An Clóchomhar Tta, 1986); Róisín Ní Mheara-Vinard, *Cé hÍ seo Amuigh* (Dublin: Coiscéim, 1992).

47. Léon Ó Broin, *Emmet* (Dublin: Sáirséal agus Dill, 1954); Tomás Ó Néill, *Fiontán Ó Leathlobhair* (Dublin: Cló Morainn, 1962); Seán Ó Lúing, *Ó Donnabháin Rossa*, vol. 1 (Dublin: Sáirséal agus Dill, 1969) and vol. 2 (Dublin: Sáirséal agus Dill, 1979).

48. Liam P. Ó Caithnia, *Scéal na hIomána* (Dublin: An Clóchomhar Tta, 1980); Ó Buachalla, *Aisling Ghéar*; Pádraig Ó Siadhail, *An Béaslaíoch* (Dublin: Coiscéim, 2007).

49. Máire Mhac an tSaoi, *Scéal Ghearóid Iarla* (Inverin: Leabhar Breac, 2011); Darach Ó Scolaí, *An Cléireach* (Inverin: Leabhar Breac, 2007); Liam Mac Cóil, *Fontenoy* (Inverin: Leabhar Breac, 2005); Seán Mac Mathúna, *Hula Hul* (Inverin: Leabhar Breac, 2007).

50. There were 160 blogs containing 3.5 million words in Irish and 278 blogs containing 5.9 million words in Welsh; data recovered from Kevin Scannell's "Indigenous Blogs" website (http://indigenoustweets.com/blogs) accessed November 15, 2014.

51. John Harris, "Irish in the Education System" in Caoilfhionn Nic Pháidín and Seán Ó Cearnaigh (eds.), *A New View of the Irish Language* (Dublin: Cois Life, 2008).

52. These are pooled figures for the Republic of Ireland and Northern Ireland; they were taken from the website of Gaelscoileanna (http://www.gaelscoileanna.ie/about/statistics/) accessed November 15, 2014.

53. Conchúr Ó Giollagáin and Seosamh Mac Donnacha, "The Gaeltacht Today," in Nic Pháidín and Ó Cearnaigh, *New View of the Irish Language*, pp. 108–120.

54. Brian Ó Curnáin, "An Ghaeilge iarthraidisiúnta agus an phragmataic chódmheasctha thiar agus theas" in Ciarán Lenoach, Conchúr Ó Giollagáin, Brian Ó Curnáin (eds.), *An Chonair Chaoch: An Mionteangachas sa Dátheangachas* (Inverin: Leabhar Breac, 2012).

CHAPTER 14

IRELAND *and* EMPIRE

Jill C. Bender

O VER THE COURSE OF FOUR centuries, the Irish played a significant role in the expansion, maintenance, and decline of Britain's empire. The complex nature of this role is well illustrated with the story of two brothers: Frank Hugh and Charles James O'Donnell. Both were born in the 1840s to Irish parents (Sergeant Bernard MacDonald and his wife, Mary, *née* Kain), both were educated at Queen's College Galway, and both pursued prominent careers that engaged with the British Empire. The eldest, F. H. O'Donnell, entered the House of Commons in 1874 as a member for Galway (borough). He quickly lost his seat on petition, but was elected three years later as member of parliament (MP) for Dungarvan and held his seat until 1885. While in office, F. H. O'Donnell proved to be a colorful and unpredictable character. (His colleagues referred to him as "Crank Hugh O'Donnell.") Historians, too, have found him difficult. In his two-volume *History of the Irish Parliamentary Party*, O'Donnell promotes his own role in Irish parliamentary nationalism to fantastical degrees. Regardless, his interest in both Irish nationalism and the Empire appeared genuine. Starting with his maiden speech in 1874, O'Donnell expressed an interest in the British Empire (specifically India). And, throughout his political career, he encouraged the globalization of Irish nationalism, arguing that Ireland had a responsibility to intervene in British politics on behalf of colonized peoples.

While F. H. O'Donnell argued for imperial reform from the Empire's metropole, his younger brother did so from the Empire's periphery. In 1872, Charles James O'Donnell secured an appointment in the Indian Civil Service (ICS) and began a nearly thirty-year career in India. Earning the moniker, "l'enfant terrible of the ICS," O'Donnell recognized his position as an opportunity to challenge British imperial policies and advocate for reform from within the system. He is perhaps best known as the author of two pamphlets, *The Black Pamphlet: the Famine of 1874* and *The Ruin of an Indian Province*, both of which offered scathing criticisms of British rule in India. Following his retirement from the ICS, O'Donnell entered politics and served as MP for the London constituency of Walworth from 1906 to 1910.

Although unique historical figures in their own right, the O'Donnell brothers also exemplify the complicated relationship between Ireland and the modern British Empire. Both men looked to the Empire for employment, and likely benefited personally from the imperial connection. Both men also used their positions in parliament and the ICS to challenge British imperial rule and advocate for change. Neither man was against empire, *per se*. Rather, both argued for a federated empire, in which the colonies (including Ireland) would be on equal status with one another as well as with Britain. Both men, in other words, remind us that British imperialism was not a black-and-white conflict between colonizer and colonized. Furthermore, they remind us that the British Empire had an impact on the Irish—whether at home or overseas—and that the Irish, in turn, had an impact on the British Empire.

In recent years, the study of Ireland and Empire has received sustained academic attention.[1] Initially this interest focused on Ireland's colonial status. Determining whether Ireland was or was not a colony proved to be a difficult task for scholars. At first glance, the island certainly appears to be a colony in all but name. English, Scottish, and Welsh settlers had been present on the island since the late sixteenth century. And by the close of the seventeenth century, "English legal, political, and administrative" norms had been put in place. Furthermore, "all landed and commercial transactions were now recognizably English."[2] In 1800, however, both the Irish and British parliaments passed legislation to abolish the 300-member Irish parliament. In its place, 100 Irish MPs took up seats at Westminster. As a result, under the 1801 Act of Union, Ireland became a part of the United Kingdom. It did not, however, become an equal partner. Economic and administrative integration was never complete. Questions regarding trade, currency, and taxation remained, and the island was administered by a chief secretary and lord lieutenant based in Dublin, an executive arrangement that would later inform British rule in India. Britain's conquest of Ireland, therefore, never appeared entirely straightforward or complete.

To further complicate the matter, even while they seemed to be colonized by the British, Irish people also played a significant role in the expansion of Britain's empire. The British Empire offered ready employment, and the Irish seized the opportunities. As noted above, Frank Hugh O'Donnell held a seat in the imperial parliament; Charles James O'Donnell rose through the ranks of the ICS. Irish soldiers, administrators, medical doctors, policemen, clergy, missionaries, and lawyers surfaced throughout the Empire in significant numbers from the eighteenth century on. As Hilary M. Carey has aptly explained, "In short, the Irish were practical imperialists—cheap, adaptable, willing to travel, hold a gun, beat a drum, preach a sermon, and generally serve in many useful positions along the colonial frontier."[3] Initially, this Irish participation unsettled many scholars, who considered the history of the Irish as both a conquered and a conquering people to be problematic. Ireland's position in the British Empire has been deemed paradoxical or contradictory.[4] Kevin Kenny has dismissed these claims, arguing "Colonized by their more powerful neighbor, the Irish lived at the heart of world's greatest Empire; most Irish people saw themselves as a part of that Empire in some way; many participated, at a variety of levels, in its workings overseas. There is no contradiction here, merely a fact of imperial history."[5] Indeed, throughout the Empire, "colonized" individuals chose to enter imperial service for a variety of reasons. Too much emphasis on Ireland's colonial status runs the risk of casting empire in a binary light and reducing Ireland's history to one of conflict and resistance.

With this in mind, the debate regarding Ireland's colonial status has for the most part moved on. As Michael de Nie has recently explained, "a consensus that Ireland's relationship with Britain shared at least some features with those of the dominions and colonies has settled in across the disciplines of Irish studies."[6] This is not to suggest that scholars have lost interest in the subject of Ireland and Empire; they have merely begun to ask different questions. Rather than look to Ireland's participation in the Empire for insight into Ireland's colonial status, historians have begun to unpack these contributions for insight into the imperial experience. Drawing from this recent scholarship, this chapter seeks to answer the following questions: Was the Irish contribution to the Empire unique? If so, what did this Irish participation mean for British imperial expansion? How did the Irish shape the Empire? And how did the Empire shape Ireland? The first part of this chapter examines the Irish in the Empire, paying close attention to the multiple ways in which they participated and consequently contributed to the development of the modern British Empire. The more involved the Irish became in imperial endeavors, the larger the impact of imperial events on Ireland. The second part examines the ways in which the Empire came home to Ireland and the lasting repercussions for Irish nationalism. As demonstrated by the O'Donnell brothers, the Irish participated in the Empire overseas and applied lessons from this experience to events at home. For historians, thus, Ireland and Empire promises to provide insight into the nuanced experience of the Irish at home and abroad and insight into the Empire more broadly. The Irish experience demonstrates the reasons and ways in which people participated in imperial expansion, and the lasting repercussions of this involvement.

THE IRISH IN THE EMPIRE

When C. J. O'Donnell ventured overseas to seek the opportunities of the British Empire, he was by no means the first Irishman to do so. The Irish have played a significant role in the construction and maintenance of England's (later Britain's) empire since its inception under the reign of Queen Elizabeth I. In fact, perhaps the most important Irish contribution to the growth of the Empire was simply bodies. Ireland has a long history of emigration; an estimated ten million people have left the island for various destinations, including but not limited to the territories of the British Empire.[7] Initially, this Irish migration represented part of the larger movement and expansion of people throughout the Atlantic World. From the late fifteenth until the late seventeenth centuries, most Irish migrants were destined for North America or the Caribbean, and they left in numbers roughly equal to those departing Scotland and England. By the eighteenth century, however, this had changed. Approximately 30,000 English and 75,000 Scots crossed the Atlantic during the 1700s. In contrast, historians have estimated the number of Irish migrants to be close to 250,000.[8] In fact, so many made the trip that one scholar has referred to Irish migration to North America during the eighteenth century as "the earliest example of European *mass* migration overseas."[9]

The vast majority of eighteenth-century Irish migrants were Ulster Protestants, whose families had arrived in Ireland from southern Scotland only one century earlier. This previous migration experience likely made later moves easier, and encouraged "a cultural ethos of migration."[10] North America seemingly offered economic opportunities, particularly for younger sons who would not inherit land under the customs of primogeniture. At the same time, many Presbyterians also moved in search of religious tolerance—a hope that was frequently disappointed on arrival. Certainly, whether Irish migrants sought employment, religious tolerance, or reunion with family members, the move was a conscious decision and often based on hope.[11]

If the number of Irish migrants appeared high in the eighteenth century, it was completely dwarfed by that of the nineteenth century. From the 1820s on, Irish migrants were predominantly Catholic, and although most continued to flock to the United States, the territories of the modern British Empire also became increasingly common destinations. Between 1820 and 1920, for example, approximately one million Irish migrants left for Canada, Australia, and New Zealand.[12] According to David Fitzpatrick: "Census returns testify that in 1911 there were about 14,600 Irish natives in the Union of South Africa, 12,200 in the Indian Empire, 1,000 in the Maltese islands, 400 in Ceylon, 250 in the Straits Settlements, and 160 in the Federated Malay States."[13] By the close of the nineteenth century, "two out of every five Irish-born people" had made their homes overseas.[14]

Given these numbers, it is difficult to imagine British expansion without the Irish presence. And these numbers are even more astounding when viewed alongside the island's population statistics. During the eighteenth century, Ireland had (unknowingly) entered a phase of population growth. This was not the case in the nineteenth century, however. Instead, Ireland's population dropped significantly. Much of this depopulation can be traced to the mid-century Famine, during which

1.3 million people died of starvation and disease, and nearly two million more emigrated. Or, as Kerby Miller has noted, "more people left Ireland in just eleven years than during the preceding two and one-half centuries."[15] Ireland's population dropped by one-third; the numbers never recovered. Scholars have debated the impact of this mass exodus on the Irish. In his influential study of Irish migration to North America, Miller has argued that a "traditional Irish Catholic worldview" predisposed Irish emigrants to see themselves as "involuntary, non-responsible 'exiles,' compelled to leave home by forces beyond individual control."[16] More recently, historians have demonstrated that Miller's exile theory does not reflect the experience of those Irish who migrated in the boundaries of the modern British Empire. Donald Akenson, for example, firmly places Irish emigration and settlement in a larger worldwide pattern of expansion and argues that the exile theory undermines the agency of emigrants who clearly chose to leave Ireland.[17] The Irish, in other words, were not "always the passive victims of British imperialism"[18] and frequently made the conscious decision to migrate for reasons other than economic destitution. Even more recently, Angela McCarthy has turned to some 253 personal letters for insight into Irish migration to New Zealand. These individual accounts and personal stories reveal that many Irish were swayed by "the guidance of pioneering migrants" and did not feel isolated upon arrival at colonial destinations.[19] Irish migrants made deliberate, informed decisions based on the information provided through "global networks of communication."[20] After one arrived, more came. And if pushed by events at home, Irish migrants were also pulled by opportunities in the Empire.

While the Irish provided significant numbers of everyday settlers, the archetypal Irishman in the Empire was the soldier. From the eighteenth century to the early twentieth century, imperial service provided an important avenue of employment for the Irish. This was true for all Irishmen and Irishwomen, regardless of religious sympathies or socioeconomic class. By the 1770s, Irish Protestants composed approximately one-third of the British officer corps.[21] Fifty years later, in 1830, when the Irish accounted for "some 32.2 per cent of the population of the United Kingdom, there were more Irishmen than Englishmen in the British Army."[22] The Irish, in other words, enlisted in disproportionate numbers and played a prominent role in both the expansion and administration of the Empire.

Although Irish regiments were deployed throughout the Empire, India was their main destination. Following the Seven Years' War, the British presence in India became increasingly militarized. In desperate need of soldiers, both the British army and the East India Company army relaxed policies prohibiting the enlistment of Irishmen. By the start of the nineteenth century, the East India Company actively sought Irish soldiers and established recruiting depots in Belfast, Dublin, Enniskillen, and Limerick.[23] These efforts paid off. From 1825 to 1850, 47.9% of the Bengal army's European recruits hailed from Ireland.[24] By 1857, on the eve of the Indian uprising, the Irish accounted for more than 50% of the Company's European soldiers and more than 40% of the combined East India Company and British army's European regiments serving in India.[25]

In reality, it was the events of 1857 that confirmed the prominent role of the Irish soldier and administrator in India. The uprising began as a mutiny of sepoys (Indian soldiers) and quickly widened into a massive civil rebellion. Six Irish-dominated infantry regiments assisted in the suppression of the uprising, as did the numerous Irish soldiers enlisted in the British and Company armies.[26] The uprising—or more accurately, its suppression—launched the careers of more than one prominent Irishman in India. Frederick Sleigh Roberts, a young subaltern during the rebellion, went on to become commander-in-chief in India and later commander-in-chief of the British army.[27] Similarly, John Lawrence, chief commissioner of the Punjab in 1857, received numerous accolades for his role in the suppression of the uprising and went on to serve as viceroy from 1864 to 1869. Furthermore, he reportedly credited his success in India to his Anglo-Irish heritage. Sir Charles Aitchison, a friend and fellow Indian administrator, recalled that Lawrence drew inspiration from stories of the 1688–1689 Siege of Derry.[28] In his 1892 biography of the Indian viceroy, Aitchison commented that "in the height of his fame" Lawrence had "told, in a public address, how the blood of the old defenders of Derry warmed within him as he fought in India against fearful odds, and nerved him for his work."[29]

Following the 1857 uprising, the British—and by extension, the Irish—presence in India changed. The British abolished the East India Company's control in the region. The crown assumed control of the Company's regiments and created a new army, officered entirely by Europeans. These changes would have an impact on the Irish regiments. According to Alexander Bubb, the transfer of the Europeans from the Company army to the British one made the latter even "more Irish-heavy." This increasing presence of Irish culture in the British army, in turn, encouraged Irish martial race discourse—the idea that some "races" were inherently suited to warfare. "The 50 years after the rebellion saw the image of the Irishman as a soldier, with his attendant characteristics, become hegemonic."[30] While the stereotype of the "fighting Irish" became more commonplace, the actual number of Irishmen enlisted in the British army was decreasing. This decline, however, was numeric and corresponded with Ireland's falling population rates. In proportional terms, Irish enlistment remained constant until the First World War.[31]

Of course, the military was not the only opportunity open to Irishmen who wished to enter imperial service. The ICS, which represented the highest level of Indian administration, proved an increasingly enticing option throughout the nineteenth century. Initially ICS officers were recruited through Haileybury College, the East India Company institution founded in 1806 to prepare Company recruits for service in India. In 1855, however, the secretary of state for India Sir

Charles Wood introduced reforms designed to professionalize the ICS. In particular, the ICS began to recruit officers through an open and competitive exam. The changes were designed to lend a degree of equality to the application process and emphasize merit over nepotism. Irish universities responded enthusiastically, recognizing the open exam as an opportunity to groom students for positions of admirable social status. Trinity College Dublin immediately introduced chairs and courses in relevant subjects. Belfast, Cork, and Galway quickly followed suit. Although not Wood's intention, the result was a marked rise in Irish recruitment. Between 1809 and 1850, less than 5% of Haileybury appointees had been born in Ireland; between 1855 and 1863, in contrast, 24% of those recruited into the ICS had been educated at an Irish university. Furthermore, Ireland was contributing a disproportionate number of recruits. Ireland's population accounted for 20% of the United Kingdom in 1857, yet Irish universities were responsible for 33% of the ICS recruits for the year.[32]

Wood made further changes during the following decade. In 1864 he "lowered the maximum age at which candidates could compete, from 22 to 21, and redistributed the number of points attached to various exam subjects."[33] As S. B. Cook has argued, both reforms were designed to discourage applicants from the "London crammers" as well as the Irish universities, and they resulted in a decline in Irish recruits during the latter decades of the nineteenth century. According to Cook, both Wood and his successor, Lord Salisbury, were products of the mid-Victorian world. Both shared the belief that "English gentlemen were the best conceived imperial guardians" and doubted whether the Irish would make adequate rulers (of either themselves or others).[34] It was not necessarily anti-imperial or nationalist sentiments that limited Irish participation in the ICS. Rather, it was mid-Victorian, anti-Irish prejudice that pushed them out. But they did not leave overnight. Irish participation in the ICS peaked in the 1880s, when Ireland produced 15% of all ICS officers.[35]

Historians have debated the significance of Irish participation in the armed services and the ICS. Certainly the numbers reflect involvement, but how is this involvement to be understood? Why did so many Irish enlist? Initially scholars turned to Ireland's own colonial past to explain Irish enlistment in the Empire—some Irish joined out of loyalty to Britain and its empire; others enlisted to escape a dire situation at home. According to Akenson, some romantically inclined scholars have even suggested that "many of the lads of the United Kingdom military were there to gain experience so that they could one day use their military knowledge to free Ireland."[36] Many scholars have struggled with whether this involvement could or should be deemed an imperial contribution. Referring to Ronald Robinson's theory of "collaboration,"[37] for example, Akenson has argued that the Irish exemplified the notion of the "prefabricated collaborator." The island's tradition of emigration, participation in the market economy, and subordination to cultural anglicization made the Irish the perfect collaborators in the worldwide establishment of British imperial control.[38] The Irish, in other words, "behaved in a colonial context very much like other white Europeans."[39] Their history did not make them "naturally" opposed to imperialism. Rather, the Irish, too, proved capable of viewing the Empire and its opportunities as a "good thing."[40] As noted above, however, some scholars have found Ireland's history as both colonizer and colonized to be paradoxical and have sought to excuse or apologize for Irish involvement. Neither argument is particularly helpful. Trying to determine whether the Irish were or were not "imperialists" oversimplifies Ireland's situation and firmly embeds the island's history in the politics of conflict and resistance.

In reality, individuals enlisted in the armed services or took the ICS exam for a variety of reasons. Many sought to improve their economic situation or the lives of family members. The rank-and-file Irish soldier was frequently Catholic, of low income, apolitical, and drawn to the military as an occupation. For example, in 1880–1881 an Irish agricultural laborer earned approximately £25 per year, a figure that declined as the century progressed. By comparison, in 1886 the pay, food, clothing, lodging, and medical expenses for a private in the British army were valued at approximately £40 per year.[41] The East India Company army, while in existence, offered even higher pay.[42] The financial benefits of military service were widely recognized among Irish agricultural laborers.[43] As the nationalist newspaper, the *Nation*, acknowledged in 1857, "when employment fails, it is well known that the Irish talks of 'taking the shilling.'"[44] The ICS offered similar promises of economic stability for the middle classes. The economic draw was strongest in the early years of the open examination, as Ireland struggled to recover from the Famine and the island's industrial base remained limited to Dublin and Ulster. As late as 1906, the *Connaught Telegraph* recalled "the curious and joyous thrill of hope" and excitement surrounding the initial introduction of the open competition. The examination provided the opportunity for "a great, an almost incredible change of passing from obscurity to glory, from grinding poverty to wealth." Rumor suggested that the "salary began at the enormous figure of £800 per year" and sometimes "reached such gigantic and Alpine heights as several thousands a year."[45]

Family tradition could prove equally convincing. The archives are filled with the stories of Irish imperial families. The Graham family from Ulster had five members serving in India during the mid-nineteenth century. The family's patriarch, Dr. James Graham, was an army surgeon; his three sons were enlisted in the Company army; and his nephew held a position in the Commissariat. Similarly, although the only one to pursue a career in the ICS, Sir John Lawrence followed his older brothers to India; both served in the Company army. Sir Michael O'Dwyer, the infamous lieutenant governor of the Punjab at the time of the 1919 Amritsar Massacre, also followed a sibling into imperial service. Frederick Sleigh Roberts, whose father had enjoyed a distinguished career in the Company army, likely summed up the pull of familial ties best. The commander-in-chief of the British army later described his decision to enter the military as almost inevitable, recalling: "I had quite made up my mind to be a soldier, I had never thought of any other profession."[46]

The same political, cultural, and social conditions that encouraged the Irish to enter imperial service often followed them overseas—shaping both the Irish experience in the Empire as well as the Empire itself. As Barry Crosbie has noted, "Irish provincial towns were small enough for many soldiers to find common ground and in India they tended to form close networks with other men and women from their particular locality or parishes in Ireland."[47] Certainly, this was true among the rank-and-file Irish soldiers. Many Irish soldiers came from the same regions of Ireland, practiced the Catholic religion, and spoke Gaelic—all of which added "a particular Gaelic-Irish dimension to Anglo-Indian society."[48] The letters of James Graham to his sister in Lisburn indicate a similar sense of community among Irish Protestants. At the height of the 1857 Indian uprising, Graham mailed copies of the *Lahore Chronicle*, which reported the military accomplishments of their Irish townsman, John Nicholson. Furthermore, he encouraged his sister to send the clippings on to Nicholson's mother as well as the provincial newspapers.[49] The Irish, in other words, established their own cultural, economic, and familial ties or networks throughout the British Empire. And in doing so, they provided the human power, knowledge, and skills to facilitate imperial expansion. Acknowledging these contributions does not cast the Irish as "colonizer" or "colonized." Rather, it allows historians to understand the multiplicity of forces that drew together the British Empire.

These Irish networks were by no means limited to the military or to the ICS. In recent years, historians have begun to draw on the study of networks for insight into the connections that held together the disparate colonies. Scholars have noted that a host of economic, political, and cultural networks permitted people, ideas, and goods to flow from one location of the Empire to another. These connections also united the Empire as an imagined community or even multiple communities. Religion, for example, played a crucial role in knitting together the various peoples and locations of the Empire. As Hilary M. Carey has recently reminded us, the British world, composed of English-speaking settler colonies, was as much an idea as it was a set of territories. And the establishment of a religious presence in these colonies "helped shape the powerful, shared sense of British identity that suffused the British world."[50] While Carey examines the British settler colonies, Crosbie has noted a similar phenomenon among Irish Catholics in India, arguing that "strong communal bonds of a Roman Catholicism that had survived centuries of persecution tied individuals together into imperial networks centred upon the church and the activities of Irish military chaplains."[51]

Irish religious involvement in the Empire began as a Protestant affair. During the eighteenth century, Ulster Presbyterians played a prominent role in the development of educational opportunities in the North American colonies. Furthermore, many Ulster Protestants were active participants in English evangelical missions, including the London Missionary Society, the Church Missionary Society, and the British and Foreign Bible Society.[52] Although Protestant missionary efforts continued, with time Ireland's "spiritual empire" became a predominantly Catholic endeavor. Initially this Irish "spiritual empire" was not designed to convert non-believers but to provide pastoral care to Catholic emigrants or those enlisted in imperial service. In fact, in 1842 All Hallows College was established in Dublin for the express purpose of educating priests for service overseas.[53]

As the number of Catholics in the British Empire increased throughout the eighteenth and nineteenth centuries, so, too, did the imperial opportunities for the Catholic Church. As noted earlier, once British officials relaxed recruiting policies, Irish Catholics enlisted for imperial service in significant numbers. Irish chaplains, priests, and bishops were close on their heels. Similarly, the flood of Irish emigrants in the nineteenth century created new and growing Catholic populations in the settler colonies. These Irish Catholic settlers, in turn, frequently "gave their allegiance and affection to Irish clergy and bishops."[54] Of course, not all Catholics in the Empire were Irish. British economic and territorial expansion also brought more and more Catholic populations into the Empire's folds. In Canada, India, and Malaya, for example, Britain stretched its control to regions formerly held by Catholic powers and home to significant numbers of Catholic individuals.[55] However, Ireland's prominent role in the institutional expansion of the Catholic Church allowed Catholicism and "Irishness" to be more or less conflated throughout the Empire by the mid-nineteenth century.

Colin Barr has recently demonstrated that this Irish influence was intentional, the result of strategic planning, and largely directed by one man—Archbishop Paul Cullen.[56] The nineteenth-century Catholic Church was both rigidly hierarchical and rigidly episcopal, meaning that a bishop exercised nearly complete power in his diocese. Bishops were appointed by the Sacred Congregation for Propagating the Faith (Propaganda) in Rome, which supervised the Catholic Church throughout the British Empire. Propaganda initially "attempted to avoid antagonising colonial governments about ecclesiastical appointments." By the early nineteenth century, however, Rome made the appointments to the colonies directly, effectively bypassing officials in both the colonies and London.[57] Propaganda, in other words, could design the church's imperial hierarchy as it wished. And from 1830 until his death in 1878, Paul Cullen was well positioned to direct these appointments and thus shape the church's imperial presence.

Stemming from his connections in Rome, Ireland, and throughout the British Empire—connections that he forged, developed, and maintained—Cullen sat firmly at the top of Ireland's "spiritual empire" throughout the mid-nineteenth century. From this position, he regularly appointed "relatives, friends, students, and diocesan priests" to episcopal positions throughout the world.[58] And this was only the tip of the iceberg. Once in place, a Cullenite bishop "then had the power to secure additional appointments to colonial seminaries, parishes, schools, hospitals, and convents from his own contacts."[59] Through these extensive religious networks, Barr has argued, Cullen was able to ensure two things: first, an Irish-ethnic dominance of the Catholic Church in the English-speaking world and second, the spread of a more ultramontane ideology known as "Hiberno-Romanism." During the nineteenth century, in other words, "Cullen and his allies 'borrowed' the British empire and more besides to build a transnational Irish spiritual empire of their own."[60]

Despite his power, Cullen's imperial influence was largely restricted to the settler colonies. By the close of the nineteenth century, the Irish Catholic missionary movement had turned its attention from ministering to the diaspora to converting non-Christians. With this shift, Irish religious efforts spread beyond the settler colonies. Irish men and women had joined the foreign missionary orders of other countries throughout the nineteenth century. Starting with the Maynooth Mission to China in 1916, Irish Catholics established their own orders throughout Africa and Asia. Between 1916 and 1937, there was an explosion of Irish institutes "established specifically for missionary activities."[61] In fact, it was the Catholic missionary enterprise that would result in Ireland's largest and longest-lasting contribution to the Empire. The colonial missionary movement, in general, provided "a rapidly mobilised workforce" for the construction of churches, schools, and other religious institutions throughout the colonies.[62] The Irish Catholic missionary movement proved to be no different, taking responsibility for health care, establishing schools, introducing the English language, as well as attempting to shape "the moral and political views of the faithful."[63]

The impact would not be limited to the Empire, however; it would also be felt at home. During the turbulent yeas of the 1916 Rising and the Civil War, for example, Irish missionaries incorporated Ireland's colonial struggles to promote their own cause. Initially Irish missionaries argued that both the nationalist and the missionary struggles shared the common objective of freedom. As the situation in Ireland shifted and Civil War erupted, the missionary movement merely adapted its stance while retaining its role as a unifier; missionary enterprise, its proponents now insisted, represented common ground, a movement all Irish individuals could support whatever their political inclinations.[64] Ireland's historical role as "a land of saints and scholars" continued to prove unifying following independence, shaping the island's post-colonial identity. The establishment of Irish missionary organizations had provided Catholic clergy an opportunity to represent Ireland overseas. That Ireland's religious expansion was a primarily Catholic endeavor immediately distinguished the young nation from Britain. Furthermore, the expansive reach of Ireland's "spiritual empire" provided immediate global recognition, allowing Ireland "to take a place on the world stage."[65]

As the number of Irish individuals in the Empire increased, Irish knowledge of the Empire also grew. For those who remained in Ireland, letters from family members, missionary accounts, and newspapers all shaped their understanding of events overseas. Some nineteenth-century industrial developments further encouraged the spread of imperial information. In 1850 the first submarine cable was established between Britain and France, and the following decades witnessed the rapid expansion of telegraph networks and the improvement of steamship services throughout the Empire. Similarly, developments in newspaper production and distribution facilitated the transmission of imperial and colonial news. In particular, the repeal of stamp and paper duties in 1855 and 1861 allowed newspapers to be more widely accessible to Ireland's increasingly literate population. By the mid-nineteenth century, the Empire ceased to be a distant, far-off location and instead had come home to Ireland.

Throughout the latter half of the nineteenth century and much of the twentieth, the Empire provided the language to articulate Irish grievances. Irish journalists in particular seized on imperial events as an opportunity to cast opinion on Irish issues. In recent years historians, too, have turned to these publications for insight into Irish perceptions of the Empire. Newspapers have an agenda, certainly, and perhaps few have been as biased as the extremes of the mid-Victorian Irish press. Yet as disseminators of news on local, national, and international levels, these publications provide a valuable glimpse into the readership that sustained them. Although they do not "reveal what people thought," Jennifer Regan-Lefebvre has argued, newspapers "should reveal what kind of information was available to the literate public who did not have imperial knowledge through first-hand accounts."[66] Indeed, the events that colored the pages of Irish journals informed the perceptions of ordinary people. As Mark Doyle has demonstrated, the Crimean War and the 1857 Indian uprising helped shape the sectarian identities emerging in mid-Victorian Belfast, even as this Catholic and Protestant rivalry also shaped each side's response to the events overseas. In particular, he argues, "imperial events gave partisans on both sides a sort of imperial vocabulary that they could use to make sense of events at home and to draw larger lessons about the costs, benefits, and problems associated with British rule."[67]

These same imperial events also provided Irish nationalists, especially Home Rule nationalists, with a powerful rhetoric. As numerous historians have recently demonstrated, Irish nationalism did not develop in a vacuum but rather in a world concerned with empire.[68] Events overseas provided those opposing imperial expansion with a host of ready-made allies, and Irish nationalists were quick to draw affinities with others under British imperial rule. This nationalist tendency to link the Empire's colonized peoples on the pages of newspapers or in the halls of Westminster has raised questions of sincerity among historians. Were Irish nationalists truly sympathetic to the plight of others in the Empire? Or was this simply political rhetoric designed to encourage nationalist optimism? As Michael de Nie has recently reminded us, they could be both. Certainly, Irish nationalists claimed kinship with colonized peoples to bolster their cause at home. These examples, however, also reflect "a widespread anti-imperialism" that shaped the Victorian political agenda.[69] By the end of the nineteenth century anti-imperialism represented a dominant strand in Irish nationalist discourse.

Irish nationalism, of course, was anything but monolithic. Throughout the late nineteenth century a small but active group of Irish MPs worked tirelessly in the House of Commons to establish colonial alliances and promote imperial reform. Yet even these Irish parliamentarians turned to the Empire to promote a variety of political agendas. There were those like F. H. O'Donnell, who claimed that Ireland's political position provided it the opportunity to lobby on behalf of colonized peoples throughout the Empire. As Regan-Lefebvre has pointed out, O'Donnell's interventionist politics did not necessarily reflect anti-imperial sympathies but rather a criticism of the *British* Empire specifically.[70] This was true, too, of Isaac Butt, the parliamentary nationalist who advocated Union reform and federalism. Indeed, Charles Stewart Parnell adopted imperial issues to distance his brand of Home Rule politics from that advanced by Butt. Finally, Michael Davitt, the Land League revolutionary, war correspondent, and MP, turned to imperial events as a means to broaden the nationalist message from one designed to reform Ireland's relationship to Britain to one pitted against British imperial rule more broadly.

The connection between Irish nationalists and the Empire went beyond mere rhetoric, informing personal relationships across colonial boundaries. The O'Donnell brothers are a prime example. Frank Hugh O'Donnell critiqued the Empire from London; his brother, Charles James O'Donnell, pushed for reform from within the ICS. The links between the two brothers reinforced the potential impact of their arguments. At the very least, this family connection caught the attention of colonial administrators. Government officials quickly deemed Charles James O'Donnell a likely intermediary between Irish and Indian nationalists and closely monitored his activities in India.[71] Although both brothers dismissed allegations that they were attempting to spread nationalist sentiments from one colony to another, Frank Hugh O'Donnell did advocate collaboration between Irish and Indian nationalists in London. And he was not alone in his efforts. In 1883 Irish MPs, including O'Donnell and Davitt, proposed allocating an Irish parliamentary seat to Dadabhai Naoroji, a well-known and respected Indian nationalist living in London. According to Davitt, had Naoroji accepted the offer, then the Irish would have had "the honor of giving a direct voice in the House of Commons to countless millions of British subjects who were ruled despotically and taxed without votes."[72] Although Parnell dismissed the suggestion, Irish and Indian nationalists had established the foundations of a lasting partnership.

This late nineteenth-century Indian-Irish collaboration is well documented by historians.[73] Irish nationalists did not limit their attention to India, however. Carla King has demonstrated that Michael Davitt, in particular, had a wide-ranging interest in the British Empire and criticized imperial measures in India, China, and throughout Africa.[74] Similarly, Roger Casement, another Irish nationalist working outside parliament, famously turned to the press to raise awareness of imperial misconduct in the Congo Free State as well as the Putumayo region of the Amazon. Efforts to globalize the Irish cause did not cease with the end of the century; collaboration between Indian and Irish nationalists continued well after the establishment of the Irish Free State in 1921.[75]

By the twentieth century, however, Ireland's relationship with the Empire had shifted. Certainly, Ireland remained connected to the Empire. Significant numbers of Irish soldiers enlisted on Britain's behalf during the First World War. Irish missionaries continued to expand their efforts to the far reaches of Asia and Africa. And, as the Civil War demonstrated, many in Ireland were willing to remain connected to the British crown. Yet it was also clear that those Irish who disagreed with the imperial connection—whether they wished to reform it or to sever it—were not alone. In the wake of Ireland's "decolonization," colonial nationalists and colonial administrators throughout the Empire looked to Ireland with hope and suspicion, respectively. For example, Bengali nationalists who were frustrated with—or at least ambivalent toward—Gandhi's nonviolent method of nationalism, looked to Ireland as "a successful model of armed resistance," one that could be both "studied and duplicated."[76] At the same time, for those officers responsible for suppressing any resistance in Bengal, Ireland also "offered a wealth of strategies to apply—or avoid—as well as a way of understanding the 'terrorist mentality.'"[77] The Irish, once perceived as the ideal "prefabricated collaborators," had become the perfect anti-imperial nationalists.

CONCLUSION

The histories of Ireland and the Empire are intertwined—and have been for more than four centuries. Recent scholarship has shown that Ireland's relationship to Britain and its empire was not simply one of conflict and resistance. Rather, the Irish constructed economic, political, and cultural networks that drew the Empire together and solidified their place within it. They assisted in the administration, population, and spiritual upkeep of Britain's imperial territories; they also shaped twentieth-century experiences of decolonization. Exploring the island's role in the expansion and collapse of the British Empire does not cast the Irish as either "colonizer" or "colonized"; it simply sheds light on the nuanced experiences of imperialism.

Room exists for further scholarship into these nuances. For example, additional research into pro-imperial Irish opinions would be welcome. The cultural history of informal imperialism in Ireland also remains underdeveloped. Furthermore, following the work on Irish and Indian collaboration, more comparative research on Ireland and other territories of the Empire is needed. Indeed, although historians of Ireland have continued to broaden the context in which they examine the island, scholars of British imperial history have not been as inclined to include Ireland in comparative studies of imperialism. This is perhaps understandable, given the early debates regarding Ireland's colonial status. The time has come, however, to incorporate Ireland. Ultimately, the island's history promises to provide insight into the intricacies of imperialism—how empires expanded, how they were maintained, and how they collapsed. Twentieth-century Irish history provides insight into power dynamics and global relations in a world after empire. Finally, the study of Ireland and Empire reminds us that Irish history, imperial history, and history more broadly cannot be reduced to the mere labels of "us" versus "them."

FURTHER READING

Stephen Howe's *Ireland and Empire: Colonial Legacies in Irish History and Culture* (Oxford: Oxford University Press, 2000) provides a sustained analysis of debates on Ireland's colonial status and delivers a rather scathing criticism of literary theorists. For a more recent, edited collection that examines Ireland's relationship to Britain and the Empire from the mid-sixteenth century to the post-colonial era, see Kevin Kenny's *Ireland and the British Empire* (Oxford: Oxford University Press, 2004).

Keith Jeffery's *"An Irish Empire?": Aspects of Ireland and the British Empire* (Manchester: Manchester University Press, 1996) includes essays that explore Ireland's contributions to the British Empire from the mid-nineteenth century to the late twentieth century; for a book-length analysis of Ireland's development of imperial networks, see Barry Crosbie's *Irish Imperial Networks: Migration, Social Communication and Exchange in Nineteenth-Century India* (Cambridge: Cambridge University Press, 2012).

The classic treatment of the Irish Catholic missionary movement is Edmund Hogan's *The Irish Missionary Movement: A Historical Survey, 1830–1980* (Dublin: Gill and MacMillan, 1990); for an analysis of Ireland's episcopal dominance in the British Empire, see Colin Barr, "'Imperium in Imperio': Irish Episcopal Imperialism in the Nineteenth Century," *English Historical Review* 123: 502 (June 2008).

Kerby Miller's *Emigrants and Exiles: Ireland and the Irish Exodus to North America* (New York and Oxford: Oxford University Press, 1985) is a defining study of nineteenth-century Irish migration to North America; Angela McCarthy's *Scottish and Irishness in New Zealand since 1840* (Manchester: Manchester University Press, 2011) offers a comparative approach that argues against the exile motif.

Howard Brasted's "Indian Nationalist Development and the Influence of Irish Home Rule, 1870–1886," *Modern Asian Studies* 14: 1 (1980) explores the development of Irish-Indian nationalist collaboration. Jennifer Regan-Lefebvre's *Cosmopolitan Nationalism in the Victorian Empire: Ireland, India and the Politics of Alfred Webb* (Basingstoke: Palgrave Macmillan, 2009) uses the life and career of Alfred Webb as a window into the international and imperial contexts that shaped Irish parliamentary nationalism.

NOTES

1. For recent examples, see Stephen Howe, "Minding the Gaps: New Directions in the Study of Ireland and Empire," *Journal of Imperial and Commonwealth History* 37: 1 (March 2009), pp. 135–149; Michael de Nie and Joe Cleary (eds.), *Éire-Ireland* 42: 1–2 (Spring/Summer 2007); Kevin Kenny (ed.), *Ireland and the British Empire*, Oxford History of the British Empire Companion Series (Oxford: Oxford University Press, 2004).

2. Jane Ohlmeyer, "A Laboratory for Empire?: Early Modern Ireland and English Imperialism," in Kenny (ed.), *Ireland and the British Empire*, p. 58.

3. Hilary M. Carey, *God's Empire: Religion and Colonialism in the British World, c. 1801–1908* (Cambridge: Cambridge University Press, 2011), pp. 124–125.

4. Michael Holmes, "The Irish and India: Imperialism, Nationalism and Internationalism" in Andy Bielenberg (ed.), *The Irish Diaspora* (Harlow, England, and New York: Longman, 2000), p. 235; Hiram Morgan, "An Unwelcome Heritage: Ireland's Role in British Empire Building," *History of European Ideas* 19 (July 1994), p. 619; Keith Jeffery, "Introduction" in Keith Jeffery (ed.), *"An Irish Empire"?: Aspects of Ireland and the British Empire* (Manchester: Manchester University Press, 1996), p. 1.

5. Kevin Kenny, "The Irish in the Empire," in Kenny (ed.), *Ireland and the British Empire*, pp. 92–95; quote is from pp. 94–95.

6. Michael de Nie, "'Speed the Mahdi!' The Irish Press and Empire during the Sudan Conflict of 1883–1885," *Journal of British Studies* 51: 4 (October 2012), p. 883.

7. Kenny, "The Irish in the Empire," p. 100.

8. Kenny, "The Irish in the Empire," pp. 95–96.

9. James Belich, *Replenishing the Earth: The Settler Revolution and the Rise of the Anglo-World, 1783–1939* (Oxford: Oxford University Press, 2009), p. 60.

10. Belich, *Replenishing the Earth*, p. 60.

11. Kenny, "The Irish in the Empire," p. 97.

12. Kenny, "The Irish in the Empire," p. 98.

13. David Fitzpatrick, "Ireland and the Empire," in Andrew Porter (ed.), *The Oxford History of the British Empire*, vol. III: *The Nineteenth Century* (Oxford: Oxford University Press, 1999), pp. 512–513.

14. Kenny, "The Irish in the Empire," p. 100.

15. Kerby Miller, *Emigrants and Exiles: Ireland and the Irish Exodus to North America* (New York and Oxford: Oxford University Press, 1985), p. 291.

16. Miller, *Emigrants and Exiles*, p. 556.

17. Akenson notes the exception of the forced migration of criminals to Australia. Donald Akenson (ed.), *The Irish Diaspora: A Primer* (Belfast: The Institute of Irish Studies, Queen's University of Belfast, 1996), pp. 92, 37, 11.

18. Andy Bielenberg, "Irish Emigration to the British Empire, 1700–1914," in Donald Akenson (ed.), *The Irish Diaspora*, p. 215.

19. Angela McCarthy, *Irish Migrants in New Zealand, 1840–1937* (Woodbridge, Suffolk: Boydell Press, 2005), pp. 2–3.

20. McCarthy, *Irish Migrants in New Zealand*, p. 262.

21. Kenny, "The Irish in the Empire," p. 104.

22. E. M. Spiers, "Army Organization and Society in the Nineteenth Century," in Thomas Bartlett and Keith Jeffery (eds.), *A Military History of Ireland* (Cambridge: Cambridge University Press, 1996), pp. 335–336.

23. Kenny, "The Irish in the Empire," p. 104; Barry Crosbie, *Irish Imperial Networks: Migration, Social Communication and Exchange in Nineteenth-Century India* (Cambridge: Cambridge University Press, 2012), p. 85.

24. Spiers, "Army Organization and Society in the Nineteenth Century," p. 336; Thomas Bartlett, "The Irish Soldier in India, 1750–1947," in Michael Holmes and Denis Holmes (eds.), *Ireland and India: Connections, Comparison, Contrasts* (Dublin: Folens, 1997), p. 15.

25. Bartlett, "The Irish Soldier in India, 1750–1947," pp. 15–16.

26. Alexander Bubb, "The Life of the Irish Soldier in India: Representations and Self-Representations, 1857–1922," *Modern Asian Studies* 46: 4 (July 2012), p. 783; Kenny, "The Irish in the Empire," p. 105.

27. Although born in India, Frederick Sleigh Roberts (or "Bobs," as Rudyard Kipling later referred to him) was born to Anglo-Irish parents.

28. Interestingly, John Lawrence's brother, Henry Lawrence, was also said to have drawn inspiration from the stories of the Siege of Derry when fighting in India in 1857. Mortally wounded during the Siege of Lucknow, Henry Lawrence, the chief commissioner of Oudh (Awadh), reportedly instructed his men: "No surrender! Let every man die at his post, but never make terms!"—mimicking the Battle Cry of Ulster Protestants in 1689. Kenny, "The Irish in the Empire," p. 105.

29. Sir Charles Aitchison, *Rulers of India: Lord Lawrence* (Oxford: Clarendon Press, 1892), pp. 20–21.

30. Bubb, "The Life of the Irish Soldier in India," pp. 785–786.

31. Kenny, "The Irish in the Empire," p. 106.

32. Scott B. Cook, "The Irish Raj: Social Origins and Careers of Irishmen in the Indian Civil Service, 1855–1914," *Journal of Social History* 20: 3 (Spring 1987), pp. 510–511.

33. Cook, "The Irish Raj," pp. 512–513.

34. Cook, "The Irish Raj," pp. 513–514.

35. Kenny, "The Irish in the Empire," p. 103.

36. Akenson, *The Irish Diaspora*, p. 144. For more on Irish soldiers, see Peter Karsten, "Irish Soldiers in the British Army, 1792–1922: Suborned or Subordinate?," *Journal of Social History* 17: 1 (1983), pp. 31–64.

37. See Ronald Robinson, "Non-European Foundation of European Imperialism: Sketch for a Theory of Collaboration," in Roger Owen and Bob Sutcliffe (eds.), *Studies in the Theory of Imperialism* (London: Longman, 1972), pp. 117–142.

38. Akenson, *The Irish Diaspora*, pp. 142–143.

39. Bielenberg, "Irish Emigration to the British Empire," p. 215.

40. Akenson, *The Irish Diaspora*, p. 150.

41. Karsten, "Irish Soldiers in the British Army, 1792–1922: Suborned or Subordinate?," p. 39.

42. Bubb, "The Life of the Irish Soldier in India," p. 773.

43. Karsten, "Irish Soldiers in the British Army, 1792–1922," p. 38.

44. *Nation*, September 5, 1857.

45. *The Connaught Telegraph*, April 21, 1906; see also Cook, "The Irish Raj," p. 511.

46. Frederick Sleigh Roberts, *Letters Written during the Indian Mutiny* (London: MacMillan and Company, 1924), p. xvii.

47. Crosbie, *Irish Imperial Networks*, p. 87.

48. Crosbie, *Irish Imperial Networks*, p. 85.

49. James Graham to his sister, Anne, September 14, 1857, in A. T. Harrison (ed.), *The Graham Indian Mutiny Papers* (Belfast: Public Record Office of Northern Ireland, 1980), pp. 78–79.

50. Carey, *God's Empire*, p. 3.

51. Crosbie, *Irish Imperial Networks*, p. 86.

52. Kenny, "The Irish in the Empire," pp. 112–113.

53. Kenny, "The Irish in the Empire," p. 114. For more on All Hallows College, see Edmund M. Hogan, *The Irish Missionary Movement: A Historical Survey, 1830–1980* (Dublin: Gill and Macmillan, 1990), pp. 20–25.

54. Carey, *God's Empire*, p. 67.

55. Carey, *God's Empire*, p. 66.

56. Colin Barr, "'*Imperium in Imperio*': Irish Episcopal Imperialism in the Nineteenth Century," *English Historical Review* 123: 502 (June 2008): pp. 611–650.

57. Carey, *God's Empire*, pp. 119–120.

58. Barr, "'*Imperium in Imperio*,'" p. 614.

59. Carey, *God's Empire*, p. 142.

60. Barr, "'*Imperium in Imperio*,'" pp. 614, 650.

61. Hogan, *The Irish Missionary Movement*, p. 9.

62. Carey, *God's Empire*, p. 61.

63. Barr, "'*Imperium in Imperio*,'" p. 613

64. Hogan, *The Irish Missionary Movement*, pp. 146–148.

65. Fiona Bateman, "Ireland's Spiritual Empire: Territory and Landscape in Irish Catholic Missionary Discourse," in Hilary M. Carey (ed.), *Empires of Religion* (Basingstoke and New York: Palgrave Macmillan, 2008), pp. 267–269.

66. Jennifer M. Regan, "'We Could Be of Service to Other Suffering People': Representations of India in the Irish Nationalist Press, c. 1857–1887," *Victorian Periodicals Review* 41: 1 (Spring 2008), pp. 62–63.

67. Mark Doyle, "The Sepoys of the Pound and Sandy Row: Empire and Identity in Mid-Victorian Belfast," *Journal of Urban History* 36: 6 (November 2010), p. 862.

68. For examples, see Paul Townend, "Between Two Worlds: Irish Nationalists and Imperial Crisis, 1878–1880," *Past & Present* 194 (February 2007), pp. 139–174; Matthew Kelly, "Irish Nationalist Opinion and the British Empire in the 1850s and 1860s," *Past & Present* 204 (August 2009), pp. 127–154; De Nie, "Speed the Mahdi!" pp. 883–909.

69. De Nie, "Speed the Mahdi!", p. 895.

70. Jennifer Regan-Lefebvre, *Cosmopolitan Nationalism in the Victorian Empire: Ireland, India and the Politics of Alfred Webb* (Basingstoke: Palgrave Macmillan, 2009), p. 135.

71. Crosbie, *Irish Imperial Networks*, pp. 243–246.

72. Michael Davitt, *The Fall of Feudalism in Ireland or The Story of the Land League Revolution* (London: Harper and Brothers Publisher, 1904), p. 447.

73. For a recent example, see Regan-Lefebvre, *Cosmopolitan Nationalism in the Victorian Empire*.

74. Carla King, "Michael Davitt, Irish Nationalism and the British Empire in the Late Nineteenth Century," in Peter Gray (ed.)., *Victoria's Ireland? Irishness and Britishness, 1837–1901* (Dublin: Four Courts Press, 2004), pp. 125–126.

75. Kate O'Malley, *Ireland, India and Empire: Indo-Irish Radical Connections, 1919–64* (Manchester: Manchester University Press, 2008).

76. Michael Silvestri, "'The Sinn Fein of India': Irish Nationalism and the Policing of Revolutionary Terrorism in Bengal," *Journal of British Studies* 39: 4 (October 2000), pp. 461–462.

77. Silvestri, "The Sinn Fein of India," p. 455.

CHAPTER 15

WOMEN *and* GENDER *in* MODERN IRELAND

Catriona Kennedy

P RESENTING AN OVERVIEW OF THE history of gender in modern Ireland
is something of a challenge. Although *Irish Historical Studies* published its
first contribution on Irish women's history in 1987 and would only publish a further five articles on women's and gender history over the next twenty
years, in recent decades there has been a proliferation of work in this area. A
search under the term "women" in the *Irish History Online* bibliographic database
currently returns 2,617 books, chapters, and journal articles and a further 364
under the term "gender." Nearly all of these publications have been published
since 1990 and deal with the nineteenth and twentieth centuries.[1] Reflecting on
the steady accumulation of research on Irish women's history, Mary O'Dowd
and Phil Kilroy have recently observed that Irish historians can no longer justify
research on women and gender by pointing to the dearth of literature on these
topics. Arguably, having reached something like a critical mass, the historiography of women and gender may now be entering an exciting new phase in which
we can debate dominant themes and narratives and make a more forceful case for
the centrality of gender to our understanding of modern Irish history.[2]

What follows is an outline of key developments in the history of women and
gender from the eighteenth century on. Such an extended chronological framework necessarily entails a broad-brushstroke approach, but it allows us to reflect
on continuing gaps in our knowledge—Irish masculinities remains a chronically
understudied area: a search under this term on Irish History Online returns only
fourteen items. It also allows us to outline some of the overarching narratives in
the current scholarship. What, for example, are the major watershed moments in

Irish women's and gender history? Identifying historical watersheds, admittedly, tends to encourage a balance-sheet take on the past, too often framed as questions about whether the French Revolution/First World War/foundation of the Irish Free State were good or bad for women. Yet, insofar as the development and interrogation of such narratives is considered a mark of the maturity and intellectual vibrancy of a particular historical field, it remains a worthwhile exercise. In terms of dominant themes, a central and recurring issue in Irish history has been the complex ways in which gender has been imbricated in debates on national modernity. Historically, the equation of modernization with anglicization prompted resistance to "the modern" in Irish culture, at the same time as the stigma of backwardness stimulated efforts to prove Ireland's claims to meet universal standards of progress. As suggested here, gender roles and relations have often been critical to these anxieties about, and aspirations to, modernity. Changes in familial structures, sexuality, and gender roles have similarly been central to historians' analyses and explanations of Irish social and economic "modernization" since the nineteenth century. At the heart of such analyses is the apparent paradox that many of the developments typically understood as having assisted Ireland's transition from a predominantly "peasant" society to a modern nation—patriarchal family structures, the movement of women out of paid labor, rigid codes of sexual respectability—are those that would come to be seen as exemplifying the deep conservatism of the Irish gender order. A related theme in Irish culture from the eighteenth through to the late twentieth century has been the coupling of an often idealized notion of domesticity with a belief, voiced by both contemporaries and historians, that Irish domesticity has been repeatedly frustrated or undermined at various points in the country's history.

A GOLDEN AGE? PRE-FAMINE IRELAND

If gender is fundamentally about power, its distribution, and its representation, then it should come as no surprise that gender relations in pre-Famine Ireland were intimately shaped by the transfers in political, religious, and cultural authority that followed the Williamite wars of the 1690s. As a key institution in the transmission of property, a central site for the metaphorical representation of political relationships, and the bedrock on which male political authority often rested, marriage and the family were deeply implicated in the consolidation of Protestant hegemony. Among the penal laws enacted by the Irish parliament from the late seventeenth century on were several that sought to maintain Irish Protestant hegemony through the regulation of marital and familial relationships. In 1697 the first laws to prevent the intermarrying of Protestants with Papists were enacted. In the first half of the eighteenth century further penal laws relating to marriage were passed, culminating with the 1745 law annulling all marriages between Catholics and Protestants that were contracted after 1746 and rendering any children of such unions illegitimate. The primary purpose of this legislation was to prevent the transmission of property from Protestant to Catholic hands with the inhibition of the growth of Catholicism an important secondary aim.

As with other elements of the penal code, the laws on intermarriage were often irregularly enforced and quietly circumvented; nonetheless they collectively contributed to the undermining of male Catholic authority in the family and the strengthening of Protestant patriarchy.[3] The interdiction on intermarriage was only one of a series of laws that impinged directly on the family. Other penal statutes sought to disrupt the transmission of property in Catholic families, requiring that estates be divided equally among sons rather than passing directly to the eldest, allowing a son who conformed to the Church of Ireland an immediate right to his father's estates, and granting a wife who converted an entitlement to her husband's property, regardless of provisions he had made in his will. As Edmund Burke observed, the penal laws subverted the patriarchal order and undermined male power over wives and children, depriving Catholic husbands of "that source of domestic authority which the common law had left to him—that of rewarding or punishing, by a voluntary distribution of his effects, what in his opinion was the good or ill behaviour of his wife."[4]

The subversion of Catholic men's authority in the household reinforced their exclusion from the political nation, an exclusion that was understood and justified in explicitly gendered terms. In the gendered vocabulary of eighteenth-century political discourse, Catholicism was equated with servility, corruption, and dependence and contrasted with Protestant virtue and manly independence. Catholic emancipation was therefore conceived in terms of their accession to full manhood. The Irish parliament's subjection to the British was similarly understood by Protestant patriots as "unmanning."[5] Consequently, late eighteenth-century campaigns for legislative and political independence were explicitly framed in terms of the assertion of Irish masculinity, a masculinity embodied in the martial display of the Volunteers in the 1770s and 1780s and armed separatism of the United Irishmen in the 1790s. The language of classical republicanism that infused late eighteenth-century Irish patriot rhetoric was often distinctly hostile to women, who were conventionally associated with luxury, commercial excess, corruption, and covert influence. Yet, in its Irish variants, these anxieties were largely absent; women were often praised for the contribution they made to Irish economic prosperity through their fashionable consumption of domestic manufactures. Indeed, in contrast to later strands of Irish nationalism—in which, as we shall see, women often figured as custodians of national tradition—the United Irishmen, drawing on Enlightenment narratives of civilization, tended to identify women as both the agents and index of national modernity. As one of the founding members of the society, William Drennan, reflected in 1793: "Much perhaps of the perfection of which society is capable, depends on a nearer equality of the sexes and on their accumulated talents and joint endeavours."[6]

Certainly urbanization, the commercialization of leisure, and a burgeoning consumer and print culture in eighteenth- and early nineteenth-century Ireland provided an expanded sphere of engagement for (mostly) Protestant Irish women. Though the culture of politeness, with its emphasis on mixed sociability and the commerce of the sexes, may have had a delayed impact on Ireland, theaters, assemblies, and pleasure gardens proliferated. Largely excluded from the homosocial world of masonic lodges, clubs, and coffeehouses, women nonetheless engaged in Irish associational life as members of the Dublin Society; as patrons of literary, scientific, and antiquarian research; and through such philanthropic organizations as the Magdalen Asylums.[7]

Women's economic prospects also expanded with the growth of towns and commercial life. The rapid expansion of the Irish textile industry in the eighteenth century increased the opportunities for remunerative work. In Dublin by the mid-eighteenth century, more than ten thousand men and women were employed in the silk and woolen trades.[8] In many pre-Famine Irish households women's spinning was central to the family economy. The gendered division of labor in the household meant that it was often a wife's earnings from spinning that provided a family's cash income, while her husband's agricultural work provided the family with food.[9] In Ulster's booming "linen triangle" the household economy for much of the eighteenth century was based on the bi-occupations of weaving and farming and a further sex-linked allocation of roles so that women spun and men wove. During the Napoleonic wars, however, the shortfall in male labor prompted the region's linen merchants to "break the link of man to the loom and woman to the spinning wheel" as women were actively incentivized to enter the weaving workforce. It was a move that, as Anne McKernan has argued, also severed the connection between farming and weaving, paving the way for the transformation of independent farmer-weavers into rural proletarian weavers.[10]

As in Britain and elsewhere in Europe, women's involvement in the workforce was often fiercely contested by male artisans. A Dublin journeyman testified to the Committee of Trade in 1782 that "women had not a right to work at men's work, it was their inheritance."[11] Among the middling and merchant classes, women were often jointly responsible for managing small family businesses with their husbands or sons, and the evidence of Irish merchants' wills shows that family businesses were often equally divided between wife and children with no regard to sex.[12] Women also established and ran businesses in their own right, one of the best-known examples being the Belfast sisters Mary Ann and Margaret McCracken's muslin manufacturing business, which operated from the 1790s to 1815. In this case, the motivation to engage in business did not derive from necessity—the McCrackens came from a comfortable background—rather it drew on a tradition of radical Protestant dissent that identified industry with virtue, and as a religious, moral, and civic obligation.[13] In contrast, Catholic women of the middling classes tended to be less likely to trade in their own right and, as Mary

O'Dowd speculates, widows may have been discouraged by a conservative religious ethos from assuming responsibility for their husbands' businesses.[14]

The relatively high levels of female engagement in remunerative work prior to the Famine has led the eighteenth and early nineteenth centuries to be identified as something of a "golden age" for women in rural Ireland, a viewpoint that can be expanded to describe the status of women in Ireland more generally.[15] It offers an Irish version of one of the most contested narratives in gender history in which the late eighteenth and early nineteenth centuries are understood as inaugurating a significant transformation in understandings of masculinity and femininity; a more thorough gendering of domestic, economic, and public life; and the intensified regulation of sexual behavior. In British and European history the resilience of this narrative, despite its critics, derives in part because it can be linked to so many different social, intellectual, and economic transformations. For Britain, the United States, and parts of continental Europe, the emergence of separate and gendered spheres has been understood as a function of the formation of middle-class cultural identity and industrialization.[16] The progressive banishment of women from the public sphere is correspondingly traced to the conservative backlash that followed the ideological upheavals of the French Revolution.[17] The rise of evangelical religion, meanwhile, supposedly encouraged an ideology of domesticity and sexual prudery.

In Ireland the forces of accelerating urbanization, intensive industrialization, and the triumph of the bourgeoisie that underpinned the "golden age to separate spheres" narrative are much less evident. Yet it is possible to construct a similar narrative for this period, albeit one that emphasizes different drivers and patterns of change. In Protestant communities the rise of evangelical religion had ambivalent implications for women. Although evangelical emphasis on domestic virtues and repression of sexuality imposed certain personal and social constraints on women, it also simultaneously opened up an expanded sphere of action through philanthropic work and related religious endeavors.[18] Under the penal laws, the suppression of Catholic worship rendered it, to a certain extent, a "domestic" religion, with religious teaching and practice concentrated on the home, meaning that women were accorded a more significant role in church organization. With the relaxation of the penal code beginning in the 1770s, however, an increasingly confident Catholic hierarchy endeavored to control the activities of laywomen. The 1805 apostolic brief that brought Nano Nagle's Presentation Sisters under ecclesiastical control and imposed a rule of enclosure that greatly restricted its members' engagement with the wider world has been identified as bringing to an end the "matriarchal era" in Irish Catholicism.[19] In the wake of the 1798 rebellion, women's involvement was seized on by conservative commentators as emblematic of the rebellion's unnatural, perverse character. The women of 1798—in the loyalist historian Samuel McSkimmin's account—were likened to the bloodthirsty fishwives and "unsexed amazons" of the French Revolution.[20] A more distinctively

Irish version of the "golden age" narrative identifies sexual prudery and increasingly rigid gender roles as an alien imposition and product of anglicization.[21] In a playful reading of *Caoineadh Airt Uí Laoire* ("The Lament for Art O Laoghaire," ca. 1770s), Declan Kiberd suggests that O'Laoghaire represented a type of Gaelic masculinity that was able to reconcile male and female elements, in contrast to the macho posturing of the planter class.[22] Yet even though Gaelic poetry of the eighteenth century was sometimes characterized by an exuberant sexual frankness and was often sympathetic to female desires and aspirations, we still know too little about gender roles and relations in eighteenth-century Ireland to be able to clearly demarcate Gaelic from anglophone gender norms.[23]

THE FAMINE, REVIVAL, AND REVOLUTION, 1850–1921: DOMESTICITY AND MODERNITY

If there is one aspect of the "golden age" narrative that is distinctive to Ireland, it is the role of the Great Famine (1845–1852). In an influential article first published in 1978, J. J. Lee claimed that the Famine "drastically weakened the position of women in Irish society."[24] A series of significant changes in the Irish economy contributed to the erosion of women's status. The crippling of the Irish domestic textile industry, already in decline since the 1820s, removed the principal source of independent income for women. The exception here was Ulster, where factory-based cotton and flax production was heavily dominated by women, who made up 76.6% of the workforce in Belfast in 1891.[25] In agriculture, the shift from tillage to less labor-intensive pastoral farming reduced women's role in farm work, while the increasing complexity of domestic management confined women to the house. With the loss of female economic independence, women became, according to Lee, increasingly vulnerable to male dominance. The ubiquity of dowries in the post-Famine marriage market functioned as a telling marker of women's perceived economic redundancy after marriage.[26]

As with other aspects of nineteenth-century Ireland, the question of whether the Great Famine merely accelerated existing trends in gender roles and relations or constituted a watershed moment remains open to debate. Nonetheless, there is broad agreement that in the second half of the nineteenth century, changes in the social structure, land inheritance practice, and patterns of nuptiality tended to reinforce a patriarchal order characterized by the subordination of women to male authority and the subordination of sons to the dominant farmer-father. Among the conservative small farmers who came to dominate rural Ireland, this "patriarchalism" was promoted by close identification of the family name with the land and with the male line. Under a system of impartible, patrilineal inheritance, land was transmitted to a single male heir, who often lived with his wife and parents in a "stem" family household.[27]

According to Lee, the conservative rural values embodied in the farming classes reinforced an unequal gender order, whose precepts were diffused through the nation by a clergy drawn from the countryside.[28] Even though this late nineteenth-century Irish ideology of domesticity may have had its roots in a conservative, Catholic rural culture, its elaboration and dissemination were indicative of what Clair Wills has identified as the complex relationship between the forces of innovation and conservatism in Ireland. The "domestication" of the Irish of all classes was dependent on an alliance between Protestant middle-class gentility and a Catholic nationalism, which "so far from valorizing tradition" was intent on "the modernization of Irish society in the face of the waywardness of popular culture."[29] For proponents of Irishwomen's domestic education, the lack of pride in and attachment to the home on the part of the Irish peasantry was understood as anomalous, a sign of the nation's backwardness. For Horace Plunkett, the founder of the co-operative movement, in contrast to the proverbial Englishman whose home was his castle, there was "a singular and significant void in the Irish conception of a home," a void that Plunkett identified as a serious obstacle to social and economic progress. In *Ireland in the New Century* (1904), Plunkett traced the Irishman's lack of regard for home and the comforts of home to the country's turbulent history of colonial and religious conflict:

> The Irish had hardly emerged from the nomad pastoral stage, when the first of that series of invasions ... made settled life impossible.... The penal laws, again, acted as a disintegrant of the home and the family; and, finally, the paralyzing effect of the abuses of land tenure, under which evidences of thrift and comfort might at any time become determining factors in the calculation of rent ... were calculated to destroy at its source the growth of a wholesome domesticity.[30]

From the 1890s on, such reform agencies as the Congested Districts Board, the Irish Agricultural Organization Society, and the Department of Agricultural and Technical Instruction instituted nationwide courses in housewifery. These initiatives often aimed at more than simply the displacement of women from the rural economy. In certain congested districts in the west of Ireland, the Congested Districts Board's appraisal that women were the more financially responsible sex resulted in the active promotion of female enterprises, such as lace- and crochet-making. With women earning a significant proportion of the family cash income and male wages often intermittent or dependent on seasonal migration, it was wives who tended to control the family budgets in such households, portioning out allowances to their husbands for drink or tobacco.[31] Nonetheless, even where female enterprise was encouraged, the emphasis was on domestic industries rather than employment outside the home. The proportion of the family income generated by female employment steadily declined in the early twentieth century, as would women's control of household budgets. In 1891, 27% of women in Ireland were classified as employed; by 1911, this number had dropped to 19%. The percentage of women engaged in housework, meanwhile, rose from 65% in 1881 to 85% by 1911.[32]

The relationship between women's participation in paid employment and their subjective assessment of their own status and well-being is necessarily complicated. As Mary Daly has observed, a significant proportion of those women recorded as working in the 1841 census were "engaged in a struggle for survival, begging, engaged in casual dealing, or performing intermittent back-breaking tasks in agriculture at a fraction of the going male rate."[33] Joanna Bourke has similarly argued that those Irish women who withdrew from the paid labor force to become housewives were not simply passive recipients of a prevailing ideology of domesticity but rational actors who accepted the intensified gendered division of labor, because they saw it as a way to maximize their personal and economic power. Housewifery, Bourke points out, granted women a degree of autonomy over their own time and the household budget. The increasing technical skill required for housework—a specialization reflected in the state provision of classes in bread-baking, bed-making, table-setting, and personal and household cleanliness—meant that men were progressively excluded from domestic tasks, and women were able to assert their eminence in the household and increase their bargaining power.[34] Irish men, however, were never completely alienated from the domestic sphere. As Bourke also notes, the increasing significance accorded to the home involved a form of male domesticity and masculine housework centered on household repairs and decoration. Moreover, the increase in all-male households and the decreasing availability of domestic servants in the late nineteenth century meant that many men had to perform essential domestic tasks, such as baking, cooking, and washing.[35]

As childcare became a more intensive and extended maternal responsibility, women were able to derive a degree of power from the control they exercised over their children and from their place as "the emotional centre of their families."[36] Whereas the post-Famine devotional revolution involved the suppression of various aspects of popular belief and practices in which women had played a leading role, the newly domesticated mother, according to Tom Inglis, played a crucial part in the social and economic development of Ireland. Mediating between the Catholic Church and the family, the Irish mother inculcated the moral and personal restraints on which the consolidation of the Catholic farmer class depended:

> It was she who, through a variety of subtle strategies and practices, persuaded her children to emigrate, postpone marriage, or not marry at all. It was she who, through inculcating these practices and a rational regulation of life in her family, provided the vital force necessary for the restructuring of Irish rural life in the late nineteenth and early twentieth centuries.[37]

Although a reformed home and domestic life may have been understood by religious, nationalist, and unionist reformers alike as the engine of national development, the form of domesticity championed by the Catholic Church and promoted by the socioeconomic structures of Irish rural life was often remote from the domestic ideal as it was elaborated in Britain and elsewhere in this period. By the late nineteenth century this ideal had become increasingly centered on the concept of companionate marriage, a union based primarily on romantic attachment, though not without regard to material concerns. The relationship between husband and wife was understood as an intimate and affectionate partnership of opposites.[38] This was very much a middle-class model of marriage, but one that British Victorian and Edwardian reformers sought to extend to both the working classes and the wider Empire. In late nineteenth-century British India the idea of the companionate marriage was vigorously promoted by British officials and often enthusiastically embraced by both male and female nationalists.[39] In contrast, in rural Ireland the continued significance of dowries and matchmakers made it impossible to present marriage as an affair of the heart; it remained an economic arrangement designed to ensure the continuity of settlement on land. That is not to say that all arranged marriages were loveless: as a Gaelic *seanfhocal* put it, *Is fearr an grá a fhásann ná an grá a fhuarann* (the love that grows is better than the love that grows cold).[40] Love, however, was not understood as essential to marriage. The Catholic Church was particularly anxious to decouple ideas of romance and love from the institution of marriage. Eager to promote the tenets of order, hygiene, and respectability that derived from a well-regulated domesticity, the church simultaneously wished to inhibit the individualism that flowed from the conjugal intimacy and interiority associated with the bourgeois family.[41]

The church's disapproval of affective individualism was linked to a broader anxiety about its potentially disruptive effects in a society where many men and women renounced marriage altogether. In 1911, 27% of Irish men and 25% of Irish women aged between forty-five and fifty-four had never married. This compared with unmarried rates in England and Wales in 1911 of 12% for men and 16% for women. The high rate of nonmarriage in Ireland can be attributed to the rigid structures governing inheritance and marriage: the marriage prospects of sons who would not inherit and undowered daughters were slim. Marriage, though, was also eschewed by those who seemingly could afford it. One explanation for this advanced by contemporary and later commentators was the pervasive influence and example of the celibate Catholic clergy. Yet Protestants too proved to be poor marriers. Some of the highest proportions of single women in 1881 and 1911 were to be found in Antrim, Armagh, Down, and Londonderry, while the heaviest concentration of single women in Ireland was in the largely Protestant and urban south county Dublin.[42]

This distinctive demographic profile resulted in the paradoxical situation whereby a model of femininity centered on the idealized housewife and mother was culturally dominant yet unattainable to a large section of the female population. The unmarried daughters of farmers could find unpaid employment in the family household or as a domestic manager for unmarried male relatives, but this role tended to be viewed as one of frustrating dependence. The outlook for single women was not, however, entirely bleak. The withdrawal of young girls from agricultural labor after the Famine meant that increasing numbers were educated to primary level, because girls were less likely to be kept from school to work. By 1860, equal numbers of boys and girls were in attendance at primary schools. This was accompanied by a sharp rise in female secondary education in the late nineteenth century. By 1914 the proportion of girls in Irish secondary schools was only exceeded in England, Wales, and Norway, and no country, except Finland, had a higher percentage of women university students. In recognition of the fact that many women would remain single, their education was often geared toward employment. In the period before the First World War opportunities for white-collar work for women expanded: by 1911 almost 30% of clerks in the civil service and business were women. The expansion of convents over the course of the nineteenth century further opened up the single-largest professional vocation for women of the Catholic middle classes.[43]

The preponderance of well-educated young women in post-Famine Ireland is closely related to one of the other distinctive features of modern Irish demography: the unusually high levels of female emigration. This has been linked to low marriage rates. Female emigration came to exceed male emigration in the 1890s, at a time when, Donald Akenson notes, it would have been increasingly clear that "about half the women of marriageable age were not finding a match."[44] Yet there was a perhaps even stronger correlation between levels of female emigration and female education. Those areas of the country where girls demonstrated higher levels of attendance and more years of schooling than boys were also areas where female emigration was highest.[45] The horizon-widening experience of education and local and familial ties to emigrants across the world would, David Fitzpatrick speculated some decades ago, have heightened Irishwomen's consciousness of the limitations that an archaic family structure imposed on them:

> The cumulative impact of emigration was to Americanise the mentality of the Irish female whether or not she left Ireland. The contradiction between the growing rigidity of Irish social institutions and the growing cosmopolitanism of their members tended to bring about fragmentation discontent and depopulation. The Irish female was "modernised" in the sense that she grew increasingly conscious of making a practical choice between remaining "Irish" and becoming "modern."[46]

Whether emigration offered Irishwomen an escape from oppressive gender relations still requires further investigation. Perhaps an even more interesting question is how the transnational links that were forged and sustained through emigration acted as vectors for the transmission of alternative ideas about gender roles and relations.

Though the campaign to "domesticate" Irish womanhood may have limited the parameters of female activity, the authority that women derived from their status as "home rulers" could also justify their intervention in public and national debates. The *United Irishwomen*, founded in Enniscorthy in 1910 as a nonsectarian—and, despite its name, purportedly nonpolitical—organization, joined the campaign to "brighten Irish rural life" promoted by George Russell (whose pseudonym was "AE") and Horace Plunkett in the journal *Irish Homestead*. As well as organizing classes in domestic education for women and establishing milk depots for school children, the *United Irishwomen* actively promoted women's participation in local government, women having been eligible to stand as both Poor Law Guardians and members of Local Government Boards since 1898.[47] It was precisely because of their shared avocations as wives, mothers, and caregivers, claimed Ellice Pilkington in 1911, that women were able to forge a cross-class, cross-religious solidarity that often eluded Irishmen, separated as they were into different occupations by the division of labor. "Patriotism for women," wrote Pilkington, "is a thing of deeds, not words.... The most magnificent theories of men and the constructive work that they do cannot create national prosperity unless women help them in the domestic details."[48] Pilkington envisioned an expanded feminine public sphere for women, in which their voices would be heard and contributions valued in discussions regarding health, education, and rural improvement. Even women's organizations more closely associated with advanced nationalism and feminist politics, such as Inghindhe na hÉireann (Daughters of Ireland), often presented their political interventions as a form of maternal activism: Maud Gonne successfully campaigned for free school meals, and in the Irish-language movement women's role in transmitting the "mother tongue" to their children was deeply prized. The dangers of such "maternalist" rhetoric were sharply exposed by the Irish feminist Hannah Sheehy Skeffington when she denounced the national movement for only recognizing Irishwomen's importance in their capacity as "mother and housewife, not as individual citizen."[49]

In addition to the tensions generated by claiming a public role derived from their domestic responsibilities, Irishwomen with nationalist sympathies at the beginning of the twentieth century had to navigate the contradictory poles of tradition and modernity. In nationalist discourses from the nineteenth-century on, it was men who were regarded as the bearers of progress, whereas women were viewed as the authentic and atavistic embodiments of national tradition.[50] In the home and through the family, women were identified as the transmitters of national language, customs, and culture. Yet the relationship between gender, tradition, and modernity during the Irish revival was complicated. Publications like *Bean na hÉireann*, the journal of the radical nationalist organization Inghinidhe na hÉireann often "moved seamlessly between tradition and modernity," urging its readers to buy Irish-made clothes, jewelry, and crafts "even as they assiduously reminded readers that such traditions were actually the latest look for the modern Irish woman."[51]

Though the Irish revival and the "revolution" of 1913–1921 promised the potential emergence of alternative, more fluid gender roles, the trajectory of Irish political masculinity in this period tended to short circuit such possibilities. Joseph Valente has identified Irish masculinity from the nineteenth century on as beset by a double bind. Were nationalists to adopt a position of self-restraint and self-discipline consistent with Victorian and Edwardian code of manliness, they risked being accused of feminine passivity, thereby proving the Celt's unfitness for self-governance. The deployment of physical force, however, would confirm the stereotype—most commonly associated with *Punch* magazine—of the bestial, simianized, violent Irishmen.[52] The Gaelic Athletic Association's promotion of a vigorous disciplined physicality was, in part, an effort to replace such negative stereotypes with a more positive image of Irish manhood. Although it may have substituted an Irish model of manliness based on "Catholic communalism" for the British Protestant version based on "class and elitism," the debt that this form of "muscular Catholicism" owed to late nineteenth-century British imperial discourses of "muscular Christianity" is clearly evident.[53] At the beginning of the twentieth century a "Cuchulanoid" hyper-masculinity nourished by the heroic myths of the Gaelic sagas fused with the martial masculinity of the republican tradition and a broader pan-European culture of militarism that prevailed in the years leading up to the First World War. Despite the involvement of transgressive uniform-wearing and revolver-wielding figures like Constance Markievicz and Margaret Skinnider, the militarization of Irish politics in this period reaffirmed the association between maleness and political citizenship. This militarization and masculinization of political life was not restricted to the nationalist movement. In Ulster too, the campaign against Home Rule, the foundation of the Ulster Volunteer Force in 1913, and the "blood sacrifice" of the 36th Division at the Somme in 1916 produced a hegemonic unionist masculinity characterized by fraternalism, militarism, and an "adversarial fractiousness."[54] This legacy of militarization combined with a dominant culture of Catholic and Protestant puritanism to ensure that after 1922, gender politics both north and south of the border remained marked by a deep conservatism.

THE FREE STATE TO THE CELTIC TIGER, 1922–2008: COMELY MAIDENS TO A CRISIS OF MASCULINITY

The curtailment of women's freedoms following the establishment of the Irish Free State is one of the most well-studied episodes in Irish gender history. Although all Irishwomen over the age of twenty-one, unlike their British sisters, were given the right to vote in 1922, this was followed by a tranche of legislation that progressively eroded women's position in public life. In 1925 women's eligibility for civil-service examinations was significantly restricted. In 1927 women were "exempted" from jury service. From 1932 women teachers were forced to retire upon marriage, a policy that was soon extended across the civil service. In 1935 the Criminal Law Amendment Act prohibited the sale and importation of contraceptives. This effort to legislate women out of public life would culminate in the 1937 Constitution, Article 41 of which committed the Free State to defending women's special place in the home. There are several possible explanations for the conservative patriarchalism of the Irish Free State. Though the cause of Irish independence held out the prospect of a radical rethinking of women's role in the new nation, as with other revolutionary moments once the conflict had ended, the established gender order was viewed as a ballast that would secure national stability and security in the aftermath of upheaval and violent change. The efforts of the Free State's leaders to exert control over women, Maryann Valiulis suggests, stemmed from a fundamental frustration at their lack of control in other areas, the limited resources available to the state, and the leaders' inability to defeat their enemies. For the new state, the chasteness and domestic virtues of Irish women formed a badge of respectability and proof of the nation's moral superiority.[55]

This view of women as defined primarily by their maternal and domestic roles was not unique to the Free State. Several countries in Europe also introduced bans on married women's employment during the inter-war years, and in Northern Ireland the possibility of exempting women from jury service had also been given serious consideration. As with the Famine, the extent to which the establishment of the Free State constituted a significant reversal in the fortunes of Irishwomen is questionable. In focusing too much on 1922 as a "watershed" moment, there is a risk that both the advances made by women in the years prior to independence and the repression they experienced afterward are exaggerated, while longer-term economic patterns are downplayed. Women's rate of secondary and university education relative to men's remained high in the decades immediately after independence. The foundation of the Free State also created new opportunities for female employment, with low-grade clerical work in the civil service expanding significantly. In the 1930s tariff protection and the program of industrialization resulted in the establishment of light manufacturing industries and the proliferation of what were generally thought of as women's jobs: by 1936, 31.3% of the manufacturing workforce was female, compared with 25.6% in 1926.[56]

The anti-modern impulses of the new state's leaders have long been stressed. Women were central to the nation's "backward look" and the insistence that traditional, rural, and Gaelic values and customs could be preserved in the midst of economic modernization. This was a vision exemplified by de Valera's 1943 St. Patrick's Day speech and its evocation of a rural idyll populated by "bright and cosy homesteads" and "comely maidens."[57] Women were also the focus of anxieties about modernity and associated concerns on the part of religious commentators and social reformers about foreign influences. The figure of the young female flapper was invoked as the quintessential symbol of moral degeneracy and sexual deviance and was considered the antithesis of virtuous Irish womanhood. Yet discourses of femininity in the decades after independence were, like other aspects of Irish life in this period, more complex than a simple emphasis on repression, restriction, and regulation allows. Though characterized by religious piety, cultural censorship, and sexual prudery, Irish society was also exposed to modernizing influences through the cinema (Ireland recorded the highest per capita cinema attendance of any nation in the inter-war years), in the dance halls, and through the proliferation of consumer goods and desires. As Louise Ryan has shown in her analysis of *The Modern Girl and Ladies Irish Home Journal*, which was published monthly during the 1930s, it was possible to elaborate a discourse of femininity in this period that reconciled being Irish with being a "modern girl," which resonated with the experiences and concerns of the reasonably affluent white-collar women workers in Dublin in the 1930s. Segueing from articles on the latest Hollywood hairstyles to pieces extolling Irish clothing and fabrics and imagining the modern Irish girl living in a Dublin bachelor flat and working in an office, the journal constructed a version of an Ireland that could "embrace modernizing influences while retaining its own unique identity."[58]

Feminist critics of the 1937 Constitution were quick to point out the paradox of the state insisting that women's role was primarily maternal and domestic, when marriage rates in Ireland remained exceptionally low.[59] The marriage rate per thousand population between 1936 and 1945 was 5.37, while in Northern Ireland in 1946 it was 7.4, and in England and Wales it was 9. The demographic implications of these low levels of nuptiality were partly offset by the high levels of fertility in marriage. In 1946 Irish couples who had been married for twenty years had on average twice as many children as their British counterparts.[60] In the absence of legally available contraception or the adequate provision of maternal health care, the experience of successive, uninterrupted childbirths was often extremely physically harrowing for women. Diarmaid Ferriter and others have questioned the depiction of mid-century Ireland as anomalous in its sexual frigidity and repression; nonetheless the prevailing culture in which significant proportions of the population remained unmarried with little prospect of sexual fulfillment outside of marriage, and sex was commonly viewed as shameful and sinful, encouraged an "acute sense of Irish sexual uniqueness."[61] In anthropologist Nancy Scheper-Hughes's controversial 1977 study of a rural community in the Kerry Gaeltacht, she concluded that the Catholic Church's hostility to sexuality was the cause of widespread mental breakdown and marital and familial decay.[62] In a country in which the sacred place of the family in national life was enshrined in the constitution and the indissolubility of marriage underwritten by a ban on divorce until 1995, marriage itself was seemingly marred by a lack of intimacy and understanding between the sexes.

If Irishwomen in the first half of the twentieth century were associated with the nation's backward glance, the changing status of women from the 1960s has come to be seen by historians and social scientists as a crucial marker of the modernization of Irish society.[63] The economic policies of the Lemass government from 1959, the expansion of the education system in the 1960s, the development of the Irish women's movement in the 1970s, and Irish accession to the European Economic Community in 1973 had a transformative impact on attitudes toward women and the opportunities available to them. In 1973 the bar to the promotion and employment of married women in the civil service was lifted. Between 1971 and 1983 the number of women in the workforce grew by 34%, and the number of married women in the workforce increased by 425% in the same period.[64] Contraception was made legally available to married couples in 1979. The rapidity of social and cultural change created "particularly violent pressure points in Irish society." Gender roles, the structure of the family, and female sexuality became the sites on which many of "the major battles between tradition and innovation" were fought.[65] Nowhere was this contest more clearly illustrated than in the 1990 presidential candidacy of Mary Robinson, who, in her career as a barrister, had been a prominent advocate of women's rights. The election campaign was explicitly represented as a choice between past and present, tradition and innovation.[66] Robinson represented, in the words of the Irish feminist Ailbhe Smyth, "a new force capable of breaking free from the strangle-hold of the historical narratives of Ireland and Irishness."[67]

Liberalization, however, was by no means linear or unimpeded. The 1983 abortion referendum saw a constitutional amendment passed by a margin of two to one that committed the state to defending the life of the "unborn." A referendum on divorce in 1986 delivered a no vote of 61%, and only with a narrow margin of 50.5% was the constitutional ban on divorce finally lifted in 1995. As the *Irish Times* journalist Carol Coulter pointed out shortly after the 1995 divorce referendum, the anti-divorce campaigners who repeatedly invoked "family values" as a reason for their opposition were expressing nostalgia for an Irish familial and domestic life of the 1940s and 1950s that had never truly existed: "large numbers of people did not marry at all, and Ireland had one of the lowest, and latest, marriage rates in Europe.... The family was then, to a great extent, a single-parent family."[68]

Those who were ambivalent about—or actively hostile to—the social, cultural, and economic transformations of the 1990s often made the reconfiguration of gender roles associated with these changes the focal point of their critique. Most notably, the journalist John Waters, in a series of columns for the *Irish Times*, railed against what he dubbed a "feminazi" conspiracy intent on denigrating and discriminating against Irish males. This feminist backlash and related claims about a widespread "crisis of masculinity" were not unique to Ireland in the late twentieth century. But in Waters's columns and those of other commentators, they intersected in a distinctive way with a broader critique of the excesses of the Celtic Tiger era and the dominant neo-liberal economic agenda, which, it was claimed, had replaced a culture of restraint, communality, and spiritualism with one predicated on greed, individualism, and materialism. Those Irish feminists who campaigned for state-funded childcare provision were, in Waters's opinion, aligning themselves with the desires of the market economy against the welfare of the family, the "integrity and autonomy" of which was being sacrificed to the "increasingly insatiable Celtic Tiger."[69] Writing in the aftermath of the economic crisis of 2008, Waters claimed that Irishwomen's economic emancipation was not just a symptom but the cause of the nation's ills. It was the entry of women into the workplace in ever-increasing numbers, he argued, that had broken the long-standing correlation between house prices and the average annual income of male workers. The consequent introduction of mortgages based on dual incomes had fueled the house-price boom of the 1990s and led ultimately to the spectacular crash of the Celtic Tiger economy.[70]

Though Waters may have been articulating a minority view, he nonetheless tapped into a long-standing set of Irish discourses in which women and the domestic realm have variously figured as a diagnostic for the nation's ills and a repository for the nation's hopes and anxieties. At different moments in modern Irish history these discourses have been in tension with one another or have been internally contradictory: nationalist movements have figured women as both agents of modernity and custodians of tradition; the Free State championed a domestic ideal to which a significant proportion of the never-married population could never aspire; the family structure and gendered division of labor that would later be viewed as emblematic of Ireland's archaic, conservative, puritanical culture, had in fact been central to its economic and social "modernization." Typically associated with the timeless, unchanging essence of the nation, women were nonetheless central to the construction of Irish Catholic modernity and to the nation's narrative of modernization from the 1970s on. Gender has been crucial to how transformations in Irish society have been managed, imagined, and explained over the past three centuries.

Although Waters's comments can thus be set in a longer history of commentaries on women, modernity, and the Irish nation, they reveal as much (if not more) about a particular moment in the history of Irish masculinities, a moment that, because of the relative dearth of research on this topic, is much more difficult to set in a longer historical perspective. Indeed, though the study of masculinities has long been directly or indirectly central to the agenda of women's history, an explicitly gendered history of Irish men remains one of the most promising avenues for future research. Such research might cover not only the different concepts of masculinity that have underpinned various political movements and ideologies but also the demographic trends, economic structures, and religious beliefs that have shaped the lived experiences and gendered subjectivities of Irish men and women. As well as studying the impact of domestic ideologies on women, we might also—following research by John Tosh for Britain and suggestive work by Joanna Bourke for Ireland—explore the roles and identities that Irish men assumed in the family and home.[71] In addition to further research on the experiences of female religious orders, we also need fuller studies of clerical masculinities.[72] To the study of the large proportion of never-married Irish women should be added research on that equally dominant figure in post-Famine Irish history, the Irish bachelor. And if the boom and bust of the Celtic Tiger can be understood as provoking a crisis of Irish masculinity, we might also ask what other moments in Irish history can be understood in such terms.

FURTHER READING

The indispensable starting point is now Máirín Ní Dhonnchadha, Margaret Mac-Curtain, Siobhán Kilfeather, Angela Bourke, Maria Luddy, Mary O'Dowd, Gerardine Meaney, and Clair Wills (eds.), *The Field Day Anthology of Irish Writing: Irish Women's Writing and Traditions*, vols. IV and V (Cork: Cork University Press, 2002). Alan Hayes and Diane Urquhart (eds.), *The Irish Women's History Reader* (London and New York: Routledge, 2001) and Maryann Gialanella Valiulis (ed.), *Gender and Power in Irish History* (Dublin: Irish Academic Press, 2009) contain key articles in the field, and Clair Wills offers an excellent overview of core themes and narratives in "Women, Domesticity and the Family: Recent Feminist Work in Irish Cultural Studies," *Cultural Studies* 15: 1 (2001), pp. 33–57.

Helpful survey histories of women and gender from the eighteenth to the twentieth century include Mary O'Dowd, *A History of Women in Ireland, 1500–1800* (Pearson: Harlow, 2005); Myrtle Hill, *Women in Ireland: A Century of Change* (Belfast: Blackstaff Press, 2003); and Rosemary Cullen Owens, *A Social History of Women in Ireland, 1870–1970* (Dublin: Gill and Macmillan, 2005).

Mary Daly and Joanna Bourke have offered bracing and empirically rigorous counterpoints to narratives of women's progressive economic marginalization in the post-Famine era: Joanna Bourke, *Husbandry to Housewifery: Women, Economic Change and Housewifery in Ireland 1890–1914* (Oxford: Clarendon Press, 1993); Mary E. Daly, "Women in the Irish Free State, 1922–39: The Interaction between Economics and Ideology," *Journal of Women's History* 7: 1 (1995) pp. 99–116.

The history of sex in Ireland, both transgressive and quotidian, has only recently become the subject of book-length studies. Two important recent works are Diarmaid Ferriter, *Occasions of Sin: Sex and Society in Modern Ireland* (London:

Profile, 2009) and Maria Luddy, *Prostitution and Irish Society, 1800–1940* (Cambridge: Cambridge University Press, 2007). Ireland's demographic peculiarities have been more widely researched. See, in particular, Mary E. Daly, *The Slow Failure: Population Decline and Independent Ireland, 1920–1973* (Madison: University of Wisconsin Press, 2006).

It is likely that there will be an increasing number of works on gender and the "revolutionary generation" in the next decade. The pioneering work is by Margaret Ward, *Unmanageable Revolutionaries: Women and Irish Nationalism* (London: Pluto Press, 1983) and Catherine Innes, *Woman and Nation in Irish Literature and Society, 1880–1935* (London: Harvester Wheatsheaf, 1993). More recent studies are by D.A.J. MacPherson, *Women and the Irish Nation: Gender, Culture and Irish Identity, 1890–1914* (Basingstoke: Palgrave Macmillan, 2012) and Karen Margaret Steele, *Women, Press, and Politics during the Irish Revival* (Syracuse, NY: Syracuse University Press, 2007).

Masculinities remain an underexplored subject in Irish history, but there is increasing work in this area. See, for example, Padhraig Higgins, *A Nation of Politicians. Gender, Patriotism, and Political Culture in Late Eighteenth-Century Ireland* (Madison: University of Wisconsin, 2010); various chapters in Marilyn Cohen and Nancy J. Curtin (eds.), *Reclaiming Gender: Transgressive Identities in Modern Ireland* (New York: St. Martin's Press, 1999); Joseph Valente, *The Myth of Manliness in Irish National Culture, 1880–1922* (Urbana, Chicago, and Springfield: University of Illinois Press, 2010); and J.G.V. McGaughey, *Ulster's Men: Protestant Unionist Masculinities and Militarization in the North of Ireland, 1912–1923* (Montreal and Kingston: McGill-Queen's University Press, 2012).

NOTES

1. *Irish History Online* (IHO), http://iho.ie/index.php, accessed August 12, 2013.

2. Mary O'Dowd and Phil Kilroy, "Thoughts on Gender History," in Maryann Gialanella Valiulis (ed.), *Gender and Power in Irish History* (Irish Academic Press: Dublin, 2009), pp. 12–13.

3. See Mary O'Dowd, *A History of Women in Ireland, 1500–1800* (Pearson: Harlow, 2005), pp. 253–254.

4. Edmund Burke, "Tracts Relative to the Laws against Popery in Ireland," in Matthew Arnold (ed.), *Letters, Speeches and Tracts on Irish Affairs* (London: Macmillan, 1881), p. 10.

5. Padhraig Higgins, *A Nation of Politicians. Gender, Patriotism, and Political Culture in Late Eighteenth-Century Ireland* (Madison: University of Wisconsin, 2010), p. 162.

6. William Drennan, "Plan of Parliamentary Representation for Ireland." National Archives of Ireland, Dublin, 620/20/1. Catriona Kennedy, "'A Gallant Nation': Chivalric Masculinity and Irish Nationalism in the 1790s," in Matthew McCormack (ed.), *Public Men. Masculinity and Politics in Modern Britain* (Basingstoke: Palgrave Macmillan, 2007), pp. 73–92.

7. Toby Barnard, *Making the Grand Figure. Lives and Possession in Ireland, 1641–1770* (New Haven, CT: Yale University Press, 2004), pp. 353–358.

8. O'Dowd, *History of Women*, p. 115.

9. Mary E. Daly, "Women in the Irish Workforce from Pre-Industrial to Modern Times," reproduced in Alan Hayes and Diane Urquhart (eds.), *The Irish Women's History Reader* (London and New York: Routledge, 2001), p. 193.

10. Anne McKernan, "War, Gender, and Industrial Innovation: Recruiting Women Weavers in Early Nineteenth-Century Ireland," *Social History* 28: 1 (Autumn 1994), pp. 109–124.

11. Cited in Imelda Brophy, "Women in the Workforce," in David Dickson (ed.), *The Gorgeous Mask: Dublin 1700–1850* (Dublin: Trinity History Workshop, 1987), p. 57.

12. O'Dowd, *Women in Ireland*, p. 115.

13. Nancy Curtin, "Women and Eighteenth-Century Irish Republicanism," in Margaret Mac-Curtain and Mary O'Dowd (eds.), *Women in Early Modern Ireland* (Edinburgh: Edinburgh University Press, 1991), p. 141.

14. O'Dowd, *History of Women*, p. 121.

15. J. J. Lee, "Women and the Church since the Famine," in Margaret MacCurtain and Donnchadh Ó Corrain (eds.), *Women in Irish Society: The Historical Dimension* (Dublin: Arlen House, 1978), pp. 37–45.

16. Leonore Davidoff and Catherine Hall, *Family Fortunes. Men and Women of the English Middle Class, 1780–1850* (London: Routledge, 1987).

17. Anna Clark, "1798 as the Defeat of Feminism: Women, Patriotism and Politics," in Terry Brotherstone, Anna Clark, and Kevin Whelan (eds.), *These Fissured Isles. Ireland, Scotland and British History, 1798–1848* (Edinburgh: John Donald, 2005), pp. 85–104, 97.

18. David Hempton and Myrtle Hill, *Evangelical Protestantism in Ulster Society, 1740–1890* (London and New York: Routledge, 1992), p. 129.

19. Rosemary Raughter, "Eighteenth-Century Catholic and Protestant Women" in Angela Bourke et al. (eds.), *The Field Day Anthology of Irish Women's Writing* (Cork: Cork University Press, 2002), vol. IV, pp. 491–493.

20. Samuel McSkimmin, *Annals of Ulster from 1790–1798*, E. J. McCrum (ed.) (Belfast: N.D., 1906 [1849]), p. 38.

21. Lee, "Women and the Church since the Famine," p. 40.

22. Declan Kiberd, *Irish Classics* (London: Granta, 2000), p. 174.

23. Meidhbhín Ní Úrdail, "The Representation of the Feminine: Some Evidence from Irish-Language Sources," *Eighteenth-Century Ireland/Irish an dá Chultú* 22 (2007), pp. 133–150.

24. Lee, "Women and the Church since the Famine," p. 37

25. Caitriona Clear, *Social Change and Everyday Life in Ireland, 1850–1922* (Manchester: Manchester University Press, 2007), p. 26.

26. Though, as Joanna Bourke notes, the argument that sees the increased importance of the dowry as reflecting the diminished economic importance of women relies on a very narrow understanding of what "economic labor" may actually consist of and ignores the contribution that housework makes to the economy.

27. Rita Rhodes, *Women and the Family in Post-Famine Ireland. Status and Opportunity in a Patriarchal Society* (New York and London: Garland, 1992), pp. 85–95.

28. Lee, "Women and the Church since the Famine," p. 136.

29. Clair Wills, "Women, Domesticity and the Family: Recent Feminist Work in Irish Cultural Studies," *Cultural Studies* 15: 1 (2001), pp. 33–57, 34.

30. Horace Plunkett, *Ireland in the New Century* (Dublin: Irish Academic Press, 1983 [1905]), pp. 53, 57–58.

31. Ciara Breathnach, "The Role of Women in the Economy of the West of Ireland, 1891–1923," *New Hibernia Review* 8: 1 (Spring, 2004), pp. 80–92.

32. Joanna Bourke, "'The Best of all Home Rulers': The Economic Power of Women in Ireland, 1880–1914," *Irish Economic and Social History* 18 (1991), pp. 34–47, 36.

33. Mary E. Daly, "Women in the Irish Free State, 1922–1939: The Interaction between Economics and Ideology," *Journal of Women's History* 6: 4/7 (Winter/Spring 1995), pp. 99–116, 104.

34. Joanna Bourke, *Husbandry to Housewifery. Women, Economic Change and Housework in Ireland, 1890–1914* (Oxford: Clarendon, 1993).

35. Joanna Bourke, "The Ideal Man: Irish Masculinity and the Home, 1880–1914," in Marilyn Cohen and Nancy J. Curtin (eds.), *Reclaiming Gender. Transgressive Identities in Modern Ireland* (New York: St. Martin's Press, 1999), pp. 93–106.

36. Rhodes, *Women and the Family*, p. 190.

37. Tom Inglis, *Moral Monopoly. The Catholic Church in Modern Irish Society* (Dublin: Gill and Macmillan, 1987), p. 188.

38. John Tosh, *A Man's Place. Masculinity and the Middle-Class Home in Victorian England* (Yale University Press: New Haven, CT, and London, 1999), p. 28.

39. Dipesh Chakrabarty, "The Difference—Deferral of (a) Colonial Modernity: Public Debates on Domesticity in British Bengal," *History Workshop Journal* 36: 1 (1993), pp. 1–34, 2.

40. Clear, *Social Change and Everyday Life*, p. 86.

41. Wills, "Women, Domesticity and the Family," p. 47.

42. Clear, *Social Change and Everyday Life*, pp. 77–78.

43. Daly, "Women in the Irish Free State," pp. 106–107. Caitríona Clear, "The Re-emergence of Nuns and Convents, 1800–1962," in A. Bourke et al. (eds.), *The Field Day Anthology of Irish Writing*, vol. IV (Cork: Cork University Press, 2002), p. 518.

44. Donald Harman Akenson, "From Women and the Irish Diaspora: The Great Unknown," in Alan Hayes and Dian Urquhart (eds.), *The Irish Women's History Reader* (London and New York: Routledge, 2001), pp. 161–167, 162.

45. Janet Nolan, "The National Schools and Irish Women's Mobility in the Late Nineteenth and Early Twentieth Centuries," *Irish Studies Review*, 5: 18 (1997), pp. 23–28, 25.

46. David Fitzpatrick, "The Modernisation of the Irish Female" in Patrick O'Flanagan, Paul Ferguson and Kevin Whelan (eds.), *Rural Ireland, 1600–1900: Modernisation and Change* (Cork: Cork University Press, 1987), pp. 162–180, p. 163.

47. D.A.J. Macpherson, *Women and the Irish Nation. Gender, Culture and Irish Identity, 1890–1914* (Basingstoke: Palgrave Macmillan, 2012), pp. 51–86.

48. Ellice Pilkington "The United Irishwomen—Their Work" in Horace Plunkett, Ellice Pilkington and George Russell (AE), *The United Irishwomen. Their Place, Work and Ideals* (Dublin: Maunsel and Company, 1911), p. 33.

49. Hannah Sheehy Skeffington quoted in Margaret Ward, *Unmanageable Revolutionaries. Women and Irish Nationalism* (London: Pluto Press, 1995 [1989]), p. 72.

50. Anne McClintock, "'No Longer in a Future Heaven': Gender, Race and Nationalism," in Anne McClintock, Aamir Mufti, and Ella Shohat (eds.), *Dangerous Liaisons: Gender, Nation and Post-Colonial Perspectives* (Minneapolis: University of Minnesota Press, 1997), p. 92

51. Karen Margaret Steele, *Women, Press and Politics during the Irish Revival* (Syracuse, NY: Syracuse University Press, 2012), p. 111.

52. Joseph Valente, *The Myth of Manliness in Irish National Culture, 1880–1922* (Urbana, Chicago, and Springfield: University of Illinois Press, 2010), p. 11.

53. Patrick F. McDevitt, "Muscular Catholicism: Nationalism, Masculinity and Gaelic Team Sports, 1884–1916," *Gender & History*, 9: 2 (August 1997), pp. 262–284.

54. Jane G.V. McGaughey, *Ulster's Men. Protestant Unionist Masculinities and Militarization in the North of Ireland, 1912–1923* (Montreal & Kingston: McGill-Queen's University Press, 2012), p. 4.

55. Maryann Gialanella Valiulis, "Power, Gender and Identity in the Irish Free State," *Journal of Women's History*, 6, 4 (Winter/Spring, 1995), 117–136, pp. 128–129.

56. Daly, "Women in the Irish Free State," pp. 100–101, 107, 110.

57. Tricia Cusack, "Janus and Gender: Women and the Nation's Backward Look," *Nations and Nationalisms*, 6, 4 (2000), pp. 541–561, 551.

58. Louise Ryan, "Constructing 'Irishwoman': Modern Girls and Comely Maidens," *Irish Studies Review*, 6, 2 (1998), pp. 263–272, 271.

59. Valiulis, "Power, Gender and Identity," p. 124.

60. Diarmaid Ferriter, *Occasions of Sin. Sex and Society in Modern Ireland* (London: Profile, 2009), pp. 297, 318.

61. Marjorie Howes, "Public Discourse, Private Reflection, 1916–70," in Bourke et al., *Field Day Anthology of Irish Women's Writing*, vol IV, 923–930, p. 926.

62. Nancy Scheper-Hughes, *Saints, Scholars and Schizophrenics. Mental Illness in Rural Ireland* (University of California Press: Berkeley, Los Angeles, 1979).

63. See, for example, Roy Foster, *Luck and the Irish. A Brief History of Change, c. 1970–2000* (Allen Lane: London, 2007), pp. 37–66.

64. Sinéad Kennedy, "Irish Women and the Celtic Tiger Economy," in Colin Coulter and Steve Coleman (eds.), *The End of Irish History. Critical Reflections on the Celtic Tiger* (Manchester: Manchester University Press, 2003), pp. 95–109, 96.

65. Ursula Barry and Clair Wills, "The Republic of Ireland: The Politics of Sexuality, 1965–2000," Bourke et al., *Field Day Anthology of Irish Women's Writing*, vol. V, 1409–1415, p. 1409.

66. Myrtle Hill, *Women in Ireland. A Century of Change* (Blackstaff Press: Belfast, 2003), pp. 234–237.

67. Ailbhe Smyth, "'A Great Day for the Women of Ireland': The Meaning of Mary Robinson's Presidency for Irishwomen," *Canadian Journal of Irish Studies*, 18: 1 (1992), pp. 61–75, p. 62.

68. Carol Coulter, "Hello Divorce, Goodbye Daddy" (1997), Bourke et al. (eds.), *Field Day Anthology*, vol. V, pp. 1465–1469, p. 1469.

69. John Waters, "Looking after Our Children," *Irish Times*, September 26, 2005.

70. John Waters, "A Modest Proposal for the Rebirth of the Boom," *Irish Times*, April 5, 2013.

71. John Tosh, *Masculinity and the Middle-Class Home in Victorian England* (New Haven, CT, and London: Yale University Press, 1999); Bourke, "The Ideal Man."

72. Joseph Nugent's work on late nineteenth-century Catholic masculinities provides some indication of the direction that such research might take. Joseph Nugent, "The Sword and the Prayerbook: Ideals of Authentic Irish Manliness," *Victorian Studies* 50: 4 (2008), pp. 587–613.

CHAPTER 16

POLITICAL VIOLENCE

Marc Mulholland

B Y EUROPEAN STANDARDS—AND FOR LARGE swaths of its modern history, even by the standards of the United States—popular violence was a
marginal phenomenon in Ireland. There are few countries, however, with
such a continuous tradition of honoring political violence. The legitimacy of government has often been weak, and the heroic reputation of revolutionaries enduring. This is not to say that the Irish dispensation was entirely insular. Ireland
could never field conventional armies against Britain, but there were always those
hoping for international conflicts in which England's difficulty would be Ireland's
opportunity, as the saying went. While the depredations of fascist and communist
militias destroyed the reputation of paramilitary politics in post-war Europe, it
continued as a live tradition in Ireland up to the end of the twentieth century.
Political violence is an ineradicable theme of modern Irish history.

In 1688–1689, international war came to Ireland. James II's French-supported
defense of his crown was defeated by William III, the Dutch king of England.
There followed the era of the penal laws, designed to prevent a resurgence of the
defeated Catholic power in Ireland. These laws symbolized the annihilation of any
remnants of the feudal Catholic ruling class. Irish Jacobitism—loyalty to the de-
throned Stuart dynasty of England—was gradually replaced by a Hibernian patriotism. Dynastic warfare was superseded by armed actions arising from subordinate classes and motivated by civil society ideals. This is how "political violence"
is defined in this chapter.

FROM UNITED IRISHMEN TO YOUNG IRELAND

The patriotic Volunteer movement of 1778–1782 was not rebellious, but it did use
armed intimidation to press for an Irish parliament freed from British government

control. This Irish parliament, entirely Protestant, in 1782 won its legislative equality with Westminster in London. The Irish government was still controlled from England, however. "Patriotism" inspired a far more radical form of Hibernianism, notably among Ulster's and especially the city of Belfast's Presbyterians, who chaffed at the Church-of-Ireland landed Ascendancy. They took the lead in a republican and separatist conspiracy in the 1790s, the United Irishmen. In this they were inspired by the American and French revolutions but also by Protestant optimism that the power of Catholic "idolatry" and authoritarianism was fatally in decline. Confidence in this belief was rendered ever more problematic as the Catholic masses were in turn mobilized and politicized. Their peasant-based Defender organization, espousing a combination of revolutionary republicanism, social leveling, and Catholic millenarianism, formed a coalition of convenience with the United Irishmen.

Until the end of the 1790s, the armies of the French republic appeared as a powerful and emancipatory ally for separatists in Ireland. The record of British arms, other than the Royal navy, was not impressive. Only bad weather prevented a French landing at Bantry Bay in 1796. This had an electrifying impact on the movement. Jemmy Hope, a hard-headed Ulster Presbyterian weaver and United Irishman, wrote that "The appearance of the French in Bantry Bay brought the rich farmers and shopkeepers into the [revolutionary] societies, and with them all the corruption essential to the objects of the British ministry."[1] The government, indeed, was struck both by acute fear and a sense of opportunity to be grabbed. Its leaders determined to use brutal methods to break the subversive conspiracy, or to provoke it into premature rebellion before foreign aid could arrive. "Means were taken," said Castlereagh, the strongman in the crown's Irish government, "to make the United Irish system explode."[2] The yeomanry and militia were unleashed, to hunt out arms and smash presses. While a certain decorum regulated treatment of gentlemen United Irish, torture was regularly employed against common-born rebels. The government paid spies and agent provocateurs to work on the divisions inherent in the United Irish movement. They sponsored the Orange Order, established in 1795, as a counterrevolutionary movement of the agrarian lower orders of the Church of Ireland locked in sectarian competition with their Catholic neighbors. Given extreme provocation, it is no surprise that the 1798 United Irish rising was a bloody debacle. French aid, in small numbers, arrived only after the rebellion had been crushed. The Presbyterian-led rising in the north failed to link up with the Catholic rising in southern and western Ireland; the latter was scarred by Catholic assaults on Protestant property and persons. The myth of an "enlightened" Catholic people, entertained by Protestant patriots, seemed discredited beyond repair.

The 1790s, therefore, saw an explosion of violence as separatists attempted to emulate the republicanism of France. Attempts by the French to open up an Irish front in the European war were frustrated by their failure to land an expeditionary force of sufficient size. The crown mobilized not only German mercenaries and Church-of-Ireland loyalists to put down the rising but also Irish-speaking peasants cut off from discourses of "liberty." About ten thousand rebels and six hundred soldiers were killed in the fighting and massacres. Popular violence would never reach nearly this level again. In the aftermath of the 1798 rebellion, there was scattered guerrilla activity in the Wicklow hills until 1803, but the attempted rising coordinated by Robert Emmet, though it had substantial support among the artisans of Dublin, was betrayed and snuffed out. Emmet, in his speech from the dock, made clear that Irish revolutionary faith in the goodwill of France, now firmly under Bonaparte's control, had all but ebbed away.

In the first half of the nineteenth century, the Irish peasantry was widely acknowledged as not only the most impoverished in Europe but also the most restive. Great numbers were involved in the constitutionalist agitation of the 1820s for Catholic emancipation (a campaign to allow Catholics to take seats in the UK parliament of Great Britain and Ireland) and in the "monster meetings" of the 1840s in support of repeal of the 1800 Act of Union and restoration of an Irish parliament. The leadership of constitutionalism was mostly middle class, with support from the Catholic clergy. Daniel O'Connell, who led the Emancipation and Repeal campaigns, had little hesitation in employing militant language: "Are we to be called slaves? Have we not the ordinary courage of Englishmen? Are we to be trampled on?" he asked an audience in 1843.[3] But on principle O'Connell opposed resort to revolutionary violence. In 1846 he enforced on his followers an "utter & total disclaimer of the contemplation of physical force."[4] Armed revolution would lead to a bloodbath, and O'Connell had lively memories of the horrors of the 1790s. He knew himself to be a restraint on the Irish urge to insurrectionary violence. If the British government has sense, O'Connell reasoned, it would support his moral authority by granting concessions. But Britain remained wary that reform could quickly escalate into revolution.

With a substantial number of Irish in the crown's armed forces, and the population of Ireland amounting to one-third of the population of the United Kingdom, a war of independence was not inconceivable. However, there existed in Ireland no martially inclined gentry class in sympathy with rebellion, such as could be found in Poland or Hungary. Landowners, in contrast, were seen—and to some extent saw themselves—as a pro-British "garrison-class." A middle-class-led rebellion supported from outside by sympathetic Great Powers, on the model of the Belgian Revolution of 1830, was ruled out by the constellation of international forces in restoration Europe. Britain's rivals ranged themselves in the Holy Alliance, which was firmly opposed to revolution and favored overseas interventions only in legitimist causes. In domestic terms, therefore, pre-Famine Ireland was best prepared for revolutionary war, but since the defeat of Bonaparte the international context was entirely unpropitious.

Nonetheless, the revolutionary tradition, though it reached low ebb in the first half of the nineteenth century, did not entirely evaporate. The sustained propaganda of Walter Cox helped keep alive bitter recriminations over government repression in the 1790s, even as the Ulster Presbyterian republican bulwark turned decisively in favor of the Union and British monarchy for fear of an intolerant Catholic democracy. The Irish peasantry was active in its own behalf in "agrarian outrage," a form of intimidation calculated to inhibit evictions of tenant farmers and, occasionally, to gain better conditions for rural laborers. Michael Beames writes that "peasant outrage was an expression of a particular 'class' consciousness, underwritten by widely held beliefs and accepted customs relating to land and the community."[5] This "Whiteboy" activity always had a certain political content, however, being somewhat protonationalist and often religiously sectarian. It was given a fillip around 1820 by circulation of the prophecies of Pastorini, promising the extirpation of Protestantism in Ireland. The movement against the payment of tithes by a Catholic peasantry for the upkeep of the Protestant Church of Ireland involved considerable violence between 1830 and 1836 (the "Tithe War"). The central swath of Ireland was the area of greatest agricultural change and thus of peasant violence.

Legal nationalist agitation reached a dead end in 1843, when Robert Peel, the British prime minister, promised to wage one-sided war if necessary to maintain Britain's hold on Ireland. From 1845 the Great Famine put Ireland on the rack. Considerable state repression was employed to maintain order and to ensure that relief efforts should not undermine this providential opportunity to enforce a rationalization of farming on Ireland by shifting it from labor-intensive to a more capital-intensive agriculture. Food riots petered out as hunger sapped the strength of the starving.

The European revolutions of 1848, for the first time since the beginning of the century, made rebellion in Ireland appear credible. Since 1847 the Young Ireland wing of O'Connell's movement had argued that, in principle, a rebellion in Ireland was justifiable. Their argument was essentially historicist: a nation has a right to assert its sovereignty in arms. O'Connell had opposed any alliance with the British Chartist movement, and the Young Ireland faction, including even the radical Irish Confederation, also stayed aloof. Much more attractive was the prospect of international solidarity from the French republic declared in February 1848. A delegation from the Irish in Paris met with Alphonse de Lamartine, the French minister of foreign affairs, on March 17, 1848, and accepted the Irish tricolor as a symbol of republican solidarity. Lamartine, however, quickly rowed back, offering Young Ireland no active support for fear of alienating Britain. In Ireland, the crown moved to preempt Young Ireland plans, and its leading propagandist, John Mitchel, was arrested in April 1848 and sentenced to transportation for treason-felony. In retrospect, this appeared to have been the best moment for an armed outbreak, but it was allowed to pass. When the rising did take place, led by the Protestant gentryman William Smith O'Brien, it lacked both élan and ruthlessness. By holding the family of the widow McCormack hostage, an Irish Constabulary detachment dissuaded the rebels from engaging in battle at Ballingarry, south Tipperary. The outbreak soon dissolved. "We were routed without a struggle and have been led into captivity without glory. We suffer not for a rebellion, but for a blunder," one leader reflected miserably.[6] The tradition of political violence dissipated.

FENIANISM AND LAND WAR

Constitutionalism, however, simultaneously reached a low ebb. Economic collapse during the Famine decimated the ranks of the property-based electorate, and this was not fully restored until the Representation of the People Act of 1868. A mid-century outburst of anti-Catholicism in Britain tended to reinforce the sectarian divide in Irish politics, notwithstanding the Tenant League of the 1850s that briefly united Presbyterian farmers in Ulster with Catholic farmers elsewhere. The absorption of the Irish Party's leadership in the lower reaches of the government in 1852 mightily reinforced the idea that Westminster was not an outlet for Irish constitutionalist ambitions so much as a source of corruption. At the parliamentary level, Irish politics mirrored the Whig/Tory divide of Britain, but it lacked popular legitimacy.

The deficit in the legitimacy of parliamentarianism allowed for the emergence of the Fenian movement, particularly in urban areas. This revolutionary organization was committed to a separate Irish republic achieved by armed rebellion. Fenianism had an important American dimension. Many Catholic Irish emigrants to the United States found themselves confronted by a White Anglo-Saxon Protestant establishment that looked down on their religion as irredeemably reactionary and antidemocratic in ethos. The Irish "Celtic" race was strongly identified with dissolute dependence, poverty, and criminality. Fenianism allowed Irish immigrants to carve themselves a niche in American society by turning the tables on the "WASP" establishment. By seizing on the U.S. civic religion of republicanism and the universal prejudice against the former colonial power, and applying them to the dream of revolution back in Ireland, Fenians asserted for the Irish immigrants a more thoroughgoing commitment to American ideals than that of their critics. General Philip Sheridan, a Union commander in the American Civil War, was not untypical in thinking that "An American by birth, I love liberty; an Irishman by descent, I hate oppression; and if I were in Ireland, I should be a Fenian."[7] The United States' Irish diaspora, for many years, reinforced Irish nationalism not only with money but also with visceral anti-British sentiments and republican ideals.

Back in Ireland, enthusiastic patriotism was taken up by many young men keen to cut a figure in their locality. By one estimate, the Fenians organized up to fifty thousand men in Ireland by the mid-1860s.[8] As rebellion was predicated on the outbreak of war between Britain and one of its geopolitical rivals—preferably America or France, but even autocratic Russia could be an ally of opportunity— the perils of risking life and limb in military action unsupported by foreign allies seemed remote. The Fenians attempted, with some initial success, to infiltrate the British army, but as the Irish proportion of the United Kingdom population dropped steadily and steeply, the chances for a rising without outside help were acknowledged as slim. Nonetheless, the Fenians talked themselves into a corner, and by 1866 it seemed necessary to attempt a rebellion even without overseas allies if revolutionary credibility was to be maintained. The rebellion of 1867 was from the outset compromised by informants and went off half-cocked. Bloodshed was minimal.

In honor of their role in putting down the rebellion, the Irish Constabulary was awarded the prefix "Royal." Though repression in Ireland was rarely acute, the constabulary was organized along semi-military gendarme lines, often made use of suspension of normal law, and was explicitly political (one of the Constabulary's functions was to monitor and report on all political activity, whether legal or not). State functions can therefore be seen as a mode of political violence, even if it was generally not egregious.

The Fenian pattern was to be repeated in the future. A number of young males (predominantly) would be drawn into revolutionary activity on the expectation of ideal circumstances for insurrection presenting, only for their committed cadre to be forced into militant action under circumstances far from ideal, so as to preserve their reputation. Fenianism was important for establishing republican separatism as the ideal maxima of Irish nationalism. It did not, as such, establish a tradition of ongoing political violence. In 1873 the Fenian Irish Republican Brotherhood adopted the position that no rising should be attempted until there was a clear public mandate. In the meantime, however, Fenianism ran arms and operated as a secret society, testing the vigilance of the law and habituating a cadre to the idea that only military action met the exigencies of British rule in Ireland.

Constitutional nationalism reemerged after the wreckage of the Fenian movement, but it was never quite entirely at odds with the revolutionary tradition. Isaac Butt founded the Home Rule movement in 1870. On the face of it Home Rulers never asked for more than something like state's rights, a devolved parliament for Irish domestic affairs within the United Kingdom. Butt had launched himself, however, as a national leader by campaigning for an amnesty for Fenian prisoners. The Fenians evinced some sympathy for Butt and at first refrained from attacking the Home Rule movement as parliamentarian. In the localities, meanwhile, Fenians began to involve themselves in agrarian agitation against the landlord system.

The rapid decline of the laborers as a proportion of the rural population in general reduced the extent of agrarian outrages, and the violence of the Tithe War was never again reached. Intimidation of farmers to dissuade them from taking over land from which tenants had been evicted—or from paying excessively high "rack rents" that would tend to increase rents for everyone—remained a subterranean current. Very occasionally even landlords might be targeted for assassination. Between 1879 and 1881, and sporadically thereafter, Fenians involved themselves in large numbers in a concerted campaign to prevent evictions and withhold excessive rents in a campaign known as the "Land War." "Moonlighting," the tactic of nighttime raids on farmers threatening the solidarity of anti-landlord agitation, was to a degree spontaneous, but it certainly involved Fenian activists. Moonlighters were reported as being organized as "bands" or "companies," each under a captain. Their depredations were concentrated in the impoverished and rural west of Ireland. They were "as a rule farmers' sons," according to one police officer; "occasionally there were labourers among them, and people also belonging to the shop keeping class."[9] The constitutionalist face of this Land War was the Irish National Land League, which was directed by a coalition of Fenians and Home Rule members of parliament (MPs) led by Charles Stewart Parnell. Parnell and his lieutenants clearly appreciated the use of intimidation in holding the movement together. They were genuinely opposed to violent excesses, particularly murder and the maiming of animals.

The dramatic eruption of terrorism from the Fenian milieu, with the assassination of the lord lieutenant and chief secretary in 1881, and the waging of a skirmishing bombing campaign in London in the mid-1880s clearly discomfited most Fenians. This kind of violence could not easily be assimilated to the preferred (if largely impractical) model of open warfare on the field, or even acts of desperation from the oppressed. Still, there remained a substantial respect for the perpetrators, who faced the likelihood of hanging or long spells in prison for their acts (if they could not escape to America, as many did). The martyrology of the felon was exceptionally resonant in Irish nationalism and could soon efface the gravity of the crime for which the martyr was convicted.

Even as constitutionalist nationalists despaired at excessive use of political violence, they were willing to use the threat of uncontrolled moonlighting as a weapon in their negotiations with the government. Political violence was still quite rare in Victorian Ireland, but its influence was greater than might appear at first glance. The ever-present possibility of political violence meant that politicians must perforce utilize it in pressing their goals. Either violent tendencies would be ascribed to opponents, or more insidiously, government would be warned that failure to make concessions to constitutionalists would empower the violent extremists. As the Home Rule politician and firebrand agitator William O'Brien put it: "violence is the only way of securing a hearing for moderation."[10]

The centrality of violence to the historicist narrative of nationalism should be added to such pragmatic considerations. British rule was described as being a product of bloody conquest, and armed revolutionaries of even quite recent vintage were lionized as idealists, even if perhaps misguided ones. Political violence, therefore, pervaded the language of constitutional nationalism. It could not have been otherwise, so long as there existed substantial reservoirs of support for armed action against what many saw as an illegitimate occupation government that was itself prepared to use main force for political ends.

If the violence of the Moonlighters and the Fenian terrorist colored Irish nationalism in the 1880s, Protestant resistance in Ulster to Home Rule occasioned severe outbreaks of rioting, notably in Belfast and Derry in 1886. Political riots were double-edged weapons for unionists. In 1864 a Belfast Protestant newspaper opined during riotous community tension that "Protestants of all denominations must be prepared to stand together and to give tangible proof, not only of their strength, but of their readiness to combine, if need be, in defence of the Throne, the Union and their liberties."[11] Rioting achieved this at a popular level, but it also ran the risk of delegitimizing loyalism, particularly as the association of nationalism and crime was a central trope of the anti-Home Rule case. However, concentrated bouts of mass violence provided ample warning of what might happen should Great Britain abandon the Protestant community in Ireland. The riots themselves were often presented as atavistic outbursts, but this was at least partly strategic. If reaction to nationalist aggression could be depicted as instinctive rather than calculated, then political leaders need not accept any responsibility for it, and it was all the easier to argue that Catholic democracy in Ireland could never be finessed to overcome Protestant antipathy.

The entry of Irish nationalism into alliance with the British Liberal Party on a common platform of Home Rule in 1885 sharply circumscribed the influence of revolutionists on the broader political spectrum. Still, Fenianism remained a current on the fringes throughout the 1890s, and the hundredth anniversary commemorations of the 1798 rebellion allowed constitutionalists to appeal to the glories of past insurrections. "We are rebels in sentiment, and should occasion offer we be rebels in act and deed," said one Home Rule MP in 1898.[12]

THE WAR OF INDEPENDENCE

Evocations of violent revolutionism redeveloped in the early years of the twentieth century. Ironically, now that rural agitation and violent Fenianism had substantially died down, it was motivated to a great extent by the lack of overt British oppression. It outraged nationalists that Britain's rule appeared to be consensual, with few radicals in prison and the Irish Parliamentary Party in alliance with one of the great parties of state. One leading cultural nationalist, Pádraic Pearse, published a poem in 1913 titled "The Rebel." This verse ostensibly ended on a bathetic note, condemning the British in descending notes of vituperation: "Tyrants ... hypocrites ... liars!" But in so doing it captures quite nicely the texture of nationalist outrage that the world took at face value Britain's apparently benign rule of a passive Ireland. British hypocrisy and deceit, for nationalists, were the unkindest cuts of all. Pearse's 1915 oration over the grave of a dead Fenian expertly probed at the sore of nationalist humiliation. Britain was acknowledged to have "worked well in secret and in the open": "They think that they have pacified Ireland.... They think that they have foreseen everything, think that they have provided against everything; but the fools, the fools, the fools!—they have left us our Fenian dead, and, while Ireland holds these graves, Ireland unfree shall never be at peace."[13] Pearse powerfully conjured the specter of nonrational violence to prick Britain's cold-blooded liberalism.

The passage of the Home Rule bill though the Westminster House of Commons in 1912, delayed two years by the House of Lords, notoriously reintroduced the gun into Irish politics. Strikingly, the British army, with the Curragh "mutiny" of 1914, showed every sign that if the government tried to use it to pass Home Rule, the army would refuse orders. The British government capitulated and assured the public that it had "no intention whatever of taking advantage of its rights to crush political opposition to the policy or principles of the Home Rule Bill."[14]

In the nine counties of Ulster, much of the male Protestant population of military age was organized from 1912 into the anti-Home Rule Ulster Volunteer Force (UVF). The mass UVF was designed to act as a tripwire force. Its existence meant that Home Rule could not be introduced in Ireland without the British government running the severe risk of warfare breaking out in Ulster. It was a high-risk strategy for the unionists. Should the UVF engage with the forces of the crown, or lead an anti-Catholic riot arms in hand, widespread sympathy for their cause in Great Britain would quickly melt away. The UVF was supposed to maintain order, prevent untimely outbursts of rioting, and force the government to draw the sword if it wished to force a Catholic democracy on Ireland. As a moral force, it would work best if it were never deployed.

That so many Irish "advanced nationalists" applauded the arming of the Ulstermen, even in a cause diametrically opposed to their own, speaks volumes for the militarization of Irish politics in this period. Drilling, preparing for warfare, and forming intense masculine bonds had been long established on mainland Europe, but had been resisted in the British Isles as essentially destructive of the liberal ethos. Now, however, it was argued that volunteering was an essential spine to any self-determining people. The Irish Volunteers, set up in 1913 in emulation of the UVF, was clearly conceived of as the core of a future army (and perhaps police force) for a Home Rule Ireland tending toward ever greater independence. The existing state apparatus—the semi-military and overtly political

Royal Irish Constabulary and the British army garrison—were seen, understandably enough, as a potential Trojan horse, owing its allegiance to a foreign power. It was not anticipated, however, that the Irish Volunteers would see action during the Home Rule crisis itself. At most, its function was as a counterbid in the political high stakes of the period. If the UVF circumscribed the ability of the government to peacefully introduce Home Rule for all of Ireland, the existence of the Irish Volunteers meant that failure to introduce Home Rule would itself run the risk of sparking an armed reaction.

It is unlikely that Home Rule was ever really emotionally satisfying to most Irish nationalists. Few ballads were written about the glories of devolved government under the crown, and the unofficial anthem of the constitutionalist movement—"God Save Ireland"—celebrated the heroism of four Fenians executed by the British in 1867 for their part in the death of a policeman during an attempt to liberate felons. The advantage of Home Rule was that it seemed winnable in an era when armed revolution appeared to be completely out of the question. It was modest and arguably equivalent to established practice in the settler colonies of the Empire so that a British government might concede it without thereby feeling it was imperiling geopolitical security or imperial dignity. There was little nationalist expectation that Irish and particularly Ulster Unionists could be won around to Home Rule in advance. But by maintaining the Union, and countenancing provisions to protect the Protestant interest, it was expected that unionists would at length accept an Irish parliament—once enacted—as a fait accompli, compatible with their legitimate interests if not with their long-established privilege. Finally, although the imperial connection was hardly a matter of nationalist celebration, it at least did not seem to impinge very directly on those Irish unwilling to participate. Britain, after all, had built its empire in the nineteenth century without the use of conscription.

The outbreak of the Great War changed all these calculations. The unionists had been far more militant than expected. The government in 1914 placed Home Rule on the statute book, but guaranteed that provisions would be made for Ulster before it came into force. It was becoming disconcertingly clear that the price of Home Rule would be something like the "mutilation" of partition. The cost of the Union, moreover, was now clearly one of blood, with Irish people expected to fight and die for the empire in Europe, and the threat of actual conscription both real and actively reviled. The constitutional nationalists, nonetheless, hoped for a blood sacrifice, whereby Irish nationalists would fight alongside their Ulster brethren in the Great War, thus proving both the military capabilities of the nation and its loyalty to the liberal empire.

The advanced nationalists—a combination of traditional Fenians with Gaelic revivalists, socialists, and assorted fringe progressives—saw both a threat that the war would finally assimilate the Irish nation to a federalized greater Britain and an opportunity, for at last Irish nationalism had a potential foreign ally in Germany.

The aim of the Easter Rising of 1916 was to get an army in the field in Ireland, so that an Irish Republic would have earned a seat at a Central Powers–dominated post-war peace congress expected by many no later than 1917. When, however, attempts to land German matériel failed, it was decided to launch the rising even with the near certainty of failure, so that at least it could not be said that an un-free Ireland willingly absorbed itself into Britain's war machine.

The Rising of Easter 1916 was surprisingly successful, holding the center of Dublin for a week. This in itself was a political achievement effacing past humiliations. A Dublin resident wrote during the rebellion that "There is almost a feeling of gratitude towards the volunteers because they are holding out for a little while, for had they been beaten the first or second day the City would have been humiliated to the soul."[15] Still, the rising was inevitably put down. A total of 466 people were killed, of whom 132 were British soldiers. Public opinion anticipated that the rebels would be accorded prisoner-of-war status, and when instead their leaders were executed as traitors there was a mass revulsion not only at the bloodshed but also at Britain's pretension that it had the right to treat Ireland as nothing more than a province. Pearse was seeking self-reassurance when he said, before his execution, that "We seem to have lost. We have not lost. To refuse to fight would have been to lose; to fight is to win. We have kept faith with the past, and handed on a tradition to the future."[16] In fact, his own generation was soon pitched into a new tumult.

In the aftermath of the rising young men flooded into the reconstituted Volunteers. In the short run, the Volunteer movement was seen—yet again—as a trip-wire limiting the government's room for maneuver. This time the intention was to prevent the imposition of conscription, which was now a stated government intention. In England, refusal to join the forces promised young men white feathers, social ostracism, and humiliation. In Ireland, one could avoid any pressure to go and fight the German army by drilling for Ireland with the Volunteers in one's local town. It was a satisfyingly easy way to earn stature. The Russian Revolution and entry of the United States into the war in 1917, moreover, explicitly committed the Great War Allies and Associates to the emancipation of small nations. Even if this was mostly understood as a means of dismembering the enemy Central Powers, it also changed the politics of separation. Home Rule had made sense in an age of empires, when it seemed sufficiently balanced to convince the British to coerce unionists into acceptance. With precious little chance of this happening, particularly after the sacrifice of the 36th Ulster Division, formed from the UVF, in the 1916 Battle of the Somme, it seemed to make much more sense to drive toward full independence in accordance with the spirit of President's Wilson's Fourteen Points. This, of course, would make partition a virtual certainty. One of the founders of the post-1916 Sinn Féin party, Father Michael O'Flanagan, appreciated this, but most nationalists preferred to occlude the point.[17]

With the end of the Great War the threat of conscription lifted, and men drifted out of the Irish Volunteers again. This left a hardened core that, as they confronted soldiers and police in endless scuffles over drilling and arms running, drifted into an illegal life on the run. In 1918, meanwhile, Sinn Féin swept the constituencies of nationalist Ireland, and its elected representatives took their seats not at Westminster, but in a self-constituted parliament for an independent Ireland, Dáil Éireann.

Despite the Dáil's Declaration of Independence, Sinn Féin traced the realization of the Republic not to the democratic mandate of 1918 but to the rising of 1916. This created circumstances highly conducive to elitism among the Volunteers, now known as the Irish Republican Army (IRA). They felt obliged to act in protection of the Dáil government, democratically mandated, and against a British government that was now clearly lacking any consensus for its rule. However, the IRA felt authorized not by decision of the Dáil civilian government (which indeed did not take official responsibility for the IRA until 1921) but rather by the tradition of self-sacrificing rebels stirring the weak-willed lump of fickle Irish public opinion from its torpor.

Éamon de Valera, president both of Sinn Féin and Dáil Éireann, had said in 1917: "England pretends that it is not by the naked sword, but by the good will of the people of Ireland that she is here. We will draw the naked sword to make her bare her naked sword."[18] This was indeed the historical function of the IRA military campaign. The War of Independence took off in 1920. This was a small war. About 1,400 were killed: 363 police personnel, 261 regular British army, about 550 IRA volunteers (including 14 official executions), and about 200 civilians. That it evolved as a guerrilla war made it all the easier for British Prime Minister Lloyd George to dismiss the IRA as nothing more than "murder gangs." IRA military operations were usually conducted on a fairly makeshift basis, but this was advantageous, in that it prevented too rapid an escalation beyond the limits of what public opinion could stomach. Crown forces were particularly prone to retaliatory actions, mostly burnings of rebel houses and extrajudicial executions, which were sufficiently brutal to alienate the nationalist population without being oppressive enough to break the IRA's will.

Michael Collins, the chief strategist on the republican side, was particularly concerned to protect his forces from informers while penetrating the government apparatus in Ireland with his own agents. Great controversy has attached to the question of to what extent IRA attacks crossed the line into sectarian malice. It is certainly the case that IRA persecution of loyalists, for giving crown forces information or other types of aid, was driven primarily by their own security requirements. They also officially and repetitively condemned sectarianism as contrary to basic republican principles. As most loyalists were also Protestant, however, it wasn't difficult to satisfy base sectarian motives in the course of identifying, isolating, and punishing "traitors" to the national struggle. Outside the systematic burning of Catholic residential areas by Protestant loyalists in Ulster, however, it is difficult to identify any general campaign to extirpate communities on the basis of their religion.

Éamon de Valera, the political leader of the Dáil, would have preferred the IRA to concentrate on fewer, large-scale engagements with crown forces. "You are going too fast," he wrote his comrades from a propaganda tour of the United States. "The odd shooting of a policeman here or there is having a bad effect, from a propaganda point of view, on us in America. What we want is one good battle about once a month with about 500 men on each side."[19] Such a strategy was un-realistic, but it caught the necessity of defining the conflict internationally as a war rather than an outburst of criminality. Indeed, the high-risk operations of Tom Barry's IRA Flying Column in County Cork—the ambush and extermination of a heavily armed police Auxiliary patrol at Kilmichael in November 1920, and a running battle with the army at Crossbarry in March 1921—did help move the British government toward acceptance of the need to negotiate with "gun-men."

The subsequent negotiations between British and Irish representatives look rather odd from our perspective. Britain's insistence that the six predominantly Protestant counties of Northern Ireland should not be forced out of the United Kingdom had the merit of respecting the self-determination of a cohesive national grouping, but at the time partition was a major embarrassment for the British. Across the empire and farther afield, Ireland was assumed to be one nation, and its breaking-up was easily depicted as an act of colonial vandalism. Indeed, Brit-ain refused negotiations with Dáil representatives until Northern Ireland was fully established and partition could be presented as a fait accompli. The repub-licans had no expectation that they could coerce Ulster's Protestants, and even if they reserved an abstract right to do so, most did not believe that it would be justifiable at the cost of civil war. Still, during the treaty negotiations, the British side was extremely anxious not to be seen as breaking on the issue of partition. If a break was to come, they preferred it to be on the continued formal subordina-tion of Ireland to the crown. This was an overtly a colonialist and anti-democratic demand, but given the continued authority of the British monarchy over one-fifth of the globe, Irish intransigence on the point would be seen as blockheaded, and Britain's willingness to wage war to defend the integrity of its monarchy was internationally accepted as a respectable *raison d'état*.

De Valera well knew that the Irish Republic was not winnable, but he was anx-ious to convince the IRA that confrontation with the British had been as pushed as far as possible by testing the negotiations. He therefore held himself in reserve, sending as plenipotentiaries a negotiating team led by Michael Collins. His in-tention, probably, was to intervene at the eleventh hour to negotiate amendments that would avoid renewal of war. As a strategy, it was not dissimilar to Parnell's testing the Land Act of 1881, threatening the British with a wave of moonlight-ing in the absence of an acceptable settlement, and then striking a deal based on an amended Land Act in the "Kilmainham Treaty" that ended the Land War. In the 1880s, this had left agrarian radicals with at least the sense that all resources had been stretched and ultimate victory—the abolition of landlordism—was simply beyond reach. A similar approach may well have paid dividends in the 1921 negotiations. If the IRA had been convinced that their political representatives had gone to the wire, they might have more easily accepted that the Republic could not be achieved in one go. Collins, however, was not enthusiastic about doing all the heavy lifting of the negotiations, and making the painful concessions, leaving de Valera as the hero who won the final agreement. He and his colleagues signed the treaty on their own cognizance without consulting with de Valera. This made Collins the de facto leader of the new state, and de Valera reacted violently to his own marginalization by condemning the treaty as inadequate (his proposed alternative treaty left the border in place but replaced membership of the British Empire with "association").

The IRA was, as de Valera might well have predicted, demoralized and angered in the belief that what had been effectively won in fighting had been lost by politics. It was left in a difficult situation. Its volunteers were committed to the Republic, but as agents of the Irish Free State were expected to swear fealty to the British crown. Most IRA volunteers probably preferred retirement from service to this perjury, but since the truce they had already emerged into the public, and as crown forces departed they were authorized to occupy barracks and strongpoints. The choice was to abandon the principles for which they had fought, leaving the state to a new Free State army equipped by the British, or to defy the public's evident desire for a compromise peace and to impose a military dictatorship and renewed war with Britain. In effect, the IRA fell somewhere between these stools. Minorities fused with the Free State army or followed the leadership of the IRA into outright armed opposition to the new state. The ensuing Civil War was brutal—government forces suffered eight hundred fatalities and perhaps as many as four thousand people were killed in total. Still, there was a discernible unwillingness to fight to the knife on both sides. Most volunteers preferred to avoid military action of any kind.

The Civil War of 1921–1923 split Sinn Féin, reducing it to a militaristic and marginalized rump—which was probably a bonus in that it prevented independent Ireland from turning into a one-party state—and soured the mood of independence, but it didn't shatter the unity of the nation. Within a few years, moderates from the losing side in the Civil War democratically formed a government, and piece by piece dismantled the impositions of the treaty. Had the IRA not been alienated from the fruits of its victory, it is most likely that it would have been absorbed into the new state apparatus. That it did not do so was a favorable happenstance, as it meant that the Free State army, having no direct relationship with the War of Independence, never had much authority. As a consequence, Irish political culture quickly demilitarized. Civilian rule became the norm, and after a long tradition of people-versus-state, the Irish polity became notably pacific and law-abiding.

The IRA, which was perceived as having "won" the War of Independence, now moved underground. The organization had the aura of proven effectiveness, revolutionary fortitude, principled opposition to mere politicking, and incorruptibility. It was a heady brew to feed a cult of political violence. These were wasting assets, however, even if sufficient to maintain a "military" structure of training, gun-running, and intelligence gathering. They were an irritant in the Southern Irish body politic in the 1930s, when they fought with the proto-fascist Blue Shirts, and in the 1940s when they attempted cooperation with the Wehrmacht. But their public prestige was ebbing fast. In 1941 the *Irish Independent* devoted only a short single-column story to the death of an IRA man on hunger strike compared to 104 lines to the death of an 89-year-old bishop.[20]

NORTHERN IRELAND AND THE TROUBLES

The early 1920s had seen very considerable violence in Ulster, particularly in the six counties that in 1920 became Northern Ireland. In the two years up to July 1922, 157 Protestants and thirty-seven members of the security forces were killed, compared to 257 Catholics. After that, the advantage swung more clearly to the Protestant unionist side.

The IRA carried out a campaign against crown forces, including the newly formed Royal Ulster Constabulary and its auxiliary forces, the A-, B-, and C-Specials. Anti-state violence by the IRA was, however, at a rather lower level than in much of the south of Ireland, partly because of operational difficulties, partly for fear of loyalist retaliation. Loyalist paramilitarism, which overlapped to a degree with unofficial police depredations, was certainly extensive. Many Catholics were expelled from their homes and jobs, and death squads practicing "representative violence," in which targets in the enemy community were picked at random as a warning to all, was frequent. In contrast to 1912, unionist political restraint on at least riotous affray was notably lacking. The idea was to give the message to Britain that any attempt to sell out the Northern Protestants would lead to an orgy of violence. In this, loyalist violence was largely successful.

In Northern Ireland, loyalist volunteering was mostly absorbed by the B-Specials, which remained in existence as an entirely Protestant force. The IRA also continued in existence, though as a minuscule remnant. Its volunteers were largely kept out of action in the IRA's small 1940s and 1950s campaigns so as not to expose them or the Catholic nationalist communities of Northern Ireland to loyalist revenge attacks. When sectarian violence did break out, the IRA stepped up partly as a defensive force, partly as a provocative purveyor of "deterrent violence."

When the civil rights movement in Northern Ireland broke out in 1968, loyalists saw it from the outset as a challenge to the legitimacy of unionist rule, if not to partition itself. At first the Royal Ulster Constabulary, with the support of the unionist-controlled devolved government at Stormont, attempted to peg civil rights marchers into Catholic districts, so as to define them as anti-partitionist and subversive. When this led to embarrassing exposure of police violence against protesters on television, loyalist counter-demonstrators took up the slack by blocking civil rights marchers from "neutral" or Protestant territory. This pattern of territorialism soon picked up its own momentum, and the IRA reemerged as "defenders" of Catholic areas by 1970 at the latest. It was the youth of working-class areas who flocked into IRA ranks. Lord Chalfont, a British politician, uncharitably described Provisional volunteers as "social rejects or young tearaways in search of escape from the grinding urban squalor of Derry and Belfast."[21] During the subsequent thirty years or so of insurgency and violent reaction—the Troubles—3,523 people were killed: Irish nationalist republican paramilitary groups, chiefly the Provisional IRA, accounted for 2,055 victims. Pro-British loyalist paramilitary groups killed 1,020, and the security forces 368.

Following a split in the IRA in 1969–1970, with the militant Provisional wing taking the lead, republicanism developed a concerted strategy to employ intercommunal tensions to delegitimize the Unionist state. The British army in August 1969 had been deployed in a peacekeeping role, but it was also required to bolster the authority of the Unionist government at Stormont, and as such it was rapidly dragged into punitive raids on Catholic areas to disarm their defenders. These Catholic defenders were now mostly arrayed in the IRA, given the inability of alternative gun-running routes or vigilante organizations to operate outside the law (arms imports from sections of the Irish government were in 1970 exposed and forbidden, while the Catholic Ex-Serviceman's Association lacked the IRA's long experience in evading state surveillance). The IRA's reputation as a people's army, a legacy still just about surviving from of the War of Independence period, was reanimated. A Catholic nurse from a working-class district in Belfast, speaking in 1971, told an interviewer that, "They're not necessarily the good, brave boys, but the IRA is something to believe in, and at least you'll be safe as long as they're in existence."[22]

The IRA, for its part, never saw "defenderism" as more than a first stage in its revolutionary offensive against British sovereignty. It did not accept that a Protestant majority in Northern Ireland legitimized partition of the island. One Provisional brusquely dismissed Protestant unionists in 1972:

The fact is that if a section of the Protestant working class sides with the enemy, it is the enemy. So does this mean we must be held to ransom?... What does the revolutionist who accepts physical force do? Does he try to accommodate himself to the establishment, or does he help tear the whole fucking system down and rebuild it? You can't apologise.[23]

In the early 1970s, the Provisionals formulated a three-pronged offensive plan. This was strikingly effective in that each stage was by itself eminently achievable if violence could sufficiently destabilize the North. The first aim was to bring down Stormont. This was achieved in March 1972, when direct rule from Britain was introduced. The second stage was to bring the British to negotiation. This was achieved in July 1972, though the talks quickly collapsed and were disavowed by the British. The third stage was to prevent any attempt at a settlement that excluded republicans. This was achieved with the collapse of the 1974 Sunning-dale Power-Sharing Agreement (which was brought down by a loyalist general strike, but republican violence was a crucial determinate of Protestant alienation from the agreement).

From 1970 to about 1975, therefore, the IRA strategy was to maintain a high volume of mayhem, even if the cost to its own volunteers was substantial (which it was). "Accidental" atrocities killing civilians were inevitable, though given the limited destructive power at their disposal, and a militarist ideology that rejected attacking noncombatants on principle, they were not as frequent as might have been. Loyalists, in contrast, launched a campaign of murder against Catholic civilians from 1972. The intention behind these was primarily to send a message to the British government that betrayal of the British in Ulster would lead to a sectarian bloodbath. Indeed, by 1974 the British had concluded that withdrawal was an impossibility without unleashing civil war and furthermore, any attempt to impose a constructive solution would be impossible against loyalist reaction.

This put the republicans in a quandary. There was no prospect of a new British initiative in the foreseeable future, and so no medium-term goal to drive toward. Rather than abandon the armed campaign, which would have been logical if dispiriting, the IRA from about 1977 restructured for a "long war." This involved more counter-intelligence work, rigorous screening and training of recruits (particularly to resist interrogation), and a lower level of activity to reduce attrition on IRA forces. The idea was to prove over a span of years that violence in Northern Ireland would not simply fade away if the British refrained from stirring the pot by introducing bold new initiatives. Eventually, it was assumed, the British would be forced to reengage with republicanism politically. "The mandarins of Whitehall [have] a scenario for British withdrawal packed away in some filing cabinet," the republican leader Gerry Adams mused, "and one day it will be used."[24] The IRA's long-war strategy was possible because British security policy remained within the broad limits of liberal legality, so disabling it from striking crippling blows against the IRA. The long war also satisfied republican mythologies of armed struggle as a good in itself, in so far as it showed Irish national aspiration to be unconquerable and the British presence in Ireland to be incompatible with real peace.

With Britain more or less limiting itself to containment, and the intensity of the IRA campaign much diminished, loyalism became much less active, particularly after an attempt to force a return of unionist hegemony through a general strike in 1977 was faced down by the government. The IRA, meanwhile, became an increasingly professional organization. But this came at the heavy cost of a shift in its modus operandi from a street-fighting "revolutionary" organization to one much more classically terroristic. Particularly from the early mid-1980s, when security-force body armor was much improved, the IRA was increasingly forced to inflict casualties either by door-step assassinations of locally recruited police and army members out of uniform, or by use of massive bombs with their concomitant risk of high civilian casualties.

The eruption of anger against Britain during the 1981 Hunger Strikes, when ten republican prisoners starved themselves to death in protest at the government's criminalization policy and in pursuit of political status, made clear the failure of Britain's decision to refrain from political initiatives in the hope that benign neglect would see community polarization and nationalist alienation slowly drain away. The governments in London and Dublin negotiated the Anglo-Irish Agreement in 1985, which was designed to isolate republicans from the wider nationalist constituency and to force the unionists into negotiating credibly for a return to devolved government. At first the IRA's reaction was extremely hostile—unsurprisingly, as it was sold by the governments as a step toward sidelining the organization. About the same time, the IRA began to shift from its strategy of attritional long war to a more propagandist struggle to create "liberated zones." They hoped to secure sustainable No Go areas excluding the security forces in some country areas, and planned for dramatic seizures of public space in "Tet Offensive" type operations. These latter were not put into practice for lack of matériel, but the attempt to up the ante was reflected in a dramatic switch to very large-scale bombs, some of which were used in attacks on the financial City of London.[25]

Loyalism also picked up momentum after the 1985 Anglo-Irish Agreement, responding to British government activism perceived as threatening the partition settlement with its usual attacks on Catholic civilian soft targets. This time, however, the British government was chivvied into maintaining its reformist momentum by clear indications that the IRA was working its way toward an unarmed strategy. In the 1990s a political settlement was negotiated between parties that laid out a path for republicans toward a share of political power, though without an end to partition. The IRA declared a ceasefire in 1994. This was shattered in February 1996 by a spectacular IRA bomb attack at Canary Wharf in London (killing two civilians)."The conflict is ongoing," Gerry Adams had told Irish radio. "Every so often there will be some spectacular to remind the outside world."[26] But this tactic seems to have been a gambit, largely successful, to demonstrate to IRA hardliners that the use of armed struggle had been tried in all viable permutations and pushed to its limit of efficacy. The cessation of violence was re-established more durably (if not quite perfectly) in 1997. Clever finessing effectively expatriated the British military establishment, as the British army left the streets and the Police Service's "political" functions were handed over to MI5, the British secret service. This allowed republicans to recognize the new Police Service of Northern Ireland as "nonpolitical" (much as the regular Dublin Metropolitan Police had been treated as noncombatants during the War of Independence).

In 2005 the IRA formally ended its armed campaign, and in 2007 Sinn Féin entered the devolved government of Northern Ireland (loyalism failed to develop a substantial political wing). Rejectionist republicans were marginalized, but sufficiently numerous to suggest the embedded glorification of political violence. Loyalist psychology remained defensive, aggrieved, and brittle, with obvious potential for violent acting out. Violence in pursuit of coherent political goals seemed exhausted, but the lure and tradition of the patriotic murder, if attenuated, remained.

FURTHER READING

As unionist histories were generally dismissive of popular violence, relevant accounts until quite late in the twentieth century tended to be nationalist and hagiographic. Particular mention should be made of R. R. Madden's *The United Irishmen: Their Lives and Time* (second series, 2 vols., London: J. Madden and Co., 1843), an uncritical but devoted act of reclamation saving testimony much of which would otherwise have been lost. No subsequent rebellion was at such risk of oblivion as the 1798.

C.H.E. Philpin (ed.), *Nationalism and Popular Protest in Ireland* (Cambridge: Cambridge University Press, 1987) is a compelling collection of articles on the phenomenon of rural violence in the nineteenth century, seeking to restore agency to the submerged masses. Charles Townshend, *Political Violence in Ireland: Government and Resistance since 1848* (Oxford: Oxford University Press, 1984) is a landmark study, arguing that the British government had insufficient moral legitimacy either to suppress popular violence completely or to govern without repression itself. R. V. Comerford, *The Fenians in Context: Irish Politics and Society, 1848–82* (Dublin: Wolfhound, 1985; second ed., 1998) provocatively argues that Irish enthusiasm for revolutionary violence was as much the bluster of young men seeking social outlets as deadly earnest. M. J. Kelly, *The Fenian Ideal and Irish Nationalism, 1882–1916* (Woodridge: Boydell, 2006) demonstrates the overlap between constitutional nationalism and revolutionary traditions.

Peter Hart, *The I.R.A. and Its Enemies: Violence and Community in Cork, 1916–1923* (Oxford: Oxford University Press, 1998) launched an irreverent trend in revolutionary historiography, focusing on the victim of violence rather than the perpetrator. Charles Townhend, *The Republic: The Fight for Irish Independence,*

1918–1923 (London: Allen Lane, 2013) makes revealing use of IRA operational reports to paint a compelling picture of the War of Independence and Civil War period. T. K. Wilson, *Frontiers of Violence: Conflict and Identity in Ulster and Upper Silesia, 1918–1922* (Oxford: Oxford University Press, 2010) breaks new ground—insufficiently followed up as yet—by putting Irish popular violence into an international comparative context.

The standard volume on the Provisional IRA, making much use of interviews by observer-participants, is Richard English, *Armed Struggle: The History of the IRA* (London: Macmillan, 2003). Ed Maloney, *A Secret History of the IRA* (London: Allen Lane, 2002) relies heavily on republicans unhappy with the movement's peace strategy, but it is indispensable. Perhaps the single best study of paramilitarism in Northern Ireland concerns loyalism: Steve Bruce, *The Red Hand: Protestant Paramilitaries in Northern Ireland* (Oxford: Oxford University Press, 1992).

NOTES

1. John Newsinger (ed.), *United Irishman: The Autobiography of Jemmy Hope* (London: Merlin, 2001), p. 57.

2. W. J. Fitzpatrick, *Secret Service Under Pitt* (London: Longmans and Co., 1892), p. 69.

3. *Shaw's Authenticated Report of the Irish State Trials* (Dublin: Henry Shaw, 1844), p. 33.

4. Oliver MacDonagh, *O'Connell: The Life of Daniel O'Connell, 1775–1847* (London: Weidenfeld and Nicolson, 1991), p. 573.

5. M. R. Beames, "Rural Conflict in Pre-famine Ireland: Peasant Assassinations in Tipperary, 1837–1847," in C.H.E. Philpin (ed.), *Nationalism and Popular Protest in Ireland* (Cambridge: Cambridge University Press, 1987), p. 278.

6. Arthur Griffith (ed.), *Meagher of the Sword: Speeches of Thomas Francis Meagher* (Dublin: M. H. Gill and Son, 1916), p. 182.

7. Godfrey Locker Lampson, *A Consideration of the State of Ireland in the Nineteenth Century* (London: Archibald Constable and Co., 1907), p. 266.

8. R. V. Comerford, *The Fenians in Context* (Dublin: Wolfhound, 1985), pp. 123–125.

9. *The Special Commission Act, 1888: Report of the Proceedings before the Commissioners Appointed by the Act*, 4 vols., (London: George Edward Wright, 1890), I, p. 510.

10. Charles Townshend, *Political Violence in Ireland: Government and Resistance since 1848* (Oxford: Oxford University Press, 1984), p. 107.

11. *Belfast Weekly News*, August 13, 1864.

12. Marc Mulholland, "'Not a Historical but a Prospective Application'? The 1798 Rising as Recalled in the Irish Popular Press of 1898," in D. George Boyce and Alan O'Day (eds.), *The Ulster Crisis, 1885–1921* (Basingstoke: Palgrave Macmillan, 2006), p. 169.

13. Pádraic Pearse, *Political Writings and Speeches* (Dublin: Talbot Press, 1966), p. 137.

14. Denis Gwynn, *The Life of John Redmond* (London: G. G. Harrap and Co., 1932), p. 297.

15. James Stephens, *The Insurrection in Dublin* (Dublin: Maunsel and Co., 1916), p. 52.

16. Sean Farrell Moran, *Patrick Pearse and the Politics of Redemption* (Washington, DC: Catholic University of America Press 1994), p. 169.

17. Michael Laffan, *The Resurrection of Ireland: The Sinn Féin Party, 1916–1923* (Cambridge: Cambridge University Press, 2004), pp. 78–79.

18. Dorothy Macardle, *The Irish Republic* (Dublin: Irish Press, 1951), p. 217.

19. Tim Pat Coogan, *De Valera: Long Fellow, Long Shadow* (London: Hutchinson, 1993), p. 198.

20. Hugh Oram, *The Newspaper Book: A History of Newspapers in Ireland, 1649–1983* (Dublin: MO Books, 1983), p. 202.

21. Lord Chalfont, "The Balance of Military Forces," in J. C. Beckett (ed.), *The Ulster Debate: Report of a Study Group of the Institute for the Study of Conflict* (London: Bodley Head, 1972), p. 56.

22. W. H. Van Voris, *Violence in Ulster: An Oral Documentary* (Amherst: University of Massachusetts Press, 1975), p. 222.

23. Van Voris, *Violence in Ulster*, p. 253.

24. Padraig O'Malley, *Northern Ireland: Questions of Nuance* (Belfast: Blackstaff Press, 1990), p. 62.

25. Ed Maloney, *A Secret History of the IRA* (London: Allen Lane, 2002), pp. 21–22; Tony Geraghty, *The Irish War* (London: HarperCollins, 1998), pp. 192–203; Marc Mulholland, "Irish Republican Politics and Violence before the Peace Process, 1968–1994," *European Review of History* 14: 3 (2007), pp. 409–414.

26. *Irish Times*, March 11, 1994.

CHAPTER 17

FAMINE

Ciara Boylan

THE GREAT FAMINE (1845–1852) WAS one of the most convulsive events in modern Irish history. An ecological shock on an exceptional scale, it resulted in the deaths of one million people and the loss of a further one and a quarter million through emigration, generating extensive economic and social changes. If the Famine was calamitous in historical terms, it has proven controversial in historiographical terms. One of the more notable aspects of Irish historical scholarship is the relative paucity of academic research on the Famine for much of the twentieth century.[1] The appearance of a number of works in the 1980s heralded something of a scholarly awakening, though what followed in the 1990s was remarkable and unprecedented.[2] The 150th anniversary of the Famine in 1995 became the eye of a historiographical hurricane. Articles, monographs, lectures, and conference papers swirled around the sesquicentenary commemorations as though the storm had been building for years, waiting to be unleashed. The pace of publication has eased since the turn of the millennium, and recently some works have presented accessible overviews of the Famine drawing on this rich body of material.[3]

This apparent historiographical silence between the 1930s and the 1980s is often interpreted as reflecting the ascendancy of revisionism, which in its efforts to de-mythologize and undermine unreconstructed nationalist and popular histories, at times downplayed key events in the nationalist historical canon.[4] The sesquicentenary commemorations created an opportunity for the reintegration of the Famine as a central event in the historical narrative of modern Ireland and for its emergence as a discrete area of teaching and scholarship. Recent histories of the Famine have, by and large, attempted to navigate the choppy waters between the populist-nationalist view of the Famine as a callous and calculated British plot and a revisionist history that has been accused of inappropriate generosity and restraint when considering the British state's response to the crisis.

According to Margaret Crawford, but for the Great Famine, "it is doubtful that Ireland would be regarded as more famine-prone than other European countries."[5] Between 1300 and 1900 there were up to thirty cases of severe famine in Ireland, with episodes of famine and subsistence crises clustered in the first half of the fourteenth century, the first half of the seventeenth century, and the first half of the eighteenth century. Most instances of famine and food scarcity were caused by climatic conditions: bad weather resulting in crop failures. The other major precipitating cause was war. Though often part of European-wide episodes, Irish conditions could affect the severity of a subsistence crisis. One of the worst famine events to affect Ireland was the great northern European famine of 1315–1318 caused by three exceptionally wet years that resulted in massive and repeated crop failures. This event coincided with Edward Bruce's invasion of Ireland in the summer of 1315, which brought in its wake deliberate crop destruction and other disruptions that "must have ensured that Ireland experienced some of the most severe effects of the famine."[6] Overall, in Ireland as elsewhere, truly calamitous famines involved a set of extraneous factors—war, plague, or economic crashes—which turned scarcities into disasters.[7] The famine of 1740–1741, known as "Blaidhain an air" (the year of the slaughter), is worthy of particular mention, as it was the first potato crisis and the most devastating famine of the eighteenth century.[8] The loss of life may have been equal or proportionally greater than that of the Great Famine, with perhaps 12.5–16% of the population dying of famine-related causes.[9] The "gap in famines" between 1740 and 1845 noted by K. H. Connell in fact included a series of smaller famines or subsistence crises, and Ireland in this period broadly conformed to a pattern of gradual decline in food shortages and famines notable in England.[10]

In the midst of the numerous shortages of the eighteenth and early nineteenth centuries, the state developed a variety of relief strategies for dealing with food shortages.[11] These included embargos on grain exports, bounties on imports of grain, and the importation of corn sold at subsidized prices. Public works were also established as a relief mechanism during the subsistence crisis of 1816–1817, when a Relief Commission was established and public works designated as the key relief mechanism. During the crisis of 1821–1822 the public works program was extended and placed on a more permanent footing. Kinealy has concluded that "the period of scarcities before the Great Famine demonstrated a long history of state involvement in famine relief. This intervention took a variety of forms which were frequently innovative and effective."[12] Echoing this, Ó Gráda suggests that one reason famine deaths decreased over time was the increasing effectiveness of relief measures in the pre-Famine period.[13]

"WHAT HOPE IS THERE FOR A NATION THAT LIVES ON POTATOES?"

In the century before the Famine, Ireland underwent a period of explosive demographic growth.[14] A population of four million in 1790 had climbed to five million by 1800; it had reached seven million by 1821; and by 1846 it is estimated to have peaked at about 8.5 million.[15] Sharp regional variations existed, with increases that were more dramatic across parts of the west and northwest. Between 1815 and the Famine, the rate of Irish population growth was slowing down.[16] Emigration was an important factor here: about 1 million people left the country between 1821 and 1841. Again, there were important regional variations. Most notably, poorer western areas, those that would be worst affected by the Famine, continued to show high levels of growth. As Ó Gráda notes, "the [demographic] adjustment was most radical where it was least needed."[17] Ireland's population may have expanded rapidly, but was the country overpopulated and hurtling toward an inevitable Malthusian crisis? Contemporary historiography has argued convincingly that "the decades before the famine show clearly that increasing population pressure did not dominate the Irish economy. More was at work than just diminishing returns."[18] The vulnerabilities in the Irish economy lay elsewhere, most obviously in the reliance on one staple food.

The diffusion of the potato was both earlier and more extensive in Ireland than anywhere else in Europe.[19] From inauspicious beginnings as a seasonal garden crop in the seventeenth century by the early eighteenth century, the potato had become a winter food for the poorest in Munster, and after 1750 it became the full-year staple food of the poorest in all areas. The potato had certain advantages: "No other crop has such a high yield that it can afford sustenance to an entire family on such a small area of ground," while it is "virtually the only food that can be eaten exclusively all year round without leading to serious nutritional deficiency."[20] On the eve of the Famine, just less than three million people, or about one-third of the population, were almost entirely dependent on the potato for subsistence and up to one-third of the entire tillage area of Ireland was given over to potatoes. For the poorest section of society reliant on the potato, the average daily intake was more than 2 kilograms per man, woman, and child. To throw some comparative relief on these numbers, in France the daily potato intake was 165 grams in 1852, and in the Netherlands it was about 800 grams in the 1840s.[21] Moreover, the potato diet was dominated by one particular variety: the lumper, valued for its ability to produce high yields on marginal ground. The dependence was absolute. Other food outputs were either exported or priced too high for the rural poor: there was no food to trade down to in the event of a shortage.

Contemporary accounts of pre-Famine Ireland in official reports and the writings of visitors alike present a country mired in endemic poverty, with modernization and development hampered by an apparently entrenched backwardness and

chronic social instability. Recent work on the pre-Famine economy has complicated this narrative, pointing to various economic indicators ranging from income levels to comparative measurements of the physical height of the peasantry
in Ireland and elsewhere. In one summation, "by almost every measure of economic activity, such as average income, trade, consumption patterns, development
of banking and communications, steady if unspectacular progress was evident in
the 1830s and early 1840s."[22] However, the progress that was made did not affect
the population equally. The Poor Law Inquiry Commission reporting in 1836 calculated the number of individuals out of work and in distress during thirty weeks
of the year at 585,000, which, when estimated dependents were included, produced a total of 2,385,000 destitute poor. The commissioners, in rejecting a poor
law for Ireland, noted: "we see that the labouring class are eager for work, that
work is not there for them, and that they are therefore, and not from any fault of
their own, in permanent want."[23] As these figures suggest, Ireland's population
growth was concentrated on the lower end of the social scale. The potato and the
extensive practice of land subdivision together created the necessary conditions
for the existence (and growth) of a large and cheap workforce for Ireland's labor-
intensive tillage economy, producing grain as a cash crop for the British market.
At the pyramidal base of Irish society were about 300,000 cottier households and
more than 600,000 laborer households, and above them about 250,000 individual
smallholders on plots averaging about 20 acres.[24] Cottiers and laborers were paid
a "potato wage": they rented small subsistence plots on which they grew potatoes,
which they paid for with their labor. Rents were high in a land-hungry economy
with a rapidly increasing population. The prevailing conditions explain "the paradox of a rapidly expanding agrarian economy, co-existing with decreasing living
standards for a proliferating social base."[25] The Devon Commission, which in-
quired into Irish land occupation, described the plight of the Irish laborer:

> the agricultural labourer of Ireland continues to suffer the greatest privations
> and hardships ... he continues to depend on casual and precarious employment
> for assistance ... he is badly housed, badly fed, badly clothed, and badly paid for
> his labour.... We cannot forbear expressing our strong sense of the patient
> endurance which the labouring classes have generally exhibited under suffer-
> ings greater, we believe, than any other country in Europe.[26]

A recurring feature of such accounts was that Irish poverty was of "a special
and exceptional character"; that it was so widespread, chronic, and pernicious
that there was no comparable counterpart.[27] The other key motif of official and
contemporary accounts of the conditions in Ireland was the turbulence of the
country and the ever-present threat of a breakdown in social order. Conflict between competing economic interests—landlords and tenants; large farmers and
smallholders; and farmers, cottiers, and laborers—was frequent in the decades
before the Famine.[28] The lack of security was seen as a serious check on capital

investment, and much of the conciliatory politics of the period were directed at pacifying the country.

The challenge posed by Ireland's economic and social problems inspired a range of analyses and remedies, many of which revolved around the assimilation of Irish institutions to an English model.[29] The dominant prescription of classical political economists involved the introduction of large-scale capitalist farming based on the English model, central to which would be a reorganization of Irish landholding around the tripartite division of labor into landlord, large tenants, and wage laborers. More radical versions associated with Manchester School economics saw Ireland as a potentially very wealthy country if a "free trade in land" could be initiated to replace the privileged caste of Irish landowners with a set of agricultural entrepreneurs.[30] Irish landlords were often criticized by would-be reformers. Charged with the same carelessness, recklessness, and indolence as their tenants, in this paternalistic moral order they were often blamed for any equivalent failings on the part of their social inferiors. However, there was a strong political reluctance to interfere with the rights of property, despite evidence that many in the propertied class in Ireland were at worst negligent and exploitative, and at best inefficient. That Irish smallholders might challenge the rights of landlords and large tenants during periods of rural unrest was seen as evidence of Ireland's untutored lack of civilization and chronic social instability rather than as reflecting a logic of protest against exploitation. The state, for its part, legislated for a number of *ad hoc* expedients—a centralized police force, a Board of Public Works, and a national system of education among them—in response to what was seen as the exceptional circumstances of the country.[31] This tension between prescriptions based on assimilation and the imposition of English models of development and the necessary expedients of dealing with an intractable and exceptional country was thrown into sharp relief during the Famine in the response of the state.

"THEY *ARE* REALITIES, AND MANY OF THEM FEARFUL ONES"

The proximate cause of the Great Famine was the fungal disease *Phytophthora infestans*, known at the time as "blight."[32] Transported from the United States, where it had been present in previous seasons, the blight first appeared in Belgium in late June 1845 and spread from there across northern and central Europe.[33] It was first observed in Ireland on August 20 of that year by Dr. David Moore of the Botanic Gardens in Dublin's Glasnevin. At the time, all but one of the most influential botanists incorrectly diagnosed the disease as a kind of dry rot. Although the late arrival of the blight in 1845 limited its impact, approximately one-third of the potato crop was destroyed in that first season. The following year, the blight attacked early and savagely. In the summer of 1846, with fields of blackened stalks and rotten tubers emitting a putrid stench, the almost total destruction of the crop was assured. In August, Father Theobald Mathew recounted the speed with which the disease wreaked its destruction: "On the 27th of last month I passed from Cork to Dublin, and this doomed plant bloomed in all the luxuriance of an abundant harvest. Returning on the 3rd instant, I beheld, with sorrow, one wide waste of putrefying vegetation."[34] By the spring of 1846 reports were converging from all parts of Ireland warning of an imminent catastrophe: "The greater part of population subsisting on potatoes perfectly black, and which will shortly be consumed"; "Many out of provisions, having neither potatoes to eat nor potatoes for seed; numbers lying sick in fever, deprived of sustenance."[35] The potato acreage planted in 1847 was one-seventh of what it had been in 1846. The yield in 1847 was good, as weather conditions that summer did not favor the spread of blight. However, the blight struck severely for a second time in 1848, leading to a further reduction in 1849. To take a clear measure of the destruction of potato yields: in 1844 a total of 2.4 million acres were sown, producing a crop of about 15 million tons. In 1845, the blight cut this to approximately 10 million tons. In 1846 this was cut catastrophically to less than 3 million tons of edible potatoes. In 1847, the total crop was only 2 million tons, and in 1848 it was 3 million tons. Underlining the scale of the ecological shock, Peter Solar's analysis has concluded that the failures of 1845 and 1848 were "at the limits of actual experience," and the loss in 1846 was "far out of the range of actual or likely western European experience."[36]

The major cause of death was famine-related diseases like typhus, relapsing fever, and dropsy, rather than starvation.[37] Most parts of the country experienced the onset of epidemic fever in the winter and spring of 1846–1847. The social dislocation associated with the Famine—the movement of countless thousands across the countryside and into towns, cities, and ports in search of sustenance or escape; the neglect of hygiene; the overcrowding of displaced families and individuals in vacant cabins, workhouses, and jails; the intermingling of the infected, convalescent, and healthy at soup kitchens, public works, and food depots—all spread disease effectively. About one hundred fever hospitals had been established by the time of the Famine. Overrun, additional accommodation was provided in wooden sheds and tents often pitched on the grounds of the hospitals. However, in many parts of the country no medical institutions existed and so attempts were made to isolate the infected in "fever huts," mostly "wretched structures of mud or stone which were hastily thrown up at the side of a road, the corner of a field, or the edge of a bog."[38] Others were quarantined at home, though any such procedure was made very difficult in the one-room cabins of the poor, where the infected were placed at one end of the house.

The workhouses, of which there were 118 on the eve of the Famine, began to fill up through 1846. By the end of 1846 more than half were full and were refusing further admittance; by spring 1847 three-quarters were full. The overcrowded and unsanitary conditions in the workhouses were highly conducive to the spread of disease, and mortality rates were high.[39] If people were not flocking to the workhouse, they were crowding onto emigrant ships. By "Black '47" emigration had become a flight of refugees. Conditions on the notorious "coffin ships" were appalling:

> Hundreds of poor people, men, women, and children, of all ages ... huddled together, without light, without air, wallowing in filth, and breathing a fetid atmosphere, sick in body, dispirited in heart; the fevered patients lying between the sound.... The supply of water, hardly enough for cooking and drinking, does not allow washing. In many ships, the filthy beds, teeming with all abominations, are never required to be brought on deck and aired.[40]

The nightmare of Grosse Île—fourteen thousand emigrants trapped in quarantine on a grim battery of ships stretching down the St. Lawrence, the dead lying among the living for days on board—and the appalling death toll of twenty thousand became emblematic of the worst horrors of Famine emigration. The combined mortality of the coffin ships to North America came to just under fifty thousand.[41] However, nearly all of the two million who emigrated between 1845 and 1855 survived their journeys.

Compounding the exodus were the mass evictions or "clearances" of the Famine years. Driven by default of rents, a desire to evade poor rates, and a recognition that the future of Irish agriculture lay not in labor-intensive tillage but in pasture farming on large consolidated farms, landowners and large tenants ejected tens of thousands of cottiers and smallholders. If some landlords assisted tenants to emigrate, these were the exception. Estimates for evictions vary considerably, but they soared in 1847, peaked in 1850, and remained at a high level for 1851 and 1852. Constabulary records indicate that 48,740 families were permanently dispossessed between 1849 and 1854, amounting to about 250,000 individuals.[42] The full figure is undoubtedly much higher, and Donnelly concludes that from 1846 to 1854, the number of people evicted from their holdings almost certainly exceeded half a million.[43]

No macro-analysis can capture the scale or intensity of the human misery wrought by the Famine, which becomes apparent in contemporary accounts recorded by relief workers, newspapers, clergymen, and medical professionals. To take one example, William Bennett, a Society of Friends worker, described conditions in County Mayo, Belmullet, in March 1847:

> We entered a cabin. Stretched in one dark corner, scarcely visible from the smoke and rags that covered them, were three children huddled together, lying there because they were too weak to rise, pale and ghastly; their little limbs, on removing a portion of the filthy covering, perfectly emaciated, eyes sunk, voice gone, and evidently in the last stage of actual starvation.... On some straw,

saddened upon the ground, moaning piteously, was a shrivelled old woman, imploring us to give her something.... We entered upwards of fifty of these tenements. The scene was invariably the same.... They did but rarely complain. When we enquired what was the matter, the answer was alike in all: "Tha shein ukrosh" [we are hungry].[44]

"GOD GRANT THAT WE MAY RIGHTLY PERFORM OUR PART"

Despite some very notable examples of intervention, in general the response of the state to Famine relief was characterized by a reluctance to interfere in the Irish economy.[45] The circumscribed level of state intervention has been explained by reference to a complex nexus of opinions, tenets, and doctrines, the most important of which were an adherence to the assumed dictates of classical political economy, in particular the doctrine of laissez-faire; a providentialist belief that the Famine represented an act of Divine will; prejudicial views on the moral failings of Irish landlords and tenants alike; and a perception that the Famine represented an opportunity to accelerate economic and social regeneration in Ireland. Repeatedly aired concerns over the sanctity of the operations of the free market were voiced alongside warnings that a country already suffering from a severe want of industry and self-reliance might be corrupted and debased even further by the provision of gratuitous and profligate relief. As such, it was not merely the objective laws of the market that had to be obeyed, but the particulars of Irish conditions.

The first set of relief measures was undertaken by the Conservative government of Robert Peel, which held office from the first appearance of the blight until June 1846. Drawing on considerable Irish experience, Peel's cabinet recognized the imminent dangers of a potato failure in Ireland and acted promptly. A special relief commission was appointed in November 1845 to coordinate the efforts of local relief committees throughout the country. These numbered about 650 by August 1846. The relief initiatives focused on two main objectives: controlling food prices and the provision of employment. Providing employment on public works was, as noted, an established response to food shortages, though on this occasion it was organized on a larger scale. In the case of schemes organized by the Board of Works, half the cost was covered by a government grant, the other half was to be repaid by local landowners as "country cess" over a period of years. Relief schemes were also organized by local committees, and here the government provided a loan to cover the cost. An estimated 140,000 people found work on relief schemes in the first distressed season.

To control price inflation, a stock of maize (Indian corn) worth £100,000 was secretly purchased in November 1845. This arrived in Ireland in early 1846 and was parceled out to food depots. Between March and June 1846, as growing distress sparked food and employment riots, special food depot operations began. Concerned about excessive interference in the food market, the Treasury—headed by that most vigilant of political economists, Charles Trevelyan—issued regulations governing the depots. Local committees were only to purchase food from the depots once food prices began rising in the area. Committees were to sell the food at cost price and were only to distribute it free to the unemployable, when the local workhouse was full. Peel, showing no small amount of political opportunism, used the Famine to set about repealing the Corn Laws, in the process splitting the Conservative party. To some extent, this measure was based on a genuine hope that the Irish might be weaned from the potato on to alternative foodstuffs.[46]

The policies of the Peel government attracted growing criticism. There were concerns over the apparent reluctance of the Irish landed class to meet their share of the costs and complaints that landlords were exploiting the public works to improve their estates at the expense of the Exchequer and that abuses of administration were resulting in landlords overlooking the most deserving in favor of their own tenants. A growing perception was that the relief policies in the first year had been overly generous. Appeals from O'Connell and others to temporarily suspend grain exports were ignored by Peel and his successors in office. The image of ships leaving Ireland laden with grain at a time of severe food shortages became, in the nationalist imagination, an emotive symbol of what John Mitchel described as "a nation perishing of political economy." Exports undoubtedly augmented the privations of the "starvation winter" of 1846–1847, particularly in the most destitute areas, but an embargo "could have served only as a temporary device to win time," and ultimately the enormous shortfall created by the decimation of a crop that was providing 60% of the nation's food needs on the eve of the Famine could not have been filled by means of an export embargo.[47]

In June 1846 John Russell's Whig government came to power, inaugurating a notably different phase of Famine relief marked by a much more doctrinaire adherence to the principles of political economy. Peel's special relief commission was wound up and its powers transferred to central government, and the Board of Works was relaunched under much more official scrutiny, reflecting a change in the center of gravity of relief provision. Under pressure from grain merchants, the importation of maize was discontinued by the government as an unnecessary interference in the food trade. A Treasury minute from August 1846 noted the need to "keep in check, as far as possible, the social evils incident to an extensive system of relief."[48] Although food depots with additional stocks would be retained, new rules were applied. For example, food from the depots was to be sold at market value rather than cost price, as had been the case previously. In the event, the purchase of a limited quantity of maize was unavoidable, but the government was slow in purchasing supplies, and compliance with the litany of administrative conditions laid down meant that it was close to Christmas before many depots began to operate, by which time many individuals had already starved in the west.[49]

The provision of employment through a reorganized public works scheme became the principal relief measure in the second half of 1846. Two changes from the earlier operation of the public works give an indication of the new orthodoxy. First, the works were now to be funded exclusively by property owners in the distressed districts (half directly by local taxpayers and the other half indirectly by government loans). Second, while Peel's administration had focused on productive works—principally on roads and drainage schemes—the Whigs showed a much greater concern with the dangers of individual profiteering, and cesspayers were expected to support works of little investment value. Despite the enormous outlay of £5 million in 1846–1847, the works were a failure by almost every measure. Wages, often required to support entire families, were paid in accordance with the exertions of the laborer, which—though rationalized as a stimulus to hard work—in the winter of 1846–1847 was tantamount to punishment for those most in need. The more malnourished the worker, the less his wages would be. Wages were often delayed, and with grain prices rising to double the normal average in early 1847, were insufficient. Weakened and malnourished, workers began to die in large numbers on the works in early 1847. The major problem was one of scale: the Board of Works felt able to cope with 100,000 laborers. In October 1846, there were 250,000 on the scheme, and in March 1847 this number had reached 714,390.

By the end of 1846 it had been decided to wind up the works and resort to an emergency provision of direct relief in the form of soup kitchens. Aside from the evident failures of the public works, the cost was becoming prohibitive. Soup kitchens were in operation in almost every poor law union by the summer of 1847. In August, three million people were receiving daily rations of "stirabout" porridge of maize, rice, and oats, the vast majority gratis. This has been judged a remarkable achievement; proof that the Victorian state was possessed of a bureaucratic and administrative armory of considerable power, which in this case was deployed to full effect. Nonetheless, the soup kitchens had never been intended as anything other than a temporary emergency measure. From autumn 1847 responsibility for relief was unburdened on an amended Irish poor law. The Poor Law Amendment (Ireland) Act introduced, for the first time, outdoor relief for certain classes of paupers and for the "able-bodied" poor, provided the workhouses were full. As a concession to landlords, an amendment known as the "Gregory Clause" was also introduced, excluding anyone on a holding of more than one quarter of an acre from relief, an adjunct that became a further agent of eviction and clearance.

The Poor Law Amendment Act was in large measure seen as an act of popular justice directed against an Irish landed class who were deemed by their many British critics to have been "so neglectful of their duties and so oppressive over many generations that they had created the conditions that led to the famine."[50] The progress of the Famine saw popular opinion crystalize around a set of assumptions about the Irish character, with *The Times* noting in March 1847 the difficulty of the challenge facing the British government in Ireland: "We have to change the very nature of a people born and bred from time immemorial in inveterate indolence, improvidence, disobedience, and consequently destitution."[51] By 1847 a mythology of British sacrifice and Irish intransigence had been established in the British consciousness, a fact reinforced by the Young Ireland rebellion of 1848. The increased visibility of Irish paupers streaming—ragged and infected—from emigrant ships into the great British cities seemed to propel opinion toward a solution that transferred responsibility for relief onto Irish landowners. An editorial in the *Liverpool Mail* from January 1847 gives an impression of the prevailing attitudes:

> We think the parish authorities have evinced a proper degree of forbearance in allowing the innumerable swarms of Irish beggars to infest the streets of Liverpool so long. But there is a limit to everything.... Instead of having the pride or the honesty to maintain their own poor, as the poorest parish in England does, [the Irish gentry] export them in ship-loads to prey upon the humanity of this country.... Give these beggars, we therefore say, a loaf of bread and send them home.[52]

It was in this context that *Punch* began advocating a complete reliance on a reformed Irish Poor Law, whereby Ireland would be left to "shift for herself for a year."[53] It was argued that the recourse to the poor law would operate as a forcible agent of modernization: in Gray's words, "a coercive stick to force Irish landowners into developmental expenditure, and to facilitate the bankruptcy and replacement of those who could not or would not comply with their developmental vision."[54]

The results were that the workhouses were rapidly overrun, and the numbers seeking outdoor relief swelled.[55] By 1848, 800,000 destitute people were receiving "outdoor" relief, and by September 1849, 250,000 were receiving "indoor" relief in the workhouses. Local ratepayers, or at least their representatives on the local poor-law committees, introduced cost-saving measures that undoubtedly increased suffering and mortality rates. Rations issued to those in the workhouse or on outdoor relief were often minimal, while some were denied relief on the slightest pretext. In May 1849 a "rate in aid" measure was passed, imposing a tax on the entire country and permitting the Poor Law Commission to transfer levies from wealthier districts to the more distressed western and southern unions; in 1850 the Treasury provided a loan of £300,000 to bail out indebted unions.

An Encumbered Estates Court was established in 1849. The aim was to initiate a "free trade in land" by speeding up the sale of encumbered states and thereby introducing of a new class of entrepreneurial landlord to Ireland. In the event, only a small number of capitalistic British investors took over Irish estates. Most were sold to existing gentry families seeking to clear debts and extend their holdings. Though it has often been assumed that many landlords were forced by Famine pressures of reduced rents and increased poor rates to unload their estates, most of the estates transferred through the Court were heavily indebted before 1845, and in this sense the Famine acted as catalyst in getting rid of landlords who were already doomed.[56]

The relief efforts of both the Peel and Russell administrations were bounded by a belief that the "natural" laws of the market ought to prevail if at all possible, and by 1847 it had become official policy to allow the Famine to "run its course." What bolstered this stance was not only interpretations of the tenets of political economy or vexations over the moral failings of the Irish noted above. Providentialism, an evangelical faith in the machinations of God in the affairs of humans and the market, exerted a profound influence on the shaping of the state's responses to the Famine.[57] As an eschatological framework of understanding, providentialism allowed for various interpretations. In the premillennial worldview of the more extreme wing of evangelicalism, the Famine was interpreted along sectarian lines as a chastisement directed at Catholics or at the British people for an overtolerance of Catholicism reflected in the granting of Catholic emancipation and the increase to the Maynooth seminary endowment in 1845. A more prevalent reading, Gray notes, interpreted the visitation as "a warning against personal and national pride and extravagance," a view that the state appeared to endorse with its "national day of fast and humiliation" held in 1847.[58] However, without being wedded to a more robust set of ideas, providentialism may not have influenced government policy to a significant degree. For high-ranking politicians and civil servants—including Peel, Russell, Charles Wood, George Grey, and Charles Trevelyan—providentialism combined with Christian political economy to create a potent ideological mixture. The result was a moralistic reading "that put the blame for the state of Irish society squarely on the moral failings of Irishmen of all classes."[59] Politicians bounded by this interpretation often cautioned against intervention on the grounds that only the suffering and atonement of the Irish people could bring salvation from this act of divine justice and reprobation.

The argument that either nature or an all-encompassing providence had delivered a unique opportunity for Irish economic and social regeneration was expressed by many of these same politicians and civil servants. Allowing the Famine to "run its course" was viewed as the most effective means of facilitating the long-term improvement of Irish society. In 1848, assuming the Famine to have ended, Trevelyan published his apologia for the government's Famine policy, *The Irish Crisis*. "Unless we are much deceived," he surmised, "posterity will trace up to that famine the commencement of a salutary revolution in the habits of a nation long singularly unfortunate, and will acknowledge that on this, as on many other occasions, Supreme Wisdom has educed permanent good out of transient evil."[60] Signs of improvement were not wanting: "the cultivation of corn [grain] has to a great extent been substituted for that of the potato"; "conacre [the "potato ground" leased by cottiers and laborers], and the excessive competition for land, have ceased to exist"; "the small-holdings, which have become deserted, owing to death, or emigration ... have, to a considerable extent, been consolidated with adjoining farms"; and "the much-desired change in ownership of land appears also to have commenced."[61] In effect, by eliminating Ireland's surplus population, destroying dependence on the potato, and shocking the population into recognizing the importance of self-reliance and the benefits of industry, the Famine had made possible a reform of Irish agriculture without the need for extensive government intervention. The idea that Ireland was undergoing a savage, punitive, but necessary regeneration provided ample support to those committed to a policy of limited intervention.

"A DEEP SYMPATHY WAS AROUSED"

Though precise figures relating to private charitable donations are difficult to calculate, it has been estimated that private contributions from all sources amounted to about £2 million.[62] When it is considered that the state expended just over £10 million, half of which was in the form of loans, the importance of private charity becomes clear.[63] Various charitable organizations were set up in response to the Famine, the most important of which were the General Central Relief Committee for All Ireland, the British Association for the Relief of Distress in Ireland and Scotland, and the Central Relief Committee of the Society of Friends.[64] Worthy of particular mention are the efforts undertaken by the Society of Friends, which established its Central Relief Committee in Dublin in November 1846 to coordinate the work of local auxiliary committees already dispensing relief.[65] Quaker relief was remarkable for several reasons: the dedication of the relief workers, the absence of any attempts at religious conversion, and the deployment of the group's considerable business acumen and links to coreligionists in England and America.[66] The Society often targeted areas where no other assistance was available and notably plugged the gap between the winding up of public works and the opening of the government soup kitchens.

In both folk memory and nationalist reconstructions, landlords have been condemned for their heartlessness during the Famine. In reality, the response of landlords varied greatly. The efforts of landlords in providing relief included the establishment of private soup kitchens, the importation of grain, rent reductions, and the provision of employment.[67] Some landlords also engaged in schemes of assisted emigration, though here they might find themselves castigated for attempting to export "the culled stock of his human farmyard" or denounced by Catholic clergy for deliberately ridding the country of Catholics.[68] The role of landlords in the mass evictions during the later Famine years came to overshadow any benevolence shown to tenants.

Aid came from Britain, the United States, Canada, Australia, South Africa, Argentina, and India, and prominent figures like Queen Victoria, the sultan of

Turkey, the tsar of Russia, and the pope made personal donations. The response of impoverished groups with no obvious connection to Ireland, such as former Caribbean slaves and the Choctaw Nation of America demonstrated both the raw humanitarianism of the response as well as the global reach of the nightmare story of what was unfolding on the Irish land. The significant contributions raised in England disproved Peel's early fear that "There will be no hope of contributions from England for the mitigation of the calamity. Monster meetings, the ungrateful return for past kindness, the subscriptions in Ireland to Repeal rent and the O'Connell tribute, will have disinclined the charitable here to make any great exertions for Irish relief."[69]

By 1847, however, most of the funds had dried up. The premature declaration by the government that the Famine had ended ensured that much of the momentum behind the philanthropic exertions was lost and that the crisis did not garner the same level of attention from that point on. This decline in funding was also reflective of "famine fatigue," a mixture of hardened attitudes and impatience. The visible influx of fever-infected Irish migrants to both Britain and the United States from 1847 and the Young Ireland rebellion certainly had an impact on attitudes. A belief had also grown up that subscriptions were not reaching the distressed but had been used to assist ratepayers. Impatience that Ireland was not improving, despite the outpouring of generosity, was echoed in Russell's frustrated remarks to Clarendon in 1849 that the British people "have granted, lent, subscribed, worked, visited, clothed the Irish; millions of pounds worth of money, years of debate etc.—the only return is calumny and rebellion—let us not grant, clothe etc. any more and see what they will do."[70]

Clergymen of all denominations were active at parish level throughout the Famine.[71] Notwithstanding evidence of interfaith cooperation, old tensions and animosities flared around the administration of relief.[72] The "Second Reformation" of the 1820s, a concerted drive to convert the Catholic population, provided a context for much of this sectarian strife. Claim and counterclaim were hurled across the spiritual barricades. There were charges that "whichever ecclesiastical body had control of relief supplies, its priests or ministers would and did give help primarily to their own adherents."[73] Perhaps the most serious charge was that of "souperism," the accusation that Protestant clergy and relief workers were providing food relief to the desperate in exchange for conversion. Irene Whelan has argued that with the onset of the blight "a new wave of proselytism was unleashed which involved a more explicit and intense campaign of evangelisation."[74] That the Famine represented an opportunity in this regard was made clear in a statement by the General Reformation Society: "If ever there was a time for England to make a great effort for the evangelising of Ireland it is the present ... the great distress has softened the heart of the poor. A famine shows the poor Romanist the incapacity and tyranny of their priest and the humanity and integrity of the Protestant clergy."[75] Missions appeared in Connacht and elsewhere, and a vigorous new organization, The Society for the Irish Church Missions to the Roman Catholics, was founded in March 1849. Conversions did take place in 1848–1850, but the numbers never amounted to more than several hundred in areas where missionary activity was most intense.[76] Nonetheless, the counterattack by the Catholic Church when it came in the early 1850s, involving episcopal tours, parish missions, and the founding of convents and monasteries across the west, demonstrated the seriousness with which this conversion effort was treated.

"I THINK I SEE A BRIGHT LIGHT SHINING IN THE DISTANCE"

Although no part of the country escaped the miseries of those years, the impact of the Famine showed considerable regional and class variation.[77] The Famine wreaked its worst effects in those counties where dependence on the potato was greatest and land subdivision most acute; that is, the counties of the west and southwest. The laboring and cottier class, existing at subsistence level, were the main victims of Famine mortality. The cost of emigration was prohibitive for the very poorest, and as such emigrants were drawn mainly from the ranks of the smallholding class, who may have had some available savings or assets to sell for their passage. Various statistical indicators bear out the uneven class impact of the Famine. Overall, the labor force declined by 19.1% between 1841 and 1851, but although there were 14.4% fewer famers, there were 24.2% fewer laborers.[78]

The collapse in population had a significant impact on landholding, as farmers and landlords consolidated smaller holdings in the wake of death, evictions, and emigration. Holdings of 1–5 acres, which made up 45% of all landholdings in 1841, had dropped to 15.5% of the total in 1851. In contrast, holdings of more than 30 acres had risen from 7% to 26% over the same period.[79] With the elimination of potato plots, the dominance of the potato in the Irish diet was broken: yields were almost half their pre-1845 level in the 1860s and 1870s.[80] It was in this context that the class of large tenant farmers came to consolidate their economic position and loom large over the economic, political, and social life of post-Famine Ireland. Although it has been argued that the move from pasture to tillage farming was under way before 1845, the loss of the large labor force that had sustained tillage in effect forced landowners into the consolidation of holdings and the creation of large pasture farms. The argument that much of the post-1850 economic adjustment would have taken place regardless of the Famine—that the Famine merely accelerated processes already under way— has not held up to the scrutiny of more recent findings, which argue instead that the Famine represented a watershed in nineteenth-century Irish economic history.[81]

Emigration had been an important feature of the Irish economy before 1845, and in this sense the Famine did accelerate existing trends. However, the Irish attitude toward emigration was transformed and a new demographic dynamic created by the exodus of those years. What had been a last-resort option before the Famine became a viable and readily applicable recourse for the poor. The large Famine emigration, concentrated in a small number of countries and cities, created networks and support mechanisms for those who followed. The Famine therefore did more than simply accelerate existing demographic trends: large-scale emigration became a permanent feature of the Irish economy, which, when combined with increased rates of late marriage, resulted in long-term population decline. Although the Irish language had been in decline before the Famine for a number of reasons, the Famine nonetheless dramatically accelerated this process by removing more than one million Irish speakers through death or emigration. In 1845 about half the population could speak Irish; by 1851 this had dropped to 23%.[82]

The Repeal movement collapsed in the face of the Famine and the death of O'Connell in 1847.[83] By exposing the inequalities of the Irish land system, the Famine did much to fuse the land question into nationalist politics. In the immediate post-Famine period, land politics revolved around calls for the legalization of the "3 Fs"—fair rents, fixity of tenure, and free sale—more commonly known as the "Ulster Custom." This was the basis on which the Tenant League was founded in 1850, and it had some electoral success with the Independent Party. However, the party had collapsed by 1859, while the recovery of agricultural incomes in the mid-1850s put paid to the effective need for the League. There was an optimism during the 1850s that the Famine had, indeed, ushered in a new era of prosperity. However, a series of poor harvests from 1859 to 1864, accompanied by falling prices, reduced living standards, the outbreak of disease, and increased emigration, shook this earlier optimism, though it did not lead to any collective action. Though the Fenian movement of the 1860s did not prioritize land issues, Gladstone's Land Act of 1870, in legislating for a watered-down version of the Ulster Custom, aimed to negate nationalist influence. By conceding something to customary rights, the Land Act also reflected the evolution of British policy from one based on the imposition of English economic models to one that recognized the historicist principle that Irish circumstances (or exceptionality) required Irish solutions. In the later 1870s and 1880s, a sustained agricultural recession resulted in the politicization of the countryside under a new and organized political leadership, which attracted considerable funding from a Famine diaspora alarmed at the return of poor harvests and large-scale evictions.

CONCLUSION

Single convulsive historical events can become historiographical behemoths, incapable of domestication by the academy and unleashing their force across popular history writing, public commemoration, national politics, and popular culture. It is difficult at times to avoid a sense that the Famine has been burdened with a weight and a set of meanings that can serve as much to obscure as to illuminate our understanding of it. Much has been written about the way in which the Famine has been remembered.[84] Nationalist memory of the Famine was being formed even as the crisis unfolded, notably in the pages of the *Nation*, where certain motifs—in particular the export of food and mass evictions—emerged as representations of deliberate British policies of extermination; these themes resurfaced in the later writings of John Mitchel, Michael Davitt, and others.[85] The Famine became a potent symbol of the malevolence of British government, and the nationalist construction of the Famine, often myopic in its interpretation of events, was influential in fermenting and spreading anti-British hostility both in Ireland and among the diaspora community. Though academic history has done much to temper this version of events, it was nonetheless a visible component of the commemorations in the 1990s and continues to be espoused. The folk memory of the Famine has yet to be fully integrated into the narrative of the Famine, and if the contents of the Irish Folklore Commission Archive "give a vivid picture of a society both remembering and refusing to remember a harrowing catastrophe in its recent past," Niall Ó Ciosáin has at least suggested a way to approach sources that academic scholarship has tended to judge according to its own exacting standards of truth.[86] One of the lessons of the folk memory, as well as of the academic historiography, is that the experience and suffering of the Famine were not shared equally. Nonetheless, the idea of a collective Famine memory was popularized during the sesquicentenary commemorations by President Mary Robinson, among others, with some commentators alluding to the repression of a collective trauma. However, the validity of the collective memory thesis is questionable, as well as coming worryingly close to a form of cultural and political hijacking at times.[87]

If the Great Famine "brought the era of famines to a cataclysmic end," it is as well to reflect on the reasons that the events of 1845–1852 were, in world-historical terms, a major famine event.[88] The dependence on the potato of the mass of impoverished Irish laborers, cottiers, and smallholders was the key vulnerability. However, two factors served to render the shock, when it came, catastrophic. The first was the scale of the devastation: three years of failure—1845, 1846, and 1848—were either at the limits of or far out of the range of European experience.[89] Second, the Famine took place in a very severe and unforgiving ideological climate that ultimately, because of a fervent adherence to the "natural laws" of God and the market and a determination to force modernization on a recalcitrant nation, meant that relief measures were inadequate to the task facing them.

FURTHER READING

Two early (and contrasting) classics of Famine literature are R. Dudley Edwards and T. Desmond Williams, *The Great Famine: Studies in Irish History, 1845–52* (New York: New York University Press,1957) and Cecil Woodham-Smith's *The*

Great Hunger: Ireland, 1845–1849 (London: Hamilton, 1962). More recent accessible narrative accounts include James Donnelly, *The Great Irish Potato Famine* (Thrupp, Stroud: Sutton Publishing, 2001); Cormac Ó Gráda, *Black '47 and Beyond* (Princeton, NJ: Princeton University Press, 1999); Christine Kinealy, *This Great Calamity* (Dublin: Gill and Macmillan 1994); Ciarán Ó Murchadha, *The Great Famine* (London: Continuum, 2011); and Enda Delaney, *The Curse of Reason* (Dublin: Gill and Macmillan, 2012). Works by economic historians taking a cliometric approach include Joel Mokyr's *Why Ireland Starved* (London: Allen and Unwin, 1983) and Austin Bourke, *"The Visitation of God?"* (Dublin: Lilliput Press, 1993). The politics of the Famine, and an exposition of the influence of providentialism, are laid out in Peter Gray's *Famine, Land and Politics* (Dublin: Irish Academic Press, 1999). Edited volumes of essays contain a wealth of contributions covering all aspects of the Famine from potatoes to policy. The monumental achievement of *Atlas of the Great Irish Famine* (Cork: Cork University Press, 2012) edited by John Crowley, William J. Smyth, and Mike Murphy combines insightful essays with wonderful and informative illustrations and maps. Other key collections include Cormac Ó Gráda (ed.), *Famine 150* (Dublin: Teagasc and University College Dublin, 1997); Póirtéir (ed.) *The Great Irish Famine* (Cork: Mercier, 1995); Richard Hayes and Chris Morash (eds.), *Fearful Realities: New Perspectives on the Famine* (Dublin: Irish Academic Press, 1996). Comparative work on the Famine is contained in Cormac Ó Gráda, Richard Paping, and Eric Vanhaute (eds.), *When the Potato Failed* (Turnhout, Belgium: Brepols, 2007).

NOTES

1. Until the 1980s the main work of academic Famine scholarship was R. Dudley Edwards and T. Desmond Williams (eds.), *The Great Famine: Studies in Irish History, 1845–52* (New York: New York University Press, 1957).

2. See J. S. Donnelly, Jr.'s contributions to W. E. Vaughan (ed.), *A New History of Ireland, V, Part 1: Ireland under the Union, 1801–70* (Oxford: Clarendon Press, 1989), pp. 272–371; Cormac Ó Gráda, *The Great Irish Famine* (Dublin: Gill and Macmillan, 1989); Cormac Ó Gráda, *Ireland Before and After the Famine: Explorations in Economic History 1800–1925* (Manchester: Manchester University Press, c. 1988); Mary E. Daly, *The Famine in Ireland* (Dublin: Published for the Dublin Historical Association by Dundalgan Press, 1986); Joel Mokyr, *Why Ireland Starved: A Quantitative and Analytical History of the Irish Economy, 1800–1850* (London: Allen and Unwin, 1983)

3. See in particular: John Crowley, William J. Smyth, and Mike Murphy (eds.), *Atlas of the Great Irish Famine, 1845–52* (Cork: Cork University Press, 2012); Enda Delaney, *The Curse of Reason: The Great Irish Famine* (Dublin: Gill and Macmillan, 2012); and Ciarán Ó Murchadha, *The Great Famine: Ireland's Agony, 1845–1852* (London: Continuum, 2011).

4. For a discussion of this "silence," see Niall Ó Ciosáin, "Was There 'Silence' about the Famine?," *Irish Studies Review* 13 (Winter 1995–1996), pp. 7–10. For accounts of the historiography of the Famine, see Christine Kinealy, *A Death-Dealing Famine: The Great Hunger in Ireland* (London: Pluto Press, 1997), pp. 1–15; James S. Donnelly, Jr., "The Great Famine and Its Interpreters, Old and New," *History Ireland* 1: 3 (Autumn 1993), pp. 27–33; Cormac Ó Gráda, "Making History in the Ireland of the 1940s and 1950s: The Saga of the Great Famine," *Irish Review* 12 (Spring/Summer 1992), pp. 87–102.

5. E. Margaret Crawford, "Famine," in S. J. Connolly (ed.), The *Oxford Companion to Irish History* (Oxford: Oxford University Press, second ed., 2002), p. 194. For work on historic Irish famines see E. Margaret Crawford (ed.), *Famine: The Irish Experience* (Edinburgh: John Donald Publishers, 1989); and L. A. Clarkson and E. Margaret Crawford, *Feast and Famine: Food and Nutrition in Ireland, 1500–1920* (Oxford: Oxford University Press, 2001).

6. Mary C. Lyons, "Weather, Famine, Pestilence and Plague in Ireland, 900–1500," in Crawford (ed.), *Famine: The Irish Experience*, p. 42.

7. David Dickson, "The Other Great Irish Famine," in Cathal Póirteir (ed.), *The Great Irish Famine* (Cork: Mercier, 1995), p. 51.

8. For work on the 1740–1741 famine, see David Dickson, "1740–41 Famine," in Crowley, Smyth, and Murphy (eds.), *Atlas of the Great Irish Famine*, pp. 23–27; Dickson, "The Other Great Irish Famine," pp. 50–59; Michael Drake, "The Irish Demographic Crisis of 1740–41," *Historical Studies* 6 (1968), pp. 101–124.

9. Cormac Ó Gráda, *Ireland Before and After the Famine: Explorations in Economic History, 1800–1925* (Manchester: Manchester University Press, second ed., 1993), p. 3; Dickson, "The Other Great Irish Famine," p. 55.

10. K. H. Connell, *The Population of Ireland, 1750–1845* (Oxford: Clarendon Press, 1950); David Dickson, "The Gap in Famines: A Useful Myth?" in Crawford (ed.), *Famine: The Irish Experience*, pp. 96–111; Cormac Ó Gráda, *Black '47 and Beyond: The Great Irish Famine in History, Economy, and Memory* (Princeton, NJ: Princeton University Press, 1999), p. 231.

11. Dickson sees 1740–1741 as the beginning of this process, with fears of social disorder in particular prompting "the gradual extension of the state into preventive and emergency procedures when confronted by harvest failure and the threat of a re-run of 1740." Dickson, "The Other Great Irish Famine," p. 58. For an outline of the evolution of state relief mechanisms, see Kinealy, *A Death-Dealing Famine*, pp. 42–48.

12. Kinealy, *A Death-Dealing Famine*, p. 47.

13. Ó Gráda, *Ireland Before and After the Famine*, p. 5.

14. Quote in section head is from Charles Trevelyan, *The Irish Crisis* (London: Longman, Brown, Green and Longmans, 1848), p. 2.

15. William J. Smyth, " 'Mapping the People': The Growth and Distribution of the Population," in Crowley, Smyth, and Murphy (eds.), *Atlas of the Great Irish Famine*, p. 13.

16. Cormac Ó Gráda and Joel Mokyr, "Poor and Getting Poorer? Living Standards in Ireland before the Famine," in Cormac Ó Gráda (ed.), *Ireland's Great Famine: Interdisciplinary Perspectives* (Dublin: University College Dublin Press, 2006), p. 35.

17. Ó Gráda, *Ireland Before and After the Famine*, p. 8.

18. Mokyr, *Why Ireland Starved*, p. 64; Ó Gráda and Mokyr, "Poor and Getting Poorer?" p. 46.

19. Austin Bourke, *"The Visitation of God?": The Potato and the Great Irish Famine* (Dublin: Lilliput Press, 1993). For further work on the potato, see John Feehan, "The Potato Root of the Famine," in Crowley, Smyth, and Murphy (eds.), *Atlas of the Great Irish Famine*, pp. 28–37; David Dickson, "The Potato and Irish Diet Before the Famine," in Cormac Ó Gráda (ed.), *Famine 150: Commemorative Lecture Series* (Dublin: Teagasc and University College Dublin, 1997), pp. 1–27; Leslie Dowley, "The Potato and Late Blight in Ireland," in Ó Gráda (ed.), *Famine 150: Commemorative Lecture Series*, pp. 49–65.

20. Ó Murchadha, *Great Famine*, pp. 6–7.

21. Cormac Ó Gráda, "Ireland's Great Famine," in Ó Gráda (ed.), *Ireland's Great Famine: Interdisciplinary Perspectives*, p. 7.

22. Delany, *Curse of Reason*, p. 41.

23. *Third Report of the Commissioners for Inquiring into the Condition of the Poorer Classes in Ireland, with Appendix and Supplement*, Parliamentary Papers 1836 (43), XXX, p. 5.

24. Ó Murchadha, *Great Famine*, pp. 5–6.

25. Kevin Whelan, "Pre and Post-Famine Landscape Change," in Póirtéir (ed.), *Great Irish Famine*, p. 20.

26. *Digest of Evidence Taken before Her Majesty's Commissioners of Inquiry into the State of the Law and Practice in Respect to the Occupation of Land in Ireland, Part II* (Dublin: Alexander Thom, 1848), p. 1116.

27. Gustave De Beaumont, *Ireland: Social, Political, and Religious* (London: Belknap Press of Harvard University Press, 2006), p. 130.

28. See Maura Cronin, *Agrarian Protest in Ireland, 1750–1960* (Dublin: Economic and Social History Society of Ireland, 2012).

29. See R. D. Collison Black, *Economic Thought and the Irish Question, 1817–1870* (Cambridge: Cambridge University Press, 1960).

30. Peter Gray, "Ideology and the Famine," in Póirtéir (ed.), *Great Irish Famine*, p. 90.

31. Oliver MacDonagh, *Ireland: The Union and Its Aftermath* (London: G. Allen and Unwin, revised and enlarged ed. 1977), pp. 34–38, 42.

32. Quote in section head is from Asenath Nicholson, *Lights and Shades of Ireland* (London: William Tweedie, 1858), p. iii.

33. For the Irish experience of famine in 1845–1850 in a comparative European perspective, see Cormac Ó Gráda, Richard Paping, and Eric Vanhaute (eds.), *When the Potato Failed: Causes and Effects of the Last European Subsistence Crisis, 1845–1850* (Turnhout, Belgium: Brepols, 2007).

34. Father Theobald Mathew to Charles Trevelyan, August, 7, 1846 cited in *Correspondence, from July, 1846, to January 1847, Relating to the Measures Adopted for the Relief of the Distress in Ireland.* Board of Works Series. (London: Clowes and Son, 1847), pp. 3–4.

35. Reports included in letter from Sir Randolph Routh to Charles Trevelyan, July 31, 1846, cited in *Correspondence Explanatory of the Measures Adopted by Her Majesty's Government for the Relief of Distress Arising from the Failure of the Potato Crop in Ireland* (London: Clowes and Sons, 1846), p. 223.

36. Peter M. Solar, "The Great Famine Was No Ordinary Subsistence Crisis," in Crawford (ed.), *Famine: The Irish Experience*, pp. 114–118.

37. For an outline of the relationship between famine and fever in Ireland, see Laurence M. Geary, "Famine, Fever and the Bloody Flux," in Póirtéir (ed.), *The Great Irish Famine*, pp. 74–85. See also Laurence M. Geary, "What People Died of during the Famine," in Ó Gráda (ed.), *Famine 150*, pp. 95–109; and Cormac Ó Gráda, "Mortality and the Great Famine," in Crowley, Smyth, and Murphy (eds.), *Atlas of the Great Irish Famine*, pp. 170–179.

38. Geary, "What People Died of during the Famine," pp. 104–105.

39. For conditions in the workhouses during the Famine, see James S. Donnelly, Jr., *The Great Irish Potato Famine* (Thrupp, Stroud: Sutton Publishing, 2001), pp. 103–110.

40. Stephen de Vere's report on a voyage to Canada in spring 1847, cited in Noel Kissane, *The Irish Famine: A Documentary History* (Dublin: National Library of Ireland, 1995), p. 162.

41. Donnelly, *Great Irish Potato Famine*, p. 181.

42. Donnelly, *Great Irish Potato Famine*, pp. 139–140.

43. James S. Donnelly, "Mass Eviction and the Great Famine: The Clearances Revisited," in Póirtéir (ed.), *The Great Irish Famine*, p. 156.

44. "Report by William Bennett on Conditions in Co. Mayo, Belmullet, 16th of the Third Month, 1847," in *Transactions of the Central Relief Committee of the Society of Friends during the Famine in Ireland, in 1846 and 1847* (Dublin: Hodges and Smith, 1852), pp. 163–164.

45. Quote in section head is from Trevelyan to Monteagle, October 9, 1846, cited in Peter Gray, *Famine, Land, and Politics: British Government and Irish Society, 1843–1850* (Dublin: Irish Academic Press, 1999), p. 232.

46. Gray, *Famine, Land, and Politics*, pp. 115–116.

47. P.M.A. Bourke, "The Irish Grain Trade," *Irish Historical Studies* 20 (1976), p. 165. Bourke, *Visitation of God?*, p. 52. This question is also addressed with careful statistical analysis in Peter Solar, "The Great Famine Was No Ordinary Subsistence Crisis." For an alternative view, see Kinealy, *Death-Dealing Famine*, pp. 77–91.

48. Treasury minute regarding relief policy, c. August 21, 1846, cited in Kissane, *Irish Famine*, p. 49.

49. Gearóid Ó Tuathaigh, *Ireland before the Famine, 1798–1848* (Dublin: Gill and Macmillan, 2007), p. 190.

50. Donnelly, *Great Irish Potato Famine*, p. 92.

51. Cited in James S. Donnelly, Jr., "'Irish Property Must Pay for Irish Poverty': British Public Opinion and the Great Irish Famine," in Richard Hayes and Chris Morash (eds.), *Fearful Realities: New Perspectives on the Famine* (Dublin: Irish Academic Press, 1996), p. 74.

52. Editorial from *Liverpool Mail*, January 30, 1847, cited in Kissane, *Irish Famine*, p. 159.

53. Cited in Peter Gray, "British Public Opinion and the Famine," in Brendán Ó Conaire, (ed.), *The Famine Lectures* (Boyle: Cómhdáil an Chraoimbhín, 1995–1997), p. 91.

54. Peter Gray, *The Making of the Irish Poor Law, 1815–43* (Manchester: Manchester University Press, 2009), pp. 335–336.

55. For the operations of the poor law during the Famine, see Christine Kinealy, "The Role of the Poor Law during the Famine," in Póirtéir (ed.), *The Great Irish Famine*, pp. 104–122.

56. Cormac Ó Gráda and Andrés Eiríksson, "Bankrupt Landlords and the Irish Famine," in Ó Gráda (ed.), *Ireland's Great Famine: Interdisciplinary Perspectives*, pp. 48–62.

57. See Gray, *Famine, Land, and Politics*; Gray, "British Public Opinion and the Famine," pp. 77–106; Gray, "Ideology and the Famine," pp. 86–103.

58. Gray, "Ideology and the Famine," pp. 91–92.

59. Gray, "Ideology and the Famine," p. 92.

60. Trevelyan, *The Irish Crisis*, p. 1.

61. Trevelyan, *The Irish Crisis*, pp. 194–196.

62. Quote in section head is from *Transactions of the Central Relief Committee of the Society of Friends*, p. 31.

63. Christine Kinealy, *The Great Irish Famine: Impact, Ideology and Rebellion* (Basingstoke: Palgrave, 2002), p. 89.

64. For the operations of charitable organizations, see Christine Kinealy, *Charity and the Great Hunger in Ireland: The Kindness of Strangers* (London: Bloomsbury Academic, 2013); Christine Kinealy, "Potatoes, Providence and Philanthropy: The Role of Private Charity during the Irish Famine," in Patrick O'Sullivan (ed.), *The Irish World Wide: History, Heritage, Identity. Volume 6: The Meaning of the Famine* (London: Leicester University Press, 1997), pp. 140–171.

65. See Daly, *Famine in Ireland*, pp. 89–92. For more on Quaker relief during the Famine, see Helen Hatton, "The Largest Amount of Good: Quaker Relief Efforts," in Crowley, Smyth, and Murphy (eds.), *Atlas of the Great Irish Famine*, pp. 100–107.

66. Food shipments from the American Society of Friends provided almost two-thirds of all of their relief supplies. Daly, *Famine in Ireland*, p. 90.

67. Kinealy, *Great Irish Famine*, p. 65.

68. *Limerick and Clare Examiner*, cited in David J. Butler, "The Landed Classes during the Famine," in Crowley, Smyth, and Murphy (eds.), *Atlas of the Great Irish Famine*, p. 267.

69. Peel, cited in Kinealy, *Great Irish Famine*, p. 62.

70. Russell, cited in Kinealy, *Great Irish Famine*, p. 88.

71. For work on clergy during the Famine, see Donal Kerr, *The Catholic Church and the Famine* (Blackrock: Columba Press, 1996); Donal Kerr, *A Nation of Beggars?: Priests, People, and Politics in Famine Ireland, 1846–1852* (Oxford: Clarendon Press, 1994). For work on Presbyterian response to the Famine, see David W. Miller, "Irish Presbyterians and the Great Famine," in Jacqueline Hill and Colm Lennon (eds.), *Luxury and Austerity* (Dublin: University College Dublin Press, 1999), pp. 165–181. Detailed work on the response of the Church of Ireland, apart from the activity of evangelical missionaries, is still wanting.

72. Desmond Bowen, *The Protestant Crusade in Ireland, 1800–70: A Study of Protestant-Catholic Relations between the Act of Union and Disestablishment* (Dublin: Gill and Macmillan, 1978), pp. 177–192.

73. Bowen, *Protestant Crusade*, p. 185.

74. Irene Whelan, "The Stigma of Souperism," in Póirtéir (ed.), *Great Irish Famine*, p. 141.

75. Bowen, *Protestant Crusade*, p. 191.

76. Whelan, "Stigma of Souperism," p. 149.

77. Quote in section head is from Trevelyan to Monteagle, October 9, 1846, cited in Gray, *Famine, Land and Politics*, p. 232. For the regional variations in mortality and emigration rates, see Cormac Ó Gráda, "Mortality and the Great Famine," in Crowley, Smyth, and Murphy (eds.), *Atlas of the Great Irish Famine*, pp. 170–179; William J. Smyth, "'Variations in Vulnerability': Understanding Where and Why the People Died," in Crowley, Smyth, and Murphy (eds.), *Atlas of the Great Irish Famine*, pp. 180–198; William J. Smyth, "Exodus from Ireland—Patterns of Emigration," in Crowley, Smyth, and Murphy (eds.), *Atlas of the Great Irish Famine*, pp. 494–503.

78. Cormac Ó Gráda, "Famine, Trauma and Memory," in Ó Gráda (ed.), *Ireland's Great Famine: Interdisciplinary Perspectives*, p. 219.

79. Ó Tuathaigh, *Ireland before the Famine*, p. 184.

80. Ó Gráda, *Black '47*, p. 227.

81. See Kevin O' Rourke, "Did the Irish Famine Matter?" *Journal of Economic History* 51: 1 (1991), pp. 1–22.

82. Gearóid Ó Tuathaigh, "Language, Ideology and National Identity," in Joe Cleary and Claire Connolly (eds.), *The Cambridge Companion to Modern Irish Culture* (Cambridge: Cambridge University Press, 2005), pp. 42–58. Mairéad Nic Craith, "Legacy and Loss: The Great Silence and Its Aftermath," in Crowley, Smyth, and Murphy (eds.), *Atlas of the Great Irish Famine*, pp. 580–587.

83. For an account of politics during the Famine, see S. J. Connolly, "The Great Famine and Irish Politics," in Póirtéir (ed.), *Great Irish Famine*, pp. 34–49.

84. On the literature of the Famine, see Chris Morash, *Writing the Irish Famine* (Oxford: Oxford University Press, 1995); Margaret Kelleher, "Irish Famine in Literature," in Póirtéir (ed.), *Great Irish Famine*, pp. 232–247. For the Famine in visual culture, see Emily Mark-FitzGerald, *Commemorating the Irish Famine: Memory and the Monument* (Liverpool: Liverpool University Press, 2013). On commemoration, see: Cormac Ó Gráda, "Famine, Trauma and Memory," in Ó Gráda (ed.), *Ireland's Great Famine: Interdisciplinary Perspectives*, pp. 217–233; Peter Gray, "Memory and the Commemoration of the Great Irish Famine," in Peter Gray and Kendrick Oliver (eds.), *The Memory of Catastrophe* (Manchester: Manchester University Press, 2004), pp. 46–64; Niall Ó Ciosáin, "Famine Memory and the Popular Representation of Scarcity," in Ian McBride (ed.), *History and Memory in Modern Ireland* (Cambridge: Cambridge University Press, 2001), pp. 95–117.

85. See Seán Ryder, "Reading Lessons: Famine and the *Nation*, 1845–1849," in Hayes and Morash (eds.), *Fearful Realities*, pp. 151–163; Donnelly, *Great Irish Famine*, pp. 209–245.

86. Niall Ó Ciosáin, "Approaching a Folklore Archive: The Irish Folklore Commission and the Memory of the Great Famine," *Folklore* 115: 2 (2004), p. 224.

87. See Ó Gráda, "Famine, Trauma and Memory," p. 217.

88. Cormac Ó Gráda, *Famine: A Short History* (Princeton, NJ: Princeton University Press, 2010), p. 38.

89. Solar, "The Great Famine Was No Ordinary Subsistence Crisis," pp. 114–118.

CHAPTER 18

ECONOMY *in* INDEPENDENT IRELAND

Andy Bielenberg

W HEN THE IRISH FREE STATE was established, two conflicting views
were discernible among the new political elite. The prevailing view
was that the state's economic interests would be best served by the
maintenance of free trade and the traditional financial links with Great Britain,
which had been vitally important historically to both the Irish agricultural sector
and those engaged in trade and commerce more generally. In contrast, the aim to
achieve greater economic self-sufficiency and autonomy from Britain chimed well
with the prevailing views of revolutionary and cultural nationalism, and popular
support for this position was clearly articulated by the Fianna Fáil party (established in 1926), which quickly developed an effective opposition to the prevailing
views of the economic establishment. Protectionism had already featured strongly
in Arthur Griffith's writings, the leading advocate of economic nationalism prior
to independence.[1]

In this respect, one of the most significant aspects of the treaty signed in December 1921, from an economic perspective, was that the new state subsequently
acquired full fiscal autonomy from the United Kingdom, facilitating the adoption
of protectionism subsequently. But the expediency of introducing tariffs and protectionism was initially firmly rejected by the 1923 Fiscal Inquiry Report. The
whole issue was then put in the hands of a Tariff Commission, which introduced
very limited protection on specific items in the 1920s, which collectively made
little impact on the economy at large but had a major impact in specific sectors,
such as tobacco.

Broadly speaking, economic policy in the 1920s remained outward looking and
sought to exploit Ireland's comparative advantage in pastoral agriculture. The

maintenance of free trade was also supported by the larger export-oriented industrialists like Guinness stout, Jacobs biscuits in Dublin, or the Ford Motor Car Company in Cork, whose trade focused heavily on the British market. Despite a professed ideological commitment to laissez-faire, the Cumann na nGaedheal government did intervene in the economy for pragmatic reasons when it became clear that private-sector investment would not be forthcoming. The most dramatic example was the construction of the great hydroelectric station off the river Shannon at Ardnacrusha between 1925 and 1929 and the establishment of the Electricity Supply Board in 1927 to centralize and organize the supply and distribution of electricity through a national grid.[2] This was the first of a series of semi-state bodies that would have a significant impact on subsequent economic development. Another example of state intervention was the establishment in 1927 of the Dairy Disposal Company to cut down excess capacity in the creamery sector. Other examples of state intervention—such as land reform (notably the 1923 Land Act) and the activities of the Department of Agriculture—essentially followed enlightened reformist initiatives, which were already well under way prior to independence.[3]

When a major world recession hit in 1929, many countries erected tariffs to protect their industry and agriculture, and Cumann na nGaedheal began gradually to abandon its commitment to Free Trade.[4] When Fianna Fáil took office in 1932 a policy of full-scale industrial protectionism was implemented, and the government embarked on an "economic war" with Britain from July 1932, when it refused to pay the annual land annuities, which were paid to the British government under the terms of the Land Acts. The British reacted by putting heavy duties on Irish cattle imported to Britain. In retaliation, the Irish government placed heavy duties on British coal, cement, electrical goods, iron and steel manufactures, and sugar. The dispute was damaging, as 96% of Irish exports went to the United Kingdom and Free State cattle exports fell from £12.7 million in 1931 to £4.3 million in 1934.[5] Moves toward reconciliation in the economic war started in 1935 with the Coal-Cattle Pact, whereby coal and cattle were exchanged on a pound-for-pound basis. This led to some recovery in the cattle trade at least. The economic war finally came to an end in 1938 with the Anglo-Irish Agreement. Neville Chamberlain, in return for a lump sum of £10 million, agreed to waive all further British claims to Irish land annuities, while tariff restrictions were relaxed.[6]

The first Fianna Fáil government took a much more interventionist stance than their predecessors had done in the sphere of industrial development. Although agricultural output actually fell during the 1930s, Fianna Fáil had some success in expanding the industrial sector, in the short term at least. The Department of Industry and Commerce acquired the power to impose tariffs, of which there were already 1,900 in operation by 1936.[7] More semi-state companies were established, including the Irish Sugar Company in 1933, and by 1938 it produced 80% of domestic sugar demand, displacing imported cane sugar. Aer Lingus, the

Irish Tourist Board, Irish Life Assurance Board, Chemici Teo (which produced industrial alcohol), and the Irish Turf Board were all set up in the 1930s, in addition to an organization established for the purpose of extending credit to industrialists, the Industrial Credit Corporation. This public investment took place in areas where specific social goals were seen to be important for which no private investment was forthcoming; collectively these institutions created a more mixed economy. But overall, most of the development in the industrial sector during the 1930s was carried out by private companies, which were given favorable tariffs to reduce foreign competition.[8] After the first push for greater industrialization in the 1930s, the industrial sector failed to achieve significant growth.[9]

Forty-eight percent of the employed population in 1936 still worked in agriculture. Owing to the drop in prices, and the impact of the economic war, agricultural output declined by more than a third between the end of the 1920s and the mid-1930s.[10] The predominance of ailing small farms in a mostly rural economy could hardly provide the basis for a dramatic expansion of domestic consumption to drive industrial development in a relatively small market. At the extreme end of the spectrum, the literature of the Blasket Islands reminds us that a tenuous semi-subsistence–oriented lifestyle was still a reality for many in parts of the western seaboard.[11] But the more frugal comfort that the American anthropologists Arensburg and Kimball described on a small farm on County Clare was perhaps somewhat more typical of this extensive small-farm sector.[12]

During the interwar years, the performance of the Irish economy was poor by international standards. The decline in international trade in the 1930s was detrimental to an economy that was fundamentally unsuited to protectionism. The outbreak of the Second World War had significant negative implications for the Southern Irish economy, which had virtually no merchant marine, relying largely on British-owned vessels to sustain trade. This left Éire very much at the mercy of the British government, which took the view that they had no special obligations to their smaller neutral neighbor.[13] The reduction in shipping space on British ships available for Irish trade dramatically curtailed economic activity, creating the biggest crisis in the economy at any time since independence. The volume of exports to Britain from the Irish Free State was almost halved between 1938 and 1943, while imports fell by more than two-thirds.[14] It was in response to this crippling situation that Seán Lemass decided in 1941 to establish Irish Shipping to maintain essential supplies, most notably the wheat supply, which constituted the bulk of its cargoes for the rest of the war.[15] To make up for the shortfall in supplies, the Department of Supplies was given sweeping powers to control imports and exports, and the storage, movement, sale, and distribution of goods. In addition, the government placed a freeze on wages with the introduction of a trade union bill in 1941 and a wages standstill order. For the remainder of the war, prices rose considerably because of supply shortages, and consequently real living standards declined.

Trade restrictions also had serious implications for Irish agriculture during the war years. But arable farming was increased through compulsory tillage orders. To make up for the shortfall of imported maize and wheat, oats were grown as a substitute for maize for animal feed, and wheat acreages were considerably raised. The results of the war for the industrial sector were far worse. Ireland's dependence on Britain for industrial equipment and spare parts, raw materials, petroleum, and—most notably—coal became all too apparent, and industrial output experienced a significant decline.[16]

As the British war economy gathered momentum, enlistment and employment opportunities in the United Kingdom began to increase. Recent estimates suggest that up to 79,000 people from Éire served in the British forces during the war. Many more acquired employment in the UK war economy. In 1942 it was estimated that about £4.2 million was sent by those working in Britain to Ireland, and a figure as high as £12 million has been cited for the later part of the war.[17]

As a consequence of the restrictions imposed on all forms of motoring due to petrol shortages, the Great Southern Railway experienced a renaissance of sorts, but the network suffered from total dependence on supplies of coal from Britain (largely from Welsh pits), which were drastically reduced. Consequently, passenger services were cut to a minimum, but the railways became responsible for distributing whatever freight could move in the economy, notably grain, turf, beets, and other essential foodstuffs, in addition to whatever coal could be mined in Ireland. Under emergency-powers legislation in 1942, the state took control (but not ownership) of the railways. Although Britain restricted its supply of such essential commodities as coal, oil, phosphate, and wheat to Ireland, the British made various exemptions to secure such commodities as chocolate crumb, cement, or beer, but these industries required coal, so the railways, for example (and the particular industrial plants concerned), got more coal to produce or carry foodstuffs and other more essential commodities destined for Britain.[18] Bryce Evans argues convincingly that the Second World War marks the high watermark of centralized state intervention in independent Ireland, as the state struggled to moderate the economic impact of severe supply shortages.[19] Yet despite an outward appearance of rigidity, Ireland's neutrality was reasonably indulgent to the Allied cause in economic terms.

One of the outcomes of wartime fuel shortages was a desire for greater self-sufficiency in this area, and it was in this context that Bord na Móna was established by the government in 1946 to consolidate and mechanize turf production.[20] Ireland came out of the war with its commitment to self-sufficiency relatively intact. It had escaped the war relatively lightly, with minimum material damage and human losses, so economic recovery took place somewhat more rapidly than in most of Europe.

Ireland was one of the sixteen governments that met in Paris in July 1947 to form the Committee for European Economic Cooperation (CEEC). The purpose of the CEEC was to frame a joint response to the American offer of Marshall Aid, which was ultimately approved in the U.S. Congress in April 1948. In the same month, the CEEC participants, including Ireland, established a permanent organization in response to American legislation called the Organisation for European Economic Cooperation, the OEEC,[21] which later became the Organisation for Economic Cooperation and Development (OECD). While Ireland participated in the European Recovery Program, its European connections did not go much further than that.

Brian Girvin goes so far as to suggest that the 1948 Trade Agreement with the United Kingdom was far more important in economic terms than association with the OEEC and the Marshall Plan.[22] In contrast, Bernadette Whelan suggests the Marshall Plan's influence was more significant, because it provided a range of positive influences from outside Ireland that marked the beginning of a shift in traditional thinking about the economy. The European Recovery Program, she argues, contributed to modernizing the national budgetary mechanisms by encouraging greater capital expenditure, while the state's capacity for statistical analysis was also improved with the establishment of the Central Statistics Office. It also contributed to altering mind-sets in administrative circles, increasing exposure to American economic thinking. For Ireland, participation in the OEEC was also diplomatically highly important, particularly when Ireland left the British Commonwealth and became a Republic in 1949. Participation in the ERP led to a more positive phase in Anglo-Irish and U.S.-Irish relations while also increasing contact with a number of continental European countries.[23]

In relative terms, the Irish economy slowed to a snail's pace during the 1950s, at a time when the rest of the world economy was experiencing significant growth. Ireland's performance during the 1950s was among the worst in Europe. It has been estimated that between 1949 and 1956 real national income rose by only 8% at a time when the average increase in Europe was about 40%. This goes a long way to explaining why emigration from Ireland reached record levels by the mid-1950s.[24] In rural areas the increasing introduction of the tractor in agriculture[25] and rural electrification (which facilitated the greater application of milking machinery, for example) reduced the demand for labor, further contributing to the rising tide of emigration.

Despite the relatively poor performance of the economy between independence and the 1950s by European standards, several important initiatives were taken by the state in this period that would prove to be collectively significant for future development. The national electricity grid was established in the 1920s, and rural electrification got under way after the Second World War and had been partially completed by 1962, so a growing number of rural households had electricity, although many still had no running water. Only one household in eight in rural Ireland had running water at the beginning of the 1960s.[26] The development of the state's electricity infrastructure was a central feature of modernization. The consumer and media revolution that took place beginning in the 1960s would simply not have been possible without the completion of the national grid. The number of televisions in the state rose rapidly from about seven thousand in 1956 to about 450,000 by 1970, reflecting the growth of a far more consumer-oriented culture.[27] Gradual yet continual urbanization contributed to these developments; by 1971 those living in urban settings with a population of more than 1,500 accounted for more than 60% of the population.[28]

Another silent revolution (though as yet unheralded by economic historians) was the surfacing of the roads in the half century or more after independence. The adaption of roads to the needs of motorized cars and trucks was a long-drawn-out process that was critical for the expansion of intra-regional trade and greater commercialization. By 1930 only 5,000 miles of road had been surfaced. Slowly over the following decades improvements were made, so that by 1950 there were more than 14,000 miles surfaced, rising dramatically thereafter to 55,000 miles by the 1980s.[29] Yet Irish investment in roads still remained very low by European standards, even though that investment in automotive transport as a proportion of gross national product was relatively high by the mid-1970s. From the 1980s European Union (EU) transfers for road development helped increase the levels of capital investment.[30] From the late 1980s and during the 1990s increased development of motorways, such as the M50 ring road around Dublin—and more recently the gradual linking of all major cities by motorway—significantly advanced the quality and extent of the Irish road system.[31] The growth of car usage in the state from fewer than 10,000 in 1923 to almost 1.9 million by 2007 reveals the growing significance of motoring in Irish society and its increasing influence in both urban and rural contexts.[32]

In policy terms, the establishment of the Industrial Development Authority (IDA) in 1949 was to be very important in the longer term. In 1952 An Foras Tionscal (the Underdevelopment Areas Board) was established to promote industries in the west and southwest, which worked jointly with the IDA to promote indigenous industries in underdeveloped areas in the west. In 1952 Córas Tráchtála (the Irish Export Board) was also set up to help exporters improve their marketing with the view to boosting exports to North America. In 1956 the introduction of the Industrial Grants Act permitted the IDA to assist industrial undertakings all over the country. The single most important initiatives in attracting foreign enterprise in the longer term was the Export Profits Tax Relief Scheme of 1956, introduced by the interparty government, which gave a complete tax exemption for a period of ten years.[33] This act, pushed through by the Department of Industry and Commerce, was to be critically important for attracting multinationals subsequently. So while protectionism essentially continued protecting native industry, encouragement was also given to foreign companies engaged in exportation to invest in building plants in the Republic of Ireland.

A major turning point in state planning has generally been attributed to the publication in 1958 of T. K. Whitaker's report, *Economic Development*, which contained the basic outlines of an alternative, more outward-looking development plan to be implemented over a five- to ten-year period. Although the role of agriculture in Irish economic development still featured more strongly in this program, greater recognition was given to the role of industrial development and exports than in the past. When a new Fianna Fáil government took office in 1957, under the influence of Lemass, it extensively utilized Whitaker's document in the First Programme for Economic Expansion in 1958.[34] However, many of the elements of this reform process (most notably the Export Profits Tax Relief Scheme) predate this program, and indeed economic performance had already improved. Moreover, the government failed to pursue many of the strategies outlined,[35] so there are few grounds to support the widely held view that state planning, driven by Lemass and Whitaker, was responsible for the general upturn in the fortunes of the Irish economy from the late 1950s.

In 1961 Ireland sought membership of the European Community (EEC) for the first time, and even though this particular bid failed in 1963, and again in 1967, the objective of entry had been firmly set, and important groundwork was laid that convinced the existing members of the EEC that Ireland was a credible candidate. The positive performance of the economy during the 1960s, as tariffs were reduced and outside influences and connections multiplied, significantly increased confidence in the capacity of the economy to survive on a wider European stage, and the Republic of Ireland finally joined the EEC in 1973, which marked the opening of a new chapter in Irish economic history. When Ireland entered the Common Market, foreign policy became far more centered on issues of trade; entry fundamentally altered the conditions of trade, which subsequently transformed the relative performance of the Irish economy.

The gains for farmers from entry were substantial, even though net agricultural output actually fell between 1972 and 1978. The price of agricultural produce trebled during this period, keeping well ahead of the cost of living. Land prices also trebled between 1972 and 1978, reflecting the growing confidence in agriculture. The impact of the European Common Agricultural Policy (or CAP, as it was known) was greater than in any other member state. By the late 1970s transfers resulting from the CAP averaged an equivalent of about 4% of the Republic's gross domestic product (GDP).[36]

EEC entry brought farmers and the government closer together, as both had a vested interest in maximizing subsidies from Brussels. Eighty-one percent of all EEC funding for Ireland in the 1970s went to agriculture, benefiting capital-intensive large farmers and dairy producers in particular. The CAP lead to a five-fold increase in milk prices, for example, while access to the French market from 1978 dramatically improved the prospects for Irish sheep farmers.[37] The CAP was committed to intensive commercial farming, which ultimately altered the nature of Irish agriculture and the social landscape of rural Ireland, broadly favoring the interests of large productive farmers over small farmers. Initially the major impact of EEC entry on the profile of agriculture was that it increased cattle and milk production, which collectively accounted for about 75% of gross agricultural output by 1980. The agri-based industries connected with milk and meat processing increased significantly as a result of EEC entry, performing well in the international market with the emergence of a number of Irish food companies of international significance. This trend has continued to the present day. Exports by 1988 accounted for about 65% of Irish agricultural output.[38]

By the mid-1980s CAP was absorbing 70% of the EEC budget, which was out of line with the economic and social significance of agriculture in the EEC population in terms of the numbers engaged in farming. The imposition of quotas in 1984 on milk production put the brakes on the most dynamic sector in Irish agriculture. Under the guidance of the MacSharry reforms, environmental considerations also brought further restrictions in Irish agriculture. Nonetheless, productivity in farming and agri-based industries rose in the 1990s, making some contribution to the boom. Agri-based industries, notably food processing, remained the most significant indigenous development in the manufacturing sector as a whole.

The contraction in the numbers engaged in farming continued. By 2011, the numbers engaged in agriculture had fallen to a mere 4.7% of the total labor force (see table 18.1). This phenomenon is common in all industrializing countries, as a whole range of new, productivity-raising inputs are applied to agriculture, such as larger and more powerful machinery, improved seed varieties, chemicals, pesticides, and fertilizers. Income and output in farming has become ever more concentrated in the large farm districts, in areas with good land that have been more amenable to restructuring and rationalization, and where the benefits of new technologies and higher capital inputs are easier to reap.

By the late 1990s, the total average income of farm households was above the national average. But subsidies were also a big factor in improving relative living standards. The influence of subsidies on farm incomes is evident from the fact that EU direct payments as a percentage of total farm incomes rose from 22% in 1992 to almost 70% in 2002, and in particular sectors, such as beef, sheep, and cereals, it was even higher than this.[39] There had also been a notable scaling up in terms of average farm size from 26 to 31 hectares between 1991–2000, while the number of farms in this period declined by 17%. The number of dairy farms has decreased even more spectacularly, from more than 86,000 in 1984 (before quotas were introduced) to only 25,000 by 2005. EU subsidies are no longer going predominantly to agriculture. By 2003 agriculture took only 45% of EU subsidies coming into the state, so it had become relatively less important than it had been in the decades after entry. However this was still a large amount of money,

Year	Agriculture share of total employment	Industry share of total employment	Services share of total employment
1926	51.8	14.5	33.7
1936	48.0	15.4	36.6
1946	46.0	14.7	39.3
1951	40.5	19.1	40.4
1961	35.7	24.2	40.1
1966	31.1	26.9	42.0
1971	25.8	29.9	44.3
1981	15.9	32.6	51.5
1983	16.8	29.4	53.8
1986	15.5	28.8	55.7
1989	15.0	28.0	57.0
1992	13.6	27.8	58.6
1995	11.5	27.9	60.6
1998	9.0	28.7	62.3
2001	7.1	28.9	64.0
2004	6.4	27.6	66.0
2007	5.1	26.9	68.0
2009	5.0	20.9	74.1
2011	4.7	18.6	76.7

Sources: Central Statistical Office Ireland (CSO) census data, available at http://www.cso.ie/en/census/index.html; CSO Statistical Abstracts, available at http://www.cso.ie; CSO Statistical Yearbook (Dublin: CSO, 2002, 2008, 2012).

and larger farmers living in the wealthier agricultural areas remain the major beneficiaries.[40]

Although a small minority of the Irish rural population now worked in farming, the food industry remained the largest Irish-owned industry in the economy in 2006, when farming and agri-based industries taken together employed 9% of the total workforce and accounted for about 10% of GDP. The food industry still accounted for 55% of Irish-owned exports.[41] Farmers, who dominated Irish society at independence, have become merely a small minority group, but in contrast to other minorities, they still have a powerful voice due to their tradition of mobilization, their institutional presence with a department in the administration, and the economic significance of agriculture historically. The continuous contraction and erosion of the agricultural population has been one of the central stories of the social and economic history of independent Ireland. Yet Matthews makes the important point that agriculture and forestry still account for 70% of the land area and thus continue to shape the landscape and environment of rural Ireland, remaining the "most substantial contributor to the economic and social viability of rural areas."[42]

The modern industrialization of the Irish Republic got under way in the 1960s, effectively making it one of the late industrializing countries of Europe. The decade was characterized by a less restrictive fiscal stance and a commitment to more outward-looking policies. Trade liberalization considerably improved Ireland's economic performance and helped raise living standards. The removal of restrictions on investment and ownership in Irish companies in the External Investment Act in 1958 and the progressive reduction of protectionism helped open up the economy, so that it became possible to exploit the upturn in global trade. The fixed capital investment of export-orientated foreign firms in Ireland, which had been merely £250,000 in 1955, had risen to £42.4 million by 1971.[43]

The Republic of Ireland clearly benefited from this general increase in transnational investment by multinational companies. In the decade leading up to 1968, about five hundred new factories were established in the state by Irish and foreign industrialists.[44] Although industry made an important contribution to growth in the Irish economy, industrial employment gains remained modest, rising from 169,000 in 1959 to 212,000 in 1972. The new jobs created were in industries with higher levels of capital investment and productivity. The United Kingdom remained the most important country of origin for foreign capital coming into Ireland through the 1960s, still accounting for more than 45% of foreign firm employment as late as 1973. However, in the following decades the United States surpassed the United Kingdom, and by 1986 U.S. firms accounted for 48% of foreign firm employment in the state, compared with only 17% for the United Kingdom.[45]

Entry into the EEC had important implications for industrial development, contributing to the expansion of foreign investment. One of the major upsides of entry was that multinationals continued to invest in building plants in Ireland, because they wanted duty-free access to the EEC market. Entry tariffs against other member states exporting into Ireland were gradually lifted during a brief transition period, and tariffs on Irish exports into the same countries were also removed. Conversely, a number of native industries experienced decline during the decade after entry, notably textiles, clothing, and footwear, as these firms ceded market share to foreign imports. A country that had made much of its own clothing in 1960 imported 77% of the clothing consumed by 1980. In the 13 years after EEC entry three-quarters of the clothing firms in the state and two-thirds of the textile firms had closed down.[46] Despite the social costs of employment losses in these sunset industries, in economic terms the decline in these indigenous industries was more than offset by the significant growth in chemicals; mechanical and electrical engineering; and the native food, drink, and tobacco industries.

The relative importance of foreign companies in the Irish industrial sector became markedly stronger in the 1980s; by 1988, foreign-owned companies accounted for 44% of manufacturing employment, 55% of manufacturing output, and 75% of manufactured exports. Further integration into the EU market made it more attractive for non-EU industrial companies to locate in the Republic of Ireland, which became the biggest exporter of computer software in Europe in the 1990s. The arrival of Intel (in Leixlip near Dublin), which committed to coming to Ireland in 1989, was a major milestone for the IDA. By 1998 Intel had invested 1.8 billion Irish pounds, employed 3,500 staff, and had helped put Ireland on the map as a leading location for software development. This large technically advanced microchip factory (the largest in the world at that time) attracted many other significant companies, resulting in the development of a whole cluster of computer and software companies in Dublin in particular.

The multinational sector, engaged in computers, software development, and pharmaceuticals, experienced a significant growth in U.S. investment, as a consequence of the general upturn in the American economy and the desire of American multinationals to expand their European sales. This enabled Ireland to fulfill the potential offered by the Single European Market from 1992. By 1996 there were about three hundred computer and electronic firms operating in the Irish Republic.[47] By 1997 software employment was split equally between foreign and indigenous firms, and the Republic of Ireland emerged as the undisputed European leader in adapting U.S.-developed software for European localization. Electronics, software, and computers had a stronger impact on the Irish economy than did previous multinational investment.[48] According to Frank Barry, by 2000 foreign multinationals accounted for one in every two manufacturing jobs in the state and one out of every five jobs in services, which was far higher than elsewhere in Europe and in most other parts of the world.[49]

The level of employment in multinationals rose in the 1990s so that by 1999 there were 135,000 jobs in about 1,200 overseas manufacturing or internationally traded service companies, with a particular concentration in pharmaceuticals, health care, software, and tele-services.[50] By 1998 American investment accounted for 78% of foreign direct investment in the Republic of Ireland. There is little doubt that this was of immense importance in contributing to the levels of growth achieved in the 1990s. By 1997 the Republic was attracting about 24% of all U.S. manufacturing investment in Europe, and in one industry, electronics, between 1980 and 1997 Ireland took 40% of all U.S. investment in Europe. The consequence was that by 1995 about one-third of all the computers sold in Europe had been made in Ireland. Foreign companies by 2006 accounted for more than half of industrial employment in Ireland, or 153,000 jobs, compared to 151,000 in indigenous firms. If employment levels were broadly similar, it is there that the comparison ends. The value of output of Irish firms was just under €10 billion, compared to multinationals for whom the value of output was a little more than €50 million, or almost 84% of total output.[51]

Rising labor costs have led to the departure of a number of multinationals in the past decade or more, notably within the Irish information and communication technologies sector, where there has also been a marked shift from manufacturing to service provision. This led to the departure of major computer hardware manufacturers like Dell, for example, who moved operations from their Limerick plant to eastern Europe, where labor costs were cheaper. As comparative advantage shifted in hardware production to locations like China and central and eastern Europe, about a third of the jobs in the Irish hardware sector were lost between 2000 and 2004 alone. Some of these employees were re-employed in the expanding sector engaged in service functions in areas like sales, logistics, and technical support,[52] contributing to the declining numbers engaged in manufacturing and a rise in service-related employment. Computer services experienced significant export growth between 2003 and 2009, accounting for more than 30% of total service exports by 2009.[53] Labor costs are somewhat less significant in the major surviving success story in Irish manufacturing, the pharmaceutical sector, in which employment continued to expand after 2000.[54] But the high share of industrial output now accounted for by pharma has made the economy more vulnerable to negative factors impacting on this sector, such as the expiration of patents for profitable drugs. The marked contraction in industry in the past decade is evident from the falling employment share of industry in the Irish economy (including construction).

Industrial employment had reached an impressive 28.9% of total employment in the economy by 2001, and up to this point industrial employment (excluding construction) had also been growing in absolute terms from the early 1990s. Since 2001 the share of employment in industry (excluding construction) contracted, while employment in construction has experienced even more rapid decline since 2007. As a consequence the whole profile of the economy has altered, with industrial employment (including construction) falling dramatically from 28.9% of total employment in 2001 to merely 18.6% by 2011 (see table 18.1).

The second phase of the Celtic Tiger from about 2002 to 2007, in contrast to the first phase (1993–2002) was not based on manufacturing competitiveness, but increasingly on a credit-fueled property and construction boom. As Irish banks acquired easier access to credit, more people were prepared to pay for larger mortgages in contexts where employment in the economy was relatively buoyant and household income was rising. Between 1996 and 2005 more than 550,000 housing units were built, and by 2007 the Republic of Ireland was producing more than twice the European unit level per year. Construction alone by 2006 accounted for 10.4% of gross national product[55] and 14% of total employment.[56] Because of adoption of the euro, Irish banks were far more willing than in the past to indulge a new frontier of construction and property development, with relatively lax regulation mechanisms, until mortgage demand began to fall in mid-2006. Then in the autumn of 2008 when Anglo-Irish Bank (the most profligate lender) experienced a full-scale meltdown, a deep economic crash occurred, with excessive bank lending to developers and builders at the eye of the storm.[57] Thereafter, employment in construction contributed to the rapid contraction of industrial employment recorded in table 18.1.

Conversely the services share in total employment in the economy has continued to rise from 64% in 2001 to 76.7% in 2011 (see table 18.1). This growth in the relative significance of services has brought the employment profile of the Irish economy more closely into line with the larger European economies. When the state was established in the 1920s services accounted for only about one-third of the total labor force.[58] The Irish Free State had a relatively high level of services by European standards even up to the 1950s. This was partially a function of the relatively insignificant contribution made by industry. It was also because of the country's close historical association with the more wealthy United Kingdom economy, with the consequence that the legal, medical, professional, transport, and banking infrastructure of the Irish Free State and its public administration were perhaps more developed than in other countries in Europe with a comparable level of economic development.

Service-sector employment rose very gradually from just more than 33% of total employment in the economy in 1926 to almost 40% by 1961, accelerating in the 1960s and 1970s as the structure of the Irish economy changed. Office-based white-collar work increased dramatically in this period as both the state and the economy at large became more bureaucratized.[59] Significant growth of public services took place in the 1960s and 1970s; by 1978 government services accounted for about 30% of service-sector output, largely reflecting the expansion of expenditure in health, education, and public administration.[60] There was also a revolution in the nature of retailing and distribution, notably in relation to the scale and size of outlets with the emergence of supermarkets, big department stores, shopping centers, bulk purchasing, and wholesaling.[61] Distribution and retailing already accounted for a large share of service-sector output between the 1950s and 1970s, which amounted to as much as a quarter of output and employment in services. But Irish road services remained poor in much of the country, and freight and haulage services were slow and relatively uncompetitive. Irish ports were relatively unmechanized by European standards, but containerization and the growth in carrying capacity improved matters in the 1960s and 1970s.

The growing openness of the Irish economy by European standards since entry in the EEC in 1973 and the resultant dramatic growth of trade have further increased the role and significance of transport in the economy at large. Growth in industrial exports in the 1980s and 1990s, and imports of consumer goods and food all contributed to increasing the volumes transported. Air services also expanded rapidly with increased carrying capacity in this period. The links between transport and tourism were also strong. Deregulation had dramatic impacts on services by increasing competition. The Dublin to London air route, for example, witnessed a major fall in fares between 1986 and 1993, when traffic increased from 900,000 to 2.4 million persons per year. This liberalization of air travel from 1987 on boosted tourism in particular and witnessed the emergence of Ryanair as a major international player in the European aviation industry and one of the major Irish service-sector company success stories. By 1994 tourism accounted for more than 7.5 % of total employment in the Irish economy, also becoming Ireland's fifth-largest export.[62] This expansion continued during the Celtic Tiger era, so that by 2005, tourism accounted for 198,000 direct and indirect jobs and almost 10% of total employment.[63] This increase illustrates the growing significance of tourism in particular and of services in general in the Irish economy at large in recent decades. Although state policy has not provided benefits to services in the same way as to industry and agriculture (because prior to the 1980s services were not generally seen as a major agent of development), some service-sector industries were assisted and protected from competition, notably Aer Lingus and CIE in the transport sector and Bord Fáilte in the tourism sector.

Policy modifications in the state's development strategies are discernible in 1980s as a consequence of the Telesis report in 1982, which advocated a greater focus on indigenous development. As part of these new initiatives, software and financial services were added to the list of targeted sectors for development. Another important advance was the upgrade of the entire telecommunications system in the early 1980s. By the mid-1990s it had been entirely digitized, so that Ireland had a relatively sophisticated telecommunications network by European standards, which was important for high-tech industries.[64] This revolution in telecommunications and the increased expenditures by the state on information technologies increased the efficiency of service provision. The growing use of computers revolutionized communications, but as late as 1998 only a quarter of all houses with computers in the state were connected to the internet; by 2004 this number had risen dramatically to more than 80%.[65] The significance of online transactions has increased subsequently.

The Financial Services Centre in Dublin was established in 1987 with major tax breaks. It became a major new source of employment and led the way in the development of financial services in the following decades. Support for financial services and tourism in recent decades in particular indicates the greater focus of the government on specifically developing and assisting the growth of traded services over nontraded services, reflecting the greater importance attached to services that earn foreign exchange.[66] Of total Irish exports by 2004, 34% were tradable services largely made up of software and business and financial services.[67]

During the first phase of the Celtic Tiger era, services associated with property and development—such as finance, insurance, real estate, and other business services—expanded dramatically from 1991, when they employed fewer than 90,000 persons, to 2002, when they employed almost 222,000 people.[68] Yet the most significant area of employment in services remained the public sector, which employed almost 342,000 by 2007 and constituted about a quarter of total employment in services. The most important categories were health and education, which collectively accounted for well over half of total employment in the public sector.[69]

The major expansion of employment in education got under way following the revolutionary educational reforms of the 1960s. The introduction of free secondary education in 1966 dramatically improved access to schooling and facilitating greater upward social mobility and economic growth in subsequent decades. Before the 1960s Ireland had low secondary-school attendance relative to other European societies, which was a significant factor reinforcing social disadvantage and inhibiting upward social mobility in Irish society. Less than 10% of the children of semi-skilled and unskilled people acquired a secondary education prior to 1966. University education in Ireland remained an elite preserve. In 1964 there were still merely 12,000 students in third level.[70] The extent of the major revolution in third-level education, and the major upgrading in second level to facilitate this, is evident from the increase in the number of students enrolled in tertiary education to 183,000 by 2009.[71] If the attainment of third-level education was relatively low by European standards in the early 1960s, among younger adult age cohorts it is now relatively higher than the European average.

Another major consequence of entry into the EEC/EU has been a gradual transition in the state's macroeconomic management. At the time of entry in 1973 the Irish pound had long traded on parity with British sterling. In an attempt to stabilize European currency fluctuations, the European Monetary System (EMS) was established in 1979; Ireland joined this system, abandoning the long-established link between the Irish pound and sterling. However, because the EMS did not encompass sterling, it was not initially a great success in the Irish case, since in 1979 more than 46% of Irish exports went to the United Kingdom, which also accounted for 50% of Irish imports. Indeed the break with sterling from 1979 contributed to the general instability in the Irish economy in the 1980s.[72] But the new Irish punt in the longer term at least provided the option of devaluation, a monetary instrument that helped make exports more competitive. For example, after the forced devaluation of the Irish punt by 10% in the EMS at the beginning of 1993, Ireland's competitive position improved dramatically. It has been argued that the improvements in the macroeconomic and fiscal management of the state in the 1990s contributed in some measure to the dramatic improvement in economic performance in the 1990s.[73]

Once Ireland joined the European Monetary Union in 1999, the value of the punt became locked into a fixed exchange rate with all the countries then entering the eurozone. Macroeconomic management was then centralized in the eurozone area, creating a somewhat less flexible environment for Irish economic management, which has become particularly apparent following the property and financial crash in 2008. When the government provided a guarantee on most bank liabilities in October 2008, without a complete picture of their full extent, it essentially socialized bank losses (bank lending in the state, which had been the equivalent of about 60% of national income in 2000, had risen dramatically to the equivalent of about 200% of national income by 2008).[74] This action in turn created a sovereign debt crisis, which forced the state in November 2010 into an €85 billion bailout (underwritten by the EU Commission, the European Central Bank, and the International Monetary Fund), which effectively converted bank debt into sovereign debt, thus totally protecting all bank bondholders at the expense of Irish taxpayers. Between 2008 and 2010 the economy was hit by a property, banking, fiscal, and financial crisis, with real GDP falling by 3% in 2008 and 7% in 2009. Meanwhile public debt, which had fallen to as low as 24.8% of GDP in 2007, shot up again to 105% of GDP by 2011, which was not far below the level to which it had risen in the last major economic crisis (109% in 1987). The lack of financial regulation in an Irish context, both in the eurozone and at the national level, was one of the major flaws of the new monetary architecture of the eurozone, which was thus not in a good position to cope with the international financial tsunami that broke in 2008. In the first comprehensive overview of the crisis, Donovan and Murphy have argued there were few other plausible options for the government to take with respect to both the bank guarantee in 2008 and bailout in 2010.[75] Regardless of this assessment, it was arguably well within the authority of the government to limit and finesse the extent of the guarantee in 2008. In addition, the government could have made the commitment of public money to the bailout in 2010 conditional on a far greater degree of burden sharing with bank bondholders (as occurred in the more recent instance of Cyprus, for example). The terms of the Irish bailout in November 2010 appear to have been more concerned with stanching further European financial losses and fully protecting bank bondholders and European Central Bank liquidity[76] at the expense of Irish taxpayers.

Although the resulting austerity measures have not been popular, from a longer-term perspective, the impact of entry into the EEC/EU since 1973 has been far more positive than negative for Irish economic development. Entry enabled the Republic of Ireland to gradually reduce its trade dependence with Britain; the United Kingdom accounted for almost 61% of Irish exports in 1972 but had fallen to less than 16% by 2010. Much of Irish growth since EEC entry was trade based; exports grew by a factor of twenty between 1970 and 2000, largely because of multinationals, and imports were eight times greater by 2000 than they had been in 1970. Ireland became one of the most open economies globally.

Although this enabled the economy to benefit more from upswings in the international economy, conversely it has also made the Republic's economy much more vulnerable to international recessions.[77]

CONCLUSION

The general rise in living standards has been one of the more significant features of the economic history of independent Ireland. Recent estimates suggest that per capita income (measured in fixed prices) was eleven times higher in 2008 than it had been in 1922.[78] Growth was exceedingly limited until the 1960s, and the economy performed poorly relative to both the United Kingdom and most of continental Europe. The Irish economy was uniquely unsuited to protectionism. Moreover, continued trading and financial dependence on the United Kingdom limited growth prospects from independence to the 1950s. British companies accounted for much of the investment made in the protectionist era, while Britain also became the main destination for Irish migrants, who departed from an economy where growth in urban employment was insufficient to offset the labor exodus from agriculture as Irish farming became increasingly mechanized.

The gradual liberalization of trade from the 1960s—first in connection with the United Kingdom through the Anglo-Irish Trade Agreement in 1965 and then with entry into the EEC in 1973 (undoubtedly the major watershed in Irish economic history since independence)—improved Irish economic performance, increased trade, and raised Irish living standards. According to the estimates of Crafts and Toniolo, Irish GDP growth rates were the best in Europe between 1973 and 2005, after having languished at the bottom of the European league between 1950 and 1973.[79] However, following the crash in 2007, the Republic of Ireland experienced negative GDP growth between 2008 and 2010, in stark contrast to its stellar performance in the preceding decade or more.[80]

Judging simply by economic performance alone (until the recent crash, at least), clearly the economy of the Republic of Ireland was able to benefit more from the economic and political relationships developed between the state, the EEC, and the United States than it had from the more dependent economic relationship it had with Great Britain between 1922 and 1973 or the efforts during the protectionist era to dilute that relationship through greater economic self-sufficiency. There is little doubt that the state played a formative and positive role in achieving this transition. Its far less impressive performance in handling the economy since the advent of the euro (and during the second phase of the Celtic Tiger era) have left a malign legacy of public debt, but this major crash since 2007 needs to be placed in the context of the exceedingly challenging economic and political environment in Europe and beyond that stems from the events of 2007.[81]

The most striking transformation in the economic history of independent Ireland has been the radical shift in its employment profile from one in which agriculture accounted for more than half of all employment in the 1920s to one in which it occupies a negligible share of employment today. Conversely the services sector has steadily grown from accounting for just more than a third of total employment in the 1920s to more than three-quarters in 2011(see table 18.1). These figures encapsulate the major transformation since independence from a predominantly rural economy and society to one that has become predominantly urban.

FURTHER READING

The 1970s witnessed something of a new awakening in the field of Irish economic history, not least with the birth of the journal *Irish Economic and Social History* in 1974. Since its inception the journal has annually published a detailed and useful select bibliography of publications in Irish economic and social history, which constitutes a vital guide. Earlier in the decade, James Meenan, *The Irish Economy since 1922* (Liverpool: Liverpool University Press, 1972) provided a pioneering survey of the Irish economic history since independence, while L. M. Cullen, *An Economic History of Ireland since 1660* (London: Batsford, 1972) was a more wide-ranging synthesis over a longer time frame, which marked something of a new departure for the discipline at large across the island, since it challenged the more pessimistic assessments of Irish economic history generated in the nationalist tradition. Since then several general surveys have been published by economic historians, including in chronological order: Kieran Kennedy, T. Giblin, and D. McHugh, *The Economic Development of Ireland in the Twentieth Century* (London: Routledge, 1988); David Johnson, *The Inter War Economy in Ireland* (Dundalk, Ireland: Dundalgan, 1989); Liam Kennedy, *The Modern Industrialization of Ireland 1940–1988* (Dundalk, Ireland: Dundalgan, 1990); Cormac Ó Gráda, *A Rocky Road: The Irish Economy since the 1920s* (Manchester: Manchester University Press, 1997). The assessment of the performance of the Irish economy since independence by Kieran Kennedy et al. marked a return to a more pessimistic appraisal, which became more common in the recessionary 1980s. In contrast, D. S. Johnson and Liam Kennedy, "The Two Economies in Ireland in the Twentieth Century," in J. R. Hill (ed.), *A New History of Ireland, VII, Ireland 1921–1984* (Oxford: Oxford University Press, 2003) provides an altogether more upbeat and optimistic assessment. The most recent general survey, Andy Bielenberg and Raymond Ryan, *An Economic History of Ireland since Independence* (London: Routledge, 2013) contains a comprehensive bibliography of the economic history of independent Ireland.

NOTES

1. R. P. Davis, *Arthur Griffith and Non-violent Sinn Féin* (Dublin: Anvil Books, 1974), pp. 127–144.

2. Andy Bielenberg (ed.), *The Shannon Scheme and the Electrification of the Irish Free State* (Dublin: Lilliput Press, 2002). For a general history of the ESB, see Maurice Manning and Moore McDowell, *History of the ESB* (Dublin: Gill and Macmillan, 1984).

3. Mary Daly, *The First Department; A History of the Department of Agriculture* (Dublin: Institute of Public Administration, 2002); T. Dooley, *"The Land for the People," The Land Question in Independent Ireland* (Dublin: University College Dublin Press, 2004).

4. David Johnson, *The Inter-War Economy in Ireland* (Dundalk, Ireland: Dundalgan Press, 1989).

5. Johnson, *The Inter-War Economy in Ireland*, pp. 13–17.

6. David Fitzpatrick, *The Two Irelands 1912–1939* (Oxford: Oxford University Press, 1998), p. 152.

7. Brian Girvin, *Between Two Worlds; Politics and Economy in Independent Ireland* (Dublin: Gill and Macmillan, 1989), pp. 89–91.

8. Mary Daly, *Industrial Development and Irish National Identity, 1922–1939* (Syracuse, NY: Syracuse University Press, 1992), p. 65.

9. Girvin, *Between Two Worlds*, pp. 118–119.

10. Cormac Ó Gráda, *A Rocky Road: The Irish Economy since the 1920s* (Manchester: Manchester University Press, 1997), p. 147.

11. See Muiris MacConghail, *The Blaskets; People and Literature* (Dublin: Town House, 1987), pp. 43–56 for a bibliography of the relevant literature and a chapter on the island's economy.

12. Conrad M. Arensburg and Solon T. Kimball, *Family and Community in Ireland* (Cambridge, MA: Harvard University Press, 1940).

13. Joseph T. Carroll, *Ireland in the War Years 1939–1945* (Newton Abbot, England: David and Charles, 1975), pp. 78–79.

14. L. M. Cullen, *An Economic History of Ireland since 1660* (London: Batsford, 1987), p. 181.

15. Carroll, *Ireland in the War Years*.

16. Liam Kennedy, *The Modern Industrialization of Ireland 1940–1988* (Dundalk, Ireland: Economic and Social History Society of Ireland, 1990).

17. Brian Girvin, *The Emergency; Neutral Ireland 1939–45* (London: Macmillan, 2006), pp. 179, 231–264. Richard Doherty, *Irish Men and Women in the Second World War* (Dublin: Four Courts Press, 1999), pp. 9–10, 23–26, 46.

18. Peter Rigney, *Trains, Coal and Turf: Transport in Emergency Ireland* (Dublin: Irish Academic Press, 2010), pp. 1–51.

19. Bryce Evans, *Ireland during the Second World War: Farewell to Plato's Cave* (Manchester: Manchester University Press, 2014), p. 1.

20. Donal Clarke, *Brown Gold: A History of Bord na Mona and the Irish Peat Industry* (Dublin: Gill and Macmillan, 2010).

21. D. J. Maher, *The Tortuous Path* (Dublin: Institute of Public Administration, 1986), pp. 22–24.

22. Brian Girvin, "Irish Agricultural Policy, Economic Nationalism and the Possibility of Market Integration in Europe," in R. T. Griffith and B. Girvin (eds.), *The Green Pool and the Origins of the Common Agricultural Policy* (London: LP, 1995), pp. 239–259.

23. Bernadette Whelan, *Ireland and the Marshall Plan 1947–57* (Dublin: Four Courts Press, 2000).

24. Kieran Kennedy, T. Giblin, and D. McHugh, *The Economic Development of Ireland in the Twentieth Century* (London: Routledge, 1988), p. 55.

25. J. A. Walsh, "Adoption and Diffusion Processes in the Mechanization of Irish Agriculture," *Irish Geography* 25 (1992), pp. 33–53.

26. Mary Daly, "Turning on the Tap, the State Irish Women and Running Water," in Mary O'Dowd and Maryann Valiulis (eds.), *Engendering Irish History* (Dublin: Wolfhound Press, 1997); Michael J. Shiel, *The Quiet Revolution: the Electrification of Rural Ireland, 1946–1976* (Dublin: O'Brien, 1984).

27. Henry Patterson, *Ireland since 1939* (Dublin: Penguin Ireland, 2006).

28. William G. Shade, "Strains of Modernization; The Republic of Ireland under Lemass and Lynch," *Eire-Ireland* 14: 1 (1979), p. 30.

29. G. Quinn and P. Lynch, "The Latest Phase in Irish Transport," in K. B. Nowlan (ed.), *Travel and Transport in Ireland* (Dublin: Gill and Macmillan, 1973), p. 158; S. D. Barrett, *Transport Policy in Ireland* (Dublin: Irish Management Institute, 1982), p. 176.

30. Barrett, *Transport Policy in Ireland*, p. 159.

31. Arnold Horner, "The Tiger Stirring: Aspects of Commuting in the Republic of Ireland 1981–96," *Irish Geography* 32 (1999), pp. 99–111.

32. Aisling Reynolds-Feighan, "Accessibility, Transportation, Infrastructure Planning and Irish Regional Policy: Issues and Dilemmas," in E. O'Leary (ed.), *Irish Regional Development: A New Agenda* (Dublin: Liffey Press, 2003); Nicola Commins and Ann Nolan, "Car Ownership and Mode of Transport to Work in Ireland," *Economic and Social Review* 41 (2010), pp. 43–75.

33. Kennedy, Giblin, and McHugh, *Economic Development of Ireland*, p. 63. Also see Frank Barry, "Foreign Investment and the Politics of Export Profits Tax Relief 1956," *Irish Economic and Social History* 38 (2011) pp. 54–73.

34. John F. McCarthy, *Planning Ireland's Future: The Legacy of T. K. Whitaker* (Dublin: Glendale Publishing, 1990).

35. Anthony J. Leddin and Brendan M. Walsh, *The Macroeconomy of the Eurozone: An Irish Perspective* (Dublin: Gill and Macmillan, 2003), pp. 86–89.

36. Ó Gráda, *A Rocky Road*, pp. 160–161.

37. Roy Foster, *Luck and the Irish: A Brief History of Change c. 1970–2000* (London: Allen Lane, 2007), pp. 22–24

38. Andy Conway, "Agricultural Policy," in Patrick Keatinge (ed.), *Ireland and EC Membership Evaluated* (London: Pinter, 1991).

39. J. A. Walsh, "Agriculture in Transition," in Brendan Bartley and Rob Kitchin (eds.), *Understanding Contemporary Ireland* (London: Pluto, 2007), p. 161.

40. Ethel Crowley, *Land Matters: Power Struggles in Rural Ireland* (Dublin: Lilliput Press, 2006), pp. 28–36.

41. Walsh, "Agriculture in Transition," p. 158.

42. Alan Matthews, "The Agri-Food Sector," in J. O'Hagan and C. Newman (eds.), *The Economy of Ireland* (Dublin: Gill and Macmillan, 2011), pp. 295–297.

43. John Kurt Jacobson, *Chasing Progress in the Irish Republic: Ideology, Democracy and Dependent Development* (Cambridge: Cambridge University Press, 1994). pp. 76, 89.

44. Maher, *The Tortuous Path*.

45. David Jacobson and Bernadetee Andresso, "Ireland as a Location for Multinational Companies," in Anthony Foley and Michael Mulreany (eds.), *The Single European Market and the Irish Economy* (Dublin: Institute of Public Administration, 1990), p. 311.

46. Denis O'Hearn, *The Atlantic Economy: Britain, the US and Ireland* (Manchester: Manchester University Press, 2001), p. 146.

47. Diarmaid Ferriter, *The Transformation of Ireland 1900–2000* (London: Profile Books, 2004), p. 671.

48. Denis O'Hearn, *Inside the Tiger: The Irish Economy and the Asian Model* (London: Pluto, 1998), pp. 68–78, 156.

49. Frank Barry, "Some Political Economy Lessons from Ireland's Boom and Bust," *Journal of Irish and Scottish Studies* 2 (2009), p. 29. On the significance of multinationals, see Frank Barry "FDI and the Host Economy: A Case Study of Ireland," in G. B. Navaretti and Anthony J. Venables (eds.), *Multinational Firms in the World Economy* (Princeton, NJ: Princeton University Press, 2004), pp. 187–216.

50. Patrick Gunnigle and David McGuire, "Why Ireland? A Qualitative Review of the Factors Influencing the Location of US Multinationals in Ireland with Particular Reference to the Impact of Labour Issues," *Economic and Social Review* 32 (2001), pp. 43–67.

51. Peadar Kerby, *Celtic Tiger in Collapse: Explaining the Weaknesses of the Irish Model* (Basingstoke: Palgrave, 2010), p. 7.

52. Frank Barry and Chris Van Egeraat, "The Decline of the Computer Hardware Sector: How Ireland Adjusted," *Quarterly Economic Commentary* (Spring, 2008), pp. 38–57.

53. Anne O'Brien, *The Politics of Tourism Development: Booms and Busts in Ireland* (Basingstoke: Palgrave Macmillan, 2011), p. 190.

54. Chris Van Egeraat and Frank Barry, "The Irish Pharmaceutical Industry over the Boom Period and Beyond," *Irish Geography* 42, (2009), pp. 23–44.

55. Rob Kitchin, C. O'Callaghan, M. Boyle, and J. Gleeson, "Placing Neoliberalism: The Rise and Fall of Ireland's Celtic Tiger," *Environment and Planning* 44 (2012), p. 1308.

56. Sebastian Dellepiane Avellaneda and Niamh Hardiman, "The European Context of Ireland's Economic Crisis," *Economic and Social Review* 41: 4 (2010), p. 484.

57. Morgan Kelly, "What Happened to Ireland?" *Irish Pages* 6: 1 (2009), pp. 7–13.

58. Desmond Gillmor, "Land and People, c. 1926," in J. R. Hill (ed.), *A New History of Ireland, VII, Ireland 1921–1984* (Oxford: Oxford University Press, 2003), p. 68.

59. Proinnsias Breathnach, "The Services Sector," in Brendan Bartley and Rob Kitchin (eds.), *Understanding Contemporary Ireland* (London: Pluto, 2007) p. 148.

60. D. J. Cogan, *The Irish Services Sector: A Study of Productive Efficiency* (Dublin: Stationery Office, 1978), p. 3.

61. Breathnach, "The Services Sector," p. 155.

62. James Deegan and Donal Dineen, "Irish Tourism Policy: Targets, Outcomes and Environmental Considerations," in Barbara O'Connor and Michael Cronin (eds.), *Tourism in Ireland* (Cork: Cork University Press, 1993).

63. O'Brien, *The Politics of Tourism Development*, p. 190.

64. Sean O'Riain, *The Politics of High Tech Growth: Developmental Networks States in the Global Economy* (Cambridge: Cambridge University Press, 2004), pp. 55, 71–72, 93.

65. Breathnach, "The Services Sector," p. 155.

66. John Fingleton, "Competition and Efficiency in the Services Sector," in John O'Hagan (ed.), *The Economy of Ireland* (Dublin: Gill and Macmillan, 2005), pp. 296–328.

67. Breathnach, "The Services Sector," p. 156. On the growing importance of internationally traded services, see Seamus Grimes and Mark White, "The Transition to Internationally Traded Services and Ireland's Emergence as a Successful European Region," *Environment and Planning* 37 (2005), pp. 2169–2188.

68. Breathnach, "The Services Sector," p. 151.

69. F. O'Toole, "Services, Competition and Regulation," in J. O'Hagan and C. Newman (eds.), *The Economy of Ireland* (Dublin: Gill and Macmillan, 2008) p. 238.

70. Ferriter, *The Transformation of Ireland*, pp. 596–597.

71. *Europe in Figures: Eurostat Yearbook*, (Luxembourg: Eurostat, 2012), p. 215.

72. Maher, *The Tortuous Path*, pp. 366–367.

73. Patrick Honahan and Brendan Walsh, "Catching up with the Leaders: The Irish Hare," *Brookings Papers on Economic Activity* 1 (2002), pp. 1–57.

74. Kelly, "What Happened to Ireland," p. 9.

75. Donal Donovan and Antoin Murphy, *The Fall of the Celtic Tiger: Ireland and the Euro Debt Crisis* (Oxford: Oxford University Press, 2013), pp. 1–16, 196.

76. Sebastian Dellepaine and Niamh Hardiman, "Governing the Irish Economy: A Triple Crisis," in Niamh Hardiman (ed.), *Irish Governance in Crisis* (Manchester: Manchester University Press, 2012), pp. 83–109.

77. Michael J. O'Sullivan, *Ireland and the Global Question* (Cork: Cork University Press, 2006), p. 75.

78. Andy Bielenberg and Raymond Ryan, *An Economic History of Ireland since Independence* (London; Routledge, 2013), p. 189. A more detailed development of many of the arguments made and the sources used in this article can be found in this volume. I acknowledge the work and contribution of my co-author, Dr. Raymond Ryan, in that project and his consequent influence in this much-briefer survey.

79. Nicholas Crafts and Gianni Toniolo, "Aggregate Growth, 1950–2005," in S. Broadbury and K. H. O'Rourke (eds.), *The Cambridge Economic History of Modern Europe, volume 2, 1870 to the Present* (Cambridge: Cambridge University Press, 2010), p. 301.

80. Donovan and Murphy, *Fall of the Celtic Tiger.*

81. Donovan and Murphy, *Fall of the Celtic Tiger.*

CHAPTER 19

NATIONALISMS

Matthew Kelly

NATIONALISM IS AN IDEOLOGY OF liberation. Nationalism is an ideology of imperial expansion and colonial conquest. Nationalism includes and excludes. Nationalists seek to create nation-states; successful states or failing states can create or intensify nationalist sentiment. Nationalism is the most powerful mobilizing force in modern political history, but its origins often lie in pre-modern communal identities and it can coexist with supra-national political arrangements and institutions. Nations are impersonal political communities that are imagined but are not imaginary; nation-states have a materiality that can be anatomized but a profoundly unstable ontological status. Nations, like their nationalisms, invite epigrammatic assertion but are best treated as historically contingent political entities.

Between 1801 and 1921, the island group sometimes known as the North Atlantic Archipelago was politically organized as a state called the "United Kingdom of Great Britain and Ireland." Although a unitary state with a sovereign government based in London, it comprised four nations—England, Scotland, Wales, and Ireland—widely considered to be of medieval origin. Peter Mandler suggests that the shared "ethnocentric liberalism" of the English, Welsh, and the Scottish made them accepting of one another but chary about the development of a British nation-state,[1] whereas much of the Irish population, whether resident on the island of Ireland, the island of Britain, or in the growing global diaspora, overtly rejected the idea that the Union could ever evolve a form of nationhood. This reflected Ireland's long history of English and British conquest, expropriation, and settlement, which had created by the modern period an Irish population ostensibly

I am grateful to Richard Bourke, Ultán Gillen, Ian McBride, and James McConnel for their comments on an earlier version of this chapter.

divided into a dispossessed "native" Catholic population and a "settler" Protestant population, whose property-based interests were predicated on the confessional divide. Although neither group was homogenous—the distinction between the Anglo-Irish or Anglican "Ascendancy" and the Presbyterians of Ulster was particularly significant—Ireland was nonetheless a majority Catholic country in an Anglican state dominated by a landed and professional Anglican elite.

In the late eighteenth century, a "patriot" Anglican politics helped dilute but not dissolve the confessional foundations of the state, but this was insufficient for a generation of radical Presbyterians raised in the civic culture of Belfast and excluded from the formal structures of the Anglican political establishment. Impatient with the pace of change and inspired by the French Revolution, they formed the United Irishmen, a separatist republican movement under the leadership of Theobald Wolfe Tone. The genesis of one strand of modern Irish nationalism is to be found in their propagation of the idea that political sovereignty resided in the people of Ireland, be they Anglican, Catholic, or Dissenter.

In conjunction with the agitation of the Catholic Defenders and an international context shaped by war, the United Irishmen fostered a revolutionary situation. The violent outbreaks of 1798, motivated by a mix of republican idealism and sectarian bitterness, were the most sustained in modern Irish history before 1919–1923 and 1969–1998. Britain's brutal campaign of pacification, galvanized by an imperial nationalism intensified by involvement in the French Revolutionary Wars, culminated in the Irish parliament's acquiescence in the Act of Union (1801) and its absorption by the Westminster parliament. Crucially, the new state denied full political rights to Ireland's Catholic population. Daniel O'Connell's campaign for Catholic emancipation, finally achieved in 1829, and the subsequent campaign for the repeal of the Act of Union, which collapsed in 1843, mobilized the politically unenfranchised Catholic masses, creating in them a powerful sense that they exclusively constituted the Irish nation. Later legislation, including the disestablishment of the Church of Ireland, reform to land tenure, and the widening of the franchise, undermined the political, spiritual, and material bases of Anglo-Irish power and authority in Ireland. The popular pressure and passions that forced the government to adopt these reforms reinforced the confessional basis of Irish political identities, and as the oligarchic politics of the eighteenth century gave way to the increasingly democratic politics of the nineteenth, so Irish political identities became territorialized. Irish unionism was gradually marginalized, and an Ulster Protestant variant, torn between an intense attachment to its "narrow ground" and a wider British identity, arose in its place. Electoral politics saw Home Rule and Unionist party politics supersede Liberal and Tory in the 1870s, broadly Irish political agendas supplanting a politics subordinate to British imperial interests.

As this account suggests, it is possible to write the history of modern Ireland in terms of competing nationalisms and unionisms, with the British government implicitly cast as the somewhat hapless "honest broker" confounded by the perversities and violent tendencies of Irish politics. This obscures the degree to which Ireland was the site of conflict between three protean political forces, each of which bore the hallmarks of nationalism, albeit in markedly distinct ways. Most obviously, there was an Irish nationalism predicated on the conviction that Irish sovereignty was distinct from British and should be exercisable according to the wishes of the people of Ireland. To this end, Irish nationalists pursued various devolutionist and separatist strategies across the nineteenth century, which at times were subordinate to efforts to mold the Irish people according to cultural nationalist dictums. Efforts to displace the Catholic communalism of O'Connellism with more pluralist conceptions of the Irish nation were one aspect of this cultural nationalism; nurturing an "Irish Ireland" predicated on the revival of the Irish language was another.

British power was manifest in the Union state in Ireland, as evident in the executive power of Dublin Castle and the quasi-military character of the Royal Irish Constabulary. These semi-colonial governing structures reflected conventional British thinking throughout the nineteenth century and much of the twentieth, which held that the British Empire's strategic, military, and commercial interests would be damaged by Ireland's secession. When in the late nineteenth and early twentieth centuries British Liberal politicians attempted to create a devolved government in Ireland, they did not concede Ireland's right to self-determination but aimed to accommodate its nationality within the governing structures of the Union and British Empire. The most farsighted commentators, including a group of influential but politically marginal Conservative thinkers, imagined the British Empire evolving into a federation of nations, to whom the British would relinquish formal political control as a notional British political culture became ascendant throughout. Only in the late twentieth century did British governments declare they had no strategic or economic interest in the retention of any part of Ireland.

Liberal moves toward Irish Home Rule intensified in most Irish Protestants a religious-political identity based on personal loyalty to the monarch as the embodiment of the Protestant Act of Settlement (1701), and an obedience to the state conditional on the resolve of the British government to uphold the Act of Union as guarantor of Protestant liberties. When this resolve was perceived to falter, Ulster Protestants, recognizing the territorial realities of unionism's electoral power, claimed that their ethno-cultural distinctiveness constituted their right to determine Ulster's future political status. It is tempting to argue this was nationalism, for its claims were predicated on a historic claim to sovereignty over Ulster rooted in the coalescence of territory and communal self-interest. But Ulster Unionists did not identify as nationalists. They sometimes toyed with the "two nations" theory of Irish history as its ultimate *explanans*, but an expressly Ulster nationalism, particularly in a secessionist form, never achieved sustained traction among Ulster Protestants. Rather, the historic achievement of the Protestants of Ulster was rhetorically loyalist and instrumentally unionist: their aggression ensured that successive British governments were forced to recognize that establishing an independent state sovereign throughout Ireland would be more politically costly than the United Kingdom's retention of a sizable part of Ulster.

Throughout the modern period, the politics of land, religion, and democracy made Ireland the site of conflict between Irish nationalism, a notional unionist nationalism, and British nationalism, all of which were conditioned by Ireland's uncertain status as imperial possession and integral part of the Union state. If in what follows the focus falls on the shifting perspectives, changing contexts, and evolving objectives of Irish nationalism, a sense of its dynamic relationship with its competitor nationalisms should not be lost. Nor should Irish nationalism's role in the global struggle against empire, in which the British state, in spite of its liberal foundations, was for a time the most successful imperial hegemon.

THE NINETEENTH CENTURY

> It's whisper'd too, that freedom's ark
> And service high and holy
> Would be profaned by feelings dark
> And passion vain or lowly,
> For Freedom comes from God's right hand
> And needs a godly train,
> And righteous men must make our land
> A nation once again!

This is the third stanza of Thomas Davis's "A Nation Once Again!," the most enduringly popular of the ballads published in *The Spirit of the Nation*, the Young Ireland anthology of 1845.[2] Its simple rhythms, rhymes, and final exultant cry belie its complexity, for these few lines sound not inevitable triumph but toll a warning, a whispered doubt that Ireland's nationalists might fall short of what freedom demands. It's not just that "service" is contrasted favorably with "passion," drawing a distinction between instrumental reason and ineffective emotion, but, Davis suggests, shows of passionate intensity might reflect less sincere commitment and more self-aggrandizement. Believing a true commitment to freedom was integral to religious faith made Davis part of the European nationalist mainstream. This sacerdotal interpretation of freedom acquired political significance in the closing couplet. In the injunction to "make our land / A nation," Davis followed classical Enlightenment thinking that to be free is to fulfill God's will, adding that this godly quality of freedom could only be achieved within the "ark" of a particular political arrangement, namely, self-governing nationhood. True nationhood, whatever its outward political institutions, was only possible as a godly enterprise.

Just as late nineteenth-century Gaelicists questioned whether the outward trappings of political independence would be of value in the absence of a concomitant revival of the Irish language, so Davis thought Ireland's national status could only be recovered as part of a broader restoration of the moral and spiritual dimensions of Irish life. Contemporary British thinkers like Thomas Carlyle, John Stuart Mill, and Matthew Arnold said much the same thing of Britain, and Carlyle's influence on Davis's fellow Young Irelanders is often noted. Davis's emphasis on Ireland's unrealized capacity to determine its own future through sub-state individual and collective action proved a malleable theme in Irish nationalism, reaching its apogee in the first years of the twentieth century with the emergence of the self-help movement and Arthur Griffith's Sinn Féin. Civic activism, overcoming ingrained habits of subservience and deference and developing a proper independence of mind and body (often referred to as "manliness"), were the dominant motifs of a nationalist language of self-respect and self-determination.

And a restoration it would be, for embedded in Davis's famous cry was the historical claim that Ireland had previously been a nation and so might be "once again." Nationalists held up various points in Ireland's past as evidence of this ancient nationhood, but that which most directly shaped nineteenth-century nationalism was an idealized memory of the late eighteenth. If Ireland's seventeenth-century history of conquest, massacre, and settlement, reinforced by anti-Catholic penal laws, loomed large in the nationalist imagination as evidence of British brutality and sectarianism, as significant was the belief that during the eighteenth century Irish society became more settled, experiencing an economic recovery; a dignifying measure of political independence in "Grattan's parliament"; and a religious tolerance, which, in Wolfe Tone's famous words, began to see the substitution of "the common name of Irishman in the place of the denominations of Protestant, Catholic and Dissenter."[3]

Nationalist historiography identified the 1798 rebellions as not merely a consequence of Britain's self-interested refusal to respond generously to the United Irish and patriot agenda but also Britain's determination to destroy that budding unity. With the United Irish rebellion crushed, Ireland pacified, sectarian passions stoked, the Irish parliament translated to Westminster, and the sectarian state reconstituted, a declensionist historical narrative of economic stagnation, depopulation, anglicization, and Protestant self-interest—all the deliberate outcome of British policy—was quickly established to describe Ireland's experience *under* the Union. In these unfinished nationalist stories, description and prescription became one, providing incontrovertible material and cultural reasons why Ireland should be self-governing once again.

The Davisite optimism of "a nation once again" disguised deep uncertainties. Would the people inhabiting Ireland only become an Irish nation through the achievement of independent statehood? Could nationalists be confident that Irish nationality was a form of self that sometimes lay dormant in the people of Ireland? Or were nations developmental projects that could succeed or fail—and fail ultimately? If some nationalists struggled to define their object because they had a weak conception of the possible distinction between nation and state, the Young Irelanders, acutely sensitive to the Irish people's incapacity to exercise the agency essential to meaningful nationhood, increasingly doubted that nationhood could exist passively. Davis's call for a nationality reified through righteousness provided a stirring antidote to the failure of late O'Connellism and the ineffectual power of the Irish crowd, but the revolutionary ferment of 1848 quickly left a nationality of moral uplift seeming inadequate. Would the reputation of Irish nationalists in Europe fade if their "constant proclamations" were not matched by action?[4] If the Irish were merely a people of boastful words rather effective deeds, could they be counted among the *struggling* nations?

Nationalist commentators reflecting on Ireland's year of failed revolution lamented less the humiliations of the March 1848 rising and more the destruction rent by the Famine on "the temperance reformation, the political training of the people, the labours of years, and pride of generations." The destruction of its political movements left Ireland without "an embodied public opinion" and, as such, the capacity to be a national and a political people.[5] Post-Famine attempts to revive a nationalist politics based on a strictly reformist parliamentary strategy amounted to little, generating the famous *Nation* editorial of 1855 decrying the "coma of Irish politics," its "indifferentism," and the "lethargy in the public mind."[6] In the decade or so that followed, the inner failure of Irish nationalism found outward expression in numerous editorials speculating about how continental events would have a favorable effect on Irish nationalism. Much hope was invested in Napoleon III, the likelihood of a Franco-British war, and the possible dividends to be paid by the historic affinity nationalists believed existed between Ireland and France.[7] The Indian "revolution" of 1857, Italian unification, and the Polish rebellion in 1863 suggested strong parallels with Irish experiences, reassuring nationalists that their own struggle was part of a historic pan-national effort to bring about the dissolution of the European empires and inaugurate a golden age of fraternal nationality.[8] Despite this, Ireland's nationalists were justifiably anxious that their brethren in continental Europe did not consider them engaged in a comparable struggle, not least when continental radicals, operating in an increasingly authoritarian atmosphere, celebrated Britain as a liberal haven and the Irish, despite their priest-ridden and pro-papal politics, as among Europe's more fortunate subject peoples. Irish nationalists, distressed by this celebration of perfidious Albion, experienced the 1850s and 1860s as a protracted crisis of representation, which generated in turn an acute sense of isolation.[9]

None of this should obscure the degree to which some found it plausible that the British state might deliver "justice for Ireland." Irish liberals wedded to an "improvement" agenda found common cause with Catholic churchmen alert to how their corporate interests might be served by Liberal governments keen to see Ireland become a stable and prosperous society. Peel's Maynooth Grant in 1845, designed to shield the Irish clergy from radical continental ideas by improving the training available in Ireland, saw the interests of the British government align with those of a Catholic hierarchy anxious about continental infidelity, secret societies, and other secularizing tendencies. Paul Cullen, Ireland's dominant Catholic churchman in the two decades after 1848, preached a providential message promising salvation through devotion that celebrated an O'Connellism limited to the achievement of Catholic emancipation and insisted that "the country"—never "the nation"—could be best served through hard work and quiet service to family, community, and the church.[10] Cullen's sense that the gullible Irish needed to be shielded from foreign subversion and charismatic Irish-Americans spreading revolutionary ideas generated a politics rooted in a mix of clerical paternalism and social elitism that expressly minimized the role to be played by the "plain people" of Ireland.

In contrast, Fenianism, as organized from 1858 through the Irish Republican Brotherhood, insisted, first, that sovereignty lay in "the people," which could be only exercised through an active citizenry, and, second, that there was an instrumental relationship between state and nation. Without access to the levers of the state, it would be impossible for the Irish to build a nation of their choosing. Fenians rejected reformist politics on the grounds that dependency on the goodwill of another nation—not least the subjugating nation—was fundamentally at odds with the exercise of national sovereignty. And though in the late 1850s, they recognized that an Anglo-French war might create an opportunity for Ireland to achieve its nationhood, the popular notion that a French intervention in Ireland might secure Ireland's independence was at odds with the Fenian understanding of sovereignty: nationhood could only be willed into being when "the Irish people" overcame carefully nurtured divisions and a proper separation of church and politics was established. As such, the Fenians, contemptuous of O'Connellism's Catholic politics, believed that the existence of their secret organization virtually established an Irish republic, because it constituted a free act of sovereignty by the Irish people: although republican, as democrats the Fenians contended that the Irish people could only decide how they would like to be governed after full sovereignty was restored.

Where Fenians proffered the link between nationhood and sovereignty as indefeasible, the Home Rule movement re-articulated the pragmatics of O'Connellism for the age of parliamentary reform. At its most circumscribed, Home Rule politics sought the supersession of the "moral force" of the crowd and the civic activism of the proto-citizen by the disciplined voter and machine politics. Rejecting Fenian absolutism, Home Rulers argued that if Ireland were granted a measure of self-government within the Union commensurate with its dignity and capacities as a nation, it would voluntarily pool a measure of its sovereignty in the interest of the Empire of which it was part and potentially a beneficiary. Criticized by its nationalist opponents as "a transacting party," it was the case that the successful passage of a Home Rule bill—even if the consequence of Irish political pressure—would constitute an act of sovereignty by the Westminster parliament rather than of the Irish people. Nonetheless, when framed as the restoration of Ireland's constitutional rights, albeit in a context shaped by Catholic emancipation and a widened franchise, Home Rulers could project their politics as high political principle.

For a brief moment in the early 1870s, it seemed that Irish elites, Protestant and Catholic, might find Home Rule and a strictly parliamentary politics acceptable.[11] This quickly changed thanks to the high visibility of Fenian entryists, whose rhetoric did not heed the conciliatory or imperial dimension of early Home Rule, and the intensifying agrarian politics of the late 1870s and early 1880s, which foregrounded the material dimension of popular nationalism and the consequences of democratization.[12] The notion that the fulfilment of Irish nationhood meant reversing the conquest placed Irish nationalism on a collision course with the vested interests sustained by the Union, as every eviction backed by the forces of the state and every imprisoned Land Leaguer demonstrated. At the same time, the modus operandi reached between the Home Rule party and the post-Cullenite Catholic Church on denominational education in the early 1880s affirmed the confessional dimension of Home Rule politics. As such, although Home Rule's breakthrough election came in 1874, the movement matured following the passage of the Representation of the People Act in 1884 and the extraordinary polling by Home Rule candidates during the 1885 general election.

Despite the efforts of the Protestant Home Rule Association, the mold was set. For the next thirty years, Irish politics was shaped by the politics of Home Rule and unionist reaction. Electoral outcomes were determined by religious demographics, with constituencies in parts of Ulster and affluent parts of Dublin returning unionist candidates and Home Rule candidates returned everywhere else. The Home Rule party's periodic organizational fragility and uncertain political achievements at times emboldened Fenians frustrated by a nationalist politics reduced to casting votes, approving resolutions, and paying dues, but the party's ascendancy before the Great War was never really in doubt.

REVOLUTION AND ANTI-PARTITIONISM

I am glad that the Orangemen have armed, for it is a goodly thing to see arms in Irish hands. I should like to see the A.O.H. [Ancient Order of Hibernians] armed. I should like to see the Transport Workers armed. I should like to see any and every body of Irish citizens armed. We must accustom ourselves to the thought of arms, to the

sight of arms, to the use of arms. We may make mistakes in the beginning and shoot the wrong people; but bloodshed is a cleansing
and sanctifying thing, and the nation which regards it as the final
horror has lost its manhood. There are many things more horrible
than bloodshed; and slavery is one of them.[13]

This notorious passage from Patrick Pearse's essay "The Coming Revolution"
was first published in November 1913. Pearse reflected on the significance to
Irish nationalism of the formation in January 1913 of the Ulster Volunteer Force,
whose purpose was to resist the implementation of Home Rule. The Ulster Volunteer Force was formed at a very particular juncture in the history of Home
Rule. Gladstone's first Home Rule bill had been defeated in the House of Commons in June 1886; his second Home Rule bill fell in the House of Lords in September 1893; the third Home Rule bill, introduced by Prime Minister Asquith in
April 1912, passed its third reading in the Commons in January 1913, only to be
defeated in the Lords later that month. Thanks to the passage of the Parliament
Act (August 1911), this did not kill the bill, for now the Lords could exercise only
a two-year suspensory veto over a non-money bill passed by the Commons three
times. With a Liberal government in office, unionists could no longer rely on
their unelected allies in the House of Lords to veto the passage of a Home Rule
bill. By guaranteeing that the will of the Commons would prevail, the Parliament
Act moved the theater of struggle from Westminster to Ireland.

Nationalists dismissed the unionist mobilization as posturing until the government began to contemplate amending the bill to allow the temporary or permanent exclusion of parts of Ulster from Home Rule. Irish Republican Brotherhood
irreconcilables and a younger generation of neo-Fenians and Gaelic revivalists
were impressed less by the effectiveness of unionist political pressure—common
enough in the context of the Union—and more by unionist means. Keeping faith
in the parliamentary process when faced with vigorous unionist activism, particularly when urged to do so by Home Rulers identified with John Redmond's brand
of imperial Home Rule, was intolerable to "advanced" nationalists. Consequently,
rather than read the unionist mobilization as an appalling subversion of the democratic process or, indeed, as another example of unionist mob rule, Pearse saw a
section of the Irish people cast off their political culture of dependency and become the active citizenry of republican virtue. As such, the passage of the Parliament Act forced unionists to take responsibility for their own future, and by doing
so they became Ireland's first citizens, providing inspiration to a nationalist population told by their leaders to passively wait on events. In the transition from the
cavalier "shoot the wrong people" to the chilling "bloodshed is a cleansing and
sanctifying thing," Pearse did not presage the "Vertigo of Self Sacrifice" that propelled the 1916 rising,[14] but he eschewed the proxy wars emasculated Irishmen
fought through the high politics of the Liberal and Conservative parties: as the

site, the subjects, and the object of Irish conflict coalesced, so Pearse imagined a revolutionary alchemy making a nation of the Irish—nationalist and unionist, Catholic and Protestant alike.

Events did not develop as Pearse anticipated. The Irish Volunteers attracted overwhelming political support only when the Redmondites took control of the organizing committee in June 1914 and permitted the great mass of Irish nationalists to participate; the split following Redmond's committal of the movement to the imperial war effort in September exposed the weakness of the advanced nationalists. In the meantime, the government amended the Home Rule bill to allow the exclusion of parts of Ulster and then suspended its operation on the outbreak of the First World War, revealing the control it retained over the political process and the Irish population's passive acceptance of its authority. Thousands of Irishmen, nationalist and unionist, joined the British army, particularly in the optimistic first months of the war, when Redmondites and unionists, each preaching a blood sacrifice of their own, competed to demonstrate their imperial loyalty.[15] Some hoped shooting Germans might reconcile Irish ready to shoot one another. In response, on Easter Monday, 1916, a small group of prominent dissidents mobilized some 1,600 men and women, occupied a number of prominent buildings in central Dublin, and declared an Irish Republic. By treating the adage "England's difficulty is Ireland's opportunity" as an instruction, the rebels validated their identification with the separatist tradition. To a world trumpeting empire loyalty, be it British, German, Habsburg, or Ottoman, they represented the integrity of Irish nationhood and the self-determining capacity of Irish masculinity and, to an extent, femininity.

Anxious mid-nineteenth-century nationalists, worried that they were not counted among the struggling nations, had been succeeded by a new vanguard buoyed by an extraordinary faith in fraternity and convinced that they were at the forefront of history. Britain's lax security regime allowed an empowering sense of impunity to develop, but of greater significance were the ideological convictions and attitudes nurtured by peacetime political activism. In particular, the political separatism of some Gaelic revivalists was reinforced by John Redmond's enthusiasm for the British Empire, which allowed a new language of anti-imperialism to be grafted onto neo-Fenian homiletics. In this way, the separatists established clearly and forcefully what differentiated their politics from that of the Home Rulers, who—until the period of high Redmondism—had been good at presenting their politics as Fenianism by other means. None of this gave the rebels a mandate from the Irish people, but as the representatives of a figurative Irish nation uncontaminated by compromise this was scarcely needed: "Ireland, through us, summons her children to the flag and strikes for her freedom," read the proclamation. Celebrated for its progressive dimension—it addressed "Irishmen and Irishwomen" and talked of the nation cherishing all its children equally—it was also distinctly authoritarian: "the Irish republic is entitled to, and hereby claims, the allegiance of every Irishman and Irishwoman."[16]

What followed is well known. The martyring of the rebel leadership, mass internment, the militarization of the British government in Ireland, Britain's double-dealing and unionist sabotage of efforts to reach an agreement on Home Rule, and the progressive radicalization of nationalist opinion culminated in Sinn Féin's landslide victory in the December 1918 general election. When Sinn Féin declared the newly constituted Dáil Éireann (Irish parliament) the government of an independent Irish Republic, they retroactively made the 1916 proclamation the foundational moment of the new nation-state. This genealogy, the construction of which was taken to be an indefeasible act of sovereignty, would confound British-Irish relations for decades to come.

Following the UK government's failure to recognize the new Irish Republic, the Irish Republican Army (IRA), a new component of the Sinn Féin movement, commenced a series of violent actions against representatives of British power in Ireland that rapidly escalated into a cycle of attack and counterattack salted with vengeance killings on all sides. During the conflict, the Pearsean logic that "arms in Irish hands" would diminish Irish divisions proved hopelessly optimistic. Catholics bore the brunt of intercommunal violence in Ulster and British reprisal attacks in the south; in some parts of Ireland Protestants had reason to fear the sectarian dimension of IRA violence; and only the most isolated guerrilla fighter could doubt the ascendant political and coercive power of the British state.[17] A parallel component of this revolutionary struggle was the creation of a parliament, cabinet, and judicial system, evidence of aspirant nation-statehood. In 1920 Britain unilaterally partitioned Ireland, creating the Home Rule states of Northern Ireland and Southern Ireland. Sinn Féin's refusal to recognize either state was expected, but agreeing to a truce a year later and sending plenipotentiaries to London to negotiate a measure of independence that would apply only to the South saw Sinn Féin accept that it could not exercise an untrammeled Irish sovereignty.

The circumstances accompanying the foundation of the Irish Free State were thus unpropitious. Though signed by plenipotentiaries, the Treaty had to be approved by the Dáil before the government could draw up a constitution that reflected its articles. Debate was acrimonious, seeing principled acquiescence pitched against principled opposition. Partition rankled, but ideological cover was provided by the Treaty's provision of a commission charged with adjusting the border; it was the oath of loyalty to the crown required of all elected representatives and state officials that saw many break with the treatyite leadership. The bloodshed of the Civil War, partly a consequence of this "symbol," should not obscure the humiliation this crude expression of British nationalism imposed on the legislators of the new state. As Éamon de Valera later explained, Ireland was not offered Dominion status as a settler colony reaching political maturity, but as a

"Mother Country" seceding from the Union following a war against the British.[18] His perspective was consistent with the old nationalist notion that Ireland was not a colony of Britain but a nation subject to imperial despotism. Still, with the treaty approved, the aspirant parliament of a thirty-two–county Irish republic was transformed into the sovereign parliament of the twenty-six–county Irish Free State. Adhering to Sinn Féin's abstentionist principles, de Valera led the anti-treatyites out of the debating chamber and the new state into civil war. This signaled a rejection by part of revolutionary Ireland that access to the levers of state would allow an electorally successful Sinn Féin to develop institutions that functioned according to its political principles.

The execution of seventy-seven "irregulars" before arms were downed in April 1923 substituted judicial terror for effective civil authority and saw the new state conduct something akin to a purge. These actions provided the foundational violence of the Irish Free State, inaugurating a fragile twenty-six–county nationalism whose state-building enterprise was necessary to justify shooting the "wrong people." A decisive shift in the discursive frameworks shaping Irish nationalism thus occurred. Whereas the men and women of 1916 had acted in the name of the nation, hoping to catalyze their fellow citizens through inspiring example, a new language of democratic legitimacy was made integral to the expression of Irish nationhood, albeit on the basis of profoundly different readings of what constituted democratic authority.[19] Republicans believed the only free elections that occurred were those held across Ireland in November 1918 and May 1921, the latter creating the second Dáil. They judged the general election of June 1922 and the comfortable victory won by pro-treaty candidates as illegitimate, because it was conducted under Britain's threat of war. The Free Staters, many of whom were republicans by conviction, built a state that paid due obeisance to the revolutionary struggle of 1916–1921 but rejected the notion that there was a binding moment of national purity they must live up to. They treated nationality, to borrow Renan's influential formulation, as a daily plebiscite, which they initially sought to win by securing the state and its citizens from the threat posed by internal republican enemies.

Deference to the all-Ireland ideal became an essential component of post-independence statecraft, but for the first half century of independence, no change to the status quo was a serious proposition. Grassroots pressure ensured Fianna Fáil and Fine Gael leaders made anti-partition gestures, such as the formation of the Anti-Partition League of Great Britain in 1938, but neither party—like their British counterparts—could be persuaded to destabilize the status quo by organizing in Northern Ireland. The Pearsean orthodoxy that a British withdrawal from Ireland would allow the people of Ireland to resolve their differences enabled nationalist politicians to focus their efforts on fruitless lobbying of the British government rather than on the more difficult task of persuading the majority population of Northern Ireland of the benefits of a single Irish state. Sporadic talk of a federal approach suggested one alternative to established orthodoxies, but economic underperformance in the South and hefty fiscal transfers from London to Belfast made the case unpersuasive, particularly once the Northern Irish government adopted the post-1945 structures of the British social-democratic state.

Political pressure on both sides of the border and at Westminster ensured the consolidation of the two Irish states. Fear that a protracted dispute over the border would rouse dissident republicans and the unwillingness of the Unionist government and Conservative backbenchers to make any concessions saw the Boundary Commission effectively abandoned in 1925. Cross-border complicity was reinforced by the Free State's acceptance of the decision by Northern Ireland's government to dismantle proportional representation, thereby abandoning the Catholics of Northern Ireland to unionist electoral hegemony. The full significance of the Free State's political status became evident in 1931, when the Statute of Westminster brought an end to the British government's right to make laws for the Dominions and permitted the Dominion governments to pass laws "repugnant" to British acts of parliament, past, present, or future. In power from 1932, Fianna Fáil removed the monarchical components of the Free State constitution, abolished the oath, and, with the External Relations Act of 1937, made the British monarch a diplomatic functionary of the Free State. With the passage of a new constitution that same year, the Irish nation, comprising the "whole island of Ireland, its islands and the territorial seas," was distinguished from the state encompassing the twenty-six counties of "Ireland" (or "Éire," as the Free State was renamed). Embedding a territorial claim to Northern Ireland in the constitution meant that in official usage "Ireland" signified not the twenty-six–county state but an aspirational thirty-two–county nation-state, a variant on the old Fenian ideal that their existence made the Republic "virtually established." The international standing of the newly constituted state was validated a year later when its territorial sovereignty was extended by Neville Chamberlain's agreement to give up the three treaty ports retained by the British.

In 1927 Seán Lemass described Fianna Fáil as "slightly constitutional," a notorious statement that alluded not to the party retaining the right to resort to physical force but its relationship to the Free State as a republican party. By 1938 Fianna Fáil had created an Irish state whose anti-partitionist ethos, embodied in its constitution, had been effectively recognized by its historic enemy. The lack of compunction shown by de Valera in moving against dissident republican groups reflected his conviction that the constitutional claim to Northern Ireland meant there was no moral reason republicans should not with dignity submit to the authority of the state, including its right to a monopoly on violence. Éire's neutrality during the Second World War, broadly supported throughout the state, was the most significant exercise of Irish sovereignty in the history of the twenty-six–county state. When de Valera rejected British overtures to trade participation in the Allied war effort for a pledge to address the partition question after the war, he affirmed the principle that the rights of the Irish nation were indefeasible rather than negotiable. By recognizing how domestic political pressures, not least from dissident republicans, conjoined with the logics of Irish nationalist state-craft, this seemingly obtuse and morally dubious decision can be understood.

TROUBLES

I who have stood dumb
when your betraying sisters,
cauled in tar,
wept by the railings,

who would connive
in civilized outrage
yet understand the exact
and tribal, intimate revenge.

These lines close "Punishment," a poem from Seamus Heaney's *North* (1975),[20] a collection that explored the rituals of the Northern Ireland "Troubles" through reflections on the ancient cadavers preserved in peat bogs found in northern Europe in the post-war period. Here Heaney contemplated the fate of an adulteress, comparing her punished body to the Northern Irish Catholic women brutally humiliated by other women for "fraternizing" with British soldiers deployed in Northern Ireland. Punishing the transgressing body was so essential a part of the conflict that it is easily missed, but more challenging is Heaney's notion that the violence of the Troubles, which in 3,526 cases led to death, was roused by atavistic instincts stemming from a collective primitivism that transcended class boundaries. As Heaney admitted, outward displays of respectability often masked inward emotional convulsions. By this reading, nationalism and unionism, modern political ideologies both, provided the fragile carapace for a conflict compelled by the intensely territorial pre-political tribal divisions inherent in Northern Irish society. "Punishment" had its cognate in an earlier poem exploring the emotional response to an earlier transgressive political act. In "Easter, 1916," W. B. Yeats imagined thinking of a "mocking tale or gibe" to share with a similarly socially situated "companion" that might put some knowing distance between him and the affecting "terrible beauty" of the 1916 rebellion. Both poets—one elegiac, one confessional—used their chosen form to address how political communities were consolidated and intensified by emotional reactions to violence.

Although Heaney's preoccupation with the coded behavior and guardedness that shaped life in Northern Ireland suggested the divisions were fundamental, the Troubles were not their inevitable consequence but a function of political failure. As has recently been argued, polarization "was the product of violence rather than a cause of it."[21] Northern Ireland's transition from dysfunctional stability to apparently intractable instability had multiple causes, which included the agency of resurgent nationalist movements.

From the 1920s through to the 1960s, mainstream Irish nationalist politicians in Northern Ireland largely refused to cooperate with the Stormont regime, their position reflecting the long-established idea that to engage was to legitimize. In contrast, Irish republicans maintained their armed struggle, explaining their actions as continuous with earlier efforts to free Ireland from British imperial rule. Accordingly, the consolidation of the twenty-six–county Irish state marked at best a tactical move in a longer-term process and at worst a self-interested betrayal of a higher ideal. Indeed, republicans, constitutional or otherwise, were outraged when the Inter-Party government dominated by Fine Gael, keen to shore up its nationalist credentials, declared Éire a republic in 1948 (and exited the Commonwealth), thereby subverting the logic of the 1937 constitution. With political leaders such as this, it thus befell an enlightened minority—as in 1848, 1867, 1916, and 1919—to sustain the struggle, seeking to exploit what opportunities came its way. Classically, Irish republicans hoped that if England encountered serious difficulties in its foreign affairs, the opportunity might arise to "strike a blow for Ireland," possibly with external assistance. Moreover, the opportunistic notion that my enemy's enemy is my friend held true for some republicans, as the pro-Nazi activities of some right-wing IRA members made clear.

From the 1920s, the IRA struck their blows by raiding police barracks for arms, attacking the security infrastructure in Northern Ireland, and, most concertedly, launching a bombing campaign in England following the IRA's declaration of war on Britain in January 1939. Although the latter generated a wave of terror, the effect was largely symbolic: a British government spokesman recognized that "the attempt was against property and not against human life."[22] When IRA men Peter Barnes and James McCormick were sentenced to be hanged for the bungled operation in Coventry on August 25, 1939, a campaign for clemency attracted widespread support in Ireland. De Valera made a fruitless appeal to Anthony Eden, explaining the "exclusively political character" of the crime, insisting that "neither of the men was of the criminal type."[23] The immediate political significance of this moment was short-lived, but it exposed the resilience of the nationalist view that the British legal system was the partisan agent of a vindictive state. Something comparable accompanied the IRA's otherwise ineffective border campaign of 1956–1962, when again an emotional spasm provoked by the death of two activists, this time during a raid, had a political effect: four republicans were returned in the Irish general election of March 1957.[24] The republican hunger strikes of 1980–1981, conducted in a more fraught political situation, were similarly affecting, arousing a generalized Catholic sympathy where close political allegiances were often wanting.

In the early 1960s, the IRA's limited capacity to conduct an effective asymmetric war was subject to internal questioning. Cathal Goulding, IRA chief of staff from 1962, queried the validity of "armed struggle" according to conventional vanguardist republican thinking. Was striking a blow for Ireland justifiable if it was unlikely to lead to any meaningful political progress and—as had occurred during the hundred or so actions of border campaign—people were killed, whether republican activists, members of the security forces, or civilian bystanders? And in what ways was the IRA's campaign helping to fulfill the republican ambition of creating a common Irishness throughout the island? Goulding and his followers cautiously steered the IRA toward a more overtly nonsectarian and leftist political orientation. Establishing a network of Wolfe Tone Societies offered an alternative to paramilitary republican activity and the prospect of a revolutionary movement based on mass mobilization. The Gouldingites, deriving their thinking from James Connolly and broader currents of leftist radicalism, thought partition would cease to be meaningful when the Protestant and Catholic working class overcame the false consciousness fostered by British imperialism and maintained by the churches. Neo-Connollyism offered a more intellectually sophisticated alternative to the Pearsean faith in the healing power of a violent conflagration, but its insistence that the Irish question was principally symptomatic of a continuing British imperialism rather than a set of socio-political dynamics largely internal to Northern Ireland would prove no less problematic.

The neo-Connollyite belief that a new nationalist movement could be built on the everyday grievances of the population of Northern Ireland—an echo of the role played by the Land Question in the nineteenth century—dovetailed with the emergence in the mid-1960s of new moves to reform the Northern Irish state. Although the distribution of public housing and gerrymandering were the most contentious issues, because they enhanced unionism's electoral position, campaigning also focused on more everyday discontents and frustrations, including "poor television reception, rent increases, resettlement grants, vandalism, new water charges, road safety, policing and inadequate midwifery."[25] The emergence of the civil rights movement was conditioned by the loosening of the traditional rigidities of Irish politics in the 1960s. Terence O'Neill and Seán Lemass, respectively the Northern Irish prime minister and the Irish taoiseach, were less constrained by unionist and nationalist orthodoxies and recognized that practical gains could result from closer cooperation between the two states. Pressure from the British government, whose previous negligence had let the problems develop, was felt in Belfast; northern nationalists were encouraged by Dublin to respond constructively to O'Neill's sometimes clumsy but well-meaning ecumenical gestures; and initiatives like the Londonderry Area Plan (1968) suggested that material grievances could be addressed by technocratic solutions, reviving the old Tory optimism that nationalism could be killed "with kindness."[26]

Essentialist unionists, often fiercely evangelical in their Protestantism, thought O'Neill's reformism endangered the Northern Irish state by emboldening the recalcitrant nationalism of its "Papist" population. By organizing counterdemonstrations intended to create conflict between the civil rights movement and the police, loyalists calculated that instability would stymie reform and expose the supposedly nationalist realities of the civil rights movement, which often did feature traditional anti-partitionism and a visible republican presence. At the same time, a nationalist activist cadre, looking to destabilize the state, predicted that violent confrontations on the streets would generate highly partisan policing. This would expose the sectarian reality of the state and draw more people into the movement. Both sides quickly became locked into a "strategy of tension," their calculations proving correct.

What neither side anticipated, however, were the transformative events of August 1969, when British troops were deployed in Derry following an intercommunal riot that culminated in the residents of the Catholic Bogside fighting the Royal Ulster Constabulary to a standstill. Sectarian fury had marginalized the progressive agendas of the neo-Connollyites and the civic reformers, and in the months that followed the assumptions that underpinned traditional nationalist and unionist identities were systematically reaffirmed. Republican agency proved decisive. First, elements in the republican movement rejected the Gouldingite agenda on the grounds that deprioritizing armed struggle left the IRA unable to fulfill its elementary obligation to protect the Catholic population. Second, with a part of Ireland once again having British troops on the street, the republicans were gifted with a legitimate enemy against whom a blow could be struck. As such, a pre-political desire to retaliate coalesced with a revived anti-imperialism, republicans identifying themselves with the anti-colonial struggles of the post-war world.[27] Just as IRA activists had to start shooting policemen in early 1919 to create the dynamic of attack and counterattack that would catalyze the Irish revolution of 1919–1921, the Provisional IRA, a breakaway faction of the republican movement, soon initiated a war with the British enemy on Irish streets. When "direct rule" was introduced in 1972, the Provisionals claimed it put "the 'Irish question' in its true perspective—an alien power seeking to lay claim to a country for which it has no legal right."[28] For the next twenty-five years, republican, unionist, and British political violence reinforced Northern Irish divisions, and though the Troubles were not in any sense static, a brutal equilibrium—sustained by painful loss and bitterness, the institutional needs and ideological rigidities of the warring factions, and a felt need to vindicate earlier actions and losses through continuing struggle—was not successfully disrupted until the 1990s.

Nationalist opinion south of the border responded to the Northern conflagration with ambivalence. Nationalist sentiment provoked by the fiftieth anniversary of the 1916 rising gave a temporary fillip to anti-partitionist sentiment, but a complacent twenty-six–county patriotism provided the base note in 1966. Although in August 1969 Jack Lynch (taoiseach) said the Irish government could "no longer stand by" and watch Catholic Irish being burned out of their homes by Protestant vigilantes, and although criminal collusion between senior Fianna Fáil cabinet ministers and the Provisional IRA embarrassed the government, significant actions did not follow, and public opinion, sporadically roused by the malaise north of the border, tended to retreat into a Know Nothingness. Behind the scenes, civil servants made it clear to ministers frustrated by their helplessness that unification was impossible. The Republic could neither afford to maintain the state according to British standards nor hope to hold it peacefully against unionist resistance. Much of this found implicit expression in July 1970, when Lynch gave a talk on radio that at once affirmed and subverted classic nationalist nostrums. Contrary to the Provisional IRA's interpretation of the conflict, he claimed there was "no real invader here," insisted it was an essentially "Irish quarrel," spoke of "Anglo-Irish friendship" ("Our peoples know and like each other"), and expressed his sympathy for young British soldiers caught up in a conflict "which must to them seem inexplicable."[29] Above all, Lynch made it clear that re-unification could only come about with the consent of the Northern Irish people, thereby committing to a principle that would underpin the peace process of the 1990s.

Lynch's revisionism reflected a growing ambivalence about the anglophobia of traditional nationalism. It was at odds with lived experience and practical politics. During the debate preceding the passage of Britain's restrictive Commonwealth Immigrants Act (1962), any suggestion that the Irish in Britain were "immigrants" or "foreign" offended Irish public opinion;[30] Ireland's economic dependence on Britain could hardly be gainsaid, as evident in 1973 when Ireland entered the European Common Market on Britain's coattails; and in 1973 the Irish government supported the Sunningdale Agreement, which attempted to restore self-government to Northern Ireland by institutionalizing Nationalist-Unionist coalition government and cooperation between Belfast and Dublin. What the Irish government could not countenance was any dilution of the constitutional claim to the North, which provided loyalists a principled reason to wreck the new arrangements; the Provisional IRA opposed the Agreement as counterrevolutionary and continued its armed struggle.

In the early 1980s Fine Gael leader and taoiseach Garret Fitzgerald's "constitutional crusade," partly a defensive response to the sympathy garnered by republican hunger strikers, culminated in the *New Irish Forum Report* (1984), a peculiar mix of constitutional nationalist orthodoxy and a mild revisionism. Although the *Report*'s claim that its formulators represented the four principal constitutional nationalist parties in Ireland and therefore a majority of Ireland's people was conventionally anti-partitionist, its insistence that a reconstituted Irish state needed to recognize the range of political identities shaping Irish life signaled a cautious move toward the "two nations" reading of Irish history that had underpinned partition. Moreover, Fitzgerald had come to believe that by separating the Irish nation from the most substantial part of its Protestant minority, partition had facilitated the development of an Irish state too narrowly predicated on Catholic nationalism. If Fianna Fáil's role in the discussions inhibited a sharp critique of the twenty-six–county state, the *Report* nonetheless offered in embryonic form the idea of "parity of esteem," which held that the states of Ireland should be neutral arbiters between the island's various political traditions. With the "principle of consent," parity of esteem became one of the key principles established during the peace process of the 1990s.[31]

On May 18, 1998, David Trimble, leader of the Ulster Unionist Party, and John Hume, leader of the Social Democratic and Labour Party, joined Bono of the Irish rock band U2 on stage in front of an audience of Belfast A-level students. This impromptu but carefully staged event occurred on the eve of dual referendums, one in Northern Ireland and one in the Republic of Ireland. The former sought endorsement of the Belfast Agreement and the latter revision of the Irish constitution. For the Agreement to come into effect, "yes" votes were needed on both sides of the border. At issue in the Republic was whether the population would approve the removal from the constitution of the territorial claim to Northern Ireland and accept its replacement with an aspiration to unite the peoples of the island through democratic means, albeit on the explicit understanding that the two jurisdictions constituted separate electorates. The revised constitution would also recognize the "entitlement and birthright of every person born in the island of Ireland, which includes its islands and seas, to be part of the Irish Nation."[32] From a nationalist point of view, this proposed revision was significant, because the principle was endorsed by the British government and was included in comparable clauses in the Belfast Agreement. With the successful passage of both referendums, Irish nationality would achieve an unprecedented status throughout the island of Ireland. Henceforth, agitating through constitutional means for Irish unity would be upheld as a right in Northern Ireland, and nationalists could expect the state to shield them from aggressive displays of loyalist or unionist sentiment.

In the Republic, 94% voted "yes," but turnout was only 56%, suggesting on the part of some a reluctance to actively endorse the constitutional revision but a readiness to acquiesce in its implications. Irish nationalists in Northern Ireland overwhelmingly endorsed the Agreement, not least because the "no" campaign orchestrated by recalcitrant loyalists underlined the significance of the concessions wrought by the process. Furious at what they regarded as the excessive efforts to conciliate nationalism, loyalists were also profoundly disturbed by Britain's decision to abandon its unconditional support for the continuing existence of Northern Ireland as a separate state.

The Provisional IRA was not directly party to the Agreement, but Sinn Féin, its political wing, was. Abandoning armed struggle and putting their arms "beyond use" was central to the progress of the peace process. These developments had complex causes, which included Britain's increasingly effective security operation, the determination shown by constitutional nationalists to bring the republicans in from the cold, the revulsion generated by actions like the Provisional

IRA's Enniskillen bombing of 1987, the British government's gradual recognition that peace would only be possible if its actions were overtly and deliberately nonpartisan, and the persuasive powers of an American president. Also significant were shifts in generational experience. The Battle of the Bogside, Internment, and Bloody Sunday propelled a generation of young working-class Catholic men into the movement in the early 1970s; something comparable albeit on a smaller scale occurred in the early 1980s following the deaths of thirteen republican hunger strikers; nothing similarly seminal occurred in the early 1990s. But this was not all. Actual political power is attractive, and following some significant teething problems, Sinn Féin has thrived in the new political dispensation North and South.

In the 1990s political thinkers prophesized a post-nationalist Ireland, suggesting that the development of a federal Europe would bring the progressive homogenization of the continent's polities and the gradual diminution of the importance of borders, making it possible to imagine the traditional relationship between national identity and the state withering away.[33] Early twenty-first century anxiety about unrestricted population movement within the European Union generated a new wave of xenophobia across the continent, which, intensified by the economic crisis, belied this optimism. Nonetheless, the new politics of Northern Ireland suggest that changes in formal political structures can help institutionalize a more tolerant and harmonious political culture, though as Belgium's recent travails suggest, only the most historically naïve believe in once-and-for-all settlements. It remains to be seen whether the current governing structures of Northern Ireland are capable of surviving a significant reduction in the Westminster subventions that subsidize the communal divide by sustaining parallel provision in public services, education, and health care.

South of the border, unsustainable national debt and the evident power of the European Central Bank and the German government strengthened the contempt for a political class already mired in corruption. Nonetheless, the diminution in sovereignty evident in externally imposed austerity did not generate a resurgent nationalism. Or, where it did, it was of a muted kind, drawing on notions of Irish resilience in the face of historic forces outside the control of a small nation stranded on an exceptionally beautiful rock in the mid-Atlantic. Prediction is a dangerous game, but it seems likely Ireland's "decade of commemoration" will continue to be marked less by nationalist laments for the unfinished revolution and more by reflection on how far Ireland has come in the meantime. Whereas the quiescence of Ulster unionism is likely to depend on whether the Union continues to serve their interests, the British of Britain, prone to take comfort in the symbolism of past imperial power at odds with its declining global clout, will remain largely oblivious. If restless Scottish nationalists remain restless, determined Britishers would do well to catch up on their Irish history.

The notes to this chapter point the reader either to sources for the quotations or recent specialist texts. Good general works on the history of Irish nationalism include D. G. Boyce, *Nationalism in Ireland* (London: Routledge, 1995); Alvin Jackson, *Home Rule: An Irish History 1800–2000* (Oxford: Oxford University Press, 2003); and Richard English, *Irish Freedom: The History of Nationalism in Ireland* (London: Pan Macmillan, 2009). Stimulating monographs on the period before 1914 are Nancy J. Curtin, *The United Irishmen: Popular Politics in Ulster and Dublin 1791–1798* (Oxford: Oxford University Press, 1994); David Dwan, *The Great Community: Culture and Nationalism in Ireland* (Dublin: Field Day, 2008); R. V. Comerford, *The Fenians in Context: Irish Politics and Society 1848–82* (Dublin: Wolfhound Press, 1998); and James McConnel, *The Irish Parliamentary Party and the Third Home Rule Crisis* (Dublin: Four Courts Press, 2013). Readers might also look at M. J. Kelly, *The Fenian Ideal and the Irish Nationalism, 1882–1916* (Woodbridge: Boydell and Brewer, 2006). Venerable work on the Home Rule party is still a good place to start on that subject, including Conor Cruise O'Brien, *Parnell and His Party* (Oxford: Oxford University Press, 1957) and F.S.L. Lyons, *Charles Stewart Parnell* (Dublin: Gill and Macmillan, 2005); not to be missed is James Loughlin, *Gladstone, Home Rule and the Ulster Question, 1882–93* (Dublin: Gill and Macmillan, 1986). On the revolutionary and post-revolutionary period, Michael Laffan, *The Resurrection of Ireland: The Sinn Féin Party 1916–1923* (Cambridge: Cambridge University Press, 1999) and Charles Townshend, *Easter 1916: The Irish Rebellion* (London: Allen Lane, 2005) are indispensable. Although Peter Hart's *The IRA and Its Enemies* (Oxford: Oxford University Press, 1998) cannot but be read in the light of the controversy it provoked, its historical achievement is greater than the weight of criticism it has borne. Kevin Matthews, *Fatal Influence: The Impact of Ireland on British Politics, 1920–1925* (Dublin: University College Dublin Press, 2004) is particularly rewarding, while Stephen Kelly, *Fianna Fáil, Partition and Northern Ireland 1926–1971* (Dublin: Irish Academic Press, 2013) offers much fascinating material quarried from the archive, though it doesn't fully displace John Bowman's elegantly written *De Valera and the Ulster Question, 1917–73* (Oxford: Oxford University Press, 1989). Recommended reading on the Northern Ireland Troubles is detailed in chapter 16 by Marc Mulholland in this volume, though special mention should be made of Allen Feldman's brilliant *Formations of Violence: The Narrative of the Body and Political Terror in Northern Ireland* (Chicago: University of Chicago Press, 1991).

NOTES

1. Peter Mandler, "Nation and Power in the Liberal State: Britain c. 1800–1914," in Len Scales and Oliver Zimmer (eds.), *Power and Nation in European History* (Cambridge: Cambridge University Press, 2005), p. 365.

2. *The Spirit of the Nation* (Dublin: James Duffy, 1845), p. 274.

3. Marianne Elliott, *Wolfe Tone* (Liverpool: Liverpool University Press, 2012), p. 395.

4. *Nation*, March 4, 1848.

5. *Nation*, September 8, 1849.

6. *Nation*, August 11, 1855.

7. Matthew Kelly, "Languages of Radicalism, Race and Religion in Irish Nationalism: The French Affinity, 1848–1871," *Journal of British Studies* 49: 4 (2010), pp. 801–825.

8. Matthew Kelly, "Irish Nationalist Opinion and the British Empire in the 1850s and 1860s," *Past & Present* 204 (August 2009), pp. 127–154.

9. Matthew Kelly, "Irish Nationalism," in David Craig and James Thompson (eds.), *Languages of Politics in Nineteenth Century Britain* (London: Palgrave Macmillan 2013).

10. Matthew Kelly, "Providence, Revolution and the Conditional Defence of the Union: Paul Cullen and the Fenians," in Dáire Keogh and Albert McDonnell (eds.), *Cardinal Paul Cullen and His World* (Dublin: Four Courts Press, 2011).

11. See David Thornley, *Isaac Butt and Home Rule* (London: MacGibbon and Kee, 1964); and Joseph Spence, "Isaac Butt, Irish Nationality and the Conditional Defence of the Union," in D. George Boyce and Alan O'Day (eds.), *Defenders of the Union* (London: Routledge, 2001).

12. See Donald E. Jordan, Jr., *Land and Popular Politics in Ireland: County Mayo from the Plantation to the Land League* (Cambridge: Cambridge University Press, 1994); and James McConnel, " 'Fenians at Westminster': The Edwardian Irish Parliamentary Party and the Legacy of the New Departure," *Irish Historical Studies* 34: 133 (May 2004).

13. Quoted in Joost Augusteijn, *Patrick Pearse. The Making of a Revolutionary* (Basingstoke: Palgrave Macmillan, 2010), p. 242.

14. The phrase is W. B. Yeats's, quoted in R. F. Foster, *W. B. Yeats. A Life. II. The Arch-Poet* (Oxford: Oxford University Press, 2003), p. 46.

15. See David Fitzpatrick, "The Logic of Collective Sacrifice: Ireland and the British Army, 1914–1918," *Historical Journal* 48: 4 (December 1995), pp. 1017–1030; and James McConnel, "Recruiting Sergeants for John Bull? Irish Nationalist MP and Enlistment during the Early Months of the Great War," *War in History* 14: 4 (2007), pp. 408–428.

16. The proclamation is quoted in R. F. Foster, *Modern Ireland 1600–1972* (London: Allen Lane, 1988), pp. 597–598.

17. See Charles Townshend, *The Republic. The Fight for Irish Independence, 1918–1923* (London: Allen Lane, 2013); and Robert Lynch, "The People's Protectors? The I.R.A. and the Belfast Pogroms, 1920–22," *Journal of British Studies* 47: 2 (2008).

18. Quoted in Brian Girvin, *The Emergency. Neutral Ireland, 1939–45* (London: Macmillan, 2003), p. 15.

19. See Tom Garvin, *1922: The Birth of Irish Democracy* (Dublin: Gill and MacMillan, 2005); but compare John M. Regan, *The Irish Counter-Revolution 1921–36* (Dublin: Irish Academic Press, 1999).

20. Seamus Heaney, *Opened Ground. Poems 1966–1996* (London: Faber and Faber, 1998), p. 118.

21. Simon Prince and Geoffrey Warner, *Belfast and Derry in Revolt. A New History of the Start of the Troubles* (Dublin: Irish Academic Press, 2012), p. 95. See also the pioneering analysis developed in Richard Bourke, *Peace in Ireland. The War of Ideas* (London: Random House, 2003).

22. Richard English, *Armed Struggle. The History of the IRA* (London: Pan Macmillan, 2003), p. 61.

23. Quoted in Girvin, *The Emergency*, p. 59.

24. English, *Armed Struggle*, p. 74

25. Prince and Warner, *Belfast and Derry in Revolt*, p. 39.

26. On O'Neillism, see Marc Mulholland, *Northern Ireland at the Crossroads: Ulster Unionism in the O'Neill Years, 1960–69* (Basingstoke: Macmillan, 2000).

27. On the complexities of republican motivations, see English, *Armed Struggle*, pp. 120–133.

28. Quoted in Paul Bew, *Ireland. The Politics of Enmity 1789–2006* (Oxford: Oxford University Press, 2007), pp. 508–509.

29. Quoted in R. F. Foster, *Luck & the Irish. A Brief History of Change 1970–2000* (London: Allen Lane, 2007), pp. 113–114.

30. Enda Delaney, *The Irish in Post-War Britain* (Oxford: Oxford University Press, 2007), pp. 78–83.

31. The New Ireland Forum report is discussed in Paul Arthur, *Special Relationship: Britain, Ireland and the Northern Ireland Problem* (Dublin: Blackstaff, 2000), pp. 186–205.

32. The Irish Constitution can be accessed online. (http://www.taoiseach.gov.ie/eng/Historical _Information/The_Constitution/).

33. See Richard Kearney, *Postnationalist Ireland: Politics, Culture, Philosophy* (London: Routledge, 1997).

CHAPTER 20

FEMINISM

Maria Luddy

MARY WOLLSTONECRAFT, CONSIDERED THE EARLIEST of modern feminists, published her *Vindication of the Rights of Woman* in 1792, perhaps the most influential text on the ideas informing the nineteenth-century women's movement. A review of the book appeared in the Belfast newspaper the *Northern Star* in December 1792, where it was noted as a work that "abounds with ingenious observations … it affords a variety of judicious instruction for the early management of the female mind, and frequently, and pertinently, corrects the assumptions of the *tyrant man*."[1] Martha McTier encouraged her brother, the United Irishman William Drennan, to read the book. On January 5, 1793, she wrote to ask "Have you read Mrs Wollstonecraft? I suppose not, or surely you would have mentioned her to me—you ought, even as a politician, and she too conspires to make an important change. I wish they would order her book to be burned." McTier realized that to order a book burned would immediately increase its sales.[2]

As defined by the *Oxford English Dictionary*, "feminism" refers to "the doctrine of equal rights for women, based on the theory of the equality of the sexes." The origin of the word "feminist" is still disputed, and as a term it was in use only from the late nineteenth century.[3] Using the *Dictionary* definition this chapter explores the ideas that shaped feminism and feminist action in Ireland from the late eighteenth to the twenty-first centuries. The history of feminism incorporates women's fight for educational equality, economic opportunity, political inclusion, legal recognition, and control over their bodies. Throughout the period feminist arguments and actions always provoked a backlash.

The late eighteenth century witnessed a revival of discussions on the place of women in society and the rights that should be made available to them. Revolutions in America and France had opened up new possibilities about reshaping society, introducing radical ideas about politics and the role of the individual in the state. Radical ideas were also put forward about how men and women might relate to each other. Mary Wollstonecraft was not the only significant feminist of the period. Such French women as Olympe de Gouges and Pauline Leon also drew attention to the issue of the rights of women. The American Declaration of Independence (1776) and the French Declaration of the Rights of Man and of the Citizen (1789) were deemed by many women to be relevant to them. They began to argue for the rights of women and for social and political change that would allow women equality with men. It was in the context of these debates that feminists called for a new role for women. Although Irishwomen were not without a public voice in Ireland from the eighteenth century, that public visibility was strongly shaped by patriotism, not the advocacy of women's rights.[4] Whereas the 1790s was a time when the rights of Irish men were constantly being urged there was little public concern in Ireland with the rights of women. But we can see this period as one where modern feminist ideas are being discussed, at least privately, through correspondence and to a limited extent in the press.

Wollstonecraft's publications were clearly known to some Irish women of the period.[5] There were several Irish editions of Wollstonecraft's *Vindication of the Rights of Woman*, and it is referred to in particular by a contemporary of McTier's, Mary Ann McCracken.[6] McCracken was a keen advocate of women's rights. In a letter from March 1797 to her brother Henry Joy McCracken, imprisoned for his United Irishmen activities, Mary Ann noted the existence of societies of United Irishwomen and argued for the rights of women. It is evident that her ideas were influenced by the writings of Wollstonecraft. McCracken's letter is the fullest articulation yet discovered relating to the rights of women in late eighteenth-century Ireland.

> I have a great curiosity to visit some female societies in this town [Belfast] (though I should like them better were they more promiscuous as there can be no other reason for having them separate but keeping the women in the dark, and certainly it is equally ungenerous or uncandid to make tools of without confiding in them). I wish to know if they have any rational ideas of liberty and equality for themselves or whether they are contented with their present abject and dependent situation, degraded by custom and education beneath the rank in society in which they were originally placed, for if we suppose woman was created for a companion to man she must of course be his equal in understanding, as without equality of mind, there can be no friendship and without friendship there can be no happiness in society.[7]

Even in the ranks of the radical United Irishmen there is only slight evidence of any concern with the rights of women. Thomas Russell was one of the few United Irishmen, if not the only one, who gave some consideration to the place of women in society. Or at least it appears so from the evidence of some jottings in his journal.

"Should," he pondered, "women be made learn[e]d? Is there a difference of mind? Why not as of body? Has it ever occur[r]ed to anatomists to observe is there any difference in the brains of men and women children [*sic*]? [Are] women in public offices as clever as men[?]"[8]

Although McTier was sympathetic to the views of Wollstonecraft, she was not an advocate of women's rights in the same way that McCracken was. Drennan was also blind to any demand for women's rights. Indeed, there appears to have been relatively little sympathy for rights being extended to women. The moderate reformer the Reverend William Bruce observed in 1792 that in the light of the rights that were being demanded for Irish men, and particularly for Catholics, "if we follow without restriction, the *theory* of human rights, where will it lead us? In its principle it requires the admission of women, of persons under age, and of paupers, to suffrage at elections; to places of office and trust, and as members of both Houses of Parliament."[9] It was a common argument to be made for decades by those who opposed women's rights.

How personal experiences could shape feminist thought and action can be seen clearly in the case of Anna Doyle Wheeler (1785–18??), an important figure in early feminism and socialism. Wheeler was from an upper-class Irish Protestant background. She had been married at fifteen, and had given birth to six children, two of whom survived infancy. She separated from her abusive husband and divorced him in 1812. As a consequence of her separation and divorce, she had no financial protection. It was her experiences as a wife that helped develop her ideas about motherhood, economic dependence, and marriage. Between 1818 and 1824 she moved back and forth from London, Dublin, Caen, and Paris. She became closely involved with the Saint-Simonians[10] and was particularly attracted by their feminist ideas. She was also a friend of Robert Owen, William Thompson, and Flora Tristan.[11] The collaboration of William Thompson and Anna Wheeler produced the important feminist tract *Appeal of One Half of the Human Race, Women, against the Pretensions of the other Half, Men, to Retain Them in Political and Thence in Civil and Domestic Slavery; in Reply to a Paragraph of Mr Mill's Celebrated "Article on Government"* (London, 1825). Although Thompson authored the book and dedicated it to Wheeler, he declared, probably with a great deal of justification, that it was she who was primarily responsible for its ideas. *The Appeal* was written in response to James Mill's argument that the franchise need not be extended to women, because their rights were satisfactorily taken care of by their husbands and fathers. Like Wheeler, Thompson was an Owenite, who believed that complete equality could only be achieved through developing a system of cooperative labor and ending competitive capitalism. The *Appeal* was initially concerned with arguing for women's right to vote. But having argued for female suffrage, the *Appeal* goes on to launch a much more radical attack on society. It argued that formal rights, although necessary, were insufficient to bring about sexual equality. How could women achieve equality with men when their duties as wives and mothers prevented them from earning an equal income and thus rendered them economically dependent? Only through the introduction of the Owenite system of cooperation could this evil be overcome. Wheeler and Thompson argued that happiness was the fundamental right of each person, that in contemporary society women were oppressed by their domestic and marital situations, and that rights are necessary for the development of self-respect and self-government.

It had long been argued that one of the reasons women were treated differently in society, and before the law, was the fact that they were different from men. The "nature" argument decreed that women were fit only to be wives and mothers in society. Women's "nature" then did not allow them to take part in public life or politics. Wheeler and Thompson refuted these beliefs. They argued that women's "nature" was a construction, something that was made up by society. They argued that women deserved equal freedom with men. Women must have equal rights with men if the greatest happiness of women and men was to be ensured. Wheeler was disillusioned by the failure of the 1832 Reform Bill to give women the vote and despaired that men would ever relinquish any power to women in the way, for example, that Mary Wollstonecraft had hoped. She also complained that most women were unreceptive to feminist ideas, marveling that women's strength often manifested itself in their willingness to endure oppression, rather than in fighting against it.

There was a common Western belief that women had particular attributes—their maternal instinct, their sensitivity—which made the home, or the domestic sphere, their natural environment. That was to be their world; politics was the concern of men. Once women's duties to their husbands and families were safeguarded, they could spend their time engaged in charitable works. From the late eighteenth century many Irish women, of the middle and upper classes, engaged in philanthropic endeavors motivated by religious beliefs and humanitarian concerns. In Ireland there were two strands in nineteenth-century women's philanthropy, a benevolent strand that attempted to alleviate the symptoms of poverty without questioning the underlying causes of that poverty, and a reformist tradition that attempted to initiate legislative measures to improve the lot of the poor.[12] In Ireland there was a clear sectarian division in philanthropic work. Among Catholic women most charitable work was left to nuns, and the dominance of religious women in such work relegated lay Catholic women primarily to a fundraising role. In consequence lay Catholic women were less likely to become active in campaigns for social change in comparison with their Protestant and nonconformist counterparts. Protestant and nonconformist women, who had direct experience of active charity work, were most moved to engage in political campaigns to alter the position of women in society. In establishing, managing, and fundraising for a range of charitable organizations, women, especially Protestant and nonconformist women, developed an awareness of social problems and a critique of public welfare institutions, such as workhouses, where they did not play a managerial role. Involvement in philanthropy allowed these women to develop skills in networking and lobbying, which they were to use in extending their political role in society.

The 1860s saw the beginnings of a range of feminist activism in Ireland. In the late 1860s a branch of the London-based Married Women's Property Committee was established in Belfast and Dublin to fight for changes in married women's property acts. A prime mover in this campaign in Ireland was Isabella M. S. Tod (1836–1896), an individual of unique importance in the women's cause in nineteenth-century Ireland.[13] Tod was the only woman to give evidence to a select committee of the House of Commons on this subject in 1868. Feminists, such as Tod, believed that working women could not maintain themselves and their families, because their husbands took their wages from them or more frequently, these husbands ran "up debts at the public houses which the women must discharge, at least under the threat of having their furniture and other property taken to pay it, and the consequences are very bad for all the family."[14] Feminists believed that women in control of their finances would bring immense benefit to their families and particularly to their children.

Education was a major preoccupation of activist women in the nineteenth century. Before the 1830s, the range of education available to girls in Ireland, as in other European countries, was haphazard. Some were educated in mixed pay-schools, where the emphasis was on reading, writing, and arithmetic. The introduction of the National School system of education in 1831 eventually opened up education to the majority of children in the country. In 1892–1893 the Irish Education Act allowed for free and compulsory education at the primary level.[15] Only a small proportion of the population had access to secondary education in the nineteenth century. Nuns led the way in catering to the needs of the emerging Catholic middle classes who wanted their daughters educated. Feminist activists sought the provision of an education for girls of the middle classes that would allow them some form of employment.

Although convents provided the most extensive secondary education available, it was women from Protestant backgrounds who fought for improvements in the education available for middle-class girls. Activists had to fight to have girls included in the benefits of the Intermediate Education Act; they also had to fight for access to university education. Historians argue that the introduction of the Intermediate Education (Ireland) Act of 1878 "revolutionized" girls' secondary education. Religious as well as academic rivalry increased the numbers of females studying at second and third levels. Catholic middle-class parents pushed for changes to the education their daughters were receiving in the convent schools. Competition among lay and convent schools forced convent schools to meet the new demands.[16] Again it was women of Protestant and nonconformist backgrounds who led the campaign for access to universities in Ireland.[17] Many activists argued that education would make women better wives and mothers and enable them to fulfill their social and moral duties better. But in effect it was these newly educated middle-class women who were to be an important force in shaping early twentieth-century Ireland.[18]

Educational advances in women's education were not always well received. Too much study, it was argued, would put a huge strain on women's nervous and reproductive systems. Feminists argued that without a proper and fitting education, one that would develop their intellectual capacities, women could not play their proper role in society. Parents feared that a daughter so educated might "shape a novel path in life for herself."[19] For activists, education for girls could only be of benefit to society in many different ways. It would strengthen the religious and moral aspects of a woman's life. The equality of education for men and women would "allow different but harmonizing modes of action" on social problems. One other great advantage of education for women, it was argued, was that it would also benefit women of the lower classes. As Tod noted, "Who can tell how great an amelioration may take place in the painful conditions of women of the lower classes, when not merely a few, but most, of those in the classes above them have not only the will, but the power, and the knowledge [of] how to help them."[20] Not only was education necessary to develop the full intellectual and spiritual potential of an individual but it was also to serve a social purpose. It was further argued that a proper education for girls would allow them to work and support themselves. In a number of speeches Tod noted the "unreasonableness of the prejudice against change" whether in relation to the secondary or higher education of women. "Before an argument of any kind is offered to us," she noted in 1875, "we are met with an advanced guard of horrified ejaculations."[21] In answer to the arguments that higher education would damage women's health or refinement, she observed that "the great features of the human mind are the same in both men and women, and that they need the same nutriment, though the development of the natures so fed will differ according to their capabilities." Against the charge that women were presumptuous in looking for higher education, she stated it to be a "nonsensical charge ... [for] if self-preservation be the first law of savage nature, self-improvement is the first law of civilised nature, and we have no notion of disobeying it."[22]

Like many feminist campaigns, that to change women's education took place over a long time span. From the 1860s mainly Protestant and Quaker women were involved in this campaign, but as more rights were won, convent schools began to take advantage of the new opportunities. In 1877 medical degrees of the Royal College of Physicians and Surgeons were opened to women on the same terms as men. In 1879 the Royal University of Ireland (RUI) degrees were also opened to women. Alexandra and Victoria colleges opened university departments to prepare girls for higher education. These new collegiate departments prepared girls older than eighteen for the Arts examination of the RUI. One hundred fifty-two women graduated from the RUI between 1884 and 1892. Women students were admitted to Trinity College in 1904. Though women were admitted to the colleges, they did not essentially have equal status with men. Staff appointments and appointments to governing bodies were, as Eibhlin Breathnach points out, still "jobs for the boys."[23]

Another major campaign for feminist activists of the nineteenth century was that organized to repeal the Contagious Diseases Acts that were introduced in the 1860s. These acts had been initiated to control the spread of venereal diseases among the soldiery. In effect the acts subjected prostitutes who were on the street to arbitrary and compulsory medical examinations and, if infected, to incarceration in a lock hospital or the lock ward of a hospital until they were cured. Feminists opposed the Acts on a number of grounds, but mainly because they applied solely to women, leaving the men untouched. For them the implementation of the Acts marked the legitimation of the double standard of sexual morality that existed in society. In Ireland the areas designated as "subjected" districts were Cork, Cobh, and the Curragh. By 1871 three branches of the Ladies' National Association for the Repeal of the Contagious Diseases Act were formed in Ireland at Belfast, Cork, and Dublin. Although the Association was small, it marked a new departure for Irish women. For the first time they were willing to discuss openly matters pertaining to sexual morality and to initiate a public campaign to question and attempt to alter the sexual double standard that existed. It was not until the 1970s that women publicly discussed issues relating to sexuality and began campaigns around issues relating to fertility and other matters regarding women's bodies. The women who were active in the Contagious Diseases Act movement in Ireland were predominantly Quakers.[24]

The demand for suffrage was the principal means whereby women fought for political involvement on the same terms as men in the late nineteenth and early twentieth centuries. A sizable majority of those women who originated the suffrage campaign in Ireland had activist roots in various philanthropic organizations. It was inevitable that women's regenerative work in philanthropic organizations should lead to a call for the extension of the franchise. With the vote women would regenerate society from a new power base. Their activism ensured that some legislative progress in regard to women's rights was made before the turn of the nineteenth century. Women who were active in the suffrage campaign also fought for women's rights in local elections. In Belfast women householders gained the municipal franchise in 1887, before women of other towns in Ireland. This had come about through the introduction of a plan to improve the drainage system of Belfast. Because this scheme would affect every ratepayer, local members of parliament (MPs) argued that the municipal franchise should be extended to all ratepayers, including women. The original bill would have given this vote to women in all municipal authorities in Ireland. However, there was considerable opposition to this in parliament, and eventually only Belfast women won the right to the municipal vote, largely owing to the lobbying efforts of women like Isabella Tod. In 1894 women in the Dublin townships of Dun Laoghaire and Blackrock won the same right. It was not until 1898 that women in the rest of Ireland were enfranchised under the Local Government Act. This Act allowed women the right to vote for local councils and to sit on district councils but not on county councils.[25] Through their activism in such campaigns, women became astute lobbyists and created possibilities for change.

In 1896, after a long campaign, and years after English women, Irish women finally received the right to sit as Poor Law Guardians (Poor Law Guardians managed the workhouses that were the main institutions of relief for the destitute poor in nineteenth-century Ireland). By 1899 ten thousand women were qualified to be Poor Law electors, but certain property qualifications had to be met before they could vote. In arguing for such voting rights, arguments based on women's supposed moral superiority and domestic skills were used. Women were believed to have particular qualities that would enable them to make good Poor Law Guardians. One commentator noted in 1896 that "there was a strong feeling in Ireland, especially in Ulster, that there was a certain sphere of work in which the services of women on boards of guardians would be of great value. Thus they could look after pauper women and children, the training of girls for service, and the food and sanitary arrangements far better than men."[26] Women, it was believed (and indeed women themselves argued), could transfer their domestic and maternal qualities from the home to the workhouse, using the rhetoric of domesticity to further their role in public politics. What is clear in all these campaigns is that nothing was easily won for women. It was only through determined lobbying and campaigning that they were able to impress politicians with their demands.

In 1866 the first suffrage petition asking for female suffrage had been presented to the House of Commons by John Stuart Mill. Of the 1,499 women who signed the petition, 25 were Irish women. One of those signatories was Anna Haslam, a Quaker, who in 1876 was to be the cofounder, with her husband, Thomas, of the Dublin Women's Suffrage Association.[27] Both men and women could and did become members of this suffrage society. In the north of Ireland, Isabella Tod had already established a suffrage society in 1872 in Belfast. The suffrage campaign reached its height in the years just before the outbreak of the Great War in 1914. The women involved in these early suffrage societies were middle class, Protestant, and nonconformist. Many of the early suffragists did not desire the vote for all but demanded that women property owners had as much right to the vote as did male property owners. This demand for citizenship did not then extend in practical terms to all women, but all women, it was believed, would benefit from even a limited suffrage. Haslam's organization's name changed a number of times to reflect its current campaign. Eventually it became the Irishwomen's Suffrage and Local Government Association (IWSLGA) in 1901. The IWSLGA campaigned on a number of issues relating to the status of women in Irish society. The first recorded membership of the IWSLGA is available from 1896 when it numbered 43. In 1911 membership had increased to 647, its high point. Its tactics, like those of English suffragists, included petitions, public lectures, letters to the newspapers, and lobbying MPs. By the end of the 1880s the suffrage cause generally had reached a low ebb, and the issue was not debated in the House of Commons between 1886 and 1892.

In the early 1900s the suffrage cause moved into a new phase influenced in particular by the establishment of the militant Women's Social and Political Union (WSPU) in England in 1903. WSPU members were willing to adopt militant tactics, such as heckling politicians at meetings, and attracting as much publicity to the cause as possible. Eventually the WSPU was to use more violent methods to advance their cause.[28] In Ireland some frustration was also felt at the lack of progress the older suffrage groups appeared to be making. In 1908 a new suffrage organization, the Irish Women's Franchise League (IWFL), formed by Hanna Sheehy Skeffington, her husband Frank, and their friends Margaret Cousins and her husband James. The members of the IWFL were committed to a more aggressive and militant campaign than were the earlier suffrage groups. Both Hanna Sheehy Skeffington and Margaret Cousins were typical of the newer generation of women activists. They were both young graduates who had married feminists.

The formation of the IWFL was a significant development in the Irish suffrage campaign. Its militancy brought the campaign to the attention of a larger audience. Their first aim was to have votes for women incorporated into the Home Rule bill that was then being fought for by the Irish Parliamentary Party. From its inception the IWFL was open to criticism from those who felt that women's suffrage should not take priority over the nationalist cause in Ireland. This became a major bone of contention among Irish women political activists. Many nationalist women saw the IWFL as an adjunct of the WSPU. The leadership of the Irish Parliamentary Party was hostile to the suffrage cause. Sinn Féin, which refused to acknowledge the right of England to rule Ireland, also had difficulties with the suffrage campaign. Although women were represented on the executive of Sinn Féin, support for suffrage was ambivalent, as Home Rule legislation seemed threatened by the suffragists insisting on the inclusion of female franchise. Arthur Griffith declared that Sinn Féin was "not particularly interested in the suffragette movement."[29] Once again women's rights came second to national rights. Hanna Sheehy Skeffington was to note that women, like Constance Markievicz, "whose natural sympathies should have been with us," instead adopted a position of opposition in terms of priorities and strategies.[30] In Belfast the IWFL was thought to be tainted by nationalism.

Other tensions developed in the suffrage community. Irish and English suffragists had much in common; they both wanted votes for women, and they read and shared the same suffrage papers. In Ireland, however, suffragists were looking for the vote from a parliament of a different country, so the question of imperial domination was an important one. Unionist women, who opposed Home Rule for Ireland, found their loyalties sorely tested, and the campaign for the vote was often abandoned. Nationalism was also a complicating factor. Constance Markievicz argued that Irish women should first of all fight for Irish freedom rather than seek the vote from an English parliament.

Inghinidhe na hÉireann (Daughters of Ireland) was formed by Maud Gonne in 1900 and included in its membership such women as the actress Sara Allgood and Jennie Wyse Power, who had been active in the Ladies' Land League and went on to become the president of Sinn Féin and a senator in the Irish Free State government. Nationalism, rather than feminism, held the first allegiance of this group, and few of its members joined the suffrage campaign. It argued that looking for the vote from the British parliament was a betrayal of Irish aspirations for independence. Suffragists responded to these arguments by claiming that it was in the women's and the nation's best interests, as an oppressed group, to fight for the vote as a true symbol of citizenship; otherwise the new Ireland would be created without the influence of half the population, its women. Cumann na mBan (Irishwomen's Council) was formed in 1913 as an auxiliary to the Irish National Volunteers. Although some members of Cumann na mBan were feminist and had been involved in the suffrage campaign, they put their energies into the nationalist cause.

There was much public opposition to women's suffrage. Women were heckled at suffrage meetings. Many Catholic bishops and clergy opposed the cause and saw suffragettes as acting "contrary to God's law."[31] Among the horrors was that the "feminist movement created a tendency to withdraw woman from the home and plunge her into the glare and light of the world."[32] Even though Catholic women were active in the suffrage campaign it was not until 1916 that the first Catholic suffrage organization was founded; named the Irish Catholic Women's Suffrage Association, it operated "under the patronage of St. Brigid and the inspiration of Pope Leo XIII."[33] The press in Ireland was generally unsympathetic to the cause. However, one individual who became a strong suffrage supporter was the Labour leader James Connolly, who observed that "in its march towards freedom, the working class of Ireland must cheer on the efforts of those women who, feeling on their souls and bodies the fetters of the ages, have risen to strike them off."[34]

The IWFL made its voice heard through the pages of the *Irish Citizen*. The *Irish Citizen* was, in reality, the third in a line of feminist publications produced in Ireland. The first was *The Woman's Advocate*, which was published in 1874 by Thomas Haslam. This publication advocated women's suffrage, and was influential in Ireland and England. The next was *Bean na hÉireann*, which ran from 1909 to 1911 and was the weekly paper of Inghinidhe na hÉireann, edited by Helena Molony. Molony had stated that she had wanted a newspaper that would be a "woman's paper, advocating militancy, separatism and feminism."[35] The *Irish Citizen* first appeared in May 1912. It was edited by Frank Sheehy Skeffington, the husband of Hanna, and James Cousins, the husband of Margaret Cousins. Most of the contributors to the paper were women. By June 1912, after the publication of its fifth issue, the editors claimed that three thousand copies were circulated each week and that more than ten thousand people read it. The paper, which ran for eight years, was seen as a means of communication among Irish suffragists and as a means of propaganda. Through the pages of the newspaper the ideas and aims of the suffrage movement would be explained to the public. The paper contained features on the progress of the suffrage cause, particularly in England and America, and reported on meetings of local suffrage societies in Ireland. It thus linked the Irish suffrage campaign with the international suffrage movement. It covered employment issues for women and contained articles on unionism, nationalism, the Irish Parliamentary Party, Home Rule, the First World War, and the 1916 rising. All major feminist themes and issues of the day were discussed in the paper.

The suffrage campaign in Ireland, strongly urban based, claimed to have a membership of three thousand by 1914. It opened the eyes of a number of suffragists to the problems faced by women of the working classes. Louie Bennett, for example, organized the Irish Women's Reform League to draw attention to the social and economic conditions of women workers and their families. The League investigated conditions in Dublin factories, campaigned for school meals, and organized a committee to monitor legislation affecting women.[36] For feminist activists equality in the labor market was always contentious. Concern about women's paid labor in the nineteenth century was often less about their right to work than the conditions under which they worked. Thus legislation tended to focus on "protection," limiting, for instance, women's working hours and attempting to improve actual working conditions. Economic independence for women rarely surfaced as a sustained campaigning issue for Irish nineteenth-century feminists.[37] The establishment of the Irish Women Workers' Union in 1911 by Delia Larkin and her brother James was a major development in supporting women's working rights. The most notable development of the women's movement in Ireland, Louie Bennett was to observe in 1918, was the growth in trade unionism among women workers.[38] The expansion of women's trade unionism was believed to be "the best possible contribution to the whole cause of feminism. There can be no real freedom or independence for women until they are economically free."[39] The growing numbers involved in the trade-union movement allowed women to express their needs as workers, and also in many cases to successfully challenge their exploitation.

The outbreak of the Great War saw suffrage societies in Ireland and Britain faced with a major dilemma. Should they support the government war effort and suspend their political activities, or should they refuse to give up on their demands and continue the campaign? For example, the English WSPU disbanded immediately and threw its efforts into supporting the government in its war effort. Nationalist women took the view that "England's difficulty was Ireland's opportunity," and groups like Cumann na mBan increased preparations for separatist action. Many suffragists were also pacifists and were horrified at the outbreak of the war. By late 1914 Louie Bennett, for example, was fearful of the breakup of the suffrage movement in Ireland. Some suffragists continued to campaign for the cause. Louie Bennett described the three main areas of suffragist work during the war years as those engaged in relief work, those devoted to suffrage only, and those engaged in peace work. Many members of the IWFL were involved in peace work, and many were strong pacifists. Their general belief was that until women were enfranchised, it would be unacceptable to submit oneself to a "state power which excludes women from the decision making process while, at the same time, uses and exploits their services."[40]

In January 1918 the Representation of the People Act came into force in Ireland. This Act granted the vote to women older than thirty who were householders, the wives of householders, were possessed of a £5 occupation qualification, or were graduates. The Irish Parliamentary Party and the unionists opposed the extension of the 1918 Act to Ireland, but for Sinn Féin the newly enfranchised woman voter was seen as an important figure. Constance Markievicz became, while in prison, the first woman to be elected to the Westminster parliament, though she did not take her seat. Under the Irish Free State Constitution of 1922, all citizens over the age of twenty-one were enfranchised. In Britain, it was not until the enactment of the Equal Franchise Bill of 1928 that women older than twenty-one were entitled to vote.

Irish women's political activism continued through the period of the fight for independence. The nature and extent of women's activism in the struggle for independence was primarily focused on achieving independence rather than on feminist issues as such. Women's involvement in the campaign for independence would suggest that they were well placed to benefit from the roles they had played in that struggle. However, from its beginning, women's political, economic, and social rights were gradually eroded in the Free State. It was always going to be difficult to dislodge the generally held views that women's lives must remain centered around the home and the family. From the foundation of the Free State there is no doubt that both the state and the church emphatically presented women's place as being in the home and the ideal role of the Irish woman as mother. Whatever equality might mean, it was always circumscribed by this belief in the domestic nature of women.

Several feminist organizations existed in Ireland in the 1920s and 1930s. The National Council of Women of Ireland was formed in 1924 by a group of Irish feminists, many of whom had been active in the suffrage campaign. It lobbied for the appointment of women police officers whose role would be the protection of children and adolescent girls.[41] The formation of the Joint Committee of Women's Societies and Social Workers in March 1935 brought the Mother's Union, the Irish Guild of Catholic Nurses, and the Irish Women Citizens' Association along with other groups together to promote and lobby on "matters of mutual interest affecting women, young persons and children."[42] This was an important campaigning body that also sought, among other things, to secure women police for the South of Ireland. Just how entrenched views of women's place in society can be is revealed by the fact that this campaign for women police began during the suffrage period, and the first female police officers appeared on the streets of Dublin in 1959. There was criticism of these organizations, and an article in *Christus Rex*, a Catholic journal of sociology, asked whether such groups "really represent the women and housewives of the country?"[43]

Equal citizenship had been guaranteed to Irish men and women under the Proclamation of 1916. Active lobbying, particularly by women, saw all Irish citizens over the age of twenty-one enfranchised under the Irish Free State Constitution enacted in June 1922. Ideas of equality and equal citizenship became central in many women's minds to understanding their significance and place in an independent Irish State. How equality was understood, or expected to work in practice, was not always clearly articulated, and as a concept equality was often framed or understood in gendered and class terms.

Much of women's political activism in the 1920s and 1930s was informed by their understanding of both the 1916 Proclamation and certain articles in the 1922 Constitution. From the 1916 Proclamation the phrase "The Republic guarantees religious and civil liberty, equal rights and equal opportunities to all its citizens" was the standard against which government policy, particularly where it affected women, was measured. Article 3 of the 1922 Constitution, which guaranteed equality to all Irish citizens, strengthened the position outlined in the Proclamation.[44] The ideals of equality implied by both these documents held a vital place in the vocabulary of feminists in the 1920s and 1930s.[45] Invoking both the 1916 Proclamation and the relevant sections of the 1922 Constitution, women campaigned against government attempts to limit their rights as citizens and specifically their rights as workers. These phrases, particularly that from the Proclamation, offered a fundamental and irrevocable foundation for campaigns of equality. The language of equality expressed in the Proclamation, sanctified by the deaths of the 1916 rising's leaders and the campaign for independence, and consolidated in the 1922 Constitution, offered women activists an essential understanding of their status in Irish society. Although it was a status continually under attack, these phrases remained an enduring legacy for activist women.[46]

The right to work remained of central importance to women trade unionists and to feminist activists from the foundation of the Free State. Attempts to restrict women's access to employment were strongly resisted by women activists. Feminists fought significant campaigns around the Civil Service Amendment Bill (1924), the Marriage Bar, the Conditions of Employment Bill (1935), and the campaign against the draft Constitution of 1937. In 1937 the Irish Women Workers' Union organized a fourteen-week strike of women laundry workers, eventually winning the right to a two-week annual holiday for all industrial workers.[47]

The implementation of restrictive legislation in the economic and political spheres found echoes in the social sphere. For instance, divorce, previously available through an act of parliament, was banned in 1925; the 1927 Juries Act made it difficult for women to sit on juries. The 1929 Censorship of Publications Bill prohibited the advertisement of contraceptives, while the 1935 Criminal Law Amendment Act prohibited the sale of contraceptives. There was some opposition to these legislative changes from women in the Irish Senate, Jennie Wyse Power being one of the few women in either house of the Oireachtas who retained her strong feminist credentials.

In Northern Ireland women's activism from the 1950s saw a range of protests not only against the state but also about society's general understanding of women's place in it. Many women in Northern Ireland used street protests, marches, and sit-ins to get their messages across. Keenan-Thomson argues that the kind of activism evident from women in the 1950s and 1960s laid the groundwork for "second-wave" feminism in Ireland.[48] She reveals how, for instance, in 1963 working-class women from Dungannon led a housing protest and engaged in civil disobedience to draw attention to their demands. Women also became involved in street activities as the civil rights movement evolved in Northern Ireland from the 1960s. Women such as Bernadette Devlin emerged from this environment. Echoing the establishment of women's organizations in England and Ireland, lesbian groups became active from 1974, with the establishment of telephone helplines; Belfast Women's Aid was set up in 1974 to offer advice and shelter to victims of domestic violence. In 1977 the Belfast Women's Collective was formed to encourage feminists to work together on a wide range of issues.[49] Between 1978 and 1981 the Women Against Imperialism group was active, also in Belfast. But what was clear is that attempts to bring women together as feminists were undermined by the political crisis of the "Troubles." Sectarian violence and its effects made working together across the political and denominational divides difficult. The Troubles saw feminism take a backseat to other problems, and the relationship between feminism and nationalism was sorely tested during the period of the Troubles. Particular tensions surfaced in relation to the "dirty protest" conducted by women republicans in Armagh prison.[50] The Women Against Imperialism Group, for instance, believed that the Armagh women's protest was an issue that was of central importance to feminist politics. Others saw it only in terms of the women following the main protest by the men. How feminist views evolved in the unionist community has been little researched, with one commentator arguing that "the possibility of unionism accommodating any form of feminism did not take place until the early 1990s."[51]

Social issues that involved family life, reproduction, and economic equality provoked campaigns by women throughout the period from the 1920s. The Irish Housewives Association (IHA) was formed in 1942 and originally sought to demand fair prices and fair distribution of goods during the Emergency, and it proved to be an effective pressure group throughout the second half of the twentieth century.[52] Comparable organizations in Northern Ireland were the Women's Institute and the Northern Ireland Housewives League. These organizations acted as consumer advocacy groups. However, as the decades passed, the IHA became more feminist in its actions, unlike the Northern Ireland groups. In the 1950s the IHA began to campaign for women jurors. It was closely allied to the International Alliance of Women, and the IHA was later instrumental in encouraging the government to establish a Commission on the Status of Women in March 1970.[53]

In 1970 the establishment of the Irish Women's Liberation Movement (IWLM) brought a new generation of women to embrace political and social activism. The IWLM was begun by a group of twelve women, six of them journalists, and its members knew how to get media attention. The manifesto of the IWLM, "Change or Chains: The Civil Wrongs of Irish Women" (1971) demanded equal pay; an end to the marriage bar;[54] equal rights in law; rights for widows, deserted wives, and unmarried mothers; equal opportunities in education; and access to legal contraception.[55] Such demands were similar to those made by feminists in Europe, except on the subject of abortion, which continues to remain a divisive issue in Irish society. One of the major issues pursued by the IWLM was contraception, a campaign that brought it infamy and publicity, particularly when on May 22, 1971, a group of women made a trip to Belfast to purchase contraceptives, which they openly and blatantly brought back to Dublin.[56]

The pill had been available in Ireland, as a menstrual-cycle regulator, from the 1960s with a doctor's prescription. The Irish Family Planning Association was formed in 1969. Family-planning clinics were established, with one operating in Limerick city from 1976. Catholic Church leaders condemned the enterprise, as did local conservative politicians, and the *Limerick Leader*, the major local newspaper, refused to print any advertising relating to the clinic. Such local and grass-roots activism is an often forgotten feature in feminist activism in Ireland from the 1970s.[57] It was not until 1979 that anti-contraception laws were removed from the statute books.

It was difficult for any women's organization in the period to ignore the subject of contraception. Such organizations as the Irish Country Women's Association (ICA; originally founded as United Irishwomen in 1911) were concerned with developing rural life; fostering traditional arts and crafts; and providing courses on cooking, domestic skills, and public speaking for its members. The ICA did not consider itself a political or feminist organization. The ICA networked with similar international organizations and beginning in the 1950s it became an effective lobbying group. However, in 1972 the ICA conducted a survey among its members on attitudes to family planning and discovered that 80% of respondents were in favor of some form of national family-planning service.[58] This issue brought organizations like the ICA into feminist politics. With the IHA, it lobbied for the

Commission on the Status of Women, and its members later played an active role in the Council for the Status of Women, formed in response to the Commission.

The IWLM had disintegrated by September 1971, but one of its founders, June Levine, noted its achievement. "We'd broken the news. We'd told Ireland about the women's movement, we'd turned women on, we'd revealed the underground anger in women's lives, we'd blown the cover."[59]

Irish Women United (IWU) was formed in 1975 and was a more radical grouping of left-wing feminists and socialist activists. It consisted of three distinct feminist strands: radical lesbians, socialist feminists, and radical feminists.[60] This group initiated the Contraception Action Programme. IWU disintegrated under internal divisions in 1977, and many of its members went on to be active in other organizations and campaigns. Many women active in these early movements established a range of organizations to fight for women's rights. Rape Crisis Centres began to appear from 1977; Women's Aid, for domestic violence, emerged in 1974; the Well Woman Centre operated in Dublin, providing health advice to women; AIM (Action, Information, Motivation) was founded in 1972 and lobbied for family-law reform; and Cherish, which provided support to single parents, was formed in 1972. The Women's Progressive Association (later to become the Women's Political Association) was formed in 1970 to support women's attempts to forge political careers.

The Commission on the Status of Women published its final report in December 1972, outlining forty-nine areas of discrimination against women in Ireland.[61] The report provided a focus for legislative reform in several areas, including employment, social-welfare taxation, and property rights. The Council was to monitor the implementation of the Commission's recommendations and also be alert to other areas where women might face discrimination. Through vigorous campaigning the Council for the Status of Women has been influential in shaping government policy and action in areas relating to, among other issues, equality legislation and domestic abuse. [62]

What was evident in feminist activism from the 1970s was the diversity of that activism, the variety of political ideologies that shaped the discourse, and the longevity of women's activist involvement. Irish feminist activism, from its earliest period, was never insular. Women were aware of what was happening in the wider world; they created networks of feminist action with their peers in England and the United States. In Ireland, throughout the period, many feminist activists knew one another, often worked on the same campaigns, and respected one another's differences of political or social opinion. It was only during the Troubles that a constant tension developed among feminist activists. Political divisions influenced the development of the women's movement in Northern Ireland and the relationship that existed with the women's movement in the South. Feminist issues had entered the mainstream of Irish political life by the 1980s. Not only had national organizations been established to cater to aspects of women's interests and needs—such as formal political involvement or advice on health issues—but also women in rural Ireland established consciousness-raising groups that encouraged the development of local support groups. While the 1980s saw Ireland in difficult economic circumstances, the early 1990s saw real and symbolic changes in Irish feminism. The first woman president of Ireland, Mary Robinson, was elected in December 1990 after a difficult campaign: in 1997 she was followed by a second female president, Mary McAleese. Both women had had distinguished political and academic careers. Symbolically much had changed, though on the ground the campaigns continued, and for feminist activists new issues were to emerge with the rise and fall of the Celtic Tiger.

FURTHER READING

As yet no comprehensive history exists of feminism in Ireland. However, much ground relating to Irish women generally in cultural, social, economic, religious, and intellectual life can be found in Angela Bourke, Siobhain Kilfeather, Maria Luddy, Margaret McCurtain, Gerardine Meaney, Maire Nic Dhonnchadha, Mary O'Dowd, and Clair Wills (eds.), *Field Day Anthology of Irish Writing: Irish Women's Writing and Traditions*, vols. 4 and 5 (Cork and New York: Cork University Press and New York University Press, 2002.) The two volumes offer an extensive opportunity to engage with Irish women's history, culture, and oral traditions from 600 AD to the late twentieth century. The volumes take an interdisciplinary approach and provide access to original documents, many translated for the first time from the Irish language. They include biographies, bibliographies, and extensive introductions. These volumes contain sections that deal specifically with feminism.

Another useful source, which also includes original documents, charts the development of second-wave feminism in Ireland from the 1970s on is Linda Connolly and Tina O'Toole, *Documenting Irish Feminisms: The Second Wave* (Dublin: Woodfield Press, 2005).

NOTES

1. *Northern Star*, December 22, 1792.
2. Jean Agnew (ed.), *The Drennan-McTier Letters* (Dublin: The Women's History Project/Irish Manuscripts Commission, 1998–1999), 3 vols., I, pp. 460, 471. For the background, see Ian McBride, *Eighteenth-Century Ireland* (Dublin: Gill and Macmillan, 2009), pp. 387–398.
3. Karen Offen, "Defining Feminism: A Comparative Historical Approach," *Signs* 14: 1 (1988), pp. 125–126.
4. Mary O'Dowd, "Politics, Patriotism and Women in Ireland, Britain and Colonial America, c. 1700–1780," *Journal of Women's History* 22: 4 (Winter 2010), pp. 15–38.
5. Wollstonecraft took up a position as governess to the three daughters of Lord and Lady Kingsborough at Mitchelstown Castle in County Cork. Two of Wollstonecraft's sisters ran a school

in Dublin, which a daughter of Daniel O'Connell attended. See Janet Todd, *Mary Wollstonecraft: A Revolutionary Life* (London: Weidenfeld and Nicholson, 2000); Janet Todd, *Daughters of Ireland* (New York: Ballantine Books, 2004).

6. See John Gray, "Mary Ann McCracken: Belfast Revolutionary and Pioneer of Feminism," in Daire Keogh and Nicholas Furlong (eds.), *The Women of 1798* (Dublin: Four Courts Press, 1993).

7. Mary Ann McCracken to Henry Joy McCracken, March 16, 1797. The full text of the letter is available in Mary McNeill, *The Life and Times of Mary Ann McCracken 1770–1866: a Belfast Panorama* (Dublin: Allan Figgis, 1960), pp. 125–128.

8. *Journals and Memoirs of Thomas Russell*, edited by C. J. Woods (Dublin: Irish Academic Press, 1991), p. 86.

9. Quoted in Gray, "Mary Ann McCracken," p. 31.

10. Saint-Simonianism was a French social and political movement of the early nineteenth century. Its members evolved from idealists to early socialists. See Pamela Pilbeam, *Saint-Simonians in Nineteenth-Century France: From Free Love to Algeria* (Basingstoke: Palgrave Macmillan, 2014).

11. For an excellent account of Wheeler, see Dolores Dooley, *Equality in Community: Sexual Equality in the Writings of William Thomson and Anna Doyle Wheeler* (Cork: Cork University Press, 1996).

12. Maria Luddy, *Women and Philanthropy in Nineteenth-Century Ireland* (Cambridge: Cambridge University Press, 1995). See also Maria Luddy, "Religion, Philanthropy and the State in Late Eighteenth and Early Nineteenth-Century Ireland," in Hugh Cunningham and Joanna Innes (eds.), *Charity, Philanthropy and Reform from the 1690s to 1850* (London: Macmillan, 1998), pp. 148–167; Margaret Preston, *Charitable Words: Women, Philanthropy, and the Language of Charity in Nineteenth-Century Dublin* (Westport, CT: Praeger, 2004).

13. Maria Luddy, "Isabella M. S. Tod, 1836–1896," in Mary Cullen and Maria Luddy (eds.), *Women, Power and Consciousness in 19th Century Ireland* (Dublin: Attic Press, 1995), pp. 197–230.

14. *Special Report from the Select Committee on the Married Women's Property Bill*, H.C. 187–8 (441), vii, 339, pp. 74–76.

15. Deirdre Raftery and Susan M. Parkes, *Female Education in Ireland, 1700–1900* (Dublin: Irish Academic Press, 2007).

16. Anne V. O'Connor, "Influences Affecting Girls' Secondary Education in Ireland, 1860–1910," *Archivium Hibernicum* 141 (1986), pp. 83–98; Anne V. O'Connor, "The Revolution in Girls' Secondary Education in Ireland, 1860–1910," in Mary Cullen (ed.), *Girls Don't Do Honours: Irishwomen in Education in the Nineteenth and Twentieth Centuries* (Dublin: Women's Education Bureau, 1987), pp. 31–54. See also Anne V. O'Connor and Susan Parkes, *Gladly Learn and Gladly Teach: A History of Alexandra College and School, Dublin, 1866–1916* (Dublin: Blackwater Press, 1983). Alison Jordan, *Margaret Byers, Pioneer of Women's Education and Founder of Victoria College, Belfast* (Belfast: Institute of Irish Studies, 1991).

17. Judith Harford, *The Opening of University Education to Women in Ireland* (Dublin: Irish Academic Press, 2008).

18. See Senia Pašeta, *Before the Revolution: Nationalism, Social Change and Ireland's Catholic Elite, 1879–1922* (Cork: Cork University Press, 1999), which briefly explores some of the issues pertinent to the education of Catholic women at this time.

19. M. S. Tod, *On the Education of Girls of the Middle Class* (London: William Ridgway, 1874).

20. *Journal of Women's Education Union*, December 15,1875, pp. 183–184.

21. Luddy, "Isabella M. S. Tod," p. 206.

22. Luddy, "Isabella M. S. Tod," p. 203.

23. Eibhlin Breathnach, "Charting New Waters: Women's Experiences in Higher Education, 1879–1908," in Mary Cullen (ed.), *Girls Don't Do Honours: Irish Women in Education in the 19th and 20th Centuries* (Dublin: Women's Education Bureau, 1987), pp. 55–78.

24. Maria Luddy, *Prostitution and Irish Society, 1800–1940* (Cambridge: Cambridge University Press, 2007), chapter 3.

25. Virginia Crossman, *Local Government in Nineteenth-Century Ireland* (Belfast: Institute of Irish Studies, 1994), pp. 83–85.

26. Crossman, *Local Government*, p. 55.

27. Carmel Quinlan, *Genteel Revolutionaries: Anna and Thomas Haslam and the Irish Women's Movement* (Cork: Cork University Press, 2002).

28. C. J. Bearman, "An Examination of Suffragette Violence," *English Historical Review* 120: 486 (2005), pp. 369–397.

29. *Irish Citizen*, May 9, 1914.

30. Hanna Sheehy Skeffington, "Reminiscences of an Irish Suffragette," in Andree Sheehy Skeffington and Rosemary Cullen Owens (eds.), *Votes for Women: Irishwomen's Struggle for the Vote* (Dublin: n.p., 1975), p. 16.

31. *Irish Catholic*, September 28, 1912.

32. *Irish Catholic*, May 9, 1914.

33. *Catholic Suffragist* 11: 5 (May 1916), p. 46.

34. James Connolly, *Selected Writings* edited by Peter Beresford Ellis (London: Penguin, 1973), p. 195.

35. Rosemary Cullen Owens, *Smashing Times: A History of the Irish Women's Suffrage Movement, 1889–1922* (Dublin: Attic Press, 1984), pp. 45–46.

36. Rosemary Cullen Owens, *Louie Bennett*, (Cork: Cork University Press, 2001).

37. For an exception see Tod, *On the Education of Girls*.

38. *Irish Citizen*, January 1918.

39. *Irish Citizen*, October 1917.

40. *Irish Citizen*, August 15, 1914.

41. Women police officers were hired by the Royal Ulster Constabulary in Northern Ireland from 1942. See Margaret Cameron, *The Women in Green: a History of the RUC's Policewomen* (Belfast: RUC Historical Society, 1993). For the campaign for women police in Ireland, see Christopher Shepard, "A Liberalisation of Irish Social Policy? Women's Organisations and the Campaign for Women Police in Ireland, 1915–1957," *Irish Historical Studies* 36: 144 (2009), pp. 564–580.

42. Caitriona Beaumont, "Women and the Politics of Equality: The Irish Women's Movement, 1930–1943," in Mary O'Dowd and Maryann Valiulis (eds.), *Women and Irish History: Essays in Honour of Margaret McCurtain* (Dublin: Wolfhound, 1997), pp. 173–188.

43. Vigilans, "As I See It," *Christus Rex* 2 (1948), p. 75.

44. Article 3 stated that all Irish citizens "shall within the limits of the jurisdiction of the Irish Free State (Saorstat Eireann) enjoy the privileges and be subject to the obligations of such citizenship." (http://www.irishstatutebook.ie/en/constitution/).

45. For recent work on the role of women in politics in these years, see Maryann Gialanella Valiulis, "Power, Gender and Identity in the Irish Free State," *Journal of Women's History* 6: 4/7/1 (Winter/Spring 1995), pp. 117–136; Mary E. Daly, "Women in the Irish Free State, 1922–1939: The Interaction between Economics and Ideology," *Journal of Women's History* 6: /4/7/1 (Winter/Spring 1995), pp. 99–116; Caitriona Beaumont, "Women, Citizenship and Catholicism in the Irish Free State, 1922–1948," *Women's History Review* 6: 4 (1997), pp. 563–585.

46. Maria Luddy, "The Problem of Equality: Women's Activist Campaigns in Ireland, 1920–40," in Thomas E. Hachey (ed.), *Turning Points in Twentieth-Century Irish History* (Dublin: Irish Academic Press, 2011), pp. 57–76.

47. Mary Jones, *These Obstreperous Lassies: A History of the Irish Women Workers Union* (Dublin: Gill and Macmillan, 1988), pp. 177–187.

48. Tara Keenan-Thomson, *Irish Women and Street Politics, 1956–1973* (Dublin: Irish Academic Press, 2010).

49. Monica McWilliams, "Women and Political Activism in Northern Ireland, 1960–1993," in A. Bourke, S. Kilfeather, M. Luddy, M. McCurtain, G. Meaney, M. Nic Dhonnchadha, M. O'Dowd, and C. Wills (eds.), *The Field Day Anthology of Irish Writing: Irish Women's Writing and Traditions* (Cork: Cork University Press, 2001), vol. 5, pp. 374–377.

50. A "dirty protest" was begun by republican male prisoners in Long Kesh in 1978 as a protest against mistreatment by prison guards; the protest escalated through hunger strikes into a demand for "special category status." The "dirty protest" involved a refusal by prisoners to wash, use the

lavatory, or clean their cells. In 1980 republican women held in Armagh prison began a "dirty protest." See Christina Loughran, "Armagh and Feminist Strategy: Campaigns Around Republican Women Prisoners in Armagh Jail," *Feminist Review* 23 (1986), pp. 59–79.

51. Eilish Rooney, "Political Division, Practical Alliance: Problems for Women in Conflict," *Journal of Women's History* 6: 7 (1995), p. 42.

52. The Irish Women's Citizen Association (formerly the Irish Women's Suffrage and Local Government Association) was the last organization directly linking nineteenth- and twentieth-century suffrage activism. It was incorporated into the Irish Housewives Association in 1949. Also incorporated into the Housewives Association was the Women's Social and Political League formed by Hanna Sheehy Skeffington in 1937. The "Emergency" was the name given to the period of the Second World War when Ireland remained neutral.

53. *Irish Times*, April 7, 1970.

54. The marriage bar required female public servants, including school teachers, to resign from their employment when they married. The marriage bar on public service was removed in 1973.

55. See Bourke et al. (eds.), *Field Day Anthology*, vol. 5, for a range of documents and commentaries on the history of women in Ireland in the twentieth century.

56. Rosemary Cullen Owens, A *Social History of Women in Ireland* (Dublin: Gill and Macmillan, 2005), p. 314.

57. Yvonne Galligan, *Women and Politics in Contemporary Ireland: From the Margins to the Mainstream* (London: Continuum, 1998), p. 58.

58. "Family Planning Survey," MS 39,866/3, Irish Country Women's Association papers. National Library of Ireland, Dublin.

59. June Levine, *Sisters* (Dublin: Ward River Press, 1982), p. 265.

60. Pat Brennan, "Women in Revolt," Attic Press Archives, BL/F/AP/1139/35. University College Cork, Boole Library, Cork.

61. *Report of the Commission on the Status of Women* (Dublin: Government Publications Office, 1972).

62. Now known as the National Women's Council of Ireland.

CHAPTER 21

DIASPORA

Enda Delaney

L ET'S IMAGINE FOR A MOMENT Irish history without migration. That seems almost impossible to contemplate. No movement of English and Scottish settlers across the North Channel and Irish Sea to settle in Ireland throughout the sixteenth and seventeenth centuries under various schemes of plantation and settlement, and in doing so irrevocably alter the ethnic and religious composition of the island. No 1641 rebellion when Ulster Catholic resentment about dispossession and displacement boiled over into a sectarian bloodbath. And what of the mass migrations to colonial America of Ulster Presbyterians, who played such a critical role in the American revolutionary era? How would the ethnic and religious composition of the people on the island of Ireland differ, and indeed that of the major receiving societies of North America, Britain, and Australasia? And what of the alternative scenarios that can be imagined if the great diasporas of the modern era had not taken place to continental Europe, North America, Australia, Britain, Asia, the Caribbean, South America, and many other places? In a moment of fantastical excursion the revolutionary nationalist, Patrick Pearse, considered in 1913 another consequence of the absence of emigration—a huge population living on the island of Ireland.[1] For Pearse this was a desirable outcome, even though every nationalist leader since Daniel O'Connell in the 1830s has accepted that exile was the fate of a significant number of each generation born in Ireland. Even Éamon de Valera's views on emigration, when stripped of the usual rhetoric, could not deny the powerlessness of any government when it came to the movements of people.[2]

But emigration was neither inevitable nor wholly predictable. Most European societies experienced migration. Some, like Germany, England, Sweden, Norway, Scotland, Italy, and Spain, had a very high incidence of emigration at particular points in time, such as the early twentieth century or the years after the Second

World War. That said, no other Western European society has had a chronological range of movement as long as Ireland's, which stretches from the beginning of recorded human history to the present day. And, equally, no other Western European country could lay claim to the sheer geographical diversity of the settlement patterns over four centuries. Only a few places across the world have not had some contact with the "wandering" Irish, be it as navvies, soldiers, servants, merchants, colonial administrators, priests, or nuns. Why this wanderlust was so deeply embedded in Irish consciousness is clearly a matter for informed speculation. In neo-Marxist analyses the role of the periphery is to supply the metropolitan core with a bountiful supply of cheap labor, and Ireland at face value fulfills this role. More persuasively, the fate of a small island with limited supplies of national resources, peripherally located on the edge of a major landmass, may simply be to export what is arguably the greatest resource, its people. No one as yet has come up with an overarching explanation for the scale and duration of Irish emigration since 1600, perhaps because a one-size-fits-all model would never really be that useful and would only serve to conceal the inherent diversity and complexity of the history of this diaspora.

I

Few of these lofty issues concerned Owen Peter Mangan (1839–1927). Mangan had a truly remarkable life, and his experiences are broadly emblematic of the nineteenth-century world that he and his fellow migrants encountered.[3] Born in Billy Hill, County Cavan in 1839, he vividly recounted in 1912 the trials and tribulations of his everyday nineteenth-century world. Mangan's father was imprisoned after a conviction for making poteen, but he died shortly after when Owen was just two. His mother married a hedge-school teacher who was a "spoiled priest," as many were, but he was cruel to the children. Owen was left with his brother in the care of an old woman, though they soon escaped in search of their mother, who by now was living in Monaghan with her new husband. There followed an itinerant existence until he left Ireland for work in the Lancashire textile industry in 1853. After a varied series of occupations, including time as a policeman in St Helens, Lancashire, Mangan eventually ended up running his own provisions shop in the 1860s. He got caught up with the Fenian scare of the late 1860s, eventually selling the shop. Concluding, probably accurately, that he had little future in England, in 1867 he left for Philadelphia, where his brother was based. Soon after that he headed north back into the textile industry at Fall River, Massachusetts, then the center of the American clothing manufacture boom. After some time there, he moved yet again, to Rhode Island, first settling in Providence and eventually becoming a salesman for the Metropolitan Insurance Company. He lived out his days in Lynn, Massachusetts, and died aged eighty-eight years in 1927, but not before he had recounted his experiences for posterity.

Similarly, who could have predicted that one of the principals in the unfolding drama that ultimately led to the recall of the viceroy Lord Torrington from Ceylon (now Sri Lanka) in 1850 would be a Kilkenny-born Protestant doctor, Christopher Elliott (1810–1859)? Elliott had come to Ceylon in 1845, first as a government surgeon, though before long he set up his own practice in Colombo, achieving widespread respect for his medical knowledge. He became involved with a small newspaper, the *Colombo Observer*, of which he was both owner and editor.[4] After the brutal suppression of the Matale Revolution in 1848, Elliott used his network of contacts in London to raise the issue at Westminster, forcing a parliamentary investigation that ultimately resulted in the recall of the viceroy.[5]

Thousands of miles away on the northern pillar of the Arc de Triomphe, listed among France's most distinguished soldiers, is the name Dillon. Arthur Dillon (1750–1794), known as Count Dillon in France, was the last of a long line of Dillons who served in the French army in the Regiment of Dillon. The Dillons were part of the "Wild Geese," Catholics who left Ireland during the seventeenth and eighteenth centuries, fighting in the armies of Spain and France. Born and raised in England, he was the grandson of Arthur Dillon (1670–1733), the Irish Jacobite commander who founded the regiment and fought with distinction in the French army in campaigns in Spain and Italy in the early 1700s.[6] His grandson too was a courageous and talented soldier, serving as a general in the French forces during the American War of Independence; eventually he was made governor of Tobago in the 1780s. After the French Revolution in 1789, his loyalty to the new republican regime came under suspicion. Recalled to Paris to answer charges of being involved in a royalist conspiracy, he was condemned to death during the Reign of Terror and was guillotined in April 1794.

Or take another very different example: Mary Harris Jones (1837?–1930), born in Cork in the later 1830s, who emigrated to North America during the Great Famine, first arriving in Canada and then eventually settling in Chicago, where her seamstress shop was destroyed by the Great Fire of 1871.[7] In the 1890s she rose to prominence as a radical trade union leader and feminist, dubbed "Mother Jones." To this day an iconic figure for socialists, trade unionists, and feminists, she campaigned against child labor, and sought to improve working conditions for women workers, miners, and other marginalized groups. She was famously described by a district attorney in West Virginia as "the most dangerous woman in America" in 1902, after she ignored numerous injunctions banning public meetings during a miners' strike.

What connects these very different individuals is the interaction between Ireland and its massive diaspora, stretching back over the last four centuries. Since 1600, at least ten million people have left Ireland, settling in every part of the globe. Despite the links between the Irish at home and those scattered across the world, they are often completely neglected in historical accounts of modern Ireland, shunted off into oblivion and seen as in no way relevant to anything that occurred in Ireland. Yet all the major events in modern Irish history—including the 1798 Rebellion, the Great Famine of 1845–1852, the Land Question of the 1870s and 1880s, and the Irish Revolution of 1914–1923—were intimately connected with and influenced by the diaspora. To write the Irish story without the diaspora is to render a partial account. It is worth remembering that in 1910 the Irish-born population of New York at 250,000 people was only exceeded by the populations of Dublin and Belfast. In other words, the third-largest "Irish" city was across the Atlantic.[8]

II

Between 1600 and the present day the history of Ireland was profoundly shaped by the experience of migration and diasporic settlement.[9] The general patterns are well known, but it is worth reminding ourselves that the initial movement of people was of settlers who arrived as part of wider plantation and settlement policies initiated by the crown in the fifteenth and sixteenth centuries. English and Scottish settlers, some soldiers, others merely seeking land and opportunity, arrived in significant numbers, seeking to bring "civilization" to the island. Much of the settlement in east Ulster was based around the informal movement of Scots across the North Channel rather than planned migrations. Historians now view the colonization of Ireland within broader frameworks of the concerns of British policy in the wider Atlantic world.[10]

Just as people arrived, there was also the concurrent displacement and subsequent exile of the Catholic middle classes, particularly to continental Europe in the dramatic moment of the flight of the earls. These "Wild Geese," who have attracted sustained scholarly attention, settled in parts of France and Spanish Flanders, some joining the Catholic armies of Europe, even constituting themselves as separate regiments, as in the case of the Dillon regiment mentioned above.[11] The Cromwellian settlement of the 1650s resulted in the confiscation of land and the exile of thousands of Catholics, many of whom ended up in the West Indies. The movement of Catholics to Europe continued across the seventeenth and eighteenth centuries, predominantly from middle-class families involved in commerce, the clergy, or strong landholding families who managed to evade confiscation. Irish Colleges on the continent, such as the ones at Douai, Salamanca, Paris, and Leuven, provided training for young clerics and acted as centers for Gaelic scholarship and learning, now largely displaced from Ireland itself under penal legislation.[12] But it was not just clerics who spent time in Europe. Middle-class Catholics had extensive trade and mercantile contacts with continental Europe and indeed North America, especially with Newfoundland, and these also proved highly versatile migration pathways.

One remarkable cache of more than 125 letters seized from a ship traveling from Bordeaux to Dublin in 1757 gives a unique insight into an Irish diasporic community in France at a time of crisis due to the outbreak of the Seven Years' War the previous year. What emerges from these letters are the diverse religious identities of the correspondents, including John Black, a Protestant merchant who was a central figure in the Irish community at Bordeaux and who recounted stories to his son told to him by his grandmother of the massacres of Protestants during the 1641 rebellion.[13] But the principal concerns were the more immediate ones of family and kin, and the correspondence shows just how important maintaining these relationships was, regardless of distance. A son, for instance, excused his lack of communication as "nothing but a bad habit that I got here."[14] Such remarkable sources are rare glimpses into conversations about essentially quite mundane yet vital matters for the individuals involved.

The life and career of Richard Hennessy (1729–1800) is a fascinating example of the tensions that existed in eighteenth-century Ireland and of how emigration was an avenue for opportunity.[15] Hennessy was born in 1729, near Mallow, County Cork, where his family had managed to hold on to their lands. A second son, he was a childhood friend and schoolmate of Edmund Burke, and later married Burke's first cousin in 1765. Despite the widely held view that he entered the French army as a senior officer in 1748, in fact he was just an ordinary soldier. He traveled to Ostend, where his uncle had a brandy-exporting business, but there were no opportunities for him there. He then moved to Cognac, where a number of Irish people were involved with the brandy trade, and his first business venture there failed. Then he moved to Bordeaux. After a series of family tragedies including the death of his wife and two sons in 1781, he decided to return to Cognac where his son, James, had been running a cognac house for another Irishman, James Saule. Saule's death in 1788 provided the opportunity for father and son to establish the partnership of Jas. Hennessy and Sons, today a global brand. The Hennessys were a shrewd and versatile pair, and during the Revolutionary Wars of the 1790s served in the local National Guard and were fortunate enough to secure very profitable contracts to supply the French armed forces. Richard maintained close links with Ireland throughout his life in France, not least because it was good for business. On a visit to London in 1791–1792, he visited his childhood friend, Edmund Burke, at his estate in Beaconsfield, Buckinghamshire. When he contemplated returning to Ireland on this visit, he concluded that such a trip would "I think be attended with more pain than pleasure."[16]

But the most important element of eighteenth-century emigration was the remarkable movement of Ulster Presbyterians to the "land of liberty." While arriving at precise numbers of those who left is highly problematic, at least 250,000 people emigrated from Ireland before 1775.[17] Roughly three-quarters of those who left Ireland between 1700 and 1776 were Irish Protestants, mainly but not exclusively Ulster Presbyterians.[18] That said, an increasing proportion of Protestants from Leinster and Munster also left Ireland for the New World. Much has been written about the role that the Scots-Irish (or "Scotch-Irish," as they came to be known) played in colonial and revolutionary America in virtually every sphere of life. The image of the Scots-Irish as pioneers working to bring "civilization" to the more remote regions of the American colonies is an enduring one, but this often had terrible consequences for Native Americans who thwarted these plans, and historians are now paying a great deal more attention to the often catastrophic encounters between colonial Americans and indigenous peoples.[19] The contribution of the Scots-Irish to the American Revolution has been raised to hagiographic proportions, yet there is no doubt that many Ulster Scots were wholeheartedly supportive of the impetus to end English "tyranny." "Call this war by whatever name you may," observed a German officer, "only call it not an American rebellion; it is nothing more or less than a Scotch Irish Presbyterian rebellion."[20] That Irish Protestants contributed to a disproportionate degree was largely due to a political and religious culture that stressed liberty and freedom, and equally the particular conditions that they encountered in the American colonies.[21]

As with most migrants who left Ireland after 1600, their subsequent histories were shaped in part by their Irish background and culture but also formed in response to the environments that they subsequently inhabited. One of the key issues for scholars has been to explore how ideas, especially political ideologies, were modified or remade through the process of movement. Nowhere is this seen more clearly than in the transmission of radicalism in both directions across the Atlantic in the later eighteenth century, associated with the French and American Revolutions and ultimately the 1798 Irish rebellion. Painstaking reconstruction of the diffusion of ideas among radicals in Ireland, Britain, Europe, and North America demonstrates the complexity and intensity of these connections across oceans.[22]

Contrary to the widespread assumption that mass Catholic migrations began with the Great Famine, in the years between the end of the Napoleonic Wars and the arrival of potato blight in Ireland in September 1845, approximately a million people left Ireland for North America, and perhaps half that number traveled to Britain, with thirty thousand obtaining state assistance to go to Australia on their own volition, and another forty thousand sent as transported criminals.[23] Several distinguishing features of this era are particularly noteworthy, not least the increasing number of middle-class Catholics leaving and the emergence of Britain as the destination of choice, especially for the poorer Irish who did not possess the resources to fund an expensive passage across the Atlantic. As David Fitzpatrick has observed, "for the intending emigrant from Ireland, Britain's attraction was largely negative: the costs of getting there, and indeed of returning home, were relatively low."[24] When the poor inquiry was undertaking its work in the early 1830s, it commissioned George Cornewall Lewis to conduct a survey of the Irish in Britain, which he did with characteristic thoroughness. What Lewis's investigations showed was that many of the Irish living in British cities had come over in the 1820s, and the principal attraction was the availability of large numbers of industrial jobs with good wages created by the booming industries.[25]

The Great Famine changed everything. First, it led to an uncoordinated exodus, especially from 1846 on, when many took the harsh and dangerous winter voyage to Canada rather than stay in Ireland. The year 1847 was even worse, and the enduring image of the "coffin ship" stems from that year, when on-board mortality on ships carrying refugees from the crisis was high. Stricter regulation of conditions on ships lowered the death rates substantially in the following years. At least one million left Ireland during the Famine, another million in the five years that followed, in what was one of the most dramatic movements of population in recorded history.[26] In 1851 more than a quarter of a million people were recorded as having left the country for "overseas" destinations.[27] Throughout the 1850s and 1860s, there was a roughly one-in-three chance that a child born in Ireland coming of age would emigrate.[28] Emigration became a stage then in the life cycle of young people, with profound consequences for Irish society. Irish movement across the Atlantic in the later nineteenth century was unusual in two respects: first, it was a movement of individuals rather than family groups, and second, females left in roughly equal numbers as males. This exodus had its peaks and troughs over the following fifty years, before the onset of the First World War temporarily cut off the option of emigration.[29]

Once the "normal" business of emigration resumed, the two new Irish states faced the prospect of the continuance of large-scale emigration in the 1920s, which may well have suited the political elites ruling the newly established entities. Those living in Northern Ireland could obtain financial support to fund journeys to Canada, Australia, and New Zealand. Ironically, short-distance movement predominated in the outward flows from the southern state, especially to Britain after the economy there improved in the mid-1930s. Britain was the new America with some startling consequences. For those who did leave in the 1930s, it was usually only intended to be a short stay, even if life created some unexpected twists and turns that eventually led to permanent settlement in Britain.[30]

The Second World War and the post-war building boom in the 1940s created many opportunities for younger migrants, and by the 1950s emigration was again reaching epidemic proportions, causing acute embarrassment to the government of the day. It was estimated in the mid-1950s that on average fifty thousand people left Ireland each year, mostly traveling to Britain. The newly independent Irish state was one of the few countries in the world to have experienced a declining population from the 1850s until the 1960s, wholly as a result of emigration. Even though rates of emigration from Northern Ireland were nowhere near the southern levels, the Stormont government does not seem to have been especially interested in emigration, perhaps because it disproportionately affected lower-skilled Catholics in West Ulster. By the 1970s improvements in the Irish economy led to a movement into the country, primarily of people who left in the 1950s and

1960s. Emigration again resumed its traditional role when a severe recession hit Ireland in the 1980s.

The mid-1990s marked a turning point in the long history of Irish migrations. The rapid economic growth and attendant prosperity associated with the "Celtic Tiger" created sufficient employment opportunities for generations coming of age for the first time since the establishment of the independent Irish state. That does not mean that emigration ceased—even at the high point of the Celtic Tiger era in 2006, people still left—but it did fundamentally alter the context. As soon as the Celtic Tiger collapsed in 2008–2009 and unemployment rose dramatically in the following years, emigration again became the safety valve that it had been for the previous 160 years. The "new" Irish left in large numbers, opting for Australia, Canada, New Zealand, and the more traditional route to Britain. For a generation that never expected to have to leave the country, it was a traumatic moment.

Meanwhile, one unanticipated consequence of rapid economic growth created a movement of people that in time will prove to be as significant as the arrival of English and Scottish settlers in the sixteenth and seventeenth centuries. For the first time in modern Irish history, large numbers of people who were born outside Ireland came to live in the country, and immigration, which was virtually unheard of prior to the 1990s, developed as a significant component of population change. In 2007 just before the crash, more than 150,000 immigrants arrived in Ireland, some Irish-born, most not. Under European Union (EU) legislation, citizens of other member states could travel without restriction, and they settled in Ireland in large numbers, mainly coming from the new EU accession countries who joined the EU in May 2004, especially Poland. Another distinct flow of migrants was from outside the EU from places as diverse as China and Africa. The most recent estimates indicate that more than 500,000 people living in Ireland were born outside the country: in other words roughly one in eight of the state's population was a "non-Irish national," to use the crude official terminology.[31] In less than two decades the ethnic composition of the population living in independent Ireland has been transformed from a homogenous white Irish-born one to a multicultural and multi-ethnic identity. For this reason, historians may well see the 2000s as a pivotal turning point in the evolution of modern Ireland in the twenty-first century.

III

The decision to leave Ireland was based on a complex set of factors, involving assessment of future life chances, economic and social opportunities, and an overall sense of whether life would be better elsewhere. Much the same reasons dominated the calculations of those who settled in Ireland over the past four centuries. For instance, the 1690s, one of the harshest decades in Scottish history, generated quite significant migration to Ulster. The movement of fifty thousand Scottish Presbyterians partly laid the foundations for the exchange of cultures and people that two centuries later would make possible the emergence of Ulster unionism.[32] At the other end of the chronological spectrum, the 1950s were for independent Ireland years of deep economic recession, and mass migration reached heights that were matched only by the Famine years of the 1840s. But this could also work the other way around when potential destinations were in the grip of recession, as occurred during the recession in the American economy of the 1870s. The best example is, of course, the so-called Celtic Tiger era, when a society completely unaccustomed to inward migrations found that, largely to its surprise, that one of the consequences of economic prosperity was that people would come to live in your country.

There were, needless to say, times when such finely calibrated decisions mattered little. During the Cromwellian era the transportation of Irish Catholics as indentured servants to the Caribbean and elsewhere was a forced movement in a time of great upheaval. Equally the Famine exiles who left in the 1840s and early 1850s for North America and Britain were essentially refugees fleeing starvation and death, many of whom subsequently nurtured bitter memories of the role of the British government in failing to prevent starvation or, more critically, large-scale evictions by heartless landlords. Political revolutions such as the 1798 uprising and the Young Ireland revolt of 1848 produced small but very active and vocal exile communities. More controversially the flight of southern Protestants in the midst of the violent conflict and sectarian tensions of the Irish Revolution has been described as a forced exodus.[33] At the time, and subsequently thereafter, huge symbolic significance was attached to the movement of relatively small numbers of Protestants, since this was a barometer of how minorities would be treated in the new emerging nationalist Ireland. Again there was a parallel with the expulsion of Belfast Catholics in 1922, many of whom made their way across the border into the Irish Free State.[34]

The migration of minorities more generally has received some treatment by historians. People on the margins of the orthodoxy of Irish society have consistently seen emigration as a pathway to emancipation, or more fundamentally, to acceptance. Young unmarried pregnant women who went to Britain to have their children or those who because of their sexual orientation were unable to continue living in the country equally perceived themselves as exiles, as did the defeated republicans who left the country in large numbers in the early 1920s heading to the United States, sensing retribution by the victorious Free State government.[35] Another vocal minority were the creative writers, for whom displacement was both a rite of passage and a state of consciousness, most famously represented in the work of the best-known exile, James Joyce. But there were also such writers as Patrick MacGill and Michael McGowan, who wrote eloquently of their own experiences of emigration in Britain and the United States, blending personal memoir with essentially the collective autobiography of generations of exiles, most of whom left little by way of a historical trace.[36]

So even though economic considerations were one of the principal reasons for leaving Ireland, they were by no means the only cause of emigration. This is neatly encapsulated in the issue of gender, or rather the relative parity of male and female departures from nineteenth- and twentieth-century Ireland. For a variety of reasons, including the nature of the national education system—which tended to promote skills such as speaking English—Irish females were well equipped to compete in what was effectively an international labor market. So whether it be personal service in the expanding northeastern cities of the United States, or factory work in wartime Britain, Irish women could be assured of opportunities. Even though earning money was understandably a consideration, so too were autonomy and escaping the rigid control that was such a feature of life in rural Ireland. One young woman captured this nicely when she was asked whether she would return home to Ireland; the response was that she had "a better life in Croydon than Sligo."[37]

Few historians now frame migration in a "push-pull" list of factors, seeing such a dichotomy as unable to capture the complexities of the human experience. If economists are wont to speak of human capital, labor as a commodity, and cost-benefits analysis of migration, historians seek now to understand, recover, and explore the context in which people left Ireland. Such contextual readings challenge older traditionalist accounts, which stress poverty in Ireland and abundant opportunities in North America or Britain. The best recent scholarship moves away from clichéd understandings of modern Ireland and pays equal attention to the complexities of the Irish environment from which people left, and the new worlds they inhabited, focusing on the relationship between the two. Such transnational approaches reflect broader trends in the writing of global migration history but have a particular Irish dimension, because most of the leading scholars who have worked on Irish migration—such as D. H. Akenson, David Fitzpatrick, and Kerby A. Miller, and the late Patrick O'Farrell—are also recognized as distinguished specialists on the history of modern Ireland. The result is a number of hugely influential studies since the 1980s that have dominated the field and have set out the parameters for future scholarship.[38] This body of scholarship has then integrated the diaspora with historical writing on the evolution of modern Ireland. A new generation of scholars has now emerged who sees the connections between Irish migrants and their homeland as shaping a whole range of topics from ethnic identity and political violence to attitudes toward land.[39]

One of the unresolved issues in the history of the Irish diaspora is the changing preference for short- or long-distance migrations over time. In other words, why did Britain prove the destination of choice in the twentieth century, yet the majority of eighteenth- and nineteenth-century exiles departed for North America? In the seventeenth century continental Europe was the favored haven for exiles from Ireland, yet after 1850 only political exiles made their way to Paris to conspire and plot treason. How do we explain the distance movement to Australia and New Zealand, which peaked in popularity at certain points in the nineteenth century, and is today one of the favored migration patterns? Where do South America, the Caribbean, and Asia fit into the overall framework? Or why did the aspiring Catholic middle-class bureaucrat choose the Indian civil service over the opportunities available in metropolitan London? Needless to say, there is no obvious explanation about why one person chooses to settle in Liverpool over Philadelphia in the 1850s. And structural approaches—while explaining much about the wider political, economic, or social contexts—do not satisfactorily explain the behavior of individuals.

So historians tend to emphasize the interaction of individual aspirations, hopes, and fears with broader factors, such as the economic conditions in the sending and receiving societies, the knowledge about opportunities and living conditions that was transmitted across oceans by letters or people, and the role of social networks in enabling and supporting individual moves. Just as Ulster Presbyterians set off in search of religious toleration in the "land of liberty" during the eighteenth century, so too did the lure of America capture many Irish imaginations in the later nineteenth century. Less is known about the extent to which individuals who left Ireland as part of an institution had detailed information or much by way of choice. For religious missionaries, knowledge of the intended place of settlement was critical, and one Catholic seminary, All Hallows College in Dublin, was established in 1842 to produce priests for the missions. That these missionaries were deeply implicated in the colonial project of British Victorian imperialism is not especially novel, yet the extent to which the Irish Catholic Church exploited opportunities available in the British Empire for its own evangelical ends is a less palatable element for generations of Irish Catholics brought up on the images of suffering and destitution in modern Africa.

What emerges from a plethora of fine-grained studies of Irish migration and settlement is that it was far less of a move from the known to the unknown. Potential migrants could often cite chapter and verse the conditions in faraway and distant places. This was encapsulated in a conversation that the liberal Unionist and agricultural reformer Sir Horace Plunkett had with a farmer in County Galway at the turn of the twentieth century. When Plunkett asked why the farmer's daughter chose to emigrate to the United States rather than move within the county where work was available, the response was "because it is nearer," meaning that she knew more about New York from friends and family than any part of Ireland, apart from her locality.[40] These studies are often based on detailed historical reconstructions of particular groups of migrants from Ireland or on examining unfamiliar or less-known sites of settlement, which demonstrates the importance of complexity in understanding the history of the Irish diaspora. For example, a fascinating study of migrants from a single parish of Inistioge, County Kilkenny, to Newfoundland between the 1780s and 1840s involves painstaking genealogical research on the Irish backgrounds of the migrants.[41] Likewise Bruce Elliott's book on families of Protestants from south Leinster who settled in Upper Canada is an impressive work of innovative scholarship.[42] More recently Tyler Anbinder's findings on the lives of the Famine Irish who settled in New York City as examined through the prism of their savings habits again manages to confound conventional wisdom by demonstrating the patterns of wealth accumulation over decades.[43] What each of these studies shows is contingency and the ability to be flexible when circumstances dictate. Like the Irish at home, the diasporic Irish had to adapt to the worlds that they now inhabited, and all the better if this could be done quickly.

However, adaptation does not equate with assimilation. In the 1960s and 1970s historians and social scientists were preoccupied with immigrant assimilation—the now largely discredited process by which migrants become American, British, or Australian. It was not a question of if but when did the Irish assimilate for an older generation of scholars. More recent work rejects such arguments based on a linear model that eventually leads to one-sided assimilation.[44] The key concern now is explaining the construction and articulation of an Irish ethnic identity, and how this varied over time and space. Most of the accounts focus on the first generation or those born in Ireland, but a few pioneering accounts, such as the work of Timothy J. Meagher, explore the construction of ethnic identity over several generations.[45]

One of the most productive ways of exploring ethnic identity is through the analysis of first-hand testimonies. Migrant letters and diaries are a unique body of source material that essentially involves "eavesdropping" on a conversation that occurred over thousands of miles. A classic work of scholarship is David Fitzpatrick's investigation of Irish migration to Australia through the analysis of 111 personal letters sent by family members. Other scholars have examined the Irish in New Zealand, Argentina, and Australia, again using letters and other forms of personal testimony. Kerby A. Miller and his associates have likewise broken new ground in the study of the American Irish by collecting a wide range of little-known materials in the form of autobiographies, memoirs, and other first-hand accounts for the period between 1675 and 1815.[46] Published autobiographies are harder to decode, given that the author always intended this material for publication, though a recent critical anthology shows just how much potential these types of sources have for the historian of the diasporic Irish.[47] Finally, the most authentic and unmediated type of source material is the words of the migrant themselves as recounted in oral history interviews. Studies that have made use of such oral histories often rightly dwell on the interpretative issues raised by using such first-hand testimonies to tell a migration story, but in terms of the vividness and richness of the materials, few documentary sources can match oral histories.[48]

What does all this mean for the student of modern Irish history? The significance of migration and diaspora for an understanding of modern Ireland should be readily apparent. Insular approaches, focusing on essentially the domestic history of the island, can no longer assume they capture the full range of the Irish historical experience. To write generations out of this history simply because they or their ancestors had to leave is to establish a hierarchy of national identity based solely on place of birth. Even such well-known political figures as the first chief of staff of the Provisional IRA, Seán Mac Stíofáin, defy this narrow definition of national identity. Mac Stíofáin confounded all the stereotypes of Irish republicans: he was English by birth, originally Protestant by religion, but baptized a Catholic at the age of seven.[49] Irishness was never circumscribed by place of birth, as hundreds of studies of the diaspora clearly show, even if the venerable inhabitants of the "motherland" are sometimes less than keen to acknowledge this.

The major political movements in modern Ireland also had a diasporic dimension, more so for Irish nationalism than for unionism. The diaspora was a critical component for Irish nationalists from the 1798 rebellion on, providing moral and financial support, volunteers, weapons, political muscle, publicity, and experience. One recent study demonstrates how revolutionary Irish nationalism in the later nineteenth century was shaped by its transnational dimensions.[50] Nationalist leaders from Charles Stewart Parnell to John Redmond and Éamon de Valera and even up to the present-day Gerry Adams have long recognized the political power of the diaspora, particularly in the United States but also in Australasia and Britain. Irish and then Ulster unionism appealed less to the huge numbers of people of Protestant descent across the globe.[51] The reasons are not entirely clear, though one factor is that the Protestant Irish did not nurture the same sense of grievance that fostered expatriate Irish nationalism. Another explanation may lie in the reactions to different streams of Irish migrants. The Protestant Irish rarely attracted much public attention in the principal receiving societies, and in places where they were numerically significant—such as Canada, Australia, and New Zealand—they quickly established such organizations as the Orange Order and Masonic Lodges to assert their allegiance to crown and country.[52] Only when communal Orange and Green violence broke out—as it did famously in New York City in 1870 and 1871—was attention focused on the "Orange" diaspora.[53]

Nativism suffused with anti-Catholicism, which was especially virulent in the mid-nineteenth century, encouraged the emergence of an identity that was in the first instance defensive and then broadened out into a more open form of ethnic pride and patriotism. An important theme that emerges in much of the work done on Irish-American nationalism is that although the homeland was obviously important, local, regional, and national concerns in the United States also shaped the politics and outlooks of the American Irish.[54] This is especially apparent in the range of American Irish ethnic organizations that developed in the later nineteenth century that had as much to do with asserting middle-class respectability as with diasporic nationalism. Ironically in a competitive multi-ethnic society, becoming American inevitably involved articulations of Irishness, and nowhere is this better seen that in the campaign to establish a "hibernarchy" in the American Catholic Church and the machine politics of the Irish in the Democratic party.

Often neglected in accounts of Irish diasporic identity is the changing context with respect to the arrival of other migrant groups. Whereas the Famine Irish who landed in the 1840s and 1850s were seen as a threatening menace to the stability of both American and British society—perceived as bringing with them poverty, disease, and the even more pernicious influence of Catholicism—by the end of that century the gaze was no longer on the Irish, as southern and Eastern European immigrants dominated the fears of Americans, and Eastern European Jews occupied British mind-sets. It is no coincidence that when the first substantive piece of legislation to restrict entry to the United States was introduced in 1924, the Irish received a generous quota of visas, which incidentally was never filled in the interwar years.[55] Likewise in Australia, the middle-class Irish quickly established themselves in the emerging nineteenth-century elite, and over time the Catholic Irish assumed positions of leadership in the Catholic Church (most famously in the cases of Cardinal Patrick Francis Moran and Archbishop Daniel Mannix), the political system, the labor movement, and many other elements of Australian life. In post-war Britain the large numbers of Irish who arrived in the 1940s and 1950s were completely overshadowed by the small numbers of black immigrants from the "new" Commonwealth, who attracted much public comment. At one time the Irish were seen as "marginal Britons," but up to the outbreak of the civil conflict in Ulster they were viewed as essentially part of British society, even if the Irish had very different views themselves. The Troubles changed all this—especially the bombing campaigns in England, which provoked a resurgence of anti-Irish hostility and prejudice that only diminished in the wake of the Belfast Agreement of 1998.[56]

One of the most intriguing developments in recent scholarship is exploring the cultural encounters that mass migration generated. A study by Mo Moulton of the Irish-English interchange of ideas, cultures, values, and prejudices in the interwar years maps out the potential of such an approach. Although these encounters generated conflict and dissonance, what is noteworthy is how "hybridity" (to borrow a term from cultural studies) characterizes the meeting of two profoundly different cultural outlooks. Similarly, work by Bernadette Whelan and Stephanie Rains has investigated the Irish-American encounter in popular culture in the twentieth century.[57] What emerges from this fascinating and original work is how deeply embedded American values were in popular culture in twentieth-century Ireland. These were disseminated by frequent contact with relatives and friends living in the United States, by mass media (especially the cinema), and by that ubiquitous figure in rural Ireland, the returned "Yank."[58]

An additional dimension relates to material culture and the physical manifestations of the diaspora. Earlier work by the historical geographer John Mannion on the material culture of the Newfoundland Irish especially has been supplemented by more recent accounts of the Du Pont Irish in Delaware, mostly Ulster Catholics, and the things they collected, consumed, and sought out. Dress was another prominent marker of material culture.[59] In John B. Keane's play, *Many Young Men of Twenty* (1961), a searing indictment of emigration from post-war Ireland, one of the characters back from England shows his prosperity by the quality of his clothing. Even fashion trends current in Britain or America could make their way into unexplored corners of rural Ireland, as the migrants returned home on holidays, looking smart and becoming what one contemporary identified as the best advertisement for emigration. Fashionable clothing could end up in some unusual places: parcels of secondhand clothing were sent to many families in Ireland by relatives and friends living in the United States.[60]

V

Migration and diaspora are fundamental to the understanding of modern Irish history. As David Fitzpatrick has reminded us, only with an appreciation of its significance is it possible to grapple with the complexities of Irish history over the past four centuries:

> Emigration was also one of the great formative factors in modern Irish history. Without studying emigration, one could scarcely hope to explain Ireland's peculiar blend of archaism and modernity as manifested in its economy, demography, social structure and political culture. Majority emigration means, moreover, that the study of Irish history must not be limited to Ireland.[61]

The hallmark of the Irish migrations since early modern times is diversity, and the challenge is to fuse the overall context with the many microstudies of individuals, communities, and regions. At one time migration studies was a deeply quantitative enterprise, essentially collecting and analyzing information about groups collected by the authorities in Ireland and elsewhere, not least in the censuses. And while that still is an important element, historians have turned to other techniques, some—as is the case for detailed textual analysis of letters and other forms of personal testimonies—derived from other disciplines, such as literature and linguistics. The other dimension is that there is a move away from the well-studied sites of the Irish diaspora, such as North America, Britain, Western Europe, and Australia, to lesser-known yet equally revealing flows to parts of the British Empire in Africa, Asia, and the Caribbean as well as to Eastern Europe and South

America. Finally, scholars no longer see Irish emigration as exceptional or indeed even unique: the pressing need, as with many other areas of Irish history, is to place the Irish experience within transnational and comparative contexts, showing how Ireland was connected to its diaspora, and how other countries with similar levels of mobility fared. Only then can we say with any certainty what was different, if anything, about the Irish diaspora.

FURTHER READING

There is no satisfactory single-volume study of the Irish diaspora since 1600. For the early modern period, Nicholas Canny, "Ireland and Continental Europe," in Alvin Jackson (ed.), *The Oxford Handbook of Modern Irish History* (Oxford: Oxford University Press, 2014) is the most up-to-date survey, but see also L. M. Cullen, "The Irish Diaspora of the Seventeenth and Eighteenth Centuries," in Nicholas Canny (ed.), *Europeans on the Move: Studies on European Migration, 1500–1800* (Oxford: Oxford University Press, 1994). The relevant chapters by David Noel Doyle, David Fitzpatrick, and Patrick O'Farrell in W. E. Vaughan (ed.), *New History of Ireland* (Oxford: Clarendon Press, 1989 and 2006), volumes 5 and 6, are excellent studies of the Irish emigration and the Irish in Britain, North America, and Australasia. D. H. Akenson, *The Irish Diaspora: A Primer* (Toronto: P. D. Meany, 1993) is a pioneering study with a global focus, questioning received wisdoms, and is mostly concerned with the period after 1820. By far by the most original and most significant book to be published in the last half century is Kerby A. Miller, *Emigrants and Exiles: Ireland and the Irish Exodus to North America* (New York: Oxford University Press, 1985); another masterpiece is on Irish migrations to Australia: David Fitzpatrick, *Oceans of Consolation: Personal Accounts of Irish Migration to Australia* (Ithaca, NY: Cornell University Press, 1994). More modest overviews can be found in David Fitzpatrick, *Irish Emigration, 1801–1921* (Dublin: Economic and Social History Society of Ireland, 1984) and Enda Delaney, *Irish Emigration since 1921* (Dublin: Economic and Social History Society of Ireland, 2002). Single-country studies are available for most of the main destinations. The best ones include Donald M. MacRaild, *The Irish Diaspora in Britain, 1750–1939* (2nd ed., Basingstoke: Palgrave, 2011); Kevin Kenny, *The American Irish: A History* (Harlow: Macmillan, 2000); C. J. Houston and W. J. Smyth, *Irish Emigration and Canadian Settlement* (Toronto: University of Toronto Press, 1990); Patrick O'Farrell, *The Irish in Australia: 1788 to the Present* (3rd ed., Cork: Cork University Press, 2000); and Angela McCarthy, *Irish Migrants in New Zealand, 1840–1937: "The Desired Haven"* (Woodbridge: Boydell Press, 2005).

1. Ruth Dudley Edwards, *Patrick Pearse: The Triumph of Failure* (Dublin: Poolbeg, 1990), p. 183.

2. See Enda Delaney, *Demography, State and Society: Irish Migration to Britain, 1921–1971* (Kingston and Montreal/Liverpool: McGill-Queen's University Press and Liverpool University Press, 2000), p. 57f.

3. Corrected typescript of autobiographical narrative, dated January 3, 1912, by Owen Peter Mangan (b. 1839 in Co. Cavan), NLI MS 22,462. This account was first brought to the attention of scholars by David Fitzpatrick, "Emigration, 1801–70," in W. E. Vaughan (ed.), *A New History of Ireland, V: Ireland under the Union, 1 (1801–70)* (Oxford: Clarendon Press, 1989), pp. 563–564.

4. Anon., "Christopher Elliott," *Tropical Agriculturalist* 13: 6 (1893), pp. 361–367.

5. Sujit Sivasundaram, *Islanded: Sri Lanka, and the Bounds of an Indian Ocean Colony* (Chicago: University of Chicago Press, 2013), pp. 310–317. He is identified incorrectly as Charles Elliott.

6. Richard Hayes, *Biographical Dictionary of Irishmen in France* (Dublin: M. H. Gill, 1949), pp. 60–62.

7. "Jones, Mary Harris ('Mother Jones')," *Dictionary of Irish Biography* (Cambridge: Cambridge University Press, 2009).

8. Enda Delaney, "Our Island Story? Towards a Transnational History of Late Modern Ireland," *Irish Historical Studies* 37: 148 (2011), p. 86.

9. For an overview, see Patrick Fitzgerald and Brian Lambkin, *Migration in Irish History, 1600–2000* (Basingstoke: Palgrave, 2008). For the historiography, see D. H. Akenson, *The Irish Diaspora: A Primer* (Toronto: P. D. Meany, 1994); Enda Delaney, Kevin Kenny, and Donald M. MacRaild, "Symposium: Perspectives on the Irish Diaspora," *Irish Economic and Social History* 33 (2006), pp. 35–52; Mary Hickman, "Migration and Diaspora," in Joe Cleary and Claire Connolly (eds.), *The Cambridge Companion to Modern Irish Culture* (Cambridge: Cambridge University Press, 2005), pp. 117–136; J. J. Lee, "The Irish Diaspora in the Nineteenth Century," in L. M. Geary and Margaret Kelleher (eds.), *Nineteenth Century Ireland: A Guide to Recent Research* (Dublin: University College Dublin Press, 2005), pp. 182–222; Kevin Kenny, "Writing the History of the Irish Diaspora," in Robert J. Savage, Jr. (ed.), *Ireland in the New Century: Politics, Culture and Identity* (Dublin: Four Courts Press, 2003), pp. 206–226; Kevin Kenny, "Diaspora and Comparison: the Global Irish as a Case Study," *Journal of American History* 90 (2003), pp. 359–398.

10. Nicholas Canny, *Making Ireland British: 1580–1650* (Oxford: Oxford University Press, 2001); Jane Ohlmeyer, " 'Civilizinge of Those Rude Partes': Colonization within Britain and Ireland, 1580s–1640s," in Nicholas Canny (ed.), *The Origins of Empire* (Oxford: Oxford University Press, 1998), pp. 124–147; Jane Ohlmeyer, "A Laboratory for Empire? Early Modern Ireland and English Imperialism," in Kevin A. Kenny (ed.), *Ireland and the British Empire* (Oxford: Oxford University Press, 2004), pp. 26–60.

11. See Nicholas Canny, "Ireland and Continental Europe, c. 1600–1750," in Alvin Jackson (ed.), *The Oxford Handbook of Modern Irish History* (Oxford: Oxford University Press, 2014), pp. 333–355.

12. Canny, "Ireland and Continental Europe," pp. 343–344.

13. L. M. Cullen, John Shovlin, and Thomas M. Truxes (eds.), *The Bordeaux-Dublin Letters, 1757: Correspondence of an Irish Community Abroad* (Oxford: Oxford University Press 2013), p. 67. For the seventeenth- and eighteenth-century patterns of movement more generally, see L. M. Cullen, "The Irish Diaspora of the Seventeenth and Eighteenth Centuries," in Nicholas Canny (ed.), *Europeans on the Move: Studies on European Migration, 1500–1800* (Oxford: Oxford University Press, 1994), pp. 113–152.

14. Cullen, Shovlin, and Truxes, *Bordeaux-Dublin Letters*, p. 96.

15. See L. M. Cullen, *The Irish Brandy Houses of Eighteenth-Century France* (Dublin: Lilliput Press, 2000).

16. "Hennessy, Richard," *Oxford Dictionary of National Biography* (Oxford: Oxford University Press, 2004).

17. Kerby A. Miller, Arnold Schrier, Bruce D. Boling, and David N. Doyle, *Irish Immigrants in the Land of Canaan: Letters and Memoirs from Colonial and Revolutionary America, 1675–1815* (Oxford and New York: Oxford University Press, 2003), p. 657.

18. Kerby A. Miller, *Emigrants and Exiles: Ireland and the Irish Exodus to North America* (New York: Oxford University Press, 1985), p. 149

19. See Kevin Kenny, *Peaceable Kingdom Lost* (New York: Oxford University Press, 2012).

20. Quoted in Miller, *Emigrants and Exiles*, p. 165.

21. David Noel Doyle, "The Irish in North America, 1776–1845," in Vaughan (ed.), *A New History of Ireland*, V, pp. 682–725; Miller, Boling, and Doyle, *Irish Immigrants In the Land of Canaan*; David Noel Doyle, *Ireland, Irishmen and Revolutionary America, 1760–1820* (Dublin: Education Company of Ireland , 1981); Patrick Griffin, *The People with No Name: Ireland's Ulster Scots, America's Scots Irish, and the Creation of a British Atlantic World, 1689–1764* (Princeton, NJ: Princeton University Press, 1999).

22. Kevin Whelan, "The Green Atlantic: Radical Reciprocities between Ireland and America in the Long Eighteenth Century," in Kathleen Wilson, (ed.), *A New Imperial History: Culture, Identity, and Modernity in Britain and the Empire, 1660–1840* (Cambridge: Cambridge University Press, 2004), pp. 216–238.

23. Fitzpatrick, "Emigration, 1801–70," p. 565.

24. David Fitzpatrick, "'A Peculiar Tramping People': The Irish in Britain, 1801–70," in Vaughan (ed.), *A New History of Ireland*, V, p. 626.

25. Fitzpatrick, "A Peculiar Tramping People," p. 627.

26. One of the best accounts remains Oliver MacDonagh, "The Irish Famine Emigration to the United States," *Perspectives in American History* 10 (1976), pp. 357–446.

27. For an attempt to write a transnational history of the Great Famine, see Enda Delaney, "Ireland's Great Famine: A Transnational History," in Niall Whelehan (ed.), *Transnational Perspectives on Modern Irish History* (New York: Routledge, 2014).

28. Fitzpatrick, "Emigration, 1801–70," p. 566.

29. For an excellent overview, see David Fitzpatrick, *Irish Emigration* (Dublin: Economic and Social History Society of Ireland, 1984).

30. See Enda Delaney, *Irish Emigration since 1921* (Dublin: Economic and Social History Society of Ireland, 2012).

31. Central Statistics Office, *Population and Migration Estimates*, April 2014 (http://www.cso.ie/en/releasesandpublications/er/pme/populationandmigrationestimatesapril2014/).

32. Alvin Jackson, *The Two Unions: Ireland, Scotland, and the Survival of the United Kingdom* (Oxford: Oxford University Press, 2012), p. 61.

33. For recent assessment, see Andy Bielenberg, "Exodus: The Emigration of Southern Irish Protestants During the Irish War of Independence and the Civil War," *Past & Present* 218 (2013), pp. 199–233

34. Peter Hart, *The IRA at War* (Oxford: Oxford University Press, 2003), pp. 241–258.

35. Gavin Foster, "No 'Wild Geese' This Time? IRA Emigration after the Irish Civil War," *Éire-Ireland* 47: 1 (2012), pp. 94–122.

36. Michael McGowan, *The Hard Road to Klondike* (London: Routledge, Kegan and Paul, 1962); Patrick McGill, *Children of the Dead End* (London: H. Jenkins, 1914); Donall Mac Amhlaigh, *An Irish Navvy: The Diary of an Exile* (London: Routledge, Kegan and Paul,1964).

37. Quoted in Delaney, *Demography, State and Society*, p. 175.

38. Akenson, *Irish Diaspora*; Fitzpatrick, *Oceans of Consolation*; Miller, *Emigrants and Exile*; Patrick O'Farrell, *The Irish in Australia: 1788 to the Present* (Cork: Cork University Press, third ed., 2001).

39. Whelehan (ed.), *Transnational Perspectives on Modern Irish History*.

40. Horace Plunkett, *Ireland in the New Century* (London: John Murray, revised ed., 1905), p. 56.

41. John Mannion and Fidelma Maddock, "Old World Antecedents, New World Adaptations: Inistioge Immigrants in Newfoundland," in William Nolan and Kevin Whelan (eds.), *Kilkenny: History and Society* (Dublin: Geography Publications, 1990), pp. 345–404.

42. Bruce S. Elliott, *Irish Migrants in the Canadas: A New Approach* (Kingston and Montreal: McGill-Queen's University Press, 1988).

43. Tyler Anbinder, "Moving beyond 'Rags to Riches': New York's Irish Famine Immigrants and Their Surprising Savings Accounts," *Journal of American History* 99: 3 (2012), pp. 741–770.

44. Mary J. Hickman, "Alternative Historiographies of the Irish in Britain: A Critique of the Segregation/Assimilation Model," in Roger Swift and Sheridan Gilley (eds.), *The Irish in Victorian Britain: The Local Dimension* (London: Four Courts Press, 1999), pp. 236–253.

45. Timothy J. Meagher, *Inventing Irish America: Generation, Class and Ethnic Identity in a New England City* (Notre Dame, IN: University of Notre Dame Press, 2000).

46. Miller, Boling, and Doyle, *Irish Immigrants in the Land of Canaan.*

47. Liam Harte, *The Literature of the Irish in Britain: Autobiography and Memoir, 1725–2001* (Basingstoke: Palgrave, 2009).

48. See Enda Delaney, *The Irish in Post-war Britain* (Oxford: Oxford University Press, 2007), pp. 7–8.

49. "Mac Stiofáin, Sean," *Dictionary of Irish Biography* (Cambridge: Cambridge University Press, 2009).

50. Niall Whelehan, *The Dynamiters: Irish Nationalism and Political Violence in the Wider World, 1867–1900* (Cambridge: Cambridge University Press, 2012).

51. See Andrew J. Wilson, "Ulster Unionists in America, 1972–1985," in *New Hibernia Review* 11: 1 (2007), pp. 50–73; Lindsey Flewelling, "Ulster Unionism and America, 1880–1920" (Dissertation, University of Edinburgh, 2012).

52. David Fitzpatrick, "Exporting Brotherhood: Orangeism in South Australia," in Enda Delaney and Donald M. MacRaild (eds.), *Irish Migration, Networks and Ethnic Identity since 1750* (London: Routledge, 2007); Donald M. MacRaild, *Faith, Fraternity and Fighting: The Orange Order and Irish Migrants in Northern England, c. 1850–1920* (Liverpool: Liverpool University Press , 2005), pp. 286–320; Donald M. MacRaild, "Wherever Orange Is Worn: Orangeism and Irish Migration in the Nineteenth and Early Twentieth Century," *Canadian Journal of Irish Studies* 28: 2 (2002), pp. 98–117; William Jenkins, "Between the Lodge and the Meeting-House: Mapping Irish Protestant Identities and Social Worlds in Late Victorian Toronto," *Social and Cultural Geography* 4 (2003), pp. 75–98; Eric Kaufmann, "The Orange Order in Scotland since 1860: A Social Analysis," in M. J. Mitchell (ed.), *New Perspectives on the Irish in Scotland* (Edinburgh: John Donald, 2008), pp. 159–190.

53. Michael A. Gordon, *The Orange Riots: Irish Political Violence in New York City, 1870 and 1871* (Ithaca, NY: Cornell University Press, 1993).

54. See Kevin Kenny, *The American Irish* (Basingstoke: Macmillan, 2000).

55. Delaney, *Demography, State and Society*, pp. 43–44.

56. Gary McGladdery, *The Provisional IRA in England: The Bombing Campaign, 1973–1997* (Dublin: Irish Academic Press 2006).

57. Gerardine Meaney, Mary O'Dowd, and Bernadette Whelan, *Reading the Irish Woman: Studies in Cultural Encounter and Exchange, 1714–1960* (Liverpool: Liverpool University Press, 2013), chapter 4; Stephanie Rains, *The Irish-American in Popular Culture, 1945–2000* (Dublin: Irish Academic Press, 2007).

58. For an older but still useful account, see Arnold Schrier, *Ireland and the American Emigration, 1850–1900* (Minneapolis: University of Minnesota Press, 1958), pp. 129–143.

59. John Mannion, *Irish Settlements in Eastern Canada: A Study of Cultural Transfer and Adaptation* (Toronto: University of Toronto Press, 1974); Margaret M. Mulrooney, *Black Powder, White Lace: The Du Pont Irish and Cultural Identity in Nineteenth-Century America* (Hanover: University of New Hampshire Press, 2002).

60. Hilary O'Kelly, "Parcels from America: American Clothes in Ireland, c. 1930–1980," in Alexandra Palmer and Hazel Clark (eds.), *Old Clothes, New Looks* (Oxford: Berg, 2005).

61. Fitzpatrick, *Irish Emigration*, p. 1.

INDEX

of, 276; on Hume's history of England, 277; on lost age, 228; on penal laws, 205; *Philosophical Enquiry*, 199–200; political philosophy of, 209–11; *Reflections on the Revolution in France*, 194, 202, 275; *Vindication of Natural Society*, 201–2

Burke, Ray, 264

Burridge, Ezekiel, 196

Butlers, 4, 25

Butt, Isaac, 92–93, 95, 107n112, 222, 224, 355

Butterfield, Herbert, historian, 273–74

Byrne, Edward, 59

Byrne, Gay, 258–59, 267

Caillard, Gaspar, 204

Cambrensis, Giraldus, 24

Cambridge Modern History, 271

Cameron, David, 176

Canny, Nicholas, historian, 284

Cantillon, Richard, 208–9

Cardinal Secrets (TV series), 176–77

Carey, Hilary M., historian, 351

Carlyle, Thomas, 222–23, 451

Carpenter, Archbishop John, 306

Carson, Edward, 143–44, 145

Carswell, John, 327

Casement, Roger, 356

Casey, Bishop Eamon: broadcasts of, 258; scandal of, 265–66

Castlereagh, Viscount, 78–79; conversion of, 80; support of for Catholic emancipation, 81–82

Catholic Association, 84, 304

Catholic catechism, Irish-language, 331–32

Catholic Church: challenge to orthodoxy of, 312–13; collapsing authority of, 176–78; concerns about television of, 257–58; devotional revolution of, 306–9; imperial opportunities for, 352–53; internalization of doctrine of, 305–6; marriage and, 369; scandals in, 176–78, 265–66, 293; in seventeenth-century Ireland, 28–29; as shadow state, 304; as stabilizing influence, 305; state and, 310–12; women in, 365–66; in women's education, 474; women's suffrage and, 479

Catholic Committee, 67

Catholic communalism, 372

Catholic Convention, 67–68

Catholic elites: conversions in, 58–59; protection of, 53–55

Catholic Emancipation, 9–10, 77–78, 81–82, 384, 453; opposition to, 84–85

Catholic Ex-Serviceman's Association, 397

Catholic middle classes, displacement and exile of, 493

Catholic Relief Act (1792), 48, 85

Catholicism: cultural preoccupation with, 294; in early modern Ireland, 296; in Europe, 304; laws repressing, 362–63; matriarchal era in, 365; in post-war Ireland, 127–28; reversion to, 31; revival of, 305–9

Catholics: disaffection of, 6–7; discrimination against, 13–14; dispossessed, 447–48; distribution of in Ulster in 1911, xvii; forced transportation of, 498; land confiscated from, 40; lands owned by, xiv; loyalty of, 59, 276–77; migrations of, 495–96; in Northern Ireland, 145–46; oppression of, 8; penal laws and, 55–58, 302–5; percentages of, 296–98

cattle raiding, 25

Caughie, Pamela, 249

Caulfield, Henry, 88–89

Celtic languages, 321

Celtic race, 386

Celtic Tiger, 131–32, 168–69, 171–74; economic crash of, 437; economic growth of, 434–36; employment opportunities in, 497; first phase of, 439; inequality in, 135–36; second phase of, 436–40; unregulated growth of, 184; women's status and, 376–77

Censorship of Publications Bill (1929), 483

Central Relief Committee of the Society of Friends, 415

Chamberlain, Neville, 426

Charitable Bequests Act (1844), 87–88

Charles II: accession of, 48; land settlements of, 49–52; religious tolerance policy of, 51

childcare, 368

Christie, Ian R., historian, 273

Church of Ireland, 7; disestablishment of, 448; efforts to disestablish, 93–94; intellectual history of, 200–205; loyalists to, 383–84; Presbyterians and, 302; reform of, 28, 303

Civil Service Amendment Bill (1924), 482

Civil War (1922–1923), 13, 14, 118–19, 395–96, 457–58

Clandeboye estates, 37

Clann na Poblachta, 126

Clarendon, Earl of, 52

Clarke, Aidan, historian, 40

Clarke, Austin, 246

Clarke, Samuel, 198

Clayton, Robert, 202

Irish nationalism of, 218, 219, 221, 223, 225, 450–52; "A Nation Once Again!", 450–51; on social fragmentation, 222

Davitt, Michael, 12, 355, 356

Dawkins, Richard, *The God Delusion*, 292

de Beaumont, Gustave, 9

de Gouges, Olympe, 471

de Lamartine, Alphonse, 385

de Nie, Michael, 345, 355

de Paor, Louis, 249

de Saint-Just, Louis Antoine Léon, 10

de Valera, Éamon, 117, 120, 121, 124–25, 169; anti-partition position of, 457–58, 459–60; broadcast media and, 254–55; Catholic Church and, 311; clemency appeal of, 461; Constitution of, 123–24; economic war of, 122; on emigration, 490; IRA and, 394; and Irish independence, 393, 395; *The Irish Press* and, 259; St. Patrick's Day speech of, 373; television and, 257

de Villette, Charles-Louis, 199, 214n21

Declaratory Act (1720), 63, 206; repeal of, 65

Defenders, 68, 383, 448

Deism, 200–205

Derry, Siege of, 53–54, 359n28

Derry Citizens Defence Association, 150

Desmond, Barry, 178

Desmond, earl of, rebellion of, 25

Devlin, Bernadette, 483

Devlin, Denis, 244–45

Devoy, John, 93

Dewards, David, 34

diaspora: political power of, 502–3; reasons for, 497–501; shaping of Irish history by, 493–97, 504–5; significance of, 501–4

Dicey, A. V., 95

Dickson, David, historian, 421n11

Dillon, Arthur, 492

Dillon, John, 97

Dinneen, Patrick, 336–37

Disraeli, Benjamin, 82, 91–92

Dissenters, anti-Union, 80–81. *See also* Presbyterians

divorce: liberalization of views on, 133, 178, 311, 375; prohibition of, 311, 483

domestication campaign, 367–71

Donnelly, James, historian, 177, 409

Donough, Earl of Thomond, 29

Doolan, Lelia, 257, 262

Down, County, colonization of, 37

Doyle, Mark, 354

Drennan, William, 66, 83, 205, 211, 363, 470

Droysen, Johann Gustav, 272

Dublin Drama League, 247–49

Dublin lockout (1913), 113

Dublin media community, 261

Dublin Penny Journal, 219

Dublin Society, 62

Dublin Women's Suffrage Association, 477

Duddy, Brendan, 158

Duffy, Charles Gavan, 89, 91, 217, 219, 224

Dunne, Ben, 265

Durcan, Mark, 175

Durcan, Paul, 257

earldoms, establishment of, 4

earls, flight of the, 327, 493

East India Company, 347–49

Easter Proclamation, 482

Easter Rising (1916), 10, 96, 111, 114, 312, 391–92, 456; Great War and, 114–16

Ecclesiastical Title Bill (1852), 90

economic boom, 131–32; construction sector during, 173–74; social partnerships during, 172–73. *See also* Celtic Tiger

economic crisis, 181–86

economic liberalization (1948–1972), 7, 110–11, 126–30; industrialization in, 129–30; international influences in, 129; political support for, 129

economic patriotism, 60, 62

economic policy: of Free State in 1920s, 425–26; of interwar years, 427–28; post-WWII, 428–29; protectionist, 13; of 1930s, 426–27; during World War II, 428. *See also* political economy

economic theory, 205–11

economy: of 1950s, 429–30; state planning of, 430–32

Edgeworth, Maria, novels of, 78–79, 103n20

Edgeworth, Richard Lovell, 77

education: expansion of employment in, 439; in post-war Ireland, 128–29; in promoting anglicization and Protestantism, 29–30; of women, 474–76

Edwards, Robert Dudley, historian, 274

Egan, Desmond, 155

elites: anti-Unionism of, 79–80, 454; corruption of, 110; landed, 33–38, 384

Elizabeth I, 22; founding of Trinity College, 29; Nine Years' War of, 26–27

Elizabeth II, visit of, 176

Elliott, Bruce, 501

Elliott, Christopher, 492

Elliott, Marianne, historian, 283

Emancipation and Repeal campaign, 384

emigration, 490; to British Empire territories, 346–47; in Celtic Tiger era, 497; changing destination preferences for, 499–500; by county (1951–1911), xvi; economic reasons for, 498–99; gender disparity in, 499; individual aspirations and, 500; mass, 10; reasons for, 491; as recourse for poor, 417–18; of women, 370–71

Emmet, Robert, 384

Encumbered Estates Acts (1848–9), 12

Encumbered Estates Court, 413–14

enfranchisement: of Catholics, 205; mass, 11, 280–81, 282

English common law, introduction of, 31–33

English language: domination of, 327; introduced to Ireland, 323–24; legislation promoting, 27–28

Equal Franchise Bill, 481

Ervine, St. John, 97

Established Church: conversion to, 28, 297–98, 332, 333; dominance of, 58, 202–3, 210

ethnic identity. *See* Church of Ireland

Europe: Catholicism in, 304; dissolution of empires of, 452; famines in, 404; migrations of populations in, 5–6, 490–91; 1948 revolutions in, 385–86; Protestant Interest in, 303; reconstruction of after fall of Rome, 14–15

European Central Bank (ECB), 182–83

European Common Agricultural Policy (CAP), 431–32

European Common Market, Ireland's entry into, 464

European Economic Community (EEC): Ireland's bids to join, 13; economic expansion with membership in, 434–41; Ireland's entry into, 375, 431–35

European Monetary System (EMS), 439–40

European Monetary Union, 440

European Recovery Program, 429

European Union (EU), 179–81; emigration in, 497

Evangelical Society of Ulster, 309

evangelicalism, 309–10; and missionary activity, 352

Evans, Bryce, 428

Exclusion Crisis, 51

Explanation, Act of (1665), 50; repeal of, 53

External Relations Act (1937), 459

family: laws regulating relationships of, 362–63; marriage and, 369; women in, 367–70

Famine, Great, 10, 60, 89–90; Catholic revival after, 307–8; cause of, 407–8; charitable response to, 415–17; church response to, 416–17; depopulation during, 346–47; disease during, 408; effects of, 92–93; evictions during, 409; explanation of, 224; historical research on, 403–4; and mass migration, 409, 417–18, 495–96; misery caused by, 409–10; nationalist construction of, 419; population collapse with, 416; poverty and, 413–14; public works measures for, 412; regional impacts of, 417; restructured rural society after, 308–9; sectarian interpretation of, 414; social and political importance of, 284; soup kitchens in, 412; state response to, 410–15, 421n11; workhouses during, 408–9

famines: in Ireland and Europe, 404; relief strategies for, 404

feasting, in medieval Ireland, 27

federalism, 88–89, 92–93, 105n84

femininity, in Free State, 373–74

feminism, 470; definition of, 470; in nineteenth century, 472–75; organizations of, 481–82; political activism and, 481–83, 485–86; second-wave, 483; social issues and, 483–84; suffrage campaign and, 476–81

Fenian Rising (1867), 93–94

Fenianism, 93–95, 97, 224, 386–89, 453–54

Fenton, Sir Geoffrey, 35

Ferns Report (2005), 177

Ferriter, Diarmaid, historian, 374

Fianna Fáil government, 120; anti-partition policy of, 458–60; constitutionalism of, 459, 464–65; economic policy of, 426–27; in modernization, 130, 131; nationalist-populist appeal of, 122–23; political power in, 169–71

filí (bardic) poetry, 324–26

Financial Services Centre, 438

financial services industry, 438–39

Fine Gael, 170, 171, 458, 461, 464–65

First World War: domestic impact of, 125; Irish conflict and, 114–16

Fitt, Gerry, 156–57

FitzGerald, Desmond, historian, 121

Fitzgerald, Edward, 69

FitzGerald, Garrett, 132, 178, 184, 311, 335, 464–65

Fitzgerald, Gerald, 325

Fitzgibbon, John, conversion of, 58–59

FitzPatrick, Brian, 34

Fitzpatrick, David, historian, 283, 499, 501;
on Irish emigration, 346, 370, 495, 501,
504
Fletcher, Andrew, 211
flight of the earls, 327, 493
Flood, Henry, 65
Foley, Donal, 260
food riots, 385
foreign investment, 131, 172, 255, 434
Foster, Roy, historian, 77, 78, 168, 172, 219;
Vivid Faces, 138n24
Fox, Charles James, 77, 83, 209
France: Irish diasporic community in, 494;
republicanism of, 383–84. *See also* French
Revolution
Free State, 13; austerity measures in, 440–41;
Catholic Church in, 176–78; credit crisis in,
14; economic crash of, 168, 181–86, 466;
economic expansion of, 168–69, 172–74;
economic growth and modernization of,
429–30; economic liberalization of, 126–30;
economic policy of in 1920s, 425–26;
employment statistics for, 433; European
Union and, 179–81; financial services
growth in, 438–39; fiscal autonomy of, 13,
425; foreign investment in, 434; GDP of,
440; gender relations in, 372–77; industrial
development in, 434–37; liberalization of,
375–76; macroeconomic management of,
439–40; modernization of, 130–36; neutrality of, 125–26; 1987 Constitution of,
374–75; 1950s economy in, 429–30; 1930s
economy in, 426–27; open economy of,
437–39; post-WWII economy of, 428–29;
real estate development in, 439; revolutionary period of, 111–19; service sector
employment in, 437; shifting employment
profile in, 441–42; stability of, 119–20;
state building in, 119–26; state economic
planning in, 430–32; tourism in, 438; war
economy of, 428
Free State army, 395–96
free thought, 201–2
free trade, 64–66, 121, 126, 130, 131, 255, 259;
in land, 407, 413; in 1920s, 425–26
French Declaration of the Rights of Man and
of the Citizen, 471
French Revolution: British involvement in,
448; Edmund Burke on, 209–10; ideas of,
8; impact in Ireland of, 205, 209–11; Irish
politics and, 66–67; religion and, 305
Froude, James Anthony, 279

Gaelic Athletic Association, 113; adaptation
of to global media, 267–68; foreign game
policy of, 134; and promotion of physical
discipline, 372
Gaelic chieftains, surrender and regrant
agreements with, 34
Gaelic customary law, 32
Gaelic Irish dynasties, 24–25
Gaelic League, 113, 336
Gaelic Revival movement, 98
Gaelic Union, 336
Gaeltacht, Kerry, 374
Gaeltacht communities, 338–39
Gagby, Douglas, 259–61
Gailey, Andrew, historian, 96
Gallagher, James, 333
Garda Siochána, 120
Garvin, Tom, historian, 179, 293
Gate Theatre, 248–49
gender, 361; dearth of literature on, 361–62;
power and, 362–63
gender relations: during the Great Famine,
366–71; from partition to economic boom,
372–77; in pre-Famine Ireland, 362–66;
during revival and revolution, 371–72.
See also masculinity; women
General Central Relief Committee for All
Ireland, 415
General Reformation Society, 416
George, David Lloyd, 114
George III: mental incapacitation of, 66; oppo-
sition to Catholic Emancipation of, 78
Geraldines, 4, 25
German Romantics, 220
Gibbon, Peter, historian, 283–84
Gibbons, Luke, critic, 262
Gilmore, Eamon, 170
Gilmour, Raymond, 154
Girvin, Brian, historian, 178, 429
Gladstone, William, 92, 93–94, 280–81; Home
Rule bill of, 95–96, 455; Parnell and, 96–98
Glorious Revolution, 196, 203, 209
Gonne, Maud, 371, 479
Goulding, Cathal, 461–62
Gouldingites, 462–63
Government of Ireland Act, 13
Gracious Declaration of November 1660,
49–50
Graham, James, 350, 351
Graham family, 350
Grattan, Henry, 7, 65, 206
Gray, Peter, historian, 90, 413, 414

MacGill, Patrick, 498–99
MacGreevy, Thomas, 245
Machiavelli, Niccolò, 3–4
MacNeill, Eoin, 274, 332–33
MacSharry reforms, 432
Maguire, Lord, conspicuous consumption of, 40
Mahon Report, 184
Mandler, Peter, historian, 447
Mangan, Owen Peter, 491
Mannion, John, historical geographer, 504
Marianism, 177, 258, 307, 312
market, "natural" laws of, 410–14
market-based economy, 38, 180, 181–85, 208, 263–64, 349–50, 376
Markievicz, Constance, 372, 478–79, 481
marriage: laws regulating, 362–63, 482–83; middle-class model of, 369; Protestant-Catholic, 362–63; in Protestant conversions, 30–31
Marriage Bar, 482
Married Women's Property Committee, 474
Marshall Plan, 429
martial law, 32–33
Martin, John, 94
Martyn, Edward, 237
masculinity, 361; crisis of, 376; Irish, 363, 366, 372
Mason, Roy, 159, 160
Mason, William Shaw, 296
Mathew, Father Theobald, 408
Matthews, Alan, 434
Maume, Patrick, historian, 86, 95
Maxwell, John, 215n66
Maynooth Act, 88
Maynooth Grant, 81–82, 453
McAleese, Mary, 176, 486
McBride, Ian, historian, 57
McBride, John, 203, 204
McCabe, Conor, 184, 185
McCafferty, Nell, 260
McCann, Eamon, 174
McCarthy, Angela, 347
McCormick, James, 461
McCracken, Margaret, 364–65
McCracken, Mary Ann, 364–65, 471
McDonnell, Joe, 161
McGahern, John, *The Dark*, 313
McGowan, Michael, 498–99
McGreevy, Thomas, 237
McGuinness, Martin, 155, 175, 176, 247
McKernan, Anne, 364
McKneight, James, 91

McNamara, Angela, 263
McQuaid, Archbishop John Charles, 295; criticism of TV by, 258; political influence of, 127, 293, 311–12, 313–14
McSkimmin, Samuel, 365
McTier, Martha, 211, 470, 472
Meagher, Timothy J., historian, 501
media: deregulation of, 264–65; global, 267–68; Irish identity discussion in, 262; in 1960–1970s, 261–62; public debate about, 262–63; scandals and corruption revealed in, 265–66. *See also* broadcasting; newspapers; radio; television
medieval Ireland: feasting in, 27; fighting in, 24–27; nobility in, 24–26; Protestant peers in, 23; religious conformity in, 22–23
Melbourne government, conciliation policy of, 86–87
Methodist mission, 309
Middle Irish period, 322–23
migration: assimilation and ethnic identity and, 501; cultural encounters generated by, 503–4; in Europe, 5–6, 497; reasons for, 497–501; Irish history shaped by, 493–97, 504; significance of, 501–4. *See also* emigration
Mill, John Stuart, first female suffrage petition of, 477
Miller, Kerby, historian, 347, 501
missionaries, Irish, 299, 303, 309–10, 352–53
missions, religious, 351–52
Mitchel, John, 92, 220, 223, 385–86, 411; war on Mammon of, 228
Mitchell, George, 162–63
modernism, 236; alienation and, 243–44; characteristics of, 237–38; Irish-language literature and, 249; realism and, 238–39; rural landscape and, 237–38; theater and, 247–49; transnational, 249–50; urban focus of, 237
modernization, 130–36; church and, 314–15; economic growth and, 128, 429–30; education in, 128–29; poverty and inequality with, 135–36; scandals and, 135; women's status and, 375–77. *See also* industrialization; liberalization
Molesworth, Robert, 193, 198, 204, 206, 207
Molony, Helena, 479
Molyneux, William, 7, 62, 193, 196, 207, 277; *The Case of Ireland's Being Bound by Acts of Parliament in England, Stated,* 206
monetary theory, 208–9
Montgomery, Hugh de Fellenberg, 94

Yelverton, Barry, 59
Young, Sir Arthur, 150
Young Ireland, 10, 91, 385–86; anthology of,
450–51; antiquarian revival and, 219;
Benthamism and, 222–23; cultural program of, 221–22; Griffith's model of,
228–29; historical significance of, 217;
model of nationhood of, 226–27; nationalism and, 88–89, 92, 94, 225–28, 451;
political economy and, 227–29; political
ideals of, 219–21, 222–24; rebellion of,
217–18; Yeats and, 224–26